Baby and Child Care

by DR. BENJAMIN SPOCK

New Revised and
Enlarged Edition

Illustrations by DOROTHEA FOX

A POCKET BOOK EDITION published by
Simon & Schuster of Canada, Ltd. • Markham, Ontario, Canada
Registered User of the Trademark

BABY AND CHILD CARE

POCKET BOOK edition published July, 1946
Revised POCKET BOOK edition published September, 1968
27th printing..........November, 1974

This book is a new version of *The Pocket Book of Baby and Child Care,* originally published under the title *The Common Sense Book of Baby and Child Care* by Duell, Sloan & Pearce. In its previous paper-bound editions, Dr. Spock's book had 179 printings and is the best-selling new title issued in the United States since 1895, when best-seller lists began.

This revised and enlarged POCKET BOOK edition is printed from brand-new plates made from completely reset, clear, easy-to-read type. POCKET BOOK editions are published by POCKET BOOKS, a division of Simon & Schuster, Inc., 630 Fifth Avenue, New York, N.Y. 10020. Trademarks registered in the United States and other countries.

L

To Jane

Contents

	Page
A Letter to the Reader of This Edition	XV
The Parents' Part	3
Trust Yourself	3
Enjoy Your Baby	4
Strictness or Permissiveness?	7
What Are Your Aims in Raising a Child?	10
Parents Are Human	17
Parental Doubts Are Normal	23
The Father's Part	28
Relations with Grandparents	31
Callers and Visitors	35
Help for the Mother	36
Equipment and Clothing	39
Equipment You'll Need	39
The Clothes He Needs	41
Bedclothes	44
Equipment That May or May Not Be Necessary	45
Formula Equipment	46
Medical and Nursing Care	49
The Visiting Nurse	49
The Baby's Doctor	49
The Hospital	55
Infant Feeding	58
What Feeding Means to the Baby	58

Page

Schedules 60
Giving the Feeding 67
Getting Enough and Gaining Weight 68
Breast Feeding 72
The Values of Breast Feeding 72
Questions About Breast Feeding 73
Getting Started at Breast Feeding 78
When the Breast Milk Seems Insufficient . . . 87
Special Problems of Breast Feeding 94
Manual Expression and Breast Pumps 100
Weaning from the Breast 103
Bottle Feeding 108
Various Milks 108
Various Sugars 113
Formulas for Emergency Use 114
Preparing a Formula 116
Formula Refrigeration 119
Giving the Bottle 120
Adding Vitamins and Water 127
Vitamins in Infancy 127
Drinking Water for a Baby 128
Changes in Diet and Schedule 131
Adding Solid Foods 131
Changes in Schedule and Bottle 142
Weaning from Bottle to Cup 150
Readiness for Weaning 150
Wean Him Gradually 152
Daily Care 154
The Bath 154
The Navel 158
The Penis 159
The Fontanel 161
Clothing, Fresh Air and Sunshine 161

Page

Sleep 166
Play Periods 169
The Bowel Movements 172
Diapers 175
Inoculations 177
Problems of Infancy 183
Crying in the Early Weeks 183
Spoiling 191
Common Kinds of Indigestion 197
Constipation 199
Diarrhea 202
Rashes 205
Mouth and Eye Troubles 209
Swollen Breasts 211
Breathing Troubles 211
Common Nervous Symptoms 213
Comforters and Thumb Sucking 215
Six-Month Independence and the Need for
    Comforters 215
Thumb Sucking 218
Pacifier 224
Rhythmic Habits 227
Your Baby's Development 229
Watching Him Grow 229
Teething 242
Toilet Training 249
Bowel Training 249
Urine Training 260
The One-Year-Old 265
What Makes Him Tick 265
Avoiding Accidents and Fears 266
Independence and Outgoingness 270
How to Handle Him 272

Page

Nap Hours Are Changing 278
He's Apt to Change His Eating Habits 278
Elements in the Diet 288
Protein 288
Minerals 289
Vitamins 289
Water and Roughage 292
Fats, Starches, Sugars 292
Sensible Diet 293
Foods and Meals 295
Milk 295
Meats, Fish, Eggs 297
Vegetables 298
Fruits 299
Cereals and Suppers 300
Less Valuable and Undesirable Foods 302
Frozen Foods 305
Feeding Between Meals 305
Meals 306
Managing Young Children 308
Play and Outgoingness 308
Early Childhood 313
The Father As Companion 320
Going to Bed 322
Duties 324
Discipline 328
Jealousy and Rivalry 339
The Two-Year-Old 350
What He's Like 350
Worries Around Two 351
Contrariness 356
Stuttering 358
Nail-biting 360

Page

Three to Six 361
Devotion to the Parents 361
Curiosity and Imagination 366
Fears Around Three, Four and Five 368
Different Causes for Handling the Genitals . . . 372
"The Facts of Life" 376
Nursery School 383
From Six to Eleven 388
Fitting into the Outside World 388
Self-Control 393
Television, Movies and Comics 395
Stealing 397
Schools 400
What a School Is For 400
Trouble with Lessons 405
Child Guidance 411
Puberty Development 414
Physical Changes 414
Psychological Changes 419
Problems of Feeding and Development . . . 435
Thin Children 435
Feeding Problems 436
Fat Children 445
Glands 449
Undescended Testicles 450
Posture 451
Illness 453
Fever 453
Giving Medicines and Enemas 458
Handling an Invalid 461
Going to the Hospital 463
Diet During Illness 466
Colds 469

Page

The Handling of a Child with a Cold 475

Ear Infections 478

Bronchitis and Pneumonia 479

Croup 480

Sinusitis, Tonsillitis and Swollen Glands . . . 482

Tonsils and Adenoids 484

Allergies 485

Skin Diseases 491

Measles, German Measles, Roseola 494

Chicken Pox, Whooping Cough, Mumps . . . 496

Scarlet Fever, Diphtheria, Poliomyelitis . . . 501

Quarantine 503

Tuberculosis 504

Rheumatic Fever 507

Urinary Disturbances 510

Vaginal Discharge 517

Stomachaches and Upsets 518

Hernias, Ruptures, Hydrocele 523

Eye Troubles 525

Convulsions 527

First Aid 529

Cuts, Hemorrhage and Burns 529

Sprains, Fractures, Head Injuries 535

Swallowed Objects and Choking 538

Artificial Respiration 539

Objects in the Nose and Ears 540

Poisons 540

Special Problems 543

Traveling with a Baby 543

The Premature Baby 546

The RH Factor 552

Twins 553

Separated Parents 560

Page

The Working Mother 563
The Fatherless Child 568
The Handicapped Child 571
Adopting a Child 585
Emergencies 593
Index 593

A Letter to the Reader of This New Edition

Most of you have a doctor you can consult. He knows your child, and therefore he is the only person in a position to advise you wisely about how you should treat him. By glancing at a rash or asking a couple of questions over the telephone, he can usually get to the solution of a problem that reading would only get you more mixed up about. This book is not meant to be used for diagnosis or treatment; it's only meant to give you a general understanding of children, their troubles and their needs. It is true that in certain sections there is emergency advice for those very few parents who are out of reach of a doctor. It's better for them to have book advice than no advice at all. But book advice is never so helpful or so safe as real medical assistance.

I want to apologize to the mother and father who have a girl and are frustrated by having the child called him all through this book. It's clumsy to say him or her every time, and I need her to refer to the mother.

The most important thing I have to say is that you should not take too literally what is said in this book. Every child is different, every parent is different, every illness or behavior problem is somewhat different from every other. All I can do is describe the most common developments and problems, in the most general terms. Remember that you know a lot about your child and that I don't know anything about him.

There are hundreds of small changes in this third edition, twenty-two years after the book first appeared and eleven since the publication of the second edition. Many of them were made necessary by scientific advances, such as the Sabin oral polio vaccine, measles vaccine, cold-mist humidifiers for croup and colds. Then there are the new ideas that have proved workable, such as the feeding of formula at room temperature or even as it comes out of the refrigerator; prepared, sterilized formula in bottles that can be thrown away after the feeding; taking temperatures in the armpit.

The **material on adolescence** has been increased a great deal. It doesn't cover all the details, but it touches on the main areas that cause concern to parents—demands for more freedom and privileges, disagreeableness toward parents, messiness, dating regulations, disobedience and defiance—and indicates my general philosophy of how to cope with them; there's a brief overall view of delinquency and the use of drugs.

The principal change that has occurred in my own outlook on child rearing has been the realization that what is making the parent's job most difficult is today's child-centered viewpoint. I don't merely refer to the few parents who kowtow to their tyrannical children or the larger number who have been intimidated by all the advice they've received from us pediatricians, psychologists, psychiatrists and pedagogues, and are hesitant to give their children the firm leadership they need, for fear they might do the wrong thing. I mean the tendency of many conscientious parents to keep their eyes exclusively focused on their child, thinking about what he needs from them and from the community, instead of thinking about what the world, the neighborhood, the family will be needing from the child and then making sure that he will grow up to meet such obligations. Even to hear this latter point of view expressed is a little startling to many Americans.

I think we've brought up our children not only less ready to do their part in solving the world's urgent problems but actually less happy in the sense of less fulfilled. For human beings, by and large, can only be really happy when they feel they are part of something bigger than themselves and when a lot is expected of them and when they are living up to these expectations.

But the reason why, as parents and professionals, we haven't taught our children their place in the world and their obligation to it is that most of us have not been at all clear about our own place in the universe or about the meaning of human existence, the way people were in earlier centuries.

I give my answers in "What Are Your Aims in Raising a Child?" (Sections 10–14).

My debt is now tremendous to all the physicians and other experts, including mothers, who have advised me through three editions of the manuscript, and the skillful, patient secretaries who have typed and retyped.

C. Anderson Aldrich, M.D., Abram Blau, M.D., Gordon M. Bruce, M.D., Clement B. P. Cobb, M.D., John R. Cobb, M.D., Ralph De Palma, M.D., Edwin Eigner, M.D., Lewis Fraad, M.D., David Friedman, M.D., Edwin Gerrish, M.D., Harry Gold, M.D., Hiram Hardesty, M.D., William W. Heroy, M.D., Frederick C. Hunt, M.D., Frances L. Ilg, M.D., Donald Jackson, M.D., John Kaster, M.D., John Kennel, M.D., Milton I. Levine, M.D., Samuel Z. Levine, M.D., John Montgomery, M.D., Hamden C. Moody, M.D., Charles O'Regan, M.D., Marian Putnam, M.D., John Reinhart, M.D., Oscar M. Schloss, M.D., Milton J. E. Senn, M.D., Carl H. Smith, M.D., Samuel Spector, M.D., Marion Stranahan, M.D., Irving Sunshine, M.D., William Wallace, M.D., Myron E. Wegman, M.D.

Barbara Biber, Ph.D., Sylvia K. Bingham, Velma Davies, R.N., Mary S. Fisher, Ph.D., Mary Hamm Flumerfelt, Sidonie M. Gruenberg, Mary Lescaze, Betty N. Richmond, Jessie Stanton, Sophie van S. Theis, A.B., L.H.D., Caroline B. Zachry, Ph.D.

Carol Colbert, Norma Nero, Lois Woodyatt.

Jane Cheney Spock has contributed endless work, patience, much of the practicality in the detailed directions in the book, wonderful judgment. Her most essential contribution of all has been to give up graciously most of the evenings of the week for many years now, while I wrote, erased and wrote again.

Warning: Salesmen for children's encyclopedias, sets of books on child care, nursery furniture, children's clothing and equipment sometimes claim that I am intimately connected with their enterprises in some way, or at least endorse their products. All such claims are fraudulent and entitle you to threaten to call the authorities in order to get rid of the salesman. I have no connection with any such enterprise and never endorse a commercial product. I have authored or co-authored several separate books but they are sold only through regular bookstores or paperback outlets, never door to door. I write for one magazine only, a regular column.

Baby and Child Care

The Parents' Part

TRUST YOURSELF

1. You know more than you think you do. Soon you're going to have a baby. Maybe you have him already. You're happy and excited, but if you haven't had much experience, you wonder whether you are going to know how to do a good job. Lately you have been listening more carefully to your friends and relatives when they talk about bringing up a child. You've begun to read articles by experts in the magazines and newspapers. After the baby is born, the doctor and nurses will begin to give you instructions, too. Sometimes it sounds like a very complicated business. You find out all the vitamins a baby needs and all the inoculations. One mother tells you that egg should be given early because of its iron, and another says that egg should be delayed to avoid allergy. You hear that a baby is easily spoiled by being picked up too much but also that a baby must be cuddled plenty, that fairy tales make children nervous, and that fairy tales are a wholesome outlet.

Don't take too seriously all that the neighbors say. Don't be overawed by what the experts say. Don't be afraid to trust your own common sense. Bringing up your child won't be a complicated job if you take it easy, trust your own instincts and follow the directions that your doctor gives you. We know for a fact that the natural loving care that kindly parents give their children is a hundred times more valuable than their knowing how to pin a diaper on just right or how to make a formula expertly. Every time you pick your baby up, even if you do it a little awkwardly at first, every time you change him, bathe him, feed him, smile at him, he's getting a feeling that he belongs to you and that you belong to him. Nobody else in the world, no matter how skillful, can give that to him.

It may surprise you to hear that the more people have

studied different methods of bringing up children, the more they have come to the conclusion that what good mothers and fathers instinctively feel like doing for their babies is usually best, after all. Furthermore, all parents do their best job when they have a natural, easy confidence in themselves. Better to make a few mistakes from being natural than to do everything letter-perfect out of a feeling of worry.

Prenatal classes for expectant mothers and fathers are provided in many communities by the Visiting Nurse Association, the Red Cross or the city health department. They are very helpful in discussing the questions and problems that all expectant parents have concerning pregnancy, delivery and care of the baby.

ENJOY YOUR BABY

2. Don't be afraid of him. You'd think from what some people say about babies demanding attention that they come into the world determined to get their parents under their thumb by hook or by crook. This isn't true. Your baby is born to be a reasonable, friendly human being.

Don't be afraid to feed him when you think he's really hungry. If you are mistaken, he'll merely refuse to take much.

Don't be afraid to love him and enjoy him. Every baby needs to be smiled at, talked to, played with, fondled—gently and lovingly—just as much as he needs vitamins and calories. That's what will make him a person who loves people and enjoys life. The baby who doesn't get any loving will grow up cold and unresponsive.

Don't be afraid to respond to other desires of his as long as they seem sensible to you and as long as you don't become a slave to him. When he cries in the early weeks, it's because he's uncomfortable for some reason or other—maybe it's hunger or indigestion, or fatigue, or tension. The uneasy feeling you have when you hear him cry, the feeling that you want to comfort him, is meant to be part of your nature, too. Being held, rocked or walked may be what he needs.

Spoiling doesn't come from being good to a baby in a sensible way, and it doesn't come all of a sudden. Spoiling comes on gradually when a mother is too afraid to use her common sense or when she really wants to be a slave and encourages her baby to become a slave driver.

Everyone wants his child to turn out to be healthy in his

habits and easy to live with. But each child himself wants to eat at sensible hours and later to learn good table manners. His bowels (as long as the movements don't become too hard) will move according to their own healthy pattern, which may or may not be regular; and when he's a lot older and wiser, you can show him where to sit to move them. He will develop his own pattern of sleep according to his own needs. In all these habits he will sooner or later want to fit into the family's way of doing things, with only a minimum of guidance from you.

3. **Enjoy him as he is—that's how he'll grow up best.** Every baby's face is different from every other's. In the same way, every baby's pattern of development is different. One may be very advanced in his general bodily strength and co-ordination, an early sitter, stander, walker—a sort of infant athlete. And yet he may be slow in doing careful, skillful things with his fingers, in talking. Even a baby who is an athlete in rolling over, standing and creeping may turn out to be slow to learn to walk. A baby who's advanced in his physical activities may be very slow in his teething, and vice versa. A child who turns out later to be smart in his schoolwork may have been so slow in beginning to talk that his parents were afraid for a while that he was dull; and a child who has just an ordinary amount of brains is sometimes a very early talker.

I am purposely picking out examples of children with mixed rates of development to give you an idea of what a jumble of different qualities and patterns of growth each individual person is composed.

One baby is born to be big-boned and square and chunky, while another will always be small-boned and delicate. One individual really seems to be born to be fat. If he loses weight during an illness, he gains it back promptly afterward. The troubles that he has in the world never take away his appetite. The opposite kind of individual stays on the thin side, even when he has the most nourishing food to eat, even though life is running smoothly for him.

Love and enjoy your child for what he is, for what he looks like, for what he does, and forget about the qualities that he doesn't have. I don't give you this advice just for sentimental reasons. There's a very important practical point here. The child who is appreciated for what he is, even if he is homely, or clumsy, or slow, will grow up with confidence in himself, happy. He will have a spirit that will make the best of all the capacities that he has, and of all the opportunities that come his way. He will make light of any handicaps. But the child who has never been quite accepted by his parents, who has always felt that he was not quite right, will grow up lacking confidence. He'll never be able to make full use of what brains, what skills, what physical attractiveness he has. If he starts life with a handicap, physical or mental, it will be multiplied tenfold by the time he is grown up.

4. He isn't frail. "I'm so afraid I'll hurt him if I don't handle him right," a mother often says about her first baby. You don't have to worry; you have a pretty tough baby. There are many ways to hold him. If his head drops backward by mistake, it won't hurt him. The open spot in his skull (the fontanel) is covered by a tough membrane like canvas that isn't easily injured. The system to control his body temperature is working quite well by the time he weighs 7 pounds if he's covered halfway sensibly. He has good resistance to most germs. During a family cold epidemic, he's apt to have it the mildest of all. If he gets his head tangled in anything, he has a strong instinct to struggle and yell. If he's not getting enough to eat, he will probably cry for more. If the light is too strong for his eyes, he'll blink and fuss. (You can take his picture with a flashbulb, even if it does make him jump.) He knows how much sleep he needs, and takes it. He can care for himself pretty well for a person who can't say a word and knows nothing about the world.

5. A baby at birth is usually disappointing-looking to a parent who hasn't seen one before. His skin is coated with a soft white wax, which, if left on, will be absorbed slowly and will lessen the chance of rashes during the hospital stay. His skin underneath is apt to be very red. His face tends to be puffy and lumpy, and there may be black-and-blue marks from forceps. The head is misshapen from "molding" during labor— low in the forehead, elongated at the back, and quite lopsided. Occasionally there may be, in addition, a hematoma, a localized hemorrhage under the scalp that sticks out as a distinct bump and takes weeks to go away. A couple of days after birth there may be a touch of jaundice, which is visible for about a week. (Jaundice that comes the first day or is very noticeable or lasts more than a week should be reported to the doctor.)

The baby's body is covered all over with fuzzy hair, which is usually shed in about a week. For a couple of weeks afterward there is apt to be a dry scaling of the skin, which is also shed. Some babies have black hair on the scalp at first, which may come far down on the forehead. The first hair, whatever its color or consistency, comes out, and the new hair that grows back, sooner or later, may be quite different in all respects.

STRICTNESS OR PERMISSIVENESS?

6. This looms as a big question for many new parents. A great majority of them find the right answer in a little while. For a few parents it remains a worrisome question, no matter how much experience they've had.

I may as well let the cat out of the bag right away as far as my opinion goes and say that strictness or permissiveness is not the real issue. Good-hearted parents who aren't afraid to be firm when it is necessary can get good results with either moderate strictness or moderate permissiveness. On the other hand, a strictness that comes from harsh feelings or a permissiveness that is timid or vacillating can each lead to poor results. The real issue is what spirit the parent puts into managing the child and what attitude is engendered in the child as a result.

7. We've been through a big transition. It's hard to get any perspective on this topic without taking a historical view. Styles in strictness vary from one period to another. The Victorian Age was quite strict, for instance, about manners and modesty. In the twentieth century, especially after World War I, a reaction set in. Several factors pushed it along. The great American pioneers in educational research, like John Dewey and William Kilpatrick, showed that a child learns better and faster with a method of teaching that makes allowance for his particular readiness to progress and that recognizes his eagerness to learn if the subject matter is suitable. Freud and his followers showed that harsh toilet training or frightening a child about sex can distort his personality and lead to neurosis. Studies of delinquents and criminals revealed that most of them had suffered more from lack of love in childhood than from lack of punishment. These discoveries, among others, encouraged a general relaxation in child discipline and a greater effort to give children what they seemed to need as individuals. Several wise leaders in American pediatrics, Aldrich and Powers and Gesell, began to introduce a similar philosophy into the medical care of babies and children. But physicians remained strict about infant feeding right into the 1940's, because they still feared that irregular schedules and irregular amounts of formula might bring on the severe diarrheal diseases that used to cause so many infant deaths. Then the experiments of Dr. Preston McLendon and Mrs. Frances P. Simsarian with the "self-demand" schedule, published in 1942, helped to convince doctors that most babies can do very well choosing their own feeding times and will remain healthy. Since then, there has been a rapid and widespread shift in medical practice. Today a majority of American babies are being put on more or less flexible schedules at first.

Doctors who used to conscientiously warn young parents against spoiling are now encouraging them to meet their baby's needs, not only for food, but for comforting and loving.

These discoveries and these changes of attitudes and methods have benefited most children and parents. There are fewer tense ones, more happy ones.

But it's not possible for a civilization like ours to go through such a change of philosophy—it really amounts to a revolution —without raising doubts in many parents' minds and without getting some parents thoroughly mixed up. It's basic human nature to tend to bring up your children about as you were brought up. It's easy enough to pick up new ideas about vitamins and inoculations. But if your upbringing was fairly strict in regard to obedience, manners, sex, truthfulness, it's natural, it's almost inevitable, that you will feel strongly underneath about such matters when raising your own children. You may have changed your theories because of something you've studied or read or heard, but when your child does something that would have been considered bad in your own childhood, you'll probably find yourself becoming more tense, or anxious, or angry than you imagined possible. This is nothing to be ashamed of. This is the way Nature expects human beings to learn child care—from their own childhood. This is how different civilizations have managed to remain stable and carry on their ideals from generation to generation.

The reason that most parents have been able to do a good job with their children during the past fifty years of changing theory is that they themselves had been brought up reasonably happily, were comfortable about raising their children the same way, and didn't follow any new theory to extremes. When doctors were emphasizing regularity, confident parents followed a regular schedule in general (and most babies adjusted to it most of the time), but they weren't afraid to make an occasional exception when the baby became painfully hungry ahead of time, because they felt in their bones that this was right.

When doctors more recently have been emphasizing flexibility, confident parents haven't carried this to extremes, either. They don't let a sleepy but obstinate baby refuse to be put to bed, because they know very well (mostly from their own childhood) that bedtime is bedtime and that theories of flexibility have very little to do with this situation.

8. Parents who become confused with new theories are often of two kinds. There are, first of all, those who have been brought up with too little confidence in their own judgment. If you don't dare trust yourself, you have to follow what someone else says, willy-nilly. A second group are those parents who feel that they were brought up too severely. They remember the resentment they felt toward their parents at times, and they don't want their children to feel that way about them. But this is a very difficult approach. If you want to raise your children the way you were raised, you have a definite pattern to follow. You know just how obedient, how helpful, how polite, you want them to be. You don't have to stop and think. But if you want to treat them quite differently than the way you were treated—more indulgently, for instance, or more as equals—you don't have any pattern of how far to carry it. If things begin to get out of hand—if, for example, your child begins to take advantage of your permissiveness—it's harder to find your way back onto the right track. The child makes you mad, all right, but the madder you get the guiltier you feel for fear you'll step into the very pattern you were determined to avoid.

Of course, I'm making all this sound too black or white. We all start out as young parents partly agreeing, partly disagreeing, with the methods our parents used. It's a matter of degree. And most of us find a compromise that works reasonably well. I have been exaggerating in order to make clear the difficulty that some parents have had.

9. Stick to your convictions. I think that good parents who naturally lean toward strictness should stick to their guns and raise their children that way. Moderate strictness—in the sense of requiring good manners, prompt obedience, orderliness—is not harmful to children so long as the parents are basically kind and so long as the children are growing up happy and friendly. But strictness is harmful when the parents are overbearing, harsh, chronically disapproving, and make no allowances for a child's age and individuality. This kind of severity produces children who are either meek and colorless or mean to others.

Parents who incline to an easygoing kind of management, who are satisfied with casual manners as long as the child's attitude is friendly, or who happen not to be particularly strict—for instance, about promptness or neatness—can also raise children who are considerate and cooperative, as long as the parents are not afraid to be firm about those matters that do seem important to them.

When parents get unhappy results from too much permissiveness, it is not so much because they demand too little, though this is part of it. It is more because they are timid or guilty about what they ask or because they are unconsciously encouraging the child to rule the roost.

WHAT ARE YOUR AIMS IN RAISING A CHILD?

The rearing of children is more and more puzzling for parents in the twentieth century because we've lost a lot of our old-fashioned convictions about what kind of morals and ambitions and characters we want them to have. We've even lost our convictions about the purpose of human existence. Instead we have come to depend on psychological concepts. They've been helpful in solving many of the smaller problems but they are of little use in answering the major questions.

You may not be conscious of these changes—because you are so much a part of these times or because you grew up in an unusually stable family.

10. Other countries and times. In the past it was assumed in many countries that man's main function in the world—over and above making a living—was to serve God, by carrying out his purposes as revealed by religion. That's why in the Middle Ages the churches were by far the most imposing buildings. Much the same was true in America in the Colonial period. Children never had any idea that life was for their fulfillment. They were constantly exhorted to overcome their base natures in order to grow up to be pleasing in God's eyes.

In other places, especially in the past hundred years or so, it has been taught that man's purpose is to serve his country. This was true to a degree of France in Napoleon's time, the British empire, the German empire. It has been even more true of some modern states, not only of a Communist state like the Soviet Union but of a democratic one like Israel. Parents and teachers are in agreement with leaders about what virtues are to be encouraged in children: cooperativeness, studiousness, dedication to the specific principles of the nation. Parents don't have to keep wondering and worrying—about whether they are doing the right thing.

In even more parts of the world, it has always been assumed that children are born and raised to serve the aims of the family—what sociologists call the extended family or the clan. In childhood and youth they are to prepare themselves for work at the jobs which are considered the valuable ones by their particular family. They must as children and later as grown-ups revere and defer to their elders. Even in marrying, in many countries, they can't be allowed to be carried away by their foolish hearts but must accept marriages that are arranged by their parents for the purpose of advancing the family's welfare.

11. Child-centered America. In America very few children are raised to believe that their principal destiny is to serve their family, their country or God. Generally we've given them the feeling that they are free to set their own aims and occupations in life according to their inclinations. In a majority of cases these aims are visualized mainly in material terms.

The tendency is for American parents to consider the child at least as important as themselves—perhaps potentially more important. An English anthropologist said that whereas in other countries children are taught to look up to their parents as rather distinguished superior people, whatever their actual place in the society, the remarkable thing about America is that a father will say to his son, "Son, if you don't do better than I've done, I won't think much of you." This is an upside-down respect. This is why America has often been called child-centered.

In other lands young parents gain confidence about aims and methods for rearing their children from family traditions and from having the grandparents nearby to advise and help them. These comforts have often been lacking in America. Our ancestors left their homelands because they were impatient with old ways and had the courage to try the unknown. Their descendants ever since have been restlessly moving from place to place in search of opportunity, often raising their children hundreds of miles away from any relatives. So they've had to turn to professional advisers and books and new theories for the help they needed.

I want to give a couple of small examples of how the child-centered, psychological approach can leave parents in the lurch unless it is backed up by a moral sense. Jealous quarreling between brothers and sisters has recently been tolerated **much more** than it was in previous generations. The psychological reasoning has been that jealousy is normal; if it is inhibited too severely, by making a child feel excessively guilty, it can cause various distortions of the personality. Parents shouldn't be badgering their children over **every little** thing anyway. There is considerable truth in these concepts. But when parents have followed them too exclusively, without consideration for the rights of the family or the ethics of society, the jealous child has been allowed to be much too mean to the younger one, has kept the family in an uproar and ended up with a guilty conscience anyway, because of the cruelty he has gotten away with.

A student of 19 is becoming increasingly rude and even verbally abusive toward his mother, who is a highly conscientious person. She has come to the guilty conclusion—incorrectly—that she must have failed him somehow, so she responds submissively to his reproaches. He senses that it is not right for him to pick on his mother just because he is out of sorts in some other department of his life yet, instinctively, he behaves worse and worse in order to get her to crack down.

You can see that psychological concepts don't help unless they are backed up by a sense of what's right and proper; they can seriously interfere with the operation of the parents' good sense; they can create further problems.

I doubt that Americans will ever want their children's ambitions to be subordinated to the wishes of the family or the needs of the country. However, I think that more of our children would grow up happier and more stable if they were acquiring a conviction, all through childhood, that the most important and the most fulfilling thing that human beings can do is to serve humanity in some fashion and to live by their ideals. (This does not preclude their earning a living or seeking advancement.) This is why human beings behave better, feel more purposeful, have better mental health during wartime, when they have a common purpose. And statistics show that there is less crime and less suicide during financial depressions, when people face a greater challenge. It's also much easier for the parents themselves, in meeting the hundred issues that come up every day with children—for instance, about politeness, chores, quarreling, schoolwork, dating—if they have their own principles. Then the answers to the detailed questions come more readily.

12. We are disillusioned. Fortunate are the parents with a strong religious faith. They are supported by a sense of conviction and serenity in all their activities. Usually they can pass on their faith to at least a majority of their children.

Many of the people who have no religious faith are doubly deprived today, because they don't have much belief in man either. We live in a disenchanted, disillusioned age—not about things, but about human beings.

This has been evident in the increasing tendency in literature, plays and movies in the past fifty years to play down the kindly and spiritual aspects of man and to focus on his crude, animal side. Manners in social life have been coarsened, especially among women. Even greeting cards, instead of wishing invalids and relatives well, jeer at them. Art rarely shows attractive people; it omits them altogether or makes them hideous. Many youths cultivate dishevelment as if they are ashamed to be human and a few of them withdraw from society altogether.

The disenchantment has been caused in part by the rapid strides in the sciences of biology, psychology and sociology, which have seemed to stress man's closeness to other animals, the crudeness of his basic instincts, the mechanicalness of his behavior patterns. Perhaps even more basic has been the weakening of the authority of religion in the minds of many people, caused by the increased authority of the sciences. This has greatly diminished man's former feeling that he was a very special and noble creature created in God's image.

The realization that the Biblical description of Creation cannot be taken literally has made many people question whether religious teachers have a solid basis for prescribing man's conduct and aims.

I believe that man's disillusionment is based on a mis-understanding of his nature. It's true he is related by evolution to other animals. But he is also vastly different. He is idealistic in his aspirations. His relationships are predominantly spiritual. His capacity for abstract reasoning has enabled him to dis-cover much of the meaning of the universe. He has invented fantastic machines. He has created beauty in all the arts. All this has been made possible by the aspirations kindled in him in early childhood by his adoration of his parents. Whether or not man has religious faith, he can believe in the power of love and in man's potentialities for good, if he understands the spiritual development of a child.

13. How man gets his aspirations. In the 3-to-6-year-old period a child matures by means of an intense adoration of his parents—not the parents as the neighbors see them but glorified. He overestimates their wisdom, power and attractive-ness. The boy yearns to be like his idealized father and spends all day practicing, in activities and manner. At the same time he develops a strong romantic attachment to his mother and idolizes her as his feminine ideal. As such she will strongly influence his choice of a wife when he grows up.

For the girl it's the other way around. She yearns to be like her mother—in occupation and in having babies of her own. She forms a possessive romantic attachment to her father.

Because children are so very aware at this dependent age of how much their parents' love means to them, they are now inspired with a similar capacity to love generously their par-ents and other people. Out of this will eventually grow their devotion to their own children and their altruism toward humanity.

In this same age period several other significant psycho-logical developments take place. Both girl and boy become fascinated with marriage and having babies. It is hard to convince boys that they can't grow babies inside themselves. Their frustrated rivalry with girls about this is believed to be one of the strongest sources of the compensatory creativity of the male in all the arts, inventions and machines.

In Nature's scheme of things the intense attachments to the two parents, having served their purpose of setting the child's ideals and advancing his maturity, must then be greatly diminished, so that he can begin the next big step—between

6 and 12 years—of becoming emotionally more independent of his parents and oriented instead toward the outside community and its ways of doing things. This is brought about by a dramatic shift in his feelings toward each parent.

The child's romantic attachment to the parent of the opposite sex gradually arouses in him increasingly uncomfortable feelings of rivalry with the parent of the same sex. This forces him eventually, by about the age of 6 or 7, to suppress guiltily his possessiveness toward the first parent and, along with it, fascination with marriage, with having babies and with sex differences. He is able to sublimate (transform) these interests into impersonal, abstract pursuits such as the 3 R's, science, nature study. He turns away impatiently from both his parents as his idols. Instead he reveres God, government authorities, laws and the heroes of history, fiction and the comics.

It is fascinating to realize that what distinguishes man so sharply from other creatures are these attitudes he develops soon after the age of 5: his inhibition and sublimation of sexuality, his interest in symbols, abstractions, systems and rules, his capacity for being inspired by heroes, God and spiritual ideals. These very human characteristics are brought out in him first by his special loves for each of his parents and then by having to give up his romantic attachment to one because of fear of rivalry with the other.

The glandular pressures of adolescence break up this impersonal, middle-childhood adjustment. The child's sexual and romantic drive now insists on some form of expression and it gradually breaks through the old inhibitions. Nevertheless, part of it will still be held in reserve and invested in idealistic aspirations—to the degree that the parents have these. The boy's romantic adoration of his mother, suppressed for years, veiled, disembodied, now lends mystery, chivalry and spirituality to his awakening love for a girl. He will want to protect, please, idolize her.

Men's idealization of woman also combines with their drive to create (Section 513) and these are the main inspiration for their creativity in architecture, engineering, technical inventiveness, scientific discovery, literature, drama, music, painting. A classic example is Dante's *Divine Comedy* which was inspired by and dedicated to Beatrice, a woman the poet had only seen, never known. To tie together this spiritual sequence: man can build a magnificent reality in adulthood out of what was only an illusion in early childhood—his loving, joyous, trusting, ingenuous, unrealistic overidealization of his two parents.

These capacities in man are developed highly in a few individuals, moderately in many, hardly at all in others. The capacity—for idealism, creativity, spirituality—is latent in every child. Whether he will realize them all will depend on his parents. At 3 and 4 years he will overidealize his parents anyway. If they have aspirations, if they have a respect for themselves, for each other and for him, he will continue to be inspired by their pattern, even after he appears to turn away from them in later childhood. If on the other hand they have no interests beyond their bodily needs, their child's estimation of them will gradually shrink down to life size and he won't try to go beyond that level himself.

14. Why we need idealistic children. If you raise a child who has idealism he will have no lack of opportunities to apply it. There are enormous, frightening problems in our country and in the world. Through our reliance on initiative and materialism we have accomplished technological miracles. But as our physical needs are met it becomes embarrassingly evident that we have made no progress in human relations, in spiritual serenity or in world security. Our rates of divorce, suicide and crime are among the highest in the world. Our race relations are barbaric—a disgrace to a nation that pretends to believe in freedom, equality and God. We have areas of poverty and demoralization in our own country that could be well on the way to solution in a year if we had the decency to face our responsibilities. Millions of dollars are spent persuading us to buy automobiles with five times the necessary horsepower and to buy cigarettes, which cause cancer.

We know how to produce food with fantastic efficiency but are holding production down at a time when there are more hungry people in the world than ever before in history.

We have an overwhelming supply of the most powerful weapons the world has ever known. Yet we are in imminent danger of annihilation, with no solution remotely in sight and no sense of security. Because of our power we are interfering arrogantly in the affairs of other nations and arousing worldwide resentment. We are spending billions each year on a race to the moon.

Our only realistic hope as I see it is to bring up our children with a feeling that they are in this world not for their own satisfaction but primarily to serve others. Children are proud to think that they can be truly useful and will rise to the challenge. This can begin very young. A baby of 9 months shouldn't be allowed to get the impression that it's all right to pull his mother's hair or bite her cheek but that he owes her respect. Between 1 and 2 years he shouldn't be allowed deliberately to break his own possessions nor to make a deliberate mess with them. By 2 he can be expected to go through the motions of helping his mother pick up his playthings. By 3 he should have such small chores as helping to set the table or empty the wastebaskets, even though they don't save his mother much work. By 7 or 8 he should be carrying out genuinely useful jobs each day.

In family conversations children should hear their parents' concern about problems of the community, the nation, the world. They should see that their parents are contributing directly to the solutions—by participating in the work of churches and welfare committees, for instance, belonging to concerned groups, making sizable contributions of money.

In school children should be studying not only the great accomplishments of their nation but its deficiencies and mistakes. Their schools should contain children from various races and backgrounds, not just out of fairness to minority groups but so that all kinds of children can learn to appreciate and get along with each other. High school and university students, while they are preparing for their eventual occupations, should spend time analyzing the unsolved problems in their own chosen fields—the human as well as the technical problems. It's also important, I think, for youths while they are still in school to volunteer or work for pay in part-time jobs where they can serve people who have serious unmet needs, then discuss these problems in class so that they won't acquire critical or condescending attitudes toward those different from themselves.

PARENTS ARE HUMAN

15. They have needs. Books about child care, like this one, put so much emphasis on all the needs that children have —for love, for understanding, for patience, for consistency, for firmness, for protection, for comradeship, for calories and vitamins—that parents sometimes feel physically and emotionally exhausted just from reading about what is expected of them. They get the impression that they are meant to have no needs themselves. They can't help feeling that an author who seems to be standing up for children all the time must be critical of parents when anything goes wrong.

It would be only fair if this book had an equal number of pages about the genuine needs of parents, the frustrations they constantly meet not only in the home but outside it, how tired they get, how much help their children could be if they were more considerate. The fact is that child rearing is a long, hard job and that parents are just as human as their children.

16. Some children are a lot more difficult than others. There is considerable evidence that different children are born with quite different temperaments. Parents can't order what they want. They take what they get. But parents have well-formed personalities, too, which they can't change overnight. One gentle couple might be ideally suited to raise a girl with a sweet, compliant nature, able to give her the freedom she needs in order to develop into an independent, capable person. They may not be nearly so ready for an energetic, assertive boy. They may find him uncomfortable, baffling and challenging, no matter how much they love him. Another couple may handle a spunky son they call Butch with ease and joy but be quite disappointed with a quiet one. Parents do the best they know how with the kind of child they receive.

17. At best, there's lots of hard work and deprivation. There is an enormous amount of hard work in child care—preparing the proper diet, washing diapers and clothes, cleaning up messes that an infant makes with his food and that an older child makes with his play, stopping fights and drying tears, listening to stories that are hard to understand, joining in games and reading stories that aren't very exciting to an adult, trudging around zoos and museums and carnivals, responding to pleas for help with homework, being slowed down in housework, yard work and cellar work by eager helpers, going to parent-teacher association meetings on tired evenings.

Children's needs account for a good part of the family budget, from the high rent or mortgage on a large enough house to the shoes that wear out or are outgrown in no time at all.

Children keep parents from parties, trips, theaters, meetings, games, friends. The fact that you prefer having children, wouldn't trade places with a childless couple for anything, doesn't alter the fact that you still miss your freedom.

Of course, parents don't have children because they want to be martyrs, or at least they shouldn't. They have them because they love children and want some of their very own. They also love children because they remember being loved so much by their parents in their own childhood. Taking care of their children, seeing them grow and develop into fine people, gives most parents—despite the hard work—their greatest satisfaction in life. This is creation. This is our visible immortality. Pride in other worldly accomplishments is usually weak in comparison.

18. Needless self-sacrifice sours everybody. But some conscientious young people facing the new responsibility of parenthood feel inside that they are called on to give up all their freedom and all their former pleasures, not as a matter of practicality, but almost as a matter of principle. Even if they do sneak off when a good chance comes, they feel too guilty to get full enjoyment. A little of this tendency is natural enough in the first few weeks of the first baby's life—it's all so new and overwhelming. But too much self-sacrificing is not good for parents or child. Parents become so preoccupied and tense that they're no fun for outsiders or for each other. They chafe at the imprisonment, despite the fact that it's self-imposed They can't help resenting the child, even though he hasn't asked for this amount of devotion As a result, they expect too much from him in return Everything gets lopsided. In theory, balance is achieved by giving your child what he needs most but keeping for yourselves such other interests and pleasures as won't hurt him at all. In this way you'll be able to love him more and show it more easily when you're with him.

19. Parents should expect something from their children. Since having children does mean giving up so much, good parents naturally do, and should expect something from their children in return: not spoken thanks for being born or being cared for—that's too much—but considerateness, affectionateness and willingness to accept the parents' standards and ideals. The parents want these qualities in their children not only selfishly, for themselves, but because they want their children to grow up to live cooperatively and happily with others.

If parents are too hesitant in asking for reasonable behavior —because they have misunderstood theories of self-expression, because they are self-sacrificing by nature, or because they are afraid of making their children dislike them—they can't help resenting the bad behavior that comes instead. They keep getting angrier underneath, without knowing what to do about it. This bothers the child, too. It makes him feel guilty and scared, but it also makes him meaner and all the more demanding. If, for example, a baby acquires a taste for staying up in the evening and his mother is afraid to deny him this pleasure, he may, over a period of several months, turn into a disagreeable tyrant who keeps her walking for hours. She's bound to dislike him for his tyranny. If she can be encouraged to be firm, it's amazing how fast he'll sweeten up and she will, too.

In other words, parents can't feel right toward their children in the long run unless they can make them behave reasonably, and children can't be happy unless they are behaving reasonably.

20. Parents are bound to get cross. I think that idealistic young people approaching parenthood assume that if they are the right sort they will have unlimited patience and love for their innocent baby. But this is not humanly possible. When your baby has been crying angrily for hours, despite all your patient efforts to comfort him, you can't go on feeling sympathetic. He seems like a disagreeable, obstinate, unappreciative person, and you can't help feeling angry—really angry. Or your older child has done something that he knows very well he shouldn't have done. Maybe he was so fascinated with a breakable object of yours or so eager to join some children on the other side of the street that he couldn't resist the temptation. Or maybe he was cross at you for having denied him something or angry at the baby for receiving so much attention. So he misbehaved from simple spite. When a child disobeys a well-understood and reasonable rule, you can't simply be a cool statue of justice. Any good parent feels strongly about right and wrong. You were taught to feel that way back in your own childhood. It's your rule that has been broken. It's probably your possession that has been damaged. It's your child, about whose character you care a great deal, who has done wrong. It's inevitable that you feel indignant. The child naturally expects this and is not hurt by it if your reaction is fair.

Sometimes it takes you a long time to realize that you are losing your temper. The child may have been putting on a series of irritating acts from the time he appeared at breakfast—making disagreeable remarks about the food, half deliberately knocking over a glass of milk, playing with something forbidden and breaking it, picking on a younger child—all of which you have tried to ignore in a supreme effort to be patient. Then at the final act, which perhaps isn't so bad, your resentment suddenly boils over, and it shocks you a little with its vehemence. Often when you look back over such a series of exasperating actions, you can see that the child has really been asking for firmness or punishment all morning and that it was your well-intentioned efforts at overpatience that made him go from one provocation to another, looking for a check.

We all get cross with our children, also, because of the pressures and frustrations we are feeling from other directions altogether. A sort of comic-strip example that's true to life concerns the father who comes home on edge from troubles that he's having in his work; he criticizes his wife, who then snaps at the older boy for something that ordinarily brings no disapproval, and he in turn picks on his younger sister.

21. Better to admit crossness. So far we have been discussing the inevitability of parental impatience and resentment from time to time. But it's just as important to consider a related question, Can the parent comfortably accept his cross feelings? Parents who aren't excessively strict with themselves are always able to admit their irritation. A natural, outspoken good mother whose child has been bedeviling her is able to say to a friend, half jokingly, "I don't think I can stand being in the house with him for another minute," or, "I'd enjoy giving him a thorough walloping." She may not carry out any of these thoughts, but she isn't ashamed to admit them to a sympathetic friend or to herself. It relieves her feelings to recognize them so clearly and to blow them off in talk. It also helps her to see what she has been putting up with and to be firmer in putting a stop to it.

It's the parents who set impossibly high standards for themselves, the parents who have angry feelings at times but can't believe that good parents should, who really suffer from them. When they detect such emotions stirring in themselves, they either feel unbearably guilty or try strenuously to deny them. But if a person tries to bury such feelings they only pop up somewhere else—as tenseness, for example, or tiredness or headache. Another indirect expression is overprotectiveness. A mother who can't ever admit that she feels antagonism toward her child imagines instead all the awful things that could beset him from other directions; she worries excessively about germs, or traffic. She tries to ward off these dangers by hovering over the child, and this tends to make him too dependent.

I'm not pointing out the problems created by denying crossness in order merely to relieve the uncomfortable feelings of parents. In general, what makes a parent miserable makes the child miserable, too. When a parent believes that antagonistic feelings are too horrible to admit, the child absorbs the same dread of them. In child guidance clinics, we see children who develop fears of imaginary dangers—fear of insects, fear of going to school, fear of being separated from their parents—that prove on investigation to be disguises for ordinary angry feelings toward their parents that these perfectionistic children dare not recognize.

To put it the other way around, a child is happier around parents who aren't afraid to admit their anger, because then he can be more comfortable about his own. And justified anger that's expressed tends to clear the air and leave everyone feeling better. I am talking not about being rough on children but about admitting your feelings. And I don't mean that all the antagonism expressed toward children is justified. Here and there you see a harsh, unloving parent who abuses his child all hours of the day, verbally or physically, with little excuse and no shame. What I have been discussing is the irritation of parents whose conscientiousness and devotion to their children is plain to see.

A loving parent who feels angry most of the time (whether it's expressed openly or not) is suffering from a real emotional strain and deserves help from a psychiatrist or a social worker (Section 577). The anger may be coming from some entirely different direction.

22. Children like to be kept good. I've probably given a false impression by focusing so much on irritation. Most of us, when family life is running with fair smoothness, get cross or angry only during occasional crises, though, as we all know, there are more of these on some days than others. The way we avoid irritation the rest of the time, whether we realize it or not, is by keeping our children under reasonable control and by being extra firm or sufficiently disapproving when things first threaten to go wrong. Such firmness is one aspect of parental love. Firmness, by keeping children on the right track, keeps them lovable. And they love us for keeping them out of trouble.

PARENTAL DOUBTS ARE NORMAL

23. Mixed feelings about pregnancy. We have an ideal about motherhood that says that a woman is overjoyed when she finds that she is going to have a baby. She spends the pregnancy dreaming about him. When he arrives she slips into the maternal role with ease and delight. This is all true to a degree—more in one case, less in another. But it is of course only one side of the picture. Medical studies have brought out (what wise women have known all along) that there are normal negative feelings connected with a pregnancy, too, especially the first one.

To some degree, the first pregnancy spells the end of carefree youth—very important to Americans. The maidenly figure goes gradually into eclipse, and with it goes sprightly grace. Both eclipses are temporary but very real. The woman realizes that after the baby comes there will be distinct limitations of social life and other outside pleasures. No more hopping into the car on the spur of the moment, going anywhere the heart desires and coming home at any old hour. The same budget has to be spread thinner, and her husband's attention, all of which has gone to her at home, will soon be going to two.

24. Feelings are different in every pregnancy. The changes to be expected because of the arrival of one more child do not look so drastic after you have had two or three, but medical experience shows that a good mother's spirit may rebel at times during any pregnancy. There may be obvious reasons why one pregnancy is more strained—perhaps it came unexpectedly soon, or the father is having tensions in his work, or there is serious illness on either side of the family, or there is disharmony between mother and father. On the other hand, there may be no explanation visible to the naked eye.

An obstetrician I know says he sometimes senses an inner

crisis with the second or third pregnancy in parents who are genuinely looking forward to a family of five or six children. A mother who really wants more children may still be disturbed subconsciously, during any one pregnancy, with sudden doubts about whether she will have the time, the physical energy or the unlimited stores of love that she imagines will be called for in taking care of another and another. Or the inner doubts may start with the father, who feels somewhat neglected as his wife becomes more and more preoccupied with the children. In either case, the blueness or grumpiness of one spouse soon has the other one feeling disappointed, too. To put it another way, each person, in order to keep on giving, must feel he is receiving something, too.

I don't want to make these reactions sound inevitable. I only want to reassure you that they do occur in the very best of parents and that in the great majority of cases they are temporary. The child when he arrives proves to be less of a challenge than the parents had anticipated subconsciously, probably because they have grown in spirit in response to the need.

25. Love for the baby comes gradually. Many a woman who is pleased and proud to be pregnant finds it hard to feel a personal love for a baby she's never seen or felt. But when he begins to move, it helps her to believe that he's a real person, after all. As the pregnancy progresses, her thoughts turn more realistically to him, to what it will mean to care for him.

A great majority of those who admit that their first reaction to pregnancy was predominantly one of dismay (and there are plenty of good people who feel this way) are reassured to find that their acceptance of the pregnancy and their fondness for the baby reaches a comfortable level before he is born.

But even when the anticipation is all that could be desired, there is often a letdown for the inexperienced mother when the baby actually arrives. She expects to recognize him immediately as her own flesh and blood, to respond to him with an overwhelming rush of maternal feeling. But in many cases this doesn't happen the first day or even the first week. Instead it is a gradual process that isn't complete until she has been home with him a little while.

Most of us have been taught that it's not fair to a coming baby to hope and expect that it will be a girl or a boy, in case it turns out to be the opposite. I wouldn't take this too seriously. We can't really begin to imagine and love a future baby without picturing it as being one sex or the other. That's the very first step. I think that all expectant parents have a preference for a boy or girl during each pregnancy, even though most of them will be quite ready to love a baby who turns out to be the opposite. So enjoy your imaginary baby and don't feel guilty if another kind arrives.

26. Why feelings are different for different children. Are parents meant to love all their children equally? This question worries a lot of conscientious parents because they suspect that in some ways they don't. When they reproach themselves about this, I think they are expecting the impossible of themselves. Good parents love their children equally in the sense that they are equally devoted to each. They want the best out of life for each and will make any necessary sacrifice to achieve this. But since all children are quite different, no parent can feel just the same about any two of them, either in the sense of enjoying their special charms or being displeased by their special faults.

It's the feeling of particular irritation toward one child that makes parents feel most guilty, especially if there is no clear reason for it. A mother says, "This one always rubs me the wrong way. Yet I'm constantly trying to be sweeter to him and to overlook his bad behavior."

27. Some causes of dissatisfaction. The reasons why parents sometimes get off on the wrong foot with one child are quite varied and are usually hidden under the surface. Two possible factors were mentioned in Section 24: the parents may not have felt ready for this pregnancy or there may have been unusual family tensions during it. The baby himself may have got the parents off to the wrong start by being completely different from what they had been secretly expecting —a boy when they were looking for a girl, or a very homely baby when they were anticipating a beauty, or a frail infant compared to their other husky children. The infant may cry for several months with colic and seem to spurn his parents' efforts to comfort him. The father may be disappointed when his son turns out to be no athlete, no scrapper; the mother because he's no student. It doesn't matter that the parents are intelligent people who well know that they can't order the kind of baby they want most. Being human, they have irrational expectations and can't help feeling let down.

As a child becomes a little older he may remind us, consciously or unconsciously, of a brother, sister, father or mother who made life hard for us at times. A mother's son may have traits like her younger brother, who used to be always in her hair—and yet she may have no conscious realization that this is the cause of a lot of her irritation.

A father may be excessively bothered by some particular characteristic in his young son—timidity, for instance—and never connect it with the fact that as a child he himself had a terrible time in overcoming timidity. You'd think that a person who has suffered a lot in trying to overcome some fault would be more sympathetic with it in his child. Usually it doesn't work that way.

28. Impatience and approval are part of child rearing. The very human tendency to react intensely to our children's behavior works positively for us, too: we strongly foster in our children the good traits that our parents fostered in us. We do it automatically, without having to think, because we learned our ideals so thoroughly in childhood. Otherwise, rearing our children would be ten times as hard as it is.

So it's human and normal and inevitable that we should feel quite differently about each of our children, that we should be impatient with certain characteristics in certain ones of them and proud of others. All these mixed attitudes are only different aspects of our deep feeling of obligation to bring up our children properly.

But if we feel too guilty about our chronic impatience with one child or another, it may produce increasing complications in our relations with him. Our guiltiness then gets to be harder on him than our irritation. This is discussed in Section 480.

29. The blue feeling. It's possible that you will find yourself feeling discouraged for a while when you first begin taking care of your baby. It's a fairly common feeling, especially with the first. You may not be able to put your finger on anything that is definitely wrong. You just weep easily. Or you may feel very bad about certain things. One woman whose baby cries quite a bit feels sure that he has a real disease, another that her husband has become strange and distant, another that she has lost all her looks.

A feeling of depression may come on a few days after the baby is born or not till several weeks later. The commonest time is when a mother comes home from the hospital, where she has been waited on hand and foot, and abruptly takes over full care of baby and household. It isn't just the work that gets her down. She may even have someone to do all the work, for the time being. It's the feeling of being responsible for the whole household again, plus the entirely new responsibility of the baby's care and safety. Then there are all the physical and glandular changes at the time of birth, which probably upset the spirits to some degree.

The majority of mothers don't get discouraged enough in this period to ever call it depression. You may think it is a mistake to bring up unpleasant things that may never happen. The reason I mention it is that several mothers have told me afterward, "I'm sure I wouldn't have been so depressed or discouraged if I had known how common this feeling is. Why, I thought that my whole outlook on life had changed for good and all." You can face a thing much better if you know that a lot of other people have gone through it, too, and if you know that it's just temporary.

If you begin to feel at all depressed, try to get some relief from the constant care of the baby in the first month or two, especially if he cries a great deal. Go to a movie, or to the beauty parlor, or to get yourself a new hat or dress. Visit a good friend occasionally. Take the baby along if you can't find anyone to stay with him. Or get your old friends to come and see you. All of these are tonics. If you are depressed, you may not feel like doing these things. But if you make yourself, you will feel a lot better. And that's important for the baby and your husband as well as yourself. If the depression does not lift in a few days or if it is becoming worse, you should promptly get in touch with a psychiatrist, through your regular doctor. A psychiatrist can be of great assistance and comfort at such a time.

When a mother feels blue and thinks that her husband seems indifferent, there are two sides to consider. On the one hand, anyone who is depressed feels that other people are less friendly and affectionate. But on the other hand, it's natural for a father, being human, to feel left out when his wife and the rest of the household are completely wrapped up in the baby. So it's a sort of vicious circle. The mother (as if she didn't have enough to do already!) has to remember to pay some attention to her husband. And she should give him every chance to share the care of the baby.

30. Other feelings. Most women find that they are more anxious than usual the first few weeks at home. They worry about the baby's crying and fretful spells, suspecting that something is seriously wrong. They worry about every sneeze and every spot of rash. They tiptoe into the baby's room to see whether he is still breathing. It's probably instinctive for mothers to be overly protective at this period. I suppose it's Nature's way of being sure that the millions of new mothers throughout the world, some of whom may be immature and careless, take their new responsibility seriously. A little worrisomeness might be a good thing for some irresponsible types. But of course it hits hardest the very conscientious ones who need it least. Fortunately it wears off.

Another kind of mood shift sometimes occurs. At first, in the hospital, a woman may feel very dependent on the nurses and grateful for the care they give the baby. Then comes a quick change of heart: she becomes confident she can take care of the baby herself and secretly resents the fact that the nurses don't let her take over. If she has a practical nurse at home, she may go through these two stages again. It certainly is normal for a mother to want to take care of her own baby by herself. The main reason she may not have this feeling at the start is because she is convinced she is inadequate. The stronger the sense of inferiority, the stronger will be the determination to assert her competence when she gains the courage.

THE FATHER'S PART

31. Men react to their wife's pregnancy with various feelings: protectiveness of the wife, increased pride in the marriage, pride about their virility (that's one thing men always worry about to some degree), anticipatory enjoyment of the child. But there can also be, way underneath, a feeling of being left out (just as a small boy may feel rejected when he finds his mother is pregnant), which can be expressed as grumpiness toward his wife, wanting to spend more evenings with his men friends, or flirtatiousness with other women. These reactions are no help to his wife, who craves extra support at the start of this unfamiliar stage of her life.

The father is apt to feel particularly left out during the hospital period with his first baby. He helps to get his wife safely to the hospital, where there are dozens of people to take care of her. Then he's really alone, with nothing to do outside of working hours. He can sit in the waiting room with some old magazines and worry about how the labor is going, or he can go to his unbelievably lonely home. It's no wonder that a man may take this occasion to drink in company at a bar. Where he works he gets some attention, but an awful lot of it is kidding. When he goes to see his wife and baby, the hospital doesn't make him feel like the head of the family; he's just another visitor who's tolerated at certain hours. When the time comes to take the family home, the concern of the mother (and of the grandmother or other helper, if any) is

*The father is apt to get the mistaken idea that he's
unimportant.*

all for the baby, and the father's function seems mainly to be that of porter. I don't mean by all this that a father expects the limelight or should have it at this time, but that he's apt to feel less important than usual and therefore let down.

32. The father's opportunity in the early weeks at home. A father shouldn't be surprised if he finds that he has mixed feelings at times toward his wife and toward his baby— during the pregnancy, during all the commotion of the hospital stage, and after they are all home again. Nevertheless, he can remind himself that his feelings are probably not nearly so churned up as his wife's, especially after the homecoming. She has been through the equivalent of an operation. She has been through an intense glandular change. If it's her first baby, she can't help feeling anxious. Any baby will make great demands on her strength and spirits at first. In a majority of cases, a woman's feelings are nearer the surface than a man's, more keenly felt. What all this adds up to is that most women need a great deal of support and comfort from their husbands at this time. To be able to give a lot to the baby, they must receive more than usual. Partly it's practical help—with the care of the baby, with the housework. Even more it's moral support: patience, understanding, appreciation, affection. The father's job may be complicated by the fact that if his wife is tired and upset she won't have the spirit to be charming and appreciative of his efforts. In fact, she may be complaining. But if he realizes how much she needs his help and love, it will encourage him to give it anyway.

33. The father and his baby. Some fathers have been brought up to think that the care of babies and children is the mother's job entirely. But a man can be a warm father and a real man at the same time.

We know that the father's closeness and friendliness to his children will have a vital effect on their spirits and characters for the rest of their lives. So the time for him to begin being a real father is right at the start. It's easiest then. The father and mother can learn together. In some cities, classes in baby care are given for fathers, too. If a father leaves it all to his wife for the first two years, she gets to be the expert and the boss as far as the children are concerned. He'll feel more bashful about pushing his way into the picture later.

Of course, I don't mean that the father has to give just as many bottles or change just as many diapers as the mother.

But it's fine for him to do these things occasionally. He might make the formula on Sunday. If the baby is on a 2 A.M. bottle in the early weeks, when the mother is still pretty tired, this is a good feeding for the father to take over. It's nice for him, if he can, to go along to the doctor's office for the baby's regular visits. It gives him a chance to bring up those questions that are bothering him and that he doesn't think his wife understands the importance of. It pleases the doctor, too. Of course, there are some fathers who get gooseflesh at the very idea of helping to take care of a baby, and there's no good to be gained by trying to force them. Most of them come around to enjoying their children later "when they're more like real people." But many fathers are only a little bashful. They just need encouragement. There's more on fathers in Sections 467–470, 483, 514–516.

RELATIONS WITH GRANDPARENTS

34. Grandparents can be a great help to young parents in all kinds of ways. They can also derive enormous pleasure from their grandchildren. They often ask wistfully, "Why couldn't I have enjoyed my own children the way I enjoy my grandchild? I suppose I was trying too hard and feeling only the responsibility."

In many parts of the world grandmothers are considered experts, and a young mother takes it for granted that when she has a question about her baby or needs a little help with him she'll ask her mother. When a mother has this kind of confidence in the grandmother, she can get not only advice but comfort. In our country, though, a new mother is often more inclined to turn to her doctor first, and some women don't ever think of consulting their mothers. This is partly because we are so used to consulting professional people about our personal problems—doctors, guidance counselors in school, marriage counselors, social workers, psychologists, ministers. Also, we take it for granted that knowledge advances rapidly, and so we often think that anyone who knew how to do a job twenty years ago is behind the times today. A more basic reason is that many young parents still feel too close to adolescence. They want to prove to the world and to themselves that they can manage their own lives. They may be afraid that the grandparents will want to tell them what to do, as if they were still dependent, and they don't want to put themselves back in that position.

35. Tensions are normal. In some families, all is harmony between parents and grandparents. In a few, disagreements are fierce. In others, there is little tension, most commonly concerning the care of the first child, but it wears off with time and adjustment.

The fortunate young woman who has lots of natural, comfortable self-confidence can turn easily to her mother for help when she needs it. And when the grandmother makes a suggestion on her own, the mother finds she can accept it if it seems good, or she can tactfully let it pass and go her own way.

But most young parents don't have that amount of assurance at first. Like almost everybody else in a new job, they are sensitive about possible inadequacies, touchy about criticism.

Most grandparents remember this well from their earlier days and try hard not to interfere. On the other hand, they have had experience, they feel they've developed judgment, they love their grandchildren dearly, and they can't help having opinions. They see surprising changes from the time when they cared for babies—flexible feeding schedules, early feeding of solid foods, perhaps later toilet training—and these are hard to get used to. Even when they accept new methods, they may be bothered by what seems to them to be excessive zeal in carrying them out. (When you are a grandparent yourself, you'll probably understand better what I mean.)

I think that if young parents have the courage, they can keep relations most comfortable by permitting or even inviting the grandparents to speak up about their opinions. Frank discussions are usually, in the long run, more comfortable than veiled hints or uneasy silences. A mother who is pretty sure she is managing the baby properly can say, "I know that this method doesn't seem quite right to you, and I'm going to discuss it again with the doctor to be sure that I've understood his directions." This doesn't mean the mother is giving in. She certainly reserves the right to make her own decision in the end. She is only recognizing the grandmother's good intentions and evident anxiety. The young mother who shows reasonableness will reassure the grandmother not only in regard to the present problem but also in regard to the future in general.

A grandmother can help the mother do a good job by showing her confidence in her and fitting in with her methods as far as possible. This puts the mother in a mood to ask advice when she is in doubt.

When the children are left in the care of the grandparents, whether for half a day or for two weeks, there should be frank understanding and reasonable compromising. The parents must have confidence that the children will be cared for according to their beliefs in important matters (that, for instance, they won't be compelled to eat food they don't like, be shamed for bowel accidents, or be frightened about policemen). On the other hand, it's unfair to expect grandparents to carry out every step of management and discipline as if they were exact replicas of the parents. It won't hurt a child to be a little more respectful to the grandparents, if that's what they want, or to have their meals on a different schedule, or to be kept cleaner or dirtier. If the parents don't feel right about the way the grandparents care for the children, of course they shouldn't ask them to take care of them.

36. The parent who is sensitive about advice. More than average tension may arise if the young mother (or father) has felt a lot of parental criticism throughout her childhood. This inevitably leaves her inwardly unsure of herself, outwardly impatient of disapproval, and grimly determined to prove her independence. She may take to new philosophies of child rearing with unusual enthusiasm and push them hard. They seem like a wholesome change from what she remembers. They are also a way to show the grandparents how old-fashioned they are and to bother them a bit. It's really fun to battle about theory when you're mad at the opponent. The only trouble is that it's the child's upbringing that provides the ammunition on both sides. All I'm suggesting is that parents who find that they are constantly upsetting grandparents should at least ask themselves whether they might be doing some of it on purpose, without quite realizing it.

37. The managerial grandmother. Occasionally there is a grandmother so constituted that she has always been too managerial with her daughter and she can't stop now even though the daughter is now a mother. Such a young mother may have a tough time at first keeping her perspective. She dreads advice. When it comes, it makes her angry, but she dare not express her feelings. If she accepts the advice, she feels dominated. If she turns it down, she feels guilty. How, then, can the beginning mother in this situation protect herself? It sounds as if she'd have to lift herself by her bootstraps. In a way she does have to, but it can be done gradually, with practice. In the first place, she can keep reminding herself that she is the mother now and that the baby is hers to take care of as she thinks best. She should be able to get support from the doctor or the public health nurse when she has been made to doubt her own method. She is surely entitled to the support of her husband, especially if it's his mother who is interfering. If he thinks that in a certain situation his mother is right, he should be able to say so to his wife, but at the same time he can show his mother that he stands with his wife against interference.

The young mother will come out better if she can learn gradually not to run away from the grandmother and not to be afraid to hear her out, because both these reactions reveal, in a way, that she feels too weak to stand up to her. Harder still, she can learn how not to get boiling mad inside or how not to explode outwardly in a temper. You might say she's entitled to get angry, which is true. But pent-up anger and explosions are both signs that she has already been feeling submissive for too long, out of fear of making the grandmother mad. A dominating grandmother usually senses these indirect signs of timidity and takes advantage of them. A mother shouldn't feel guilty about making her mother mad, if it must come to that. Actually, it shouldn't be necessary to blow up at the grandmother—or at least not more than once or twice. The mother can learn to speak up for herself right away, in a matter-of-fact, confident tone, before she gets angry ("Well, the doctor told me to feed him this way," "You see, I like to keep him as cool as possible," "I don't want him to cry for long"). This calm, assured tone is usually the most effective way to convince the grandmother that the mother has the courage of her convictions.

In these occasional situations that contain a lot of continual tension, it is often helpful for the parents, and perhaps the grandparents, to consult a professional person—wise family doctor, psychiatrist, social worker, sensible minister—preferably in separate interviews, so that each can present the picture as he sees it, even though they may all come together for a final discussion. In any case it should be understood that, in the end, the responsibility and the right to make the decision are the parents'.

CALLERS AND VISITORS

38. Limit the visitors at first. The birth of a baby is an occasion that brings relatives and friends flocking, to congratulate the parents and to see the baby. This is gratifying to the parents and fills them with pride. However, too much of it may be exhausting to the mother. How much is too much? It's very different in different cases. Most mothers tire easily the first few weeks at home. They have just gone through the equivalent of an operation and in addition have felt the effects of some intense glandular changes. Perhaps more important still are the emotional shifts that are called for, especially with the first baby, which are discussed in Section 29.

Visitors are pure pleasure to some people—relaxing, distracting, rejuvenating. To most of us, however, only a few old friends have such a good effect. Other visitors, to a greater or lesser degree, make us somewhat tense, even when we enjoy seeing them, and leave us somewhat fatigued, especially if we aren't feeling well. When a new mother becomes tired out, it gets her off on the wrong foot at the time of the most important transition in her life, and this is too bad for everybody. I think a new mother should set strict limits for visitors right from the start, see how it goes, and then increase the number very gradually if she finds she has plenty of strength left over. It helps a mother to get the doctor's agreement to strict limits. Then she doesn't have to feel that she's being inhospitable; she's just following doctor's orders. I'd tell each person who calls up, "The doctor says I can see only one visitor a day for fifteen minutes, beginning tomorrow. Can you come Tuesday about four P.M.?" There are lots of additional reasons that can be thrown in to strengthen the point; extra-long labor, breast feeding, slowness in getting strength back.

To people who appear at the house without a telephone call, you can act pleased but guilty: "The doctor wants me to see only one visitor a day for the next week, but come in for just a minute, anyway."

One mother found it helped to tack on her front door a notice saying she didn't want life insurance for the baby, photographs of the baby, nursery equipment, or sets of books, so she would not have to answer the door for salesmen.

39. Visitors playing with the baby. Most visitors get all excited when they see a baby. They want to hold him, joggle him, tickle him, jounce him, waggle their heads at him and keep up a blue streak of baby talk. Some babies can take a lot, some can't take any, and most are in between. A mother has to use her judgment about how much is wise and then be very firm. This is hard to carry out, though, because it's one of the great pleasures of parenthood to have people enjoy the baby. Most babies are easily tired, too, by strange places and strange happenings, as visits to the doctor's office prove.

HELP FOR THE MOTHER

40. Arranging for extra help in the beginning. If you can figure out a way to get someone to help you the first few weeks you are taking care of the baby, by all means do so. If you try to do everything by yourself and get exhausted, you may have to get help and have it for longer in the end. Besides, getting tired and depressed starts you and the baby off on the wrong foot.

Your mother may be the ideal helper, if you get along with her easily. If you feel she is bossy and still treats you like a child, this is not the time to have her. You will want to feel that the baby is your own and that you are doing a good job with him. It will help to have a person who has taken care of babies before, but it's most important of all to have someone that you enjoy having around.

If you can afford to hire a houseworker or a practical baby nurse for a few weeks, there will be the advantage over a relative that you can let her go if she doesn't work out right. In one way, a houseworker is best—the mother can have the satisfaction of taking complete care of her baby from the start —but a houseworker is hard to find. Next best is a practical nurse who will do part of the housework, who is willing to fit in with your way of doing things, who will let you feel that the baby is yours, and who has a relaxed, agreeable personality. If you find that you have a practical nurse who acts as if the baby were hers rather than yours and criticizes everything you do, for goodness' sake get rid of her right away and take a chance on finding a better one.

How long should you engage a helper for? It will depend, of course, on your finances, on your desire to take over, and on your strength. Each day as your strength increases, take over a little more of the work. If, when 2 weeks are nearly up, you find that you still get tired easily, then by all means keep the helper, whether you can really afford her or not. She is not a luxury, under these circumstances, but a necessity. If you take over before you are strong enough, it will cost more in the end, financially and spiritually, than if you keep her on for another week or two.

Most expectant mothers feel a little scared at the prospect of taking sole charge of a helpless baby for the first time. If you have this feeling, it doesn't mean that you won't be able to do a good job or that you have to have a nurse to show you how. But if you feel really panicky, you will probably learn more comfortably with an agreeable practical nurse—or relative, if this can be arranged.

If you can't have regular help, you may be able to afford and find a woman to come in once or twice a week to do the cleaning, help you catch up on the housework, and watch the baby for a few hours while you go out for a visit.

Whether or not you have your own help, you should arrange to have a visiting nurse come in for a visit or two. See Section 74.

41. Practical aids. If you are going to be washing the baby's diapers yourself, now is the time to get an automatic washer and dryer if you can possibly afford them. They save hours of work each week, and precious energy. They are somewhat less essential if you can get diaper service but still very worthwhile.

New mothers find it a great help to send out the regular laundry, at least temporarily during the early months of baby care. This is a good time to simplify housework by putting unnecessary furniture and furnishings in a storeroom for a couple of months or a couple of years. Learn to use more of the easily prepared foods for a while.

42. Sitters are a boon to parents and can help a child to develop independence. You and your child should know your sitter well. For night sitting with a baby who doesn't waken, it may only be necessary for her to be sensible and dependable. But for babies who waken and for children above the age of a year who might waken, it's important for the sitter to be a person they know and like while awake. It is frightening to most children to waken and find a stranger. If the sitter is to care for the child or even just put him to bed, you should be sure from seeing her in action with your child that she understands and loves children and can manage them with kindliness and firmness. So try to engage the sitter a few times while you and she will be there together for a while. Then the young child can get used to her before she has to do too much for him directly. As the child gradually accepts her, she can do more for him.

It is certainly important that you stick to one or two sitters as much as possible. You can learn about capable sitters or about a reliable agency through a friend whose judgment you trust.

Young or old? It's a matter of maturity and spirit rather than years. I've occasionally seen a girl as young as 14 who was extremely capable and dependable, but it's unfair to expect such qualities in most girls that age. And some grown women may prove unreliable or harsh or ineffectual. One older woman has a knack with children. Another is too inflexible to adapt to a new child or is so nervous that she makes child and parent uneasy.

To keep things straight, it's sensible to have a permanent notebook for the sitter, listing the child's routine, some of the things he may ask for (in his words), the telephone numbers of the doctor and of a neighbor to call in an emergency if you can't be reached, bedtime hours, what the sitter may help herself to in the kitchen, the whereabouts of linen, night-clothes, and other things that may be needed, how to turn the furnace up or down.

But most of all, know your sitter and know that your child trusts her.

There is more on the qualities of a mother's substitute in Section 778.

Equipment and Clothing

EQUIPMENT YOU'LL NEED

43. Getting things ahead of time. Some women don't feel like buying anything until they have their baby. The advantage of getting and arranging everything ahead of time is that it lightens the burden later. A certain number of mothers feel tired and easily discouraged at the time they begin taking care of the baby themselves. Then a little job like buying half a dozen nipples looms as a real ordeal. Mothers who have gotten depressed have said to me afterward, "The next time, I'm going to buy everything that I need way ahead. Every pin and nightie is going to be in its place."

What do you really have to have, in the way of equipment, to take care of a new baby? There are no exact rules, but here are some suggestions:

44. A place to sleep. You may want to get a beautiful bassinet, lined with silk. But the baby doesn't care. All he needs is sides to keep him from rolling out, and something soft but firm in the bottom for a mattress. A crib, a clothes or market basket, a box or bureau drawer will do. Mattresses made of foam rubber or hair keep their shape best, but they are more expensive. (Occasionally hair, principally pig's hair, causes allergy in a susceptible child in an allergic family. This risk can be avoided by enclosing the mattress in an airtight casing made for this purpose.) You can make a mattress by folding up an old blanket and tufting it. Don't use a soft pillow for a mattress. There's a slight risk of the baby's smothering in one. The sides of a small bassinet will probably have to be lined to keep the baby from hurting his hands.

He doesn't need a pillow for his head, and it's better not to use one.

45. Something to bathe him in and dress him on. The baby can be bathed in the kitchen sink, a plastic tub (get one with a wide edge to rest your arm on), a dishpan or a washstand. You can bathe and dress the baby on a low table, at which you sit (a card table with steady legs is a good size), or on the top of a fairly high bureau, at which you stand. You can sit on a high stool at the sink.

A folding, fabric bathtub is a convenience if you can afford it and have room for it. The tub part is made of waterproof material hung from a frame on high legs. It is high enough so that you don't break your back bathing the baby. When the bath is finished, a flat canvas top covers the tub, and on this the baby can be dried, dressed and changed.

46. Other Equipment

Safety pins.

Child's nose syringe, rubber with a glass tip, to remove mucus during colds.

Mouth thermometer, to take axillary (armpit) temperatures.

Absorbent cotton. A pound roll of sterile absorbent cotton. You make soft swabs for removing dried mucus from the nose and for cleaning the outer ear by firmly rolling a small piece of cotton between moist finger and thumb.

Vitamin drops, usually containing vitamins A, C and D. Ask your doctor which preparation to get.

Soap. Any mild soap is satisfactory. A soap with hexachlorophene helps to prevent infection.

Diaper pail. This should hold 3 gallons, be nonrusting and have a cover. You can use a plastic bag for a liner to prevent rusting. Some mothers like two, one for wet and another, containing soapy water, for soiled diapers. If you are going to use a diaper service, they will provide a container.

An inclined plastic seat in which the baby can be strapped, carried short distances, set down almost anywhere, and from which he can watch the world go by, is a most useful accessory.

THE CLOTHES HE NEEDS

47. Knitted nightgowns are entirely practical and can be worn also during a baby's period awake and even during visits.

The mittens on the end of the sleeves, which are to keep him from scratching himself, can be worn open or closed. The long gowns make it harder for the baby to kick off his coverings, the short ones may be preferable for a hot climate. Buy 3 or 4 anyway. It would be convenient to have 2 or 3 more, especially if you don't have a washer and dryer. They come in only the newborn size.

48. Shirts: There are 2 styles of undershirt: pullover and snap closing. The latter is slightly easier to put on a small, limp baby. Medium weight and short sleeves should be sufficient unless a baby will live in an unusually cold house. Some brands have tabs to pin diapers to, which will help an inexperienced mother to keep the diapers from falling down. Start with the 1-year size; or if you are fussy about fit, the 6-month size. Buy 3 or 4 anyway. It would be convenient to have 2 or 3 more, especially if you don't have a washer and dryer.

49. Stretch suits of nylon or orlon, sometimes combined with cotton, or of terry, are increasingly popular for daytime wear for babies but can also be used for sleeping. They snap from neck down one or both legs.

50. Sacks and kimonos are short jackets and long gowns, front opening, usually of flowered cotton flannelette, to be worn over shirt or nightie for a dressier appearance; not essential, often a shower present.

51. Sweaters, of orlon, are useful in a cold house, a cold sleeping room or outdoors in cold weather, to add extra warmth over or under the other clothes when the baby is up, under other coverings when in bed. Be sure that the neck opening has sufficient give or that there are shoulder snaps or buttons.

52. Outer clothes, for outings in cold climates.

A bunting or pram bag is a zippered bag in which the baby is encased up to the shoulders.

A pram suit has a coverall shape and also encloses the feet and may come in one or two pieces. It should zip or snap from neck to foot.

These outer garments may be either quilted, or of acrylic blanketing, or, for the older child, of wool.

53. Bibs

Small round bibs are useful for keeping drool off the clothes. For the mess that a baby or child always makes with his solid food he needs a large bib of plastic or terry (or a combination), preferably with a pocket along the lower edge to catch the food that comes running down. Plastic is easily rinsed but just looks uncomfortable to the adult. Be sure there is a cloth binding around the neck. A terry bib can also be used for wiping the face if you can find a dry corner. Bibs are gift items.

54. Diapers. If you live in a city, you will probably want to use a diaper service if you can afford it. It saves time, effort and drying space. The company supplies the diapers as well as launders them.

The most popular materials for diapers are gauze, cotton flannel and bird's-eye. The gauze diapers are quicker drying but do not hold as much of the urine when the baby is larger. Two dozen will cover your needs if you wash them every day and don't use too many for sheets, towels, etc. Six dozen will cover all possible needs. Get the large size.

55. Diaper liners (not essential). There are diaper liners, made of paper, to put in the diaper at the times of day when bowel movements are expected, to keep the diaper from becoming soiled.

There are also liners made of treated nylon that are meant to keep the baby's skin less wet.

56. Waterproof pants over the diapers are a special help when you are going places with the baby. Whether you use waterproof pants at home depends on how well the baby's skin stands up. When a baby has no waterproof pants on, a lot of the urine in the diaper is absorbed into the surrounding clothing and evaporated. With waterproof pants the diapers stay much wetter and warmer. This favors diaper rash. As long as your baby's skin is clear in the diaper region, you can use pants as much as is convenient. When there is diaper rash, leave them off. Wash them each day.

Pants come in pull-on and snap-on styles. Waterproof silk or nylon pants stay soft longer than plastic plants. The elastic at the edges is less irritating when enclosed in a soft binding.

57. Bed or sleep bags and walkers. By 6 months, when babies can move about in their cribs, most mothers find it more practical to put them to bed in sleep bags or walkers than to try to keep blankets over them. (They simply crawl out from under their covers.) The bags are shaped like long nighties, which cover the feet and have sleeves. The bed walkers are shaped like coveralls or snowsuits, enclosing each leg separately, including the foot. (The sole of the foot may be of tough, nonskid material.) These bed bags and walkers come in a wide range of materials to provide different degrees of warmth: plissé, cotton flannel, cotton blanketing, 75% acetate plus 25% acrylic, 100% acrylic. There is also "thermal" material. Many of the bags of blanketing can be let out in the length and shoulders as a child grows.

If a baby or child is going to sleep in a room which is warm enough so that his mother would be comfortable wearing a cotton dress or sleeping under a cotton blanket, his bag or walker shouldn't be warmer than cotton blanketing. If his room will be cold enough so that an adult would require a good wool or acrylic blanket for covering, he will need an acrylic bag or walker.

Incidentally, a baby or child doesn't need more in the way of clothing or covering than an adult; if anything, less.

It is most convenient when the zipper on a bed walker goes from neck to foot.

58. Other clothes. Knitted wool caps are all right for going outdoors in the kind of weather that makes grownups put on overcoats, or for sleeping in an equally cold room. For milder weather, caps are unnecessary; most babies don't like them anyway. You don't need booties and stockings, at least until your baby is sitting up and playing around in a cold house. Dresses make a baby look pretty, but are unnecessary otherwise, and bothersome to the baby and the mother.

BEDCLOTHES

59. Blankets. Even if you use bed bags or walkers as the baby's principal bed covering, you will probably need a couple of blankets for certain occasions or for extra covering when it's cold. A knitted shawl is a particularly convenient form of blanket for a baby because it wraps around him so easily when he is up, and stays tucked when it is over him in bed. Acrylic blankets and shawls are both warm and washable. Blankets should be large enough to tuck well under a crib mattress.

Cotton "receiving blankets," which have little warmth, are useful for wrapping around the baby who would otherwise kick off his bed coverings or for tightly swaddling the young baby who is only comfortable and secure when held immobile (Section 290).

60. Waterproof sheeting of plastic or rubber. Most popular is sheeting that has a flannelette backing on both surfaces. It stays in place, and the sheet does not slip on it. It is more comfortable in case the baby happens to get in contact with it. Since it allows some circulation of air under the baby, there is usually no need to cover it with a quilted pad, and this makes a saving in laundry. However, in hot weather you may still need a pad, too. The sheeting should be washed (it will go in the machine) each day if it gets wet with urine, so you will need two.

The waterproof sheeting should preferably be large enough to tuck in around the mattress. Otherwise the edges of the mattress may get wet at times. Incidentally, the plastic cover that comes on most new mattresses is not sufficient by itself. Sooner or later urine gets into the air holes and makes it smell.

Additional small squares of flannel-backed sheeting will save more laundry. Place one under the baby's hips. It will keep the bedsheet dry if the baby stays in one place. The mother can use one as a lap protector.

61. Pads. If you are using plain waterproof sheeting (without flannel backing), you will need to cover it with a quilted pad. This is to absorb moisture and allow some circulation of air under the baby's body; otherwise the skin stays too hot and wet. The number of pads you will need will depend on how often the laundry is done, how much the baby wets, how much he spits up. You will need 3 anyway, and 6 are more convenient.

62. Sheets. You will need 3 to 6 sheets. If you are using a small bassinet at first, you can use diapers for sheets. For anything larger, the best sheets are made of cotton stockinette. They are easy to wash, quick to dry, spread smoothly without ironing and do not feel clammy when wet. Fitted sheets can be bought to cover the crib mattress.

EQUIPMENT THAT MAY OR MAY NOT BE NECESSARY

63. Scales. If a baby is doing well and is seen by his doctor regularly, there is no real need to have scales at home. You can rent good scales at a children's store or hospital equipment store if your doctor thinks them necessary.

64. A carriage (pram) is used primarily by mothers in the Northeastern part of the United States to take their babies on daily outings in or to give them naps in, on the porch. They often buy the finest and handsomest carriage they can afford and get a lot of satisfaction out of it. But in most parts of this country mothers don't think about carriages—or outings. A stroller is a handy way to take a young child shopping and on other errands, especially for those in cities who don't have a car at their disposal.

Families with cars usually find that a canvas car bed for the baby, which attaches to the car securely, is a necessity.

There are contrivances for carrying a baby a few months old strapped to the mother's back or side so that her hands can be free during work, walks and shopping.

65. Bottle warmer. It isn't considered necessary any longer to warm a baby's bottle. It can of course be warmed in any kind of container. An electric warmer is very handy when the hot water supply is undependable. There is a special warmer that plugs into an automobile cigarette lighter.

66. Bath thermometer. Not necessary, but a comfort to the inexperienced mother.

67. Toiletries

Baby Lotion. Not really necessary unless the skin is dry, though mothers enjoy applying it. A lotion with hexachlorophene helps to prevent mild skin infections.

Baby oils, most of which are made of mineral oil, have been used extensively, for dry or normal skin or for diaper rash. But tests have shown that mineral oil itself may cause a very mild rash in some babies. So it is sensible not to use it routinely unless a mother finds by testing that it has more advantage than disadvantage in her baby's case.

Baby powder. Helps a little to avoid chafing, but it is not necessary in most cases. (Zinc stearate powder is not considered safe for babies, because it is irritating when breathed into the lungs.) Any powder should be applied fairly carefully (shake it into your hand first), so that there isn't a cloud of it around the baby's face.

Zinc ointment. In tube or jar, to protect the skin when there is a diaper rash.

FORMULA EQUIPMENT

68. Nursing bottles. If you know ahead of time that you are not going to breast-feed the baby, buy at least 9 of the 8-ounce bottles. You will use 6 to 8 a day in the beginning for the formula, and you will surely break a few eventually. If you expect to breast-feed, buy at least 3, for occasional formula feedings, water and juice.

The nipple fits into a plastic screw-on cap. Except when the baby is nursing. the nipple is stored upside down in the bottle and a plastic disk covers the opening.

Pyrex bottles are more expensive but don't break because of too rapid heating or chilling. In the long run they are probably an economy for most mothers.

Plastic bottles don't break when adults or babies drop them. Water and juice can be given just as well from 8-ounce bottles, even though they are unnecessarily large. But some mothers prefer 4-ounce bottles for this purpose. Two or 3 of these will be enough.

There are also disposable bottles of thin flexible plastic that come in a long strip already sterilized. The mothers who use them swear by them.

69. Nipples. A dozen if the baby will be bottle-fed, a half dozen if breast-fed. You have to have a few extra in case you drop one on the floor or are having trouble making the nipple holes the right size.

Nipples made with silicone are more expensive but don't deteriorate from boiling and milk fat.

Most people use nipples with one or more holes in the top. If you have trouble with clogged nipples, you can buy those with "cross-cut" openings or you can cross-cut your own (Section 190).

70. A pail, kettle or roaster with lid for sterilizing the bottles, preferably 8 inches high and 9 inches in diameter so that it will hold 8 bottles vertically in a wire bottle rack. There are electric sterilizers but they are an unnecessary expense.

71. A container for mixing formula, marked in ounces. A glass quart measure marked in ounces is very convenient.

If you don't want to buy a quart measure, you can use any measuring cup marked in ounces and then mix in any saucepan or pitcher that holds a quart. In a pinch you can use a nursing bottle for a measure, but it is inconvenient to pour into.

72. A funnel is helpful in getting the formula into the bottles. A **jar brush** and a **nipple brush** are essential.

73. The other equipment you will need for making a formula does not need to be bought specially.

Long tablespoon for stirring.

Set of measuring spoons for measuring the sugar or syrup.

Knife to level the sugar in the measuring spoon. (Not necessary if you use syrup.)

Can opener for evaporated milk. A beer-can opener is easiest.

Tongs, rubber-coated in the part that grips a bottle, are good for handling hot bottles; but if you follow the method in Section 183, you'll let the bottles cool before handling them.

Medical and Nursing Care

THE VISITING NURSE

74. Whether or not you have help at home, you ought to try to get a visiting nurse or public health nurse to come in once or twice in the early days. She will show you how to make the formula, bathe the baby and follow other directions of the doctor. And you can always call her later when you have questions and problems. There are visiting nurses or public health nurses in most cities and in many country districts. Ask the doctor or the nurse in the hospital, telephone the Visiting Nurse Association or local health department, or write the state health department.

THE BABY'S DOCTOR

75. Regular visits. The way to be sure that your baby is doing well is to have him checked by a doctor regularly. The visits should be once a month in the early months, and at least once every 3 months during the second year. The doctor will want to weigh and measure the baby to see how he's growing, examine him to see that he's developing well, give him his inoculations. The mother will have five or ten questions that she wants to ask, with her first baby anyway. It's a good idea to have a little notebook that's always handy for writing down questions when they come to your mind at home, and also for noting developments, such as teething or a rash, that you may want to know the date of later. Of course, some families live so far away from a doctor that they can't plan to visit him monthly. In some cases the mother and doctor can keep in touch by telephone. Naturally, every baby won't get into trouble just because his doctor doesn't see him regularly.

But experience has shown that the monthly visit is vitally important for the occasional baby who is not doing well and a worthwhile and comforting precaution for all the rest.

76. Who's to be the doctor? In many cases the family physician who has delivered the baby will go on seeing him afterward. A family doctor who is used to taking care of babies can do just as good a job as the specialist, unless some unusual problem comes up. In large cities the mother may have been delivered by a specialist in obstetrics who doesn't take care of the baby afterward. Then she will want to find a children's specialist (known as a pediatrician or pediatrist). One mother gets along best with a doctor who is casual, not too fussy about details. Another feels right only if she gets every direction down to the last period. You may have more confidence in an older man or feel that you are imposing less on a younger man, or you may prefer a woman. If you have definite feelings about what kind of doctor you want, discuss the matter with your obstetrician. He will know the children's specialists who are available.

77. The child-health conference. A city baby whose parents can't afford regular visits to a private doctor can and should attend a "well-baby clinic" or "child-health conference" at a hospital or child-health station. These have been established in many country districts, too. If you live in the country, write ahead of time to the state health department to find where the nearest clinic is. In a city you can find the nearest clinic by telephoning the city health department or the Visiting Nurse Association. On the staff of the well-baby clinic or child-health conference are doctors and nurses who work as a team. The doctor examines the baby at regular intervals, gives inoculations and advises the mother. The nurse helps the mother in carrying out his recommendations and in dozens of other practical child-care matters. She can make a home visit soon after the mother and baby leave the hospital and at other times when the mother has a problem that won't wait until the next clinic visit.

78. Getting along with a doctor. In most cases the parents and the doctor soon come to know and trust each other and get along fine. But occasionally, since they are all human beings, there may be misunderstandings and tensions. Most of these are avoidable or easily cleared up with frankness on both sides.

Unless expense is no concern, it's a good idea to discuss charges when first engaging a physician. It's easier at the start than later. Though this may embarrass you, remember that it's an old story with the doctor and he should be able to take it. Many physicians will lower their fees for people with less-than-average income and are glad to know of the need ahead of time.

Most new parents are bashful in the beginning about asking questions about baby care that they are afraid are too simple or silly. It's foolish to worry about this. If there's any kind of question on your mind, you're entitled to an answer— that's what doctors are for. A doctor is pleased to answer any questions that he can; the easier, the better.

Even if you feel sure that your doctor will be grumpy about something that is probably not serious but that you are nonetheless concerned about, call him anyway. Your child's health is more important than the doctor's feelings or your own feelings.

It often happens that a parent asks about a problem and the doctor explains part of it but gets sidetracked before he has answered the parent's most important question. If the mother is bashful, she may hesitate about coming back to that point and go home somewhat unsatisfied. She should encourage herself to be bold, to make clear exactly what she wants to know, so that the doctor can give her the answer or, if it is out of his line, refer her to some other professional person.

79. Office visits for illness. Most parents remember that when they were sick as children the doctor made home visits. It seems wrong to them to take a sick child out to the doctor's office. Of course, the office visit is more convenient for the busy doctor. But he wouldn't advise it if it had not proved entirely safe, in these days of heated cars, and definitely beneficial in many illnesses. With many throat infections it is now important to take a throat culture to discover whether a streptococcus is the cause. If it is, the use of antibiotic medication is essential. If not, it is better not to prescribe it. It is often helpful during an illness which is still undiagnosed to get a urine specimen or a blood count. After an injury an X ray is often desirable. In these situations and many others the doctor can do a better job in his office.

80. Asking for a consultation. If your child has some illness or condition that worries you intensely and you would like another expert opinion, it is always your right to ask freely for a consultation. Many parents are hesitant about doing so, fearing that this would express lack of confidence in the present doctor and hurt his feelings. But it is a regular procedure in the practice of medicine, and the doctor should be able to take it in his stride. Actually, a doctor, like any other human being, senses uneasiness in the people he deals with, even when it is unspoken, and it makes his job harder. A consultation usually clears the air for him as well as for the family.

81. Frankness works best. I think the main point in all these situations is that if you are unsatisfied with your doctor's advice or care, you should try to bring it out into the open right away, in the most matter-of-fact manner you can muster. An early meeting of minds is easier for him and you than allowing your tension and irritation to accumulate inside you.

Sometimes, though, a patient and doctor find that they just can't get along together, no matter how frank and cooperative they try to be, and then it's better all around to admit it openly. Every doctor, including the most successful, has learned that he doesn't suit everybody, and he takes this philosophically.

82. The time for telephone calls. Find out from your doctor what time of day he prefers phone calls, particularly about new illness that may require a home visit. A majority of illnesses in children first show definite symptoms during the afternoon, and most doctors would like to know about them as early in the afternoon as possible so that they can plan their visits efficiently. Naturally, if the symptoms that worry you don't come on till later, that's the time you have to call the doctor.

83. When to call the doctor. After you've raised a couple of babies, you'll have a good idea of which symptoms or questions require prompt contact with the doctor and which can wait till tomorrow or the next visit. But new parents often ask for a list. Even if they never consult the list, they feel more comfortable having one.

No list can be anywhere near complete. There are, of course, hundreds of different diseases and injuries. You always have to use your own common sense. The following discussion contains only a few general guides.

By far the most important rule, as I see it, is to consult the doctor promptly, at least by telephone, if a baby or child **looks different** (in general appearance) or **acts differently**. By this I mean such signs as unusual paleness, unusual tiredness, unusual drowsiness, lack of interest, unusual irritability, anxiousness, restlessness, prostration.

Fever is discussed in Section 618. How high or low it is is less important than whether the child seems really sick. A high fever often accompanies a mild infection after the age of 1 or 2 years, and a young baby can be quite sick with little or no fever. As a general rule, consult the doctor if the baby has a temperature of 101° or more. You don't have to call him in the middle of the night if the baby has only a mild cold with 101° and otherwise seems happy; call him in the morning. But if the baby looks sick or has more serious symptoms with a fever of 101°, call promptly.

Colds. In general, you call the doctor if the cold is more than mild, or if there are any new symptoms, or if the child looks sicker. What to be concerned about in **colds** is discussed in Sections 642–644; **coughs**, in Section 650; **earaches**, in Section 649.

Hoarseness of voice, difficulty in breathing (Sections 652–654, 663, 664), should always be reported immediately.

Pain or suspicion of pain should be reported when it first appears. (Colic that occurs every evening for weeks doesn't need to be reported every time, of course.) **Ear infection** is discussed in Section 649; **stomachache**, in Sections 705, 706; pain in the **urinary tract,** Sections 699–702; **headache** should be reported promptly in a small child.

Sudden decrease in appetite is sometimes a sign of illness. It doesn't need to be reported if it occurs only once and if the child is as comfortable and happy as ever. But if the child acts differently in other respects, the doctor should be called.

Vomiting of any unusual type should be reported promptly, especially if the child looks sick or different in any other way. This does not apply, of course, to the spitting up after meals that is so common at first. See Sections 305, 306, 705, 706.

Diarrhea of the more serious sort, in infants, which should be reported to the doctor immediately, and the milder kinds which should be reported within a few hours are discussed in Section 315. Diarrhea of children should be reported soon (Section 705).

Blood in the bowel movements (Sections 315, 705, 270), blood in the vomitus, should be reported promptly.

Inflammation of the eye or injury to the eye should be reported promptly (Section 711).

Injury to the head should be reported if the baby isn't happy and health-looking in 15 minutes (Section 730).

Bulging of the soft spot should be reported.

Injury to a limb should be reported if the baby is not inclined to use it normally or shows pain on using it (Sections 728, 729).

Burns should be reported if blisters appear (Section 725).

Poisons. If your child has eaten anything that might possibly be dangerous (Sections 735–738), you should reach your doctor or another immediately.

Cuts are discussed in Sections 719–723.

Nosebleeds are discussed in Section 724.

Rashes. Of course, the commonest rashes in the first year are diaper rash (Section 319) and rough patches on the cheeks or a few small raised pink spots on the face (Section 320), none of which is an emergency. Babies are protected against contagious diseases like measles, German measles, and scarlet fever (but not chicken pox) for the first half year anyway, if the mother has had them. Cradle cap is very common but unimportant (Section 322). Eczema occurs occasionally (Section 666) and should be reported within a day or so. Impetigo is uncommon after a baby leaves the hospital but should be reported the first day (Section 672). If a child seems sick with a rash or if the rash is extensive, you should call the doctor right away.

84. Finding a doctor in a strange city. If you need a doctor for your child in a strange town, find the name of the best hospital. Telephone, and ask for the name of a pediatrician on the staff or a general practitioner who takes care of children. If there is any hitch, ask to speak to the physician in chief (who will probably not be a children's specialist). He will give you the names of one or two suitable doctors.

85. Things to have in your medicine cabinet. A box of sterile gauze squares, or "dressings," 3 inches square (each dressing remains sterile in a separate envelope). Two rolls of sterile bandage 2 inches wide, two rolls 1 inch wide. A roll of sterile absorbent cotton. A roll of adhesive plaster 1 inch wide. You can make narrower strips by cutting the end with scissors and then tearing. A box of small prepared bandages. A good pair of splinter forceps (tweezers to remove splinters).

Ask your doctor what antiseptic he recommends. A package of bicarbonate of soda (baking soda). A tube or jar of petroleum jelly or some other preparation that your doctor recommends for the emergency treatment of burns. A bottle of aspirin tablets for babies (each tablet contains 1¼ grains). If you live far away from medical help, ask your doctor if he recommends your having a bottle of syrup of ipecac to cause vomiting in a case of serious poisoning.

A mouth thermometer, to take axillary temperatures. A hot-water bottle. A rubber nose syringe with a glass tip, for clearing out a baby's nose during a cold.

THE HOSPITAL

86. Hospital impressions. Nowadays most babies in this country are born in a hospital. There the doctor is closer at hand when needed, and he is assisted by interns, nurses, technicians and consultants. A hospital offers all the complicated equipment, like incubators and oxygen tents, to cope with sudden emergencies. All this makes the mother feel very safe and well cared for. But it also has mild drawbacks, which are part and parcel of its virtues. The babies are usually in a nursery some distance from the mothers, where they can be efficiently watched and cared for by the nurses and won't disturb their mothers' rest. But it isn't quite natural, from the new mother's point of view, to have her baby somewhere else and taken care of so completely for a number of days. It may give her a feeling underneath of being somewhat ignorant and useless. A mother who has had several children might laugh at this and say, "It's wonderful to have that long rest in the hospital and not have to worry about the baby."

But it's different for her; she has a lot of confidence in herself as a mother and takes the hospital in her stride.

A man, too, may get the wrong first impression of himself as a father when his baby is born in a hospital. The mother at least knows that she is the center of attention. The poor father is a complete outsider. If he wants to see his baby, he has to stand outside a nursery window and look beseechingly at the nurse. Viewing a baby through glass is a poor substitute for holding him in your arms. Of course, the hospital is right in guarding his baby and all the others from any outside germs. But it gives the father the feeling that he is not considered a suitable companion for his child.

Both parents, I know, can get the wrong idea from the masks that are worn in many maternity hospitals. It makes them think of themselves as a menace to their baby. They wonder whether they ought not to be wearing them at home. The reason the masks are worn in hospitals is that so many adults and babies are gathered there in close quarters. A new germ brought in by anyone could spread easily and cause a lot of trouble. But in a family group there is very little risk of infection unless some member has a fresh cold or sore throat.

87. Rooming-in. In an effort to overcome some of the unnatural drawbacks of the maternity hospital, doctors and nurses have been experimenting in recent years with what's called the rooming-in plan. The baby's bassinet, instead of being in a nursery, is close to the mother's bed. She is encouraged by the nurses to begin taking care of him as soon as she is able—holding him, feeding him, diapering him, bathing him. She has the chance to practice these things while she is among experienced people who can explain things to her and help her. She learns about her baby's hunger patterns, his sleep, his cry, his bowel movements, so that he is not a stranger when she takes him home. This is of particular advantage to the inexperienced mother. An irregular feeding schedule, governed by the baby's need, is no problem, and this favors the success of breast feeding. The father when visiting feels he is a part of the family, and he can hold the baby and practice a bit of baby care himself.

Though rooming-in has always been practiced in some other parts of the world and though it was practiced in the United States many years ago, it has only recently been revived here, in a few hospitals, in an experimental way. It is safe. Most first-time mothers who have rooming-in are very enthusiastic and many want to have subsequent babies the same way. Other experienced mothers, with no time or way to get a vacation, prefer the luxury of full rest in the hospital.

Rooming-in is not easy to establish in a hospital. It involves many changes in hospital administration and philosophy. Getting it started usually requires research funds and a long period of planning and testing. If you hoped to have rooming-in but find it unavailable, don't feel that all is lost. You'll be able to make up for the lack of it after going home, especially in these days when the hospital stay is so short.

Infant Feeding

WHAT FEEDING MEANS TO THE BABY

88. **He knows a lot about diet.** You might get the idea, in case the hospital has given you a formula slip, that feeding a baby is something like chemistry. You take so many ounces of milk and water, mix them this way, cook them that way, put 3½ ounces into each of 6 bottles, and feed at 6 A.M., 10 A.M., 2 P.M., 6 P.M., 10 P.M., 2 A.M. The formula slip is concerned with the details; it forgets to tell you that the food is for a human being who has strong feelings about how much he wants and when he's hungry again. It's true that you have the responsibility of making the formula carefully. The amounts have been calculated by the doctor on the basis of the baby's weight and what he seemed to want in the hospital. But the baby is the one who knows how many calories his body needs and what his digestion can handle. If he's regularly not getting enough, he'll probably cry for more. Take his word for it and get in touch with the doctor. If there's more in the bottle than he feels like, let him stop when he wants to.

Think of the baby's first year this way: He wakes up because he's hungry, cries because he wants to be fed. He is so eager when the nipple goes into his mouth that he almost shudders. When he nurses, you can see that it is an intense experience. Perhaps he breaks into perspiration. If you stop him in the middle of a nursing, he may cry furiously. When he has had as much as he wants, he is groggy with satisfaction and falls asleep. Even when he is asleep, it sometimes looks as if he were dreaming of nursing. His mouth makes sucking motions, and his whole expression looks blissful. This all adds up to the fact that feeding is his great joy. He get his early ideas about life from the way feeding goes. He gets his first ideas about the world from the person who feeds him.

When a mother constantly urges her baby to take more than he wants, he is apt to become steadily less interested. He may try to escape from it by going to sleep earlier and earlier in the feeding, or he may rebel and become more balky. He's apt to lose some of his active, positive feeling about life. It's as though he got the idea: "Life is a struggle. Those people are always after you. You have to fight to protect yourself."

So don't urge a baby to take more than he is eager for. Let him go on enjoying his meals, feeling that you are his friend. This is one of the principal ways in which his self-confidence, his joy in life and his love of people will be firmly established during the first year.

89. The important sucking instinct. A baby nurses eagerly for two separate reasons. First, because he's hungry. Second, because he loves to suck. If you feed him plenty but don't give him enough chance to suck, his craving for sucking will go unsatisfied and he will try to suck something else—his fist, or his thumb, or the clothes. It's important to give him a long enough nursing period at each feeding and to have a sufficient number of feedings each day. All this is taken up in detail in Section 338–349, on thumb sucking. The thing to watch for in the beginning is not whether the baby is actually sucking his thumb, but whether he looks as if he is trying to.

90. Babies normally lose weight in the beginning. A good-size baby who gets formula from the start usually begins to gain it back in 2 or 3 days, because he can drink and digest well. The small or premature baby loses weight longer and regains it more slowly, because he can take only small feedings at first. It may take him several weeks just to get back to birth weight. This delay doesn't handicap him. Eventually he will gain rapidly to make up for it. The breast-fed baby is naturally going to be slower than the bottle-fed baby in regaining his birth weight, because his mother won't be able to supply him with much milk until he's 4 or 5 days old, and even then the milk is apt to come in slowly.

Some parents worry unnecessarily about the initial weight loss. They can't help feeling that it's unnatural and dangerous for the weight to be going down instead of up. They also may have heard that if a baby loses excessive amounts of weight, he may develop fever from becoming dehydrated (dried out).

It's for this reason that some hospitals give water for the first few days to the babies who get no formula and whose mother's milk has not come in yet. But the chance of dehydration fever is small, and it can always be cured immediately by giving fluid.

Concern about the early weight loss not only may upset a mother needlessly but may also cause her to abandon breast feeding before it has been given a fair chance. Some hospitals, to keep the mother from worrying, don't tell her the daily weight of the baby, but this method doesn't always work. The mother who is anxious imagines the worst. It's better for the mother to realize how natural the weight loss is and to resolve to leave the whole matter in the doctor's hands.

SCHEDULES

Your doctor will talk to you about your baby's feeding schedule. It will depend on your baby's size, hungriness, wakefulness and on what the doctor thinks will suit you and the baby best. What follows is a general discussion of the principles involved.

91. What regularity and flexibility are all about. During the first half of this century in this country, babies were usually kept on very strict, regular schedules. A newborn 7-pounder would be fed at exactly 6 A.M., 10 A.M., 2 P.M., 6 P.M., 10 P.M. and 2 A.M.—no earlier, no later, regardless of when he seemed hungry. Doctors did not know for sure the cause of the serious intestinal infections that afflicted tens of thousands of babies yearly. It was believed that these infections were caused not only by the contamination of milk (from carelessness in the dairy or in making the formula at home, or from insufficient refrigeration) but also by wrong proportions in the formula **and** by irregularity in feeding.

Strictness was preached and practiced everywhere—on the dairy farm, in the commercial dairy and in the home. Doctors and nurses feared irregular feeding so strongly that they came to disapprove of it psychologically, too, and taught mothers that it would lead to spoiling the child. In the general enthusiasm for strictness, mothers were usually advised to ignore their baby except at feeding time. Even kissing was frowned on by a few.

Strict regularity worked well enough with a majority of babies. When they took an ample feeding at breast or bottle, it lasted them for about 4 hours just because that is the way a young baby's digestive system usually works. But it's also a fact that we are creatures of habit at any age, and if we are always fed at exactly the same hour we soon learn, inside, to become suddenly hungry right at that moment.

But there were always a few babies who had trouble adjusting to regularity in the first month or two—babies whose stomachs couldn't seem to hold 4 hours' worth of milk, babies who went to sleep halfway through feedings, restless babies, colicky babies. They would cry miserably for shorter or longer periods each day, but their mothers and doctors dared not feed them (or even pick them up) off schedule. It was hard enough on the babies. I think it was harder still on the mothers, who had to sit listening, biting their nails, wanting to comfort their babies but not allowed to do so. You don't know how lucky you are to be able to be natural and flexible.

Anyway, the serious diarrheal diseases almost disappeared. The chief factor was the pasteurization of milk in the commercial dairy, but care in preparing the formula and better refrigeration helped, too. But it took many more years before doctors dared to begin experimenting with flexible schedules. When they did, they found that flexibility did not lead to diarrhea or indigestion, nor did it lead to spoiling, as many had feared.

The first experiments were carried out by Dr. Preston McLendon and Mrs. Frances P. Simsarian, a psychologist and a new mother, with Mrs. Simsarian's new baby. They wanted to find out what kind of schedule a baby would establish if he was breast-fed whenever he seemed hungry. The baby waked rather infrequently the first few days. Then, from just about the time the milk began to come in, he waked surprisingly often—about 10 times a day—in the second half of the first week. But by the age of 2 weeks he had settled down to 6 or 7 feedings a day, at rather irregular intervals. By 10 weeks he had arrived at approximately a 4-hour schedule. They called this an experiment in "self-demand" feeding, and this term has become well known. (I don't happen to like it for general use because it suggests the picture of a demanding baby, which isn't correct.) Since that experiment led the way, in 1942, there has been a general relaxation in infant feeding schedules, which has had a wholesome effect on babies and parents.

92. Misunderstandings about self-demand. I think, though, that there has been a certain amount of misunderstanding. Some young parents, eager to be progressive, have assumed that if they wanted to get away from the rigid scheduling of the past they must go all the way in the opposite direction, feed their baby **any** time he woke and **never** wake him for a feeding, just as if **they** were conducting a scientific experiment, or as if there were a fundamental superiority in irregularity.

This may work out well enough if the baby is a peaceful one with a good digestion, if the mother doesn't have to worry about her own schedule, and if she doesn't mind being waked between midnight and 6 A.M. But if the baby happens to be a restless, fretful one, it can lead to a great many feedings and very little rest for the parents, for several months. And in a few cases it encourages the baby to be still waking for a couple of night feedings even at the end of the first year.

When some mothers follow self-demand to inconvenient extremes, it makes other mothers shy away from it like the plague. In a group of mothers talking about schedules, one will say in a superior tone, **"My** baby is on self-demand," and another will answer rather indignantly, "Well, mine **isn't!"** When parents act as if the schedule is a matter of belief, like a religious or political conviction, it seems to me that the real point has been lost.

The main purpose of any schedule is to do right by the baby. But another purpose is to enable the parents to care for him in a way that will conserve their strength and spirits. This usually means getting down to a reasonable number of feedings at predictable hours, and omitting the night feeding as soon as the baby is ready. Otherwise the parents won't be able to do as good a job with him in other respects. What's good for them will be good for him, and vice versa.

Now that it's no longer necessary to stick to a rigid schedule, you and the baby are free to start with what he seems to need and then to move toward what is convenient for all.

If a mother **prefers** to feed her baby on an irregular schedule for many months, there is certainly no harm done to his nutrition. It does no harm to the mother, either, if she's a person who just hates to do anything by the clock. But if she's fairly regular about the rest of her life and has other things to get done, I only worry that she has gotten the idea that the more she gives up for the baby the better it is for him, or that she has to prove she is a good mother by ignoring her own convenience. These attitudes tend to create difficulties in the long run.

93. General guide to scheduling. The main consideration for the baby is that he does not have to cry with hunger for long periods. He doesn't mind at all being waked up for a feeding after an interval of 3 or 4 hours.

Every baby has a tendency to develop regular habits of becoming hungry, and these will come much more rapidly if his mother guides him a bit.

Also, babies tend to gradually lengthen the interval between feedings as they grow bigger and older. A 5- or 6-pounder usually needs to be fed about every 3 hours. Most 8- or 9-pounders are happy to average 4 hours between feedings. They come to realize that they don't need the late-night feeding, and most of them give it up by 1 or 2 months of age. Somewhere between the fourth and eight months, a majority of babies show a preference for a 5-hour interval, and during this period they become able to sleep through the evening feeding, too.

In all these tendencies—to more regular feedings and to fewer feedings—the baby can be greatly influenced by the mother's management. If she wakes him whenever he's still asleep 4 hours after the last feeding, she helps him to establish a 4-hour hunger habit. If, when he stirs and whimpers a couple of hours after the last feeding, she holds back for a few minutes and gives him a chance to go to sleep again, or if, when he gets crying steadily, she tries to comfort him with a pacifier or a bottle of water, she helps his stomach to adjust to a longer interval. If, on the other hand, she always picks him up and feeds him promptly when he stirs, even though it's only a couple of hours after the last feeding, she keeps him accustomed to short intervals and small feedings.

Individual babies differ widely in how soon they can comfortably settle down to regular schedules. A great majority of the ones who are good feeders, who are reasonably relaxed and who are getting plenty to drink from breast or bottle can be eased into a smooth 4-hour schedule and will give up the 2 A.M. feeding within a month after birth. On the other hand, if a baby is a listless, sleepy feeder at first, or a restless, fretful waker (Sections 139, 193–195, 290–292), or if the breast-milk supply is not yet well established, it will be more comfortable for all concerned to go more slowly. But even in these cases, there will be less perplexity on the part of the mother every day—about whether to give a feeding right away or to wait—and an earlier settling down on the part of the baby, if the mother is always working gently toward more regular feedings, as close as possible to every 4 hours.

94. Specific suggestions for working toward a regular schedule. A relaxed baby who weighed 7 or 8 pounds at birth usually is able to last 3½ to 4 hours on a full stomach and wants 6 or 7 feedings in the 24 hours at the start. The parents can keep in mind, as a rough guide, a 4-hour schedule (6 A.M., 10 A.M., 2 P.M., 6 P.M., 10 P.M., 2 A.M.), but be quite willing to feed him early if he really seems hungry— 1 hour early if he is taking good amounts from the bottle; as much as 2 hours early if he is breast-fed and the supply is not yet well established.

If your baby is still asleep when one of these regular feeding hours comes around, you can wake him up. You won't have to urge him to eat. A baby who is waked up 4 hours after his last feeding will usually be starving hungry in a few minutes. But suppose he wakes an hour early for his next feeding. You don't have to feed him the first minute he whimpers. He's not sure himself he's hungry. But if in 10 or 15 minutes he's crying hard with hunger, I wouldn't wait any longer. What happens to the 4-hour schedule? He may make up the difference and sleep long enough before the next feeding to get back on schedule. If he doesn't make up the time during the day, he may make it up at night. If he's always waking early, nearer to every 3 hours, maybe he isn't getting enough to last him 4 hours. If he is being breast-fed, let him nurse more often—even after 2 hours if he seems very hungry—expecting that the more frequent emptying of the breast will stimulate it to supply more milk in the next few days. When he gets a larger amount, he will be able to last longer. If he is on the bottle, draining every one and regularly waking early, consult the doctor about increasing the formula.

95. Just how early should you give another feeding? I have been saying that if the baby who generally can go 4 hours wakes after 3 or 3½ hours and seems really hungry, it is all right to feed him then. But suppose he wakes an hour or so after his last feeding. If he finished his usual bottle at his last feeding, the chances are against his being hungry again so soon. It is more likely that he has been waked by indigestion or colic. You can try burping him again, or see whether he will be comforted by a couple of ounces of water or a pacifier. I would not be in a rush to feed him again, though you may decide to try it in a little while if nothing else works. You can't be sure it's hunger just because a baby tries to eat his hand or starts to take the bottle eagerly. Often a baby who is having colic will do both these things. It seems the baby himself can't distinguish between colic pains and hunger pains. This is discussed in Section 292.

In other words, you don't **always** feed a baby when he cries. If he is crying at the wrong times, you have to study the situation and perhaps discuss it with your doctor.

96. Other hours for a 4-hour schedule. Can you aim for a 4-hour schedule with hours other than the usual 6 A.M., 10 A.M., 2 P.M., 6 P.M., 10 P.M., 2 A.M.? You certainly can, if the baby is willing. The commonest substitute is 7 A.M., 11 A.M., 3 P.M., 7 P.M., 11 P.M. (with or without 3 A.M.). The only hitch is that most young babies always want to start the day between 5 and 6 A.M., no matter when they were last fed during the night. Once in a while, a lucky mother gets a baby who is on the usual 10-2-6-10 schedule but is willing to wait until 7 A.M. for his first feeding, even when he is quite young. This is all right, too.

97. A 3-hour schedule. If your baby is getting all the milk he wants but usually wakes in about 3 hours in the day-time, it will probably be more convenient to stick to a 3-hour schedule for the time being.

It's mostly babies weighing under 7 pounds who need to be on a 3-hour schedule. But this is not an absolute rule. Some 6-pounders are willing and able to go 4 hours. And an occasional 8-pounder can't hold enough to last more than 3 hours for the first couple of weeks.

Most babies who need a 3-hour schedule during the day-time are able to go 4 hours at night if they weigh as much as 5 pounds. The feedings usually work out about as follows: 6 A.M., 9 A.M., 12 noon, 3 P.M., 6 P.M., 10 P.M., 2 A.M.

98. The 2 A.M. feeding. The easiest rule for the 2 A.M. feeding is not to wake the baby but to let him wake you if he wants to. A baby who still needs that feeding usually wakes surprisingly close to the hour of 2. Then some night, probably when he's between 2 and 6 weeks old, he will sleep through until 3 or 3:30 A.M. You feed him then, and count it as a 2 A.M. feeding. He'll probably be awake and hungry again between 6 and 7 A.M. The next night he may sleep till 4:30 or 5 A.M. You feed him then, but this time you count it as a 6 o'clock feeding and hope that he'll be happy until somewhere near 10 A.M. When a baby gets ready to give up the 2 A.M. feeding, he usually does it in a hurry, within two or three nights. Then you divide his total formula into 5 bottles instead of 6.

99. Omitting the 2 A.M. feeding. If a baby has reached the age of 1 month and weighs 9 pounds and still is waking for a 2 A.M. feeding, I think it's sensible for the parents to try to influence him to give it up. Instead of hurrying to him as soon as he stirs, you can let him fuss for 15 or 30 minutes and see if he won't go back to sleep. If he doesn't quiet down, try him on a couple of ounces of warm water. If he's crying furiously at the end of half an hour, it will be easier all around to give him breast or formula, but try again in another week or two. From a nutritional point of view, a 9-pounder who's eating well during the day doesn't really need a 2 A.M. feeding.

100. The 10 P.M., or evening, feeding is the one that you can probably time to your own convenience. Most babies, by the time they are a few weeks old, are perfectly willing to wait until 11 or even midnight for it. If you want to get to bed early, wake the baby at 10 or even a little before. If it is more convenient to feed him late, suit yourself, as long as he is willing to stay asleep.

If a baby is still waking for a 2 A.M. feeding, I would advise against letting him sleep through the 10 or 11 P.M. feeding, even though he's quite willing. When he's ready to give up one of them, you'll want him to give up the 2 A.M. feeding first, so that your sleep won't be interrupted.

If your baby is already off the 2 A.M. feeding but is still quite irregular about his daytime feeding hours, I'd continue to wake him at 10 or 11 P.M., provided he's willing to be fed. This at least ends the day on schedule, helps very much to avoid a feeding between midnight and 4 A.M., and tends to start him off somewhere between 5 and 6 the next morning.

Omitting the 10 P.M. feeding is discussed in Section 223.

GIVING THE FEEDING

The details of giving breast feedings are discussed in Sections 114–127. Some of the problems of babies who do not nurse well in the early weeks and are slow to settle into a schedule are described in Section 139.

Giving the bottle is discussed in Sections 187–195. This includes some of the difficulties in the early weeks.

101. Refusal to nurse in later months. Once in a while a baby between 4 and 7 months old acts queerly at his feedings. The mother will say that he nurses hungrily at breast or bottle for a few minutes. Then he becomes frantic, lets go of the nipple and cries as if in pain. He still seems very hungry. But each time he goes back to nursing he becomes uncomfortable sooner. He takes his solid food eagerly. I think that this distress is caused by teething. I suspect that as the baby nurses, the suction engorges his painful gums and makes them tingle unbearably. You can break each nursing period into several parts and give the solid food in the intervals, since the distress comes on only after a number of minutes of sucking. If he is on a bottle, you can enlarge the holes in a few nipples so that he gets the bottle in a shorter time. (Use these easy nipples only while the trouble lasts, since they will prevent the baby, in the long run, from getting sufficient sucking satisfaction.) If the baby's discomfort is excessive and comes on very promptly, you could, for a few days, give up the bottle altogether. Give him his milk from the cup, if he is skillful enough, or from a spoon, or mix a large amount of it with his cereal and other foods. Don't worry if he doesn't get his usual amount.

An ear infection, complicating a cold, may cause enough pain in the jaw joint so that a baby will refuse to nurse even though he may be able to eat solids pretty well.

An occasional baby will decline to take the breast during the mother's menstrual periods. He can be given formula during those days. It will be necessary for the mother to express the breast milk manually to relieve the fullness and to keep the supply going. The baby will resume the breast when the period is over and will usually be able to revive the breast-milk supply if the mother rapidly eliminates the bottles.

102. Getting up the air bubble. All babies swallow some air while they are drinking their milk. It collects as a bubble in the stomach. An occasional baby's stomach becomes uncomfortably full before he is halfway through his feeding, and he has to stop. Most never swallow enough to interrupt the meal. A few, especially breast-fed babies, don't even have a bubble at the end of a feeding. There are a couple of ways to bubble a baby, and you can find which works best for you. The first is to sit him upright in your lap and gently rub his stomach. The other is to hold him up against your shoulder and massage or pat him in the middle of the back. It's a good idea to put a diaper over your shoulder in case he spits up a little. One kind of stomach lets go of the bubble very easily and promptly. The other kind seems to want to hang on to it. When the bubble doesn't come up easily, it sometimes helps to put the baby in a lying position for a second and then bring him back to your shoulder again.

You need to bubble your baby in the middle of a feeding only if he swallows so much air that it stops his nursing. But you should at least try to get the bubble up at the end of the feeding. Most babies will become uncomfortable in a little while if put to bed with the bubble still in the stomach. Some babies even get colic pains from it. On the other hand, if your baby is hard to bubble and if he always seems just as comfortable whether he has burped or not, there is no need for you to try for more than a few minutes.

This is as good a place as any to mention the fact that when a young baby has taken a full feeding, his abdomen bulges to an extent that's apt to worry the inexperienced mother. This is only because the amount he needs to drink at each feeding is much larger in comparison to the size of his abdomen than it is in an adult. You'd look full if you weighed 110 pounds and drank 2 quarts of milk at a meal.

GETTING ENOUGH AND GAINING WEIGHT

103. An infant usually knows how much food he needs. If he is outgrowing his present formula, or if his mother's breast-milk supply has decreased temporarily because of fatigue or tension, he will probably begin to wake earlier and earlier before each feeding and cry with a cry that you now recognize as one of hunger. He will be finishing all his bottles to the last drop and looking around for more. He may try to eat his hands. If you are weighing him, you may find that he is gaining less than he did before. Sometimes a baby who is getting hungry will become constipated, also. If he is getting **really** hungry, he may cry at the end of some of his feedings, too.

If your baby is showing some of these signs of dissatisfaction and if he is on a formula, it is time to get in touch with your doctor to see about an increase. If you are unable to consult a doctor and are using the formulas in this book, it is time to change to the stronger formula. In fact, you don't have to wait this long. It's reasonable to increase the formula just as soon as a baby is regularly finishing all his bottles, even before he's showing any signs of dissatisfaction. There's one caution: if you give him an increase on such slight provocation, he probably won't be ready to take it all. So be careful not to urge him.

If a baby is being breast-fed and waking early, you can nurse him early, even though this might mean an extra feeding a day. The more frequent feedings will help to satisfy him, and the more frequent emptying of the breasts will stimulate them to produce a larger supply if that is possible. If you have been nursing at only one breast a feeding, give both breasts at each feeding for a while.

104. How much weight should your baby gain? The best that you can say is that he should gain at the rate that he seems to want to gain at. Most babies know. If they are offered more food than they need, they refuse it. If they are given less, they show their hunger by waking earlier before feedings and eating their fists.

We can talk about average babies if you remember clearly that no baby is average. When a doctor talks about an average baby, he means only that he has added together the fast gainers and the slow gainers and the medium gainers. One baby is **meant** to be a slow gainer, and another is **meant** to be a fast gainer.

If a baby is gaining slowly, that doesn't mean for sure that he was meant to. If he is hungry all the time, that is a pretty good sign that he is meant to be gaining faster. Once in a while slow gaining means that a baby is sick. A slow gainer particularly needs to be seen regularly by a doctor to make sure that he is healthy. Occasionally you see an exceptionally polite baby who is gaining slowly and who doesn't seem too hungry. But if you give him more to eat, he takes it quite willingly and gains more rapidly. In other words, not every baby yells when he is being fed too little.

The average baby's weight is a little over 7 pounds at birth, and 14 pounds at 5 months. That is to say, the average baby doubles his birth weight at about 5 months. But in actual practice, babies who are small at birth are more apt to grow faster, as if trying to catch up, and babies who are born big are less apt to double their birth weight by 5 months.

The average baby gains close to 2 pounds a month (6 or 8 ounces a week) during the first 3 months. Of course, some healthy ones gain less, and other more. Then he slows down. By 6 months the average gain is down to a pound a month (4 ounces a week). That's quite a drop in a 3-month period. In the last quarter of the first year, the average gain is down to ⅔ pound a month (2 or 3 ounces a week), and during the second year to about ½ pound a month.

As the baby grows older, you can see that he gains more slowly. He also gains more irregularly. Teething, for instance, may take his appetite away for several weeks, and he may hardly gain at all. When he feels more comfortable, his appetite revives and his weight catches up with a rush.

You can't decide too much from how a baby's weight changes from week to week. What he weighs each time will depend on how recently he has urinated, how recently he has moved his bowels, how recently he has eaten. If you find, one morning, that he has gained only 4 ounces in the past week, whereas before he had always gained 7, don't jump to the conclusion that he is starving or that something else is wrong. If he seems perfectly happy and satisfied, wait another week to see what happens. He may make an extra large gain to make up for the small one. Always remember, though, that the older he gets, the slower he will gain.

105. How often do you need to weigh the baby? Of course, most mothers don't have scales, and most babies get weighed only when they go to see their doctor, which is plenty often. When a baby is happy and doing well, weighing more frequently than once a month serves no purpose but to satisfy curiosity. If you have scales, don't weigh more often than once a week. Once in 2 weeks is even better. If you weigh your baby every day, you encourage yourself to get too wrapped up in his weight. On the other hand, if he is crying a lot, or having indigestion, or vomiting a great deal, frequent weighing may help you and your doctor in deciding what is the matter. For instance, if he is crying excessively but gaining rapidly, it points toward colic, not hunger.

Breast Feeding

THE VALUES OF BREAST FEEDING

106. Breast feeding is natural. On general principle, it's safer to do things the natural way unless you are absolutely sure you have a better way. Breast feeding has definite advantages that we know of, and it may have others that we haven't learned yet. It helps the mother physically. When the baby nurses, the muscle wall of the uterus contracts vigorously. This hastens its return to normal size and position.

You may have heard that the baby gets some protection against disease from the colostrum (the fluid that comes in before the real milk). It may well be so, though it has not been conclusively proved. Breast-fed babies have somewhat fewer bowel upsets than bottle-fed babies. A big advantage of breast feeding is that the milk is always pure; a baby can't catch an intestinal infection from it. From a purely practical point of view, it saves hours of time every week, because there are no bottles to sterilize, no formulas to mix and cook, no refrigeration to worry about, no bottles to warm. You appreciate this particularly if you ever have to travel. Of course, breast feeding saves money, too. There is another advantage that isn't often mentioned: it's more adapted to satisfying the baby's sucking instinct. At the breast he can suck as long as he feels the need. I think that there is less thumb-sucking among breast-fed babies, for that reason.

The most convincing evidence of the value of breast feeding comes from mothers who have done it. They tell of the tremendous satisfaction they experience from knowing that they are providing the baby with something no one else can give him, from seeing his devotion to the breast, from feeling his closeness. It is too seldom mentioned that after a couple of weeks the act of nursing becomes definitely pleasurable for the mother—it's intended to be. A woman doesn't get to feel like a mother, or come to enjoy being a mother, or feel the full motherly love for her child just from the fact that a baby has been born to her. With her first infant particularly, she becomes a real mother only as she takes care of her child. The more success she has in the beginning in doing her part and the more visibly her baby is satisfied by her care, the sooner and the more enjoyably she slips into the role. In this sense breast feeding does wonders for a young mother and for her relationship with her baby. She and her baby are happy in themselves and feel more and more loving to each other.

However, fewer babies have been breast-fed in recent years, especially in cities. The chief reason is that bottle feeding has gotten to be safe and easy. Another reason is custom. If most of the women in a community use bottle feeding, it seems like the most natural thing to the new mother.

QUESTIONS ABOUT BREAST FEEDING

107. The mother's figure. Some mothers shy away from breast feeding for fear it will spoil their figure. You certainly don't have to eat excessively or get fat in order to make milk. A nursing mother needs enough extra to keep her own body from being depleted. She does not need to gain an ounce above her regular weight.

But what about the effect of nursing on the shape and size of the breasts? They enlarge during pregnancy and will stay somewhat enlarged as long as nursing continues; then they return to approximately their previous size. There is no one answer to the question whether nursing several children will cause the breasts to become flattened or to sag. There are women who have nursed babies and whose breasts have become flatter with the years, but there are others whose breasts have flattened without their ever having nursed a child. I know from my own medical experience that many women breast-feed several babies with no deleterious effect on their figures. Others end up with even better figures.

There are two precautions that are probably important. First, the mother should wear a well-fitting brassiere that supports the breasts, not only while she is nursing but also during the later part of pregnancy, day and night, when the breasts are definitely enlarged. This is to prevent stretching of the skin and of the supporting tissues in the breast during the time the breasts are heavier. For many women it is advisable to change to a larger brassiere by the seventh month of pregnancy. It is well worthwhile to buy nursing brassieres that have changeable, washable pads in them to absorb any milk that may leak between feedings (of course, cotton may be used instead), and the fronts of which can be opened for nursing (get the kind that can be opened easily with one hand).

The other precaution during pregnancy and nursing is to avoid putting on excess weight. After all, the breasts may sag from obesity, quite apart from pregnancy.

108. Size of breasts is of no importance. Some women with small breasts assume that they will be less able to produce milk in sufficient quantity. There is probably little basis for this belief. When a woman is not pregnant and not nursing, the glandular tissue is quiescent and constitutes only a minor part of the breast. The greater part is composed of fat tissue, which is apparently concentrated there for purposes of beauty. The larger breast has more fat tissue; the smaller breast has less. As a woman's pregnancy progresses, secretions from the ovaries stimulate the glandular, milk-producing tissue to develop and enlarge. The arteries and veins that serve the glandular tissue enlarge, too, so that the veins become prominent on the surface of the breast. The milk, when it comes in a few days after delivery, causes further enlargement of the breasts. Doctors who have cared for nursing mothers agree that even women who have unusually small breasts before pregnancy may produce copious amounts of milk.

109. Does it tire the mother? You occasionally hear it said that breast feeding "takes a lot out of a woman." Many women do feel fatigued in the early weeks of nursing, but so do many who are feeding by bottle. They are getting their strength back after the delivery and hospitalization. The nervous tension from caring for a new baby is tiring. But it's also true that the breasts are requiring a goodly number of calories each day for the baby, and a mother must eat considerably more than usual just to keep her weight up. In the long run there is no more reason for a woman to feel exhausted from breast feeding than from a vacation on which she is taking a lot of exercise in the form of walks or swimming. Our bodies soon adapt to increasing or decreasing energy needs, and our appetites go up or down accordingly in order to keep our weight stationary. If a nursing mother is healthy and happy, her appetite will naturally take care of the need for extra calories for the baby's milk. Some nursing mothers are amazed at the amount of food they crave and can eat without gaining weight. Sometimes the appetite overdoes it, though, and then the woman has to call on her will power and the help of the doctor, public health nurse and perhaps nutritionist to keep from gaining too much.

A woman who feels that nursing takes too much out of her may be a worrisome person whose concern about the new baby depresses her appetite or her spirits. Or she may be an individual who has never had much confidence in her health and strength and therefore feels that any unusual demand on her system is a threat, even though her body is actually handling the situation well. Or, least likely of all, she may be in poor physical health. Needless to say, a nursing mother who is not feeling well or is losing weight should consult her doctor promptly.

Some women, usually because of the way they were brought up, feel deeply uncomfortable at the prospect of breast feeding—it may seem too immodest or too animal-like. If such a feeling is strong, I think it is preferable for the mother not to try, no matter how much she wants to do right by her baby.

Quite a few fathers, including some very good ones, object to breast feeding—they can't help feeling jealous. Then the mother has to use her best judgment.

110. The working mother. What about the woman who hesitates to nurse because she has to go back to work? The answer depends on her working hours and how soon she must get back to the job. If she has to be out of the home only 8 hours a day, she can still nurse her baby except for one feeding. Even if she can't nurse after she resumes work, it would still be worthwhile to breast-feed the baby temporarily if she has a month or two.

111. There are other ways to show affection, too. Suppose you want to breast-feed your baby but don't succeed. Will the baby suffer, physically or emotionally? No, you can't put it that strongly. If you make the formula carefully and if you keep in touch with the doctor, the chances are great that the baby will prosper from a bodily point of view. And if, when you give him his bottle, you cuddle him in your arms, he will be nourished spiritually, much as if he were at the breast. Mothers who have read what psychologists and psychiatrists say about the importance of breast feeding sometimes get the idea that it has been shown that bottle-fed babies turn out to be less happy than breast-fed babies. Nobody has proved that.

To put it in other words, there are hundreds of ways in which a mother shows her devotion to her baby and builds his trust in her. Breast feeding is one way, and a very good one, but certainly not essential. Giving flowers is one way a man may show his love for his wife. But no sensible wife who has other proofs of her husband's love will despair just because he's not a flower giver. You may think I'm laboring this point. I give it this emphasis because there are conscientious young women who, as a result of what they've studied or heard, set their hearts on being able to breast-feed. Then, if it doesn't work, they feel that they have deprived their babies and failed as women. This great buildup of the importance of nursing is not justified by the facts, and the reaction to lack of success is unnecessarily hard on the mother and, indirectly, on the baby. After all, he needs a cheerful mother more than he needs breast milk.

It's well to remember that the production of milk depends on the glandular secretions in the mother's body and on the hospital routines, over neither of which the mother has control, as well as on her own efforts. Therefore, failure in breast feeding should not be a matter for self-reproach.

So think of breast feeding not as a test of your devotion to the baby (plenty of undevoted mothers in past ages have nursed their babies) or as a test of your physical and emotional adequacy as a woman (which it hardly is at all), but simply as a good thing if you really enjoy it and it works, but no cause for despair if not.

A majority of women who are eager to nurse find that they do better with each succeeding child, probably as a result of increasing experience and confidence.

112. The mother can lead a normal life. Some mothers hesitate to nurse their baby because they have heard that they will have to give up too much. Generally speaking, this is not so. There is no evidence that it will harm the baby if the mother drinks coffee or tea, smokes, uses alcoholic beverages in moderation, or goes in for athletics. The nursing mother can usually continue to eat all the foods she is accustomed to. There is no reason to believe, for instance, that if she eats prunes it will make the baby's bowels loose, or that if she eats fried food it will give the baby indigestion. Once in a while, it is true, a baby seems to get upset every time his mother eats a certain food. Naturally, if this happens several times in succession, she can give up that particular food. Some drugs get into the milk, but usually not in large enough quantities to affect the baby. A mother can take milk of magnesia, mineral oil, aspirin, barbiturates, codeine, morphine, sulpha drugs, antibiotics, without affecting the baby. She should not take bromides, atropine, cascara, ergot.

When a nursing mother becomes nervously upset, it sometimes cuts down, for the time being, the amount of milk she can produce. Occasionally it seems to make the baby feel out of sorts, too. Some women never menstruate so long as they continue to nurse. Others menstruate regularly or irregularly. Once in a while a nursing baby will be mildly upset during his mother's menstruation or refuse to nurse.

There is no reason a nursing mother shouldn't let the baby have a bottle once in a while, even once a day, in case she wants to be away from home for longer than 4 hours.

113. The mother's diet. A nursing mother does need to be sure that her diet contains plenty of the elements that the baby is withdrawing in the milk. A large amount of calcium (lime) is excreted in the milk, to enable the baby's bones to grow rapidly. If the mother takes in too little, the breasts will withdraw it from her bones. It used to be thought that she would loose calcium from her teeth, too, but this is probably not so. She should take as much milk as the baby is getting from her, plus a little extra for her own needs, in any beverage that she likes, or cooked into cereals, soups, puddings, or in the form of cheese (Section 438).

Her daily diet should include the following elements (even if she has to limit her diet otherwise to keep her weight down): Milk—at the very least, a quart a day, and preferably a quart and a half. It can be the usual fresh milk or it can be evaporated, powdered or skimmed, and it can be served in any form. Fruits and vegetables—6 servings a day. (This may sound like too much until you realize that the juice of 2 oranges, a salad, a green or yellow vegetable, and potatoes twice add up to 6 servings.) To include enough vitamin C, 2 of these servings should be raw and 2 should be oranges, grapefruit, tomatoes, raw cabbage or berries. For the sake of vitamin A, there should be one dark-green, leafy vegetable or a deep-yellow one. Potatoes are valuable aside from their calories. Fruits and vegetables can be fresh, canned, frozen or dried. **Meat, poultry, fish**—at least 1 generous portion, preferably 2. Liver is especially valuable and should be included occasionally. **Eggs**—1 a day. **Cereal and bread**—3 servings a day, whole grain or enriched (to contain the B vitamins). **Butter or fortified margarine** for vitamin A. If your weight won't stand these, eat more green, leafy vegetables and deep-yellow ones. A **vitamin-D preparation**, prescribed by the doctor, to make sure you are utilizing the calcium in your diet.

If a nursing mother is gaining unwelcome weight, she can drink skimmed milk, hold down on butter, keep the cereal and bread portions small (but use whole-grain products to provide B vitamins), limit strictly or omit such high-calorie foods as candy, pastries, cakes, cookies, soda-fountain drinks. (It's too bad that these high-calorie sweets are the foods that weight-gainers crave most.) But she should not cut down on the milk, vegetables, fruit, meat and vitamin D.

GETTING STARTED AT BREAST FEEDING

114. The mother's position and relaxation. Some mothers prefer, even in bed in the hospital, to nurse sitting up. Others find it easier, while still in bed, to nurse lying down. To do this, lay the baby beside you on the bed and lie on your side, facing him. Move closer until the nipple touches his lips. You may need to prop yourself up on your elbow to bring the nipple to the right position. When he feels the nipple near his mouth he will "root around," trying to get hold of it. At times you may need to put a finger on the breast to give him breathing space for his nose, though this isn't usually necessary. If you let your finger touch his face, he may go for it.

When you are able to sit up, in the hospital or later at home, you can find the position that suits you best. Some mothers prefer to nurse lying down; most sit up. Those who have used a rocking chair for nursing swear by it. The height of the arm of the chair is really important for resting your arms. A pillow or cushion there may help. Anyway, get comfortable so that you can relax and rest your muscles.

After a mother has become accustomed to nursing and is relaxed at that time, she may fall asleep if she nurses lying down, especially at 2 A.M. or 6 A.M., when she is sleepy. Then there is a slight risk of obstructing the baby's breathing with her breast or arm. For this reason it's better for her to nurse sitting up in bed or in a chair in the early-morning hours or at any other time when she feels sleepy, unless a nurse or other helper is in the room.

You'll probably notice that the state of your feelings has a lot to do with how easily the milk comes. Worries and tenseness can hold the milk back. So try to get troubles off your mind before beginning. If possible, lie down for 15 minutes before you expect the baby to wake and do what is most relaxing, whether it's shutting your eyes, or reading, or listening to the radio.

After you have been nursing for a few weeks, you may notice a distinct sensation of the milk being "let down" or "coming in" at nursing time. It may start leaking from the breasts when you hear the baby beginning to cry in the next room. This shows how much feelings have to do with the formation and release of the milk.

(There are nursing pads to place inside the brassiere, either disposable or reusable.)

115. Getting the entire areola into the baby's mouth. A baby does not get the milk simply by taking the nipple into his mouth and sucking. The milk is formed in the glandular tissue throughout the breast. It then passes through small ducts toward the center of the breast, where it collects in a number of "sinuses." These sinuses, or storage spaces, are located in a circle right behind the areola, the dark area around the nipple. A short duct leads from each sinus through the nipple to the outside (there are a number of openings in each nipple). When a baby is nursing properly, most or all of the areolar area is in his mouth, and the principal action is the squeezing of the sinuses (behind the areola) by the baby's gums. This forces the milk, which has collected in the sinuses, through the nipple and into his mouth. The sucking action of the baby's tongue is not so much to draw the milk through the nipple into his mouth as to keep the areola drawn into his mouth and also to get the milk from the front of his mouth back into his throat. If a baby takes only the nipple into his mouth, he gets almost no milk. And if he chews on the nipple, he is apt to make it sore. But if he takes the entire areola into his mouth, his gums squeeze the areola and cannot hurt the nipple. It may help him get the entire areola into his mouth if the mother or nurse will compress it or flatten it a little between thumb and finger. If the baby starts to mouth and chew on the nipple alone, he should be stopped promptly. Slip your finger into the corner of his mouth to break the suction, or between his gums if necessary. (Otherwise you would have to pull him off the breast, which is hard on the nipple.) Then reinsert the aerola in his mouth. If he persists in chewing the nipple, stop the feeding for good.

116. Different babies behave differently at the breast. A physician who has studied the behavior of hundreds of babies when first put to breast has, with a sense of humor, pointed out the different types. The **eager beaver** draws the areola in avidly and sucks vigorously until satisfied. The only problem is that he may be too hard on the nipple if he is allowed to chew it. The **excitable** baby may become so agitated and active that he keeps losing the breast and then, instead of trying again, he screams. He may have to be picked up and comforted for several minutes before he is calm enough to try again. After a few days he usually settles down. The **procrastinator** can't be bothered to nurse the first few days; he is waiting until the milk comes in. Prodding him only makes him balky. He does well when the time comes. The **taster** must, for a little while, mouth the nipple and smack his lips over the drop of milk he tastes, before he settles down to business. Efforts to hurry him only make him angry. The **rester** wants to nurse a few minutes and then rest a few minutes before starting again. He can't be rushed. He usually does a good job in his own way, but it takes him longer.

117. There are two things that often make a balky baby angrier. The first is to hold his head, in trying to direct it toward the breast. A baby hates to have his head held; he fights to get free. The other is to squeeze him across the cheeks to get his mouth open. A baby has an instinct to turn toward anything that touches his cheek. This is to help him find the nipple. When you squeeze him on both cheeks at the same time, you baffle and annoy him.

When a baby is refusing to take the breast and carrying on, a mother can't help feeling spurned, frustrated and irritated. She shouldn't let her feelings be hurt by this inexperienced but apparently opinionated newcomer. If she can keep trying for a few more feedings, the chances are that he will find out what it's all about.

118. The early schedule. A baby is put to breast sometime in the first 18 hours after birth. This interval varies a lot in different hospitals, and it doesn't make a great deal of difference. For the first 2 or 3 days no real milk is produced, only a small amount of a fluid called colostrum. Fitting in with this lack of milk is the fact that most babies are quiet, sleepy and unhungry for the first 2 or 3 days, so they don't mind waiting. Usually the length of time at breast is limited during this period (perhaps to 5 minutes at each feeding) so that the mother's nipples will not get too much use until they have become somewhat toughened. The 2 A.M. feeding is often omitted during these days so that the mother can catch up on her rest.

Whether the baby is then put to breast on a regular schedule or according to his own waking-and-hunger pattern depends on whether the baby is in a newborn nursery and can be brought to the mother only at specified times or whether mother and baby are in a rooming-in unit, close together, so that she can watch him and can feed him whenever he seems to need to be fed. A rooming-in arrangement and a flexible schedule are particularly handy for breast feeding, because the baby will get to breast when he is ready and eager to nurse. If the breast-milk supply has not caught up with his hunger, he wakes and empties the breasts more frequently, which is the principal means of stimulating the breasts to produce more milk.

119. When the milk comes in. There is considerable variation in the time and manner in which the milk comes in. It most often starts to come in on the third or fourth day of the baby's life. It tends to come earlier in mothers who have had a child before, later in new mothers. Sometimes it comes so suddenly that the mother can name the hour. In other cases the progress is much more gradual. And it's on about the third or fourth day that a majority of babies become distinctly more wakeful and hungry. This is one of the many examples of how smoothly Nature works things out. Studies of babies who have been breast-fed whenever they appeared hungry have shown that a majority of them want to nurse unusually often between the third and sixth days, commonly up to 10 or 12 times a day. (The stools may become frequent on these days, too.) Mothers who are particularly anxious to make a success of breast feeding are apt to feel disappointed by this frequency, assuming that it means the breast-milk supply is inadequate. This is unnecessarily pessimistic. It's more sensible to think that the baby is now settling down to the serious business of eating and growing, and that he is providing the breasts with the stimulation they must have if they are to meet his increasing needs. It is during this latter half of the first week, too, that the breasts are receiving the strongest stimulation from the hormones (the glandular secretions that make the milk come in in the first place). It is no wonder that in the first few days the breasts sometimes become too full, and that sometimes there isn't enough to satisfy the newly hungry baby. Still, the system is generally efficient, much better than you or I could design. The hormone factor calms down at the end of the first week. Then it is how much the baby demands that determines how much the breasts produce. In the changeover period (the second week) there may not be quite enough until the breasts adjust to the demand. The baby's hunger teaches the breast how much to produce, not just in the second or third week, but on through the succeeding months. In other words, the supply may still be increasing when the baby is several months old, if he wants more.

120. Increase the nursing time gradually. To protect the nipples, the time a baby is allowed to nurse at each feeding is increased gradually: not more than a total of 5 minutes each feeding for the first 3 days; perhaps 10 minutes on the fourth day; 15 the next; then 20 minutes for several days. If after 10 days it is clear that the nipples have no tendency to become sore, the length of time the baby nurses can be left to his wishes and the mother's convenience. It may vary a lot from day to day and from feeding to feeding. Most babies are satisfied after between 20 and 30 minutes, and there is no point in going beyond 40 minutes.

121. The schedule in the hospital. In a rooming-in unit the baby is nursed whenever he is hungry. In a hospital in which all babies are in a nursery and are fed by the clock, full-sized babies are taken to the mother every 4 hours day and night (6 feedings in 24 hours) after the milk has come in. By this time the baby is hungry in the middle of the night, the mother is reasonably rested and the nighttime stimulation of the breasts is important. A small baby may be put temporarily on a 3-hour schedule by day and probably a 4-hour at night, making 7 feedings in the 24 hours.

Back in the prewar days, when many mothers stayed in the hospital for two weeks and when practically all babies were kept in the nursery and brought in to the mother only on a 4-hour schedule, it was often a problem to satisfy a baby's hunger and give the breasts sufficient stimulation between the third and fourteenth days of the baby's life unless the mother was an unusually copious milk producer. Nowadays, when the lying-in period is usually less than a week, the mother who has not yet been able to supply enough milk to satisfy her baby on a strict 4-hour schedule can shift to a flexible (self-demand) schedule just as soon as she gets home, and it will probably not be too late for the breasts to respond to the more frequent nursing.

122. One or both breasts? In very natural, "uncivilized" parts of the world, where nursing is the only way babies are fed, where mothers carry their babies around with them in slings while they work and where schedules are unknown, babies tend to wake and be put to breast frequently. They nurse relatively briefly, at one breast, and then fall asleep again. In our civilization, which runs pretty much according to the clock and in which babies are put in a crib in a quiet room after a feeding, the tendency is toward fewer and larger feedings. If a mother produces ample amounts of milk, a baby may be quite satisfied with one breast at each feeding. Each breast receives the stimulation of very complete emptying, even though this occurs only once in about 8 hours. In many cases, however, the amount in one breast does not satisfy the baby, and both breasts are given at each feeding, the left breast being offered first at one feeding, the right breast first at the next. Some mothers and doctors advocate both breasts anyway. To ensure complete emptying of one breast, the baby might be kept on the first breast for 12 to 15 minutes, if he is willing, and then allowed to nurse on the second breast for as short or as long a period as he wishes. A baby who sticks to business will take the greatest part of the milk in 5 or 6 minutes and will have pretty well emptied the breast in 10 or 15 minutes. (The breasts will always be producing a little new milk, so he will always taste something.) Therefore, there is no need for a mother to prolong breast feeding beyond a total of 20 to 40 minutes, depending on how eager he is to continue and how much time she has to spare. Stop after 30 minutes if the baby is willing. Bringing up the bubble is discussed in Section 102.

123. How do you know whether the baby is getting enough? This question is likely to baffle the new mother. You certainly can't tell from the length of time the baby nurses. He goes on nursing after he's already obtained most of the milk —sometimes for 10 more minutes, sometimes for 30—because he's still getting a small trickle of milk, or because he enjoys sucking, or because he's still awake and having a good time. Even if you weighed him before and after each feeding so that you knew exactly how much milk he obtained, it wouldn't tell you about his satisfaction. Careful observations of slightly older babies have shown that the same baby will appear to be entirely satisfied by 3 ounces at one feeding and by 10 ounces at another.

124. You can't tell from the appearance of breasts or milk. Most women with experience have decided that they can't tell from the apparent fullness of the breast before feeding how much milk is there. In the first week or two, the breasts are noticeably full and firm as a result of glandular changes, but after a while they normally become softer and less prominent, even though the milk supply is increasing. A baby can get 6 or more ounces from a breast that to the mother does not seem full at all. You can't tell anything from the color and appearance of the milk. Breast milk always looks thin and bluish compared to cow's milk, and there are no important variations in the composition of the milk from time to time in the same mother, or from one mother to another.

125. You can't tell by the baby's crying alone. You can't be sure that the baby who fusses a lot after feeding is hungry, because in the early weeks babies who are fretful or colicky or have what I call "irritable crying" characteristically cry after certain feedings, even when these feedings are unusually large.

126. The best guide is the combination of weight gain and satisfaction. Generally speaking, you and the doctor decide the question on the basis of the baby's behavior over a number of days and on the basis of his weight-gaining. Neither alone is conclusive. A baby who is happy and gaining fast is obviously getting enough. A baby who cries hard every after-noon or evening but is gaining weight at the average rate is probably getting plenty to eat but having colic. A baby who gains slowly but is quite contented is, in most cases, a baby who is meant to be a slow gainer. However, there are a few babies who don't protest even when they are not gaining at all. It's the baby who is gaining very slowly and acting hungry most of the time who's probably not getting enough.

So it's best to assume that the baby is getting enough in the long run unless the baby and the doctor definitely tell you differently. Certainly at any one feeding you should be satisfied if the baby seems satisfied.

127. Don't throw away your confidence. The doubt about sufficiency of the milk supply is natural enough in the new mother, who has had no proof yet of her adequacy. The doubt also arises in mothers who have had more experience but who have never had much self-confidence. Usually when the mother is worrying about the amount, the doctor finds that there is no insufficiency of milk, only an insufficiency of confidence. Worry only discourages the milk supply.

It's good to remember that throughout the largest part of the world, in which there are no scales and no doctors, the mother simply assumes that the baby is receiving plenty if he acts contented and looks well, and that this system works well in at least nine out of ten cases.

128. Care of nipples. Some doctors recommend regular massage of the nipples during the last month of pregnancy, to toughen them. After the baby is born and begins to nurse, no particular care of the nipples, no wiping or ointment should be necessary. It is sensible for the mother to wash her hands with soap before fingering her nipples (to massage or examine them), since infection can enter the breast through the nipple and since babies can easily pick up thrush, a mild fungus in-fection of the mouth. But hand-washing should not be neces-sary before an ordinary nursing.

Some experienced mothers are convinced that the most helpful step in healing sore nipples, and in keeping them healthy, is to allow them to dry in the air for 10 or 15 minutes before closing the nursing flaps of the brassiere, or to leave the flaps open between feedings. Nipples will also stay drier and healthier if there is no waterproof lining in the brassiere.

129. How to try extra hard. You hear of women who want to nurse their babies but don't succeed. People talk about how complicated our civilization is and how it makes mothers too tense to nurse. There's no doubt that nervousness works against breast feeding, but I don't think most women are nervous. Breast feeding most often fails because it isn't given a good trial.

There are three factors that make a big difference: (1) keeping away from formula, (2) not getting discouraged too early, (3) sufficient stimulation of the breasts after the milk has begun to come in.

If a baby is given formula for the first 3 or 4 days of life, the chance of successful breast feeding is diminished. The baby who is satisfied by plenty of formula doesn't try so hard at breast. (Water, which is sometimes given during this period to make sure he doesn't become too dried out, is not likely to interfere with his hunger at breast.) After the mother's milk has begun to come in, it's wise to avoid formula, too, if the baby can be kept fairly well satisfied and is not continuing to lose weight.

Sometimes a mother becomes discouraged just at the moment when her milk is coming in, or a day or two later because she isn't producing very much. This is no time for her to quit. She hasn't given herself half a chance. It is certainly worth continuing if she is producing as much as 1 ounce at any feeding on about the fifth day. If a mother has a practical or baby nurse at this stage, it's a great help to have one who is encouraging and cooperative.

The night nursings, which will probably come at about 10 P.M. and 2 A.M., are as important as the daytime nursings in giving the breasts regular stimulation at first. If the breasts are not supplying a sufficient amount of milk to keep the baby satisfied for 3 or 4 hours, it helps to let him empty them more frequently, as often as every 2 hours (including both breasts at each feeding), provided the nipples aren't sore. This is the way the baby and the breasts would adjust to each other in a faraway spot where there was no cow's milk. The frequent emptying of the breasts stimulates them to produce more milk. Then the baby is able to go for longer periods again. Of course, a baby cannot be kept off formula indefinitely if he remains miserably hungry for many days, or continues to lose weight, or develops fever from insufficient fluid. Frequent nursing shouldn't be carried to the point where the nipples become cracked or the mother is exhausted from having no time to rest.

If a mother is able to keep in frequent touch with the doctor, he will help her decide at each step such questions as how many days the baby can go on an insufficient amount of breast milk without resorting to formula, how much nursing the mother's nipples can stand, how frequently to nurse. The point is, though, that the doctor is influenced in many of these decisions by the mother's attitude toward nursing. If she makes it clear that she is eager to succeed, it helps him in giving the directions that will make it possible.

WHEN THE BREAST MILK SEEMS INSUFFICIENT

130. Trying to increase it after getting home (if you cannot consult the doctor regularly). Suppose that in the hospital your baby was nursed as frequently as possible and received both breasts at each feeding, but still did not get enough. The doctor decided that he had to have some formula, too. Let's say that the baby was averaging less than 2 ounces from both breasts and required a 2-ounce bottle in addition at each nursing. You decided after talking it over with the doctor that you wanted to continue the breast feeding after going home, with the hope of eventually getting the baby entirely breast-fed.

Sometimes the mother feels so much more relaxed and natural after a couple of days at home that the breast-milk supply increases without any other encouragement, and the baby is so satisfied that he isn't particularly interested in the bottle. In that case the mother should stop offering the bottle right away. Usually, however, the baby enjoys the bottle so much that he continues to take it and so has less appetite for the breast. Therefore, in most cases the mother must deliberately cut down on the formula and count on the baby's increasing hunger to give more stimulation to the breasts. Here is one method: For the first couple of days at home continue to give the formula after nursing, as in the hospital, but don't give a drop more than the baby demands. (The breast-milk supply often does not increase the first day or two at home, and it sometimes decreases temporarily because of the mother's fatigue.) After 2 days, begin to reduce the amount in each bottle by ¼ ounce each day until you are down to no bottle at all. What will happen? As you cut down the formula, the baby will probably get hungry earlier. You nurse him when he becomes hungry, whether it's after 4, or 3, or even 2 hours. This sounds like an awful lot of work, but it won't be forever. You are hoping that the frequent emptying of the breasts will stimulate them to produce more and more milk. When this happens, the baby will begin to sleep for longer and longer periods again. In a week or two he may work himself back onto approximately a 4-hour schedule. (I remember one baby who never got more than an ounce at a time from the breast in the hospital, and who worked up to 5 ounces in 2 weeks at home. Of course, this won't happen in every case.) If you try it for 5 or 6 days and the baby gets hungrier all the time and fails to gain weight, then you may have to go back to the formula temporarily. But even then, if you want to keep on trying, you can offer only 2 ounces of formula after each breast feeding, and in a few days, when you feel more rested, try gradually reducing this amount again.

As a general rule it is not sensible to nurse more often than about every 2 hours. The mother is apt to become tired and irritable (from the nervous strain) and the nipples may become sore.

Some doctors recommend manual expression of any milk that remains in the breast after the baby has finished nursing, as an excellent temporary method of increasing the supply (Sections 149, 150).

131. Fluids for the mother. It's most important during this trial period that the mother take wonderful care of herself, avoid getting tired at all costs, let the housework go, forget about outside worries and obligations, keep visitors down to one or two comfortable friends, eat and drink well. A good time to drink something is 10 or 15 minutes before you expect a nursing. Some women who enjoy beer find it a very pleasant means of taking extra fluid and achieving relaxation.

There are two sides to the matter of fluids. There's no good to be gained from drinking more fluid than feels comfortable, because the body promptly gets rid of excess water through the urine. On the other hand, a new, excited, busy mother may forget to drink as much as she needs and go thirsty through absentmindedness. This will cut down the milk supply.

132. Don't let friends discourage you. Perhaps this is as good a time as any to mention that in these days, when breast feeding is the exception rather than the rule, a mother who is attempting it may occasionally be subjected to a surprising amount of skepticism on the part of friends and relatives who are otherwise quite sympathetic. There are remarks like: "You aren't going to breast-feed, are you?" "Very few can make the grade." "Why in the world are you trying to do that?" "With breasts like yours you'll never succeed." "Your poor baby is hungry. Are you trying to starve him to prove a point?" The milder remarks can perhaps be blamed on surprise, but the meaner ones strongly suggest jealousy. Later on, if there is any question about continuing to nurse, you'll find several friends who'll urge you to stop.

133. When the breast milk seems to decrease later. A good percentage of mothers who are eager to breast-feed are successful in the hospital and for a number of days or weeks afterward (with the possible exception of the first day or two at home when the supply often decreases temporarily). Then too many of them feel that they are failing and give up. They say, "I didn't have as much milk," or "My milk didn't seem to agree with the baby," or "As he grew bigger my milk was no longer sufficient."

Why is it that throughout most of the world a mother's milk takes care of the baby for many months and that it's only in bottle-feeding countries like ours that the breast-milk supply seems to fail so early in a majority of cases? I don't believe that American mothers are that nervous. They are certainly as healthy as any. I think there is one main reason. The mother here who is trying to breast-feed, instead of feeling that she is doing the most natural thing in the world and assuming that she'll succeed like everyone else, feels that she's attempting to do the unusual, the difficult thing. Unless she has tremendous self-confidence, she keeps wondering whether she won't fail. In a sense, she's looking for signs of failure. If her baby cries one day a bit more than usual, her first thought is that her milk has decreased. If he develops indigestion or colic, or a rash, she is quick to suspect her milk. Her anxiety makes her feel sure that the bottle is the answer. And the trouble is that the bottle is always available. Probably she was given formula directions when she left the hospital ("just in case"), or she can call the doctor or the public health nurse and get directions. Babies on the breast who begin to receive ample amounts of formula several times a day practically always nurse less eagerly at breast. And milk left in the breast is Nature's method of signaling to the glands, "Make less, make less."

In other words, the combination of a mother lacking confidence in her ability to breast-feed and the availability of bottles of formula is the most efficient method of discouraging breast feeding.

To put it positively: the way to make breast feeding a success is to go on breast feeding and keep away from formula (except possibly for one relief bottle a day after the breast supply is well established). See Sections 135, 136.

Under normal conditions the amount of milk supplied by the breasts is not a stationary quantity. The breasts are ready at any time gradually to decrease or increase the amount, depending on whether the baby wants less or more. As a baby grows and his appetite increases, he empties the breasts more completely and sometimes more frequently. This is the stimulation that encourages a larger supply.

134. Hunger is not the commonest reason for crying. The most common reason for a mother to start worrying is that her baby begins to fret right after feedings, or between feedings. Her first thought is that her milk supply is failing. But this assumption is not correct. The fact is that almost all babies—especially first babies—have fretful spells, most often in the afternoon or evening. Bottle-fed babies fuss as much as breast-fed babies. Babies who are getting all the milk they can possibly hold have crying spells just the same as babies who are receiving less. These fretful spells are discussed in Section 292, on colic, and Section 290, on general fretfulness. If a mother realizes clearly that most of the fussing in the early weeks is not caused by hunger, she won't be so quick to lose confidence in her breast-milk supply.

Though it is much less likely, it is, of course, possible that a baby is beginning to fret because he's hungry. However, hunger is much more apt to wake a baby a little earlier for the next feeding than to bother him in the first hour or two after the last feeding. If he is hungry it may be because his appetite has taken a sudden spurt or it may possibly mean that his mother's milk has decreased slightly because of fatigue or tension. In either case the answer is the same: take it for granted that he'll wake and want to nurse more frequently and more vigorously for a day or for a few days until the breasts have adjusted to the demand. Then he will probably go back to his previous schedule.

In case the fussing was not due to hunger at all, the extra nursing has done no harm.

The treatment of fretfulness seems clear to me. Any thought of giving a bottle of formula should be postponed for at least a week or two. The baby should be allowed to nurse as often as every 2 hours, for 20 to 40 minutes. If he makes a reasonable weight gain in that week or two, consideration of formula should again be put off, for at least 2 more weeks. The baby can be comforted during his fretful periods with a pacifier or with a bottle of water or possibly sugar water (Sections 201, 202). The mother may occasionally want to nurse him even more frequently than every 2 hours. It certainly won't do the baby any harm. I'm only thinking of the mother: she can't help becoming frantic if she's nursing all day long, and it won't do that much good. Emptying the breasts 10 times a day will give them about as much stimulation as they can use. It is also necessary for the mother to have some rest and relaxation.

135. A relief bottle is all right. Does all this mean that a mother who wants to continue breast feeding must never give a bottle under any circumstances? No, it isn't that crucial. Most of the mothers who want to give a relief bottle regularly once a day find that they can do so without discouraging the breast-milk supply, provided the supply has been well established for a few weeks and provided it's only one bottle a day. And certainly a mother who has not been giving a bottle regularly can give one occasionally. Perhaps she must be away for a feeding. Or perhaps she has become extremely tired or upset and the baby has acted entirely dissatisfied with one feeding. One bottle doesn't stop breast feeding. What I have been advising against is regularly giving a complementary bottle (a bottle given in addition to a breast feeding) 2 or 3 times a day, if you hope to continue with breast feeding.

136. A relief bottle. The relief bottle can be given every day if desired, at the 10 A.M., 2 P.M., or 6 P.M. feeding. (When the baby is off the 2 A.M. feeding, the mother will usually be too uncomfortable to omit either the 10 P.M. or the 6 A.M. nursing, since this would leave the breasts full for 12 hours. Also, such a long interval might discourage the breast-milk supply.)

If a mother plans to wean her baby from breast to bottle sometime between 2 and 6 months, it's a good idea to offer a relief bottle at least twice a week, even though she could nurse just as well. The reason is that some babies become so set in their ways during this age period that they will refuse to take a bottle of milk if they have not been used to it, and this may make quite a struggle. A baby rarely gets this opinionated before the age of 2 months. And after 6 months he will probably be weaned directly to the cup.

It is sometimes recommended that all breast-fed babies get a bottle once or twice a week, even though the mother is planning to nurse her infant until he is weaned to the cup. This is on the theory that the mother might have to stop nursing for some unexpected reason. You can decide for yourself, balancing the inconvenience of making the bottle against risking the baby's putting up a struggle if weaned suddenly.

Your doctor will give you a formula for a single bottle. If you cannot consult a doctor you can try the following: 4 ounces of pasteurized whole milk (shake the bottle, if you do not use homogenized milk), 2 ounces of water, 2 level teaspoonfuls of granulated sugar. Mix, pour it into the bottle, cap it loosely, stand it in boiling water for 25 minutes.

You should end up with 6 ounces of formula. Let the baby take as much of this as he wants. A small baby won't want it all. It will be about enough for the average 10-pounder. If it's insufficient for a big baby, make it 6 ounces of milk, 2 teaspoonfuls of sugar, no water.

For most families, it is more convenient to make a formula for a single bottle from pasteurized milk than from evaporated milk, because only a very small amount of the can of milk is used. However, if you don't have pasteurized milk, or if you can use up the rest of the evaporated milk for other purposes, you may prefer to use evaporated milk for the relief bottle. You can buy evaporated milk in small, 6-ounce cans. To make a 6-ounce formula, use 2 ounces of evaporated milk, 4 ounces of water, 2 level teaspoonfuls of granulated sugar. Mix, bottle, sterilize as in the next-to-last paragraph. A stronger formula would be 3 ounces of evaporated milk, 3 ounces of water, 2 teaspoonfuls of sugar.

137. Breast and bottle both. If a mother who can't produce enough milk to completely satisfy the baby wants to go on with a combination of breast and bottle, there is no reason why she shouldn't. However, in many cases of mixed feedings,

the breast-milk supply gradually decreases. Also, the baby
may come to prefer the bottle and reject the breast altogether.

Most women don't want to go on with both, because it
means all the trouble of formula-making and being tied
down by the nursing schedule. The most sensible thing to do
when the mother is producing a reasonable amount of milk
(say half or more of what the baby needs) is to first make a
real effort to dispense with the formula altogether (Section
130). If this does not increase the breast-milk supply sufficiently, then she can wean the baby completely to the bottle,
knowing that she has tried as hard as she could.

138. How to supplement the breast with the bottle (if
you cannot consult a doctor). Let's say that you have tried to
get along on breast feeding alone, but that it is not providing
sufficient milk. You have to give some formula to satisfy the
baby, but you want to do it in the way that is least likely to
decrease the breast-milk supply. I will discuss the subject in
different paragraphs, depending on how much extra the baby
needs, and use the word complemental to mean a bottle that
is given right after (in addition to) a breast feeding, and
supplemental to mean a bottle that is given instead of a
breast feeding. In a general way, it's more convenient to omit
certain breast feedings altogether and give supplemental
bottles instead. On the other hand, there's slightly more chance
of keeping up the breast-milk supply if you continue to give
the breast at every feeding, with a complemental bottle in
addition at certain feedings when the baby doesn't get enough
at breast.

Suppose the breasts are supplying enough at all but one
feeding. Six P.M. is apt to be the scantiest, 2 P.M. the next.
You could try giving a complemental bottle in addition to the
6 P.M. nursing. Or you could give a supplemental bottle instead of the 2 P.M. nursing; then there might be enough
breast milk stored up at 6 P.M.

Suppose the breasts are supplying less than enough at two
or more feedings. You could give complemental bottles after
the breast feedings at 10 A.M., 2 P.M. and 6 P.M. The 6
A.M. breast feeding is apt to be the largest of the day and
may supply all that the baby needs at that time. The 10 P.M.
breast feeding is also apt to be fairly large. Another method,
if the breasts are supplying less than enough at several feedings, would be to breast-feed alone at 6 A.M., 2 P.M., 10 P.M.,

and give supplemental bottles alone at 10 A.M. and 6 P.M. (also at 2 A.M. if the baby still needs to be fed then).

If the breast-milk supply is insufficient at all feedings, you will need a bottle at all feedings, whether you give the breast first or not.

How much formula do you put in each bottle, whether it is a complemental or a supplemental bottle? The answer is: As much as the baby seems to need. If your baby weighs 9 pounds or more, he may want 6 ounces in his supplemental bottle; if he is smaller, he may want less. If it's a complemental bottle after a breast feeding, he may want 2 to 3 ounces. If so, offer 3 ounces and let him take what he wants.

If your doctor has not given you a formula and you cannot reach him, you can try the formulas in this book. In Section 136 there are directions for making a formula for a 6-ounce relief bottle. You could use this for making one 6-ounce supplemental bottle, or for two 3-ounce complemental ones. If you need 12 ounces altogether, for two 6-ounce bottles or for three 4-ounce bottles, then double the quantities listed. If you need only 3 ounces altogether, use half the quantities listed. Don't worry too much about coming out even. If, for instance, you need one 4-ounce bottle a day, make a 6-ounce bottle and throw out what the baby doesn't want.

You can go on multiplying the 6-ounce relief-bottle formula as you need more, or you can turn to Section 177.

SPECIAL PROBLEMS OF BREAST FEEDING

139. The fiddler, the fusser, the sleeper and the waker. There are several patterns of behavior in the early weeks of nursing that complicate the mother's job and nearly drive her mad. The first is that of the baby who never seems to nurse very vigorously and falls asleep 5 minutes or so after starting. You don't know whether he has taken a reasonable amount or not. (A baby usually gets a major part of what's in the breast in 5 minutes of steady nursing.) It wouldn't be so bad if he'd sleep for 2 or 3 hours, but he may wake and cry again in a few minutes after he's put back to bed. We don't really know what causes this inefficient nursing or the prompt waking. One possibility is that the baby's nervous system and digestive system are not yet working well enough together. Perhaps the comfort of his mother's arms and the breast in his mouth is enough to put him back to sleep. When he's a little older and knows what it's all about, his hunger will keep him awake until he's well satisfied. In the bottle-fed baby, a contributory cause of falling asleep may be nipple holes that are too small. In the breast-fed baby, it may be that although the mother has plenty of milk, the baby cannot get it well enough.

It's probably that a mother's feelings control the ease with which the milk flows. Many mothers after a few weeks of nursing notice that as soon as they hear the baby cry with hunger, the milk starts to leak from the breasts. And feelings of anxiety or other tension probably hold the milk in. (Farmers know that cows can't "let down" the milk if they are tense.)

One baby who finds that he's getting little result from nursing goes back to sleep. Then when he's put back into the harder, cooler bed, his hunger wakes him up again. Another baby, who's hungrier or more wide awake or more assertive, reacts with irritation when he finds he can't get enough milk. He jerks his head away from the breast and yells, tries again, gets mad again.

The fact that the baby doesn't nurse well only increases the mother's uneasiness, so a vicious cycle sets in. If a mother understands this mechanism, she can use all her ingenuity in finding her own best way to relax before and during nursing. It's different with each individual. Music, a magazine, a glass of beer, a cigarette, television—whatever works best is what she should adopt.

If the baby gets sleepy or restless after a few minutes at one breast, you can try shifting right away to the other breast, to see if the easier flow of milk will help. Of course, you'd like him to work at least 15 minutes on one breast to be sure that it is well stimulated, but if he won't, he won't.

If the baby is one of those "resters," who doze, off and on, but suck well in between, let him continue. But if he doesn't resume nursing, it works better not to prolong the nursing or to keep trying to wake him up again. In the long run you only take away his enthusiasm and make him an indifferent eater.

What do you do if he wakes as soon as you put him to bed or a little later? I think it's better to assume first that if he has nursed for 5 minutes he's had enough to keep him satisfied for a couple of hours, and try not to feed him again right away. Let him fuss for a while if you can stand it. Give him a pacifier if you and your doctor approve. See if a hot water bottle will make him feel cozier (Section 293).

The purpose is to teach him that feedings come every few hours and that it's his eagerness that brings the satisfaction. To keep feeding him off and on for an hour and a half tends to teach him that feedings are always chasing him and that sometimes the only way to escape them is to go to sleep. However, the chances are that the baby will outgrow this inconvenient pattern in a few weeks, no matter how you handle it. So if he wakes as soon as he's in bed and can't be comforted and gets to crying frantically, you'd better feed him again anyway, and never mind the theory. You can at least give him a second chance. But don't go on to a third and a fourth feeding if you can help it. Make him wait an hour or two anyway.

140. Retracted nipples. If a mother's nipples are flat or retracted (drawn back into the breast by the supporting tissue), it may further complicate the business of getting a baby started at the breast, especially if he is the excitable type. If he searches around and can't find the nipple, he may cry angrily and pull his head back. There are several tactful things you can try. If possible, put him to breast when he first wakes up, before he gets too cross. If he starts crying at the first attempt, stop right away and comfort him before trying again. Take your time. It sometimes makes a nipple stand out better to massage it lightly with the fingers first. Or the baby can, for a couple of days, nurse for a minute or two through a nipple shield (Section 152), to draw the nipple out, before taking the mother's nipple directly.

Actually, the nipple is not so important in nursing (as explained in Section 115) as it is in guiding the baby to draw the entire areola into his mouth. However, the supporting tissues that retract the nipple also make it more difficult for the baby to draw the areola forward and shape it to his mouth. Probably the most valuable procedure is for the mother (or nurse) to squeeze some of the milk from the sinuses by manual expression (Sections 149, 150) so that the areolar region will be softer and more compressible. Then press the areola into a flatter shape, between thumb and finger, when putting it into the baby's mouth.

141. Pains during nursing. You may be bothered the first week or so by cramps in your lower abdomen as soon as the baby starts nursing. This is the normal reflex action by which nursing causes the uterus to contract. It is intended to

SPECIAL PROBLEMS OF BREAST FEEDING · 97

help the uterus get back to its nonpregnant size. These cramps disappear after a while.

Twinges of pain in the nipple that last a few seconds after the baby begins to nurse, for the first few days or weeks, are very common, mean nothing and will soon go away.

142. Sore or cracked nipples. Pain that persists throughout the nursing may point to a cracked nipple, and a careful search should be made. (A very few mothers are unusually sensitive and continue to feel pain even though the nipples remain healthy.) If a nipple is cracked (often because a baby has chewed on it instead of taking the whole areola into his mouth), it is usually recommended that nursing be stopped on that breast for 24 to 48 hours (or at least cut down to perhaps 3 minutes every 8 hours). The physician may prescribe an ointment for the sore nipple. Another method is to let the nipples dry for 15 minutes before closing the flaps of the brassiere; or leave them open. Remove the waterproof lining from the brassiere. One mother found successful a small tea strainer (the kind that can be detached from the handle) over the nipple, inside an ample brassiere.

To provide continued stimulation of the breast or to relieve fullness, milk can be expressed manually, 2 or 3 times in the 24 hours. The baby nurses at the other breast at each feeding.

If the nipple is much improved after 12 to 48 hours of rest, the baby may be allowed to nurse at it very briefly (perhaps 3 minutes), provided this is not painful. If all goes well, he continues to nurse a limited amount at that breast—for example, not more than 5 minutes each time the first day, 10 minutes the second, 15 minutes the third. If the crack and pain return, the rest treatment is repeated.

Another method of treating cracked nipples is to let the baby continue nursing but through a nipple shield (Section 152). This is apt to be less successful, because it does not give the mother's nipple a complete rest and because it usually produces less milk than a mother can get by manual expression.

143. Distended breasts; areolar engorgement. There are three different ways in which the breasts may become overdistended or engorged. The commonest and simplest is caused by overfilling of the sinuses, the storage spaces located behind the areola. This is not uncomfortable for the mother, but it may make the areolar region so firm and flat that the baby cannot take it into his mouth in order to compress it with his gums. The only thing he can get hold of is the nipple, and he is apt to chew on it and perhaps make it sore. It is important, therefore, for the mother or nurse to express sufficient milk from the sinuses so that the areolar region will become soft enough and compressible enough for the baby to take it into his mouth (Sections 149, 150).

It is not necessary to express much milk to soften the areolar region. Two to 5 minutes on each breast should be sufficient. Then the mother can compress the areola region from above and below as she puts the breast into the baby's mouth, to help him get started. This type of engorgement is most likely to occur in the latter half of the first week, to last 2 or 3 days, and not to return, as long as nursing continues normally.

144. Peripheral engorgement. Another type of engorgement involves not just the areolar region but the whole breast. The entire breast becomes firm and uncomfortable. Most cases are mild, but in the infrequent case that becomes severe, the breast is enlarged, surprisingly hard and very painful.

The usual mild case can be relieved promptly by having the baby nurse. It may be necessary to soften the areolar region first by manual expression if it is too firm for the baby to get into his mouth.

The severe case may require several different kinds of treatment. If the baby cannot consume enough milk to relieve the distension, the entire breast needs to be massaged, starting at the outer edges and working toward the areola. Cocoa butter or cold cream should be used during the massage to avoid irritating the skin, but the ointment should be kept off the areola, because it makes it too slippery for areolar expression, which comes next. Massage of the entire breast is tiring to the mother and should be carried on only long enough to partially relieve the engorgement. It may be performed once or several times a day. The difficulty usually lasts only 2 or 3 days. The application of cloths wet with comfortably hot water seems to help prepare the breasts for massage. If massage and manual expression cannot be used successfully because there is no one available to do it or to teach the mother how, a breast pump can be tried (Section 151). Between nursings or treatments, a firm support should be given to the breasts from all sides by a large, firm brassiere or by a binder that gives support from the shoulders. The binder should be used not to flatten the breasts against the chest but to support them firmly from below and both sides. An ice bag or hot water bottle can be applied for short periods. There are various medications that the physician may prescribe. This total engorgement practically always occurs, if at all, in the latter half of the first week. It is rare after that.

145. Caked breast and breast abscess. A third type of engorgement is similar to total engorgement in that it is outside the areolar region and is painful. But it is confined to only one segment of the breast. This type is sometimes called caked breast. It is more likely to occur after the hospital period. Treatment is similar to that of total engorgement: hot applications followed by massage of the engorged area, support by an efficient brassiere or a binder, ice bag or hot water bottle between treatments, continuation of nursing.

If a sore spot develops inside the breast, this may be an infection, or breast abscess. The skin may become red over it. You should take your temperature and get in touch with your doctor. However, with modern methods of treating infections, it may not be necessary to keep the baby from nursing at that breast, even temporarily.

146. When the mother is ill. In the ordinary illnesses during which the mother stays at home, it is customary to allow the baby to continue to nurse as usual. To be sure, there is a chance of the baby's catching the ailment, but this would be true even if he weren't being nursed. Besides, most infections are contagious before any symptoms are noticed. Babies on the average have milder colds than older members of the family.

147. Biting the nipple (when the baby gets teeth). You can't blame the baby for trying a few bites when his gums are tingling during teething or when a couple of teeth have come in. He doesn't realize it hurts. But it's not only painful; it may make the nipples so sore that nursing has to be stopped.

Most babies can be taught quickly not to bite. Instantly slip your finger between his gums and say "No" very firmly. This surprises him and usually inhibits him. If he does it again, put your finger in again, say "No" and end the feeding.

It's usually late in the feeding anyway, when a baby starts to bite.

MANUAL EXPRESSION AND BREAST PUMPS

148. The purpose. Manual expression or breast pumps are used to obtain milk for the baby when he cannot or will not nurse at the breast, although the mother has plenty of milk. A small, premature baby may be too weak to nurse, or to be taken out of the incubator. He can be fed breast milk from a bottle or medicine dropper. When an ill mother is away in a hospital, or when it is considered unwise, in the home, to expose the baby to her directly, her milk can be collected and given to the baby from a bottle (or discarded) until she can nurse him again.

When it is desired to obtain plenty of milk or to keep the breasts functioning, they are emptied at regular intervals. When the breasts are partially emptied to spare the mother pain during weaning, it is done only as often as necessary and only long enough to relieve the pressure.

The best way to learn manual expression is from an experienced nurse while you are in the hospital. It's a good idea to get some instruction even though you don't anticipate using it. Or a public health nurse or a visiting nurse can teach you at home. A mother can learn by herself, but this takes a little longer. In any case, it seems like an awkward business at first, and several practice sessions will be necessary before you become very efficient. Don't be discouraged.

The milk produced in the glandular tissue throughout the breast flows through tiny tubes toward the center of the breast and is stored in 15 to 20 sinuses, or sacs, which are located behind the areola, the dark-colored skin around the nipple. In manual expression, the milk is squeezed out of the sinuses, each of which has a small tube leading through the nipple to the outside.

If you are going to express only a small amount of milk—for instance, to relieve engorgement in the areolar area—you can use any handy cup to catch it. If you are going to express as much as you can and will be giving it to the baby right afterward, you should wash the cup with soap, rinse it and dry it with a clean towel. After expressing the milk, you pour it into a nursing bottle and cap with a nipple, both of which should have been washed with soap and rinsed since the last use. If you are going to save the milk for a number of hours—for instance, if you are delivering it once a day to the hospital for a premature baby—it should be kept as sterile as possible. Either you can express the milk into a sterilized cup and then transfer it to a sterilized bottle with cap and nipple (sterilized by boiling for 5 minutes), or you can use a washed cup, bottle, cap and nipple, and sterilize after the milk is in the bottle (Sections 181-183).

149. The finger-and-thumb method. In the commoner method of manual expression, the sinuses are repeatedly squeezed between thumb and finger. First, of course, you wash your hands with soap. To apply the pressure where the sinuses lie, deep behind the areola, it is necessary to place the tips of thumb and finger on opposite sides of the areola (just at the edge where the dark skin meets the normally colored skin). Then press thumb and finger in deeply until they meet the ribs. In this position, squeeze them rhythmically together. The right hand is usually used to express the left breast, and in this instance the left hand holds the cup that catches the milk

The main thing is to press in deeply enough and at the edge of the areola. The nipple itself is not squeezed or fingered. You may be able to get more milk with each squeeze if you not only press thumb and finger toward each other but

pull slightly outward with them (toward the nipple) at the same time, to complete the milking motion.

After a bit, the thumb and finger can be shifted, partway "around the clock," to be sure that all the sinuses are being pressed. If the finger and thumb become tired—and they will at first—you can shift back and forth from side to side.

150. The thumb-and-cup method. Another method, less commonly used but very efficient when learned, is to press the sinuses between the thumb and the inside edge of a teacup that has a flared edge (it's too hard to get the areola and the thumb down inside a cup with straight sides). If you will be saving the milk for hours, the cup should be sterilized.

First, wash your hands with soap and water. Tuck the lower edge of the cup **deep** into the left breast, at the lower edge of the areola, and tip the cup up partway, holding it with the left hand. Place the thumb of the right hand on the **upper** edge of the areola. Now the areola is being pressed between the right thumb and the rim of the cup. Press the right thumb firmly inward (toward the rim) and then downward

(toward the nipple). This squeezes the milk from the sacs into the tubes running through the nipple. When you press toward the nipple, don't slide your thumb across the dark skin; the skin moves with the thumb. It is not necessary to squeeze or even touch the nipple.

With a little practice, you will be able to press the milk out in a fine spray. The first few days your thumb may be tired and lame, but this won't last. If you are emptying a full breast, it may take 20 minutes—more if you are just learning. If you are attempting to empty the breasts completely after the baby has finished nursing, it will take only a few minutes. When the breast is full, the milk comes in a spray. When it is partly empty, it comes in drops. Stop when no more milk comes. Naturally, if you wait 10 minutes the breast will have made more milk, but you don't have to empty it again.

151. Breast pumps. The simplest, least expensive and easiest to find is of glass, with a rubber bulb to apply the suction. Then there are electric breast pumps, which can be rented from some hospitals and surgical-supply stores, and which are a lot more efficient.

152. A nipple shield consists of a rubber nipple attached to a rubber or glass cone that fits over the front of the breast. The all-rubber type is more efficient. As the baby sucks on the rubber nipple, a vacuum is created in the cone and this draws the areola into the cone and draws out some of the milk. A nipple shield is used temporarily when the mother's nipples are retracted or sore.

WEANING FROM THE BREAST

Weaning is important not only for the baby but for the mother, and not only physically but emotionally. A mother who has set great store by nursing may feel mildly let down and depressed after she stops—as if she has lost some of her closeness to the baby or as if she has become a less worthwhile person. This is an additional reason for making weaning a gradual process whenever possible.

153. Weaning when there is little breast milk. Weaning from the breast is quite easy when the mother is producing only a small amount of milk. It's usually not necessary for her to bind her breasts or limit her own fluids. She can just stop putting the baby to breast and wait. If the breasts get so full that they are uncomfortable, she can nurse him for 15 or 30 seconds. This will relieve the pressure without really stimulating the breast. If the breasts should become uncomfortable again, she can repeat this. If she is producing a moderate amount of milk, she should plan to wean more gradually. It still isn't necessary to bind the breasts or to limit fluids. Try omitting every other breast feeding. If, in a day or two, the breasts have not become uncomfortably full, stop all regular nursing, but put the baby to breast for a short period if the breasts then become uncomfortable.

If you have no doctor to advise you, use the formula in Section 177.

154. Sudden weaning from the breast (if you cannot consult a doctor). You may have to wean the baby from the breast suddenly if, for instance, you become seriously ill or you have to go out of town for an emergency. (It is not usually necessary to wean the baby because of mild or moderately severe illness in the mother. Your doctor is the one to decide this.) One method is to limit the fluids that the mother drinks and to apply a tight binder and ice bags to her breasts. This is a pretty uncomfortable business. A better way is to relieve the breasts whenever they become uncomfortably full, either with a breast pump or by manual expression. If you consult a doctor, he may recommend several days of injections with a special preparation that decreases milk production.

If you have no doctor to advise you, use the formula in Section 177.

155. Gradual weaning from breast to cup in the middle of the first year. If a mother is producing plenty of milk, how long should she plan to nurse? Best of all, most natural of all, is to nurse until the baby is ready for weaning to the cup. Most breast-fed babies are becoming bored between 5 and 6 months.

It's a good idea to begin offering a sip of milk from the cup from the age of 5 months, so that the baby gets used to it before he is too opinionated. By 6 months encourage him to hold the cup himself (Sections 231–234). If by 5, 5½ or 6 months he is nursing for shorter periods, I would assume he is ready for gradual weaning. Now offer him the cup at all his meals and increase the amount as he shows his willingness to take more, but continue to breast-feed him at the end of the meal. Next, leave out one of his daily breast feedings, the one that he seems the least interested in, giving him only the cup. This is usually at breakfast or lunch. In a week, omit another breast feeding if he seems willing, and in another week, the last one. His willingness to be weaned may not progress steadily. If he gets into a period when he is miserable from teething or illness, he may want to retreat a little. This is natural enough, and there is no danger in accommodating him.

When weaning is carried out this gradually, there is usually no problem about the mother's breasts. If, however, they become uncomfortably full at any time, the mother only needs to allow the baby to nurse for 15 to 30 seconds to relieve the pressure. Don't let him nurse for 5 minutes—that will encourage the breasts too much.

Most mothers find they are a bit reluctant to end this important emotional tie and some of them will put off weaning, week after week.

Sometimes a mother will be afraid to give up nursing altogether, because the baby is not taking as much milk from the cup as he used to take from the breast. This may postpone the weaning indefinitely. I would stop the nursing if the baby is taking an average of 4 ounces from the cup at each meal, or a total of 12 to 16 ounces a day. After the nursing is stopped, he will probably increase the amount from the cup up to a total of 16 ounces or more. This is usually enough, with all the other things he is eating.

I think it is preferable to have a baby weaned from the breast by 6 or 7 months if he seems ready for it. A child seldom demands the breast after that, and it's apt to be continued for some other reason. When breast feeding is continued way beyond the age that the child really needs it, it may become a habit that makes him unnaturally dependent on his mother.

Some other points about weaning are taken up in Sections 231–237.

156. Gradual weaning from breast to bottle in the first 4 months. There are lots of mothers who either aren't able or don't want to nurse a baby until he is ready to be weaned to the cup at about 5 or 6 months. In one case the milk supply becomes insufficient. The baby cries from hunger and fails to gain sufficient weight. A hungry baby like this seldom puts up any fuss over weaning to the bottle. How fast the weaning to the bottle goes will depend on how much the mother is producing.

If you find that your breast-milk supply is failing rapidly and the baby is quite hungry, and if you have no doctor to consult, make up a complete formula from Section 177 or 178. Give him a bottle at each feeding, after the breast, letting him take as much or as little of it as he wants. Omit the breast feeding at 6 P.M. Two days later omit the 10 A.M. breast feeding, also. Discontinue the remaining breast feedings, one every 2 or 3 days, in the following order: 2 P.M., 10 P.M., 6 A.M. (If the mother's milk is decreasing only gradually and the baby is only slightly dissatisfied, it will work better to introduce the bottles one feeding at a time, as in the third paragraph below.)

But suppose there is no problem of the milk supply giving out. Let's say a mother wants to nurse her baby for a few months to give him a good start, but not for most of the year. How long is it important to nurse? There's no hard-and-fast answer to this, of course. The physical advantages of breast milk, its purity, its easy digestibility, are most valuable to the baby at first. But there is no age at which they suddenly become of no benefit. The emotional advantages of breast feeding will not cease at any definite period, either. One sensible time to wean to the bottle is at about 3 months. By this age the baby's digestive system will have settled down. He will be about over any tendency to colic. He will be pretty husky and still gaining rapidly. But if a mother would like to stop at 1 or 2 months, those are satisfactory times to wean, too. It is a little safer not to wean in very hot weather.

If you plan to wean to the bottle at some age beyond 1 month, it is wiser to keep the baby accustomed to the bottle from the age of 1 month on, by giving him one regularly 2 or 3 times a week, every day if you prefer.

If the breasts have been producing a good amount of milk, the weaning should preferably be gradual from the beginning. First, omit one breast feeding a day, say a 6 P.M., and give a bottle instead. Let the baby take as much or as little of this as he wants. Wait 2 or 3 days until the breasts become adjusted to the change, then omit the 10 A.M. breast feeding, too, and substitute the second daily bottle. Again wait 2 or 3 days, and then omit the 2 P.M. breast feeding. Now the baby is getting the breast only at 6 A.M. and 10 P.M. and a bottle at each of the other three feedings. You will probably need to wait 3 or even 4 days each time before omitting these last two nursings. Any time the breasts become uncomfortable, even though it isn't time for a scheduled nursing, let the baby nurse for a few seconds, or use manual expression or a breast pump for a few minutes, just to relieve the pressure. Then it should not be necessary to use a binder or to limit your fluids.

157. If the baby won't take the bottle. A baby of 2 months or more who has not regularly had a bottle may balk completely. Try for a week offering him a bottle once or twice a day, before the breast or solid food. Don't force it; don't get him angry. Take it away if he refuses, and give him the rest of his meal, including the breast. In a few days' time, he may change his mind.

If he's still adamant, omit the 2 P.M. breast feeding altogether and see if this makes him thirsty enough so that he will try the bottle at 6 P.M. If he still holds out, you will probably have to give him the breast anyway at the 6 P.M. feeding, because it will be uncomfortably full. But continue to omit the 2 P.M. nursing for several days. It may work on a subsequent day, though it didn't the first.

The next step is to try omitting every other breast feeding throughout the 24 hours (nurse at 6 A.M., 2 P.M., 10 P.M.) and hold down on the solid foods so that he's pretty hungry —or omit solids altogether.

The only alternative left is to stop breast feeding entirely and starve him into capitulation. I put this last, because it is drastic for both baby and mother.

The mother can use a breast pump or manual expression (Sections 149–151) just enough to relieve the pressure and discomfort.

Bottle Feeding

VARIOUS MILKS

158. What is a formula? There is nothing mysterious about a formula. It is a mixture of cow's milk, water and sugar. (Sometimes the doctor omits sugar.) The water and sugar are put in to make the mixture more like mother's milk in composition. The cow's milk that you use may be evaporated milk, pasteurized whole milk or powdered milk. Each has its special advantages. A variety of sugars are used. The commonest are granulated sugar, corn syrup, brown sugar and mixtures of dextrins and maltose.

The reason you have to sterilize carefully the ingredients and the bottles is that germs thrive on milk, just the way babies do. If a few bacteria get into the formula when you make it on Tuesday, they may have multiplied a lot by the time the baby drinks the last of it on Wednesday, especially if the formula has not been well refrigerated. Boiling the formula also makes it more digestible.

Your doctor will prescribe the best kind of milk for your baby, taking into account his particular needs and what is available. The commonest milks used in formula-making are listed for general information.

159. Evaporated milk. Evaporated milk is canned milk from which a little more than half the water has been removed. (It should not be confused with **condensed** milk, which is heavily sweetened with sugar and is not suitable for infants.) The advantages of evaporated milk are several. It is thoroughly sterilized in the process of canning, so it is free of germs when you open it. It is, in most localities, cheaper than fresh milk. It can be kept indefinitely in the unopened can without refrigeration. It's the same wherever you buy it, so a baby who travels doesn't have to adjust to different kinds of milk. It is a little easier to digest than fresh milk and less apt to cause allergies, like eczema. It contains added vitamin D.

When you have listed all these advantages, you wonder why anyone uses fresh milk. The main reasons are custom and taste. The taste of evaporated milk doesn't appeal to some older children and adults who have become accustomed to fresh milk. But babies love it, and they rarely object to changing back and forth. There's no reason why a baby shouldn't go on drinking evaporated milk for years (Section 230).

Since evaporated milk is about twice the strength of fresh milk, you always dilute it with at least an equal amount of water.

There are many brands of evaporated milk. All are of about the same composition. You do not have to worry about switching from one brand to another.

160. Modified evaporated and powdered milks. A number of evaporated and powdered milks, with special brand names, have already been modified to make them closer to breast milk in composition, and many doctors prescribe them routinely. In all of them sugar has been added (so that the mother does not have to do this herself), and in some of them the protein has been decreased. These milks should be used on a doctor's recommendation and diluted according to directions.

161. Prepared (ready-to-use) formulas. These are ready-to-use formulas in disposable bottles or cans which are, of course, extremely convenient to use, though several times as expensive as what you can prepare yourself.

162. Pasteurized milk. If you are going to make your baby's formula from fresh rather than evaporated milk, it is very desirable that it be pasteurized. In pasteurization, the milk is heated, before being bottled in the dairy, to kill the bacteria dangerous to human beings.

163. Homogenized milk is pasteurized milk in which the fat droplets have been broken up into much smaller particles, making the fat easier to digest. The cream does not rise to the top but stays mixed throughout the milk. Homogenized milk has some advantages for a baby who digests milk poorly. It causes less scum than ordinary milk and will be helpful if you are having trouble with clogged nipples.

164. Vitamin D (pasteurized) milk is available in some localities.

165. Raw milk is unpasteurized. It is milk just as it comes from the cow. It should be boiled for 5 minutes, not only for babies but for children of all ages. This is to be sure that it does not contain bacteria that cause diarrhea, sore throat, tuberculosis or other infections. Raw milk from Jersey and Guernsey cows is apt to be richer in cream than ordinary commercial milk, and so may upset a baby's digestion. If you move to the country and get this rich milk, you should pour off a little of the cream, so that what's left looks about like commercial milk.

166. Whole milk is an expression used in formula-making. It means that the normal amount of cream is mixed throughout the milk. To obtain whole milk, you shake up the bottle of pasteurized milk, if it is not homogenized, to mix the cream with the rest of the milk. You do this before using any for the formula. If you leave the cream on top and use only the milk in the upper part of the bottle, the formula will be too rich in butter fat. On the other hand, if you are using a bottle of milk from which the top cream has already been used, the formula will be too thin. You don't have to shake homogenized milk, because the cream does not separate.

167. Half-skimmed milk, in which about half the cream has been removed, is preferred by some doctors for feeding **premature babies** until they weigh about 5 pounds, because it is more easily digested than milk with all the cream still in it. (Skimmed milk with **all** the cream removed is too weak for feeding prematures.)

You may be able to buy half-skimmed powdered milk in cans at the grocery or drugstore. Most brands are converted back to liquid half-skimmed milk by mixing in water in the ratio of 2 ounces of water to 1 level tablespoonful of powdered milk (consult the label). Directions for liquefying are in Section 169.

Some commercial dairies sell pasteurized half-skimmed milk in bottles. Or you can buy pasteurized whole milk and remove half the cream with a skimming spoon (or a round measuring spoon, the bowl of which is bent at right angles to the handle).

168. Skimmed milk (for diarrhea). Skimmed milk, or skimmed milk diluted to half strength, is often prescribed for diarrhea, because milk is easier to digest when there is no cream in it. Most dairies sell skimmed pasteurized milk.

You can probably buy powdered skimmed milk in cans at the grocery or drugstore. Most brands are converted back to liquid skimmed milk by mixing in water in the ratio of 2 ounces of water to 1 level tablespoonful of powder (consult the label), as in Section 169.

When you are making **diluted** skimmed milk for diarrhea, you use only half that amount of powder: 1 level tablespoonful of powder to 4 ounces of water.

169. Powdered milk. Powdered whole milk is useful if you are traveling with your baby, or if you are going to live in an uncivilized spot where you can't get evaporated or safe fresh milk. You can carry a large supply with you, and it won't weigh too much. It is more expensive than fresh or evaporated milk. You turn it back into liquid **whole** milk by mixing in the proportion of 1 level tablespoonful of powdered milk to 2 ounces of water. If your baby is taking a formula of 10 ounces of evaporated milk, 20 ounces of water, and 2 tablespoonfuls of granulated sugar, you use 10 tablespoonfuls of powdered milk. You mix this with 30 ounces of water and 2 tablespoonfuls of sugar.

You boil the required amount of water, and dissolve the sugar in it. When this has cooled at least to body heat, place the powder on top and beat it in with a sterilized fork or egg beater.

Powdered milk should be kept in the refrigerator after the can has been opened.

We have been talking about powdered **whole** milk. There are other varieties of powdered milk in which the proportions of the different elements have been changed. The latter should be used only under a physician's supervision.

170. Lactic-acid milk. Lactic-acid milk is a sour milk. It can be made in two ways. In a commercial dairy or in a formula room in a hospital, they put lactic-acid bacilli into pasteurized milk. The bacilli produce the lactic acid, which sours the milk.

The other way is to add the chemical **lactic acid** to pasteurized or evaporated milk. This can be done in the home.

Lactic-acid milk is more easily digested by some babies than ordinary sweet milk. Doctors often prescribe it for those who have painful indigestion, or who vomit a lot, or who have a tendency to diarrhea. Some doctors prefer to use it routinely for all babies. It discourages the growth of harmful bacteria, so it is safer than sweet milk when refrigeration is poor. The amounts of milk, water and sugar are the same as in an ordinary formula.

Lactic-acid milk is a little tricky to make in the home. The three important things are to have the milk and water well chilled, to acidify the milk very gradually, and not to get the milk too hot after it is acidified. You boil your milk in one saucepan, cool it, then chill it in the refrigerator. In a separate saucepan, boil your water and sugar, then cool and chill it. Now add 1 teaspoonful of "U.S.P. Lactic Acid" to the water and sugar. (This is the usual amount for a total formula of 24 to 30 ounces. For a smaller formula, use proportionately less.) Now add the acidified water to the milk very slowly, stirring constantly. If someone can help you, have her pour the acidified water into the milk while you stir continuously with an egg beater. You are trying to avoid getting too much acid in any one part of the milk, because that makes a large, tough curd which won't go through the nipple. That's why you add the acid to the water first, so that it will be diluted before it touches the milk. If you have a formula calling for just milk and sugar, no water, I would add the lactic acid to 1 or 2 ounces of water anyway, before adding it to the milk.

If you warm the bottle for the baby, don't heat it too rapidly or too hot. Heat it in a pan of warm water. If you prepare lactic-acid milk carefully, the curds will be fine enough to go through the ordinary-size nipple holes. If necessary, enlarge the nipple holes.

You can buy prepared whole lactic-acid milk in some large cities. It is usually quite expensive. You can also buy it in powdered form, through your druggist. In using it in a formula, you add water and sugar, the same way as in a sweet-milk formula.

171. Artificial milks, for babies and children who are allergic to real milk, are made from a mixture of foods, such as soybean flour and sugar. They require larger nipple holes.

VARIOUS SUGARS

The doctor will prescribe the sugar that he thinks best for your baby (or none at all). The usual sugars are listed here.

172. Ordinary granulated sugar is commonly used in formula-making because it is cheap, available and usually satisfactory. Being highly refined, it has nothing in it to counteract constipation, if a baby has that tendency. The largest amount usually added to a 24-hour formula is 2 or 3 tablespoonfuls.

173. Brown sugar is a less refined sugar. It is useful when the baby's stools are too dry and firm. A tablespoonful has the same food value as a tablespoonful of granulated sugar.

174. Corn syrup is also commonly used in formulas. It contains a mixture of sugar and dextrins. A dextrin is half-way between a sugar and a starch. In the intestine, it is only slowly converted into sugar, so that at any one time there is less sugar in the intestine to make gas. That's why a dextrin mixture is thought to be better for a baby who is forming lots of gas or has a tendency to looseness. However, it can be used for babies with good digestions, too. It is inexpensive. You use the same number of tablespoonfuls of it as you would of granulated sugar. The maximum for a 24-hour formula is usually 2 or 3 tablespoonfuls. The light syrup is ordinarily used, unless there is a tendency to constipation. The dark syrup, being less refined, is slightly more laxative.

175. Dextrin and maltose preparations are much like corn syrup, except that they are in powder form and are more expensive. A tablespoonful contains only half as much nourishment (calories) as granulated sugar. Therefore, if you are changing, you use 2 tablespoonfuls of a dextrin and maltose preparation in place of 1 tablespoonful of granulated sugar. The maximum for a 24-hour formula is usually 4 to 6 tablespoonfuls.

176. Lactose is the sugar that naturally occurs in human and cow's milk. It is satisfactory for formulas, but expensive. It takes 1½ tablespoonfuls of it to equal 1 tablespoonful of granulated sugar.

FORMULAS FOR EMERGENCY USE

In the next pages are a couple of formulas for parents who are completely unable to consult a doctor about a baby's feeding. If you bring your baby to a private doctor, clinic, baby-health station, or have the help of a visiting or public health nurse, you will be given formulas based on your baby's age, weight, rate of gain, and digestion. That is the only sound way to decide on the right formula. If you are completely out of reach and if your baby is healthy and normal, you can probably make out with the formulas in this book and a little common sense.

There are **prepared formulas,** ready to use, though relatively expensive (Section 161).

177. A moderately dilute formula suitable for a newborn baby or for a baby with a small appetite:

evaporated milk .... 10 ounces
water .... 20 ounces
corn syrup .... 2 level tablespoonfuls

This will make 30 ounces of formula, which will probably be more than the average baby will need in 24 hours until he weighs 9 or 10 pounds.

How many ounces in how many bottles? A 6-pounder may want about 3 ounces roughly every 3 hours during the day (6 A.M., 9 A.M., 12 noon, 3 P.M., 6 P.M.) and about every 4 hours at night (10 P.M., 2 A.M.), a total of about 21 ounces in the 24 hours.

A 7- or 8-pounder may want about 4 ounces on an average of every 4 hours day and night (6 A.M., 10 A.M., 2 P.M., 6

P.M., 10 P.M., 2 A.M.) for the first week or so, a total of about 24 ounces. But usually, by the time he is a few weeks old, he is willing, if waked and fed at 10 or 11 P.M., to sleep through the 2 A.M. feeding. Then you can put larger amounts in fewer bottles.

You can divide your total formula any way that is most convenient, depending on how many bottles your baby wants in the 24 hours and how many ounces he usually wants at each feeding.

In the early weeks, for instance, if you are making a total of 30 ounces of formula for a 7- or 8-pound baby, you can put 3¾ ounces in each of 8 bottles. If he is unusually regular and needs only 6 bottles in 24 hours, you can use the extra bottles for the first two feedings of the next 24-hour period and then make up the next formula later in the day. Or you can discard the extra bottles (or use the formula for cooking) and make up the new formula at always the same time of day.

But most babies wake somewhat irregularly at first. If your doctor has recommended a flexible schedule (feeding the baby—at least during the day—whenever he seems really hungry, regardless of the clock), the two extra bottles may well be called for by a baby who wakes more frequently than six times in the 24 hours. It is unlikely, though, that a 7- or 8-pounder will want more than 20 to 24 ounces in the 24 hours, so you can expect several bottles to be only partly finished.

If in the early weeks your baby wakes and is hungry for more feedings than you have bottles for, you can make the next formula early. If this works you back to an inconvenient hour for formula preparation, you can make formula twice in one day to catch up.

As your baby gets older and grows bigger, you can expect him to cut down gradually on the number of feedings each day, to increase the amount he wants in an average feeding, and to increase his total amount for the day. As you watch his changing pattern, you will be able to decide when to increase the amount in each bottle and cut down on the number of bottles. Thirty ounces of total formula make about 3¾ ounces in 8 bottles, 4¼ ounces in 7 bottles, 5 ounces in 6 bottles, 6 ounces in 5 bottles.

178. A full-strength formula for a baby who has become dissatisfied with the more dilute formula (probably when he weighs about 10 pounds):

evaporated milk ....13 ounces (1 can)
water (to make a total of one
   quart)..19 ounces
corn syrup... 3 tablespoonfuls

This will make about 5¼ ounces in 6 bottles, 6½ ounces in 5 bottles, 8 ounces in 4 bottles.

179. Weakening the formula temporarily. (Directions for those who cannot consult a doctor. If you can reach a doctor, he is the one to advise you about any changes.) The formula may be weakened temporarily—for example, if a baby is having a spell of indigestion or mild diarrhea or if a newborn baby has a poor appetite and is finishing only about half of each bottle.

If the bottles have already been prepared with the usual formula, pour off half the quantity, add an equal amount of boiled water. Make 1 or 2 extra bottles with the formula you are pouring off. If you are just making the formula, do it the usual way but put only half the usual amount into each bottle and then add an equal amount of boiled water. Make 1 or 2 extra bottles with the remaining formula, weakened the same way.

This method of weakening a formula may sound wasteful, but it's safer than getting all mixed up in more complicated arithmetic. Besides, it's convenient to have an extra bottle or two of formula. A baby whose formula has been weakened may suddenly get very hungry.

PREPARING A FORMULA

There are various ways of preparing a formula. Which one you use depends on what the doctor or nurse who teaches you recommends, how much special equipment you have, what you find easiest.

The method described here is called **terminal sterilization,** because the sterilizing of the formula and of the bottles takes place at the end of the preparation, after the formula is all in the nursing bottles. This method is the simplest and the safest. The only trouble is that there is apt to be more scum to clog the nipple holes, because there is no chance to strain the formula after it has been boiled.

The reason for all this sterilizing is that germs grow readily in milk, and germs added at the time the formula is prepared may multiply a lot by the time the baby drinks it if it is not well refrigerated.

180. Care of bottles and nipples after use. After the baby has finished with a bottle, rinse it, squirt a little water through the nipple to remove scum, wash the bottle, nipple, and bottle cap briefly but vigorously with cold water, detergent and a jar brush. Rinse and set to drain.

It is easier to get the equipment clean if you wash it right after use. But if you prefer, you can wash all the bottles, nipples and caps together before making formula.

If you have trouble with clogged nipples, clean each nipple hole daily by rotating a toothpick in it. See also Section 190.

PREPARING THE FORMULA

181. Equipment (see Sections 68–73 for description of equipment). Equipment should be clean but need not be sterilized ahead of time.

1. **8-ounce nursing bottles.** As many as the baby will need for taking the total amount of formula, probably 6 to 8 bottles for 24 hours in the beginning. You may want an extra bottle for water if the baby takes it.

2. An equal number of **nipples, bottle caps** and **disks.**

3. A **quart measure** of glass.

4. A **tablespoon** for stirring.

5. A set of **measuring spoons,** and if you are using a dry sugar, a knife to level the sugar in the spoon.

6. A **can opener,** for evaporated milk. (A beer-can opener is easiest.)

7. A **sterilizing pail** with **lid** and **bottle rack.**

182. Mixing the formula. Let's, for an example, assume that the formula will be:

evaporated milk...................................10 ounces
water...20 ounces
corn syrup.. 2 tablespoonfuls

with which you expect to make 7 bottles of about 4¼ ounces each.

Run faucet water (hot or cold) into the quart measure up to the 20-ounce mark.

Put the 2 level tablespoonfuls of corn syrup into the water and stir until dissolved (syrup or sugar dissolves faster in warm water).

Briefly wash the top of a 13-ounce can of evaporated milk with soap; rinse; then make two openings with the can opener on opposite sides of the top, one to let the milk out, the other to let air in.

Pour 10 ounces of the evaporated milk into the quart measure, bringing the total to 30 ounces.

Stir with the tablespoon and pour about 4¼ ounces into each of 7 bottles.

183. Sterilizing the formula. Insert the nipples upside down in the caps, cover with the disks, then screw the caps partly on. Leave the caps only partly screwed on so that there will be a space for hot air to escape as the bottles heat up, and to re-enter as the bottles cool again.

Place the bottles in the wire rack in the sterilizing pail, put an inch or two of hot water in the bottom, put the pail on the stove, and heat. The water should boil for a full 25 minutes.

It has been discovered that there will be the least clogging of the nipple holes if the formula is allowed to cool slowly without being shaken at all. (This allows the scum to form into one large firm piece.) So leave the sterilizing pail (with its cover on) right on the stove (with the heat off) for an hour or two.

When the bottles are lukewarm, screw the caps down and place the bottles in the refrigerator.

FORMULA REFRIGERATION

184. Insufficient space in refrigerator. If you don't have room in your refrigerator for 5 or 6 bottles, you can sterilize your formula in a quart bottle. Just before each feeding pour the required amount of formula into a clean nursing bottle. The nursing bottle doesn't have to be sterilized if it's been well scrubbed and if the formula will be drunk right away. Formula shouldn't remain for hours in an unsterilized bottle.

185. Saving the unused evaporated milk. When you use less than a full can of evaporated milk, you can save what is left for the next day. Leave it in the can and cover the top with a fresh piece of waxed paper held with a rubber band to keep bacteria, mold and dust particles from drifting in. Keep the covered can in the refrigerator, and use it all up the next day.

186. If you cannot keep the formula cold. If you ever get into a situation where you can't keep the baby's bottles cold until feeding time—for instance, if your refrigerator stops working—you will be pretty safe if you heat each bottle before giving it. Put the bottle in hot water, bring to a boil, boil 25 minutes, then cool it down to body temperature before giving it.

GIVING THE BOTTLE

187. The first few days. Usually the first bottle is offered about 12 hours after the baby is born, though it can be started earlier if he seems hungry. The baby is apt to want little the first few feedings. Even if he takes only half an ounce, don't try to get more into him. It's often 3 or 4 days before he wants the amounts you expect him to need, and it may take a week or more. Don't worry; it may be better for his digestion to start gradually. He'll find out what he needs when he comes more to life in a few days.

188. Giving the formula. You don't need to shake the bottle when you remove it from the refrigerator unless the formula is made from unhomogenized fresh milk—in which case the cream needs mixing in.

It has been discovered that babies enjoy just as well and do just as well on formula that is either warmed or at room temperature or right out of the refrigerator, as long as it comes at the same temperature at each feeding. I think the main reason why many mothers still warm the bottles is that they have always thought of bottles as being warmed and breast milk is warm, so it seems unkind to give a baby cold milk. If I were a mother I'd take advantage of the convenience of the new knowledge and feed always at room or refrigerator temperature, whichever was convenient.

You can warm the bottle in a saucepan or pitcher of hot water or in a washbasin. It's more convenient, if there is no hot water near the baby's room, to use an electric bottle warmer. Body temperature is the right temperature to aim for. The best way to test this is to shake a few drops on the inside of your wrist. If it feels hot, it is too hot.

If you make your formula with granulated sugar or lactose, it's a good habit to taste it before using it each day to avoid the dangerous accident that sometimes occurs of using salt or bicarbonate of soda instead. Or taste the drop of milk you shake on your wrist, at the first feeding after making formula.

Sit in a comfortable chair and hold the baby cradled in your arm. Most mothers want a chair with arms, and perhaps a pillow under the elbow. Some find a rocking chair is perfect.

Keep the bottle tilted up, so that the nipple is always full. Most babies want to work steadily until they have taken all the formula they need. There are some, though, who swallow a lot of air during nursing, and if the air bubble in the stomach gets too big, they feel uncomfortably full and stop nursing in the middle of the bottle. If this happens, bring up the bubble (see Section 102) and go on with the feeding. A few babies need to be bubbled 2 or even 3 times in the course of a bottle—others not at all. You will soon find out which type your baby is.

As soon as your baby stops nursing and seems satisfied, let that be the end of the feeding. He knows better than anyone else how much he needs.

189. Can you prop the bottle? It's good for the mother to hold her baby in her arms during bottle feedings. This is the position that Nature intends. The baby and mother are as close as can be, and they can watch each other's face. Feeding is a baby's greatest joy, by far, and it's good for him to link this with his mother's presence and his mother's face.

On the other hand, some busy mothers, with other children and a husband to take care of, have to prop the bottle at certain feedings. Most mothers of twins find it essential to prop the bottle for one or both babies at each feeding. These mothers point out that there are a number of chances every day for a mother to talk to her baby and cuddle him and that these other times may be calmer and happier than certain hectic feeding times. I agree that there are a hundred different ways to show a baby that you love him and that no single one of them is essential in itself. I agree that it does no harm for a loving but busy mother to prop some of the bottles if she can make it up to the baby in other ways. I'd still advise a mother who's not too busy not to prop.

Most mothers prop with a folded diaper, but there are bottle holders that are more efficient.

Many babies by the time they are 6 or 7 months old feel so grownup that they don't want to take the bottle cuddled in their mother's arms. They want to sit up straight and hold the bottle themselves. Of course, there's no point insisting on a baby's being in your lap when he'd prefer something else. See Section 197.

190. Making the nipple holes right. If the nipple holes are too small, the baby will get too little. He'll start fussing, or he'll become tired long before he's finished and go to sleep. If they are too large, he may choke or get indigestion; in the long run, he may get too little sucking satisfaction and suck his thumb more. For most babies, the right speed is when the bottle takes about 20 minutes of straight sucking time. The holes are generally right for a young baby if, when you turn the bottle upside down, the milk comes out in a fine spray for a second or two and then changes to drops. If it keeps coming in a spray, it is probably too fast. If it comes in slow drops from the beginning, it is probably too slow.

There are probably small holes on the rubber shoulders of the nipples you use, or some other channel for letting air into the bottle as the baby withdraws milk, to prevent a vacuum, which would collapse the nipple. (After a while babies learn by themselves to release a collapsed nipple so that air can bubble in.) This air passage is usually designed so that if you screw the nipple cap down tighter, the passage is decreased in size (or closed altogether); so there is a partial vacuum and the baby has to suck harder and take longer to finish his bottle. A looser cap allows faster drinking. See Section 341 on relationship to thumb sucking.

Many new nipples are too slow for a young baby but are right for an older, stronger one. If they are too slow for your baby, enlarge them carefully as follows: Stick the dull end of a fine (No. 10) needle into a cork. Then, holding the cork, heat the needle point in a flame until it's red-hot. Stick it a short distance into the top of the nipple. You don't have to poke it into the old hole. Don't use too large a needle or poke it in too far, until you can test your results. If you make the holes too large, you'll have to throw the nipple away. You can make 1, 2 or 3 enlarged holes. If you have no cork, you can wrap a piece of cloth around the dull end of the needle or hold it in pliers. There is also a nipple perforator with which you can make or enlarge holes.

191. Nipple holes clogged with scum. If you have trouble with clogged nipple holes, you can buy small wire strainers that fit inside the base of each nipple. Insert a strainer in each nipple before putting the nipple in bottle and then sterilize. Or you can stretch a few layers of cheesecloth or one-third of the thickness of a 2" x 2" sterile gauze square across the top of the bottle, before putting the cap on at the time of feeding. Or you may find it adequate to clean each nipple hole daily by rotating a toothpick in it.

Another way to prevent clogging is to buy nipples that, instead of having small holes, are "cross cut." This means that a small cross has been cut in the tip of the nipple. The milk does not pour out, as you might expect, because the edges of the cut stay together until the baby sucks. You can make small cross cuts in your regular nipples with a razor blade. First pinch the nipple tip to make a narrow ridge, then cut across it. Then pinch again (at a right angle to the first pinch) and make another cut.

192. Don't urge the baby to take more than he wants. The main trouble with bottle feeding, to my mind, is that the mother can see how much formula is left. Some babies always want the same quantity at every feeding of the day. But there are others whose appetites are much more variable. You mustn't get the idea that your baby has to have a certain amount at each feeding. It may help you acquire a more relaxed feeling about this to realize that a breast-fed baby may get as much as 10 ounces at the 6 A.M. nursing and as little as 4 ounces at the 6 P.M. feeding and be perfectly happy with each. If you can trust a breast-fed baby to take what he needs, you can trust a bottle-fed baby, too.

It is necessary to make this point because quite a number of children become feeding problems. They lose the natural appetite that they were born with and balk at all or many of their foods. These problems develop, in nine out of ten cases, because the mother has been trying, sometimes since infancy, to get her child to eat more than he wants. When you succeed in getting a baby or child to take a few more mouthfuls than he is eager for, it looks to you as if you have gained something. But this isn't so. He will only cut down at his next feeding. He knows the amounts and he even knows the different kinds of foods that his body is calling for. Urging your child isn't necessary, doesn't get you anywhere. It is harmful because it begins, after a while, to take away his appetite, and makes him want to eat less than his system really needs.

In the long run, urging does more than destroy appetite and make a thin child. It robs him of some of his positive feeling for life. A baby is meant to spend his first year getting hungry, demanding food, enjoying it, reaching satisfaction— a lusty success story, repeated at least 3 times a day, week after week. It builds into him self-confidence, outgoingness, trust in his mother. But if mealtime becomes a struggle, if feeding becomes something that is done to him, he goes on the defensive and builds up a balky, suspicious attitude toward life and toward people.

I don't mean that you have to snatch the bottle away for good the first time your baby pauses. Some babies like to rest a bit several times during a feeding. But if he seems indifferent when you put the nipple back in his mouth (and it's not due to a bubble), then he's satisfied, and you should be, too. You may say, "If I wait 10 minutes, he'll sometimes take a little bit more." Better not.

193. The baby who wakes in a few minutes. What about the baby who goes to sleep after he's taken 4 of his 5 ounces and then wakes up and cries a few minutes later? This is more apt to be due to an air bubble or colic or periodic irritable crying than to hunger. A baby won't notice a difference of an ounce, especially if he's gone to sleep. In fact, a baby will often sleep just as well when he's taken only half his usual amount, though he may wake a little early.

It's perfectly all right occasionally to give your baby the rest of the formula a little later, if you feel sure that he's hungry for it. But I think it's better to assume first that he is not really hungry and give him a good chance to go back to sleep—with or without a pacifier. In other words, try to postpone the next feeding for 2 or 3 hours.

194. The young baby who only half finishes. A mother may bring a baby home from the hospital and find that he stops taking his bottle and falls asleep when it's still half full. Yet they said in the hospital that he was taking it all. The mother keeps trying to rouse him, to wedge another quarter of an ounce in, but it's slow, hard, frustrating work. What's the trouble? He may be a baby who hasn't quite "come to" yet. (An occasional baby stays sluggish like that for the first 2 or 3 weeks and then comes to life with a bang.)

The constructive thing to do is to let the baby stop when he wants to, even if he's taken only an ounce or two. Won't he get hungry then, long before it's time for the next feeding? He may, or he may not. If he does, feed him. "But," you say, "I'd be feeding him all day and night." It probably won't be that bad. The point is that if you let a baby stop when he feels like it and let him come to feel his own hunger, he will gradually become more eager for his feedings and take larger amounts. Then he will be able to sleep for longer periods. You can help him to learn to wait longer and be hungrier by trying to stretch out the interval to 2, 2½, then 3 hours. Don't pick him up just as soon as he starts fussing but wait a while. He may go back to sleep. If he gets to crying hard, you'll probably have to feed him.

If you keep urging him to finish, there's a chance that he'll go right on being indifferent.

If his appetite doesn't begin to improve in a few days and he's still taking altogether only about half of his formula, and if you have no doctor to advise you, you can dilute his formula in half for a day or two (Section 179). When he's dissatisfied with that, go back to his full-strength formula.

195. The baby who fusses soon after starting a bottle or who promptly goes to sleep may be frustrated by a nipple hole that is clogged or too small. See if the milk comes in a fine spray when the bottle is first inverted. Try enlarging the nipple hole a little anyway, as an experiment (Section 190).

The older baby who refuses to nurse is discussed in Section 101.

196. How long after a bottle has been taken out of the refrigerator can you still use it? During the time when a bottle is at drinking temperature or room temperature or pleasant outdoor temperature, any bacteria that may have gotten into the formula will be able to multiply rapidly. That is why it is unwise to give a baby a bottle that has been sitting around the house or carriage or car for several hours, whether it's a full bottle or one that has been partly consumed.

If you will need to feed the baby a couple of hours after leaving home, put the bottle, as soon as you take it out of the refrigerator, into an insulated bag designed to keep things cold or wrap it in 10 layers of newspaper (which is a pretty good insulator).

If you have a young baby who sometimes goes to sleep after half a bottle and then wakes in a couple of hours for the rest, you can promptly put his half-finished bottle back into the refrigerator. I wouldn't use such a bottle more than twice.

197. Avoiding a bedtime bottle through the second year. Some parents are bothered if a baby wants a bottle far into the second year; others don't mind at all. If you care, one precaution you can take is not to get your baby used to taking his own bottle in bed. After 5 months, many babies come to feel so grown up that they don't want to be cradled in their mothers' arms at nursing time; they want to sit up. And they also want to take the bottle away from the mother and hold it themselves. A practical mother, seeing she's not much use, is apt to put such a baby in his crib, where he drinks his bottle and puts himself to sleep all in one operation. This pattern is a handy one for putting babies to sleep, but in the long run it makes it impossible for some of them to go to sleep without a bottle. (Read Section 231.) When the mother tries to withhold the bedtime bottle at 9, 15 or 21 months, such a baby will cry frantically and be unable to fall asleep for a long time. If you want your baby to be weaned from the bottle before a year of age—and I think this is preferable—let him continue to take his bottle on your lap.

If you prefer the bottle in bed as a sort of sedative and won't mind continuing to give it through a good part of the second year, then there's no harm.

Adding Vitamins and Water

VITAMINS IN INFANCY

198. Babies definitely need extra vitamin D and vitamin C. (They are discussed in Sections 428 and 429.) There are only small amounts of these in milk as it comes from the cow and in solid foods that are given early.

Breast milk may contain sufficient vitamin C if the mother's diet is rich in citrus fruits and certain vegetables (Section 421), but breast milk doesn't contain enough vitamin D. A bottle-fed baby should receive 25 to 50 milligrams a day of vitamin C in a commercial preparation until he is receiving 2 ounces of orange juice daily. It does no harm for a breast-fed baby to take this, too, and this is an extra precaution.

In the United States, pasteurized milk contains 400 units of vitamin D to the quart, and evaporated milk when diluted with an equal amount of water contains the same amount. This should be sufficient to prevent rickets in a normal baby. A breast-fed baby should receive 500 units daily in a commercial preparation.

In actual practice most physicians routinely give a 3-vitamin preparation that contains C, D and A to all babies, whether on breast or bottle. The dropper that comes with the bottle has lines showing 0.3 cc and 0.6 cc (three-tenths and six-tenths of a cubic centimeter). The fluid is drawn up to the line the doctor prescribes and then squirted directly into the baby's mouth at the beginning of one of the feedings of the day.

If you have no doctor to advise you, give 0.3 cc once a day, winter and summer, starting at 1 month or earlier. In most preparations this gives 500 units of D, 2,500 units of A and 25 milligrams of C. Some doctors prescribe 0.6 cc. You should not go beyond this amount, since excessive doses of vitamin D can be harmful.

199. "Multivitamin" preparations contain a number of B vitamins in addition to A, D and C. However, milk, cereals and the other foods that babies and children eat usually provide sufficient B vitamins. The main reason for not using one of these products routinely for children, aside from the fact that the added B vitamins are not necessary, is that they are more expensive.

200. Orange juice. When your baby is a few months old, the doctor will probably suggest adding orange juice to his diet. It can be fresh, frozen or canned. Orange juice is usually mixed with an equal amount of boiled water so that it won't taste too strong. One way is to start with 1 teaspoonful of orange juice and 1 teaspoonful of water. The next day give 2 teaspoonfuls of orange juice and 2 teaspoonfuls of water. The third day, 3 teaspoonfuls of each. And so on, up to an ounce of each. Then gradually decrease the water and increase the orange juice, until you are giving 2 ounces of straight orange juice. You strain the orange juice, so that the pulp won't clog the nipples. The baby usually takes it from the bottle until he's 5 or 6 months old; after that, from a cup or glass. Orange juice is often given before the baby's bath, because this is a time when he is always awake for about an hour before his next feeding. You can give it at room temperature or slightly warmed. Don't get it hot. Heat destroys vitamin C.

Most babies love orange juice and digest it easily. Some young babies always vomit it. An occasional baby seems to be made uncomfortable by it or gets a rash from it. Very few babies dislike it at first, but some turn against it later. If for any of these reasons your baby can't take orange juice, you can postpone it for a month or two or you can try tomato juice (4 ounces a day). Unfortunately, if a baby is upset by orange juice or dislikes it, he usually is upset by or dislikes tomato juice, too. If he doesn't take orange juice or tomato juice, he should continue with drops that contain vitamin C.

DRINKING WATER FOR A BABY

201. Some want water; others don't. It is often recommended that a baby be offered a few ounces of water between meals, once or twice a day. It is not absolutely necessary, because the amount of fluid in the formula is probably calculated to satisfy the baby's ordinary needs. It is more important to offer water during excessively hot weather or when the baby has a fever. Babies who ordinarily refuse water often take it at these times.

As a matter of fact, a lot of babies don't want any water from the time they are a week or two old until they are about a year. During this age they fairly worship anything with nourishment in it, but they feel insulted by plain water. If your baby likes it, by all means give it to him once or several times a day when he is awake between meals (not just before the next meal). You can give him as much as he wants. He probably won't want more than 2 ounces. But don't urge him to take water if he doesn't want it. There's no point in getting him mad. He knows what he needs.

If your baby takes water, boil for 3 minutes a sufficient quantity for the day; keep it in a sterilized bottle. When you need some, pour 2 ounces into another bottle.

Boil the water that your baby drinks through the first year anyway, and through the second year also if you aren't sure that the water from your faucet or well is absolutely pure.

If you are using well water, it is important to have it tested for bacteria and for nitrates before the baby arrives. (Nitrate salts in well water cause blueness of the lips and skin of babies.) Write your state health department.

202. Sugar water. If your baby won't take his water plain, you can try him on sugar water. You may particularly want him to take water if you are trying to get him off a night feeding or if he is taking little milk because of an illness or if the weather is very hot.

Add 1 level tablespoonful of granulated sugar or corn syrup to a pint of water before boiling it for 3 minutes.

203. You don't have to boil everything. You sterilize the formula and nursing equipment because germs multiply in milk. You boil drinking water because there is a chance that harmful germs will get into the reservoir or well, or into your pipes through faulty plumbing. Sometimes mothers get so scared by the care that they take in preparing the formula and drinking water that they think they have to sterilize everything that goes into the baby's mouth. You don't have to be so fussy with all the other things that your baby will eat and drink. You don't have to boil dishes and cups and feeding spoons, because germs don't get a chance to grow on clean, dry utensils. It's sensible to wash the outside of the baby's orange, since it may have been recently handled by someone with a cold. There's no need to sterilize the knife you cut it with. Germs won't multiply in orange juice that a baby is going to drink 10 minutes after it is squeezed.

You can wash with soap, when you first buy them, the teething rings, pacifiers and toys that a baby puts in his mouth. But there is no need to keep on washing them afterward, unless they fall on the floor, because the only germs on them will be the baby's own germs that he's used to.

Changes in Diet and Schedule

The doctor who is taking care of your baby and knows his digestion is, of course, the one to advise you about these changes. The specific directions in this chapter are for parents who are unable to consult a doctor regularly.

ADDING SOLID FOODS

204. There's no set age when it's important to start solid food. Fifty years ago it was begun when a baby was a year old. As the years have passed, doctors have experimented with giving it earlier and earlier, and found that babies took it and prospered. There are two definite advantages in starting in the first half year. Babies take to the idea more easily than when they are older and more opinionated. And a variety of solid foods adds to the diet substances that are scanty in milk, particularly iron.

Nowadays doctors customarily recommend the first solid food sometime between 2 and 4 months. There is no great advantage in extreme earliness. A baby usually gets all the calories he needs from milk for the first 3 months. His immature digestive system doesn't make much use of starch for several months; much of it comes out in the bowel movement.

When there is a family history of allergy, the doctor may wait considerably longer to introduce foods other than milk, because the older a baby is when he receives a new food, the less apt he is to develop an allergy to it.

The baby's hunger and digestive system may both influence the age at which the doctor suggests starting solids. A baby of 8 weeks who is not getting quite enough breast milk to satisfy him might well be started early on his solid food to avoid a supplementary formula. On the other hand, if a baby has been on the edge of looseness all the time he was on formula alone, the doctor may prefer to wait longer than usual before introducing solids, for fear of upsetting the digestion further. A big factor in giving solids earlier has been the eagerness of mothers who don't want their baby to be one day later than the baby up the street. They put strong pressure on doctors. I think it's sensible to wait till 3 months.

205. Solids before or after the milk? Most babies who are not used to solids expect their milk and want their milk first when it's feeding time. They become indignant if offered a spoonful of something solid instead. So start with the formula or the breast feeding. A month or two later, when a baby has learned that solid foods can ward off starvation just as well as milk, you can experiment with moving his solids up to the middle or the beginning of the meal. Eventually almost all babies are happy to take all their solid food first and then top if off with the beverage, the way so many adults do. Shortcuts are mentioned in Section 763.

206. What kind of spoon? A teaspoon is pretty wide for a small baby's mouth, and most spoons have a bowl so deep that the baby can't scoop all the contents out. A small coffee spoon (demitasse spoon) is better, preferably one with a shallow bowl. Some mothers like to use a flat butter spreader or wooden tongue blades—the kind that doctors use—which can be bought in bulk at the drugstore. There is a spoon with a rubber coating on the bowl for a teething baby who wants to bite on his spoon; and one in which the bowl swivels to stay level, for the 1-year-old self-feeder.

207. Cereal. The exact order in which solids are introduced is not important. Cereal is commonly given first. The only disadvantage is that its taste doesn't have great appeal for many babies. Different babies prefer different ones. There is some advantage in getting a baby used to variety.

208. Give him time to learn to like it. A doctor usually recommends starting with a teaspoonful or less and working up gradually to 2 or 3 tablespoonfuls if the baby wants it. This gradualness is to make sure the baby learns to like it and won't be upset. Just give him a taste for several days, until he shows signs of enjoying it. There's no rush.

A baby taking his first teaspoonful of solid food is quite funny and a little pathetic. He looks puzzled and disgusted. He wrinkles up his nose and forehead. You can't blame him. After all, the taste is new, the consistency is new, the spoon may be new. When he sucks on a nipple, the milk gets to the right place automatically. He's had no training in catching hold of a lump of food with the front of his tongue and moving it back into his throat. He just clacks his tongue against the roof of his mouth, and most of the cereal gets squeezed back out onto his chin. You will have to shave it off his chin and scoop it back into his mouth. Again a lot will be oozed out frontward, but don't be discouraged—some goes down inside, too. Be patient until he is more experienced.

It doesn't matter much at which meals you start the solids. Just don't give it at the feeding when he's least hungry. Cereal is usually given at the 10 A.M. and 6 P.M. feedings.

It's a good idea, if you are starting with cereal, to mix it (with formula or milk) thinner than the directions on the box say. Then it will seem more familiar to the baby and be easier for him to swallow. Also, babies and small children dislike food with a sticky consistency. If your baby is on a formula, you will use some of that to mix with the cereal. Some babies, however, miss any formula that is taken out of the bottle. In that case, or if the baby is on the breast, use pasteurized milk to make the cereal. You do not need to boil it, if your doctor agrees it is safe enough. If you have no fresh milk, use equal parts of evaporated milk and water to mix with the cereal. Of course, you can use plain boiled water, but this is less likely to appeal to the baby.

209. Which cereals? Most mothers give the precooked cereals made especially for babies, of which there is a wide variety. They are ready for eating as soon as mixed, which is a great convenience. Most of them are fortified with iron, which is otherwise apt to be lacking in a baby's diet (until he is taking egg yolk). Anemia from insufficient iron is fairly common during the first year. Sometimes, if the baby belongs to an allergic family, the doctor may prefer to start cereals at a later age than usual. Then he may start with rice, oats, corn or barley, omitting wheat for several more months, because wheat causes allergy more often than other cereals.

Also, he may delay the mixed cereals until the baby has shown he can take each of the separate kinds without trouble.

If you prefer to give the baby the same cooked cereals as the other members of the family, you can start with a white (refined) wheat cereal. This has small grains and little roughage. By the time he is 5 or 6 months old, you can branch out into whole wheat, oatmeal, hominy, rice. A few babies get loose bowel movements from the roughage of whole wheat and oatmeal until they are older. Wheat, oat and barley cereals are the most valuable in terms of vitamins and proteins. Add salt to taste.

210. The baby who balks at cereal. You will know within a few days after starting how your baby is going to take to cereal. Some babies seem to decide, "It's queer, but it's nourishment, so I'll eat it." As the days go by they grow more and more enthusiastic. They open their mouths for it like birds in the nest.

But there are other babies who decide on the second day of cereal that they don't like it at all. And on the third day they dislike it more than on the second. If your baby feels this way, be careful. Take it easy. If you try to push the cereal into him against his will, he will get more and more rebellious. You will get exasperated, too. In a week or two he may become so suspicious that he balks at the bottle, too. Offer the cereal just once a day. Give him only enough to cover the tip of the teaspoon until he is used to it. Add a pinch of sugar to see if he likes it better sweet. If in 2 or 3 days he is getting more set against it in spite of all these precautions, then stop altogether for a couple of weeks. If he still balks when you try again, report it to your doctor.

I think it's a great mistake to get into an argument with a baby about his first solid food. Sometimes a long-lasting feeding problem starts in this way. Even if it doesn't last, it's bad for mother and baby to go through an unnecessary fight.

If you have no doctor to advise you, I suggest that you start with fruit instead of cereal. Babies are puzzled by fruit, too, the first time they have it. But within a day or two practically all of them decide they love it. By the end of 2 weeks they are ready to assume that anything that comes on a spoon is wonderful. Then you can add cereal, too.

211. Starting fruit. Fruit is often the second solid added to a baby's diet, a few weeks after he has become used to cereal. Some doctors prefer it as the first solid food because babies usually take to it so enthusiastically.

For the first 6 or 8 months of a baby's life, his fruit is stewed, except for raw ripe banana. Apples, peaches, pears, apricots, prunes and pineapple are the usual fruits. You can buy the small jars of strained fruits for babies. You can use fresh or frozen fruit that you have stewed for the rest of the family, but strain or sieve it for the baby and add enough sugar to keep it from tasting sour. Or you can use canned fruit that you serve to other members of the family. Much canned fruit for adults is undesirably sweet, so pour off the excess syrup before straining it for the baby.

Fruit can be given at any one of the baby's feedings, even twice a day, depending on his appetite and digestion. The most popular time is 2 P.M. or 6 P.M.

Increase each fruit gradually as the baby learns to like it. Most babies are satisfied with half a baby jar or can. You can give the other half next day. Fruit can be kept 3 days if it is well refrigerated. Don't feed the baby out of the jar or can unless you are using it up at one meal. Saliva introduced into the container can spoil food rapidly.

Banana should be very ripe. It should have black spots on the skin and be tan-colored inside. Mash it fine with a fork. Add a little formula or milk if it seems too thick for your baby.

Fruit has the general reputation of being laxative. But most individuals, including infants, don't show any definite looseness or cramps from any of the fruits mentioned above, except for prunes or prune juice. Prunes are mildly laxative for almost all babies, and this makes them a doubly valuable food for those who have a chronic tendency to constipation. For the baby who needs it and likes it that regularly, pureed prunes or prune juice can be given at one feeding and some other fruit at another feeding each day.

If your baby's bowels become loose too easily, you will probably omit prunes altogether and give other fruits only once a day.

In the second half of the first year, you can begin adding or substituting other raw fruits besides bananas: scraped apple, pear, avocado. (Berries and seedless grapes are usually postponed till the baby is 2 years of age.)

212. Vegetables. Strained boiled vegetables are commonly added to a baby's diet 2 to 4 weeks after he has gotten used to cereal or fruit or both.

The ones usually offered are string beans, peas, spinach, tomatoes, squash, carrots, beets, sweet potatoes, celery. There are other vegetables—such as broccoli, cauliflower, cabbage, turnips, onions—which, as usually cooked, are so strong-tasting that most babies don't like them and most parents don't bother to try them. However, if your family likes some of them (and they can be made much less strong by boiling in two changes of water), there is no harm in straining some and offering it to your baby, too. Corn is not given because of the large husks on the kernels.

You can serve your baby fresh or frozen vegetables, boiled and strained, or the ones in jars or cans already pureed for babies, or the ordinary canned vegetables that you serve the rest of the family, but strained.

Babies are more likely to be choosy about vegetables than about cereals or fruits. You will probably find that there are one or two vegetables that your baby doesn't like. Don't urge them, but try them again every month or so. There's no point fussing over a few foods when we have so many to choose from. Some babies are much more enthusiastic about vegetables if a little salt is added for flavoring, and there is no harm in this.

It's common for undigested vegetable to appear in the bowel movements when the baby is first taking it. This is not a bad sign so long as there is no looseness or mucus, but increase slowly until his digestion learns to handle it. If a vegetable causes looseness or much mucus, omit it for the time being and try a very small amount in another month.

Beets may show up red in the bowel movement or color the urine, which is nothing to worry about if you can remember that it is caused by beets and not blood.

Spinach causes chapping of the lips and around the anus in some babies. If it does, omit it for several months and try again.

Lunchtime—2 P.M. for a baby still on a roughly 4-hour schedule, noon for an older baby on 3 meals a day—is the conventional time for vegetables.

Work up to several tablespoonfuls as desired or half a baby jar or can. The rest, if refrigerated, can be given the next day. If you have no refrigerator, don't keep vegetables. Cooked vegetables spoil fairly rapidly. Don't feed the baby out of the jar or can unless you are using it up at one meal. Saliva introduced into the container can spoil food rapidly.

213. Eggs. Egg yolk is important because it contains valuable iron. Babies begin to need more iron for their red blood cells around the middle of the first year, because with their rapid growth, they begin to outgrow the limited amount that was in their bodies at birth. (Milk contains practically no iron, and many other foods provide very little. However, a majority of the cereals prepared for babies contain good amounts of iron.)

Egg should be started with a little caution, because it is one of the foods that is most apt to cause allergy, especially in allergic families. The commonest form of allergy in babies is eczema, in which the skin, particularly around the face and ears, first becomes rough, red, scaly, and then may go on to oozing and crusting. It itches.

In order to lessen the chance of egg allergy, several precautions can be taken. The yolk only can be used until the baby is nearer to a year of age, since the iron is in the yolk and it's the white that usually causes the allergy. The yolk can be served hard-boiled, because thorough cooking of any food lessens the likelihood of its causing trouble. You can start by offering less than a quarter of a teaspoonful and increase gradually.

So you hard-boil an egg for 20 minutes, take off the white and crumble the yolk. Some babies dislike the taste of plain hard-cooked egg yolk. You can try adding salt to give it some flavor, or mix it with the baby's cereal or vegetable. If this makes him balk at the cereal or vegetable, don't persist.

Egg yolk is most commonly started at 5 or 6 months of age, but some doctors prefer to wait until 8 or 10 months, especially in an allergic family.

If you have no doctor to advise you, start egg yolk at 4 months unless there is allergy in the family. Better wait till 9 months to offer soft-cooked or scrambled eggs, which contain the white, and then start very gradually, as if it were a new food.

Egg can be given at breakfast, lunch or supper. When you add meat to the diet, serve the egg at breakfast or at supper.

214. Meats. Nutrition studies have shown that babies profit by meats during the first year, so many doctors recommend them as early as 2 to 6 months of age. Meats for babies are finely ground or "strained" or "scraped," so they can be swallowed easily before the baby has any teeth.

You can give your baby jars or cans of strained meats, such

as beef, beef heart, liver, lamb, chicken, veal, pork. Don't feed the baby out of the jar or can unless you are using it up at one meal. Saliva introduced into the container can spoil food rapidly. Or you can prepare the meat yourself. The simplest way to cook beef or lamb chop for a baby is to scrape it, while still raw, with a dull knife or tablespoon. Put this soft pulp in a custard cup and set it in a pan of slowly boiling water. Cook until the color changes. If desired, milk or water can be added, before cooking, to make the meat more moist. Another method is to briefly broil a piece of beef (top round, for instance) or lamb chop, to sterilize the surface, and then; grasping it firmly, scrape it with a tablespoon. This scrapes out the soft red meat and leaves the tough white fibers behind. A piece of liver can be plunged into boiling water, cooked until color changes, and then pressed through a sieve. Pork should be well cooked. Salt to taste.

After your baby has become used to strained or scraped meat, you can give him beef that you have briefly broiled and put through a fine grinder. It is preferable not to give meat ground by the butcher, because the meat surfaces that have been handled and those that have come in contact with the grinder are mixed through the rest of the meat. Also, it may contain a lot of fat and tough fiber.

By the time the baby is used to ground beef, he can also have ground or fine-minced chicken, lamb, liver, bacon, veal and pork. Pork should always be cooked through.

215. Meat soups. There are a variety of meat soups in jars or cans for babies. They usually consist of small amounts of a meat and a vegetable with a larger amount of a cereal such as rice or barley. In adding them to a meal with other foods, it is sensible to consider them as primarily a starch. Don't count on them regularly as a source of meat.

When there is a tendency to allergy, such mixtures may be confusing unless the baby has already taken each of the foods included in the mixture without reaction.

Meat soups are appropriate for occasional use any time after the baby has begun to have plain meats.

216. The meals at 6 months (if you cannot consult a doctor). By the time your baby is 6 months old, he will probably be eating cereal, egg yolk and a variety of fruits, vegetables and meats. A common arrangement for a moderately hungry baby is cereal and egg yolk for breakfast, vegetable and meat for lunch, cereal and fruit for supper. But there are no hard and fast rules. It all depends on your convenience and your baby's appetite. For instance, if he's not a very hungry baby, you could give fruit and egg at breakfast, vegetable and meat at lunch, cereal alone at supper. If he tends to be constipated, you can give him prunes every night along with his cereal, and another fruit at his breakfast or lunch. You may want to give him his meat and vegetable at supper with the rest of the family, the cereal and fruit at lunch.

217. Simple puddings if convenient. Puddings aren't as important for most babies as other foods. They don't add any new element to the diet; they take time to prepare. Fruit makes, in some respects, a more valuable dessert. However, if you are making puddings for your family anyway, you can begin giving them to the baby for lunch or supper any time after 6 months.

Puddings may be important in special cases. If, when your baby is about a year old, he loses most of his desire for milk as a drink, you can get several ounces into him each day in pudding form. Puddings may also be helpful for the rare baby who is "fed up" with each food after a few spoonfuls. He may like pudding as an extra dessert, in addition to fruit. Puddings are also helpful when a baby turns against cereal for supper. Then supper can be fruit and pudding, or vegetable and pudding.

The more valuable and common puddings are those made mainly of milk (junket), milk and egg (boiled and baked custard), milk and starch (tapioca, rice, cornstarch). The gelatin in gelatin desserts is relatively unimportant, but there is value in the fruit that is added to it.

Some puddings come in jars or cans for babies. Don't feed the baby out of the jar or can unless you are using it up at one meal. Saliva introduced into the container can spoil food rapidly. Many of the packaged cornstarch puddings that come in various flavors and are meant for family use are sweetened excessively, and it is better to avoid these.

So if your child likes fruit for dessert and digests it well, is drinking plenty of milk and is well nourished, there is no reason for you to prepare puddings regularly unless you want to. Even if you do serve puddings, it is desirable that half the baby's desserts be raw or stewed fruit.

218. Adding potato if your baby likes it and needs it. Other starch. Potatoes are good as a source of starch at lunch for a child who is hungry or in place of cereal at supper. They also contain appreciable amounts of iron, other salts and vitamin C, so that they have food values aside from the starch.

Potato, baked or boiled, can be introduced into the diet any time in the last half of the first year. A logical time is when the baby goes onto a 3-meals-a-day schedule. When his lunch is 5 hours away from his supper, the starch, which a potato is mostly made of, supplies lots of energy (calories) to last through the afternoon.

A word of caution about potato. Babies are more apt to gag and rebel against it than any other food. I don't know whether this is because it is grainy or because it is sticky. So mash it very smooth at first, make it thin by mixing with plenty of milk, and offer it in very small amounts until he gets used to it. Flavor it with salt. Don't urge it on him if he continues to gag; forget about it, at least for a month, and then try again.

If your baby is pretty fat and seems content with a lunch of green vegetable, meat, milk and perhaps fruit, leave out potato. It doesn't add anything new to his diet.

You can occasionally substitute macaroni, spaghetti, noodles or rice for potato. Strain or mash them fine at first.

219. Adding fish. By 10 or 12 months, you can also add the white, nonoily fish, such as flounder, haddock and halibut, if the child likes them. You can poach them in pieces in slowly boiling water. Or you can place small pieces in a custard cup, cover with milk, and then place the cup in a pan of boiling water until the fish is cooked through. Or you can serve the baby the fish you have boiled, baked or broiled for the rest of the family. In any case, crumble the flakes in your fingers to be sure there are no bones.

Substitute fish for meat at lunchtime. Some babies love it, and then it's a great help. But a lot of babies turn thumbs down. Don't try to force it.

The oily fish, like mackerel, are liable to be harder to digest and less appealing.

220. Finger foods. By the time a baby is 6 or 7 months old, he wants to and can pick foods up in his hand and suck and munch on them. This is good training for him as preparation for spoon-feeding himself at about a year. If a baby is never allowed to feed himself with his fingers, he's less likely to have the ambition to try the spoon.

The traditional first finger food is a crust of stale bread or toast or zwieback at 6 or 7 months. The baby sucks at it and chews at it with his bare gums (they may be tingling with teething, and in that case he'll enjoy the biting). As it softens gradually with his saliva, some of it rubs or dissolves off into his mouth, enough to make him feel he's getting somewhere. Most of it goes on his hands, face, hair and the furniture.

By 9 months you are mashing his food instead of straining it, and you can leave unmashed some of the pieces of string beans and carrots. He will want to pick up these pieces, along with particles of meat, and put them in his mouth. He can also chew on a slice of raw apple or pear.

The average baby gets his first tooth at about 7 months, and at a year may have 4 to 6 sharp biting teeth. But he probably won't get his first molars for grinding until sometime around a year and a quarter. Therefore you can't expect him to do much efficient grinding of food till then.

221. Lumpy foods by a year. Somewhere between 7 and 12 months, you want to get your baby used to lumpy or chopped foods. If he goes much beyond a year eating nothing but pureed things, it gets harder and harder to make the change. People have the idea that a baby can't handle lumps until he gets a fair set of teeth. This isn't true. He can mush up lumps of cooked vegetables or fruit and pieces of zwieback with his gums and tongue.

Some babies seem to be born more squeamish about lumps than others. But most babies and older children who gag easily on particles of food have become that way either because the mother tried to make the change to chopped foods too abruptly or too late, or because she has been forcing food when the child didn't want it.

There are two important points in shifting to chopped foods. Make the change a gradual one. When you first serve chopped vegetables, mash them up pretty fine with a fork. Don't put too much in the baby's mouth at a time. When he's used to this consistency, gradually mash less and less. The other way a baby gets used to lumps is by being allowed to pick up a cube of cooked carrot, for instance, in his fingers and put it in his mouth himself. What he can't stand is to have a whole spoonful of lumps dumped into his mouth when he's not used to it.

So start the change by 9 months. You can serve the baby the boiled vegetables and stewed fruits that you cook for the rest of the family or you can buy the chopped (junior) foods in jars or cans prepared for babies.

You don't have to make all his foods lumpy. It is necessary only that he get used to eating some lumps each day.

Meats should generally continue to be served ground or minced fine. Most small children dislike chunks of meat that don't chew up easily. They often chew on such a piece for a long time without getting anywhere. They don't dare try to swallow too big a piece, as adults do when they are desperate. This may lead to gagging or at least to a loss of appetite for this particular kind of meat.

Gagging is also discussed in Section 609.

222. Diet by the end of the first year. In case you are mixed up by all the things that have been added to the diet, here is a rough list of what babies are apt to be eating by the end of the year:

Breakfast: cereal (preferably brown), egg (whole, soft), toast, milk

Lunch: vegetable (green or yellow, in lumps), potato (or macaroni, etc.), meat or fish, fruit, milk

Supper: cereal, fruit, milk

Or he may have his "big" meal at supper with the family. Then lunch might be something starchy, such as a meat soup with starch, or potato, cereal or pudding; and a fruit or vegetable.

Fruit juice (including orange juice) is given daily between meals or at breakfast. Zwieback, toast, bread (preferably whole grain) can be given at meals or between, with a little butter or margarine. A simple pudding can be substituted for one of the fruit desserts. The fruit is stewed except for banana, scraped apple, pear, avocado.

In other words, a pretty grown-up diet.

CHANGES IN SCHEDULE AND BOTTLE

223. When to omit the 10 P.M. feeding. When you give up the 10 or 11 P.M. feeding should depend most on when the baby is ready. There are two things to consider.

The first is whether he is ready to sleep through the night. You can't be sure that he's ready just because he always has to be waked up at 10 or 11. If you don't wake him, he may wake himself around midnight. Better wait until you have had to wake him for several weeks. Then see if he sleeps through. If he wakes hungry later in the night, feed him and go back to the evening feeding for a few more weeks.

Of course, if a baby is very small or gaining slowly or having trouble with his digestion, it may be better to keep the evening feeding going a while longer, even if he is willing to sleep through without it.

Another point is whether he is sucking his thumb a lot. If he is, it may mean that he is not getting as much sucking as he'd like from breast or bottle. If you cut out a feeding at this time, you reduce his sucking time further still. However, if he continues to be a thumb-sucker in spite of all your efforts, you don't have to go on **forever** giving him the evening feeding. For one thing, as he gets older he may refuse to wake up, no matter how hard you try, or fall asleep again as soon as he has taken a couple of ounces. I'd stop the feeding by this time anyway, whether he is sucking his thumb or not.

In a general way, then, let your baby give up his 10 P.M. feeding when he shows that he can sleep through without it and get enough sucking satisfaction without it. This will probably be between the ages of 3 and 6 months. Wait till 5 or 6 months if he is sucking his thumb much and is willing to take the evening feeding.

Most babies get themselves off the evening feeding as soon as they can. But an occasional one will continue it indefinitely, especially if the mother rushes in as soon as he first murmurs. If your baby is still waking for his feeding at 7 or 8 months, I'd try to get him over the habit. At this age he certainly doesn't need nourishment at night if he is eating well in the daytime and gaining satisfactorily. Let him fuss for 20 or 30 minutes (without going to him at all) and see if he won't go back to sleep.

When you omit the evening bottle, distribute the formula into the other 4 bottles. This probably makes about 7½ ounces in each bottle. But if he wants only his usual 5 or 6 ounces, let it go at that without any urging. Twenty-four ounces a day is plenty if he's satisfied.

224. If your baby loses his appetite between 3 and 9 months. A baby may take solids eagerly for the first couple of months and then rather suddenly lose a lot of his appetite. One reason may be that at this age period he is meant to slow down in his weight-gaining. In his first 3 months he has probably gained close to 2 pounds a month. By 6 months he is apt to be down to a pound a month. Otherwise he would becomes too fat. Also, he may be bothered by teething. One baby wants to leave out a lot of his solid food; another turns against his milk.

If your baby loses a lot of his appetite, don't urge him. There are two things you can do. The first is to gradually remove the sugar from his formula (Section 225). The sugar was there in the early months principally to give him enough calories while he was on a diluted formula. He doesn't really need these sugar calories when he is eating a good helping of solid food 3 times a day. In fact, the very sweetness of the formula may be killing his appetite for unsweetened foods.

The other thing you can do is to go from the approximately 4-hour schedule during the daytime (6 A.M., 10 A.M., 2 P.M., 6 P.M.) to a 3-meals-a-day schedule (approximately 7 A.M., 12 noon, 5 P.M.), whether or not he is still on an evening feeding (Section 226).

If a baby's appetite still doesn't revive with these two measures, it's important to get him to the doctor, to be sure that he's otherwise healthy.

225. When to remove the sugar from the formula. You want to remove the sugar from the formula gradually, when your baby is somewhere between 4 and 9 months of age. The time depends on his appetite. If he goes through a phase of poor appetite at the age of 4, 5 or 6 months, that is a good time to take out the sugar. If, on the other hand, he is the kind of a baby who never seems to get enough to eat and is always hungry ahead of mealtime, then leave the sugar in until he is 7 or 8 months old.

Remove the sugar gradually, so that he doesn't notice any sudden change in taste. You can remove about a quarter of a tablespoonful a day from the formula until there is none left.

226. When to put the baby on three meals a day. This depends on when your baby is ready for it. It may be anywhere between the ages of 4 and 10 months. A 3-meal schedule means about 5 hours between meals. If your baby is starved at the end of 4 hours and crying with hunger, he isn't ready for a 3-meal schedule, no matter how old he is.

If he has to have his first feeding by 6 A.M., there's usually not much use talking about 3 meals a day.

On the other hand, your baby may show clearly at a certain stage that he is ready for 3 meals. A mother will say, "He only eats well at every other meal. If he finishes his 6 A.M. bottle, he'll eat poorly at 10, well at 2 and poorly at 6 P.M." Babies who are acting like this need to be changed to a 3-meals-a-day schedule so that they will be hungry at mealtime. Otherwise they are apt to become feeding problems.

If a baby is thumb-sucking a lot and is still ready to eat every 4 hours, this is a reason for leaving in the fourth feeding for a while longer.

Once in a while there is a baby who is no longer ready to eat every 4 hours during the daytime, but who still wakes up like clockwork for his 10 P.M. bottle. There's no problem here. You try to adjust to the baby's needs, as usual, putting him on 3 meals during the day and continuing to give the 10 P.M. feeding until he is ready to sleep through.

There's another problem that turns up occasionally. A baby seems to have outgrown the 4-hour schedule. He's not hungry for some of his meals. And yet he's still waking around 6 A.M., yelling with hunger. How do you put him on 3 meals a day and still feed him at 6 A.M.? The easiest way is to give him his milk from breast or bottle as soon as he demands it in the morning, and give him his cereal, or his cereal and fruit, a little later, as soon as it is convenient (for instance, between 7 and 8). His next meal will be lunch, around noon. Of course, the baby who is hungry early is no problem if the whole family breakfasts around 6 A.M. Some babies who wake early are quite satisfied with a bottle of orange juice for the time being. Then they can have their milk along with the rest of their breakfast, later.

Another factor is the mother's convenience. Suppose she has her hands full preparing meals for her older children, and her baby is able to go more than 4 hours between meals, even though he is still willing to eat that often. This mother naturally wants to get the baby onto the same 3 meals as the older children now, and there is no reason why she shouldn't, especially if he isn't thumb-sucking much. There are other mothers, especially with the first baby, who find the 4-hour schedule fits their own convenience better than 3 meals a day. There is no reason why these babies shouldn't stay on the 4 hour schedule longer than average as long as they remain hungry for their meals that often. In other words, there is no rule about making such a change in a baby's routine. It's just a matter of reasonableness and common sense. You see what the baby is ready for and fit it in with your convenience.

The hours at which a baby is fed when he goes onto 3 meals a day depend largely on the family's habit, somewhat on the baby's hunger. Breakfast is usually between 7 and 8, but can be later if he's willing. He gets cereal and fruit (one or the other if he has a small appetite), his milk, and probably his egg. In the middle of the morning, he probably needs something to help him last through until lunch. Orange juice, about 2 ounces, is best. If he doesn't drink orange juice, you could give him pineapple juice, prune juice or tomato juice. If he gets very hungry before meals, add a piece of zwieback or dry bread crust or plain cracker.

Lunch comes in the neighborhood of 12 o'clock. Some babies must have it by 11:30. It probably consists of a green or yellow vegetable, meat, potato and milk. Potato is usually added at the time a baby goes on 3 meals a day, to give him enough extra energy to last through the afternoon. You don't bother with it if your baby has a small appetite or is getting fat. Fruit or pudding may be given at lunch, if this is the most convenient time of day or if your baby is hard to fill up. A baby should get fruit once or twice a day, but there is no harm in 3 times a day if it agrees with his digestion.

In the middle of the afternoon, if he needs a snack, another 2 ounces of orange juice or another fruit juice. Occasionally a mother says that it suits her baby best, for the first month or two after he gets on a regular breakfast-lunch-supper schedule, to give him an extra breast or bottle feeding at about 3 P.M. Of course, this still means 4 milk feedings a day, though a baby may want only half a bottle at 3 P.M. and 6 P.M. This extra bottle or half bottle in the middle of the afternoon is called for only if the mother wants his supper to be late, around 6, and if the baby has a very large appetite. Ordinarily, milk is not given between meals, because it stays in the stomach for 3 or 4 hours and takes away the appetite for the next meal.

Supper is usually given sometime between 5 and 6 P.M. when a baby goes on 3 meals a day. Most babies can't last beyond 5 if lunch is at 12, and some need to be fed even earlier. Supper is usually cereal, fruit and milk.

When a baby is taking milk only 3 times a day, he is probably getting a smaller total for the day than formerly, because he probably does not want more than his usual 6 to 8 ounces a meal. Don't worry about this. Don't try to tuck a few extra ounces into him at odd hours to keep up to the old 30-ounce total. Most babies are quite safe if they are taking as much as 24 ounces a day. On the other hand, if your baby is the unusual one who wants as much as 10 ounces a meal, give it to him.

227. When can you stop sterilizing the formula and bottles (if you cannot consult a doctor)? The answer to this question depends on so many different things that you ought to take it up with your doctor even if you can consult him only on rare occasions. But for those who can't, I'll mention some of the factors.

There are four reasons why you have to sterilize the formula in bottles when you are making a formula that contains water and that will last for a day. (1) There may be dangerous germs in the water (especially if the supply is unreliable). (2) Germs may be introduced in preparing the formula. (3) Germs multiply rapidly in milk over a period of hours, especially if it is not well refrigerated. (4) Babies develop intestinal infections easily. (This susceptibility is not outgrown until the second year, and then only gradually.)

So, as long as you are making a 24-hour formula that contains water, you have to sterilize the formula and bottles.

228. The answer in the case of straight pasteurized milk. If a baby of 9 months, for instance, has graduated to straight pasteurized milk in the bottle (or cup), the doctor may say it is safe to stop sterilizing milk and bottles if the mother fills each clean bottle just before giving it. The few germs left in such a bottle have no chance to multiply in the few minutes it takes the baby to drink it. The pasteurized milk should have no dangerous germs in it, and no water has been added. However, a doctor may be slower to advise giving unboiled pasteurized milk if a baby is particularly susceptible to diarrhea, if the weather is hot, or if there isn't a good refrigerator in which to keep the quart container from the dairy. Raw (unpasteurized) milk should be boiled throughout childhood.

229. The answer in the case of evaporated milk. The situation is different for a baby on an evaporated-milk mixture. The milk is sterile as it comes from the freshly opened can. If the opened can is kept in the refrigerator, it is safe for 24 hours anyway. It is the water that is the more doubtful factor. Some tap water and well water is not safe enough for the doctor to recommend using it unboiled until the baby is a year or more old; and there is always at least a slight risk of contamination of any water supply under special circumstances. So the water should be sterilized before or after being mixed with evaporated milk until the doctor says it is safe to stop. However, this is no problem. A day's supply of water can be boiled in 5 minutes and kept in its container for use throughout the day. Then at each feeding the mother can combine equal parts of evaporated milk and boiled water to give to the baby, either by cup or by bottle. As explained in the previous paragraph, the cup or bottle needs only to be washed clean (a milky bottle is more easily washed with cold water and detergent), because the milk will be in it only a few minutes. (Of course, you may feel that it's just as easy to continue to boil all together the formula and bottles needed for 24 hours.)

230. When do you change from evaporated to pasteurized milk? The really sensible answer would be "Never." Evaporated milk is sterile, cheaper, easier to store, easier to digest, less likely to cause allergy. It's only slightly less convenient to serve. When the baby is off formula, you merely mix equal parts of evaporated milk and boiled water in the cup or bottle just before feeding. When your doctor says you no longer need to boil the baby's water, you can mix equal parts of evaporated milk and tap water in the cup or bottle.

With all the advantages of evaporated milk, why are most babies changed to pasteurized milk? It's rarely at the insistence of the doctor. It's usually the strong wish of the mother. I think there are several reasons for this. Proud mothers delight in seeing their babies make advances, and for some reason the change from evaporated to pasteurized milk seems as important to them as learning to walk or becoming toilet-trained or entering school. Also, some mothers who don't like the taste of evaporated milk seem to assume that the baby will turn against it, too, just as soon as he is old enough to have any discrimination. They are sure this moment has come the first time he takes less than his usual amount of formula. I don't think there is any evidence that babies prefer pasteurized milk, but I've rarely been able to convince a mother of this. Also, it seems a lot easier to a mother to pour pasteurized milk out of a quart bottle than to mix evaporated milk with water, though I don't think it takes half a minute more. Anyway, there's no medical reason why a baby needs to change, so keep him on evaporated milk as long as you are willing to.

Weaning from Bottle to Cup

READINESS FOR WEANING

231. When are babies ready for weaning to cup? For years I was baffled by the fact that breast-fed babies and some bottle-fed ones show they're beginning to be bored with suckling by 5 or 6 months. Instead of nursing eagerly for 20 minutes, as they used to, they stop after 5 minutes to flirt with their mothers or play with their bottles or with their own hands. These babies will go on being somewhat indifferent to breast or bottle at 8, 10, 12 months, though they'll take it as long as it's offered, in most cases. They like to take milk from the cup, and they continue to do so.

But there are other babies who—quite the opposite—become **more** attached to their bottles at 6, 8 and 10 months than they ever were before. The mother of one of these will say, "Oh, how he loves his bottle! He watches it all the time he's taking his solid food. When it's time, he snatches it eagerly. He strokes it lovingly all the time he's drinking it and murmurs to it. He's very suspicious about milk from the cup, though he took it willingly before 6 months." Many of these babies continue to be very dependent on the bedtime bottle until 1½ or 2 years of age—unable to settle down or go to sleep without it—and are still firmly opposed to milk in the cup or glass. (It's interesting that they are quite willing to take water or juices from the cup.)

I finally realized that it is the babies who are allowed to take their bottles to bed by themselves who become **more** attached to their bottles in the second half of the first year. The bottle becomes a precious comforter at bedtime, reminding the child of his early months, when his greatest pleasure and security came from his intensely close relationship with his mother. His bottle in this sense becomes a mother substitute. Whereas the child who is still taking his bottle in his mother's lap, at 5 or 6 or 7 months, develops no such attachment to it because his real mother is right there. So the way to keep a baby from forming a lasting dependence on the bottle is to refrain from giving him the bottle to take to bed at this stage but to wean him gradually to the cup instead. Other examples of this same kind of dependence—on a soft toy or a pacifier—are explained more fully in Section 336.

232. Starting sips of milk from the cup by five months. It's a good idea to begin offering your baby a sip of milk from the cup each day by the time he's 5 months old. You aren't going to try to wean him to the cup right away. You only want to accustom him, at an age when he's not too opinionated, to the idea that milk comes in cups, too.

Pour half an ounce of the formula into a small cup or glass once a day. He won't want more than one sip at a time, and won't get much at first, but he'll probably think it is fun. If he is a breast-fed baby, pour half an ounce of pasteurized milk (from a well-shaken-up bottle) into a cup. It isn't usually necessary to boil this if it is pasteurized, but your doctor is the one to advise you on this point.

233. Orange juice doesn't count toward weaning. You may already have begun to give your baby orange juice from a cup or glass. If not, you can start that now, too. But the thing to remember is that a baby who is getting used to orange juice from a cup isn't getting used to the idea that milk can also come that way.

234. Helping a baby to like the cup. When he's 6 months old and wants to grab everything and put it in his mouth, give him a small, narrow, empty glass or cup that he can hold easily by himself and pretend to drink from. Or a baby's mug with 2 handles. When he does it fairly well, put a few drops of milk in the cup. Increase the amount as he gains in skill. If he takes to the idea of drinking by himself at 6 months, he is much less likely to turn against the cup at 7 or 8 months. If he stops drinking from the cup by himself for a few days, resist the temptation to pick up the cup and offer it to him, as this might only make him balky. Remember in the early months of cup drinking that he'll probably want only one swallow at a time. Many babies don't learn to take several gulps in succession until they are 1 to 1½ years old.

The child between 1 and 2 who is suspicious of the old cup he has always been offered may be delighted with a new cup or glass of a different shape or color. Changing to cold milk sometimes changes his mind. If the doctor thinks it's advisable, a little flavoring or coloring in the milk may help. Some mothers have found that adding a little cereal to the cup of milk makes it different enough to be acceptable for drinking. The cereal can gradually be removed a few weeks later.

There are special cups designed for weaning that have a lid with a flat spout. The lid keeps the milk from spilling and the spout goes into the baby's mouth. The baby can later use it without lid and spout. Some mothers like them because they prevent spilling for the first few months of cup drinking, until the baby gains skill. Other mothers object that a baby may first balk at the transition from bottle to weaning cup and even object again to the change to cup or glass without a spout. There are weaning cups with two handles, which are easier for a baby to hold, and others with a weighted base.

WEAN HIM GRADUALLY

235. Take it easy and follow his lead. If your baby at 5 or 6 months is becoming a little bored with his bottle and likes milk from the cup, gradually increase the amount in the cup. Give him the cup at every meal. This leaves less and less in the bottle. Then leave out the bottle that he takes least interest in, probably the lunch or breakfast one. In a week, give up the second bottle if he's progressing, and then the third. Most babies love their supper bottle most and are slowest in giving it up. Others feel that way about the breakfast bottle.

Willingness to be weaned doesn't always increase steadily. Misery from teething or a cold often makes a baby want more of the bottle for the time being. Follow his needs. The trend that made him start to give up the bottle before will set in again when he feels better.

236. The reluctant weaner. The baby who is reluctant to give up the bottle at 6 or 8 months may take one sip from the cup and push it away impatiently. Or he may pretend he doesn't know what it's for; he lets the milk run out at the sides of his mouth, smiling innocently. He may relent a little at 12 months but it is more likely that he'll remain suspicious till 15 months or even later. Put an ounce of milk in a small glass that he can handle and just set it on his tray every day or so, hoping that he'll drink it. If one sip is all he takes, don't even try to give him two. Act as if it doesn't make any difference to you.

When a suspicious baby does start to take a little milk from the cup, you must still be patient, because it will probably take several more months before he is ready to give up the bottle altogether. This applies particularly to the supper or bedtime bottle. Many late weaners insist on a bedtime bottle till about 2 years of age.

237. Sometimes it's the mother who delays weaning. Sometimes a baby is kept on the bottle longer than he needs to be because his mother worries about the fact that he isn't taking as much from the cup as he used to take from the bottle. Let's say that at 8 months he's drinking about 6 ounces from the cup at breakfast, 6 ounces at lunch, and about 4 ounces at supper, and that he's not especially eager for the bottle but if his mother gives it to him at the end of the meal he is willing to take a few ounces more that way. I think that a baby over 6 months who is taking as much as 16 ounces a day from the cup, and not acting as if he misses the bottle, might better be off the bottle altogether. If he is kept on it now, he may become less willing to give it up at that suspicious age between 10 to 15 months.

Another problem may develop for the mother who uses the bottle as a pacifier during the second year. Whenever her child has a crying spell in the daytime or wakes at night, she kindheartedly makes another bottle for him. The child may get as many as 8 bottles in the 24 hours—a total of 2 quarts of milk. This naturally takes away most of his appetite for meals, and he is then likely to develop a severe anemia. (There's practically no iron in milk.)

It's important from a nutritional point of view that a child not take more than a quart of milk a day. And from the point of view of emotional development, he should feel that he is being encouraged by his mother to grow out of babyhood. One of the most important ways she achieves this is by helping him to give up his bottles, one by one, as soon as he feels able to do so.

Daily Care

THE BATH

238. Before any feeding. It's usually most convenient in the early months to give the bath before the 10 A.M. feeding, but before any feeding is all right (not after a feeding, because you want him to go to sleep then). The father may even enjoy bathing him before the 6 P.M. or 10 P.M. feeding. By the time your baby is on 3 meals a day, you may want to change to before lunch or before supper. If you give him his orange juice before the bath, it keeps him from getting too hungry. As the child gets older still and stays up for a while after supper, it may work out better to give the bath after supper, especially if he needs his supper early. Bathe him in a reasonably warm room—the kitchen, if necessary.

239. A sponge bath if you prefer. Though it's the custom to give a complete tub or sponge bath every day, it certainly isn't necessary more than once or twice a week in cool weather, so long as the baby is kept clean in the diaper area and around the mouth. On the days when you don't give him a full bath, give a sponge bath in the diaper area. The tub bath is apt to be frightening at first to the inexperienced mother—the baby seems so helpless, limp and slippery, especially after he has been soaked. A baby may feel uneasy in the tub at first, because he can't be well supported there. You can give him a sponge bath for a few weeks until you and he feel more secure, or even for months—until he can sit up—if you prefer. It is often advised that a tub bath not be given until the navel is healed.

You can give a sponge bath on a table or in your lap. You'll want a piece of waterproof material under the baby. If you are using a hard surface like a table, there should be some padding over it (large pillow or folded blanket or quilt) so that the baby won't roll too easily. (Rolling frightens young babies.) Wash the face and scalp with a washcloth and clear warm water. (The scalp can be soaped once or twice a week.) Lightly soap the rest of the body with the washcloth or your hand. Then wipe the soap off by going over him at least twice with the rinsed washcloth, paying attention to creases.

240. The tub bath. Before starting the bath, be sure you have everything you need close at hand. If you forget the towel, you'll have to go after it holding a dripping baby in your arms.

Take off your wristwatch.
An apron keeps your clothes drier.
Have at hand:
> soap (some doctors recommend a soap containing hexachlorophene)
> washcloth
> towel
> absorbent cotton for nose and ears if necessary
> lotion or powder if you use either
> shirt, diaper, pins, nightie

The bath can be given in a washbowl, dishpan, kitchen sink or enamelware tub. The regular bathtub is hard on a mother's back and legs. Some mothers prefer a baby's fabric tub on high legs if there is room for it. For your own comfort, you can put a dishpan or enamelware tub on a table at which you sit or on something higher like a dresser, at which you stand. You can sit on a stool at the kitchen sink. The water should be about body temperature (90°–100°). A bath thermometer is a comfort to the inexperienced mother but is not necessary. Test the temperature with your elbow or wrist. It should feel comfortably warm. Use only a small amount of water at first until you get the knack of holding the baby securely. A tub is less slippery if you line it with a diaper each time. Hold the baby so that his head is supported on your wrist, and the fingers of that hand hold him securely in the armpit. Wash his face first, with a soft washcloth, without soap, then his scalp. His scalp needs to be soaped only once or twice a week. Wipe the soapsuds off his scalp with a damp washcloth, going over it twice. If the washcloth is too wet, the soapy water may get into his eyes and sting. (There are shampoos for babies that do not sting the eyes as much as ordinary shampoos.) Then soap the rest of the body, arms and legs, using the washcloth or your hand. (It's easier to soap your hand than a washcloth when your other hand is occupied.) If the skin gets dry, try omitting the soap except for once or twice a week.

Your hand under his arm, your wrist supporting his head.

If you feel nervous at first for fear you'll drop the baby in the water, you can soap him while he is on your lap or on a table. Then rinse him off in the tub, holding him securely with both hands.

Use a soft bath towel for drying him, and blot rather than rub. If you begin giving the tub bath before the navel is completely healed, dry it thoroughly after the bath with sterile cotton. Most babies, after a few weeks' experience, have a wonderful time in the bath, so don't rush it. Enjoy it with him.

241. Ears, eyes, nose, mouth, nails. You need to wash only the outer ear and the entrance to the canal, not inside. Wax is formed in the canal to protect and clean it.

The eyes are bathed constantly by the steady flow of the tears (not just when the baby is crying). This is why it is unnecessary to put any drops in the eyes while they are healthy.

The mouth ordinarily needs no extra care.

The nails can be cut easily while the baby sleeps. Clippers may be easier than nail scissors. There are manicure scissors with ball points. [I think they have spheres on them.]

The nose has a beautiful system for keeping itself clear. Tiny invisible hairs in the cells lining the nose keep moving the mucus and dust down toward the front of the nose, where it collects on the large hairs near the opening. This tickles the nose and makes the baby sneeze or rub the collection out. When you are drying the baby after the bath, you can first moisten and then gently wipe out the ball of dried mucus with the corner of the washcloth, or with a piece of absorbent cotton that has been twisted into a point and then wet, or, if necessary, with cotton carefully wrapped around the end of a toothpick or match stick so that the wood does not protrude. You can also buy prepared cotton swabs. Don't fuss at this too long if it makes him angry.

Dried mucus obstructing the nose. Sometimes, especially when the house is heated, enough dried mucus collects in the nose of a small infant to partially obstruct his breathing. Then each time he breathes in, the lower edges of his chest are pulled inward, or "retracted." An older child or adult would breathe through his mouth, but most babies can't leave their mouths open. If your baby's nose becomes obstructed at any time of day, you can first moisten and then remove the mucus as in the previous paragraph.

242. Lotion or powder? It's fun to apply lotion or powder to a baby after his bath, and the baby likes it, too, but neither is really necessary in most cases. (If it were, Nature would provide it.) Powder is helpful if the baby's skin chafes easily. It should be dusted on your hand first—away from the baby, so that he won't breathe a cloud of powder—and then rubbed gently on his skin. It should be applied thinly, so that it won't form lumps. Any baby powder or plain talcum is satisfactory. (Don't use zinc stearate powder; it's irritating to the lungs.) A baby lotion may be helpful when the skin is dry or there is a mild diaper rash. A lotion with hexachlorophene helps to prevent infection. Baby oils and mineral oil have been less often used since it has been shown that they sometimes cause a mild rash.

THE NAVEL

243. The healing of the navel. When the baby is still in the mother's womb, he is nourished through the blood vessels of the umbilical cord. Just after birth, the doctor ties it and cuts it off close to the baby's body. The stump that's left withers and eventually drops off, usually in about a week, though it may take 3 weeks. When the cord falls off, it may leave a raw spot, which takes a number of days, occasionally a number of weeks, to heal over. If healing is slow, the raw spot may become lumpy with what's called granulation tissue, but this is of no importance. The raw spot should merely be kept clean and dry, so that harmful germs will not infect it. If it is kept dry, a scab covers it until it is healed. Nowadays most doctors recommend that no dressing be put over the navel while it heals. In this way it is likely to stay driest. It is sometimes recommended that the baby not be given a tub bath until the navel is completely healed, but this rule is not essential if the navel is wiped dry with sterile cotton. It is wise to keep the diaper below the level of the unhealed navel, so that it doesn't keep it wet.

If the unhealed navel becomes moist and discharges, it should be protected more carefully from constant wetting by the diaper, and cleaned each day with alcohol. The doctor may recommend touching it with an antiseptic powder or powdered alum to hasten drying and healing.

If the navel and the surrounding skin become red, infection is present and you should get in touch with your doctor right away. Until you can reach him, you should apply continuous wet dressings (Section 727).

If the scab on the unhealed navel gets pulled by the clothing, there may be a drop or two of blood. This amount is of no importance.

244. Umbilical hernia. After the skin of the navel heals over, there is usually still an opening in the deeper, muscular layer of the abdomen where the umbilical vessels passed through. When the baby cries, a small part of the intestine is pushed through this hole (umbilical ring) and it makes the navel puff out somewhat. This is called an umbilical hernia. When the ring is small, the protrusion of the hernia is never much larger than a pea and the ring is likely to close over in a few weeks or months. When the ring is large, it may take months or even years to close and the protrusion may be larger than a cherry.

It used to be thought that the closing of the umbilical ring could be hastened by putting a tight strap of adhesive across the navel to keep it from protruding. It is now believed that strapping makes no difference. It is much easier not to bother with the adhesive, which always became soiled, soon loosened, and left raw places in the skin.

You don't have to worry about the protrusion of the hernia. It rarely causes any trouble, as other hernias sometimes do (Section 709). There is no need to try to keep the baby from crying.

In the well-padded older child or adult, the fat over the abdomen is thick enough to make the navel appear to be at the bottom of a hole. This is rarely the case in the first 2 or 3 years of life. The folds of skin of the navel (looking something like a rosebud) stand right out on the full abdomen. This prominence of the skin folds of the navel should not be confused with a hernia. A hernia can be felt underneath the skin folds, like a small, soft balloon. A hernia makes the navel stick out farther than it would otherwise.

If an umbilical hernia is still large at 6 or 8 years, and showing no decrease, surgical repair is often recommended.

THE PENIS

245. Circumcision and other ways to care for the penis. Should a baby boy be circumcised? If not, what care should be given the penis (the genital)? There's no single answer.

Circumcision is the cutting off of the sleeve of skin (called the foreskin) that normally covers the head of the penis. The advantages of circumcision are cleanliness and practicality. A cheeselike material called smegma is secreted by the skin of the head of the penis. When the foreskin remains, there is always smegma under it. Sometimes ordinary germs get into this smegma-filled space and cause an irritation or mild infection. If the foreskin has been removed, the smegma does not collect and there is no place for infection to occur. If circumcision is performed in early infancy, there will be no risk of psychological harm from having to do it later (Section 247). I think circumcision is a good idea, especially if most of the boys in the neighborhood are circumcised—then a boy feels "regular." However, it is not necessary. It is usually done before the baby leaves the hospital.

If your baby has been circumcised, the wound will not heal for a number of days. To protect the wound and to keep the scab from sticking to the diaper, put petrolatum (petroleum jelly) or boric acid ointment on a single layer of gauze about the size of a large postage stamp and wrap this around the end of the penis. The ointment will hold the gauze in place. If the wound gets rubbed by the diaper, a few drops of blood or a pink stain appears on the diaper. This is of no importance.

Another method of keeping the penis clean is to pull back (retract) the foreskin each day in the bath and briefly wash the head of the penis. This is painful to the baby at first because of the smallness of the opening in the foreskin in infants, and is difficult for mothers to do efficiently. I think it is an unsatisfactory method, psychologically and physically.

The third method of care is to leave the foreskin alone. This is the simplest way and the one used throughout a great part of the world. Its disadvantages are the slight risk of an infection under the foreskin, and the possibility, on this account, of having to consider circumcision at a later age when the child is very likely to be made nervous by the operation.

246. Why circumcision is harmful after infancy. The question of circumcision is often raised later in childhood, either because there has been an irritating infection beneath the foreskin or because the child is masturbating. In the days before the importance of the child's emotions was recognized, it seemed logical to circumcise for either of these reasons. The parents or the doctor might say, "Maybe he's masturbating because there is discomfort from a little infection." The trouble is that this theory often puts the cart before the horse. We know now that a boy, especially between 3 and 6, often becomes nervous about his penis for fear some injury might happen to it (explained in Section 522). This worry may cause him to handle himself and produce a little irritation. If this should be the real sequence of events, you can see that an operation on the penis would be a bad thing for his fears.

The danger of psychological harm from circumcision is greatest between 1 and 6 years, but there is some risk up through adolescence. I think it's wise to avoid the operation after the baby is a few months old, especially as a treatment for masturbation. The possibility of psychological harm from a later circumcision is reason for performing the operation right after birth.

247. Erections. It is common for boy babies to have erections of the penis, especially when the bladder is full or during urination. This has no importance.

THE FONTANEL

248. The soft spot on the top of a baby's head is where the four pieces of bone that make up the top of the skull have not yet grown together. The size of the fontanel at birth is different in different babies. A large one is nothing to worry about, and it's bound to be slower to close than a small one. Some fontanels close as early as 9 months and slow ones not till 2 years. The average is at 12 to 18 months.

If the light is right, you can see that the fontanel pulsates with the beat of the heart.

Mothers worry unnecessarily about the danger of touching the soft spot. Actually, it is covered by a membrane as tough as canvas, and there is very little risk of hurting a baby there.

CLOTHING, FRESH AIR AND SUNSHINE

249. Room temperature. The hardest question for a doctor to answer, in a book or in his office, is how much covering to put on a baby. All he can give are some rough guides. A baby under 5 pounds hasn't a very good system for keeping his body at the right temperature and has to be in an incubator. Between 5 and 8 pounds, he doesn't usually need to be heated from the outside. He can take care of himself in a comfortable room, say 68° to 72°.

By the time he weighs 8 pounds, his heat regulator is working well and he is getting a layer of fat that helps him stay warm. Now his room for sleeping can be allowed to go down to 60° in cool or cold weather.

It isn't necessary to try to get a baby's sleeping room below 60° (which is mildly cold).

A room temperature of 68° to 72° for eating and playing is right for babies weighing over 5 pounds, just as it is for older children and adults.

250. Clothing. Babies and children who are reasonably plump need less covering than an adult. More babies are overdressed than underdressed. This isn't good for them. If a person is always too warmly dressed, his body loses its ability to adjust to changes. He is more likely to become chilled. So, in general, put on too little rather than too much and then watch the baby. Don't try to put on enough to keep his hands warm, because most babies' hands stay cool when they are comfortably dressed. Feel his legs or arms or neck. Best guide of all is the color of his face. If he is getting cold, he loses the color from his cheeks, and he may begin to fuss, too.

When putting on sweaters and shirts with small openings, remember that a baby's head is more egg-shaped than ball-shaped. Gather the sweater into a loop, slip it first over the back of the baby's head, then forward, stretching it forward as you bring it down past the forehead and nose. When taking it off, pull the baby's arms out of the sleeves first. Gather the sweater into a loop as it lies around his neck. Raise the front part of the loop up past his nose and forehead (while the back of the loop is still at the back of his neck), then slip it off toward the back of his head.

A cap in which to sleep in very cold weather should be of knitted wool, so that if it slips over the baby's face he can breathe through it.

251. Practical coverings. It is better to use all-acrylic blankets or bags when a baby is sleeping in a cool room (60°–72°). They have the best combination of warmth and washability. Knitted shawls tuck and wrap more easily than woven blankets, especially when the baby is up, and because they are thinner you can adjust the amount of covering to the temperature more exactly than with thick blankets. Avoid coverings that are heavy, such as solid-feeling quilts.

Sleep bags can't be kicked off, as blankets can; sleep walkers are sensible by the time a baby can stand.

In a warm room (over 72°) or in warm weather, a baby really only needs cotton covering. There are now cotton thermal blankets said to be adaptable to cold or warm temperatures.

All blankets, quilts, sheets should be large enough to tuck securely under the mattress, so that they will not work loose. Waterproof sheets and pads should either be large enough to tuck in securely or should be pinned or tied down at all corners so that they will not come loose. The mattress should be firm and flat enough so that the baby will not be lying in a depression. A carriage mattress should fit well, so that there is no space around the edge in which he might get wedged. Use no pillow in crib or carriage.

252. Fresh air. Changes of air temperature are beneficial in toning up the body's system for adapting to cold or heat. A bank clerk is much more likely to become chilled staying outdoors in winter than a lumberjack, who is used to such weather. Cool or cold air improves appetite, puts color in the cheeks and gives more pep to humans of all ages. A baby living continuously in a warm room usually has a pasty complexion and may have a sluggish appetite.

In cold weather the air contains much less moisture. When this air is heated in a house it becomes relatively drier still, especially when the temperature rises above 72°. Dry, hot air dries and hardens the mucus in the nose and parches the air passages generally. This makes the baby uncomfortable and probably lowers his ability to resist infections.

It's good for a baby (like anyone else) to get outdoors for 2 or 3 hours a day, particularly during the season when the house is heated.

When he is sleeping indoors during cold weather, I think it is preferable that his window be open wide enough (and the radiator turned off) so that the temperature falls to about 60°.

When he is awake, and with the family, the room temperature should be kept between 68° and 72°.

Most people accustomed to heated houses let the temperature gradually get hotter all winter, without noticing it, and come to demand excessive heat. One way to counteract this in a private house is with a thermostat, which turns the furnace down when the desired temperature (70°) is reached. In an apartment or private house without a thermostat, the mother should hang a house thermometer in a prominent place and glance at it several times a day until she becomes so attuned to a range of 68° to 70° that she notices a higher temperature without looking.

The problem of providing cool enough air for a baby is further complicated by the inexperienced mother's natural anxiety and protectiveness. She tends to keep her baby in a too hot room and too well covered, besides. Under these conditions some babies even develop heat rash in winter.

253. Taking the baby out of doors. I grew up and practiced pediatrics in the eastern part of the United States, where most conscientious parents take it for granted that babies and children should be outdoors 2 or 3 hours a day when it isn't raining and the temperature isn't far below freezing. Children love to be out and it gives them pink cheeks and good appetites. So I can't help but believe in the tradition. I have to admit, though, that there is no such tradition in other parts of the country.

An 8-pounder can certainly go out when it's 60° or above. The temperature of the air is not the only factor. Moist, cold air is more chilling than dry air of the same temperature, and wind is the greatest chiller. Even when the temperature is below freezing, a 12-pound baby can be comfortable in a sunny, sheltered spot for an hour or two.

In winter the best time to have the baby out is in the middle of the day (between the 10 A.M. and 2 P.M. feedings in the early months). If you live in the country or have your own yard, you can put him out for even longer than 3 hours in reasonable weather. Let the sun fall on his face for a short time if this does not make him uncomfortable (see Section 254 on sunbathing).

As he grows older, is awake for longer periods and appreciates company more, I wouldn't keep him out all by himself for more than an hour when he is awake. By the second half of the first year, a child is entitled to have people nearby most of the time he's awake, even though he's amusing himself. It's fine for him to be out for 2 or 3 hours with his mother or when he's asleep.

If you live in a city and have no yard to park the baby in, you can push him in a carriage. Long woolen or thermal underwear, or tights, slacks, woolen stockings and boots make your life a lot more pleasant during this period. If you enjoy being out and can afford the time, the more the better.

In summer, if your house gets stifling hot and you can find a fairly cool place outdoors, the longer the baby stays out when asleep the better. If your house stays cool, I would still try to have the baby out for a couple of hours a day, but in the first part of the morning and the end of the afternoon.

When your baby first goes on 3 meals a day, you may need to shift the hours outdoors somewhat to suit your and his convenience. But the general principle of trying to get him out for 2 or 3 hours a day remains the same. As he gets nearer to a year old, he becomes more interested in his surroundings. He may refuse to go to sleep after lunch if he is being pushed around in his carriage. Then you may have to let him have his nap in his crib after lunch. That leaves very little of the afternoon for an outing, especially in winter. You might keep him out for 1 to 2 hours in the morning and an hour in the afternoon. What part of the morning you take him out also depends on when he takes his morning nap. Some babies in the last part of the first year fall asleep right after breakfast, others not until the end of the morning. If your baby won't sleep while he is outdoors, you have to fit in the outings when he is awake.

254. Sunshine and sunbaths. Direct sunshine contains ultraviolet rays, which create vitamin D right in the skin. On general principles it's sensible for babies and children to be in the sun for part of the time. There are three cautions. Exposure to sunshine should be increased very gradually to avoid burns, especially where the sun is hot and the air is clear. Secondly, excessive exposure is probably unwise even when the skin has been gradually tanned. The reason the skin becomes tanned is to protect the body from the effects of too much sun. In other words, the body can't use more than a moderate amount. Excessive amounts may be harmful to the skin. Thirdly, a severe sunburn is just as dangerous as a heat burn. When you put a baby out to sleep in a carriage, you must take into account how much sunshine he will get on his skin, especially if you are putting him in a new spot in a season when the sun is bright.

In summer you can begin exposing the baby's body to the sun as soon as the weather is warm enough and as soon as he weighs about 10 pounds. This means that he is plump enough so that he won't get chilled when he is partly undressed outdoors. In cooler weather you may be able to expose his legs alone. You have to wait longer to expose his face, until his eyes are no longer bothered by the bright light. This varies in different babies. When you do expose his face, turn him so that the top of his head is toward the sun. Then his eyebrows will shield his eyes.

In winter you can, if you wish, give him sunbaths at an open window if the room is warm enough and the wind does not blow on him.

Begin with 2 minutes and increase the exposure gradually —adding 2 minutes each day is fast enough. Divide the time between back and stomach. I wouldn't suggest going beyond 30 or 40 minutes of full exposure, especially in summer. In warm weather it is important that the baby not get overheated during his sunbath. Put him on a pad on the floor or on the ground where the air will cool him, not down inside a bassinet or carriage. If he becomes flushed, he's too hot.

When the sunshine is intense, as at the beach, a baby should be in the shade all the time the first day or two, and even then he may get enough reflected glare to give his tender skin a burn. A baby old enough to sit up and crawl around needs a hat at the beach or any equally sunny place. Remember that the redness of sunburn doesn't show up until several hours after the damage is done.

SLEEP

255. How much should a baby sleep? Mothers often ask this question. Of course, the baby is the only one who can answer it. One baby seems to need a lot, and another surprisingly little. As long as a baby is satisfied with his feedings, comfortable, gets plenty of fresh air and sleeps in a cool place, you can leave it to him to take the amount of sleep he needs.

Most babies in the early months sleep from feeding to feeding if they are getting enough to eat and not having indigestion. There are a few babies, though, who are unusually wakeful right from the beginning, and not because anything is wrong. If you have this kind of baby, there's nothing you need to do about it.

As your baby gets older, he gradually sleeps less and less. You're apt to notice it first in the late afternoon. In time he becomes wakeful at other periods during the day. Each baby develops his own pattern of wakefulness and tends to be awake at the same time every day. Toward the end of his first year, he probably is down to 2 naps a day; and between 1 and 1½ years, he probably gives up one of these. It is only during infancy that you can leave the amount of sleep entirely up to the baby. A child by the age of 2 is a much more complicated being. Excitement, worries, fear of bad dreams, competition with a brother may keep him from getting the sleep he needs.

256. Going to bed. It is preferable to get your baby used to the idea that he always goes to bed and to sleep right after a meal. (An occasional baby won't fall easily into this pattern but insists on being sociable after his meals. I'd try to change his mind.) It is good, too, for him to get used to falling asleep in his own bed, without company, at least by the time any 3-month colic is over.

Most babies can get accustomed to either a silent home or an average noisy one. So there is no point tiptoeing and whispering around the house at first—you'd only be training the baby to be easily wakened by unexpected sounds. The infant and child who, awake or asleep, is used to ordinary household noises and human voices usually sleeps right through a visit of talking, laughing friends, a radio or TV tuned to a reasonable level, even somebody's coming into his room.

257. On back or stomach? A majority of babies seem, from the beginning, to be a little more comfortable going to sleep on their stomachs. This is particularly true of the baby who develops colic: the pressure on the abdomen seems to partly relieve the gas pains.

Others either don't care at first or prefer sleeping on their backs. There are two disadvantages to a baby's sleeping on his back. If he vomits, he's more likely to choke on the vomitus. Also, he tends to keep his head turned toward the same side—usually toward the center of the room. This may flatten that side of his head. It won't hurt his brain, and the head will gradually straighten out, but it may take a couple of years. If you start early, you may be able to get him used to turning his head to both sides by putting his head where his feet were the time before, each time you put him to bed. Then if there is one part of the room he likes to look at, he will turn his head in each direction half the time. Within a few weeks a baby usually develops such a strong preference for his usual position, stomach or back, that it's quite a struggle to change him.

I think it is preferable to accustom a baby to sleeping on his stomach from the start if he is willing. He may change later when he learns to turn over.

The one objection that is raised against sleeping on the stomach, by some orthopedic (bone) specialists, is that if a baby has a tendency to turn his feet in too much or out too much, this may be accentuated by his lying on his stomach. Others reply that even if this is true, the in-turning or out-turning will be outgrown in any case after the child has been walking for a while. Ask your baby's doctor.

Some physicians recommend that, to avoid the disadvantages of back or stomach sleeping, a baby should be taught to sleep on his side with the aid of firm pillows. In my experience this is very difficult to accomplish; the baby always slides away from the pillow and ends up on his back or stomach. By 6 months, however, some babies begin to sleep on their sides by preference.

258. See if you can train the baby to sleep later or be happy in his bed in the morning. In the middle part of the first year, most babies become willing to sleep a little later than that uncivilized 5 or 6 A.M. waking hour that they all love at first. However, most parents develop such a habit of listening for the baby in their sleep and jumping out of bed at the first murmur that they never give him a chance to go back to sleep if he's willing, or to become accustomed to amusing himself for a while. As a result, they may find themselves still getting up before 7 A.M. when the child is 2 or 3 years old. And a child who has been used to early company for so long will demand it.

So if you like to sleep till 7 or 8, use your alarm clock again instead of the baby. Set the alarm 5 minutes later than he usually wakes, and every few days move it 5 minutes later still. If he wakes before the alarm, he may go back to sleep without your hearing him or he may learn to stay awake contentedly for a longer and longer period. If he fusses, wait a while to see if he quiets down. Of course, if he works himself up to indignant crying and it persists, you've got to get up. But try again in another month.

259. Out of the parents' room by six months if possible. A child can sleep in a room by himself from the time he is born, if convenient, as long as the parents are near enough to hear him when he cries. If he starts with his parents, 6 months is a good age to move him. He has the strength to take care of himself pretty well, and he doesn't yet have set ideas about where he wants to be. It is preferable that he not sleep in his parents' room after he is about 6 months old. Otherwise there is a chance that he may become dependent on this arrangement and be afraid and unwilling to sleep anywhere else. The older he is, the harder it may be to move him.

Another trouble is that the young child may be upset by the parents' intercourse, which he misunderstands and which frightens him. Parents are apt to think there is no danger if they first make sure the child is asleep. But children's psychiatrists have found cases in which the child awakened and was much disturbed without the parents' ever being aware of it.

Whether a child should sleep in a room by himself or with another youngster is largely a practical matter. If it's possible, it's fine for each child to have a room of his own, especially as he grows older, where he can keep his own possessions under control and have privacy when he wants it. The main disadvantage of two young children in the same room is that they are apt to wake each other up at the wrong times.

260. Better not let the child in your bed. Sometimes when a small child is going through a period of waking up frightened at night—perhaps coming repeatedly into the parents' room, perhaps crying persistently—the parents take him into bed with them so that they can all get some sleep. This seems like the most practical thing to do at the time, but it usually turns out to be a mistake. Even if the child's anxiety improves during the following weeks, he is apt to cling to the security of his parents' bed, and there is the devil to pay getting him out again. So always bring him promptly and firmly back to his own bed. I think it's a sensible rule not to take a child into the parents' bed for any reason (even as a treat when the father is away on a business trip).

PLAY PERIODS

261. Being companionable with your baby. Be quietly friendly with your baby whenever you are with him. He's getting a sense of how much you mean to each other all the time you're feeding him, bubbling him, bathing him, dressing him, changing his diapers, holding him or just sitting in the room with him. When you hug him or make noises at him, when you show him that you think he's the most wonderful baby in the world, it makes his spirit grow, just the way milk makes his bones grow. That must be why we grown-ups instinctively talk baby talk and waggle our heads when we greet a baby, even grown-ups who are otherwise dignified or unsociable.

One trouble with being an inexperienced parent is that part of the time you take the job so seriously that you forget to enjoy it. Then you and the baby are both missing something.

Naturally I don't mean that you should be talking a blue streak at him all the time he's awake, or constantly joggling him or tickling him. That would tire him out, and in the long run would make him tense and spoiled. You can be quiet nine-tenths of the time you are with him. It's the gentle, easygoing kind of companionship that's good for him and good for you. It's the comfortable feeling that goes into your arms when you hold him, the fond, peaceful expression on your face when you look at him, and the gentle tone in your voice.

262. Companionship without spoiling. Though it's good for a baby during his play periods to be somewhere near his mother (and brothers and sisters, if any) so that he can see her, make noises at her, hear her speak to him, have her show him a way to play with something occasionally, it isn't necessary or sensible for him to be in her lap or arms or to have her amusing him much of the time. He can be enjoying her company, profiting from it, and still be learning how to occupy himself. If a new mother is so delighted with her baby that she is holding him or making games for him a good part of his wakeful period, he may become quite dependent on these attentions and demand more and more of them. See Sections 297, 298.

263. Things to watch and things to play with. Young babies begin waking earlier and earlier, especially at the end of the afternoon. At such times they want something to do and they want some companionship. At 2, 3 and 4 months, they enjoy looking at bright-colored things and things that move. Outdoors, they are delighted to watch leaves and shadows. Indoors, they study their hands, pictures on the wall. There are bright-colored plastic shapes on strings that you can suspend between the top rails of the crib. Place them just within arm's reach—not right on top of a baby's nose—for the time when he begins reaching. You can make mobiles yourself—cardboard shapes covered with colored paper that hang from the ceiling or from a lighting fixture and rotate in slight drafts (they aren't strong enough for playing with or healthful for chewing)—or you can hang suitable household objects within reach—spoons, plastic cups, for instance. Remember that eventually everything goes into the mouth. As a baby gets toward the middle of his first year, his greatest joy is handling and mouthing objects: collections of plastic objects linked together (made for this age), rattles, teething rings, animals and dolls of cloth, household objects that are safe in the mouth. Don't let a baby or small child have objects or furniture that has been repainted with outdoor paint containing lead, or thin celluloid toys that can be chewed into small, sharp pieces, or small glass beads and other small objects that can be choked on. Take the metal whistles out of rubber animals.

Each afternoon when the baby becomes bored with his crib, put him in the playpen near where you are working or sitting. If you are going to use a pen, the baby should become accustomed to it at 3 or 4 months, before he has learned to sit and crawl and before he has had the freedom of the floor. Otherwise he considers it a prison from the start. By the time he can sit and crawl, he has fun going after things that are a few feet away, handling larger objects like cooking spoons, saucepans, strainers. When he becomes bored with the playpen, he can sit in a bouncing chair or a chair-table arrangement. It's good for him to end up with some free creeping.

264. When to get a playpen. You don't have to have a playpen. Some psychologists and physicians disapprove, feeling that it prevents the creeping baby from exploring and gaining independence. I understand this theoretical objection, though I don't believe there is any proof one way or the other. I have usually suggested a playpen on purely practical grounds as a great help, especially for the busy mother. Set up in the living room or the kitchen, where the mother is working, it gives the baby the company that he can't have in his own room and a chance to see everything that is going on. Later he has fun by the hour putting toys out onto the floor and getting them back again. When he is old enough to stand up, the pen gives him a railing to hold onto and a firm foundation under his feet. In good weather he can sit safely in his playpen on the porch and watch the world go by.

The net playpens are becoming more popular than the wooden ones mainly because they are so much lighter to move around.

265. Walkers, swings. A walker or a swing is useful after a baby has learned to sit and before he learns to walk. It will keep him happy for quite a while, exercise him and keep him from getting into as much trouble as he would creeping. However, I wouldn't keep a baby in a walker or swing all the time he's up. He needs chances to creep, explore, stand, walk.

In one kind of walker with springs, a baby can jounce up and down before he learns to walk around. Some pediatricians and orthopedists object to a walker, at least if a baby toes in or out excessively when using one. Ask your doctor.

There are swings on standards, for indoors or out, some with windup motors, swings for doorways, swings with springs in which a baby can bounce.

THE BOWEL MOVEMENTS

266. The gastrocolic reflex. The bowels are apt to move soon after a meal in most individuals because the filling of the stomach tends to stimulate the intestinal tract all the way down. This hookup is called the gastrocolic reflex. The movement is more apt to occur after breakfast because of the abrupt resumption of stomach and intestinal activity after the long night's quiet.

Sometimes this reflex works too actively in the early months of life, especially in a breast-fed baby, who may have a movement after every nursing. More inconvenient still is the pattern of an occasional baby who begins to strain soon after the start of each feeding, produces nothing, but keeps straining so hard, as long as the nipple is in his mouth, that he can't nurse. You have to let his intestines quiet down for 15 minutes and try again.

267. Meconium. For the first day or so after birth, the baby's movements are composed of material called meconium, which is greenish-black in color and of a smooth, sticky consistency. Then they change to brown and to yellow. If a baby hasn't had a movement by the end of his second day, the doctor should be notified.

268. The breast-fed baby may have many or few movements. A breast-fed baby usually has several movements a day in the early weeks. Some have a movement after every nursing. They are usually of a light-yellow color. They may be pasty or they may have the consistency of thick cream soup. They are practically never too hard. Many breast-fed babies change from frequent to infrequent movements by the time they are 1, 2 or 3 months old. Some then have 1 movement a day, others a movement only every other day or even further apart. This is apt to alarm a mother who has been brought up to believe that everyone must have a movement every day. But there is nothing to worry about so long as the baby is comfortable. The breast-fed baby's movement stays just as soft, even when it is passed every 2 or 3 days.

Some of these breast-fed babies who have infrequent movements begin to push and strain a lot when 2 or 3 days have gone by. Yet the movement is like creamed soup when it does come out. The only explanation I can make for this is that the movement is so liquid that it doesn't put the right kind of pressure on the inside of the anus, where the movement comes out. Consult the doctor about this. Adding a little solid food to the diet usually helps, even though the baby doesn't otherwise need solid food yet. Two to 4 teaspoonfuls of pureed prunes daily (stewed or canned) generally work well. There is no call for cathartics in this kind of difficulty. I think it is better not to use suppositories or enemas regularly, for fear the baby will come to depend on them. Try to solve the problem with prunes or other solid food.

269. The bottle-fed baby's movements. The baby fed cow's milk usually has between 1 and 4 movements a day at first, though an occasional baby has as many as 6. As he grows older, the number tends to decrease to 1 or 2 a day. The number is unimportant if the consistency of the movement is good and if the baby is doing well.

Cow's-milk movements are most often pasty and of a pale-yellow or tan color. However, some young babies always have stools that are more like soft scrambled eggs (curdy lumps with looser material in between). This is not important if the baby is comfortable and gaining well.

The commonest disturbance of the bowel movements in the

baby on cow's milk is a tendency to hardness. This is discussed in the section on **constipation** (Section 309).

A very few bottle-fed babies have a tendency to loose, green, curdy movements in the early months. This is usually worse as more sugar is added to the formula. A severe case needs a lot of supervision by the doctor. If you are completely out of reach of a doctor, you can omit the sugar from the formula altogether. However, if a baby's movements are always just a little loose, it can be ignored, provided he is comfortable, gaining well, and the doctor finds nothing wrong.

270. Changes in the movements. You can see that it doesn't matter if one baby's movements are always a little different from another baby's, as long as he's doing well. It's more apt to mean something, and should be discussed with the doctor, when his movements undergo a real change. If they were previously pasty and then turn lumpy, slightly looser, slightly more frequent, it may be a spell of indigestion or a mild intestinal infection. If they become definitely loose, frequent, greenish, and the smell changes, it is almost certainly due to an intestinal infection (diarrhea), whether mild or severe. When a bowel movement is delayed and then comes unusually firm, it sometimes means the beginning of a cold, sore throat or other disease, but not necessarily. (The infection makes the intestine more sluggish, just as it's apt to diminish the appetite.) Generally speaking, changes in the number and color of the movements are less important than changes in the consistency and smell.

Mucus in the bowel movements is common when a baby has diarrhea, and it is just another sign that the intestines are irritated. Similarly, it may occur in indigestion. It can also come from higher up, from the throat and bronchial tubes of a baby with a cold, or of a healthy newborn baby. Some babies form a great deal of mucus in the early weeks.

When a **new vegetable** is added to the diet (less frequently in the case of other foods), part of it may come through looking just the same as it went in. If it also causes signs of irritation, such as looseness and mucus, give much less the next time. If there is no irritation, you can keep on with the same amount or increase slowly until he learns to digest it better. Beets can turn the whole movement red.

A bowel movement exposed to the air may turn brown or it may turn green. This is of no importance.

Small streaks of blood on the outside of a bowel movement usually come from a crack, or "fissure," in the anus, caused by hard bowel movements. The bleeding is not serious in itself, but the doctor should be notified so that the constipation can be treated promptly. This is important for psychological as well as physical reasons (Section 389). **Larger amounts of blood** in the movement are rare and may come from malformations of the intestines, from severe diarrhea or from intussusception (Section 705). The doctor should be called or the child taken to a hospital immediately.

Diarrhea is discussed in Sections 315–317.

DIAPERS

271. Diapering. How to fold a diaper depends on the size of the baby and of the diaper. The only important things in putting it on are to have the most cloth where there is the most urine, and not to have so much diaper bunched between the legs that they are kept widely separated. With a full-size newborn baby and the usual large diapers, you can fold as in the pictures. First fold lengthwise so that there are 3 thicknesses. Then fold about one third of the end over. As a result, half of the folded diaper has 6 layers, the other half 3 layers. A boy needs the double thickness in front; a girl needs the thickness in front if she lies on her abdomen, in back if she lies on her back. When you put in the pin, slip two fingers of the other hand between the baby and the diaper to prevent sticking him.

Most mothers change the diapers when they pick the baby up for his feeding and again before they put him back to bed.

One way to fold a diaper.

Mothers who are very busy, though, have found they can save time and laundry by changing only once at each feeding, either before or after. Most babies are not bothered by being wet. But a few are extra sensitive and have to be changed more often. If a child has sufficient covers over him, his wet diaper does not feel cold. It is when wet clothing is exposed to the air that evaporation makes it cold.

If a baby drenches himself and his bed, it may be worthwhile using 2 diapers at a time. The second one may be too bulky if put on the same way as the first. You can pin it around his waist like an apron.

Disposable diapers are handy for traveling. Some mothers for whom the added expense is not important find them ideal for every day. There are various types and sizes.

See Sections 55 and 56 on **diaper liners** and **waterproof pants.**

In cleaning the baby after a bowel movement, you can use plain water on cotton or a washcloth, soap and water (the soap should be wiped off) or baby lotion. It isn't necessary to wash the baby when changing a wet diaper.

272. Washing the diapers. You want a covered pail partially filled with water to put used diapers in as soon as removed. If it contains soap or detergent, this helps in removing stains. Be sure the soap is well dissolved, to prevent lumps of soap from remaining in the diapers later. When you remove a soiled diaper, scrape the movement off into the toilet with a knife, or rinse it by holding it in the toilet while you flush it (hold tight).

You wash the diapers with mild soap or mild detergent in washing machine or washtub (dissolve the soap well first), and rinse 2 or 3 times. The number of rinsings depends on how soon the water gets clear and on how delicate the baby's skin is. If your baby's skin isn't sensitive, 2 rinsings may be enough.

If your baby has a tendency to diaper rash, you may need to take additional precautions—at least at the times the rash appears, and perhaps regularly. Bacteria that sometimes collect in diapers manufacture ammonia from the urine. This ammonia is the main cause of diaper rash. These bacteria are not completely removed by washing. They must be destroyed if there is much diaper rash, either by boiling the diapers or by adding a special diaper antiseptic to the last rinsing water. Ask your doctor for the name of a diaper antiseptic that is safe and convenient. Some clothes washers and dryers effectively kill these bacteria depending on the heat. (Diapers that go to the diaper service are sterilized.)

Sunshine is a potent destroyer of many bacteria. There is probably less chance of diaper rash if you hang the diapers (and also the other things that are wet by the urine: nighties, shirts, sheets, pads, waterproof sheeting, waterproof pants) in the sun to dry. See Section 319 on diaper rash.

If the diapers (and other clothes) are becoming hard, unabsorbent and gray with soap deposit (the same as the ring in the bathtub) you can soften them and clean them by using a water conditioner.

INOCULATIONS

273. Keep a record with you. It's a good idea to keep a record (signed by your doctor) of all your children's inoculations (and sensitivity to drugs, if any) in your home, and to carry it with you when the family goes on trips. It's also valuable if you move or if you change doctors. To be sure, you can always write or phone the doctor who gave the inoculations, but this is often impossible to do in a hurry during an emergency. The commonest emergency is when a child away from home receives a wound that calls for extra protection against tetanus (lockjaw). Then it is very important for the attending doctor to know for certain whether the child has received tetanus inoculations.

274. Diphtheria, pertussis (whooping cough), tetanus inoculations (DPT). Inoculations against these three diseases are usually given together in a combined form (three materials in one shot). They should be started very early, preferably at 2 months of age. Three shots are given (each shot containing diphtheria, pertussis and tetanus materials), most commonly 1 month apart. However, if the interval between inoculations is longer than a month, the effect is just as good.

The protection from the three shots is usually very high, but after a few months it begins to taper off. So a booster shot is given a year later (at 15 to 18 months of age) to bring the protection back to a high level, and again at about 3 years of age. A further inoculation against tetanus and diphtheria is given at 6 years and 12 years.

These combined inoculations often cause a reaction (on

account of the whooping cough material), consisting of fever, crankiness, loss of appetite, soreness around the injection, which usually starts 3 or 4 hours after the shot. The doctor can prescribe medication to relieve the symptoms. The baby should feel better the next day. If he has a fever after that, it should not be blamed on the inoculation; it is due to some new infection. These shots do not cause cough or cold symptoms.

Doctors usually don't give these inoculations when a baby has a fresh cold or other infection. They are not usually given during a poliomyelitis epidemic for fear of temporarily lowering resistance to that disease.

It is common for a firm lump, or "knot," to remain in the buttock or arm where the child has received a shot. It remains for several months and is nothing to worry about.

Now we should discuss the three materials that go into these combined inoculations.

275. Pertussis (whooping cough) vaccine is one of the materials that go into DPT inoculations. It is made from killed whooping cough germs. It may not give complete protection from whooping cough, but if an inoculated child does catch the disease it is apt to be mild. Whooping cough is a dangerous disease for babies, and this is one reason the inoculations are started so early in infancy.

It takes two or three shots and some time before the vaccine stimulates the body to build a high resistance. So no immediate help can be expected from a first inoculation given after a child has already been exposed to the disease. Boosters are given at 15 months and 3 years.

276. Diphtheria toxoid is another of the materials that go into DPT shots. The poisonous substance from diphtheria germs, called diphtheria toxin (which is what does the damage when a person has the disease), is treated chemically so that it is changed to a nonpoisonous substance—a toxoid. Diphtheria toxoid, when injected, can stimulate the body to build protection against diphtheria toxin. It is recommended that a child have three shots in early infancy and boosters at 15 months, 3 years, 6 years, 12 years. In this way he is almost certainly protected against diphtheria.

277. Tetanus toxoid is the third material that goes into DPT shots. It is made from the poisonous substance (tetanus toxin) in tetanus germs, and when several shots are injected they stimulate the body to slowly build its own, long-lasting protection against tetanus. It must be differentiated from tetanus antitoxin, which is a horse serum that gives prompt but only temporary protection.

Tetanus, or lockjaw, is a serious infection that sometimes gets into a wound. The germs occur most commonly in soil and other places where horse manure and cow manure have been. The germs can still be found fairly regularly in city streets. A wound is more liable to be infected with tetanus if it is deep. A deep puncture from a nail in a barnyard is therefore the riskiest kind. Lots of people think that the rust on a nail brings the danger of tetanus. This is not true. The important thing is where the nail has been.

Nowadays if a child who has already built his own protection as a result of tetanus toxoid injections receives a dangerous wound, the doctor merely gives another toxoid booster to be sure the protection is high. But if the doctor has no proof that toxoid inoculations have been given, he has to give horse serum (Section 278) in order to play safe. That is why you should carry a record of a child's inoculations with you when you are away from your own doctor.

The protection a child builds up from tetanus toxoid develops slowly and reaches a safe height only after the second shot. Therefore, there is no use starting this method at the time he gets a dangerous wound. He needs a shot of horse serum to give him immediate protection.

A booster shot is given at 15 months, 3 years, 6 years, 12 years. In addition, if the child gets a dangerous wound at any time, he should have another toxoid injection. This immediately boosts his protection to a good, high level.

278. Tetanus antitoxin (horse serum). Long before we had tetanus toxoid for long-lasting protection, we had tetanus antitoxin horse serum. A horse is inoculated with tetanus germs until his blood serum contains a lot of protection against this disease. Some of this serum is injected into a person who has had a dangerous wound. The person in this way borrows some of the horse's protection, but it lasts only a few weeks. The trouble with the horse serum injection is that it is apt to produce serum sickness (hives and fever) a couple of weeks later. It may also make a person highly sensitive to horse serum. If this happens, a second injection might make him very sick indeed, unless given with extreme care.

If an injured child or adult has not already built his own

protection from toxoid inoculations, or if proof of these is lacking, it is often hard to decide whether horse serum is necessary—for instance, when a wound is not very deep and when there is a question whether any tetanus germs could have gotten in. It's a matter that has to be decided each time between the parents and the doctor. Serum isn't usually given for cuts and scratches that a child receives indoors.

279. Oral Poliovirus Vaccine (Sabin vaccine) should be given to all babies, beginning at 2 months of age or as soon thereafter as possible. It is a live virus that has been grown on living cells in a laboratory and is taken by mouth. There are three types of virus that cause polio and a person has to take three types of vaccine to be completely protected. At the time this is written (1968) some doctors give Type I, Type III, Type II in that order, 6 or 8 weeks apart. However, another method is to give a "Trivalent" vaccine (which contains all three types) 3 times in succession, at the same intervals. In either case a booster shot of Trivalent vaccine is given at 15 months and again at 6 years.

The world had to wait a long time for this vaccine. Any vaccine has to be made by growing the germs of the disease in a laboratory. Polio is caused by a virus. Viruses, unlike ordinary bacteria, grow only on living tissues, ordinarily only in man or other species which are susceptible to certain virus diseases. Three scientists, Drs. John Enders, Frederick Robbins and Thomas Weller, finally discovered how to grow polio virus in monkey tissue kept alive in test tubes. When this step was solved, Dr. Jonas Salk was able to develop a vaccine which was made safe by killing the virus with a chemical; but the immunity it created in a person was not complete and it kept decreasing unless boosters were given frequently. Then Dr. Albert Sabin found a way to attenuate (weaken) the live virus enough to make it safe, yet it created a high and long-lasting immunity.

280. Measles Vaccine is fortunately available now and should be given to every healthy child at 12 months, without exception, or as soon thereafter as possible. Though most people think of measles as harmless because they suffered no bad consequences, it can have serious complications— ear infections, pneumonia, encephalitis, even permanent brain damage. That's why the vaccine is important. The vaccine is made of live measles virus which has been rendered mild in its effect by being grown for a long time on live chick embryo. It is not given until a year of age so that the immunity which a baby may have inherited from his mother will have a full opportunity to wear off first. The vaccine stimulates the body to build its own immunity, which, it is hoped, will last for life.

Though the reactions to the measles vaccine (which is really a mild case of measles) are much less severe than having regular measles itself, still, one child in ten has fever as high as 103°, beginning about a week after the inoculation and lasting 1 to 5 days, and one child in ten has a mild rash.

281. Vaccination against smallpox. This is a must for all babies. It's best done between 12 and 15 months, when it's less apt to make him sick. Smallpox is a serious disease, and vaccination is a sure preventive. The vaccine contains the virus or germ of cowpox, and when the vaccination "takes," the baby is having a light case of cowpox. The wonderful thing about cowpox is that, though it is a very mild disease, it protects a person from getting the severe disease smallpox.

Once in a while there's a baby who shouldn't be vaccinated for the time being. If he has eczema or any other skin disease, vaccination should be postponed until his rash has cleared up (unless there are cases of smallpox in the community). Babies with eczema or other rashes sometimes get severe reactions from vaccination. Vaccination should also be postponed if a baby has been frail or sickly. It's wise not to vaccinate during a very hot spell, or when other members of the family have fresh colds, or when the baby has a cold or any other upset. It should also be postponed if there is in the family another child with eczema who has never been vaccinated. He might become accidentally inoculated from the vaccination. To be absolutely safe, a child should be revaccinated every 6 years. When cases of smallpox appear in a neighborhood, everybody should be immediately revaccinated.

The doctor puts a drop of the vaccine material on the baby's skin, and then pricks or scratches the skin through the drop. Nothing happens right away. In about 3 days a little red pimple appears, which soon gets a whitish blister on it. It gradually enlarges and is surrounded by a reddened area. It's at its worst on about the eighth or ninth day. In a mild vaccination the whole thing may be no larger than a nickel. In a moderate reaction the redness and swelling may cover an area larger than a silver dollar. When the vaccination is mild,

a baby may show no ill effects at all. If it is moderate, he feels
sick and cranky, loses his appetite and runs a fever. Don't
have your baby vaccinated when you are going to be traveling
or unusually busy a week later.

After the height of the reaction, the vaccination dries up
and turns into a tough brown scab, which takes several weeks
to fall off.

The air should not be shut out from a vaccination. A celluloid shield should never be used. It is best of all to leave the
vaccination uncovered, except by the clothing, as long as the
baby does not scratch at it. If it is on his upper arm and he
is scratching it, you can pin a square sterile gauze dressing
on the inside of his nightie or shirt, so that it lies over the vaccination. If a girl is vaccinated on the thigh (to avoid the arm
scar) and there is no clothing to protect it from scratching,
you can place a square sterile gauze dressing over the vaccination and attach it with 2 narrow strips of adhesive plaster
running up and down the thigh. Don't run adhesive plaster
around the leg or arm. It may cut off the circulation.

You don't need to do anything about the vaccination for
the first 3 or 4 days. After the blister or white top appears, the
baby is usually kept out of the tub bath, because it's better
to keep the top from being softened and broken, if possible.
Give him a sponge bath from the time the blister appears
until the scab falls off.

Even though severe reactions to vaccinations are uncommon and rarely lead to complications, you should keep in
touch with your doctor if your baby's arm is widely inflamed,
or the fever is high, or the reaction lasts after the tenth day.

If a vaccination doesn't take, it doesn't mean that the person
is immune. It shows only that the vaccine material was weak
or that it didn't get through the skin. He should be vaccinated
again and again, if necessary, until there is a take.

When a person who had a successful vaccination years before is vaccinated again, he should show some reaction on his
skin. If most of his former protection has worn off, his new
vaccination develops much like the previous one. If he still
has most of his old protection, a small pimple forms, lasts a
few days, and goes away without ever coming to a head. If
nothing shows at all, it means that the vaccine material was
weak or did not get through the skin. The vaccination should
then be repeated.

Problems of Infancy

CRYING IN THE EARLY WEEKS

282. What does it mean? This is usually an important question with a first baby. As he grows older, crying is much less of a problem because you worry less, you know what to expect from him at different times of the day, you are able to distinguish between different cries, and he has fewer causes for crying.

Several questions pop into your mind: Is he hungry? Is he wet? Is he sick? Does he have indigestion? Is a pin sticking into him? Is he becoming spoiled? Parents are not apt to think of fatigue, but it's one of the commonest causes. It is fairly easy to answer these questions, one by one.

But there is a lot of fretting and crying that can't be explained by any of these reasons. In fact, by the time they are a couple of weeks old, almost all babies—especially first babies—get into fretful periods that we can give names to but can't explain exactly. When the crying is regularly limited to one period in the evening or afternoon, we can call it **colic** (if there is pain, distension and gas) or **periodic irritable crying** (if there is no distension.) If the baby is fussing off and on, any old time of the day or night, we can sigh and say that he is just a **fretful baby** at this stage. If he's unusually tense and jumpy, we use the term **hypertonic baby.** But we don't know the meaning of these patterns of behavior. We only know that they commonly occur and that they gradually peter out—usually by 3 months of age. Maybe they are different variations of one condition. In a vague way we can sense that the age period between birth and about 3 months is one of adjustment of the baby's immature nervous system and immature digestive system to life in the outside world and that a smooth adjustment is harder for some babies to achieve.

Anyway, the important thing to remember is that these most common types of crying in the early weeks are temporary and are not a sign of anything serious.

283. Hunger? Whether you're feeding your baby on a fairly regular schedule or according to his desire, you soon get an idea of what his pattern is like—at what times of day he wants more to eat, at what times he's apt to wake early. This should help you to decide whether unusual crying is due to hunger. If a baby took less than half his usual amount at his last feeding, it may be the reason why he's awake and crying in a couple of hours instead of in 3 or 4 hours. But not necessarily. A baby who has taken much less than his usual amount may, just as often, sleep contentedly for the full 4-hour period.

If a baby took an average amount at his last feeding and wakes crying before 2 hours, it is even less likely that he is hungry. (If he wakes within an hour, especially in the evening or afternoon, it's most apt to be colic.) If it's 2½ or 3 hours after the last feeding, then consider hunger first.

Could it be that he has outgrown his formula or the breast-milk supply, or that the breast supply is decreasing? A baby doesn't outgrow his formula all of a sudden, from one day to the next. He will have been finishing every bottle for several days and looking around for more. He begins to wake and cry a little earlier than usual, not a lot. In most cases, it's only after he has been waking early from hunger for a number of days that he begins crying after a feeding.

Normally the breast-milk supply increases as the baby demands it. The more complete and more frequent emptying of the breast stimulates it to greater production. Of course, it is possible for a mother to have less breast milk occasionally if she is fatigued or worried.

I'd sum it up with the following rule of thumb: If a baby has been crying hard for 15 minutes or more and if it's more than 2 hours after the last feeding—or even if it's less than 2 hours after a very small feeding—give him another feeding. If this satisfies him and puts him to sleep, it's the right answer. If it's less than 2 hours after a full feeding, it's unlikely that he's hungry. Let him fuss or cry for 15 or 20 minutes more, if you can stand it, or give him a pacifier, and see if he won't go back to sleep. If he's crying harder than ever, there's no harm trying a feeding.

(Don't start giving a bottle the first time you suspect the breast milk is insufficient; give the breast.)

284. Is he sick? Babies catch colds and they catch intestinal infections during their early months, but these show themselves in running noses, coughs or loose bowel movements. Other infections are pretty rare. If your baby is not only crying but **looks different** in general appearance and color, take his temperature and report to the doctor.

285. Is he crying because he's wet or has had a bowel movement? A very few young babies seem uncomfortable when wet or soiled. Most don't mind at all. You can change him anyway.

286. Is it a safety pin? This doesn't happen, once in a hundred years, but you can look to be sure.

287. Is it indigestion? You can try bubbling him again even though you got a bubble up before. Indigestion with spitting and loose, curdy green stools is discussed in Section 307, colic in Section 292.

288. Is he spoiled? Though older babies can be spoiled (Section 296), I think you can assume that in the first month your baby is not crying because he's spoiled.

289. Fatigue? When a young baby has been awake an unusually long while or when he has been stimulated more than usual by being with strangers or by being in a strange place or even by being played with by his parents, he may react by becoming tense and irritable. Instead of being easier for him to fall asleep, it may be harder. If the parents or strangers then try to comfort him with more play, more talk, more jouncing, it may make matters worse.

Some young babies seem to be made in such a way that they can **never** drift peacefully into sleep. Their fatigue at the end of every period of being awake produces a tension that is a sort of hump they must get over before falling asleep. They have to cry. Some of them cry frantically and loudly. Then gradually or suddenly the crying stops and they are asleep.

So if your baby is crying at the end of a wakeful period and after he has been fed, try assuming first that he's just tired and put him to bed. Let him cry for 15 to 30 minutes if he has to. Some babies fall asleep faster if left in the crib, and this is the method to strive for in the long run. Another baby who has become overfatigued relaxes sooner if kept in gentle motion—by being pushed back and forth in a bassinet that has wheels or by being rocked in the carriage or by being held in the arms and walked quietly, preferably in a darkened room. I would try walking a baby occasionally during an unusually tense spell (or rocking him in a rocking chair), but I wouldn't go on week after week putting him to sleep this way. He might become more and more dependent on it and demand more of it. You'd surely resent it sooner or later.

290. Fretful babies. Almost all babies have at least a few fretful spells during the early weeks, especially first babies. A few babies are excessively fretful—on certain days or a good part of the time. These fretful periods may alternate with unusually long stretches during which they sleep liké a log and are almost impossible to wake. We don't really know what the cause is, whether it is indigestion because of an immature digestive system or whether it is the irritability and instability of a nervous system that hasn't settled down yet. This tendency doesn't mean anything serious and it passes with time, but it's hard on the parents while it lasts.

There are various things you can try: Try a pacifier between feedings. Try swaddling the baby snugly in a receiving blanket. Some mothers and experienced nurses insist that a fretful or tense baby is much happier if he sleeps in a small space—a small bassinet, a car bed, even a cardboard carton fitted with a folded pad or blanket for a mattress and lined with a blanket. If you have a carriage or can borrow a cradle, you can see whether motion soothes him. A car ride works like magic with many fretful babies, but the trouble may return as soon as you get home, or even at every red light. A hot water bottle may comfort him (Section 293). You can also try music. Read Section 294 on getting some relief yourself. Doctors often prescribe a sedative.

291. A hypertonic baby is one who is unusually tense and restless during the early weeks. His body doesn't relax well. He startles excessively at slight noise or on any quick change of position. If, for instance, he is laid on his back on a firm surface and rolls to one side, or if he is held too loosely in the arms, or if the person carrying him moves him too suddenly, he may almost jump out of his skin. He may hate a tub bath for a couple of months. A hypertonic baby may also have colic or periodic irritable crying.

Hypertonic babies usually do best on a quiet regime: quiet room, few visitors, low voices, slow movements in handling him, a firm hold in carrying him, a big pillow (with a water proof cover) to lie on while being changed and sponge-bathed so that he won't roll, swaddling in a receiving blanket most of the time, lying on his stomach in bed, a small confining bassinet (Sections 290 and 293). Doctors frequently prescribe a sedative.

292. Three-month colic and "periodic irritable crying." In this section I am describing two somewhat similar conditions that may be related to each other. The first is colic (sharp pains in the intestine). The baby's abdomen becomes distended with gas, he pulls up or stiffens his legs, screams piercingly, and may pass gas by rectum. The second condition I call "periodic irritable crying." The baby, even though he has had plenty to eat, cries miserably for several hours at one regular time of day without definite signs of pain or gas. He may be pacified as long as you hold him and carry him about. One baby has colic, another has irritable crying, a third seems to have a mixture. The two conditions may be related to each other, because both commonly start around 2 to 4 weeks of age and are usually over by the time the baby is about 3 months old. Both conditions cause trouble most often between 6 and 10 P.M.

The commonest story is this: The baby was said to be well behaved and quiet in the hospital, but a few days after going home he suddenly has a crying spell that lasts for 3 or 4 hours straight. His mother changes him, turns him over, gives him a drink of water, but nothing works for long. After a couple of hours, she wonders if he is hungry ahead of time, because he seems to be trying to get everything into his mouth. She warms up a bottle and he takes it eagerly at first, but before it's finished he lets go and cries again. The screaming often continues for the full 4-hour interval between feedings. After he has finished his next regular bottle, he may be miraculously relieved.

Lots of babies have just a few attacks scattered through the early months. At the other extreme is the infant who has trouble every night until he's 3 months old (that's why the severer cases have always been called 3-month colic). In a rare case severe colic can last 6 months or even longer.

One baby is very regular about his colic or irritable crying. He sleeps like an angel after every feeding but one, and always screams from 6 P.M. to 10 P.M. or from 2 P.M. to 6 P.M. Another baby spreads his unhappiness through a longer period, and the mother says, "He sleeps like a lamb all night, but cries off and on for half the day." This is not so bad as the baby who sleeps all day and cries half the night. Another starts out being restless in the day-time and then gradually shifts to night, or vice versa. The crying of colic most often begins after a feeding, sometimes right after, sometimes half an hour or so later. In this way it is different from the crying of the hungry baby, which usually occurs before the feeding.

A mother is distressed to have her baby so unhappy and thinks that something is terribly wrong. She wonders how long he can keep this up and not become exhausted She wonders how long she can stand it. The strange thing is that the colicky or crying baby usually prospers from the physical point of view. In spite of hours of crying, he continues to gain weight, not just average-well but better than average. He is a hungry baby. He gulps down his whole feeding and always seems to be demanding an increased amount.

When a baby turns colicky, the mother's first thought is apt to be that his feeding is wrong. If he is on the breast, she thinks her milk is to blame. If he is on a formula, she wonders if it needs some fundamental change—perhaps from evaporated milk to fresh milk or perhaps from granulated sugar to a fancier sugar, like the baby next door. Changing the formula may bring about improvement in some cases, but not in most. It is plain to see that the quality of the feeding is not the main cause of colic. Otherwise why should the baby be able to digest it perfectly 4 out of 5 feedings a day, and get into trouble only in the evening? Colic occurs with breast milk, with cow's milk and with all kinds of formulas. Once in a while, orange juice is suspected of being the cause.

We don't know the basic cause of most colic or irritable crying. One guess is that both conditions are due to a periodic tension in the baby's immature nervous system. Some of these babies are hypertonic all the time (Section 291). The fact that the trouble is commonest in the evening or late afternoon suggests that fatigue plays a part. Many babies up to the age of 3 months are on edge just before falling asleep. Instead of being able to slip peacefully off, they must let out at least a few piercing cries.

293. The treatment of colic. The most important thing is for the mother and father to recognize that the condition is fairly common, that it doesn't seem to do the baby any permanent harm, that, on the contrary, it occurs most often in babies that are developing and growing well, and that it will probably be gone by the time the baby is 3 months old, if not before, leaving him none the worse for wear. If the parent can accept the condition in a fairly calm and resigned way, the battle is half won.

Some colicky babies (the hypertonic ones) seem to be definitely better when they lead quiet, calm lives—sleeping in a quiet room, being handled slowly and gently, being talked to softly, not seeing any visitors (at least closely), not being tickled or rough-housed in any way, avoiding noisy places outdoors, and perhaps, in an extreme case in a city, not going outdoors at all till the colic improves. The colicky baby, like others, must have company and cuddling and be smiled at, but it can be done gently. It is important to get his bubble up after feedings. The mother should keep closely in touch with the doctor. He may prescribe a sedative or other relaxing drugs. A sedative properly prescribed is not harmful or habit forming, even if used for months.

But suppose it is not possible to get in touch immediately with the doctor. What home remedies are useful?

In many cases, a pacifier is by far the most effective remedy, but pacifiers are disapproved of by some parents and some doctors (Sections 347–349).

The colicky baby is usually more comfortable on his stomach. He may get more relief still by being laid across his mother's knees or a hot water bottle, and rubbed on his back.

Hot water bottle. You should be able to rest the inside of your wrist against the hot water bottle without discomfort. Then, as an extra precaution, wrap it in a diaper or towel before laying the baby against it or half on it.

Should you pick a baby up, or rock him gently, or carry him around while he has colic? Even if it makes him stop crying, won't it spoil him? We aren't as scared nowadays of the danger of spoiling a baby as we used to be. If a baby is comforted when he is miserable, he usually doesn't go on demanding that comfort when he isn't miserable. If a baby is screaming with colic or irritability, and picking him up or rocking him seems to help him, then do it. If, however, holding him makes him feel no better, it's just as well not to get him used to being held so much (Section 295).

Babies who are unusually miserable or unusually tense need especially to be under close medical supervision. Most of them improve steadily as they grow older, but the first 2 or 3 months may be rough on them and on their parents.

294. It's hard on the parents of a fretful, hypertonic, colicky or irritable baby. If your baby is colicky or irritable, he may be soothed when you first pick him up. But after a few minutes he's apt to be screaming harder than ever. He thrashes with his arms and kicks with his legs. He not only refuses to be comforted—he acts as if he were angry at you for trying. These reactions are painful for you. You feel sorry for him, at least in the beginning. You feel increasingly inadequate, because you're not able to do anything to relieve him. Then as the minutes go by and he acts angrier and angrier, you feel that he is spurning you as a parent and you can't help feeling mad at him underneath. But getting angry at a tiny baby makes you ashamed of yourself, and you try hard to suppress the feeling. This makes you more tense than ever.

Every parent gets angry at such times, and there's no need to feel guilty. If you can admit the feeling and laugh about it with your husband, you will be able to stand it more comfortably. The other thing to remember is that the baby is not mad at you. He doesn't know yet that you are a person or that he is a person. He's just a bundle of organs and nerves during his first month. Some kind of pain is spreading through his system, and it automatically sets all his limbs to thrashing, just as a tap on his knee automatically makes his leg kick.

If you have the bad luck to have a baby who cries a great deal from colic or irritability or fretfulness, despite your own and your doctor's efforts, you have to think of yourself, too. You may be the kind of mother who isn't bothered too much after you have found out that there is nothing seriously wrong with him and after you have done all that you can to make him happy. That's fine, if you are made that way. But many mothers get worn out and frantic listening to a baby cry, especially when it's the first. You should make a great effort to get away from home and baby for a few hours at least twice a week—oftener if you can arrange it. Hire someone, or ask a friend or neighbor to come in and relieve you. If you're like most people, you hesitate to do this. "Why should I inflict the baby on somebody else? Besides, I'd be nervous being away from him for so long." But you shouldn't think of a vacation like this as just a treat for you. It's very important for you, for the baby and for your husband that you do not get exhausted and depressed. If you can't get anyone to come in, let your husband stay home one or two evenings a week while you go out to visit or see a movie, and encourage him to take one or two nights off a week. The baby doesn't need two worried parents at a time to listen to him. Try also to get friends to come in and visit you. Remember that everything that helps you keep a sense of balance, everything that keeps you from getting too preoccupied with the baby, helps the baby and the rest of the family in the long run.

SPOILING

295. Can you spoil a baby? This question comes up naturally in the first few weeks at home if a baby is fussing a lot between feedings instead of sleeping peacefully. You pick him up and walk him around and he stops crying, at least for the time being. Lay him down, and he starts all over again. I don't think you need to worry much about spoiling in the first month or even the first 2 months. The chances are great that such a young baby is feeling miserable inside If he stops fussing when picked up, it's probably because the motion and distraction, and perhaps the warm pressure on his abdomen from being held, make him forget his pains or tensions at least temporarily. Even if you decide later that he has been somewhat spoiled from an early age, you can usually undo the harm in a few days, in the first 4 or 5 months.

296. You can be a little more suspicious by 3 months. By the time babies are about 3 months old, the commonest causes of physical misery—colic, irritable crying, fretfulness— are over in a great majority of cases. (A very few babies go on having severe colic until 4 or 5 months old.) You notice that the baby who was previously colicky no longer wakes suddenly with cramps and distension. The baby who suffered from irritable crying or fretfulness no longer has distinctly miserable spells that contrast with comfortable periods. Naturally, some of these babies who have been held and walked a great deal for 3 months straight are mildly spoiled. They want their walking and their company anyway. Now it's sensible to become a little less tenderhearted. I don't mean that you should turn severe all of a sudden. But when it's bedtime you can tell your baby cheerfully but firmly that he has to sleep and that you have to go, even if he yells for a few minutes. The more severe form of this problem is discussed in Section 301.

297. A parent who's too eager to amuse. A mild kind of spoiling occurs when a mother (or father or grandmother) is so delighted with her baby that she is regularly playing with him most of the time he's awake—carrying him around or dancing with him or jouncing him on her knees or playing pat-a-cake or making him laugh. (Everyone does these a little.) Gradually he forgets how to amuse himself. He feels bored, deserted and miserable when left alone and cries for attention. What started out as fun for the mother becomes an endless chore.

298. Parents who submit too easily. If a mother is too ready to pick a baby up and carry him around whenever he fusses, she may find after a couple of months that he is fretting and holding out his arms to be carried almost all the time he is awake. If she continues to give in, he realizes after a while that he has his poor tired mother under his thumb and he becomes increasingly disagreeable and tyrannical in demanding this service. The mother can't help resenting such an unreasonable attitude and gets to dislike him heartily. But these emotions are apt to make her feel guilty, and besides, she doesn't know how to get out of the jam.

299. Some causes of spoiling. Why does a parent get involved in these ordinary types of spoiling? In the first place, it usually happens with the first baby and all of us come near it with our first. For most people a first baby is the most fascinating plaything in the world. If a man can be obsessed for a while with a new car and a woman with a fur coat, it's easy to see why a baby is all-absorbing for months. But delight is not the only factor. Parents are apt to project all the hopes and fears they've had about themselves onto their firstborn. There's the anxiety, too, the unfamiliar sense of being entirely responsible for the safety and happiness of a helpless human being. His crying makes a powerful demand on you to do something. With your second baby you have more assurance and a sense of proportion; you know that a child has to be denied some things for his own good, and you don't feel guilty about being hardhearted when you know for sure it's right.

But some parents are more easily drawn into spoiling than others—for instance, parents who have had to wait a long time for a baby and suspect that they may not be able to have another; parents with too little confidence in their own worthiness who become willing slaves to a child and expect him to be all the things they felt they never could be; parents who have adopted a baby and feel that they have to do a superhuman job to justify themselves; parents who have studied child psychology in college or nursing or medicine or worked professionally in the field and feel doubly obligated to prove their capability (actually, it's a tougher job when you know the theory); parents who are ashamed when they've felt cross at the baby and try to even things up by giving him anything he wants; parents who feel too angry or guilty when they hear a baby crying and find the tension unbearable. See also Section 503 on overprotection.

Whatever the underlying factor, all these parents are a little too willing to sacrifice their own comforts and their own rights, too anxious to give the baby anything he asks for. This might not be too bad if a baby knew what was sensible to ask for. But he doesn't know what's good for him. It's his nature to expect firm guidance from his parents. This comforts him. When they are hesitant it makes him uneasy. If they always anxiously pick him up whenever he fusses—as if it would be terrible to leave him there—he, too, gets the feeling that this would be terrible. And the more they submit to his orders, the more demanding he becomes. (A human being of any age finds himself imposing on a person who is too submissive.)

300. How do you unspoil? The earlier you detect the problem, the easier it is to cure. But it takes a lot of will power and a little hardening of the heart. To get yourself in the right mood you have to remember that, in the long run, unreasonable demandingness and excessive dependence are worse for the baby than for you. They get him out of kilter with himself and with the world. So you are reforming him for his own good.

Make out a schedule for yourself, on paper if necessary, that requires you to be busy with housework or anything else for most of the time the baby is awake. Go at it with a great bustle—to impress the baby and to impress yourself. When he frets and raises his arms, explain to him in a friendly but very firm tone that this job and that job must get done this afternoon. Though he doesn't understand the words, he does understand the tone of voice. Stick to your busy work. The first hour of the first day is the hardest. One baby accepts the change better if his mother stays out of sight a good part of the time at first and talks little. This helps him to become absorbed in something else. Another adjusts more quickly if he can at least see his mother and hear her talking to him, even if she won't pick him up. When you bring him a plaything or show him how to use it, or when you decide it's time to play with him a bit at the end of the afternoon, sit down beside him on the floor. Let him climb into your arms if he wants, but don't get back into the habit of walking him around. If you're on the floor with him, he can crawl away when he eventually realizes you won't walk. If you pick him up and walk him, he'll surely object noisily just as soon as you start to put him down again. If he keeps on fretting indefinitely when you sit with him on the floor, remember another job and get busy again.

301. Chronic resistance to sleep in infancy—Going-to-bed type: This is a difficulty that develops insidiously. In most cases it grows out of a case of colic or irritable crying. It can be thought of as a form of spoiling. A baby has been miserable with colic most evenings for his first 2 or 3 months. His mother has found that he is more comfortable when she carries him around. This makes her feel better, too. But by the time he is about 3 or 4 months old, it gradually dawns on her that he doesn't seem to be in so much pain or misery any more—his cry is now angry and demanding. He wants his walking because he's used to it and thinks he's entitled to it. He almost glares at his mother when she sits down for a well-needed rest as if to say, "Woman, get going!"

A baby who becomes engaged in a nightly struggle to keep his mother walking has to really train himself to stay awake, and he succeeds step by step as the months go by—first to 9 P.M., then to 10, 11, even midnight. His mother says that his lids often close and his head droops while she's carrying him, but that as soon as she starts to lay him down he wakes with an indignant yell.

Such a sleep problem is exhausting to baby and parents. The baby is apt to become more irritable in the daytime, too, and may eat less well. The parents can't help getting more and more irritated and resentful. A baby shouldn't be able to put adults through a performance like this every night. They know it but don't know what to do about it. Even a baby senses, I think, that he shouldn't be able to get away with such tyranny.

The habit is usually easy to break once the parents realize that it is as bad for the baby as it is for them. The cure is simple: put the baby to bed at a reasonable hour, say good night affectionately but firmly, walk out of the room, and don't go back. Most babies who have developed this pattern cry furiously for 20 or 30 minutes the first night, and then when they see that nothing happens, they suddenly fall asleep! The second night the crying is apt to last only 10 minutes. The third night there usually isn't any at all.

It's hard on the kindhearted parents while the crying lasts. They imagine the worst: that his head is caught in the slats of the crib, or that he has vomited and is lying in a mess, that he is at least in a panic about being deserted. From the rapidity with which these sleep problems can be cured in the first year, and from the way the babies immediately become much happier as soon as this is accomplished, I'm convinced that they are only crying from anger at this age. It's important not to tiptoe in to be sure the baby is safe or to reassure him that you are nearby. This only enrages him and keeps him crying much longer. See Section 503 on overprotection.

If the several nights of crying will wake other children or anger the neighbors, you can muffle the sound by putting a rug or blanket on the floor and a blanket over the window. Soft surfaces of this kind absorb a surprising amount of the sound.

It's sometimes worthwhile to explain the program to touchy neighbors in order to reassure them that it will take only a few nights and to ask their indulgence.

302. Waking-in-the-night type: In this form the baby goes to bed and right to sleep like an angel but develops a habit of regularly waking in the middle of the night. Sometimes it starts from a bad cold or ear infection that wakes him with real discomfort. This makes his parents quick to run to him again on subsequent nights when they hear a whimper, even though the cold is subsiding. Sometimes the wakefulness seems to start during a painful stage of teething. I imagine that all babies, like older people, half-wake a number of times every night to shift position. When a baby has been picked up and treated to company for a number of nights, I think he learns to rouse himself from half awake to wide awake to have more of the fun.

If the parents don't know how to put a stop to it, a baby may learn to wake not once but several times, to stay awake longer and longer each time, to demand not just company but walking, and to resist being put back to bed by furious crying. I've heard of cases in which it amounted eventually to 3 or 4 hours of walking each night. This is even more exhausting and irritating to baby and parents than a going-to-bed problem. See Section 503 on overprotection.

Most cases can be cured easily. The baby has to learn that there is nothing to be gained by waking and crying. This can usually be accomplished in 2 or 3 nights by letting him cry and not going to him at all. It is apt to be 20 to 30 minutes the first night (it may seem much longer), 10 minutes the second night, none the third.

One additional requirement is necessary, in my experience. The baby must not see the parents when he wakes up. If he sees them, even though they pretend to be asleep, this angers him and stimulates him to keep up the crying indefinitely. It is essential to put his bed in a different room from theirs, at least for a few nights, until the habit is broken, no matter how inconvenient this may be. If this is absolutely impossible, a screen or curtain can be rigged to prevent his seeing them. Read the other suggestions in the previous section.

303. The spoiled baby who vomits. Some babies (and young children) vomit easily when enraged. The mother is apt to be upset and shows it by her anxious looks, by rushing to clean up, by being more sympathetic afterward, by being quicker to come to the baby the next time he screams. This lesson is not lost on the child, and he is likely to vomit more deliberately the next time he's in a temper. And he also comes to be frightened by the vomiting he induces, because his mother is frightened by it. I think it is essential that a mother harden her heart to the vomiting if her baby is using it to bully her. If she is trying to get him over a refusal to go to bed, she should stick to her program and not go in. She can clean him up later after he has gone to sleep.

COMMON KINDS OF INDIGESTION

Consult the doctor promptly about any change in your baby's digestion. Don't try to diagnose it yourself—there is too much chance of error. There are many other causes of vomiting, cramps and loose movements besides those mentioned here. This discussion is primarily to help parents to adjust to a few common types of mild chronic indigestion of early infancy, after the doctor has made the diagnosis.

304. Hiccups. Most babies hiccup pretty regularly after meals in the early months. It doesn't seem to mean anything, and there is nothing that you need to do, aside from seeing if he has a bubble. If a drink of warm water stops him, there's no harm in giving it.

305. Spitting and vomiting are common. The word "spitting" is popularly used when the stomach contents spill gently out of the baby's mouth, usually in small amounts. The muscle valve at the upper end of his stomach just doesn't hold the contents down well, the way it does in an older child or adult. Any movement may cause the spitting: joggling the baby, squeezing him too tight, laying him down, or just the digestive motions of the stomach itself.

Most babies do considerable spitting during the early months, and this usually means nothing. Some spit several times after every feeding. Others do it only occasionally. (Milk stains can be more easily removed from sheets, diapers and clothing if they are first soaked in cold water.)

The word "vomiting" is used when the stomach contents are ejected with enough force to propel them at least a few inches away from the mouth. It alarms a new mother when her baby first vomits a large amount of milk. But this is not serious in itself if the baby seems otherwise healthy. There are a few babies who vomit a large amount as often as once a day, especially the hypertonic babies (Section 291) and especially in the early weeks. Naturally, if your baby spits or vomits regularly even though he is continuing to gain, you should discuss it with the doctor—particularly if there are other signs of indigestion. It is worthwhile taking extra care to bring up the bubble. In most cases the spitting goes right on, no matter how you change the formula or decrease the quantity.

The question occurs to you: If a baby has vomited what seems like his whole feeding, should he be fed again right away? If he seems happy enough, don't feed him, at least until he acts very hungry. His stomach may be a little upset, and it is better to give it a chance to quiet down. Remember that the amount vomited usually looks larger than it actually is. There are babies who you would swear are vomiting most of every feeding but who still go on gaining satisfactorily.

Whether or not the spit-up milk is sour and curdled is not important. The first step in digestion in the stomach is the secretion of acid. Any food that has been in the stomach for a while is acidified. The effect of acid on milk is to curdle it.

All that I have been saying about how common it is for babies to spit and to vomit occasionally doesn't mean that you never have to take vomiting seriously. A baby who begins vomiting all his feedings right after birth must be watched carefully by the doctor. Usually it's due to mucus in the stomach and clears up in a few days, but once in a great while it's more serious, especially if there is green bile in it, and requires prompt medical or surgical treatment.

306. Projectile vomiting in pyloric stenosis. Another uncommon form of vomiting is most apt to begin when the baby is several weeks old. It is called pyloric stenosis. In this condition, the valve leading from the far end of the stomach into the intestines will not open up satisfactorily to let the food through. It is more common in boy babies. The food is vomited out with great force (projectilely), so that it lands at a distance from the baby's mouth. The vomiting may occur during or shortly after the feeding. It doesn't mean that your baby has this condition if he has projectile vomiting once in a while. But if he has projectile vomiting as often as twice a day, he must be under careful medical observation. If other methods of treatment fail and if he continues to vomit most of his feedings and fails to gain, he may have to be cured by operation.

If your baby has not been a vomiter and then suddenly vomits a large amount for the first time, it's a good idea to take his temperature to make sure that he is not sick. Many different infections start with vomiting in a baby. If he has no fever and looks entirely normal, don't worry. If he seems sick in any other way or vomits again, call the doctor.

Vomiting that comes on suddenly later in infancy, especially if there is pain or if there is green bile in the vomitus, may mean obstruction of the intestines, as in intussusception (Section 705) or strangulated hernia (Section 709). It requires immediate attention.

In most babies the tendency to spitting is greatest in the early weeks and months, and decreases as they get older. Most have stopped it altogether by the time they can sit up. An occasional one goes on until he is walking. Once in a while a baby only starts his spitting when he is several months old. Sometimes teething seems to make it worse for a while. Spitting is messy and inconvenient but not important if he's gaining well and is happy.

307. Mild indigestion and gas. In 3-month colic the baby has regular spells of misery that seem to have more to do with the time of day than with what he is having to eat. But another baby may develop a spell of indigestion that's more continuous. Common symptoms are discomfort and fretting, passing gas by rectum, increased spitting and vomiting, bowel movements that are partly loose, partly curdy, and perhaps greenish. These cases are more likely to be improved by changes in the formula than are cases of 3-month colic. If you have a doctor or can reach one, you should, of course, consult him about the baby's indigestion even if the baby is gaining. It is absolutely necessary to consult a doctor if a baby is having trouble and not gaining weight.

If you are completely out of reach of a doctor and indigestion is persisting, you can try omitting all sugar from the formula. The baby may need a larger total amount of the sugarless formula to make up for the sugar calories. If he is on a weak beginning formula, you may need to increase the evaporated milk to the full can (13 ounces of evaporated milk, 19 ounces of water). If the indigestion is not improved, you can acidify the formula (Section 170). If these changes are successful, keep them up for a couple of months or until you can consult a doctor.

CONSTIPATION

308. What's constipation and what isn't? One baby always has his bowel movement at the same time of day, another at a different time each day. One is just as healthy as the other. There is no advantage to be gained by trying to make the irregular baby regular. In the first place, it can't usually be done. In the second place, there's a danger, in the long run, of upsetting the baby emotionally if you keep trying to get a movement out of him when he isn't ready.

It isn't constipation when a breast-fed baby has a movement only every other day, because the movement is still very soft, and there is no reason why a baby needs to have a movement every day. Perhaps you could call it a kind of constipation when he strains unsuccessfully to get this liquid movement out, but it's not the ordinary kind.

309. Hard movements with the bottle-fed baby. One type of constipation is when the movements of a baby on cow's milk become hard and formed. They may be uncomfortable for him to pass. Consult your doctor about this. If you cannot reach a doctor, there are two remedies you can try. The simplest is to change the sugar in the formula to one that is more laxative. If you have been using light corn syrup, change to the dark. If this is not sufficient or if the baby has been on granulated sugar, use brown sugar. (You use the same amount as you were using of granulated sugar or corn syrup.) This kind of constipation is also helped by adding prune juice or pureed prunes to the baby's diet. You can start with 2 teaspoonfuls of the prunes (stewed or canned) or of the juice (homemade, from stewed prunes, or canned prune juice) at the 6 P.M. feeding. If this isn't enough, increase to 4 teaspoonfuls of prunes or juice, or even more. Some babies get cramps from prunes or prune juice, but most take it all right.

310. Chronic constipation is less common in the older baby or child, especially if he is taking a varied diet including whole-grain cereals, vegetables and fruits. If your child becomes constipated, take it up with the doctor—don't try to treat it yourself, because you aren't sure what it is due to. It's very important, whatever treatment you use, that you do not get the child concerned about his bowel function. Don't get into serious conversations about it with him, or connect it with germs or his health or how he feels. Don't encourage him to keep track of his movements, or seem to pay too much attention to them yourself. Avoid enemas. Do what the doctor recommends as matter-of-factly, cheerfully and briefly as possible, whether it's diet, medication or exercise, without going into the whys and wherefores with the child; otherwise you may turn him into a hypochondriac.

But suppose you are unable to consult a doctor, and your child, otherwise healthy, gradually gets into a spell of constipation. (Naturally, if he has any symptoms of illness, you get him to the doctor or hospital somehow.) Give him more fruit or vegetables, if he likes either, 2 or 3 times a day. If he likes prunes or figs, serve them every day. Fruit and vegetable juices help, too. See that he has plenty of exercise. If he is 4 or 5 or older, and in spite of your efforts with diet continues to have rather constipated and irregular movements that don't hurt him, relax until you can get a doctor's help.

Mineral oil is not considered safe for a baby. If he chokes on it, some may get breathed into the lungs and possibly cause a chronic kind of pneumonia.

311. Painfully hard movements in the early years should be treated promptly. If you have a child of 1, 2 or 3 years whose movements are hurting him, it's urgent to relieve him. Otherwise he may become worried because of the pain. It's a psychological emergency (Sections 312 and 389). If you cannot reach a doctor and are compelled to treat the condition yourself, a reasonably safe thing to use is a commercial preparation made of acidophilus bacilli, mineral oil and chocolate flavoring; a teaspoonful of this each evening is usually sufficient to prevent hard movements. This is not a cathartic and does not soften up an already hard movement. You give a teaspoonful every night after supper for at least a month or until you can get advice from your doctor. If the movements are then good, cut down gradually, to ¾ teaspoonful for 3 nights, ½ teaspoonful, and so on. If the constipation starts to return, give the full dose for another month.

312. Psychological constipation. There are two varieties of constipation that are largely psychological in origin and that start most frequently between the ages of 1 and 2. If a child at this age has one or two painfully hard movements, he may tend to hold back for weeks or even months afterward for fear of being hurt again. If he holds the movement in for a day or two, it's apt to be hard again, and this keeps the problem going. It's discussed in Section 389. Occasionally when a mother goes at toilet training in too determined a manner, the small child, being in an independent stage in his development, automatically resists and holds the movement back, which leads to constipation. This is discussed in Section 380.

313. Temporary constipation is common during illness, especially if there is fever. In former days parents and doctors often felt it was the most important symptom to treat and that the child couldn't begin to recover until he was "cleaned out." Some people even believed that the constipation was the main cause of the illness. It's more sensible to realize that any disease that can make a person feel sick all over is apt to affect his entire stomach and intestinal system, slowing down his bowels, taking away his appetite, perhaps causing him to vomit. These symptoms may appear several hours before any others. The doctor may prescribe a cathartic on general principles, but if he is delayed in coming, the parent needn't feel that valuable time is being lost.

If you have to treat a sick child without a doctor, don't worry too much about his bowels. It's better to do too little than too much. If he isn't eating anything, there isn't much for his bowels to move.

314. Spastic constipation. In this kind of constipation, the movement comes out as a collection of small hard balls. It occurs on a cow's-milk formula or on a regular solid-food diet. The sections of the large intestine go into spasms and hold small pieces of the bowel movement until they become dried into little balls. Nobody knows why the intestines of some people have this tendency. It may be due to nervous tension in some cases. It is often hard to cure. Sometimes it is helped by changes in the formula or diet, but frequently not. A child may outgrow spastic constipation at any age. If there is a delay in consulting a doctor, you can try the suggestions in Section 311.

DIARRHEA

315. Diarrhea in babies. A baby's intestines are sensitive the first year or two. They may be upset not only by the germs that cause diarrhea in older individuals but by one or another vegetable, by cold germs and by other germs that don't affect older children and grown-ups at all. This is why we try to protect babies from infections in others, sterilize their milk so carefully, make formula changes gradually, add new foods slowly.

If a baby's movements have been good but suddenly turn loose, you should assume that he has an intestinal infection.

There are usually other changes, too. The stools are likely to be more numerous. The color often changes, most commonly to greenish. The odor is usually different.

Most diarrheas are mild and can be cured easily if they are treated early. A diarrhea should be considered severe if any of the following symptoms are present: watery stools; pus or blood in the stools; vomiting; fever of 101° or more; the baby looks prostrated or has sunken eyes with gray circles under them.

Even for a mild diarrhea you ought to get in touch with the doctor promptly, because the sooner treatment is started, the lighter the disease will be and the quicker over. If the baby has any of the symptoms that point to a severe diarrhea, it is vitally important to get the doctor or to take the baby to a hospital, even if this involves a long trip.

Two rare types of chronic diarrhea are discussed in Section 707.

316. Emergency treatment of mild diarrhea, until you can consult a doctor. It will often be several hours before you can get advice from the doctor, and in the rare case of a baby who is hundreds of miles from nowhere, it may not be possible to reach one at all. So the following emergency suggestions are given. But they should not encourage any mother to treat diarrhea herself if she can possibly consult a doctor.

If the baby is on the breast alone, let him continue to nurse. If he wants less than usual, so much the better. If he is taking solids, too, omit them until you can talk to the doctor or the diarrhea is cured. Most diarrheas do well with breast milk.

If your baby is on formula alone and develops a mild diarrhea, dilute each bottle in half until you can speak to the doctor (Section 179). Even better than half-strength formula is diluted skimmed milk if you can get it. See Section 168. Let the baby take as little of each bottle as satisfies him. But if on this weak formula he gets hungry more often, feed him more frequently. If you have to continue to treat him yourself, try to keep him on half-strength formula or diluted skimmed milk until his movements have been normal or nearly normal for a whole day and until he is hungry for more. If he isn't hungry enough to demand a stronger formula, it's probably a sign that he's still ill and that it's safer not to increase yet. If a mild diarrhea isn't much improved in 2 or 3 days, you should consider it more serious and make a greater effort to reach the doctor.

If a baby on both formula and solid foods develops a mild diarrhea, omit all solids until you consult the doctor or until the diarrhea is over. If the baby is not hungry for his formula or if he is not improved in a day, dilute the formula as directed in Section 179, or give diluted skimmed milk (Section 168). When he is well, get the formula back to normal first before resuming the solids. In putting the solids back, go slowly. Add only one more type of food each day. Give one-third the usual amount the first day, two-thirds the second day, the full amount the third day. Resume his usual foods in something like the following order: (1) gelatin or junket, (2) applesauce and orange juice, (3) meat and egg, (4) white cereal, (5) vegetables, (6) potato or other starch, (7) other fruits. For example, the first day you might give a third of his usual serving of junket; the second day two-thirds of his usual amount of junket and a third of his usual serving of applesauce. Naturally, you don't add any foods at this time that he was not taking before.

317. Emergency treatment of severe diarrhea, until you can reach a doctor. If a baby develops any of the symptoms pointing to a severe diarrhea (watery stools, pus or blood in the stools, vomiting, fever of 101° or more, prostration or sunken eyes), give only a special formula made without milk as follows:

water	1	quart
his usual sugar	1	level tablespoonful

Give 1 to 4 ounces every 2 or 3 hours if he is awake and wants it, until you can talk to the doctor. If you are compelled to go on treating the illness yourself, keep him on this special formula alone for 24 to 72 hours, depending on how soon the bowel movements improve in appearance. Then proceed very gradually. I will list the possible stages in increasing the diet. If he recovers fairly rapidly, advance 1 stage each day. If he's improving slowly, take 2 days for each step.

Stage 1: Give him diluted skimmed milk. This is skimmed milk diluted with an equal amount of water (Section 168). If this is not available, make a formula using half his usual amount of his usual milk, no sugar, and enough water to make the usual total volume. Put only about two-thirds of the usual amount into each bottle; use the rest to make a couple of extra bottles in case he has to be fed every 3 hours. Let him take just as little at each feeding as satisfies him; better too little than too much.

Stage 2: Use diluted skimmed milk with 1 tablespoonful of his usual sugar. If this is not available, use half the usual amount of his usual milk, enough water to make up the usual total, 1 tablespoonful of sugar.

Stage 3: Use full-strength skimmed milk and 2 tablespoonfuls of sugar. If not available, use half the amount of his usual milk, enough water to make up the usual total, 2 tablespoonfuls of sugar.

Stage 4 (if the bowel movements are normal): His usual formula.

Stage 5 and after: Add solids gradually, as in the last section.

If the movements become somewhat looser, drop back 2 stages. If the diarrhea becomes severe again, go all the way back to the special formula without milk and make a greater effort to get to a doctor.

When a diarrhea is improving, the first movement of the day is apt to look better, and a later one not so good. This in itself should not make you discouraged, but it shows that it is safer to see what the afternoon movements are like before strengthening the formula or adding to the diet. A sympathetic parent who is told to cut a baby's formula or diet way down during diarrhea is apt to cry out, "But he'll be hungry." Maybe he will be, maybe not. But it's kinder to make him a little unhappy for a day or two than to let his diarrhea get worse, for in the latter case you would have to starve him for longer in the end.

By the time a child is 2 or more, there is much less chance of severe or prolonged diarrhea. Until the doctor can be reached, the best treatment is bed rest and such fluids and soft solids as water, skimmed milk, gelatin, junket.

RASHES

Consult the doctor about all rashes. It's easy to be mistaken.

318. Bluish mottling. Babies who have pale skins often show a bluish mottling of the skin of the body when undressed.

319. Diaper rash. Most babies have sensitive skins in the early months. The diaper region is particularly apt to suffer. You may bring your baby home from the hospital with a sore behind. This doesn't mean that the hospital has been neglectful, but only that his skin needs extra care. The commonest forms of diaper rash are collections of small red pimples and patches of rough, red skin. Some of the pimples may become mildly infected and develop whiteheads (pustules) on them. If the rash is bad, raw spots may appear.

In the early months the rash is thought most often to be caused simply by the effect of constant wetness on a tender skin. Almost all babies develop a few spots of diaper rash from time to time. If it is slight and goes away as fast as it came, no special treatment is necessary. It is wise to discontinue the use of waterproof pants while there is any rash.

If a baby in the early months tends to have a persistent rash, it is necessary to discontinue the use of waterproof pants, at least while the rash remains. Try the diaper liners that keep the skin drier. After the bath or after washing the diaper area, wipe off all the soap with clear water on a washcloth. (Soap can sometimes be irritating or even favor infection when it hardens on the skin the way it hardens on the tub in a ring.) Use a soap with hexachlorophene for the bath, especially if there are whiteheads present in the rash. When the skin really needs a protective coating, use Lassar's paste or zinc oxide ointment, which are thick and relatively durable compared to powder, lotion, oil and petroleum jelly, which get wiped off easily. If the rash is worse in the folds than on the prominences it is probably a seborrheic rash; this usually responds to a steroid ointment, which your doctor may prescribe.

As a baby grows older, his skin becomes less easily irritated by urine. Diapers that go to the diaper service are sterilized there. When diapers are simply washed at home, there is no sterilization and some of the bacteria in them stay alive. There is a particular type of bacteria named "ammoniagenes" which manufactures ammonia out of urine and which is not readily killed by soap or detergent. It may accumulate in the diapers, the nightclothes and the bedclothes. The ammonia will be noticed especially in the morning when the blanket is turned back. It may even make your eyes water. When there is a bad diaper rash after 6 months of age and particularly after a year, it is usually caused by ammonia. See Section 700 for sore on the end of the penis.

If a diaper rash is severe and persists, especially if there is a smell of ammonia in the nightclothes, the most important step is to use a diaper antiseptic in the last rinse water for the diapers, the nightclothes, the bedclothes and everything that gets wet with urine. Some of the antiseptic remains in the diapers and clothes and this prevents the growth of the bacteria and the formation of ammonia. Ask your doctor for the name of a diaper antiseptic. In addition, you can use for the diapers a detergent that contains a diaper antiseptic.

Another antiseptic, simple and inexpensive, is the ordinary hypochlorite laundry bleach used in the normal manner. Another suggestion is to resume the diaper service, even though you don't need that many diapers; this doesn't take care of sterilizing the nightclothes and bedclothes though, if the rash is caused by ammonia. Drying diapers (and night and bedclothes) in the sun is a good way to kill most bacteria.

When a rash is bad, and especially if there are a lot of pustules (whiteheads), it usually works better not to use an ointment but to expose the whole diaper area to the air for several hours a day, keeping the baby in a warm room. You can cover his chest and his legs with 2 separate light blankets. Fold his diaper underneath him to catch some of the urine. Exposing a bad diaper rash to the air is the surest method of curing it, whether there are pustules or not.

If your baby has a tendency to develop bad diaper rash easily and frequently, you can experiment to see which precautions, used regularly, work best and with least effort: drying the diapers in the sun, or using a special diaper antiseptic in the last rinse, or boiling the diapers, or using ointment. Used regularly, one or the other of these or a combination may do the trick. If it seems necessary, you can change diapers not only before and after feedings but also midway between feedings.

Diapers from a diaper service are usually sterilized, so there is no point in boiling them again. Some diaper services also use a special antiseptic in the last rinse to discourage any growth of bacteria after the diaper has been wet by the baby.

Irritating bowel movements during an attack of diarrhea sometimes cause a very sore rash around the anus. The treatment is to try to change the diaper just as soon as it is soiled, clean the area with oil and apply a thick covering of zinc ointment. If this does not work, the diaper should be left off and the diaper area exposed to the air.

320. Mild face rashes. There are several mild face rashes that babies have in the first few months that aren't definite enough to have names but are very common. First of all, there are minute shiny white pimples without any redness around them. They look like tiny pearls in the skin. They will surely go away as the baby gets older. Then there are collections of a few small red spots or smooth pimples on the cheeks. These may last a long time and get a mother quite upset. At times they fade and then get red again. Different ointments don't seem to do much good, but these spots always go away eventually. Less common is a rough, red patch on the cheeks that comes and goes.

Babies in the early weeks often have white blisters in the middle part of their lips from sucking. Sometimes the blisters peel. These clear up in time and need no treatment.

321. Prickly heat. Prickly heat is very common in the shoulder and neck region of babies when hot weather first begins. It is made up of clusters of minute pink pimples surrounded by blotches of pink skin. Tiny blisters form on some of the pimples, and when they dry up they give the rash a slightly tan look. Prickly heat usually starts around the neck. If it is bad, it can spread down onto the chest and back and up around the ears and face. It seldom bothers a baby. You can pat the rash several times a day with a bicarbonate of soda solution (1 teaspoonful of bicarbonate of soda to 1 cup of clean water) on absorbent cotton. Another treatment is dusting with cornstarch powder. It is more important to try to keep the baby cool. Don't be afraid to take off his clothes in very hot weather.

322. Cradle cap. Cradle cap is a mild disorder of the skin of the scalp. It is quite common in the early months. It appears as scalp patches that look dirty. The best treatment is to keep water and soap off the scalp altogether. Instead, clean the scalp with mineral oil or baby oil on a piece of absorbent cotton. Oiling the spots twice a day softens the crusts, which can then usually be combed off with a very fine-toothed comb. If this method is not successful, consult your doctor. Cradle cap rarely persists beyond the early months.

Eczema is discussed in Section 666.

Impetigo and other common rashes are discussed in Section 672.

MOUTH AND EYE TROUBLES

323. Thrush. Thrush is a mild fungus infection of the mouth. It looks as if patches of milk scum were stuck to the cheeks and tongue and roof of the mouth. But, unlike scum, it does not wipe off easily. If you do rub it off, the underlying skin bleeds slightly and looks inflamed. Thrush usually makes a baby's mouth sore. He shows the discomfort when he is trying to nurse. A baby's mouth is more apt to become infected with thrush if the nipples are handled carelessly. But it also occurs in babies who are taken care of to perfection. If you suspect it, consult the doctor promptly for diagnosis and treatment. If there is a delay in getting medical advice, it is helpful to have the baby drink half an ounce of boiled water, or suck it from a piece of sterile absorbent cotton, after his milk. This washes the milk out of his mouth and gives the thrush fungus less to live on.

Don't be fooled by the color of the inner sides of the gums where the upper molar teeth are going to be. The skin color here is normally very pale, and is sometimes mistaken for thrush by mothers who are on the lookout for it.

Cysts on the gums. Some babies have one or two little pearly-white cysts on the sharp edge of their gums. They may make you think of teeth, but they are too round and they don't make a click on a spoon. They have no importance and eventually disappear.

324. Discharge and tearing of the eye. Many babies develop a mild inflammation in the eyes a few days after birth. This is caused by the medication that is always used right after birth, to avoid infection.

If at any later time the baby has an inflammation that makes the whites of his eyes look bloodshot or even pink, it is probably an infection, and the doctor should be called promptly.

There is another kind of very mild but chronic infection of the eyelids that develops off and on in the early months in quite a number of babies, most commonly in only one eye. The eye waters and tears excessively, particularly in windy weather. White matter collects in the corner of the eye and along the edges of the lids. This discharge may keep the lids stuck together when the baby first wakes up. The condition is caused by an obstructed tear duct. The tear duct leads from a small opening at the inner corner of the eyelids, first toward the nose, then down the side of the eye socket and into the nose cavity. When this duct is partly plugged, the tears are not drained off as fast as they form. They well up in the eye and run down the cheek. The lids keep getting mildly infected, just because the eye is not being cleansed sufficiently by the tears. The doctor should, of course, see the eyes and make the diagnosis.

The first thing to realize about this condition is that it is fairly common, not serious, and does not injure the eye. It may last for many months. The tendency is outgrown in most cases even if nothing is done. If by a year it is still bothersome, an eye doctor can clear the duct with a simple procedure. When the lids are stuck together, you can soften the crust by laying over the lids a piece of sterile cotton wet with a sterile solution of boric acid, which you can get in the drugstore. The doctor sometimes advises massage of the duct, but don't do this without his directions. A plugged tear duct does not cause inflammation of the white of the eye. If the eye is bloodshot, something else is wrong and you should call the doctor.

325. Crossed eyes. It is common for a baby's eyes to turn in or out too much at moments in the early months. In most cases they become steady and straight as he grows older. If, however, the eyes turn in or out all the time or much of the time, even in the first month, or if they are not steady by 3 months, an eye doctor should be consulted (Section 711). Many times a mother thinks her baby's eyes are crossed when they are really straight. This is because the skin area between the eyes (over the root of the nose) is relatively wider in a baby than in an older person; so the amonut of white of the eye showing on the inner side of the iris (toward the nose) is much smaller than the white on the outer side (toward the ear). Another reason a baby's eyes sometimes appear crossed is that when he is looking at something in his hand he has to converge (cross) his eyes a lot to focus on it, because his arm is so short. He is only converging his eyes normally, the way we adults do to a lesser extent. His eyes won't get stuck that way.

The main reason why it is important for an infant's eyes to be examined promptly, when there is a question about whether they are straight, is because a crossed eye or a wall-eye will gradually become blind if efforts are not begun early to make the child use it. When the two eyes do not coordinate and converge on an object, each eye will be seeing a somewhat different scene. The person will be "seeing double." This is confusing and uncomfortable for him. So automatically he learns to ignore and suppress the vision of one eye. He gradually makes that eye blind—not in the sense of a physical change—it's a psychological process. If this goes on too long, it will become impossible to ever bring back the vision in that eye. This has been called "lazy eye." The eye doctor's job is to promptly put the lazy eye back to work, usually by having the child wear a patch over the good eye a large part of the time. The doctor may prescribe glasses to further encourage the coordinated use of the two eyes. Then comes the decision whether there should be an operation, in addition. Occasionally several operations have to be performed before the result is satisfactory.

Mothers often ask whether it is safe to hang toys over a baby's crib, since he sometimes is cross-eyed looking at them. Don't hang a toy right on top of a baby's nose, but it's perfectly all right to hang it at arm's reach.

It's not uncommon in a newborn baby for the lid of one eye to droop a little lower than the other or for one eye to look smaller. In most cases, these differences become less and less noticeable as the baby grows older. The baby's eyes should be examined, to be sure that they are straight.

SWOLLEN BREASTS

326. When the baby has swollen breasts. Many babies, both boys and girls, have swollen breasts for some time after birth. In some cases a little milk runs out. This is caused by the glandular changes in the mother just before the baby is born. Nothing needs to be done for swollen breasts in the baby; the swelling will surely disappear in time. The breasts should **not** be massaged or squeezed, since this is likely to irritate and infect them.

BREATHING TROUBLE

327. Sneezing. Babies sneeze easily. Sneezing doesn't usually mean a cold unless the nose begins to run, too. It is most often caused by dust and dried mucus that has collected in a ball in the front of the nose and tickles. If the breathing is obstructed, see Section 241.

328. Faint breathing. New parents usually worry a little about a new baby's breathing because it is often irregular and at times so shallow that they can't hear it or see it. They may worry, too, the first time they hear their baby snoring faintly in his sleep. Both conditions are normal.

329. Chronic noisy breathing occurs in a certain number of young babies. In one form the baby makes a snoring noise in the back of his nose. It's just like a grown-up's snoring, except that the baby does it while he is awake. It seems to be caused by the fact that he hasn't yet learned to control his soft palate. He'll outgrow it.

The commoner type of chronic noisy breathing is caused in the larynx (voice box). The epiglottis, a fleshy structure just above the vocal cords, is so soft and floppy in some babies that it is sucked down and made to vibrate. This causes a loud rattling, snoring noise during breathing in, which doctors call stridor. It sounds as if the baby were choking, but he can breathe that way indefinitely. In most cases the stridor occurs only when the baby is breathing hard. It usually goes away when he is quiet or asleep. It may be better when he lies on his abdomen. It should be discussed with the doctor, but no treatment is necessary or does any good. Stridor goes away as the baby grows older.

Noisy breathing that comes on acutely, particularly in an older infant or child, has an entirely different significance from the chronic variety. It may be due to croup, asthma or other infection, and requires prompt medical attention.

Every baby with noisy breathing, chronic or acute, should be examined by a doctor.

Obstruction in the nose from dry mucus is discussed in Section 241; obstruction from moist mucus during a cold, in Section 642.

330. Breath-holding spells. Some babies get so furiously angry when they cry, and hold their breath so long, that they turn blue. When this first happens, it scares the wits out of the parents. It seldom means anything except that the baby has that kind of temperament. (It's often a baby who's unusually happy at other times.) The doctor should be told about it so that at the next visit he can make sure that everything is all right physically; otherwise nothing needs to be done. It's not a reason for keeping the baby from ever crying. If you pick him up every time he cries, he's likely to get spoiled.

331. The thymus gland. You hear people talking about the thymus gland with great awe. You'd think it was a very dangerous gland indeed. It is sometimes blamed on those very rare occasions when a baby dies for no apparent reason. Most of this bad reputation is not deserved at all. Every baby has a thymus gland in the upper part of his chest. A normal thymus may be large enough so that it presses slightly on the windpipe, but this almost never causes any symptoms or trouble. It is no longer considered necessary or wise to give X-ray treatment for the thymus gland.

The old idea that enlarged thymus could cause sudden death came about because of a misunderstanding about what size the gland is meant to be. Now that we know more about it, we realize that those glands that were found in cases of sudden death, and that were thought to be enlarged, were really normal-size glands. Those rare cases of sudden death are usually found, on very careful examination, to have been caused by sudden severe infection.

So don't worry about the thymus. There's no good reason why a healthy newborn baby needs an X-ray picture to show how big his thymus is.

COMMON NERVOUS SYMPTOMS

332. Babies who startle easily. Newborn babies are startled by loud noises and by sudden change in position. Some are much more sensitive than others. When you put a baby on a flat, hard surface and he jerks his arms and legs, it's likely to rock his body a little. This unexpected motion is enough to make a sensitive baby nearly jump out of his skin and cry with fright. He may hate his bath because he is held so loosely. He needs to be washed in his mother's lap and then rinsed in the tub, while held securely in both her hands. He should be held firmly and moved slowly at all times. He will gradually get over this uneasiness as he grows older. See Section 291 on the hypertonic baby.

333. The trembles. Some babies have trembly moments in the early months. The chin may quiver, or the arms and legs may tremble, especially when the baby is excited or when he is cool just after being undressed. This trembling is nothing to be disturbed about. It is just one of the signs that the baby's nervous system is still young. The tendency passes away in time.

334. Twitching. Some babies twitch occasionally in their sleep, and once in a while there is one who twitches frequently. This, too, usually disappears as the baby grows older. Mention it to the doctor so that he can check.

Comforters and Thumb Sucking

This chapter is about the wide variety of things and methods that small children use to comfort themselves with, when they are tired or unhappy: a stuffed animal or a piece of fabric to stroke, a pacifier, thumb or bottle to suck, a habit like rocking or head rolling.

From the age of 6 months onward, when they first begin to feel somewhat separate from the mother, they use these sucking, stroking or rocking habits at tired or unhappy moments to bring back the complete security which the mother formerly provided.

SIX-MONTH INDEPENDENCE AND THE NEED FOR COMFORTERS

335. The first sense of separateness. We believe that at about 6 months of age a baby begins to realize dimly that he is a separate person. Perhaps it would be more accurate to say that his unfolding instincts make him begin to insist on a slight physical separateness from his mother and on his right to do some things for himself; and that he then becomes aware of the importance of this separateness to himself. I am thinking of the way many 6-month-olds show impatience with being cuddled in their mother's arms any longer, during bottle or solid-food feedings; they try to sit up straight instead. They want to hold onto their own bottle. They may even try to get their mother's hand off it by jerking it sideways. From now on—until they are fully mature adults—children will continue to insist on a gradually increasing independence, emotional as well as physical.

336. Comforters to recapture the security of early infancy. But when the young child over 6 months old is very tired or frustrated, he craves to slip back to early infancy, when being fed in his mother's arms was all there was to paradise. (Psychologists call this tendency to retreat under stress "regression"; even the competent adult may become childishly helpless or demanding when ill.) On the other hand, he is unwilling to give up the precious bit of independence from his mother which he has achieved since he was tiny. This is where various comforters come in. By means of them, the infant attains pleasure and security without giving up independence. Thumb sucking or pacifier sucking or drinking his bottle in bed reminds him of the pleasure of being fed from breast or bottle in his mother's arms. Stroking a cuddly toy animal or a cherished blanket or diaper recalls the good sensation when he gently stroked his mother's clothing or the blanket he was wrapped in during his feeding. (Puppies and kittens have an instinct to stroke their mother's breasts when nursing, which helps to make the milk flow. The human infant's impulse to stroke while nursing is perhaps a remnant of the same instinct in our prehuman ancestors.) When he rocks himself against a stuffed chair back or rolls his head from side to side in bed, he is creating again the rhythmic soothing he experienced as a fretful young infant when his mother rocked him or walked him.

The child recreates certain comforting aspects of his mother out of the cuddly toy and his thumb for example; but it's not a mother who can envelop him or control him; it's a mother he can control. (It's interesting to see how a young child will sometimes abuse the object which is so precious to him; he will slap it crossly or slam it heartlessly against the furniture.)

Why do I make such an issue over comforters? Partly because it gives us an understanding of the great psychological importance to the child of establishing independence, which he begins to do by 6 months, and of the meaning of regression. But also, in a very practical way, it explains a number of perplexing things about early childhood. For instance, I think that thumb sucking in the first half year of infancy is simply an expression of the baby's need to suck, especially when he's hungry. But after 6 months thumb sucking becomes something else: a reminder of early infantile comfort, which the child now needs only when he's sleepy or upset. That is to say, the thumb becomes a comforter, such a precious comforter that most children won't give it up again until 3, 4 or 5 years of age.

Similarly the pacifier changes its meaning after the age of 6 months, from a satisfier of the sucking need to a comforter at regressed times of day. But the pacifier is not usually as precious as the thumb; most children will give it up at 1 or 2 years of age if the mother does not continue to encourage its use. (A child may suck thumb or pacifier, not both.)

The meaning of the bottle changes, too. I think that the reason that many a baby becomes more and more attached to the bottle after 6 months is that his mother has fallen into the habit of handing him his bottle to drink by himself in bed. In this way the bottle becomes a precious comforter; if a child becomes intensely attached to it in this way, he is apt to remain very attached to it until 1½ or 2 years of age. Whereas the bottle which a mother gives to the child while he is sitting in her lap cannot become a precious comforter in place of the mother—because the mother is right there.

Some children do not adopt any stroking comforter such as a cuddly toy or piece of cloth, nor a sucking comforter such as a precious bottle, pacifier or thumb. I don't know why. I haven't been able to see any psychological differences between those who do and those who don't. I don't know of any important reason to encourage a child to adopt a precious comforter or to discourage him, except for certain practical considerations in regard to the bottle in bed (Section 231) and the pacifier (Section 347).

337. The strokable comforter. In my experience the child who is a thumb sucker is more likely than the nonthumb sucker to become attached to a strokable comforter also. It's as if he regresses (slips back) to early infancy through the thumb-sucking pleasure and then wants to add the pleasure of stroking something, too.

Some children develop an intense attachment to an object, which lasts for several years; others develop only a mild attachment which weakens after a while; others still shift from one object to another.

When the attachment to a cuddly toy or piece of cloth is intense, it is apt to raise practical problems for the mother. The child may want to carry the object with him everywhere. It is going to become increasingly dirty and eventually tattered. Usually the child objects vigorously to a washing or cleaning of the object and he will reject a substitution altogether. If the object gets lost the child will be in real despair and will probably be unable to go to sleep for hours.

I think it is unfair (and it's usually impossible) to try to break a child's attachment to a comforter after it has been well formed. However, I've known a couple of mothers who were ingenious and firm enough to keep the problem within bounds because they felt very strongly about this: they insisted from the beginning that the object must stay in the child's room, or at least in the house.

It is better to sneak a blanket or diaper away from the child at night, at regular intervals, for washing and drying before it ever gets gray, so that it won't change so drastically in color and smell. (The smell of a comforter may be an important part of it to some children.) Better still would be to acquire a duplicate and identical toy or piece of cloth, and to keep substituting the clean one from time to time, without the child knowing. The trouble is that you usually don't realize when the toy is bought for the baby at 3 or 6 months that it's going to become priceless to him at 15 months. It is impossible to wash and dry most animals overnight. You can do a fair job of washing the surface with soap and water on a washcloth or brush. Dry with an electric fan.

Is there any harm in letting a child become dependent on a cuddly comforter and take it to bed? None that I know of except the parents' distress at its dinginess. There is no way to prevent its happening anyway. Any child will receive soft toys during his first year and it's usually not until he's 15 or 18 months old and begins to insist on carrying one object with him that his parents realize what has happened.

A child will probably outgrow his dependence at some time between 2 and 5 years of age. (A few will cling longer.) It's wise for the parent to remind him in an encouraging tone—a couple of times a year, not every week—that someday he'll be a big boy and won't need it any more. This kind of hint and confidence helps him to outgrow it as soon as he is able.

THUMB SUCKING

338. The meaning of thumb sucking. The main reason that a young baby sucks his thumb seems to be that he hasn't had enough sucking at the breast or bottle to satisfy his sucking need. Dr. David Levy pointed out that babies who are fed every 3 hours don't suck their thumbs as much as babies fed every 4 hours, and that babies who have cut down on nursing time from 20 minutes to 10 minutes (because the nipples have become old and soft) are more likely to suck their thumbs than babies who still have to work for 20 minutes. Dr. Levy fed a litter of puppies with a medicine dropper so that they had no chance to suck during their feedings. They acted just the same as babies who don't get enough chance to suck at feeding time. They sucked their own and each other's paws and skin so hard that the fur came off.

All babies aren't born with the same amount of instinct to suck. One baby never nurses more than 15 minutes at a time and yet never once has put his thumb in his mouth, and another whose bottles have always taken 20 minutes or more thumb-sucks excessively. A few begin to thumb-suck in the delivery room, and they keep at it. I suspect that a strong sucking instinct runs in some families.

You don't need to be concerned when a baby sucks his thumb for only a few minutes just before his feeding time. He is probably doing this only because he's hungry. It's when a baby tries to get his thumb just as soon as his feeding is over, or when he sucks a lot between feedings, that you have to think of ways to satisfy his sucking craving. Most babies who thumb-suck start before they are 3 months old.

I might add here that the thumb-, finger-, and hand-chewing that almost every baby does from the time he begins to teethe (commonly around 3 or 4 months) should not be confused with thumb sucking. Naturally, the baby who is a thumb sucker is sucking at one minute, chewing at another, during his teething periods.

If your baby begins to try to suck his thumb or finger or hand, I think it's preferable not to stop him directly but to try to give him more opportunity to suck at the breast or the bottle or the pacifier. The most effective method by far to prevent thumb sucking is the ample use of the pacifier in the first 3 months (Section 347), if the parents are willing. In addition there are two other matters to consider: the number of feedings, and how long each feeding takes.

339. The time to pay attention to thumb sucking. The time to pay attention to thumb sucking is when the baby first tries to do it, not when he finally succeeds. I make this point because there are lots of babies who, for the first few months of their lives, haven't much control over their arms. You see such a baby struggling to get his hands up, and searching around with his mouth. If by good luck he gets his fist to his mouth, he sucks it vigorously as long as it happens to stay there. This baby, just as much as the skillful thumb sucker, is showing a need to suck longer at the breast or bottle.

The very young baby needs help most, because the sucking need is strongest in the first 3 months. From then on it tapers off. In most babies I think it's about gone by 6 or 7 months. The thumb sucking which persists after 6 months is a comforting device, not an expression of sucking need. See Section 336.

340. Thumb sucking in breast-fed babies. I have the impression that a breast-fed baby is less apt to be a thumb sucker. This is probably because the mother is inclined to let him go on nursing as long as he wants to. She doesn't know whether her breast is empty, so she leaves it up to the baby. When a baby finishes a bottle, it's done. He stops because he doesn't like to suck air or because his mother takes away the bottle. The first question, then, about a breast-fed baby who is trying to suck his thumb is: Would he nurse longer if allowed to? If so, let him nurse for 30 or even 40 minutes at times if this is convenient for you. (To go beyond 40 minutes is too time consuming.) A baby gets most of the milk from a breast in 5 or 6 minutes; the rest of the time he's satisfying his craving to suck, lured on by a small trickle of milk. In other words, if he nurses for 35 minutes, he gets only slightly more milk than if he had nursed for 20. A breast-fed baby, allowed to nurse as long as he wants, may vary surprisingly. He is satisfied with 10 minutes at one feeding and wants as much as 40 minutes at another. This is an example of how breast feeding is adaptable to a baby's individual needs.

If a baby being nursed on one breast each feeding doesn't want to nurse any longer, there's nothing that you can do to make him. But if he is getting **both** breasts at each feeding and begins to suck his thumb, there are two methods you can try to make him nurse longer. See if he can be satisfied with one breast at each feeding, nursing as long as he will. If his hunger can't be satisfied that way, then at least let him nurse longer at the first breast. Instead of taking him off in 10 minutes, let him stay on for 20, if he will. Then put him to the second breast for as long as he wants.

341. Thumb sucking in the bottle baby. With the average bottle-fed baby, thumb sucking is most likely to begin at about the time he learns to finish his bottle in 10 minutes instead of in 20. This happens because the baby gets stronger as he gets older, but the rubber nipples get weaker. Bottles with plastic screw-on caps have nipples with a special opening near the edge for air intake. You can slow down this kind of bottle by screwing the cap on tighter. This partly blocks the air intake, keeps more of a vacuum in the bottle. The next thing to do is to get new nipples, leave the holes as they are, and see if that lengthens the bottle time. Of course, if the nipple holes are too small, some babies stop trying altogether. Try to keep the nipple holes small enough so that a bottle takes 20 minutes anyway, at least during the first 6 months. In this discussion, I am talking about the actual number of minutes that the baby is sucking. Naturally, it wouldn't help to lengthen the feeding time by pausing in the middle of the feeding.

342. With a thumb sucker, it's better to go slow in omitting feedings. It's not just the length of each feeding, but also the number or frequency of feedings in the 24 hours that determines whether a baby satisfies his sucking instinct. So if a baby is still thumb sucking even though you have made each breast or bottle feeding last as long as possible, it is sensible to go slow in dropping other feedings. For example, if a 3-month-old baby seems willing to sleep through the 10 P.M. feeding but is doing a good deal of thumb sucking, I would suggest waiting a while longer before dropping it—perhaps a couple of months, provided he is still willing to drink it when he's waked.

343. The effect on the teeth. You may be worried about the effect of thumb sucking on the baby's jaws and teeth. It is true that thumb sucking often pushes the upper front baby teeth forward and the lower teeth back. How much the teeth are displaced depends on how much the child sucks his thumb and, even more, on what position he holds his thumb in. But dentists point out that this tilting of the baby teeth has no effect on the permanent teeth that begin coming in at about 6 years of age. In other words, if the thumb sucking is given up by 6 years of age—as it is in a great majority of cases—there is very little chance of its hurting the permanent teeth.

But whether thumb sucking displaces the teeth or not, you naturally prefer to have your child give it up as soon as possible. The suggestions I have been making are the ones that I think will end thumb sucking soonest.

344. Why not use restraints? Why not tie a baby's arms down or put aluminum mittens over his hands to keep him from thumb sucking? This would frustrate him a great deal, which theoretically is not a good idea. Furthermore, it usually doesn't cure the baby who is thumb sucking a lot. We have all heard of despairing mothers who use elbow splints or metal mitts or bad-tasting paint not just for days but for months. And the day they take off the restraint, the thumb pops back in the mouth. To be sure, there are some mothers who say they have had good results from using such restraints. But in most of these cases, the thumb sucking was very mild. Many babies do a little thumb sucking off and on. They get over it quickly, whether you do anything or not. I think, myself, that restraints only make the confirmed thumb sucker do it more in the long run.

345. Thumb sucking in the older baby and child. Up to now we have been talking about how thumb sucking begins in the early months. But by the time a baby is 6 months old, his thumb sucking is turning into something different. It is a comforter that he needs at special times. He sucks when he is tired or bored or frustrated, or to put himself to sleep. When he can't make a go of things at the more grown-up level, he retreats to early infancy when sucking was his chief joy. This need for comforters is discussed in Section 336.

Even though thumb sucking satisfies a different need after the age of 6 months, it's of course the baby who first sucked his thumb to satisfy his sucking need who goes on doing it now for comfort. It's very rare for a child beyond the age of 6 months or 1 year to begin to thumb-suck for the first time.

There is no point worrying about lengthening the sucking time of the 6-month or 12-month-old. Is there anything that the parents need to do? I don't think so, if the child is generally outgoing, happy and busy, and sucks mainly at bedtime and occasionally during the day. In other words, thumb sucking by itself is not a sign of unhappiness or maladjustment or lack of love. In fact, most thumb suckers are very happy children. (And the children who are severely deprived of affection don't thumb-suck.) On the other hand, if a child is sucking a great deal of the time instead of playing, his parents should only ask themselves whether there is anything they ought to do so that he won't need to comfort himself so much. A child may be bored from not seeing enough of other children or from not having enough things to play with. Or perhaps he's having to sit in his carriage for hours. A child of 1½ may be at loggerheads with his mother all day if she is always stopping him from doing all the things that fascinate him instead of diverting him to playthings that are permissible. Another child has children with whom he can play and freedom to do things at home, but he's too timid to throw himself into these activities. He thumb-sucks while he watches. I give the examples only to make it clear that if anything needs to be done for excessive thumb sucking, it is to make the child's life more satisfying.

Elbow splints, mitts and bad-tasting stuff on the thumb only make the child miserable and don't stop the habit any more often in older children than they do in small babies. I think that they tend to prolong the habit. The same applies to scolding a child or pulling his thumb out of his mouth. I remember the story of Anne, who finally stopped sucking her thumb of her own accord at 3. Six months later her Uncle George, who had been the member of the family who used to nag her about it, came back to the house to live. Anne's thumb sucking began again the minute he entered the house. You often hear the recommendation that you give the child a toy when you see him thumb sucking. It certainly is sound to have enough interesting things around for him to play with so that he won't be bored. But if every time his thumb goes in his mouth you jump toward him and poke an old toy into his hands, he'll soon catch on. What about bribing? If your child is one of the rare ones who is still sucking his thumb at the age of 5, and you are beginning to worry about what it will do to his permanent teeth when they come in, you will have a fair chance of succeeding if the bribe is a good one. A girl of 4 or 5 who wants to get over her thumb sucking may be helped by having her fingernails painted like a lady's. But practically no child of 2 or 3 has the will power to deny an instinct for the sake of reward. You're apt to make a fuss and get nowhere.

So if your child is thumb sucking, see to it that his life is good. In the long run it will help him if you remind him that someday he will be grown-up enough to stop. This friendly encouragement makes him want to stop as soon as he is able. But don't nag him. Most important of all, try to stop thinking about it. If you keep on worrying, even though you resolve to say nothing, the child will feel it and react against it. Remember that thumb sucking goes away all by itself in time. In the overwhelming majority of cases, it is over before the second teeth appear. It doesn't go away steadily, though. It decreases rapidly for a while, and then comes back part-way during an illness or when the child has a difficult adjustment to make. Eventually it goes for good. It rarely stops before 3 years. It usually peters out between 3 and 6.

Most of the babies who go on thumb sucking until they are 1 or more years old do some kind of stroking at the same time. One rubs or plucks a piece of blanket, or diaper, or silk, or a woolly toy. Another strokes his earlobe or twists a lock of hair. Still another wants to hold a piece of cloth right up close to his face and perhaps stroke his nose or lip with a free finger. These motions remind you of how the younger baby used to be gently feeling his mother's skin or clothing when he was suckling at the breast or bottle. And when he presses something against his face, it looks as though he were remembering how he felt at the breast. These habits are discussed in Section 336.

346. Ruminating. Sometimes a baby or young child gets in the habit of sucking and chewing on his tongue until his last meal comes up (somewhat the way a cow's does), a practice known as ruminating. It's a rare condition. Some cases begin when a thumb-sucking baby has his arms restrained. He turns to sucking his tongue instead. I would certainly advise letting such a baby have this thumb back immediately, before the ruminating becomes a habit. Be sure, also, that he has enough companionship, play and affection. It is said that the meals stay down better when they consist entirely of solids. That means cooking the milk into his cereals, puddings.

PACIFIER

347. A pacifier is helpful for fretfulness or to prevent thumb sucking. A pacifier is a "blind" nipple (without a hole in it) attached to a disk that rests against the baby's lips to keep the nipple from being pulled entirely into his mouth. On the back of the disk is a ring by which the pacifier can be held by the baby, or hung on a ribbon around his neck.

One satisfactory style is made of one piece of soft rubber, which means that it won't bother the baby's face if he goes to sleep on it and, more important, he won't be able to pull the nipple off the disk and choke on it. The only trouble with this shape of pacifier is that the long nipple may reach the back of the throat and gag a young baby. There is also a pacifier that has a short nipple with a ball-shaped end.

A baby who has periods of mild irritability can often be entirely quieted by having a pacifier to suck. We don't know whether this is because the sucking soothes some vague discomfort or simply keeps the baby's mouth busy. For colic, in which the pain is much more definite, the pacifier usually gives at least partial relief.

Irritable crying and colic are about over in most cases by 3 months or so, and the use of the pacifier can then be stopped so that it won't become a long-lasting habit.

348. The pacifier, if used right, is an efficient way to prevent thumb sucking. Most of the babies who use the pacifier freely for the first few months of life never become thumb suckers, even if they give up the pacifier at 3 or 4 months.

Some would say then: What's the use of a pacifier to avoid thumb sucking when pacifier sucking is just as unattractive? The answer is that if a baby becomes a regular thumb sucker in his first 3 months (and about half of all babies do), he will continue to be a thumb sucker until 3, 4 or 5 years of age, sometimes longer. By contrast, a majority of the babies who become pacifier suckers are ready to give it up by 3 or 4 months. Whereas they used to suck it eagerly for long periods, they now spit it out soon after it's put in their mouth, or even immediately. Most of the rest give it up by 1 or 2 years of age. This is a lot younger than the thumb is given up.

Another advantage is that pacifier sucking is less likely to push the teeth out of position than thumb sucking.

349. A mother's reluctance to start and reluctance to stop the pacifier. There are two problems that interfere with the most efficient use of the pacifier. In many cases where its use would be helpful, the mother is reluctant to use it at all or, more often, comes around to trying it so late that the baby won't take to it, as he would have in the first weeks. The mother's reluctance is natural enough. A majority of people dislike the appearance of a pacifier bobbing around in a baby's face, especially when he's old enough to be walking around; and he's apt to have a faraway, "dopey" expression on his face when sucking it. But though many mothers reject the pacifier when the doctor suggests it, they often change their mind a few weeks later, after learning from a friend or relative how well it can work.

The second problem is that the mother who has used the pacifier successfully for fretfulness or colic is apt to develop such a dependence on it—for comforting the baby any time he gives a whimper—that she can't get over the habit of popping it into his mouth many times a day, even after he is old enough to be ready to give it up (usually between 2 and 4 months). Then the baby is apt to develop, at 5, 6, 7 months, a dependence that lasts until a year or a year and a half.

Pacifier sucking (like thumb sucking) up to 3, 4, 5 months of age is a way in which a baby who needs extra sucking can get it. But by 3 or 4 months the sucking need is decreasing; many babies begin to spit the pacifier out; their regular nursing apparently gives them all the sucking they want. By 5 or 6 months the sucking need is about gone (as is shown most clearly in the way breast-fed babies now express boredom with nursing). So if a mother continues to offer the pacifier after about 4 months, either because the baby is one of the minority who hasn't had enough of it yet, or because it has become a habit that the mother can't stop, the pacifier sucking becomes a comforting habit which the baby may then not be willing to give up until he is 1, 1½, 2 years of age.

If a baby isn't willing to give up the pacifier—at any age —I don't think it's right to take it away. But I think there are very good reasons to stop offering it at 3 or 4 months to a baby who is showing, by spitting it out soon after it is put in his mouth, that he really doesn't need it or want it any more. The relatives who don't approve of pacifiers will quiet down. There won't be any displacement of the teeth.

How would you use the pacifier to prevent thumb sucking? In the first place, many babies—perhaps 50%—never try to thumb-suck at all or do it only casually and for brief periods. In these, there is nothing to prevent and no need to get involved with the pacifier (unless there is colic). On the other hand, you have to decide not on the basis of what a baby is actually accomplishing, but from what he is trying to do. If he tries after meals to get his thumb in his mouth and sucks eagerly when he succeeds, then there is good reason to consider the pacifier.

What age to start? If a baby becomes used to this thumb over a period of weeks or months, the chances are that he will refuse the pacifier. He has learned to enjoy not only the sensations in his mouth but the sensations in his thumb. So if you are going to use a pacifier, start it in the first few weeks of life.

What times of day? The logical time to offer the pacifier is whenever the baby is searching around with his mouth and trying to suck on thumb, fingers, wrist, clothing or anything else he can reach. In the early months, a baby is seldom awake except before and after feedings, so these are the usual times. But if he's awake between feedings, I'd give it to him then, too. The idea is to give it to him not as little as possible, but as much as he can use it in the first 3 months, so that he will be satisfied and give it up as soon as he can.

I think it is preferable to remove the pacifier when the baby begins to be drowsy, if he doesn't object too strongly, or just as soon as he is asleep. A baby who is accustomed to having a pacifier in his mouth when asleep may, if it falls out, wake and cry unhappily until it is replaced. This can happen a dozen times a night—especially when a baby who has previously slept on his back learns to turn over on his abdomen—and it can be an awful nuisance.

In getting the baby off the pacifier when he is beginning to spit it out soon after it's put in his mouth, or when he just seems happy without it, I wouldn't try to accomplish this in one day. Take a week or two to cut down and don't be afraid to increase again for a day or two if he seems to have a special need for comforting. But decrease again when he's willing.

If your baby is still on the pacifier after 5 or 6 months and wakes several times a night because he's lost it, put several in his bed at bedtime so that there's a better chance of his finding one by himself. Or pin one to his nightie. (Don't put a long cord on a pacifier to hang it around the baby's neck. This can be dangerous.)

When a baby has a few teeth, he can pull the nipple of an old, tired pacifier off the disk or chew pieces out of the nipple. These pieces may cause serious choking if swallowed the wrong way. So buy new pacifiers when the old ones become at all weak or crumbly.

RHYTHMIC HABITS

350. Rocking, jouncing, head rolling, head banging. In rocking, a baby sitting in a chair or couch rocks hard against the back and lets it bounce him forward again. I call it jouncing when a baby gets on his hands and knees and rhythmically jounces down against his heels. This usually moves his crib across the room until it bangs monotonously against the wall. A baby may roll his head from side to side while lying on his back in bed. Head banging, in which a baby bangs the back of his head or his forehead against the head of the crib, is of all these habits the most distressing to the parents. It makes them wonder whether he has any brains to start with and whether, if he does, he'll injure them.

What's the meaning of these rhythmic movements? I don't think we know all the answers but we have some ideas. These habits usually appear in the second half of the first year in the age period when babies naturally acquire a sense of rhythm and try to sway in time to music. (Is this to help them learn the rhythm of walking?) I think they are commoner in boys, who belong to the tenser sex. They are mainly carried out, like thumb sucking or the stroking of a soft toy, when the child is tired, sleepy or frustrated. So I think they come under the heading of comforters and may represent the child's wish to regress to the period of early infancy when he was rocked and carried a lot. Read Sections 335–337.

If a baby bangs his head, you can pad his crib to keep him from bruising himself. One father solved his baby's head banging by sawing the headboard out of the crib and tacking a piece of canvas in its place. For the jouncing baby who rattles the whole house, you can put the crib on a carpet and tack the carpet to the floor, or tie some kind of homemade pads, preferably of rubber, onto the feet of the crib. Or you can put the crib against the wall, where it's going to end up anyway, and place a big wad of padding between the crib and the wall.

In any case, I would not scold the baby or try to restrain him.

Your Baby's Development

WATCHING HIM GROW

351. He's repeating the whole history of the human race. There's nothing in the world more fascinating than watching a child grow and develop. At first you think of it as just a matter of growing bigger. Then, as he begins to do things, you may think of it as "learning tricks." But it's really more complicated and full of meaning than that. Each child as he develops is retracing the whole history of mankind, physically and spiritually, step by step. A baby starts off in the womb as a single tiny cell, just the way the first living thing appeared in the ocean. Weeks later, as he lies in the amniotic fluid in the womb, he has gills like a fish. Toward the end of his first year of life, when he learns to clamber to his feet, he's celebrating that period millions of years ago when man's ancestors got up off all fours. It's just at that time that the baby is learning to use his fingers with skill and delicacy. Our ancestors stood up because they had found more useful things to do with their hands than walking on them. The child in the years after 6 gives up part of his dependence on his parents. He makes it his business to find out how to fit into the world outside his family. He takes seriously the rules of the game. He is probably reliving that stage of human history when our wild ancestors found it was better not to roam the forest in independent family groups but to form larger communities. Then they had to learn self-control, how to cooperate with each other according to rules and laws, instead of depending on the old man of the family to boss them around.

To appreciate your child's development up to 5, you ought to read *Infant and Child in the Culture of Today*, by Arnold Gesell and Frances L. Ilg.[1] They have studied hundreds of

---

[1] New York: Harper & Brothers, 1943. $4.50.

babies and children and can tell you not just what a child will probably do at different age periods, but something about what it means. Understanding what your child is up to is the first step in learning how to get along with him. As you watch your own baby grow, remember the advice in Section 3 of this book.

352. Slow developers. You watch your child grow with a mixture of strong feelings. When he is coming along speedily, you are proud of him and proud of yourself for having produced him. As he shows his delight in his new accomplishments and in discovering the amazing world around him, you live over again the pleasantest parts of your own childhood. But always you find that you are quick to worry if there are any signs that he is failing to keep up with his own progress or to keep up with other children you know about. You feel not only anxious but vaguely guilty. That's the way all good parents are made. Anything the slightest bit out of line makes them wonder whether they are caring for their child properly, whether they have given him a worthy inheritance, whether something they were made to feel guilty about in their own past is affecting him. The Bible speaks ominously of the sins of the father being visited on the children, and many of us parents were warned in similar words in our own upbringing.

Rarely does slow development have anything to do with inadequate care or inherited defects or the sins of the parents (real or imaginary).

Every child's development is different from every other child's and is a complex mixture of patterns, as was explained in Section 3. These are determined mainly by his inheritance —normal inheritance, not faulty inheritance. Slow or fast walking, teething, talking, early or late puberty development, tallness or shortness, tend to run in families. But all these characteristics vary in the same family, because each family's inheritance is a great mixture.

Motor development covers such skills as holding the head erect, sitting, creeping, standing, walking. We have average figures for each of these, but the variations are great among babies who are entirely healthy and normal.

There are a few rare diseases that interfere with motor development, but these can usually be diagnosed by a doctor. The overwhelming majority of cases of slow motor development—more than nine out of ten—are simply a matter of normal variation.

Development of intelligence. It's particularly important for parents of a child who is slow in his motor development to know that there is very little connection between this and his intelligence. More than nine out of ten of the babies who are distinctly slow in motor development turn out to have normal intelligence. Incidentally, the development tests that are sometimes given in infancy (particularly in cases for adoption) are mainly tests of motor ability and social responsiveness. They reveal whether a baby has had a disease or injury to his brain and whether he has suffered emotionally from neglect. But aside from these conditions, they do not tell in the first year anything about what his intelligence will be in the future. Intelligence, which has to do with such abilities as reasoning and memory, cannot begin to be tested reliably until about 2 years of age.

Intelligence, in contrast to motor development, has a lot more to do with environment than with inheritance. Babies born to mothers with low intelligence but adopted into average or bright families tend to develop an intelligence like that of their adopted parents.

Social and emotional development may depend somewhat on the temperament that a baby is born with—whether he is quiet or active, for instance—but most of all they depend on what experiences he has. There is no evidence that specific disturbances like alcoholism, untruthfulness, meanness and delinquency are inherited.

A baby who is slow in his development certainly needs to be checked regularly by his doctor to be sure that there is no disease or condition that needs correcting. This is especially true if he is not only slow in motor development but also unresponsive to the people and things around him. Then he should have at least one consultation with a pediatrician, an eye specialist and a hearing specialist.

353. He's wrapped up in himself the first 2 or 3 months. In the period up to 2 or 3 months, a baby hasn't much contact with the outside world. Most of the time he seems to be listening to what his insides tell him. When they tell him that all is well, he is very peaceful. When they tell him about hunger, or indigestion, or tiredness, he feels wholeheartedly wretched because there's nothing to distract him.

It's an irritable period for some babies. One has colic, another has spells of irritable crying, a third always screams for a few minutes just before falling asleep.

As a baby gets beyond the 3-month period, he takes a lot more notice of the world around him. He turns his head in all directions, all by himself, and seems pleased with what he sees.

354. He starts by using his head. It's a gradual process by which a baby learns to control his body. It starts with the head and gradually works down to the hands, trunk and legs. Just as soon as he's born, he knows how to suck. And if something touches his cheek—the nipple or your finger, for example—he tries to reach it with his mouth. He's ready to do his part in nursing. If you try to hold his head still, he becomes angry right away and twists to get it free. Probably he has this instinct to keep from being smothered.

Mothers ask, "When does he begin to see?" This is a gradual process, like everything else. As soon as he's born, he can tell light from dark. A bright light bothers him and makes him shut his eyes. In the early weeks he begins to fix his gaze on objects that are near. By the time he's 1 or 2 months old, he recognizes a human face and responds to it. By 3 months he looks around in all directions. In the early months he can't coordinate his two eyes very efficiently and often looks cross-eyed. Also, the surface of his eyes isn't sensitive, and a piece of fuzz there may not bother him at all.

A newborn baby seems to be deaf the first day or two because of fluid in his inner ear. But soon he is apt to have a sharp sense of hearing and may startle all over when he hears a loud noise. A few babies remain deaf for a number of weeks, apparently because the fluid in the ear is slow to absorb.

355. He smiles early, because he's a social being. Somewhere between 1 and 2 months of age, your baby smiles at you one day when you are talking and smiling to him. It's an exciting moment for you. But think what it means about his development. He knows little at this age; he can't use his hands or even turn his head from side to side. And yet he already knows that he's a sociable being, that it's nice to have loving people around, that he feels like responding to them. And if he's handled with plenty of affection and sensible firmness, he'll go on being friendly and reasonable just because it is his nature.

356. Using his hands. As soon as they are born, a very few babies can put their thumbs in their mouth any time they want to. But most can't get even their hands to their mouth with any regularity until they are 2 or 3 months old. And because their fists are still clenched tight, it usually takes them longer still to get hold of a thumb separately.

But the main business of hands is to grab and handle things. A baby seems to know ahead of time what he's going to be learning next. Weeks before he can actually grab an object, he looks as if he wanted to and were trying. At this stage, if you put a rattle into his hand, he holds onto it and waves it. Around the middle of the first year, he learns how to reach something that's brought within arm's reach. Gradually he handles things more expertly. In the last quarter of his first year, he loves to pick up tiny objects, like a speck of dust, carefully and deliberately.

357. Right- and left-handedness. The subject of handedness in children is a somewhat confusing one. Some babies stay ambidextrous for the first year or so and then gradually become right- or left-handed. Others show an early preference for the right or left hand that seems permanent. Others use one hand predominantly for several months and then shift to the other.

Formerly most scientists who were interested in handedness believed it was an inborn trait that would sooner or later become evident in each individual. And since many speech and reading specialists believed that changing a left-handed child to right-handed sometimes caused stuttering or reading difficulties, it seemed best not to try to influence any baby or small child, for fear of confusing a possible left-hander. More recently, Dr. Abram Blau wrote a book, *The Master Hand*, giving evidence in support of his belief that right- or left-handedness is not inborn but acquired as a habit. He recommends that parents tactfully help the baby and small child to favor the right hand from the beginning. He believes that the child who prefers his left hand despite his mother's efforts is most likely doing so because of contrariness ("negativism").

Faced with two opposite theories, what is a parent to do? I think there is a fairly safe compromise course. If a baby seems ambidextrous, as he is likely to be when he first begins to hold things in the middle of the first year, or right-handed, then assume he is right-handed, hang his first crib toy nearer his right hand, and favor his right hand as you hand him toys and finger foods and, later, a spoon. But if from the very beginning he has a definite preference for the left or if later he begins to insist on using his left, I wouldn't argue or fight with him but leave him to his preference. Even if his left-handedness is an expression of contrariness, it would only make matters worse to get him more antagonistic and obstinate.

The cue then is to guide him tactfully if he is willing to be guided but not to fight him.

358. How a baby feels about strangers. You can get an idea of how a baby goes from phase to phase in his development by watching his reaction to strangers at different ages. This is how it goes in a doctor's office. A 2-month-old baby doesn't pay much attention to the doctor. As he lies on the examining table, he keeps looking over his shoulder at his mother. The 3-month-old is the doctor's delight. He breaks into a body-wiggling smile just as often as the doctor is willing to smile and make noises at him. By about 5 months, a baby may have changed his mind. When a stranger approaches, he stops his kicking and cooing. His body freezes, and he eyes him intently, suspiciously, maybe for 10 or 20 seconds. Then his stomach begins to rise and fall rapidly. Finally his chin puckers, and he begins to shriek. He may get so worked up that he cries long after the examination is over. This is a sensitive period, when a baby may take alarm at anything unfamiliar, such as a visitor's hat or even his father's face. Probably the main cause of this behavior is that he is now smart enough to distinguish between friend and stranger. If your baby is sensitive about new people, new places, in the middle of his first year, I'd protect him from too much fright by making strangers keep at a little distance until he gets used to them, especially in new places. He'll remember his father in a while.

Some babies accept strangers in a fairly casual way until the end of the first year. But then everything changes. I think 13 months is the most suspicious age of all. The usual baby at this age scrambles to his feet when the doctor approaches and tries to climb off the table and onto his mother. He cries furiously, buries his face in his mother's neck, ostrich fashion. Every once in a while he stops just long enough to peer over his shoulder at the doctor, with looks like daggers. He usually stops crying and struggling soon after the examination is over. A few minutes later he may be happily exploring the office and even making friends with the doctor himself. There is more about handling the sensitiveness of the 1-year-old in Section 407.

359. Rolling over and sitting up. The age when babies roll over, sit up, creep, stand up or walk is more variable than the age when they get control of their head or arms. A lot depends on temperament and weight. A wiry, energetic baby is in a great rush to get moving. A plump, placid one is willing to wait until later.

A baby, by the age he first tries to roll over, shouldn't be left unguarded on a table for as long as it takes the mother to turn her back, unless he is secured with a strap (such as comes with fabric bathtubs). By the time he can actually roll over, it is not safe to leave him even in the middle of an adult's bed. It is amazing how fast such a baby can reach the edge.

Most babies learn to sit steadily (after being helped up) between 7 and 9 months. Some normal, intelligent ones wait till as late as a year. But before a baby has the coordination to succeed, he wants to try. When you take hold of his hands, he attempts to pull himself up. This eagerness always raises the question in the mother's mind: How young can I prop him up in the carriage or high chair? Doctors feel that in general it's better not to prop a baby straight up until he can sit steadily himself for many minutes. This doesn't mean that you can't pull him up to a sitting position for fun, or sit him in your lap, or prop him on a slanted pillow in the carriage, just as long as his neck and back are straight. It's the curled-over position that's not so good for long periods.

This brings up the question of a high chair. It is of greatest advantage when the baby is eating his meals with the rest of the family. On the other hand, falling out of a high chair is a common accident. If a baby is going to be eating most of his meals by himself, I think it is preferable to buy him a low chair-table arrangement. If you are going to use a high chair, get one with a broad base (so that it doesn't tip over easily) and a strap to buckle the baby in. Don't leave a baby for long periods in a high or low chair after he has learned to creep or stand. He needs more freedom.

360. A toy or food while being changed. One of the things a baby never learns is that he ought to lie still while his mother changes or dresses him. It goes completely against his nature. From around half a year, when he learns to roll over, until his mother dresses him standing up at about a year, he struggles or cries indignantly against lying down, as if he has never heard of such an outrage.

There are a few things that help a little. One baby can be distracted by a mother who makes funny noises, another by a small bit of zwieback or cracker. You can have a special fascinating toy, like a music box, that you hand him at dressing time only. Distract him just before you lay him down, not after he starts yelling.

361. Creeping. Creeping can begin any time between 6 months and a year. Some babies never creep at all; they just sit around until they learn to stand up. There are a dozen different ways of creeping, and a baby may change his style as he becomes more expert. One first learns to creep backward, another somewhat sideways. One wants to do it on hands and toes with legs straight, another on hands and knees, another still on one knee and one foot. The baby who learns to be a speedy creeper may be late in walking, and the one who is a clumsy creeper, or who never learns to creep at all, has a good reason for learning to walk early.

362. Standing. Standing usually comes in the last quarter of the first year, but a very ambitious, wiry baby may do it as early as 7 months. Occasionally you see one who doesn't stand until after a year who seems to be bright and healthy in all other respects. Some of these are plump, easygoing babies. Others just seem to be slow getting coordination in their legs. I wouldn't worry about such a child so long as the doctor finds that he is healthy and so long as he seems bright and responsive in other ways.

Quite a number of babies get themselves into a jam when they first learn to stand up but don't yet know how to sit down again. The poor things stand for hours until they are frantic with exhaustion. A mother takes pity on such a child, unhitches him from the railing of his playpen and sits him down. But instantly he forgets all about his fatigue and pulls himself to his feet again. This time he is crying within a few minutes. The best that a mother can do is to give him especially interesting things to play with while he's sitting, wheel him in the carriage longer than usual, and comfort herself that he'll probably learn how to sit down within a week. One day he tries it. Very carefully he lets his behind down as far as his arms reach and, after a long hesitation, lets go. He finds that it wasn't such a long drop and that his seat is well padded.

As the weeks go by, he learns to move around hanging on, first with two hands, then with one. Eventually he has enough balance to let go altogether for a few seconds when he is absorbed and doesn't realize what a daring thing he's doing. He is getting ready for walking.

363. Walking. Lots of factors determine the age when a baby walks alone: ambitiousness, heaviness, how well he can get places by creeping, illnesses, bad experiences. A baby just beginning to walk when an illness lays him up for 2 weeks may not try again for a month or more. Or one who is just learning and has a fall may refuse to let go with his hands again for many weeks.

Most babies learn to walk between 12 and 15 months. A few muscular, ambitious ones start as early as 9 months. A fair number of bright children, without rickets or any other physical disease, do not begin until 18 months or even later.

When a baby begins to walk, it raises a lot of minor problems, like shoes and discipline, but these are taken up in later sections.

You don't have to do anything to teach your child to walk. When his muscles, his nerves, and his spirit are ready, you won't be able to stop him. I remember a mother who got herself into a jam by walking her baby around a great deal before he was able to do it by himself. He was so delighted with this suspended walking that he demanded it all day long. Her back was almost broken.

A mother of a baby who walks early may wonder whether it won't be bad for his legs. As far as we know, a child's physique is able to stand whatever he's ready to do by himself. Babies sometimes become bowlegged or knock-kneed in the early months of walking, but this happens with late walkers as well as with early walkers.

364. Feet and legs. All babies have feet that look flat the first couple of years, partly because they haven't built their arches yet, partly because their feet are so plump. As they learn to stand and walk, they exercise the muscles that help create the arch of the foot. (See next section.)

How straight the legs, ankles and feet grow depends on several factors, including the pattern of development a baby is born with and whether he has rickets (soft bones due to insufficient vitamin D). Some babies seem to have a tendency to knock-knees and ankles that sag inward even though there is never any rickets. The heavy child is more apt to develop these conditions. Other babies seem to be born with a tendency to bowlegs and toeing in, quite apart from rickets. I think this is especially true of the very active, athletic ones. If a baby has a tendency to knock-knees, and also has soft bones due to rickets, you can see why his knock-knees will develop more rapidly and more severely. The same applies to bowlegs. Another factor may be the position a baby keeps his feet and legs in. For instance, you occasionally see a foot that becomes turned in at the ankle because the baby always sits with his foot tucked under him in that position. It is sometimes suspected that a baby has been made to toe in by always lying on his stomach with his feet pointed toward each other, or by pushing himself in a walker with the outside edges of his feet.

All babies toe out to some degree when they start to walk, and then gradually bring the front part of the feet in as they progress. One starts with his feet sticking right out to the side, like Charlie Chaplin, and ends up toeing out only moderately. The average baby starts toeing out moderately and ends up with his feet almost parallel. The baby who starts out with feet almost parallel is more apt to end up toeing in. Toeing in and bowlegs often go together.

The doctor at the regular examinations watches the baby's ankles and legs from the time he begins to stand up. This is one reason why regular visits are important during the second year. If weak ankles, knock-knees, bowlegs or toeing in develops, he may recommend corrective shoes. If there is any suspicion of rickets, he may have an X-ray picture taken.

365. Shoes: when and what kind? In most cases there's no need to put anything on a baby's feet until he's walking outdoors. Normally his feet stay cool just the way his hands do, and this doesn't bother him. In other words, there's no necessity for knitted booties or soft shoes in the first year unless the house or the floor is unusually cold.

After a baby is standing and walking, there's a real value in leaving him barefoot most of the time when conditions are suitable. A baby's arches are relatively flat at first. He gradually builds his arches up and strengthens his ankles by using them vigorously in standing and walking. (I suppose the reason that the soles of the feet are ticklish and sensitive under the arch is to remind us to keep that part arched up off the ground.) Walking on an uneven or rough surface also fosters the use of the foot and leg muscles. When you always provide a baby with a flat floor to walk on and always enclose his feet in shoes (with their smooth insides), especially if the soles are stiff, you encourage him to relax his foot muscles and to walk flat-footed.

Of course, a child who is walking needs shoes when he goes outdoors in cold weather and when he walks on pavements and other surfaces that are hazardous. But it's good for a child to continue to go barefoot indoors till the age of 2 or 3, and outdoors, too, in warm weather at the beach, in the sandbox and in other safe places.

Doctors most commonly recommend semisoft soles at first, so that the child's feet have a better chance to move. The important thing is to have the shoes big enough so that the toes aren't cramped, but not so big that they almost slip off. Socks should always be large enough, too.

Small children outgrow their shoes at a discouragingly fast rate, sometimes in 2 months, and a mother should form the habit of feeling the shoes every few weeks to make sure they are still large enough. There must be more than just enough space for the toes, because as the child walks, his toes are squeezed up into the front of the shoe with each step. There should be enough empty space in the toe of the shoe, as the child stands, so that you can get about half your thumbnail onto the tip of the shoe before running into the child's toe. You can't judge while he is sitting down; the feet don't fill as much of the shoe unless he's standing up. Naturally, the shoes should be comfortably wide, too. There are soft adjustable shoes which can be let out a full size.

If the doctor is prescribing wedges in the shoes to correct such things as weak ankles, toeing in, bowlegs, knock-knees, he may specify firm shoes. Corrective shoes don't do much good if they are limp, and they usually need to be high.

But if your baby's feet and legs are strong, you can get medium-soft shoes, even inexpensive ones if they fit well and are large enough. Sneakers are considered satisfactory by many doctors as long as they don't cause sweating. The feet are pudgy the first couple of years, and as a result low shoes sometimes do not stay on so well as high shoes.

366. Talking. Most babies begin to use a few sounds that mean something when they are in the neighborhood of a year old. But there are perfectly normal children who wait months longer. It seems to be largely a matter of temperament or personality. Your friendly, outgoing baby just naturally wants to talk young. The quiet, observer type seems to want to spend a long time solemnly watching the world go by before he feels like saying anything about it.

The atmosphere around a baby and the way he is handled are important, too. If a mother, under nervous tension, is always silent when she does things for her child, he feels the lack of communication and remains in his own shell. At the other extreme, if the adults in a family are going at a baby too hard, talking at him and bossing him continually, he may feel uncomfortable and unresponsive whenever people are around. He's not at an age when he can talk back or go out for a walk to get away from it all. People young and old feel like talking when they are around easygoing, sympathetic friends. The only difference with a baby is that he has to have more desire in order to learn the words in the first place.

It's sometimes said that a certain child hasn't learned to talk because the whole family waits on him hand and foot, gives him everything before he's had time to realize that he wants it. This kind of service might slow a baby down a little in learning new words, but I don't think it would make him silent unless the family were also keeping after him too much and squelching his outgoingness.

Once in a while you suspect that a baby is slow to pick up words because his mother talks to him in long sentences and he never has a chance to grab hold of a single word at a time to learn. This isn't common, because it comes instinctively to most people to use single words at first with a baby, or to stress the important word in a phrase.

Does slow talking point to slow mental development? This is apt to be the first awful thought that occurs to parents. It is true that some children who are mentally slow are late talkers, but plenty of them use words at the regular age. Naturally, the child who is severely retarded, who can't sit up, for instance, until he's 2, will be really delayed in his talking also. But the fact is that a great majority of late talkers, even those who don't talk much until 3, have normal intelligence, and some of them are unusually bright.

I think you can guess what to do if your child is a late talker. Don't fret about it and don't jump to the conclusion that he's stupid. Show him comfortable affection, and try not to boss him too much. Give him chances, if possible, to be around other children where he can make his own way. Talk to him with simple words in a friendly manner. Encourage him to ask for things by name, but try to avoid angry demands that he speak.

All babies start out mispronouncing most of the words that they use, and gradually improve. But one continues to have trouble with one sound and another with another. Some of these mispronunciations are apparently due to real clumsiness of the tongue or other part of the speech apparatus. After all, some grown-ups still lisp, no matter how hard they try. Other mispronunciations seem to be due to quirks in the child's feelings. He clings to the mispronunciation of one word long after he's learned to make the same sound correctly in another word. Minor delays like this are not important if the child is generally well adjusted and outgoing, and is growing up in other respects. It's all right to correct a child occasionally in a friendly way. It's a mistake to be too serious or argumentative about it.

What about the child who has such clumsy speech at 3 or 4 or 5 or older that other children can't understand him and make fun of him? In the first place, he needs to have his hearing checked by a specialist. He might go to a speech expert if there is one who knows how to get along with a small child easily and can make the lessons appeal to him. But whether or not an expert is available, such a child needs regular association with other children as close to his own age as possible, preferably in a good nursery school, until he's ready for the grades. A good teacher can protect the child with a defect from the scorn of the other children in tactful ways, and can often coach him in talking more easily than the parent because she isn't so worried about it. Some grade schools have trained speech teachers.

Deliberate baby talk comes up most often in the child who is jealous of a younger member of the family, who he feels is getting too much admiration and affection (see Section 490). There is another kind of affected baby talk in the child who has no rivals to worry about. I am thinking, for instance, of the little girl with corkscrew curls and fancy clothes who is the only child of a doting family. They are so pleased with her as a plaything that they forget she has to grow up. They keep talking baby talk to her long after it is natural, and show her that they love her best when she acts babyish and "cute." You can't blame her for playing up to them. But she will have a tough time when she gets around children her own age, because they won't think she's cute; they'll think she's awful.

TEETHING

367. Age of teething means little. Teething is quite different in different babies. One chews things, frets and drools for 3 or 4 months before each tooth comes through, and makes life miserable for the whole family. In another case, a mother discovers a tooth one fine morning without ever having suspected that her baby was teething.

One baby gets his first tooth at 3 months, another not till a year. Yet both are healthy, normal infants. It is true that certain diseases once in a while influence the age of teething. But this is rare. In a baby who is reasonably healthy, the age of teething is simply a matter of the pattern of development he was born with. In one family most of the children teethe early, in another late. You can't decide your baby is extra bright because he teethes early, that he's generally backward because he teethes late.

360. How the average baby's teeth come through. The average baby gets his first tooth around 7 months, but he has been drooling, biting and having periods of fretfulness from the age of 3 or 4 months. Since a baby gets 20 teeth in his first 2½ years, it is easy to see why he is teething most of that whole period. This also explains why it's so easy to blame every ailment on teething.

In the olden days it was the custom to blame teeth for colds, diarrheas, fevers. Of course, these diseases are caused by germs and not by teething. However, in some babies it looks as though teething lowers resistance, making it easier for an infection to start at that time. But if your baby becomes sick while he's teething, or has a fever as high as 101°, he needs a doctor to diagnose and treat the disease just as much as if he had gotten sick when he wasn't teething.

Usually the first 2 teeth are the lower central incisors. ("Incisor" is the name given to the 8 front teeth, which have sharp cutting edges.) After a few months come the 4 upper incisors. The average baby has these 6 teeth, 4 above and 2 below, when he is a year old. After this there's usually a pause of several months. Then 6 more teeth are apt to come in, without much pause in between—the 2 remaining lower incisors, and all 4 first molars. The molars don't come in next to the incisor teeth but farther back, leaving a space for the canine teeth.

After the first molar teeth, there is a pause of several months before the canines (the pointed "dog teeth") come through in the spaces between the incisors and the molars.

The commonest time is in the second half of the second year. The last 4 teeth in the baby set are the second molars. They come in right behind the first molars, usually in the first half of the third year.

369. Wakefulness with teething. The first 4 molar teeth, which in the average baby come through between a year and a year and a half, are more likely to cause a baby trouble than the others. He may be cranky and lose his appetite for days at a time. He may wake crying a number of times each night. This can be quite a problem if he doesn't fall asleep again quickly. A small bottle or cup of milk may seem to be the easiest way to pacify him. Is this risky? In most cases, the baby stops waking when the teeth are through. But an occasional baby develops a persistent habit of waking, especially if he is picked up for the bottle and given a sociable time (Section 285). Therefore, I think it's preferable not to get into the habit of giving a night feeding at this age or of picking the baby up, if he quiets down in a few minutes by himself. If you do have to give a bottle, give it in the crib, and stop it firmly when the teeth are through.

The coming of the first teeth, in the middle of the first year, may cause waking, too.

Refusal to take bottle or breast during teething is discussed in Section 101.

370. Let him chew. Sometimes a mother thinks it's her duty to keep her baby from putting things in his mouth and chewing. This notion will surely drive her and the baby frantic in time. Most babies must put things in their mouths, off and on, at least from 6 months to 15 months. The best that a mother can do is to provide chewable objects that are dull enough so that if the baby falls with them in his mouth they won't do too much damage. Rubber teething rings of various shapes are good, but any piece of rubber that the baby can hold easily will do. You have to be careful about toys made from thin celluloid. Babies sometimes break off and swallow small bits or choke on them. You also have to be careful that the baby doesn't gnaw the paint off furniture and other objects if there is any danger that the paint is made with lead. Nowadays practically all babies' furniture and painted toys are painted with leadless paint. You have to think about objects that have been repainted at home or that were never expected to be chewed by babies. Some babies prefer a certain kind of cloth for chewing on. Let him have what he seems to want as long as it's not dangerous. You don't have to fret about the germs on a teething ring or a favorite piece of cloth. They are his own germs, anyway. Of course, it's a good idea to wash the teething ring with soap after it has fallen on the floor or after the dog has gotten it. If the baby chews on a piece of cloth, you can boil it occasionally. Some babies love to have their gums firmly rubbed at times. Don't use any medicine without the doctor's recommendation.

371. What makes good teeth. The first thing to realize is that the crowns of all the baby teeth (the parts that will show) are formed in his gums before he is born. In other words, they are made from what the mother eats during her pregnancy. Research shows that among the food elements necessary to make strong teeth, the following are particularly important: calcium and phosphorus (milk and cheese), vitamin D (vitamin drops and sunshine), vitamin C (vitamin drops, oranges, other citrus fruits, raw tomatoes, cabbage). Other factors are probably necessary, too, including vitamin A and some of the B vitamins.

The baby's permanent teeth, the first of which won't appear until he is about 6 years old, already are being formed within a few months after his birth. A baby at this age is, of course. getting plenty of calcium and phosphorus from his milk diet He should get C and D vitamins by the time he is a month old. (These are usually added in the form of concentrated drops.)

372. Fluoride in the water makes stronger teeth. One element known to be valuable in the formation of a child's teeth is fluoride—a minute amount in the diet of the mother while she is pregnant, and in the diet of the baby and small child while his permanent teeth are being formed. There is much less tooth decay in those parts of the country where fluoride occurs naturally in the water. It is now added, in minute, safe amounts, to the water of many progressive communities as a public health measure. If there is no fluoride in the water, the mother's physician or dentist can prescribe a minute daily dose for the mother during her pregnancy and for the child after he is born. The dentist can give a child part of the benefit by painting fluoride on his teeth and recommending fluoride toothpaste. Whenever it is proposed that fluoride be added to a city's water supply, it makes some citizens anxious. They discover literature that claims fluoridation is harmful, and they may invite speakers from other cities, who are known as opponents of fluoridation, to testify against it. Since some of the statements are very alarming, they raise questions in the minds of all citizens. It is well to remember that intensive and extensive studies were made by responsible scientists before artificial fluoridation was ever proposed and that all the possible dangers and objections were carefully checked. Then committees of experts of the American Public Health Association, the American Dental Association, the American Medical Association and the United States Public Health Service reviewed the evidence before publicly recommending fluoridation.

It gives you a better perspective to realize that similar alarm was raised about vaccination, diphtheria inoculation and chlorination of water before these procedures became generally accepted.

373. Decay is favored by frequent contact with sugars and starches. Dental scientists haven't yet been able to find all the answers to decay (caries) of the teeth. The diet of the pregnant mother and of the baby are important in the formation of the teeth. Heredity probably plays a part.

But some teeth that look strong decay later. Dentists believe that the principal cause of tooth decay is lactic acid. This lactic acid is manufactured by bacteria that live on sugars and starches that are in contact with the teeth. The more hours of the day there are starches and sugars on the teeth, the greater the number of bacteria there are and the more lactic acid is produced to dissolve holes in the teeth. That is why frequent between-meal sucking of lollipops, eating of sticky candy and dried fruit, drinking of sodas and nibbling of cookies and crackers (which so often stick to the teeth) are particularly liable to cause decay.

Of course, most fruits contain some sugar, and even vegetables contain a little. But the sugar is dilute and as a result is washed away sooner. And the rough fibers of fruit have a brushing action on the teeth. All of us eat starches to a greater or lesser extent, but we usually take them only at meals and many of them—especially those containing roughage, such as whole grains and potatoes—don't stick long to the teeth. It's the frequent between-meal eating of sugars and starches, which stick, that is particularly hard on the teeth.

374. Care of the teeth. It is sometimes recommended that a baby's teeth be brushed when he has his first set of molars. For most babies this would be in the first half of the second year. I think, myself, that there is something to be said for waiting until the child is nearly 2. At this age, he has a passion to copy everything he sees done around him. If his mother and father brush their teeth, he one day grabs one of their brushes and insists on trying it himself. This is a good time to buy him a brush and let him go to it. Naturally, he won't be very efficient at first, but you can help him tactfully. Perhaps I am making too much of a point of this, but it's a good example of a basic truth. Three-quarters of the things that we think we must impose on children as unpleasant duties are things that they enjoy learning to do themselves at a certain stage of their development, if we only give them a chance.

The main purpose of brushing the teeth is to remove the lumps of food from around the teeth. **The logical time is after meals, 3 times a day.** (Hang toothbrushes in the kitchen as well as in the bathroom.) Most important is after supper, so that the teeth are clean for the long night period

Children want to do grown-up things.

when the mouth is quiet and the saliva is flowing slowly. There is no proof that the green film that forms on some children's teeth is harmful.

375. Dental examination twice a year from the age of 3. It's wise to begin taking a child to the dentist every 6 months, beginning when he is 3 years old. He is coming into the period when tooth decay may start. The time to fill cavities is when they are small. This saves the teeth, and it hurts the child less. Even if your child doesn't have a cavity at the 3- or 3½-year-old visit to the dentist, it is worth the expense for two reasons. It's insurance that the teeth are healthy. It gets the child used to going to the dentist without fear. This confidence makes a big difference when he has to have his first filling.

Parents sometimes think that they don't have to worry about decay of the baby teeth because they are all going to be lost anyway. This is wrong. A decayed tooth may cause the child pain, and it sometimes leads to infection of the jaw. And if a baby tooth is so decayed or causes so much pain that it has to be pulled, it leaves a space in the jaw that allows nearby teeth to grow out of position. Then there isn't enough room for the permanent tooth when it's ready to come through. Remember that the last baby teeth are not lost until the child is 12 years old. So they need just as careful care as the permanent ones.

376. The permanent teeth. The permanent teeth begin to appear when the child is about 6 years old. The 6-year-old molars come through farther back than the baby molars. The first baby teeth to be lost are the lower central incisors. The permanent incisors, pushing up underneath, destroy the roots of the baby teeth, which get loose and then fall out. The baby teeth are lost in about the same order they come in: the incisors, the molars, the canines. The permanent teeth that take the place of the baby molars are called bicuspids. The substitution of the new teeth is completed somewhere around 12 to 14 years of age. Meanwhile, the 12-year-old molars have come through behind the 6-year molars. The "18-year molars," or "wisdom teeth," come considerably later (sometimes never).

When teeth come through crooked or out of place, there is some tendency for them to straighten out later, how much one cannot tell ahead of time. Your regular dentist, who should be seeing your child's teeth every 6 months, can advise you whether he needs special treatment for this.

When the permanent teeth come in they are often behind the baby teeth and later move forward. They have jagged edges which later wear down.

Toilet Training

BOWEL TRAINING

377. What does it mean? Learning to use the toilet is an important forward step for a child—in several ways. He gains control of two apertures of his body that previously functioned automatically, and this gives him a lot of pride; in fact, he's so proud at first that he tries to perform every few minutes. He is accepting the first serious responsibility that his mother assigns to him. Their successful cooperation on this major project will give each of them a new confidence in each other. And whereas the child used to be a lighthearted messer—with his food anyway, and with his BM, too, if he ever had the opportunity to get at it—he now begins to take satisfaction in cleanliness. You may think of this shift as primarily meaning no more soiled diapers. That's important, all right. But the preference for cleanliness that a child gains at a year and a half or two means a lot more than that. It's actually the foundation for his lifelong preference for unsticky hands, for clean clothes, for a neat home, for an orderly way of doing business. It's from his toilet training that he gets some of his feeling that one way of doing things is right and another way is not; this helps him to develop a sense of obligation, to become a systematic person. So toilet training plays a part in the formation of a child's character and in building the basic trust between him and his mother.

378. What is Readiness for Training? The first year. Ease in training depends a great deal on a mother taking advantage of the stages of her child's readiness.

In the first year a baby shows very little awareness of his bowel function. And he doesn't participate—in a voluntary sense—in moving his bowels. When his rectum becomes sufficiently full, and particularly after a meal when the muscular activity of his stomach stimulates his entire intestinal tract, the movement presses against the inner valve of his anus and causes it to open somewhat. By means of a nerve reflex this stimulates a squeezing, pushing-down action of the abdominal muscles. The baby, in other words, does not decide to push, the way an older child or adult does; he pushes automatically.

During the first year there is a small amount of readiness for partial training in some babies in the sense that they always have their first movement of the day within 5 or 10 minutes after breakfast. If a mother wishes to do so, she can sit such a baby on the toilet seat every day (from the age of about 7 or 8 months, when he can sit steadily) just in time to "catch" his movement. After a few weeks of this, his nervous system becomes "conditioned," as the psychologists call it, so that he automatically begins to push as soon as he feels the toilet seat under him. This is only a small degree of training, because the baby is not really conscious of his bowel movement or of what he himself is doing. He is not cooperating knowingly.

The principal gain in this degree of training, in the first year, is that the baby becomes somewhat accustomed to sitting on the toilet and to having his bowels move there. This may help him to make progress in the voluntary control of his bowels and bladder in his second year. On the other hand, he may balk later—when he learns what is going on—just like the child who has had no early training at all.

The main limitation to any training during the first year is that a majority of babies are not regular enough to be caught. If they can't be caught, they can't be conditioned. When a mother tries to catch the movements of an irregular baby she may become quite frustrated, which is not good for her. Or she may get chronically irritated at the baby, which is not good for either of them. Or she may be tempted to keep the baby on the toilet for long periods of time, which is apt to make him very impatient eventually.

If a mother wants to start training before a year and if she can catch her baby regularly without having to make a big fuss about it, this early conditioning may help the baby and herself through the later and more important stages.

379. The first half of the second year. In the first half of the second year—approximately 12 to 18 months—

there are new developments in the child's attitude toward his movements, which may or may not aid in training. He may become somewhat conscious of the sensations that come from the passing of the movement, though probably not sufficiently aware to notify his mother. But he is very likely, if he has chances to see his BM—in the potty or on the floor or formed in his diapers—to develop a distinctly possessive feeling for it. He becomes proud of it, much as he becomes proud of his nose or his navel. If he has had a movement in the potty and his mother is in the next room, he may bring her in by the hand to admire what he has done. He may sniff the smell appreciatively as he has been taught to smell a flower.

At this age his mother will probably be using some phrase like "Did Johnny make a BM?" when she feels his diaper, or "Johnny did duty" when she cleans him up. So he is learning to associate the movement with the family word for it, though he is probably still too young to repeat the word himself.

Early in the second year there are other aspects of readiness that we don't ordinarily associate with toilet training. The child gets the idea of giving presents and takes lots of satisfaction from this. When he decides that he likes his mother's visitor, he will bring all his possessions and hand them to her, one by one. This joy in giving plays a part in his willingness to give up his movement at his mother's request. And he takes pride in his mother's approval when he has learned to do something grown up.

It's also at about a year that a baby becomes fascinated with putting things in containers. This, too, is an element in using the potty or the toilet.

These general aspects of readiness give a mother some basis for starting training at this age if she wishes to, especially if she sees some specific signs of readiness that she and the child can take advantage of. He may begin to make some sound or facial expression that gives her warning. Or if he is fairly predictable in having his first movement of the day within 5 or 10 minutes after breakfast, she can introduce him gradually to the potty chair (see Section 382) and then have him sit on it every morning for perhaps 10 or 15 minutes, while she talks about how this is the big boy's way to do a BM. (See Section 383).

Even if a child between 12 and 18 months is not very regular, his mother may still want to make an attempt to get training started by trying to catch a few movements, with the hope that the child can be made so proud of himself about these that he will want to continue. She could introduce him to the potty chair gradually and then sit him on it at the most likely time each day, talking about how grown up and comfortable it is to have movements this way. If she has no success at all in a couple of weeks, she'll probably want to quit until the child is nearing a year and a half.

There are two kinds of difficulty with training in the first half of the second year. The first concerns the child who is irregular, whose movement never is "caught" and who doesn't seem to get the idea at all. You have to wait a while with him. The second problem is the child who gets the idea of what his mother is after, all right, but declines to give up his movement to the potty. He is discussed in the next section.

380. Balking, especially between 12 and 18 months. Many a baby who has been willingly using the seat for several months suddenly changes his pattern at some time between 12 and 18 months. He sits down obediently but never has a movement so long as he stays there. Right after getting up, he moves his bowels in the corner or in his pants. A mother says, "He seems to have forgotten what it is all about." I don't believe a child forgets that easily. I think that his possessive feeling about his movements has become stronger than ever and that he's simply unwilling to give them up so readily to the potty or toilet or to his mother. Besides, he wants to do everything by himself, in his own way, at this age, and that goes for moving his bowels, too. So he just holds the movement in—at least until he can get away from the seat, which symbolizes giving it up and giving in.

If the resistance persists for many weeks and increases, the child may hold back his movement not only while he is on the seat but for the rest of the day, too, if he can manage it. This is a psychological type of constipation. It is rarely unhealthy from a physical point of view.

Since the small child at this stage may be unwilling to give up his movement because he considers it a rather precious possession, it may help to remind him that it's all right to let this one go because he will be able to make another one tomorrow and tomorrow and tomorrow.

If a baby younger than 1½ years becomes definitely balky within a few days after his mother has started his training, I think it is all right, if she prefers, to wait for further efforts until he is about 18 months old, when he is likely to have greater readiness. But if she has had a number of successes, if the child shows he understands what is being asked of him and shows that he can cooperate, then I think the mother should for several reasons, continue with the training even if the child now wants to change his mind and quit. For if his mother gives in, she implies that training is not important, which is untrue. She also makes it harder to resume training. later, because the child will have more self-confidence about foiling her. She will be frustrated by the long delay, more so because she knows the child could use the toilet if he were willing.

To persist with training a mother can sit with her child for 15 or even 30 minutes, to keep him from leaping up or forgetting what he was there for. She can talk with assurance about all the advantages of being a big boy in this respect (Section 383).

381. Greater readiness between 18 and 24 months. Time to start. In the second half of the second year—18 to 24 months—a majority of children show more definite signs of readiness. They have a greater awareness of when a movement is coming or being passed. They may stop playing for a few seconds or they may act a bit uncomfortable afterward. They may make some kind of sign or sound to the mother, to indicate that the diaper is soiled, as if they'd like to be cleaned up. This notification is more likely if the mother has been suggesting that the child let her know. Usually it takes a little longer, and some encouragement from the mother, before children will become sufficiently aware of the approaching movement—before it has been passed— to be able to notify the mother in time to be helped to the toilet.

Children may now show some degree of aversion toward the BM, acting disgusted if they get some of it on their fingers by mistake or if the smell is strong from the potty or from an accident in the pants.

It isn't only the dirtiness of the BM which may now bother the child. The aversion often spreads to include other forms of dirtiness, too. One child may be upset if he gets mud on his hands. Another may suddenly become disgusted with chocolate 'pudding. If children are offered finger paints to play with just at this stage of training, they may refuse to touch them. It's surprising to see how the delight and pride in the bowel movement, which was characteristic of the first half of the second year, can turn to slight or strong aversion within a few months. Usually, however, the shift is not complete, and much of the possessiveness will persist, alongside the disgust.

382. The regular toilet or a child's seat on the floor? Many babies become accustomed from the start to a baby's toilet seat attached to the regular toilet seat. If such an arrangement is used, it's preferable to have a footrest attached to the baby's seat so that he can feel more steady. The father should also build a steady box-shaped structure to serve as a step, so that the child can learn to climb up on the seat by himself.

It's a sensible precaution during the second year for the mother to wait until the child has gone away from the bathroom before flushing the toilet. Most 1-to-2-year-olds are fascinated with the flushing at first and want to do it themselves. But a small proportion of them later become frightened by the violent way the water flushes the movement away and then are afraid to sit on the seat. One child probably fears that he might fall in and disappear likewise. Another is apparently worried to see this object, which he considers part of himself, snatched away.

I myself think it's preferable to use a child's seat over a potty, close to the floor, up to 2½ years. A child feels more friendly toward a small piece of furniture that is his own and that he can sit down on by himself. His feet can stay on the floor, and there is no height to make him feel insecure. Until 2½ years, I'd empty the potty and flush the toilet after he has gone away.

You can buy your child a potty chair, let him get used to sitting in it playfully (with his clothes on) for a couple of days. You can also be explaining that the potty chair is for Johnny to do duty on, with his diapers off, just the way Mommy and Daddy do it on the big toilet, so that he can be getting used to this idea, too. (A child at this age is easily alarmed by being hurried or pushed into a strange situation.) Then one fine morning you remove his diaper and invite him to sit down like a big boy or a big daddy.

383. Practical steps. By the time a child is 18 months old, I believe a mother **should** begin her training efforts, even if she has not noticed any particular signs of readiness. To put it another way, I think she should make it her business now to look more carefully for signs of readiness and to take advantage of whatever there is, however slight.

Some children become so aware at this age of the sensation of a coming movement (or a full bladder) that they give a signal without any coaching. However, a child is most apt at first to notify his mother **after** the accident has occurred. This is really a sign of progress, even though it doesn't seem so to the parent. He should be praised for telling, and encouraged to tell again tomorrow—"so that we can make the BM go in the potty, so that we won't have to clean it up."

Children who don't signal but whose movements come soon after breakfast can be placed on the seat then. When the movement comes each day on the potty, you can show your pleasure and suggest that the child tell you tomorrow when he's ready. The point is that he's likely to pick up the idea more quickly at this age.

If the child is one of those who are still not regular and who are still not showing the slightest change of facial expression, you can talk to him as you're cleaning him up about how he could be a grown-up boy like Daddy, or Charlie, by using the potty; he could wear pants instead of diapers; he could stay nice and clean; there would be no bother about changing. And you can begin sitting him on the seat at the most likely time of day, giving him the same kind of talk.

384. Emphasizing the discomfort, fostering masterfulness. I think it is sensible for you to encourage the swing of the pendulum, from possessiveness to aversion, by emphasizing the uncomfortableness of having the movement in the diaper. You can explain to the child, as you clean up, that he will feel good, and be more like grown-ups, if he will tell you beforehand next time so that you can put him on the seat. But it's better not to make the child feel intensely disgusted or ashamed; that might instill too much squeamishness into his character.

You can also flatter and foster your child's masterfulness by expressing confidence in his eventual ability to stay clean— like a big boy—before he succeeds, and by congratulating him enthusiastically whenever he does succeed.

385. Imitation and pleasing the parent as aids to training. Training may sometimes be aided greatly toward the end of the second year by the child's passion to imitate everything he sees done by others. If he has an older brother or sister whom he sees using the toilet, he may become determined to do likewise. To see a parent perform is also apt to stimulate imitation. However, most child psychiatrists think it's unwise, for other reasons, for children to be observing their parents when on or at the toilet. See Section 540.

The gratification of pleasing the mother and father is certainly a powerful influence in making a child want to be trained. Your cue is to be interested, encouraging, friendly. In most cases you also have to be quite definite and persistent, because training is rarely accomplished in a few days or a few weeks, and the child usually needs a lot of guidance. You may even have to become distinctly emphatic, when you come to realize that the child knows just what he should be doing but is obviously stalling and teasing. However, it is better to avoid chronic complaining and nagging, in a tone which suggests that you expect no success.

Your main cue is to remain friendly, encouraging, and optimistic about tomorrow. You can talk about how you, Daddy, brothers, sisters, friends, use the toilet, how the child is growing bigger every day, how nice it feels to be clean and dry. I don't mean a whole sermon every day, just a reminder.

In some cases, the child can be encouraged to take a new view of training by being offered new clothes as a reward: some fancy panties for the girls instead of the plain white training pants, some costume that appeals to the boy.

386. The child who doesn't seem to understand. When the child is still irregular and showing no signs of interest or discomfort or disgust by the second half of the second year, you can leave him in no pants at all for part of the day (while he is in a room with no carpet) so that when the movement comes it will go on the floor where he can see it and realize, for the first time perhaps, what is happening. Then you can demonstrate where it belongs by scooping it into the potty or toilet. Or when you are changing a soiled diaper you can scrape the movement into the potty, with explanations. However, there is no point in giving these demonstrations more than a few times.

387. Training pants instead of diapers. As soon as a child is successful with BM's and urine part of the time, it's wise to graduate to training pants during the day—with congratulations, of course. As soon as he has any control at all, it will be increased by his going without the diaper. The lack of diaper reminds him of the importance of control. To continue to put diapers on a child who is gaining control is an expression of lack of confidence. A diaper invites wetting and soiling.

388. The final stage—doing it all by himself. When a child has reached the stage of being quite reliable about signaling to his mother, he still expects her to get him to the seat and take his clothes down. He won't really have reached the last stage of training until he does these jobs by himself, usually between 2 and 2½ years. A lot depends on whether his mother is encouraging him to take over and on how easily he can get his clothes down. Even so, there are apt to be occasional accidents—when playing outdoors, when away from home or when there is diarrhea—until he is about 3 years old. By the time a child is 2½ years old you should suggest that he begin wiping himself, even if he doesn't do this efficiently.

389. Fear of painfully hard movements. Sometimes a child gradually or suddenly gets into a spell of unusually hard movements that are painful to pass. Not all hard movements are painful. The collections of small hard pellets—the result of what is sometimes called spastic constipation—are rarely painful. It's usually the hard movement in one large piece, with a wide diameter, that is to blame. As it is passed, it may tear a tiny slit, or "fissure," in the edge of the stretched anus. When a fissure has occurred, it is likely to be stretched open again each time another movement is passed. This is quite painful, and the fissure may thus be kept from healing for many weeks. You can easily see how a child who has once been hurt may dread a repetition and fight against toileting again. It may become a vicious circle, because if the child succeeds in holding back his movement for several days, it is more likely to be hard.

It's important to notify the doctor promptly if a child begins to have hard movements, particularly in this sensitive second year, so that he can consider a change in the diet or a medication to keep them soft. Adding prunes or prune juice to the diet every day, if the child likes them, usually works. More whole grain wheat and oats in cereal, bread and crackers may help some. If you have such an emergency and cannot reach a doctor soon, you can use mineral oil, a tablespoonful each day, more or less, depending on the effect, for several months.

It helps to keep reassuring the child for a while that you know he is worried for fear another movement will hurt the way the previous one did, but that he doesn't need to worry any more because the movements are now kept soft by the medicine.

If a child remains frightened and resistant or if he seems to continue to have pain, the doctor should examine him for the possibility that a fissure has been created and is not healing. It is sometimes necessary to stretch the fissured anus while the child is under anesthesia.

390. The main cause of modern training problems. There is considerable evidence that toilet training has become increasingly difficult in the twentieth century, for some parents. I have been a member of a research team that has looked into this problem, among others, by following the emotional development of several dozen children very closely in a special clinic. In a majority of these children the training was slower and more difficult than we staff people thought necessary. To make a very long story short, it seemed that what was usually interfering was the mothers' fear that they would stir up too much antagonism in their children. Most of them had started training in the first half of the second year. But at the first sign of resistance they had stopped their efforts and postponed the business for a while. Several children, for instance, had developed the habit of withholding their movement as long as they stayed on the seat; others would become impatient to get up right away or would object to sitting down in the first place; still others would shift their bowel-moving time from morning to naptime. After a month or two the mothers would cautiously start training again, run into resistance again, stop again. They felt that any kind of resistance showed that their children were not ready for training.

However, it seemed to the staff people that despite the

various specific forms of resistance, the children were generally ready and in some ways eager for training. They showed that they were aware of the coming of a bowel movement, felt at least slightly uncomfortable when soiled, made some kind of sign before or after the movement, were proud of wearing pants, felt undignified and outraged when put back into diapers. But it seemed that the mothers, influenced primarily by their apprehension about a conflict, tended to minimize these signs of readiness. Several of them, for instance, recognized that the child was signaling for the bathroom but felt that it was a mistake to take him because he so often balked when he got there.

The staff became convinced that the commonest block to training in America today is this fear of arousing hostility in children, and that it has been created in part by the well-meant efforts of parent educators like myself to avoid the occasional open conflicts over training that occurred in past generations. It's interesting that these modern training problems occur mainly in families with college background or with a definite interest in child psychology. For in another clinic in our medical school, where few of the families are college educated or interested in psychology, the great majority of the children are trained before the age of 2 years, without severity, without struggle and without evident harm to the personality. When we ask these less sophisticated mothers the secret of their success (so that we can tell it to the others), they act surprised and say that they just watch for the child's readiness, begin sitting him on the potty chair, and in a few weeks or months he's well trained. It seems that their great advantage is that they aren't afraid of arousing hostility. And the reason is that most of them have never even heard of it.

One of the mothers in the study whose child became trained by 2 years testified spontaneously about the need for perseverance.

She said in effect to her doctor, "I'm glad now that you kept after me. Otherwise I would certainly have dropped the training—at several different stages. I had a strong inclination to shy away from any conflict. But now that my child is trained I can see how grown-up he feels about this accomplishment. And I'm surprised how much satisfaction I take in it, too. In fact, it seems to have brought us closer together—it's as if we'd found a new trust in each other."

URINE TRAINING

391. Readiness for urine training. In one sense, bladder training is more difficult or at least slower than bowel training—it's easier for a person of any age to control a movement than to control urine. Whereas most children have complete control of their bowels by about 2 years (if they have a mind to), plenty of 2½-year-olds are still wetting fairly often either in the daytime or at night. On the other hand, children rarely make an issue of daytime urination. When they are physically able to control the bladder, they are usually quite agreeable to doing so. That is to say, they don't refuse to go to the toilet or to release the urine when they get there. It seems as though urine doesn't matter to them as a possession, the way the bowel movement often does.

392. The bladder begins to retain more urine sometime between 12 and 18 months. In most babies, the bladder empties itself automatically quite often during the first year and the first few months of the second year. Then it begins to retain urine for longer periods. Often it's around the age of 15 or 16 months that a mother first notices—with surprise and pleasure—that her child is dry for as long as 2 hours, usually during the nap. This isn't due to any training efforts. It's simply the maturing of the baby's bladder. This is shown clearly in the story of the occasional baby who becomes dry at night by the age of 12 months—before the mother has ever sat him on the seat for either bowels or urine. On the average, boys are slower than girls in urine training, day or night. A few children have bladders that are still emptying frequently, every half hour to an hour, at 2 years of age.

Though many a child's bladder retains urine for 2 hours by the time he is 1¼ or 1½ years old, this does not mean, of course, that he is trained. If a mother keeps it in mind and goes at it tactfully, she may be able to catch his urine several times a day. But it's very unusual for a child of this age to keep it in mind or to make any signal. He doesn't seem to be enough aware of it.

393. Notifying between 18 and 24 months. Sometime in the latter part of the second year, many children do become enough aware of a full bladder to say a word or to make some special signal to the mother. Signaling is commoner at this age in those children whose mothers have been catching them fairly regularly; this has focused the child's attention. As a matter of fact, for the first few weeks the child often notifies his mother after he has wet. This seems pointless to some mothers and others even suspect their child is teasing them, but they shouldn't be so pessimistic. It's simply that at first the feeling of being wet is more noticeable to the child than the feeling of a full bladder. His intentions are good, he's doing his best for the time being, and soon he'll be calling in time if he sees that his efforts are appreciated.

But even after a child has begun notifying he's not solidly trained yet. He's too busy at times to notice his full bladder, so there continue to be frequent accidents except when his mother keeps the time in mind. And he still has to progress to the final stage—when he notices in time and has skill enough and sense of responsibility enough to take himself to the toilet, manage his clothes and carry out the whole job. Studies of average children show that most of them are still having frequent accidents at 2½ years and plenty aren't able to take over full responsibility until they are about 3.

394. Catching in the first half of the second year. There are two general approaches to bladder training. The mother who prefers to get at it as early as is sensible (the mother who also starts to catch regular bowel movements in the last part of the first year or the first part of the second) can start gradually to catch the urine any time when the bladder shows that it is retaining urine for a couple of hours. If you wait until you find your child dry after 2 hours, you can be reasonably sure of three things:

1. The bladder is grown up enough to cooperate. You won't be trying to train something that is nowhere near ready for training.

2. Your child's bladder will be full after 2 hours. That means that he is ready to urinate pretty soon. You won't have to keep him on the seat for long.

3. If you wait to put him on until he's been dry for 2 hours, you won't be going at his training too suddenly, because you will find him dry only every few days at first. Gradually, as the weeks pass, you'll find him dry more regularly.

This is a practical time to change to training pants.

In a majority of children, dryness first shows up at the end of the nap. A few are first found dry at another time of day. In a few, it is first discovered on waking in the morning.

395. Waiting for notification. Parents who prefer to go slow on training (who wait on bowel training for signals or imitation in the last half of the second year) are naturally waiting on bladder training, too. The child who has learned somewhere between 18 and 24 months to make a sign that a bowel movement is coming, usually, a month or so later, becomes aware enough of a full bladder to tell his mother about that, too, if she encourages him a little by saying the word and by suggesting that he can tell her about this also.

If a mother is waiting for her child to do most of the training himself (through his own desire to use the toilet just like others in the family), he will, toward the end of the second year, probably achieve most of his bowel and urine training at the same time. This can be a nuisance for a few days, because at times he'll want to go to the toilet every 10 minutes in hopes he can perform again.

I want to add again that the parent who prefers to wait for the child to start the training, with signal or imitation, shouldn't get the idea that any suggestion on her part is wrong and will spoil the method. Most children are quite ready and willing in the last part of the second year to begin to try to cooperate with a mother's wishes if she expresses them in an agreeable and encouraging manner and if she takes into account her child's readiness. To put it the other way around, it's unnecessary and sometimes confusing to a child if the mother is so afraid of interfering that she tries to keep it a secret that she wishes him to become trained.

396. Inability to urinate away from home. It sometimes happens that a child around 2 has become so well trained to his own potty chair or toilet seat that he can't perform anywhere else. You can't urge him or scold him into it. He will probably wet his pants eventually, for which he shouldn't be scolded. If he is painfully full, can't let go, and you can't get home, put him in a hot bath for half an hour. This will probably work. Keep this possibility in mind when you take him traveling, and bring along his own seat if necessary. It's better to get a child used early to urinating in different places, including outdoors. There are portable urinals for boys and for girls to which a child can be accustomed at home and which can then be taken along when he visits.

397. Standing up to urinate comes later. Parents are sometimes worried because a 2-year-old boy won't make the change to urinating standing up. It isn't necessary to make an issue of this. He'll get the idea sooner or later, when he has a chance to see older boys occasionally or his father once or twice. See Section 540 on parental nudity.

398. Staying dry at night. Many inexperienced and experienced parents assume that the only reason a child learns to stay dry through the night is that the parent picks him up late in the evening. They ask, "Now that he is reasonably dry in the daytime, when should I begin to pick him up at night?" This is a mistaken idea, and it makes night dryness sound like too much of a job. It's closer to the facts to say that a child just naturally becomes dry at night when his bladder becomes mature enough, provided he isn't nervous or rebellious (Section 694). This is shown clearly by the fact that one baby in a hundred regularly stays dry at night from the age of 12 months, although the mother has made no training effort at all and although the child wets throughout the day. And quite a few children, late in the second year or early in the third, become dry at night before they have much control in the daytime. The reason the bladder can retain urine for longer periods during sleep than in the daytime is that the kidneys automatically produce less urine when a person is quiet and asleep and make the urine more concentrated.

Most children become dry at night between 2 and 3 years of age, a smaller number between 1 and 2, a few not till after 3. Boys tend to be later than girls, high-strung children later than relaxed ones. Sometimes slowness in becoming dry seems to be a family trait.

I don't think it is necessary for parents to do anything special about night training. The natural maturing of the bladder plus the idea that the child gets in the daytime—that urine belongs in the toilet—takes care of most cases. Of course, it helps a little if the parents share in the child's pride when he begins to have dry nights.

Some parents prefer to take a more active part and begin picking the child up at 10 P.M. just as soon as he has become responsible in the daytime. It may be possible to hasten night dryness a bit in this way, since a bladder that is emptied in the evening is not so full in the early morning. Some children wake easily in the evening and perform readily. Others are hard to wake or have trouble performing or become very upset. I think that if the parents run into any trouble, they should call it off.

The One-Year-Old

WHAT MAKES HIM TICK

399. Feeling his oats. One year old is an exciting age. Your baby is changing in lots of ways—in his eating, in how he gets around, in what he wants to do and in how he feels about himself and other people. When he was little and helpless, you could put him where you wanted him, give him the playthings you thought suitable, feed him the foods you knew were best. Most of the time he was willing to let you be the boss, and took it all in good spirit. It's more complicated now that he is around a year old. He seems to realize that he's not meant to be a baby doll the rest of his life, that he's a human being with ideas and a will of his own.

When you suggest something that doesn't appeal to him, he feels he must assert himself. His nature tells him to. He just says No in words or actions, even about things that he likes to do. The psychologists call it "negativism"; mothers call it "that terrible No stage." But stop and think what would happen to him if he never felt like saying No. He'd become a robot, a mechanical man. You wouldn't be able to resist the temptation to boss him all the time, and he'd stop learning and developing. When he was old enough to go out into the world, to school and later to work, everybody else would take advantage of him, too. He'd never be good for anything.

400. The passion to explore. He's a demon explorer. He pokes into every nook and cranny, fingers the carving in the furniture, shakes a table or anything else that isn't nailed down, wants to take every single book out of the bookcase, climbs onto anything he can reach, fits little things into big things and then tries to fit big things into little things. A tired-out mother calls this "getting into everything," and her tone of voice says that he's a nuisance. She probably doesn't realize what a vital period this is for him. A baby has to find out about the size and shape and movableness of everything in his world and test out his own skill before he can advance to the next stage, just the way he'll have to go through the grades before he can go to high school. That he "gets into everything" is a sign that he's bright in mind and spirit.

Incidentally, you've probably realized by now that he is never quiet while he's awake. It isn't nervousness—it's eagerness. He's made that way so that he will surely keep learning and practicing all day long.

AVOIDING ACCIDENTS AND FEARS

401. One year is a dangerous age. Parents cannot prevent all accidents. If they were careful enough or worrisome enough to try, they would only make a child timid and dependent.

On the other hand, a great majority of serious accidents can be easily prevented if you know where the common dangers lie and are sensible in avoiding them. Here is a list:

Low chair-table combinations are safer than **high chairs**. If you use a high chair, it should have a broad base so that it won't tip, a harness to hold a climbing baby, a latch to keep him from raising the tray. A **baby carriage** should have a harness for a baby who has reached the climbing age. There should be gates at the top and sometimes at the bottom of **stairs**, including porch stairs, until the child can go up and down steadily. Upstairs **windows** should have guards, or be opened only at the top.

It is not wise to let a baby be crawling or a small child be walking around the **kitchen** during the cooking or serving of meals. There is danger from spattering grease, from the mother's tripping and spilling something hot, from the child's pulling a pot off the stove. This is the best time for the playpen or a pen made by laying chairs on their sides, or for his chair. His chair or pen should be well away from the stove. A baby can reach a surprising distance when he tries. Get in the habit of turning **pot handles** away from the front of the stove. When serving the meal, put a coffeepot or other **hot container** in the middle of the table. Avoid tablecloths that hang over the edge and so can be pulled off.

A baby or small child who still puts things in his mouth should not have small objects like buttons, beans, peas or beads to play with, or nuts or popcorn to eat, because they are easily breathed into the windpipe and cause choking. Take away a pencil or other sharp object if a small child keeps it in his mouth when he plays or runs.

As a matter of habit, always feel the temperature of a bath just before you put a child in, even if you remember doing it earlier. Hot faucets sometimes cause burns. Don't touch, or let a child touch, electrical equipment while in a bath or while holding onto a faucet. Don't leave pails of hot water on the floor.

Electric cords should be in first-class condition. Train the baby not to chew them. There are plug locks to keep wall plugs from being pulled. Cover unused wall outlets with "plug ups" made for that purpose. There are wall outlets in which the holes close automatically when a plug is pulled out. Put bulbs into empty lamp sockets if they are within reach.

There are door stops and safety knobs that will keep children from opening forbidden doors, and adaptable latches and locks for medicine and kitchen cabinets.

Keep matches in containers in high places that are impossible for even a determined 3- or 4-year-old to reach.

Keep dangerous tools and power tools out of reach. Keep children far away from a rotary lawn mower; better still, trade it in.

Never leave a small child unattended in a bathtub.

Be extremely cautious in backing a car down the driveway.

Wells, pools, cisterns should be well protected. Even shallow pools are dangerous.

At the beach or lake a child should wear a life jacket whenever he is not in bed, until he can swim a hundred feet.

Use a safety belt for a child in a car, even on short trips, and don't let him stand up on the seat.

Put broken glass, opened cans, into a covered hard-to-open receptacle. Use a can with a slot in the top for used razor blades.

Don't let a baby go close to strange dogs at an age when he is likely to startle or hurt them.

402. Now's the time to put poisons out of reach. A fifth of all accidental poisonings occur in the second year of life. Children in this exploring and tasting age will, when the spirit moves them, eat almost anything, no matter how it tastes. They especially love pills, good-tasting medicines, cigarettes and matches. You will be surprised to read the list of the substances that most frequently cause dangerous poisoning in children:

Aspirin and other drugs
Insect and rat poisons
Kerosene, gasoline, benzene and cleaning fluids
Lead in paint that a child has chewed off something.
(Most indoor paint and toy paint contains no lead. The danger is from outdoor paint on windowsills, porches, etc., and from outdoor paint that has been used at home to repaint toys, cribs and other furniture.)
Liquid furniture and auto polish
Lye, alkalis used for cleaning drains, bowls, ovens
Oil of wintergreen
Plant sprays

Now is the time to inspect your house with an eagle eye—or, rather, a baby's eye. Put all **medicines** safely out of reach **immediately after each use.** Put bold additional, clear labels on all medicines so that you won't use the wrong one. Throw away medicine after an illness is over. It's unlikely you'll use it again. It may deteriorate anyway. It's confusing to have old medicines mixed in with others still in use. Don't ordinarily change a medicine to another container. But you can buy a "child proof container" (complicated to open) in which to keep aspirin or other pills, capsules often used, especially for the children.

Don't change **any** substance from the container it came in to a container in which something else comes: plant spray in a Coke bottle, for instance, or oven cleaner in a cup. This is a frequent cause of serious accidents.

Somewhat dangerous in the bathroom are shampoos, hair tonics, home permanent and beauty preparations.

Find inaccessible places in the kitchen and utility room for cleaning fluids and powders, detergents, drain, bowl and oven cleaners, ammonia, washing soda, bleach, wax remover, metal polish, borax, mothballs, lighter fluid, shoe polish. Get rid of rat poisons, insect pastes and poisons—they are too dangerous.

In the basement or garage find truly safe places for turpentine, paint thinners, kerosene, gasoline, benzene, insecticides, plant sprays, weed killers, antifreeze, car cleaners and polishes. When discarding containers, be sure that they are completely empty and then rinse them.

403. Protect him from frightening sounds and sights. A baby at a year may become fascinated with one thing for several weeks on end—for instance, the telephone, or planes overhead, or electric lights. Let him touch and become familiar with objects that are not dangerous or disturbing. However, in some cases the child is half frightened of the object. Then it's wiser for the parents not to play up to his interest, or if it's something dangerous, not to dwell on the danger. Better to distract him with something else than to increase his awe.

At this age a baby may be frightened by strange objects that move suddenly or make a loud noise, such as folded pictures that pop up from a book, the opening of an umbrella, a vacuum cleaner, a siren, a barking, jumping dog, a train, even a vase of rustling branches.

Try not to have these startling things too close to a 1-year-old until he gets used to them. If the vacuum cleaner bothers him, don't use it for a few months, at least while he is indoors. Then try it the first time when he is some distance away.

404. Fear of the bath. Between 1 and 2 years, a child may become frightened of the bath, because of slipping under water, or getting soap in his eyes, or even seeing and hearing the water go down the drain. To avoid soap in the eyes, soap with a washcloth that is not too wet and rinse several times with a damp but not dripping washcloth. There are also special shampoos for children that don't sting the eyes. If he becomes afraid to get into the bathtub, don't force him at all. You can try a dishpan, but if he's afraid of that, give him a sponge bath for several months, until he gets back his courage. Then start with an inch of water and remove him before you pull the stopper.

If your baby, toward the end of the first year, begins to fight having the food washed off his face and hands with a cloth after meals, set a pan of water on the tray in front of him and let him dabble his hands while you wash his face with your wet hand.

Fear of strangers is discussed in Sections 358 and 407, fear of the flushing toilet in Section 382.

INDEPENDENCE AND OUTGOINGNESS

405. He gets more dependent and more independent at the same time. This sounds contradictory. A mother complains of a year-old baby, "He's getting to cry every time I go out of the room." This doesn't mean that he is developing a bad habit, but that he's growing up and realizing how much he depends on his mother. It's inconvenient, but it's a good sign.

But at the very age when he is becoming more dependent, he is also developing the urge to be on his own, discover new places, make up to unfamiliar people.

Watch a baby at the creeping stage when his mother is washing the dishes. He plays contentedly with some pots and pans for a while. Then he gets a little bored and decides to explore in the dining room. He creeps around under the furniture there, picking up little pieces of dust and tasting them, carefully climbing to his feet to reach the handle of a drawer. After a while he seems to feel the need of company again, for he suddenly scrambles back into the kitchen. At one time you see his urge for independence getting the upper hand, at another the need for security. He satisfies each in turn. As the months go by he becomes more bold and daring in his experiments and explorations. He still needs his mother, but not so often. He is building his own independence, but part of the courage comes from knowing he can get security when he feels he needs it.

I am making the point that independence comes from security as well as from freedom, because a few people get it twisted around backward. They try to "train" independence into a child by keeping him in a room by himself for long periods even though he is crying for company. I think that when the issue is being forced this hard, a child is not learning anything very good.

So the baby at around a year is at a fork in the road. If he's given a chance, he gradually becomes more independent: more sociable with outsiders (grown-ups and children), more self-reliant, more outgoing. If he's confined a great deal, kept away from others, used to having only his mother hovering over him (Section 503), he is apt to become tied to her apron strings, more timid with strangers, wrapped up in himself. How is independence encouraged?

Let him out of the carriage when he can walk. When a baby has learned to walk, it's time to let him out of his carriage on his daily outings. Never mind if he gets dirty; he should. Try to go to a place where you don't have to be after him every minute and where he can get used to other children. If he picks up cigarette butts, you have to jump, take them away and show him something else that's fun. You can't let him eat handfuls of sand or earth because it irritates his intestines and may give him worms. If he puts everything in his mouth, try giving him a hard cracker or some clean object he likes to chew on, to keep his mouth busy. Keeping an ablebodied walking baby tucked in his carriage may keep him out of trouble, but it cramps his style and hinders his development. Some parents find a harness is very practical for shopping and walks at this age. It shouldn't be used for hitching him in one place for long.

406. Let him out of the playpen when he insists. One child is willing to stay in the playpen, at least for short periods, as late as a year and a half. Another thinks it's a prison by the time he's 9 months. Most like it well enough until they learn to walk, around the age of a year and a quarter. I'd say let your baby out of the pen when he feels unhappy there. I don't mean at the first whimper, for if you give him something new to play with, he may be happy there for another hour. Outgrowing the pen is a gradual process. At first he gets sick of it only after a long spell. Gradually he gets impatient earlier. It may be months before he objects to being put in at all. In any case, let him out each time he's sure he's had enough.

407. Get him used to outsiders. At this age a baby's nature tells him to be leery and suspicious of strangers till he has had a chance to look them over. But then he wants to get closer and eventually make friends, in a 1-year-old fashion, of course. He may just stand close and gaze, or solemnly hand something to the newcomer and then take it back, or bring everything movable in the room and pile it in the person's lap.

Many adults don't have the sense to let a small child alone while he sizes them up. They rush up to him, full of talk, and he has to retreat to his mother for protection. Then it takes longer for him to work up his courage to be friendly. I think it helps for a mother to remind a visitor in the beginning, "It makes him bashful when you pay attention to him right away. If we talk for a while, he'll try to make friends sooner."

Let him out when he's had enough.

When your baby is old enough to walk, give him plenty of chances to get used to strangers and make up to them. Take him to the grocery store a couple of times a week. If possible, take him every day where other small children play. He isn't able to play with them yet, but at times he wants to watch. If he is used to playing near them now, he will be ready for cooperative play when the time comes, between 2 and 3. If he's never been around other children by 3, it will take him months just to get used to them.

HOW TO HANDLE HIM

408. He's very distractible, and that's a big help. The year-old baby is so eager to find out about the whole world that he isn't particular where he begins or where he stops. Even if he's all absorbed in a ring of keys, you can make him drop it by giving him an egg beater. His distractibility is one of the handles by which his wise parent guides him.

409. Arranging the house for a wandering baby. When you tell a mother that her baby has outgrown the playpen or the crib and that she ought to let him on the floor, she is apt to look unhappy and say, "But I'm afraid he'd hurt himself. At least he'd wreck the house." Sooner or later he must be let out to roam around, if not at 10 months, at least by 15 months, when he's walking. And he's not going to be any more reasonable or easier to control then. At whatever age you give him the freedom of the house, you have to make adjustments, so it's better to do it when he is ready.

How do you keep a year-old baby from hurting himself or the household furnishings, anyway? First of all, you can arrange the rooms where he'll be so that he's allowed to play with three-quarters of the things he can reach. Then only a quarter have to be forbidden. Whereas, if you try to forbid him to touch three-quarters of the things, you will drive him and yourself mad. If there are plenty of things he can do, he's not going to bother so much about the things he can't do. Practically speaking, this means taking breakable ashtrays and vases and ornaments off low tables and shelves and putting them out of reach. It means taking the valuable books off the lower shelves of the bookcases and putting the old magazines there instead. Jam the good books in tight so that he can't pull them out. In the kitchen, put the pots and pans on the shelves near the floor and put the china and packages of food out of reach. One mother filled a lower bureau drawer with old clothes, toys and other interesting objects and let the baby explore it, empty it, fill it, to his heart's content.

410. How do you make him leave certain things alone? This is the main problem between 1 and 2 years. There are always a few things that you have to teach him to let alone. There have to be lamps on tables. He mustn't pull them off by their cords or push tables over. He mustn't touch the hot stove, or turn on the gas, or crawl out a window.

411. "No" isn't enough at first. You can't stop him by just saying "No," at least not in the beginning. Even later, it depends on your tone of voice and how often you say it and whether you really mean it. It's not a method to rely on

heavily until he has learned from experience what it means—
and that you mean it. Don't say "No" in a challenging voice
from across the room. This gives him a choice. He says to
himself, "Shall I be a mouse and do as she says, or shall I
be a man and grab the lamp cord?" Remember that his
nature is egging him on to try things and to balk at directions.

Better to remove and distract him than just to say, "No, no!"

The chances are he'll keep on approaching the lamp cord
with an eye on you to see how angry you get. It's much
wiser, the first few times he goes for the lamp, to go over
promptly and whisk him to another part of the room. You
can say "No" at the same time to begin teaching him what it
means. Quickly give him a magazine, an empty cigarette box,
anything that is safe and interesting. There's no use tossing
him a rattle that he was bored with months ago.

Suppose he goes back to the lamp a few minutes later? Remove him and distract him again, promptly, definitely, cheerfully. Say, "No, no," at the same time that you remove him, adding it to your action for good measure. Sit down with him for a minute to show him what he can do with the new plaything. If necessary, put the lamp out of reach this time, or even take him out of the room. You are tactfully but firmly showing him that you are absolutely sure in your own mind that the lamp is not the thing to play with. You are keeping away from choices, arguments, cross looks, scoldings—which may not do the job and which are likely to get his back up.

You might say, "But he won't learn unless I teach him it's naughty." Oh, yes, he will. In fact, he can accept the lesson more easily if it's done in this matter-of-fact way. When you disapprovingly waggle a finger from across the room at a baby who hasn't yet learned that no really means no, your crossness rubs him the wrong way. It makes him want to take a chance on disobeying. And it's no better if you grab him, hold him face to face, and give him a talking-to. You're not giving him a chance to give in gracefully or forget. His only choice is to surrender meekly or to defy you.

I think of a Mrs. T. who complained bitterly that her 16-month-old daughter was "naughty." Just then Suzy toddled into the room, a nice girl with a normal amount of spunk. Instantly Mrs. T. looked disapproving and said, "Now remember, don't go near the radio." Suzy hadn't been thinking of the radio at all, but now she had to. She turned and moved slowly toward it. Mrs. T. gets panicky just as soon as each of her children in turn shows signs of developing into an independent person. She dreads that she won't be able to control them. In her uneasiness, she makes an issue when there doesn't need to be any. It's like the person learning to ride a bicycle who sees a rock in the road ahead. He is so nervous about it that he keeps steering right for it.

Take the example next of a baby who is getting close to a hot stove. A mother doesn't sit still and say, "No-o-o," in a disapproving voice. She jumps and gets him out of the way. This is the method that comes naturally if she is really trying to keep him from doing something, and not just engaging in a battle of wills.

412. Take lots of time or be masterful. A mother of a 1¾-year-old boy takes him with her every day to the grocery store. But she complains that instead of walking right along, he wanders up the walk and climbs the front steps of every house they pass on the way. The more she calls to him, the more he lingers. When she scolds him, he runs in the opposite direction. She is afraid he is turning into a behavior problem. This baby isn't a behavior problem, though he may be made into one. He's not at an age when he can keep the grocery store in mind. His nature says to him, "Look at that walk to explore! Look at those stairs!" Every time his mother calls to him, it reminds him of his new-felt urge to assert himself. What can the mother do? If she has to get to the store promptly, she can take him in his carriage. But if she's going to use this time for his outing, she should allow four times as long as if she were going alone, and let him make his side trips. If she keeps moving slowly, he'll want to catch up to her every once in a while.

Here's another tight spot. It's time to go in for lunch, but your small child is digging happily in the dirt. If you say, "Now it's time to go in," in a tone of voice that means, "Now you can't have any more fun," you get resistance. But if you say cheerfully, "Let's go climb the stairs," it may give him a desire to go. But suppose he's tired and cranky that day, and nothing that's indoors makes any appeal. He just gets balky right away, disagreeably balky. I'd pick him up casually and carry him indoors, even if he's squealing and kicking like a little pig. You do this in a self-confident way, as if you were saying to him, "I know, you're tired and cross. But when we have to go in, we have to." Don't scold him; it won't make him see the error of his ways. Don't argue with him, because that won't change his mind; you only get yourself frustrated. A small child who is feeling miserable and making a scene is comforted underneath by sensing that his mother knows what to do without getting angry.

413. Dropping and throwing things. Around the age of 1 year, a baby learns to drop things on purpose. He solemnly leans over the side of his high chair, and drops food on the floor, or tosses his toys, one after the other, out of his crib. Then he cries because he hasn't got them. An irritated mother is apt to think he's deliberately making a monkey out of her. But he isn't thinking of her; he is fascinated by a new skill. He wants to do it all day long, the way a boy wants to ride his new two-wheeler. If you pick up the object, he realizes it's a game that two can play and is more delighted. It's better not to get in the habit of picking up his dropped toys

Dropping is a new skill.

right away. Put him on the floor or ground when he gets in this mood. You can tie his favorite bed toys to the slats of his crib on strings a foot long. (A baby may become dangerously entangled in a long string.) Tie others to his carriage. You don't want him throwing food out of the high chair in any case, but he won't start until his appetite is pretty well satisfied. Take the food away promptly and firmly when the dropping begins, and put him down to play. Trying to scold a baby out of dropping things leads to nothing but frustration for the mother.

NAP HOURS ARE CHANGING

414. Naptimes are shifting in most babies around the age of a year. One who was taking a nap at about 9 A.M. may refuse it altogether or show that he wants it later and later in the morning. If he takes it late, he is unready for his next nap until the middle of the afternoon, and this probably throws off his bedtime after supper. Or he may refuse the afternoon nap altogether. A baby may vary a lot from day to day at this period, and even go back to a 9 A.M. nap that he has refused for 2 weeks, so don't come to final conclusions too soon. You have to put up with these inconveniences as best you can, realizing that they are temporary. With some babies who are not ready to sleep in the first part of the morning, you can remove the need for the before-lunch nap by putting them in their beds anyway, around 9 in the morning, if they are willing to lie or sit quietly for a while. Of course, another kind of baby only gets in a rage if put to bed when not sleepy, and nothing is accomplished.

If a baby becomes sleepy just before noon, it's the mother's cue to move lunch up to 11:30 or even 11 for a few days. Then the long nap comes after lunch. But for a while after a baby has cut down to 1 nap a day, whether morning or afternoon, he may get frantically tired before suppertime. As a doctor friend of mine put it, "There's a stage in a baby's life when 2 naps are too many and 1 is not enough." You can help your baby through this period by giving him his supper and putting him to bed for the night a little earlier for the time being.

Don't get the idea from this section that all babies give up their morning nap in the same way or at the same age. One is through with it at 9 months; another craves it and benefits by it as late as 2 years.

HE'S APT TO CHANGE HIS EATING HABITS

415. He gets more choosy for several reasons. Somewhere around a year a baby is apt to change his feeling about his food. He becomes more choosy and less hungry. This is not surprising. If he kept on eating and gaining the way he did when he was a little baby, he'd turn into a mountain.

Now he seems to feel that he has time to look the meal over and ask himself, "What looks good today and what doesn't?" What a contrast to his behavior at 8 months! In those days he felt he was starved to death when mealtime came around. He'd whimper pathetically while his mother tied his bib, and lean forward for every bite. It wouldn't matter much what she was serving him. He was too hungry to care.

There are other reasons, aside from not being so hungry, that make him choosy. He's beginning to realize that he's a separate person with ideas of his own, so he becomes definite in his dislikes of a food that he was doubtful about before. His memory is getting better, too. He probably realizes, "The meals here are served up pretty regularly, and they stay around long enough for me to get what I want."

Teething often takes away a child's appetite, especially when the first molars are on their way. He may eat only half his usual amount for days, or occasionally refuse an entire meal. Finally, and perhaps most important, there is the fact that appetite naturally varies from day to day and week to week. We grown-ups know that one day we grab a big glass of tomato juice and another day split pea soup looks better. It is the same way with children and babies. But the reason you don't see this variation more often in infants under a year is that most of the time they are too hungry to turn anything down.

416. Dr. Davis' experiments in appetite. Dr. Clara Davis wanted to find out what children would eat if left to their own desires and given a variety of wholesome foods to choose from. She didn't start with older children for fear they would have already developed prejudices about food. So she picked three babies, 8 to 10 months old, who had never had anything to eat but breast milk. She took them to live at a place where they could be watched carefully. And this is how they were fed: At each meal a nurse would place before them 6 or 8 serving dishes containing a variety of wholesome, unrefined foods. There were vegetables, fruits, eggs, cereals, meats, whole-grain bread, milk, water and fruit juices. The nurse was told, "Don't help the baby till he shows you what he wants." The 8-month-old baby would lean forward and dip his fist into a dish of beets and then try to eat it off his hand. Now the nurse was permitted to give him a teaspoonful of beets. Then she must wait until he showed his choice again. Another spoonful of beets or maybe applesauce.

Dr. Davis discovered three important things. First, babies who chose their own diet from a variety of natural foods developed very well; none of them got too fat or too thin. Second, every baby, over a period of time, chose what any scientist would agree was a well-balanced diet. Third, from meal to meal and day to day, the appetite varied a lot. Each separate meal wasn't well-balanced. For several meals in a row a baby might feed largely on greens. Then he would change about and go more heavily for starches. Sometimes he would go on a real jag and, for instance, make a whole meal of nothing but beets, perhaps four times as much beets as a grownup would consider a polite amount. And after this spree he wouldn't vomit, he wouldn't have a belly ache or diarrhea. A baby would sometimes drink as much as a quart of milk in addition to his full meal, and at the next meal want very little milk at all. One baby, on several occasions, ate as many as 6 hard-boiled eggs in addition to a full meal. Dr. Davis kept track of the beef intake of a baby over a period of many days. He would go along for a while eating an average portion of beef, and then his appetite for beef would begin to increase. He might work up to four times as much beef as we would ordinarily think proper, keep up that rate for several days, and then taper off. The way this craving for beef gradually increased and then decreased suggested to Dr. Davis that there was a real bodily need for something in that beef that influenced the appetite for days. Dr. Davis eventually carried out the experiment with many older children, too, even hospital patients, and found that the results were just as good.

417. What parents can learn from Dr. Davis. The good results from this experimental method of feeding don't prove that a mother ought to serve her child 6 or 8 dishes at each meal, like the hors d'œuvres in a Swedish restaurant. But it does show that she can trust an unspoiled child's appetite to choose a wholesome diet if she serves him a reasonable variety and balance of those natural, unrefined foods **that he enjoys eating at present.** It means that she can let him eat larger amounts than usual of a food his appetite craves without worrying about the consequences. Even more important, it means that she doesn't have to worry when he develops a temporary dislike of a vegetable.

It is hard for us moderns to have this kind of confidence in our children's appetites. We have heard so much about what the scientists say we ought to eat that we have forgotten that our bodies have known a lot about this for millions of years. Each kind of caterpillar knows for sure what sort of leaves it can eat and refuses all others. The deer travels for miles to the salt lick when his body craves salt. The robin knows what is good for him without ever attending a lecture. It is not surprising that man should also have some instinctive knowledge of what is good for him. I don't mean that a child or grown-up will always eat what's best for him, and I don't mean that parents don't need to know what makes a balanced diet. If a mother doesn't know any better than to offer her child only doughnuts and coffee at every meal, there is no chance for him to pick a well-balanced diet out of this selection, no matter how sound his instincts are. It is important for a mother to know the value of vegetables, fruits, milk, meat, eggs, whole-grain cereal, so that she can offer her child a variety that covers all his needs. But it is just as important for her to know that her child's instincts are sound to start with, that his appetite naturally varies, that he will probably try to pick a well-balanced diet in the long run if he isn't given too many prejudices.

418. Let him give up certain vegetables for a while. If he suddenly turns against the vegetable that he loved last week, let him turn against it. If you don't make a fuss today, he will probably come back to it next week or next month. But if you insist on his taking it when he seems to dislike it, you only make him set his mind that that particular food is his enemy. You turn a temporary dislike into a permanent hate. If he turns down the same vegetable twice in succession, leave it out for a couple of weeks. It is naturally irritating to a mother to buy a food, prepare it, serve it and then have it turned down by an opinionated wretch who loved the same thing a few days ago. It is hard for her not to be cross and bossy at such a time. But it is worse for the child's feeling about food to try to force or urge it. If he turns down half his vegetables for a while, as is common in the second year, serve him the ones that he does like. This is the wise and pleasant way to take advantage of the great variety of fresh and canned vegetables that we have. If he turns against all vegetables for a while but loves his fruit, let him have extra fruit. If he is taking enough fruit, milk and his vitamin drops, he is not missing anything that's in vegetables. (See Section 443 for vegetable substitutes.)

419. What to do if he is tired of cereal. Many babies get fed up with cereal sometime in the second year, especially for supper. Don't try to push it in. There are many substitutes you can offer, which are discussed in Sections 445 and 446. Even if he gives up all starches for a few weeks, it won't hurt him.

420. Don't be alarmed if he wants less milk at times. Milk is a very valuable food. It provides good amounts of most of the elements that are important for a child's diet, as is explained in Section 437. But it is helpful to remember that in the parts of the world where there are no cows or goats, children get these substances from other foods after their nursing period is over. It's also good to know that an average of a pint and a half (24 ounces) a day safely covers the needs of almost every child between 1 and 3 who is taking a reasonable diet otherwise. Many children between the ages of 1 and 2 want to cut down to this amount or less, at least temporarily. If a parent worries and sets to work to urge or force a larger amount, the child is apt to become steadily more disgusted. In the long run, he takes less milk than if he had been let alone.

Don't keep offering the cup again after he has shown that he's not interested. Every time he has to decline it makes him more determined he doesn't want it. If he drops down to an average of 8 ounces, wait a few days and see if he doesn't increase again.

If he goes on drinking less than a pint and a half, there are many other ways that milk can be used in the diet; these are discussed in Section 438. Milk in any of these forms is just as nutritious as when it comes straight from the cow.

If a child goes on for a month averaging less than a pint and a half of milk in all forms, the mother should report it to the doctor. He may prescribe calcium in some other form until the child's appetite for milk comes back.

421. Be wary of feeding problems now. The reason for discussing the natural variations in a child's appetite at this age is an important one. Feeding problems start more commonly between 1 and 2 years than at any other period. Once a child becomes balky, once a mother becomes worried and angry, the fat's in the fire. The more the mother frets and urges, the less the child eats. And the less he takes, the more anxious the mother is. Meals become agonizing. The problem may last for years. The tension that grows up between parent and child causes other behavior problems, too.

The best way to keep your child eating well is to let him go on thinking of food as something he wants. Allow him to eat a larger than usual amount of one wholesome food, less or none of another, if that's the way he feels. When making up his meals, select a well-balanced diet, but select it from among the wholesome foods that he really enjoys. Expect his taste to change from month to month. If you cannot consult a doctor about additions to his diet, look ahead to Sections 437–447 for new foods and those to substitute for the ones he is leaving out temporarily.

The chances are great that if you don't make a battle of it, your child will eat a reasonably balanced diet from week to week, though it may be somewhat lopsided from meal to meal or day to day. If it stays unbalanced for weeks, you should discuss the problem with a doctor, even if it is difficult to reach him.

422. Standing and playing at meals. This may be quite a problem even before the age of a year. It comes about because the baby is less ravenous for his food, more interested in all kinds of new activities, like climbing, handling the spoon, messing in the food, tipping the cup upside down, dropping things on the floor. I've seen a 1-year-old fed a whole meal standing up backward in the high chair, or even being followed around the house by a long-suffering mother with a spoon and dish in her hands.

Fooling at meals is only a sign that a child is growing up and that his mother is sometimes more keen about his eating than he is. It's inconvenient and irritating, and it's apt to lead to feeding problems, too. I wouldn't let it go on. You'll notice that the child climbs and plays when he's partly or completely satisfied, not when he's really hungry. So whenever he loses interest in his food, assume he's had enough, let him down from his chair and take the food away. It's right to be firm, but you don't need to get mad. If he immediately whimpers for his meal, as if to say he didn't mean he wasn't hungry, give him one more chance. But if he shows no regret, don't try to give him the meal a little later. If he gets extra hungry between meals, give him a little more than usual at his between-meal feeding, or give him his next regular meal early. If you always stop the meal casually when

Time to finish the meal.

he loses interest, he will do his part by paying attention when he is hungry.

Now I want to make a reservation. A baby around a year has a powerful urge to dip his fingers into the vegetable, or squeeze a little cereal in his hand, or stir a drop of milk around on the tray. This isn't fooling. He may be opening his mouth eagerly for food at the same time. I wouldn't try to stop the meal for this alone, and I wouldn't try to stop him from experimenting just a little bit with the feel of his food. But if he tries to turn the dish over, hold it down firmly. If he insists, keep it out of reach for a while or stop the meal.

423. Let him feed himself early. The age at which a baby feeds himself depends largely on the adult's attitude. Dr. Davis, in her experiments on what diets babies choose, found that some infants were efficiently spoon-feeding themselves before the age of a year. At the other extreme, an over-protective mother swears that her 2-year-old couldn't possibly feed himself at all. It all depends on when you give him a chance.

Most babies show an ambition to manage the spoon by a year, and if they have opportunity to practice, a lot of them can do a good job without help by 15 months.

A baby gets some preparation for spoon-feeding way back at 6 months, when he holds his own zwieback and other finger foods. Then at around 9 months, when he gets chopped foods, he wants to pick up the pieces and put them in his mouth. The baby who has never been allowed to feed himself with his fingers is apt to be delayed in taking to spoon-feeding.

Feeling is learning.

A polite baby of 10 to 12 months may just want to rest his hand on his mother's when she's feeding him. But most babies, when the urge comes, try to yank the spoon out of their mother's hand. A mother may think this has to be a tug of war, but she can give the baby that spoon and get another to use herself. The baby soon discovers that it's more complicated than just getting possession of the spoon. It takes him weeks to learn how to get a speck of food on the spoon, and weeks more to learn not to turn it upside down between the dish and his mouth. He becomes bored with trying to eat, and stirs or slops the food instead. Then it's time to move the dish out of reach, perhaps leaving a few crumbs of meat in front of him for him to experiment with.

Even when he's trying very hard to feed himself correctly, he makes plenty of accidental messes, and this you've got to put up with. If you're worried about the rug, put a big plastic tablecloth under his chair. It helps to use a hot-water plate with partitions. This keeps his food warm, is harder for him to pick up, and has straight sides to push the food against. Baby spoons with looped handles are meant to be easy to hold, but I think they are more difficult than small spoons with straight handles.

There is now a spoon in which the bowl swivels in the handle so that it will stay level.

If he can feed himself, let him take over completely. Now we come to the most important point. It isn't enough to let the baby have a spoon and a chance to use it; you've got to gradually give him more **reason** to use it. At first he tries because he wants to do things for himself. But after he sees how complicated it is, he's apt to give up the whole business if **you keep on rapidly feeding him anyway.** In other words, when he begins to be able to get a speck to his mouth, you ought to let him have a few minutes alone with the food, at the beginning of the meal when he's hungriest. Then his appetite urges him on. The better he gets at feeding himself, the longer he should have at each meal to do it.

By the time he can polish off his favorite dish in 10 minutes, it's time for you to be out of the picture. This is where mothers often go wrong. They say, "He can eat his own meat and fruit all right now, but I have to feed him his vegetable, potato and cereal still." That's a little risky. If he's able to manage one food, he has skill enough to manage the others. If you go on feeding him the ones he doesn't bother with, you build up a sharper and sharper distinction between the foods **he** wants and the foods **you** want him to take. In the long run, this takes away his appetite for **your** foods. But if you put thought into serving as well-balanced a diet as possible from among the foods he is presently enjoying and let him feed himself entirely, the chances are great that he will strike a good balance from week to week, even though he may slight this or that food at certain meals.

Don't worry about table manners. A baby wants to eat more expertly, more neatly, all by himself. He wants to graduate from fingers to spoon and from spoon to fork, as soon as he feels equal to the challenge, just as he wants to try everything else difficult that he sees others doing. Dr. Davis noticed this in the babies she was observing, and they weren't coached at all. She pointed out that puppies show the same urge to learn eating manners without teaching. In the beginning, they stand in a pan of milk and dip their faces. First, they learn to keep their feet out; next, to lap the milk without dipping their faces; finally, to lick their whiskers politely at the end.

I have been making quite a point about letting a child learn to feed himself somewhere between the ages of 12 and 15 months, because that is the age when he wants to try. Suppose a mother keeps a baby from doing it at this age, and then at 21 months declares, "You big lummox, it's time for you to feed yourself." Then the child is apt to take the attitude, "Oh no! It's my custom and my privilege to be fed." He's now reached a more advanced stage, when trying to manage a spoon is no longer exciting. In fact, his whole sense of what's proper rebels against it. His mother has lost the golden opportunity.

Don't take this all so seriously that you think there is only one right age, or worry because your baby is not making sufficient progress, or try to force him to feed himself when he's not ready or not eager. That would only create other problems. I'm only making the point that babies want to learn this skill earlier than many mothers realize, and that it is important for the parent to gradually give up feeding as the child is able to take over.

Elements in the Diet

Before we talk about the everyday foods that children can eat, we ought to discuss the more important chemical substances that foods are composed of, and what the body uses them for.

You can compare a child's body, in one way, to a building under construction. A lot of different materials are needed to build it and to keep it in repair. But a human being is also a machine that's running. It requires fuel for energy, and other substances to make it work properly, just as an automobile needs gasoline, oil, grease, water.

PROTEIN

424. Protein is the main building material of the body. The muscles, heart, brain, kidneys, for instance, are largely made of protein (aside from water). The structure of bones is protein, filled in with minerals, much the way a collar is made stiff with starch. The child needs good food protein to continually increase the size of every part of his body, and also to repair wear and tear.

Most natural foods contain protein, some much, some little. Meat, poultry, fish, eggs, milk are the foods richest in it. They are the only foods that supply "complete proteins"—that is to say, they contain the complete variety of protein elements the human body needs. That is why a child should be averaging a pint and a half of milk daily and also receiving either meat (or poultry or fish) or eggs daily, preferably both. Next in importance are the proteins in whole-grain cereals, nuts and mealy vegetables (soy and other beans, peas). These grain and vegetable proteins are only fair in amount and are "incomplete." Whole wheat, for example, contains some essential protein elements; beans contain others. If a child is eating a variety of whole grains and vegetables, they will supplement the proteins from his meats, fish, eggs, milk, but will not take their place.

MINERALS

425. Minerals of many kinds play a vital part in the structure and in the working of every part of the body. The hardness of bones and teeth depends on calcium and phosphorus. The substance in red blood cells that carries the oxygen to all regions of the body is made partly of iron and copper. Iodine is necessary in the functioning of the thyroid gland.

All natural unrefined foods (fruits, vegetables, meats, whole grains, eggs, milk) contain a variety of valuable minerals. But the refining of grains and the prolonged cooking of vegetables in a lot of water removes a great deal. The minerals most likely to be insufficient in the diet are calcium, iron and, in certain areas, iodine. Calcium occurs in small amounts in vegetables and some fruits, but plentifully in milk (and cheese). Iron (to prevent anemia) is supplied by green, leafy vegetables, meats, fruits, whole grains, but more abundantly by egg yolk and liver. Iodine is missing in some inland regions where the drinking water, vegetables and fruits lack it, and seafood is not available. Table salt is iodized for people in those areas, to prevent goiter.

VITAMINS

Vitamins are special substances that the body needs in minute amounts in order to work right, somewhat the way any machine needs a few drops of oil, or a gasoline motor depends on a tiny electric spark.

426. Vitamin A is necessary to keep healthy the linings of the bronchial, intestinal and urinary systems, and various parts of the eyes, including that which enables us to see in dim light. The body gets it plentifully from milk fat, egg yolk, green and yellow vegetables, vitamin drops. Probably the only

people who receive too little are those on really bad diets or those who cannot absorb it because of serious intestinal disease. These people may be subject to bad colds because of the deficiency. There is no reason to believe, though, that the person on a decent diet will catch fewer colds by taking more and more vitamin A.

427. Vitamin B complex. Scientists used to think that there was just one vitamin B, which had several actions in the body. But when they studied "it," it turned out to be a dozen different vitamins. However, these mostly occur in the same foods. Since the B vitamins are not yet all known or understood, it is more important for people to eat plenty of the natural foods they mostly occur in than to take them separately in pill form. The four known to be most important for human beings are called by their chemical names now: thiamin, riboflavin, niacin, pyridoxine. Every tissue in the body needs these four vitamins.

Thiamin (B_1) occurs in fair amounts in whole grain, milk, eggs, liver, meat and certain vegetables and fruits. It is destroyed by long cooking, especially when soda is used. People are apt to receive an insufficient supply of it when they eat a lot of refined starches and sugars. Lack of thiamin can cause poor appetite, slow growth, fatigue, stomach and intestinal troubles, neuritis. (However, there are many different causes of all these symptoms, and thiamin deficiency is not the most common one.)

Riboflavin (also known as B_2) occurs abundantly in liver, meat, eggs, milk, green vegetables, whole grains, yeast. So a deficiency is only likely if a person's diet consists mainly of refined starches and sugar. Deficiency causes cracks in the corners of the mouth and other lip, skin, mouth and eye troubles.

Niacin (nicotinic acid) occurs abundantly in about the same foods as riboflavin. Deficiency causes mouth, intestinal and skin troubles (it looks like a chronic sunburn which turns rough and scaly) which are part of the disease called pellagra.

Pyridoxine (B_6) is widely distributed among foods, so symptoms of deficiency (neuritis, convulsions, anemia, rash) occur only in the rare individual who has an inherited need of extra amounts.

Cobalamine (B₁₂) is widely distributed among animal foods, including milk, but absent in the vegetable kingdom. Deficiency causes pernicious anemia.

428. Vitamin C (ascorbic acid) occurs most abundantly in oranges, lemons, grapefruit, raw and properly canned tomatoes and tomato juice, raw cabbage. It occurs in fair amounts in several other fruits and vegetables, including potatoes. It is included in many vitamin preparations. It is easily destroyed in cooking. It is necessary for the development of bones, teeth, blood vessels and other tissues, and plays a part in the functioning of most of the cells in the body. Deficiency is commonest in babies living on cow's milk without orange or tomato juice or vitamin C medicine, and shows itself in painful hemorrhages around the bones and in swollen, bleeding gums. This condition is called scurvy.

429. Vitamin D is needed in large amounts for growth, particularly of the bones and teeth. It helps get calcium and phosphorus, which are in the food in the intestines, absorbed into the blood and deposited in the growing parts of the bones. That's why it should be added to the diet of children, especially in the period of rapid growth in infancy. Ordinary foods contain only a small amount. The suns rays shining on the fat in people's skins manufacture vitamin D right there, and that's how they naturally get it when they live outdoors and wear few clothes. When they live in colder climates, they cover up their bodies with clothes and live indoors. The sun's rays in these regions are more slanting and are shut off by soot in the air and by window glass. Various fish liver oils and synthetic preparations are then the best source of vitamin D. (Fish store it in their livers by eating minute plants that float on the surface of the ocean. Sunshine manufactures it in these plants.) Vitamin D deficiency results in soft, bent bones, poor teeth, weak muscles and ligaments. This is called rickets.

Fully grown people probably receive enough vitamin D from the small amounts in eggs, butter, fish, and from a little sunshine. But the child who is not getting lots of sunshine should drink milk containing vitamin D, or take a special preparation of vitamin D, summer and winter, until he has reached his full height in adolescence. Mothers need extra vitamin D during pregnancy and breast feeding.

WATER AND ROUGHAGE

430. Water provides no calories or vitamins, but it is vitally important in the makeup and working of the body. (A baby's body is 60% water.) A child should have a chance to drink water once or twice in each between-meal period, more often in hot weather. Most foods are largely composed of water, too, and that is how people receive part of their daily needs.

431. Roughage means the fibers in vegetables, fruits and grains (bran, for instance) that our intestines can't digest and absorb. The roughage passes on in the bowel movement, unused in one sense but useful in another. It provides part of the bulk in the bowel contents that helps to stimulate the intestines to function. If a person stays on a bland diet, let's say milk and broth and eggs, he is apt to become constipated from having too little substance left in his lower intestines.

FATS, STARCHES, SUGARS

432. Fuel. So far we have discussed the building materials of the body and the other substances that are necessary to make the system work right. But we haven't considered fuel. The body, being a sort of engine, requires constant fueling just as an automobile needs gasoline. When a person is asleep, the heart still beats, the intestines contract, the liver, kidneys and other organs keep working. This is like an automobile in neutral with the motor idling. When the person wakes up, moves around, works, runs, he burns more fuel just as the automobile does. Most of the food a child eats is used up daily for fuel, even when he is growing rapidly.

The fuel substances are starch, sugar, fat (and, to a slight degree, protein). A starch is composed of a chemical combination of sugars. In the intestines, it is broken up into sugars before it is absorbed into the body. Because starches and sugars are so closely related, they are lumped together under the term **carbohydrates.**

433. The body's fat. When a person eats more fat, sugar, starch and protein than he needs for fuel, the extra is converted into fat and stored under his skin. When he is eating too little "fuel," he uses up some of his own fat and becomes thinner. This "fat pad," which all people have to a greater or lesser degree, serves not only as a storehouse of fuel but helps, like a blanket, to keep a person warm.

434. Calories. The fuel value of food is measured in calories. Water and minerals have no calories—that is, they have no fuel or energy in them. Fat is rich in calories; an ounce of it has twice as many as an ounce of starch, sugar or protein. Butter, margarine, vegetable oil, which are almost entirely fat, and cream and salad dressings, which contain a lot of it, are therefore very high in calories.

Sugars and syrups are also very high in calories, because they are wholly carbohydrates and contain no water or undigestible roughage.

Grains (which we eat as cereals, breads, crackers, macaroni, puddings, etc.) and starchy vegetables (such as potatoes, beans, corn) are high in calories because of the large proportion of starch in their makeup.

Meats, poultry, fish, eggs, cheese are high in calories because of their combination of protein and fat. Most of us do not receive as many daily calories from these foods as we do from grains and starchy vegetables, because we eat them in smaller amounts. Milk is a fine source of calories because of its sugar, fat and protein and because it is easily taken in good amounts.

Fresh and stewed fruits in general provide a fair number of calories because of the natural sugar they contain. Bananas and dried fruit are richer (comparable to potatoes).

Vegetables vary from moderately high to low in calories (mostly in the form of starch and sugar). The vegetables with a moderately high number of calories are white and sweet potatoes, corn, and such beans as soy, navy, baked and lima. The vegetables that provide a fair number of calories are peas, beets, carrots, onions, parsnips, squash, beet greens. Vegetables low in calories are string beans, cabbage, cauliflower, celery, eggplant, spinach, tomatoes, lettuce, Swiss chard, broccoli, asparagus.

SENSIBLE DIET

435. Keep a balanced attitude. You don't judge foods on calories alone, or on vitamins alone, or on minerals alone. Everybody in the long run needs a balance of low- and high-calorie foods as he needs a balance in other respects in his diet. If a person takes one aspect of diet too seriously and forgets the others, it's apt to lead to trouble. An adolescent girl acquires a fanatical zeal to reduce, leaves out all the foods in which she has heard there are more than a few calories, tries to live on vegetable juices, fruit and coffee. She is bound to be sick if she keeps on. A serious-minded mother who has the mistaken idea that vitamins are the whole show and that starches are inferior serves her child carrot salad and grapefruit for supper. The poor fellow can't get enough calories out of that to satisfy a rabbit. A plump mother from a plump family, ashamed of her child's scrawniness, serves him only rich foods. These depress his appetite further. Taking them in small amounts, he is apt to be deprived of minerals and vitamins.

436. A simple guide to diet. The whole business of diet sounds complicated, but it needn't be. Fortunately, a mother doesn't have to figure out the perfect diet for her child. The experiments of Dr. Davis and others have shown that the child's own appetite seeks a well-balanced diet in the long run (Section 416), provided he hasn't been urged or given prejudices against foods, and provided he is offered a reasonable variety of wholesome, natural, unrefined foods. The parents' job is to have a general idea of the kinds of foods that combine to make a good diet, and which ones can be substituted for those that the child has lost his taste for. Roughly speaking, the following are required every day:

1. Milk (in any form), preferably 1½ to 2 pints.
2. Meat or poultry or fish.
3. Egg (extra egg can partially substitute for meat and vice versa, though it is desirable to give both).
4. Vegetable, green or yellow, 1 or 2 times, some of it raw.
5. Fruit, 2 or 3 times, at least half of it raw, including orange juice (extra fruit can substitute for vegetable and vice versa).
6. Starchy vegetable, 1 or 2 times.
7. Whole-grain bread, crackers, cereals, 1 to 3 times (enriched starches can be substituted occasionally).
8. Vitamin D (in milk or in drops).

Now we are ready to discuss actual foods.

Foods and Meals

What foods should be added to a child's diet and at what age are individual matters that his doctor should decide. It depends on how his digestion has handled various foods in the past, which ones he is refusing, which ones are available in the market.

This chapter is for the benefit of parents who are unable to consult a doctor regularly and have to depend on their own knowledge over long periods of time. If you are in this situation, use all your common sense. Avoid the idea that there is an exact age for a certain food. Start new foods gradually even in the second year. Go slow and play safe with the child who has bowel upsets easily.

Feeding Your Baby and Child, by Benjamin M. Spock, M.D., and Miriam E. Lowenberg, Ph.D.,[1] has many recipes and practical suggestions.

MILK

437. Milk after a year. Milk contains almost all the food elements that a human being needs: protein, fat, sugar, minerals and most of the vitamins. Children who are taking a well-balanced diet except for milk are likely to get enough of most of these elements from other foods. The exception is calcium. Milk is the only food that contains a lot of it. That is why you would like a child to average between 1½ and 2 pints a day, in some form.

Remember, though, that many children want less one day

[1]Duell, Sloan & Pearce, New York, 1955, $3.95. Pocket Books, New York, 1956, 50c.

or one week, more the next, and that the surest way to keep
them liking it is to let them take less temporarily when they
feel that way. If your child cuts down, don't urge him. If he
isn't back to a pint and a half in a few weeks, think of all the
other ways you can serve milk.

438. Substitutes for plain milk. Precooked and dry
cereals absorb a lot of milk in preparing. There are all the
milk puddings from junket to rice pudding. Vegetable and
chicken soups can be mixed with milk instead of water. Baked
macaroni, scalloped and mashed potatoes, and many other
cooked dishes can be made with milk.

What about flavoring milk? It is better to avoid flavoring
if the child takes a reasonable amount of milk in other forms.
But if necessary, milk can be made into cocoa or hot chocolate,
or served cold, flavored with a little chocolate syrup. However, chocolate upsets some small children, so it is preferable
to delay it until the age of 2, and to start very gradually. Milk
can be flavored with vanilla or any of the commercial cereal-
and-malt preparations sold for this purpose. With any flavoring, avoid making the milk really sweet, for fear of spoiling
the appetite. Sipping a drink through a straw or glass tube
may make it seem like a treat.

A flavored drink is likely to lose some of its appeal, anyway, when the novelty wears off. This is especially apt to
happen if the mother begins to urge it the first time the child
takes less than a glassful. It can't be repeated too often that
when a parent says, "Drink a little more of your chocolate
milk" (or anything else), it begins to take away a child's
appetite.

Cheese is a useful form of milk. An ounce of most varieties
contains about the same amount of calcium as 8 ounces of
milk. But there are two important exceptions. You need three
times as much cream cheese (3 ounces) to supply the amount
of calcium in an 8-ounce glass of milk. Cottage cheese provides still less; in fact, it takes 10 ounces of cottage cheese to
supply the calcium in 8 ounces of milk.

Cottage cheese, having little fat, is the most easily digested,
and so it can be eaten in larger amounts, salted or mixed with
grated raw vegetables or a little jelly. Other cheeses, being
rich in fat, should be started gradually, and the child will
probably want only small amounts. They can be served as
spreads, or grated into other foods, or in pieces.

If a child doesn't want to take milk in any form (or is allergic to it), he should be receiving calcium in some other form that the doctor prescribes.

Butter or fortified margarine should be added very gradually to vegetables and to bread around the age of a year. Top milk can also be introduced slowly on cereal, puddings, fruits, for the child who is hungry. The digestive system needs time to adjust to increased amounts of fat.

MEATS, FISH, EGGS

439. Meats. Most babies by the age of a year will be eating ground or fine-minced beef, chicken, lamb, liver, bacon, veal, pork when these are served to the rest of the family, or they can continue having them as junior foods from jars or cans. Bacon contains little protein so should not be counted on regularly as a meat. Most of the fat should be trimmed off pork. Pork is an excellent source of vitamins. It should be thoroughly cooked, so that it is white all through, not pink. Incompletely cooked pork is the source of the dangerous disease trichinosis. Better wait until 2 before beginning ham (not fried) or beef frankfurters.

Many young children who love the taste of meat turn against it if it isn't cut up or ground finely enough. They become a little frightened and gag easily at lumps that don't easily turn to mush. So continue to mince fine or grind your child's meats until he is 5 or 6.

440. Fish of the white, nonoily varieties, such as cod, haddock, halibut, flounder, can be started cautiously at the age of a year, baked, boiled or broiled. It should be carefully crumbled with the fingers to remove bones. The more oily fish and canned fish may be added gradually at 2. Some children love fish, and then it makes a fine substitute for meat once or twice a week. But many others stay firmly opposed even after several trials. Don't urge it.

441. Eggs. Eggs are equally valuable hard-boiled, soft-boiled, scrambled, fried, cooked into foods, or served in drinks. It is desirable for a child to have an egg a day if he likes them, for protein and iron. He can have 2 eggs a day if desired.

If a child dislikes most meats and fish, or you cannot get them, his protein needs will probably be covered by 1½ to

2 pints of milk and 2 eggs a day, since he is getting some protein in his whole grains and vegetables.

If a child dislikes eggs or is allergic to them, it is more important for him to have meat regularly.

VEGETABLES

442. Varieties of vegetables. The baby during his first year has probably had most of the following vegetables: spinach, peas, onions, carrots, asparagus, chard, squash, tomatoes, beets, celery, potatoes.

Before a year the change should have been made gradually from pureed to a coarser, lumpy consistency. (Naturally, some pureed and finely mashed vegetables can still be served.) Peas should be mashed slightly to avoid their being swallowed whole.

Sweet potatoes or yams can be used at times instead of white potatoes, beginning at a year. If you have been sticking to the easily digested vegetables up to the age of a year, you can try gradually the less popular and sometimes less digestible ones, such as lima beans (mashed), broccoli, cabbage, cauliflower, turnips, parsnips. Much of their strong taste can be removed by changing the cooking water twice, though this destroys some of the vitamins. Some children like them and digest them well, but many won't touch them. Wait until 2 years to serve corn in the kernel. Young children don't chew it; it comes through unchanged. Use only tender corn. When cutting it off the cob, don't cut too close. Then each kernel will be cut open. At 3 or 4, when you start corn on the cob, slice down the center of each row of kernels, so that they are all open.

The more easily digested raw vegetables are usually started between 1 and 2 years for the child with a good digestion. The best are peeled tomatoes, lettuce, sliced string beans, shredded carrots, scraped chopped celery. They should be well scrubbed. Go slow at first and see how they are digested. Orange juice or sweetened lemon juice, with a little salt, can be used for dressing.

Raw vegetable juices can be started at the same time. Raw vegetables and vegetable juices are not only as good as cooked vegetables for the child who digests them well—they are better, because the vitamins have not been partly destroyed by heat, and minerals and vitamins have not been dissolved out in the cooking water.

If a child has temporarily turned against plain vegetables, remember vegetable soups: pea, tomato, celery, onion, spinach, beet, corn, and the soups that contain a large amount of mixed vegetables.

443. Temporary substitutes for vegetables. Suppose a child has refused vegetables in any form for weeks. Will his nutrition suffer? Vegetables are particularly valuable for various minerals and vitamins, and also for roughage. But a variety of fruits supply many of the minerals and vitamins, and the same amount of roughage. If the child is taking vitamin drops, milk, meat and egg, he is getting the other salts and vitamins that fruits do not provide so well. In other words, if your child dislikes all vegetables but likes fruits, don't fuss about what he is missing. Serve him fruit 2 or 3 times a day and forget about vegetables for a few weeks or even months. If you don't make an issue of them, the chances are great that his appetite will swing around to them again in time.

FRUITS

444. Fruits. A baby during his first year has probably had stewed or canned applesauce, apricots, prunes, pears, peaches, pineapple and raw, ripe banana, apple, pear, avocado. By a year some of these should be served in a lumpy consistency. Canned fruits, such as pears, peaches, pineapple, put up for adults are not so desirable for children because they are heavily sweetened with syrup. At least, pour the syrup off.

Raw fruits, such as oranges, peaches, apricots, plums, seedless grapes, are usually added between the ages of 1 and 2 years for children with a good digestion. They should be thoroughly ripe. Peel them until the child is 3 or 4 years old. When the peel is left on, the fruit should be washed to remove chemicals used in spraying.

It is usually recommended to wait until the age of 2 to add cherries and raw berries (strawberries, raspberries, blackberries, blueberries, huckleberries, loganberries). Strawberries sometimes cause a rash. Small children swallow berries whole and pass them that way, so mash them until your child chews well. Remove cherry pits until he can separate them in his mouth. At whatever age you start berries, start gradually and stop if they cause upsets.

Cantaloupe, honeydew melon, watermelon can be started cautiously at 2. Begin with small amounts, mashed.

Dried fruits, such as prunes, apricots, figs, dates, can be given unstewed at 2, chopped in salads or whole for nibbling. They should be well washed unless the package states they are ready for eating raw. These dried fruits stick to the teeth for a long time, so they should not be used frequently.

CEREALS AND SUPPERS

445. Cereals. A baby at a year can be, and probably is, taking one or a variety of the precooked cereals, and also cooked oatmeal and cooked whole wheat cereals that the rest of the family eats. If he likes these, continue to serve them once or twice a day indefinitely.

Remember that young children like their foods either firm or else quite soft and runny. They are apt to dislike pasty consistencies. So keep cereal mixtures thin.

If your child gets bored with one, try another that he may not have been so keen about before. You can also serve occasionally boiled unpolished rice, hominy or one of the refined wheat cereals.

There are also all the dry cereals, which offer variety and may be appealing because older children are eating them. Whole wheat and oat cereals are the most valuable ones, because they are rich in vitamins and minerals. (Corn and rice are less valuable.)

446. Breads are cereals. If a child is sick of his ordinary cereal for breakfast, you can give him bread, toast, roll or bun made of whole, cracked, or enriched wheat, rye, oatmeal, or banana bread. A cereal in baked form is just as valuable as one that has been boiled. The fact that it is not hot makes no difference in its food value or digestibility. Spread with butter or margarine (starting with a small amount for the 1-year-old). You can also spread with pureed fruit or a light touch of marmalade if it makes the bread more appealing.

447. Lunch or supper, whichever is the simpler meal. In the family in which I was brought up the young children had a light supper at 5:30 and were in bed by 6:45. Then our parents had a quiet, dignified dinner. When I practiced pediatrics in New York City, most of the families for whom I was doctor followed this same pattern. So I automatically think of supper as the light meal for children. This is generally not true, for throughout most of this country the children have their main meal in the evening with their parents; for them lunch is the light meal.

Many mothers complain that they get in a rut about lunch or supper, can't think how to vary it. A good rough rule is to serve:

1. A filling dish with plenty of calories, and
2. Either a fruit or vegetable.

Breads and sandwiches of several kinds can be the filling dish as the baby grows older. When he's only a year old, he makes slow work of bread, and he always pulls a sandwich apart to get at the filling. But nearer to 2 years, he can handle these well. You can use rye bread, whole wheat bread, oatmeal bread, enriched white bread, banana bread to start with, and by the age of 2 add pumpernickel, nut bread. Spread with a little butter, margarine, cottage or creamed cheese. You can add a touch of jam, jelly, marmalade, honey, or a few grains of brown sugar for flavor if this is necessary to make the sandwich appealing, but I wouldn't put on a thick layer of any of these sugary substances. Sandwiches can be made with a wide variety of other foods, plain or in combination: raw vegetable (lettuce, tomato, grated carrot or cabbage), stewed fruit, chopped dried fruit, peanut butter, egg, canned fish, minced poultry and meats. Cheese can be used as a spread or grated, and later in thin slices. Creamed cheese or, after the age of 3, a little mayonnaise can be combined with many of the substances listed above.

A fairly substantial dish for occasional use is a broth or soup containing lots of barley, rice or noodles; or a vegetable soup, plain or creamed, with a couple of handfuls of toast cut into small cubes to toss in.

A poached or coddled or scrambled egg can be given (in addition to or instead of the breakfast egg) on toast or with toast crumbled into it. Or serve with crackers or bread on the side.

Simple crackers, preferably whole wheat, can be served plain, or with a spread, or in a bowl of hot or cold milk. (Graham crackers have few calories.) Bread and toast in slices or pieces, salted, can also be served in a bowl of cold or hot milk.

Potato is a good filling dish if the child is fond of it. Macaroni, spaghetti or noodles can be used occasionally.

Cooked, precooked or dry cereal for supper can be made more appealing by adding sliced raw fruit, stewed fruit, chopped dried fruit or a little brown sugar, honey or molasses.

Instead of a filling first course followed by stewed or raw fruit, you can occasionally serve first a cooked green or yellow vegetable, or a vegetable or fruit salad. Then follow with a milk-pudding dessert: custard, baked or boiled; rice, tapioca, bread or cornstarch pudding; occasionally ice cream for the older child. A banana makes an excellent filling dessert.

There are some children who never want and never seem to need much starch. They are able to get enough calories from milk, meats, fruits, vegetables to gain weight reasonably. They also get their B-complex vitamins from these foods. In other words, grains and other starches are the things you least need to worry about in your child's diet. Let him go without them for weeks if he is doing well otherwise.

LESS VALUABLE AND UNDESIRABLE FOODS

448. Cookies, cakes, rich crackers, pastries. The main objection to these foods is that they are largely composed of refined starch, sugar and fat. Being rich in calories, they quickly satisfy a child's appetite, but give him practically no salts, vitamins, roughage or protein. They are sometimes called "deprived" foods. They cheat a child by making him feel well fed when he is being partly starved, and by spoiling his appetite for better foods.

You don't have to be so suspicious of rich, refined foods that you stop your child from eating cake at a birthday party. It's the steady diet of such foods that deprives him of nutrition. But there's no sense starting them at home when there is no need.

Filled pastries, such as custard and cream pies, éclairs, cream puffs, have an additional danger. Harmful bacteria grow readily in these fillings if they are not kept well refrigerated. They are a frequent cause of food poisoning.

449. Highly sweetened foods are also undesirable in the diet. They quickly satisfy the appetite, take it away for better

foods and favor decay of the teeth. If a child likes his cereal
and fruits without extra sugar, by all means leave it off. If a
thin sprinkle of sugar or a few drops of honey or molasses
make a big difference, let him have it without an argument.
But be cheerfully firm about not letting him pour it on thick.
Jellies, jams, most canned fruits (except those put up for
babies) contain excessive amounts of sugar, and it's best not
to get in the habit of serving them. If a child enjoys his bread
and butter only when there is jam on it, put on just enough
to flavor it. If occasionally it is convenient to give him canned
peaches because the rest of the family is having them, pour
off the syrup. Raisins, dates, dried prunes and figs are also
believed to be hard on the teeth when eaten regularly because they stick to the teeth for such a long time.

450. Candy, sodas, sundaes, being sweet, "deprived"
foods, bring up special problems because they are often eaten
between meals, when they have their worst effect on appetite
and teeth, and because so many other children are eating
them. There is no reason why a child of 2 years or more
shouldn't occasionally have a serving of good ice cream or a
piece of candy at the end of a meal when the rest of the
family is enjoying it. But it's better to avoid sweets between
meals as much as possible, and to avoid candy regularly even
at the end of meals. Candy, particularly, is suspected of
favoring decay of the teeth because it keeps the mouth syrupy
for some time.

It's easy enough to keep **young** children from the candy
habit by not having it around the home, and to avoid sodas
and sundaes by not buying them. It is more difficult with the
school-age child who has found out all about these delights.
A mother hates to make her own child an exception or a sissy.
If he has the desire only once in a while, it's probably best to
let him be one of the boys. But if he craves sweets, and especially if he has teeth that decay easily, it's better for the
parents to limit him strictly to special occasions.

451. Craving for sweets is often caused by parents.
Children like sweets, for one reason, because their hungry,
growing bodies recognize the extra calories in them. But it is
not certain that unspoiled children want a lot of them. A few
small children actually dislike all sweet foods. Dr. Clara
Davis in her experiments in letting children choose their own
diets from a variety of **natural** foods found that in the long

run they wanted only a reasonable amount of the sweeter foods.

I think much of the exaggerated craving for sweets is caused unwittingly by parents. A mother, trying to get her child to finish his vegetable, says, "You can't have your ice cream until you've finished your spinach," or, "If you eat up all your cereal, I'll give you a piece of candy." When you hold back on food (or a prize of any kind), it whets the desire. This has exactly the opposite effect from what the mother wants: the child gets to despise spinach and cereal, and to want ice cream and candy more and more. I'd say jokingly that the only safe way to bribe a child about food is to say, "You can't have your spinach until you've eaten your ice cream." Seriously, though, never hold back on one food until another is eaten. Let your child go on thinking his plain foods are just as good as his sweet ones. If one day he catches sight of his dessert first and asks for it, let him have it right away, willingly.

452. Corn, rice and refined wheat are less valuable than whole wheat and oats. Corn and rice are relatively low in vitamins and valuable proteins (even before they are refined) compared with oats, rye and whole wheat. And when any grain is refined, much of its vitamins, minerals and roughage are removed in the process. Therefore, the foods to serve less frequently are refined (white) wheat cereals, white bread that is not enriched, macaroni, spaghetti, noodles, crackers (aside from whole wheat crackers), rice, corn meal, corn cereals, hominy. Then there are the desserts made from these grains: cornstarch, rice, tapioca puddings. When rice is used for cereal, puddings and as a substitute for potato, it is better to use the unpolished brown rice. Enriched white bread has had some of the original B-complex vitamins restored, but it does not contain all the values in whole wheat bread.

You may think that I am exaggerating the dangers of refined sweets and starches. I certainly don't want to turn you into a food crank who scolds his friends for serving white bread or who haunts the health-food stores looking for raw and coarse substances to munch. But there are plenty of children who get their daily carbohydrates somewhat as follows: Breakfast—a white cooked cereal (with lots of sugar) and a slice of white toast with jam. Lunch—macaroni, white bread and jam. Midafternoon—ice cream soda. Supper—corn flakes, cakes and a cornstarch pudding. Even if such a child is also taking vegetable, fruit, meat and milk, he is still getting two-thirds of his nourishment in a "deprived" form.

453. Coffee and tea are not good drinks for children because they take the place of milk and because they contain the stimulant caffeine. Most children are stimulated enough already. Flavoring a child's milk with a tablespoonful of coffee or tea may be justified if he likes it **only** in that pretend grown-up way. But in the case of most children, it's easier and safer not to get started with these beverages.

FROZEN FOODS

454. Frozen foods are just as good for children as fresh and canned foods, if used correctly. Freezing a food breaks it down chemically, just as cooking it does. It is then in a state in which both people and germs can digest it better. In other words, a cooked or a frozen food spoils more rapidly than an ordinary raw food because poisonous bacteria can live and multiply in it more easily.

Foods that spoil easily when kept long out of the refrigerator are milk, foods made with milk (puddings, pastry, fillings), vegetables, poultry, stuffing.

FEEDING BETWEEN MEALS

455. Use common sense between meals. Many young children, and some older ones, too, need a snack between meals. If it's the right kind of food, given at a sensible hour, presented in the right way, it shouldn't interfere with meals or lead to feeding problems.

Fruit juice, fruit and vegetable juice are easily and quickly digested and are least likely to favor tooth decay. Milk stays in the stomach much longer and is therefore more apt to take away appetite for the next meal. Occasionally, though, you see a child who never can eat very much at one meal and gets excessively hungry and tired before the next, he may thrive when given milk between meals. Its slow digestibility is what keeps him going, and he has a better appetite for the next meal because he's not exhausted.

Cakes, cookies and pastry have three disadvantages; they are rich in calories, poor in other food values and hard on the teeth. Even crackers and bread stick to the teeth for some time, and so are not ideal for a regular between-meal diet.

For most children the snack is best given midway between meals, or not closer than 1½ hours before the next one. Even here there are exceptions. There are children who receive juice in the middle of the morning but still get so hungry and cross before lunch is ready that they pick fights and refuse to eat. Getting a glass of orange or tomato juice the minute they get home, even though it is 20 minutes before lunch, improves their disposition and their appetite. So you see that what and when to feed between meals is a matter of common sense and doing what suits the individual child. Plenty of children can get along without any food between meals, and this is best of all for the teeth.

A mother may complain that her child eats badly at meals but is always begging for food between meals. This problem doesn't arise because a mother has been lenient about food between meals. Quite the contrary. In every case that I have seen, the mother has been urging or forcing the child to eat at mealtime and holding back on food at other times. It's the pushing that takes away his appetite at meals. After months of it the very sight of the dining room is enough to make his stomach revolt. But when the meal is safely over (though little has been eaten), his stomach feels natural again. Soon it's acting the way a healthy empty stomach is meant to act—it's asking for food. The treatment, then, is not to deny the child food between meals but to let mealtime be so enjoyable that his mouth waters then, too. What is a meal? It's food specially prepared to be appetizing. When a child finds it less appealing than snacks, something has gone wrong.

MEALS

456. Suggested guide for meals.
Breakfast
  1. Fruit or fruit juice
  2. Cereal
  3. Egg
  4. Milk

Lunch (or supper)
1. A filling dish, such as:
    cereal
        or bread or sandwiches
        or potato
        or soup with crackers, toast, barley, rice, noodles, etc.
        or an egg dish with toast
        or (less frequently) a pudding, macaroni or spaghetti
2. Vegetable or fruit, raw or cooked
3. Milk

Dinner (or lunch)
1. Meat or fish or poultry (or extra egg)
2. Green or yellow vegetable (cooked or raw)
3. Potato
4. Raw fruit, occasionally a pudding
5. Milk

Vitamin preparation daily
Fruit, or tomato juice between meals if needed
Bread (whole-grain) at meals if desired

Managing Young Children

PLAY AND OUTGOINGNESS

457. Play is serious business. When we see children building with blocks, pretending to be airplanes, learning to skip rope, we're apt to think, in our mixed-up, adult way, that these are just amusements, quite different from serious occupations such as doing lessons and holding a job. We are mixed up because most of us were taught in our own childhood that play was fun but that schoolwork was a duty and a job was a grind.

The baby passing a rattle from one hand to the other or learning to crawl downstairs, the small boy pushing a block along a crack on the floor, pretending it's a train, are hard at work learning about the world. They are training themselves for useful work later, just as much as the high school student studying geometry. A child loves his play, not because it's easy, but because it's hard. He is striving every hour of every day to graduate to more difficult achievements and to do what the older kids and grown-ups do.

The mother of a 1-year-old complains that he gets bored with hollow blocks and only wants to fit pots and pans together. One reason is that he knows already that his mother plays with pots and pans and not with blocks. That makes pots and pans more fun. It must be for this reason that 1-year-olds are fascinated with cigarettes.

458. Simple toys are best. Children usually love simple toys best and play with them longest. This isn't because children are simple—it's because they have so much imagination. There are two very different kinds of toy trains. One is made of metal painted to look real, and it's meant to run on a track. The other is made of plain, flat wooden blocks that link together easily. All that the **young** child can do with the realistic train is push one car along the floor. It's too hard to put the cars on the track or hitch them together. He can't even put anything in the passenger coach until the top breaks off. After a while he gets bored. The wooden block cars are different. He can link a string of them together and admire his long train. Two make a trailer truck. He can pile small blocks on top, call it a freight train, and make deliveries. When he is bored with dry land, the blocks become separate boats or a string of barges with a tug. He can go on like this forever.

Sometimes parents with little money to spend feel sad that they can't buy a shiny automobile for their youngster to pedal or a playhouse. But think what a child can do with a packing box. By turns it's a bed, a house, a truck, a tank, a fort, a dolls' house, a garage. Don't take this idea so seriously that you never get your child a really fine plaything. The time will come when he wants a three-wheel bike or an express cart with all his heart, and you will want to buy it for him if you can. I only mean that simple things come first. Add the fancier toys as you can afford them and as you find out what he really enjoys.

The baby, before he can use his hands, loves to watch bright-colored objects that hang on a string tied across the sides of his crib and that move slightly in the draft. In the last half of the first year, he loves objects to handle and rattle and chew, such as the newer plastic toys (small rings on a big ring, for example). There's no paint to come off, and there's no danger from chips, as there is with thin celluloid toys.

Around a year to a year and a half, the child is fascinated with putting one thing into another, and pushing or pulling it around. The block that runs on four wheels and has holes for pegs is a favorite, but a plain box with a string is as good. As a matter of fact, pushing comes before pulling, and that's why the bell on wheels, pushed with a stick, is so popular. Hollow blocks don't interest him so long as pots, pans, strainers and spoons.

Soft dolls and woolly animals are loved by most children throughout the early years. Others see no sense in them.

As the child gets toward the age of 2, he's more interested in copying. First, it's the immediate things that his mother and father do, like sweeping, washing dishes and shaving. As he grows beyond 2, his imagination becomes more creative. This is the period for dolls and dolls' furniture, trucks and cars, and above all, blocks. Blocks piled on top of each other are the Empire State Building; end to end they make a train. They can be laid out on the floor in the outline of a house or boat to sit in, and so on indefinitely. A good-size bag of wooden blocks of different shapes is worth ten toys to any child up to 6 or 8.

459. Let children play at their own level. A grown-up playing with a child often is tempted to make the play too complicated. A mother who has bought her small daughter a doll with a whole wardrobe of clothes would like to dress the doll just right, beginning with the underclothes. But the little girl may want to start with the red overcoat. A mother buys her small, sick boy a box of crayons and a book of outline pictures to color. He picks up an orange crayon and rubs it back and forth across the page, not trying to keep within the lines, not worrying that he's using orange for sky and grass. It's hard for a parent not to say, "Oh, no, not like that. See, you do it this way." Or a father who has never had enough chance to play with trains produces a whole set for his 3-year-old at Christmas. The father can't wait to get started. He fits the tracks together. But the boy has grabbed one of the cars and has shot it across the room, smack against the wall. "No, no!" says Father. "You put the car on the track like this." The child gives the car a push along the track, and it falls off at the curve. "No, no," says Father. "You have to wind up the engine and let the engine pull the car." But the poor child hasn't the strength to wind up the engine or the skill to put the cars on the track. He doesn't care about realism yet. After his father has been impatient with him for 15 minutes, he gets a strong dislike for tin trains and an uncomfortable feeling that he can't measure up to his father's expectations. He wanders off to do something that he can enjoy.

A child becomes interested in dressing dolls properly, coloring carefully, playing trains realistically, each at a certain stage of his development. You can't hurry him. When you try, you only make him feel incompetent. This does more harm than good. Your child loves to have you play with him if you are willing to play at his level. Let him show you how. Help him if he asks for it. If you've bought him a toy that is too complicated, either let him misuse it in his own way or tactfully hide it until he's older.

460. Generosity can't be forced. When children begin to play around each other at 1½, 2, 2½, they are apt to grab things from each other without much ceremony. The small child who has a possession never gives it up to be nice. He either hangs on like grim death, perhaps whacking at the attacker, or he gives it up in bewilderment. Mothers, seeing these goings on, are sometimes horrified.

If your child, around 2, always seems to be the grabber, it doesn't mean that he's going to be a bully. He's too young to have much feeling for others. Let him grab sometimes. If he's doing it constantly, it may help to let him play part of the time with slightly older children who stand up for their rights. If he always intimidates a certain child, better keep them separated for a while. If your child is hurting another or looks as if he were planning murder, pull him away in a matter-of-fact manner and get him interested in something else. It's better not to heap shame on him—that only makes him feel abandoned, and more aggressive.

If a child goes on being unusually aggressive when he's 3 or older and doesn't seem to be learning anything about co-operative play, it's time to look into his adjustment at home. It's in these early, less serious problems that a good children's psychiatrist (either a private doctor or one in a child-guidance clinic) can help a parent and child most easily and most thoroughly (Section 577).

If your child at 2 doesn't give up his possessions, he is behaving normally for this age. He will come around to generosity very gradually, as his spirit grows up and as he learns to enjoy and love other children. If you make him give up his treasured cart whenever another child wants it, you only give him the feeling that the whole world is out to get his things away from him—not just the children but the grown-ups, too. This makes him more possessive, instead of less. When a child is reaching the stage when he's beginning to enjoy playing with others, somewhere around 3, you can help to make a game of sharing. "First Johnny has a turn pulling the cart and Catherine rides in it. Then Catherine pulls the cart and Johnny has a turn to ride in it." This makes sharing fun instead of an unpleasant duty. Timidity is discussed in Section 464.

461. Helping a first child to be outgoing. Most first children grow up happy and well adjusted like most second and third and fourth children in a family. But a few of them have a harder time adjusting to the outside world.

A mother is apt to say, "The second baby is so easy. He doesn't cry. He is rarely a serious problem. He plays contentedly by himself, and yet he is so friendly if you go near him." When he's several years older, the mother says, "The second is such a friendly, outgoing child that everybody just naturally loves him. When we're walking down the street, strangers smile at him and stop us to ask how old he is. They only notice the older one afterward, to be polite. You can see that it hurts the older one's feelings. He craves attention much more than the second."

What makes the difference? One trouble is that the first baby in some families gets more fussing over than is good for him, especially after the age of 6 months, when he begins to be able to amuse himself. The parents may be noticing him, suggesting things to him, picking him up, more than is necessary. This gives him too little chance to develop his own interests. He too seldom makes the first greeting, because the parents are speaking to him first. He may be shown off to other grown-ups too much. A little of this is harmless; a steady diet of it makes him self-conscious. When the first child is sick, the parents naturally hang over his bed with more concern and anxiety than they will after they have had longer experience. When he is naughty, they are more apt to take it seriously and to make a fuss about it.

A steady flow of fussy attention toward a child tends to spoil him somewhat for the outside world in two ways. He grows up assuming that he is the hub of the universe and that everyone should automatically admire him whether he is being attractive or not. On the other hand, he hasn't been practicing how to make his own fun or how to be outgoing and appealing to people.

Of course, the answer is not to ignore a first child. He needs affection and responsiveness in good measure. But let him play his own games as long as he is interested and happy, with the least possible interference, bossing, scolding and anxious concern. Give him a chance to start the conversation sometimes. When visitors come, let him make up to them himself. When he comes to you for play or for affection, be warm and friendly, but let him go when he turns back to his own pursuits.

Another factor that sometimes seems to make a first child unsociable is too serious an attitude on the parents' part. It isn't that the parents are grim people; they can be easygoing with their friends and their later children. They are just trying too hard with the first.

You know what I mean if you have ever seen a tense person trying to ride a horse for the first time. He sits stiff as a china doll, doesn't know how to accommodate to the horse's movements and is apt to be unnecessarily bossy. It's hard work for the horse and the rider. The experienced rider knows how to relax, how to give in and conform to some of the horse's motions without losing his seat, how to direct the horse gently. Bringing up a child isn't much like riding a horse, but the same spirit works in both jobs.

A similar example is the young officer or executive who is put in charge of other people for the first time. If he isn't too sure of himself, he may be unnecessarily solemn and strict in the beginning, for fear he won't keep control. The more experienced person isn't afraid to be friendly and reasonable.

You may say, "The trouble is that I am inexperienced." But you don't have to have experience to do a wonderful job with a baby—all you need to start with is a friendly spirit. A child won't throw you the way a horse might (at least not until he's much older), and he won't laugh at you the way a squad of men might. Don't be afraid to relax, to be agreeable. Better too easygoing than too stiff.

EARLY CHILDHOOD

462. The control of aggression. Is pistol play good or bad for boys? For many years I emphasized its harmlessness. When a thoughtful mother expressed doubt about letting her son have pistols and other warlike toys, because she didn't want to encourage him in the slightest degree to become a delinquent or a militarist, I would explain how little connection there was: In the course of growing up, a child has a natural tendency to bring his aggressiveness more and more under control provided his parents encourage this. A 1- to 2-year-old, when he's angry with another child, may bite his arm without hesitation. But by 3 or 4 he has already learned that crude aggression is not right. However, he likes to pretend to shoot a pretend Indian. He may pretend to shoot his mother or father, but he grins to assure them that his gun and his hostility aren't to be taken seriously.

In the 6- to 12-year-old period, boys will play an earnest game of war, but it has lots of rules. There may be arguments and roughhousing, but real fights are relatively infrequent. At this age a boy doesn't shoot at his mother or father, even in fun. It's not that his parents have turned stricter; his own conscience has. He says, "Step on a crack; break your mother's back," which means that even the thought of wishing harm to his parents now makes him uncomfortable. In adolescence, aggressive feelings become much stronger, but the well-brought-up boy sublimates them into athletics and other competition or into kidding his pals.

In other words, I'd explain that playing at war is a natural step in the disciplining of the aggression of young boys (few girls do it); that most clergymen and pacifists probably did the same thing; an idealistic mother doesn't really need to worry about producing a scoundrel; that the aggressive delinquent was not distorted in personality by being allowed to play bandit at 5 or 10, he was neglected and abused in his first couple of years, when his character was beginning to take shape; that he was doomed before he had any toys worthy of the name.

But nowadays I'd give a mother much more encouragement in her inclination to guide her son away from violence. A number of occurrences have convinced me of the importance of this.

One of the first things that made me change my mind, several years ago, was an observation that an experienced nursery school teacher told me about. Her children were crudely bopping each other much more than previously, without provocation. When she remonstrated with them, they would protest, "But that's what the Three Stooges do." (This was a children's TV program full of violence and buffoonery which had recently been introduced and which immediately became very popular.) This attitude did not signify a serious undermining of character. But it certainly showed me that watching violence can lower a child's standards of behavior. Recent psychological experiments have shown that watching brutality stimulates at least slight cruelty in adults, too.

What further shocked me into reconsidering my point of view was the assassination of President Kennedy, and the fact that some schoolchildren cheered about this. (I didn't so much blame the children as I blamed the kind of American parents who will say about a President they dislike, "I'd shoot him if I got the chance!")

These incidents made me think of other evidences that Americans have often been too tolerant of harshness, lawlessness and violence. We were ruthless in dealing with the Indians. In some frontier areas we slipped into the tradition of vigilante justice. We were hard on the later waves of immigrants. At times we've denied justice to groups with different religions or political views. We have high crime rates. A great proportion of our adult as well as our child population has been endlessly fascinated with dramas of Western violence and with brutal crime stories, in movies and on television. We have had a shameful history of racist lynchings and murders, as well as regular abuse and humiliation. In recent years it has been realized that infants and small children are sometimes brought to hospitals with severe injuries caused by gross parental brutality.

Of course, some of these phenomena are characteristic of only a small percentage of the population. Even the others that apply to a majority of people don't necessarily mean that we Americans on the average have more aggressiveness inside us than the people of other nations. I think rather that the aggressiveness we have is less controlled, from childhood on.

To me it seems very clear that in order to have a more stable and civilized national life we should bring up the next generation of Americans with a greater respect for law and for other people's rights and sensibilities than in the past. There are many ways in which we could and should teach these attitudes. One simple opportunity we could utilize in the first half of childhood is to show our disapproval of lawlessness and violence in television programs and in children's pistol play.

I also believe that the survival of the world now depends on a much greater awareness of the need to avoid war and to actively seek peaceful agreements. There are enough nuclear arms to utterly destroy all civilization. One international incident in which belligerence or brinkmanship was carried a small step too far could escalate into annihilation within a few hours. This terrifying situation demands a much greater stability and self-restraint on the part of national leaders and citizens than they have ever shown in the past. We owe it to our children to prepare them very deliberately for this awesome responsibility. I see little evidence that this is being done now.

When we let people grow up feeling that cruelty is all right provided they know it is make-believe, or provided they sufficiently disapprove of certain individuals or groups, or provided the cruelty is in the service of their country (whether the country is right or wrong), we make it easier for them to go berserk when the provocation comes.

But can we imagine actually depriving American boys of their pistols or of watching their favorite Western or crime programs? I think we should consider it—to at least a partial degree.

I believe that parents should firmly stop children's war play or any other kind of play that degenerates into deliberate cruelty or meanness. (By this I don't mean they should interfere in every little quarrel or tussle.)

If I had a 3- or 4-year-old son who asked me to buy him a pistol, I'd tell him—with a friendly smile, not a scowl—that I don't want to give him a gun for even pretend shooting because there is too much meanness and killing in the world, that we must all learn how to get along in a friendly way together. I'd ask him if he didn't want some other present instead.

If I saw him, soon afterward, using a stick for a pistol in order to join a gang that was merrily going "bang-bang" at each other, I wouldn't rush out to remind him of my views. I'd let him have the fun of participating as long as there was no cruelty. If his uncle gave him a pistol or a soldier's helmet for his birthday, I myself wouldn't have the nerve to take it away from him. If when he was 7 or 8 he decided he wanted to spend his own money for battle equipment, I wouldn't forbid him. I'd remind him that I myself don't want to buy war toys or give them as presents; but from now on he will be playing more and more away from home and making more of his own decisions; he can make this decision for himself. I wouldn't give this talk in such a disapproving manner that he wouldn't dare decide against my policy. I would feel I'd made my point and that he had been inwardly influenced by my viewpoint as much as I could influence him. Even if he should buy weapons then, he would be likely to end up—in adolescence and adulthood—as thoughtful about the problems of peace as if I'd prohibited his buying them, perhaps more so.

One reason I keep backing away from a flat prohibition is that it would have its heaviest effect on the individuals who need it least. If all the parents of America became convinced and agreed on a toy-weapons ban on the first of next month, this would be ideal from my point of view. But this isn't going to happen for a long time, unless one bomb goes off by accident and shocks the world into a banning of all weapons, real and pretend. A small percentage of parents—those most thoughtful and conscientious—will be the first ones who will want to dissuade their sons from war toys; but their sons will be most apt to be the sensitive, responsible children anyway. So I think it's carrying the issue unnecessarily far for those of us who are particularly concerned about peace and kindliness to insist that our young sons demonstrate a total commitment to our cause while all their friends are pistol toters. (It might be practical in a neighborhood where a majority of parents had the same conviction.) The main ideal is that children should grow up with a fond attitude toward all humanity. That will come about basically from the general atmosphere of our families. It will be strengthened by the attitude toward nations and groups that we teach specifically. The elimination of war play would have some additional influence, but not as much as the two previous factors.

I feel less inclined to compromise on brutality on television and in movies. The sight of a real human face being apparently smashed by a fist has a lot more impact on children than what they imagine when they are making up their own stories. I believe that parents should flatly forbid programs that go in for violence. I don't think they are good for adults either. Young children can only partly distinguish between dramas and reality. Parents can explain, "It isn't right for people to hurt each other or kill each other and I don't want you to watch them do it."

Even if a child cheats and watches such a program in secret, he'll know very well that his parents disapprove, and this will protect him to a degree from the coarsening effect of the scenes.

463. Naughty words. Sometimes at 3, more often at 4, children go through a phase of reveling in bathroom words. They gaily insult each other with expressions like "You great big duty" and "I'll flush you down the toilet," and think they are very witty and bold. You should consider this a normal development. You can tell your child to stop it if you don't like it, or you can let him have his fun until you've had enough.

As they grow older, all normal children who have a chance (as they should) to be around other children, learn swear words and "dirty" words. Long before they know what the words mean, they know that they are naughty. Being human, they repeat them to show that they are worldly wise and not afraid to be a little bad. It's usually quite a shock to conscientious parents to hear these words coming from the mouths of their supposedly sweet innocents. What's a good parent to do? It's better not to jump out of your skin or act horribly shocked. For the timid child this has too strong an effect; it worries him, makes him afraid to be around children who use bad words. But most children who find they have shocked their parents are delighted, at least secretly. Some of them go on cussing endlessly at home, hoping to get the same rise. Others, stopped at home by threats, use all their bad language elsewhere. The point is that when you tell a child that just by making certain sounds he has the power to scandalize the whole world, it's like handing him a full-size cannon and telling him, "For goodness' sake, don't set it off." On the other hand, I don't think that you have to sit mute and just take it. You can just tell him firmly that you and most people don't like to hear those words and you don't want him to use them.

464. Timidity and sissiness. A first child who has not had much chance to play with other children is apt, at 2 years of age, to let them take his toys away from him and push him around. He may just look perplexed or he may run crying to his mother each time. This is apt to worry the father and mother. In most cases it is a temporary state of affairs caused by inexperience. If he continues to play near children regularly, the chances are great that as the months go by he will learn how to get mad and stand up for his rights. It's wise for his mother not to show too much concern or sympathy, not to fight his battles for him, not to tell him he must share, but to suggest casually that he go and get the toy back.

The second or third child in a family rarely has this problem, probably because he's had to stand up for his rights from the age of 1 year.

If there is one aggressive child who regularly bullies your child and your child is becoming more intimidated rather than less as the weeks go by, it may be wise for a couple of months to take him somewhere else to play, where he will have more chance of finding his courage.

If a child goes on past 3 or 4 being easily picked on, it's a good idea to consult a child guidance clinic or a family social agency to try to find out what's wrong.

A father may be upset if his son at 2 likes to play occasionally with dolls and doll carriages. This is too early to start worrying. Children at 2 don't make much distinction between masculine and feminine activities. By 3 they are usually beginning to show a preference for the conventional activities of their own sex a majority of the time, and by 4 this preference is likely to be stronger still. It is perfectly natural for a regular boy of 3 or 4 to play with girls part of the time, the more so if there aren't boys of his own age available, but if they are playing house he should usually be wanting to play father or son.

If a boy of 3 or 4 or 5 is avoiding boys or is regularly preferring to take the part of a mother or girl in house play, he is probably afraid of being a boy and needs child guidance help. He also needs a friendlier relationship with his father. Sometimes the mother is being too protective and enveloping.

465. Biting humans. It's natural for a baby around 1 year to take a bite out of his parent's cheek. His teething makes him want to bite anyway, and when he feels tired he's even more in the mood for it. I don't think it means much, either, when a child between 1 and 2 bites another child, whether it's in a friendly or angry spirit.

After 2 or 2½ it depends on how often the biting occurs and how the child is getting along otherwise. If he is generally happy and outgoing but occasionally takes a bite when he gets in a fight, it's of no great importance. But if he is tense or unhappy much of the time and keeps biting other children for no good reason, it's a sign that something is wrong. Perhaps he is being bossed and disciplined too much at home and is in a frantic, high-strung state. Perhaps he has had too little chance to get used to other children and imagines they are dangerous and threatening to him. Perhaps he is jealous of a baby at home and carries over the fear and resentment to all other small children, as if they were competitors, too. If the cause and the cure are not easy to see, a children's psychiatrist will be able to help (Section 577).

Some mothers who have been bitten ask if they should bite back. A mother can control her child better by staying in charge as a friendly boss than by descending to his age level to battle with bites, slaps or shouts. Besides, when you bite or slap a 1-year-old, he's apt to keep it up, either as a fight or a game. And if you just look reproachful, you bring out his meanness. The only thing you need to do is to keep from being bitten again, by drawing back when he gets that gleam in his eye, showing him clearly that you don't like it and won't let it happen.

466. Comforting a hurt child. When a child is hurt he wants to be comforted and his parent feels like comforting him. This is natural and right.

Sometimes a parent who is particularly anxious for his child to grow up brave and uncomplaining fears that comforting him will make him a sissy. But a secure child isn't made dependent by ordinary comforting. As he grows older, especially as he gets into the period beyond 6 years, he makes a great effort all by himself to be brave and not to run to his mother.

The child who is a crybaby over small hurts and aches has had a more complicated past. He may have been made generally dependent by all kinds of fussing and overprotection. Sometimes the mother is a person who, without realizing it, has a rather severe, critical attitude toward him at most times and shows her tender side mainly when he is hurt or ill. Her move here is not to be more severe when he's in trouble but to show that she enjoys and loves him when he's all right. In another case a parent has an exaggerated horror of injuries, and the child has caught some of this anxiety.

You don't need to be afraid to comfort your child while he is miserable. Merely avoid emphasizing the injury, and distract him back to his regular activities as soon as he is able.

THE FATHER AS COMPANION

467. A boy needs a friendly, accepting father. Boys and girls need chances to be around their father, to be enjoyed by him, and if possible, to do things with him. Unfortunately, the father is apt to come home wanting most of all to slump down and read the paper. If he understands how valuable his companionship is, he will feel more like making a reasonable effort. I say **reasonable** because I don't think the conscientious father (or mother, either) should force himself beyond his endurance. Better to play for 15 minutes enjoyably and then say, "Now I'm going to read my paper," than to spend all day at the zoo, crossly.

Sometimes a father is so eager to have his son turn out perfect that it gets in the way of their having a good time together. The man who is eager for his son to become an athlete may take him out at an early age to play catch. Naturally, every throw, every catch, has its faults. If the father is constantly criticizing, even in a friendly tone, the boy becomes uncomfortable inside. It isn't any fun. Also, it gives him the feeling of being no good, in his father's eyes and in his own. A boy comes around to an interest in sports in good time if he's naturally self-confident and outgoing. Feeling approved of by his father helps him more than being coached by him. A game of catch is fine if it's the son's idea and if it's for fun.

A boy doesn't grow spiritually to be a man just because he's born with a male body. The thing that makes him feel and act like a man is being able to copy, to pattern himself after, men and older boys with whom he feels friendly. He can't pattern himself after a person unless he feels that this person likes him and approves of him. If a father is always impatient or irritated with him, the boy is likely to feel uncomfortable not only when he's around his father but when he's around other men and boys, too. He is apt to draw closer to his mother and take on her manners and interests.

So a father who wants to help his small son grow up to be manly shouldn't jump on him too hard when he cries, scorn him when he's playing a girlish game, or force him to practice athletics. He should enjoy him when he's around, give him the feeling he's a chip off the old block, share a secret with him, take him alone on excursions sometimes.

The boy who hasn't got a father, temporarily or permanently, is discussed in Sections 779 and 780.

The father's part in discipline is discussed in Section 483.

There's more on the father's relations with son and daughter in Sections 512–516.

468. A girl needs a friendly father, too. It's easy to see that a boy needs a father to pattern himself after, but many people don't realize that a friendly father plays a different but equally important part in the development of a girl. She doesn't exactly pattern herself after him, but she gains confidence in herself as a girl and a woman from feeling his approval. I'm thinking of little things he can do, like complimenting her on her dress, or hairdo, or the cookies she's made. When she is older, he can show her that he's interested in her opinions and let her in on some of his. Later, when she has boyfriends, it's important for him to welcome them, even if he secretly doesn't think they are quite good enough for her.

By learning to enjoy the qualities in her father that are particularly masculine, a girl is getting ready for her adult life in a world that is half made up of men. The way she makes friendships with boys and men later, the kind of man she eventually falls in love with, the kind of married life she makes, are all influenced strongly by the kind of relationship she has had with her father throughout her childhood.

469. A little roughhousing goes a long way. Lots of fathers enjoy roughhousing with their young children, and most children love it, too. But children easily become overexcited by it, and this sometimes leads to nightmares. It's good to remember that at 2 and 3 and 4, children's loves and hates and fears get out of control easily. And young children can't distinguish too clearly between real and pretend. For them, a father who is pretending to be a bear or a prizefighter really becomes one for the time being. This is usually too much for a small child to take. So roughhousing should be mild and good-natured and brief—even when the child begs for more. Most important is that it shouldn't be a pretend fight or a pretend chase. Let it just be simple acrobatics. Stop, anyway, if a child gets worked up.

470. A father should go light on teasing. On the average, men seem to have more fierceness in them than women do. In civilized life, they have to keep this under control. When a man feels irritated at a friend or a business associate, he can't simply hit him or insult him. But according to the rules, it's all right to kid him a little. So men learn to be kidders. Then when a father feels mildly irritated at his son, he may try to work it off as kidding. A child feels humiliated when he's laughed at, and he doesn't know how to tease back. Teasing is too strong for young children.

GOING TO BED

471. Keeping bedtime happy. Three or four factors can make the difference between the child who goes to bed willingly and the one who stalls and argues.

Keep bedtime agreeable and happy. Remember that it is delicious and inviting to the tired child if you don't turn it into an unpleasant duty. Have an air of cheerful certainty about it. Expect him to turn in at the hour you decide as surely as you expect him to breathe. It's good for a child to be able to persuade his mother (or father) to change her mind once in a while about bedtime (Fourth of July, for instance). But bedtime comes too often for regular argument. It usually works best to have the nap come right after lunch, before he has had time to become absorbed in play. The relationship between supper and bedtime is usually more complicated because of the bath and the father's coming home.

Until the child is at least 3 or 4, and in any case until he is responsible enough to like to get himself to bed, lead him rather than push him with words. Carry the very small child to bed affectionately. Lead the 3- or 4-year-old by the hand, both of you still chatting about what was last on his mind.

Small children are comforted by having a certain amount of ritual about going to bed. For example, the dolly is put in her bed and tucked in. Then the teddy bear is put in the child's bed. Then the child is tucked in and kissed. Then the mother pulls down the shade or puts out the light. Try not to rush going to bed, no matter how much of a hurry you are in. (On the other hand, it isn't wise to let the child keep lengthening the rituals.) Keep it peaceful. Tell or read a story regularly if you have time. It shouldn't be scary. Most children are helped in going to bed by having a cozy toy animal or doll for company in bed.

472. How much sleep does a child need anyway? You can usually trust an infant to take what rest he needs. By the time a child is 2 or more, you can't leave it all to him to decide. He may need more sleep but be kept from getting it by tenseness of different kinds: loneliness, fear of being left alone, fear of the dark, fear of nightmares, fear of wetting his bed, excitement from stimulating experiences. He may be all keyed up from competing with an older brother, or "burned up" with jealousy of a younger sister. He may be on edge each evening because there is always a tug of war with his mother about when he is to go to bed or because he is worrying about his schoolwork or the TV thriller he has been watching. The prevention of these various troubles is discussed elsewhere. I bring them up here only to point out at the start that you can't say that the child doesn't need more sleep just because he won't take it.

The average 2-year-old needs 12 hours of sleep at night and 1 to 2 hours of nap. The nap or rest usually shortens as he grows from 2 to 6, and bedtime at night stays the same. Between the ages of 6 and 9, the average child can usually give up an hour of his night's sleep, half an hour at a time, and for instance, go to bed at 8 if he's getting up at 7. By the age of 12, he will probably have been able to clip off two more half hours and go to bed at 9. These are average figures. Some children need more, others less.

Many children stop going to sleep at naptime around the age of 3 or 4, but most of them still need a real rest or at least a quiet play period indoors after lunch until they are 5 or 6. Many wise schools provide a rest period through the sixth grade. It all depends on the individual child's temperament and activity.

Going-to-bed problems and sleep problems in infancy are discussed in Sections 301, 302; around 2 years of age, in Sections 500, 502; after 3, in Section 517.

DUTIES

473. Let him enjoy his duties. How does a child learn to perform various duties? By his very nature, he starts out feeling that dressing himself, brushing his teeth, sweeping, putting things away are exciting and grown-up things to do. If his parents succeed in keeping on good terms with him as he grows older, he enjoys going on errands, carrying wood, beating rugs, because he still wants to have a part in important jobs and to please his mother and father. Most of us (including the author) aren't able to bring up our children so well that we get cooperation all the time, but if we realize that children prefer to be helpful, we are less likely to make household tasks sound like unpleasant duties or to assign them when we're irritable.

A child can't be expected to continue indefinitely to be responsible about his duties—even at 15 years. (Most adults lapse into irresponsibility at times, too.) He has to be reminded. If you can find the patience, try to make the reminder matter-of-fact, polite, as if you were speaking to an adult. It's the nagging, belittling tone that kills all pride in a job. It also helps a lot to assign a child tasks that he can do in the company of other members of the family, whether it's dish-drying or lawn-mowing. Then the grown-upness of the task and the fun of helping spur the child on.

474. Dressing himself. Between the ages of 1 and 1½ years, a child begins to try to undress himself. (He pulls the toe of his sock directly toward his stomach, which makes it stick.) By about 2, he can do a pretty good job of stripping himself. Now he tries hard to put on his clothes, but gets all tangled up. It probably takes him another year to learn to put the easier garments on right, and another year still (till about 4 or 5) to handle the trickier jobs, like laces and buttons.

This period from 1½ to 4 years requires a lot of tact. If you don't let him do the parts he is able to, or if you interfere too much, it's apt to make him angry. If he never has a chance to learn at the age when it appeals to him, he may lose the desire. Yet if you don't help him at all, he'll never be dressed and he may get frustrated at his own failure. You can help him tactfully in the jobs that are possible. Pull the socks partway off so that the rest is easy. Lay out the garment that he's going to want to put on, so that he'll start straight. Interest him in the easier jobs while you do the hard ones. When he gets tangled up, don't insist on taking over but straighten him out so that he can carry on. If he feels that you are with him and not against him, he is much more cooperative. It takes patience, though.

475. Putting things away. When your child is very young and you still expect to pick up and put things away after he is through playing, you can do it as part of the game, with enthusiasm. "The square blocks go here, in big piles, and the long blocks go there. Over here let's pretend there's a garage, and all the cars go here to sleep at night." By the time he is 4 or 5, he has fallen into the habit of putting things away and enjoying it. Many times he does it without any reminder. But if he still needs help at times, join in sociably.

If you say to a 3-year-old, "Now put your things away," it sounds unpleasant. Even if he enjoys doing it, you are handing him a job that practically no 3-year-old has the perseverance to carry through. Furthermore, he's still at a very balky stage.

Cheerfully helping a child to put things away not only develops a good attitude in him but is easier for the mother than long arguments.

476. Dawdling. If you ever see a mother trying to get a dawdling child going in the morning, urging him, warning him, scolding him, to get out of bed, to get washed, to get dressed, to eat his breakfast, to start for school, you will vow that you will never get in that fix. The dawdling child wasn't born that way. He was made that way gradually, in most cases, by constant pushing. "Hurry up and finish your lunch." "How many times do I have to tell you to get ready for bed?" It's easy to fall into the habit of prodding children, and it builds up an absentminded balkiness in them. Parents say they have to nag or the child won't get anywhere. It's a vicious circle, but the parent starts it. More often it's the mother. She may be a somewhat impatient person with an itch to manage—especially males. She usually doesn't even realize how much initiative she tends to take away from her son.

In the early years, before a child is capable of carrying out directions, lead him through his various routines. As he gets old enough to want to take over responsibilities, step out of the picture as fast as you can. When he slips back and forgets, lead again. When he goes to school, let him think of it as his job to get there on time. It may be better to quietly allow him to be late to school once or twice, or to miss the bus and school altogether and find out for himself how sorry he feels. A child hates to miss things even more than his mother hates to have him miss them. That's the best mainspring to move him along.

You may have the impression that I think a child should not be held to any obligation. On the contrary. I think he should sit down at table when a meal is ready and get up in the morning at the proper time. I'm only making the point that if he's allowed to use his own initiative most of the time, reminded in a matter-of-fact way when he's clearly failed to do something on his own, not prodded unnecessarily in advance, not pushed too much, he usually wants to do these things.

477. Let him get dirty sometimes. A small child wants to do a lot of things that get him dirty, and they are good for him, too. He loves to dig in earth and sand, wade in mud puddles, splash in water in the washstand. He wants to roll in the grass, squeeze mud in his hand. When he has chances to do these delightful things, it enriches his spirit, makes him a warmer person, just the way beautiful music or falling in love improves an adult.

The small child who is always sternly warned against getting his clothes dirty or making a mess, and who takes it to heart, will be cramped. If he becomes really timid about dirt, it makes him too cautious in other ways also, and keeps him from developing into the free, warm, life-loving person he was meant to be.

I don't mean to give the impression that you must always hold yourself back and let your child make any kind of mess that strikes his fancy. But when you do have to stop him, don't try to scare him or disgust him; just substitute something else a little more practical. If he wants to make mud pies when he has his Sunday clothes on, have him change into old clothes first. If he gets hold of an old brush and wants to paint the house, set him to work (with a pail of water for "paint") on the woodshed or the tiled floor of the bathroom.

478. Good manners come naturally. Teaching a child to say "How d'do" or "Thank you" is really not the first step. The most important thing is to have him like people. If he doesn't, it's hard to teach him even surface manners.

The second step is to avoid making him self-conscious with strangers. We're apt, especially with our first child, to introduce him right away to a new grown-up and make him say something. But when you do that to a 2-year-old, you get him all embarrassed. He learns to feel uncomfortable just as soon as he sees you greeting somebody, because he knows he's about to be put on the spot. It's much better in the first 3 or 4 years, when a child needs time to size a stranger up, to draw the newcomer's conversation away from him, not toward him. A child of 3 or 4 is likely to watch a stranger talking to his mother for a few minutes and then suddenly break into the conversation with a remark, "The water came out of the toilet all over the floor." This isn't Lord Chesterfield's kind of manners, but it's real manners because he feels like sharing a fascinating experience. If that spirit toward strangers keeps up, he'll learn how to be friendly in a more conventional way soon enough.

The third, and probably most important, step is for a child to grow up in a family whose members are considerate of each other. Then he absorbs kindliness. He wants to say "Thank you" because the rest of the family say it and mean it. He enjoys tipping his hat to a lady when his father does, because he craves being like his father.

Certainly it is also necessary to teach a child just how to be polite and considerate. If it's done in a friendly spirit, he is proud to learn. More important, everybody likes a child with sensibly good manners and resents one who is rude or thoughtless. So the parents owe it to the child to make him likable. The appreciation he gets makes him more friendly in turn.

When you coach a child about manners, try to do it when you're alone with him rather than in the embarrassing presence of outsiders.

DISCIPLINE

479. Some common misunderstandings about discipline. A great deal of study has been given to the psychology of children in the past half century by educators, psychoanalysts, child psychiatrists, psychologists and pediatricians. Parents have been eager to read the results; newspapers and magazines have obliged by publishing them. We have learned a great deal bit by bit: that children need the love of good parents more than anything else; that they work hard, all by themselves, to be more grown-up and responsible; that many of the ones who get into the most trouble are suffering from lack of affection rather than from lack of punishment; that children are eager to learn if they are given school projects that are right for their age and are taught by understanding teachers; that some jealous feelings toward brothers and sisters and occasional angry feelings toward parents are natural and that a child does not need to feel deeply ashamed of them; that a childish interest in the facts of life and in some aspects of sex is quite normal; that too harsh a repression of aggressive feelings and sexual interest may lead to neurosis; that unconscious thoughts are as influential as conscious ones; that each child is an individual and should be allowed to be so.

All these ideas sound commonplace today, but when they

were first expressed they were very startling. Many of them ran counter to beliefs that had been held for centuries. It is not possible to change so many ideas about the nature and needs of children without mixing up a lot of parents. Parents who have had a very comfortable childhood and who are very stable people have been least confused. They may have been interested in hearing about these new ideas, and they may have agreed. But when it came to actually managing their children, they did it in much the same way they were brought up themselves. And it has been successful with their children, as it had been with them. This is the natural way to learn child care—from having been a child in a reasonably happy family.

The parents who have had more trouble with the new ideas are usually those who haven't been too happy about their own upbringing. Many of them have felt both resentful and guilty about the strained relations that existed at times between themselves and their parents. They haven't wanted their own children to feel that way about them. So they have welcomed new theories. They have often read meanings into them that went beyond what the scientists intended—for instance, that all that children need is love; that they shouldn't be made to conform; that they should be allowed to carry out their aggressive feelings against parents and others; that whenever anything goes wrong it's the parents' fault; that when children misbehave the parents shouldn't become angry or punish them but should try to show more love. All of these misconceptions are unworkable if carried very far. They encourage children to become demanding and disagreeable. They make children feel guilty about their excessive misbehavior. They make parents strive to be superhuman. When the bad behavior comes, the parents try to suppress their anger for a while. But eventually they have to explode. Then they feel guilty and bewildered. This leads to more misbehavior on the child's part. (See Section 480.)

Some parents who are very polite people themselves allow their children to be surprisingly obnoxious, not only to themselves but to outsiders as well. They don't seem to see what is going on. Some of these situations, when studied carefully, reveal that the parents had always been compelled to be much too good in their own childhood and to suppress all their natural resentments. Now they get a subtle glee from letting their own flesh and blood act out all the disagreeableness they themselves had to bottle up, pretending all the time that this is all according to the best modern theories of child rearing.

480. How feelings of guilt in the parents lead to discipline problems. There are many situations in which parents may always feel a bit guilty toward one child, or another. Some of them were mentioned in Sections 26 and 27. There are other obvious cases: the mother who goes to work without first settling in her own mind whether she will be neglecting her child; parents who have a child with a physical or mental handicap; parents who have adopted a baby and can't get over the feeling that they have to do a superhuman job to justify themselves in taking over someone else's child; parents who have been brought up with so much disapproval that they always feel guilty until they are proved innocent; parents who have studied child psychology in college or a professional school, who know about all the pitfalls, and who yet expect to have to do a superior job because of their training.

Whatever the cause of the feeling of guilt, it tends to get in the way of easy management of a child. The parent is inclined to expect too little from the child, too much from himself or herself. (It's more practical here to speak of the mother because she's usually so much more involved in child care, but the same things may apply just as well to the father.) The mother is often still trying to be patient and sweet-tempered when her overworked patience is really exhausted and the child is, in fact, getting out of hand and needs some definite correction. Or she is vacillating when the child needs firmness.

A child, like an adult, knows when he is getting away with too much naughtiness or rudeness even when his mother is trying to close her eyes to it. He feels guilty inside. He would like to be stopped. But if he isn't corrected, he's likely to behave worse and worse. It's as if he were saying, "How bad do I have to be before somebody stops me?"

Eventually his behavior becomes so provoking that his mother's patience snaps. She scolds him or punishes him. Peace is restored. But the trouble with the parent who feels guilty is that she is too ashamed of losing her temper. So instead of letting well enough alone, she tries to undo the correction or lets the child punish her in return. Perhaps she permits the child to be rude to her right in the middle of the punishment. Or she takes back the penalty before it has been half paid. Or she pretends not to notice when the child begins misbehaving again. In some situations if the child does not retaliate at all, a mother begins to subtly provoke him to do so—without realizing, of course, what she is up to.

All of this may sound too complicated or unnatural to you. If you can't imagine a parent letting a child get away with murder or, worse still, encouraging it, it only shows that you don't have the problem of guilt feelings. Actually, it isn't a rare problem. A majority of conscientious parents let a child get out of hand occasionally when they feel they have been unfair or neglectful. But they soon recover their balance. However, when a parent says, "Everything this child does or says rubs me the wrong way," it's a pretty good sign that the parent feels overly guilty and is chronically submissive and permissive, and that the child is reacting to this with constant provocation. No child can be that irritating by accident. If the parent can determine in which respects she may be too permissive and can firm up her discipline, she may, if she is on the right track, be delighted to find that her child becomes not only better behaved but much happier. Then she can really love him better, and he in turn responds to this.

481. You can be both firm and friendly. A child needs to feel that his mother and father, however agreeable, have their own rights, know how to be firm, won't let him be unreasonable or rude. He likes them better that way. It trains him from the beginning to get along reasonably with other people. The spoiled child is not a happy creature even in his own home. And when he gets out into the world, whether it's at 2 or 4 or 6, he is in for a rude shock. He finds that nobody is willing to kowtow to him; in fact, everybody dislikes him for his selfishness. Either he must go through life being unpopular, or he must learn the hard way how to be agreeable.

Conscientious parents often let a child take advantage of them for a while—until their patience is exhausted—and then turn on him crossly. But neither of these stages is really necessary. If parents have a healthy self-respect, they can stand up for themselves while they are still feeling friendly. For instance, if your child is insisting that you continue to play a game after you are exhausted, don't be afraid to say cheerfully but definitely, "I'm all tired out. I'm going to read a book now, and you can read your book, too."

If he is being very balky about getting out of the express wagon of another child who has to take it home now, though you have tried to interest him in something else, don't feel that you must go on being sweetly reasonable forever. Lift him out, even if he yells for a minute.

482. Let the child know that his angry feelings are normal. When a child is being rude to a parent—perhaps because he has had to be frustrated or because he's jealous of his brother or sister—the parent should promptly stop him and insist on politeness. But at the same time the parent can say that he knows his child is cross at him sometimes—all children get mad at their parents sometimes. This may sound contradictory to you; it sounds like undoing the correction. Child guidance work teaches us in case after case that a child is happier as well as better behaved if his parents insist on reasonably good behavior. But at the same time it helps a child to realize that his parents know he has angry feelings and that his parents are not enraged at him or alienated from him on account of them. This realization helps him get over his anger and keeps him from feeling too guilty or frightened because of it. Making this distinction between hostile feelings and hostile actions works out well in actual practice.

483. A father should share in discipline. A father who feels that in his own childhood his father was too severe with him may say, "I don't want my son to resent me as I sometimes resented my father." So he leans over backward to avoid any unpleasantness with his son and leaves all the disciplining to the mother. If the boy is doing something that makes him cross, the father tries to conceal his feelings and says nothing. This is trying too hard to be agreeable (or to pretend to be agreeable). A child knows when he has displeased a parent or broken a rule, and he expects to be corrected. If his parent tries to hide his disapproval or irritation, it only makes the child uneasy. He imagines that all this suppressed anger is piling up somewhere (which isn't too far from the truth) and worries about what will happen if it ever breaks out. Child guidance clinic studies show clearly that the boy whose father declines to do his share in maintaining discipline is much more apt to be afraid of him than the one whose father has no hesitation in controlling his child and showing indignation when it is justified. In the latter case the boy pays the price of his misbehavior, learns that though it isn't pleasant it isn't fatal, either, and the air is cleared. So a boy needs a father who's a pal at times but who's a parent all the time.

484. Don't say, "Do you want to . . .?"; just do what's necessary. It's easy to fall into the habit of saying to a small child, "Do you want to sit down and have your lunch?" "Shall we get dressed now?" "Do you want to do wee wee?" The trouble is that the natural response of the child, particularly between 1 and 3, is No. Then the poor mother has to persuade him to give in to something that was necessary anyway. The arguments use up thousands of words. It is better not to give him a choice. When it's time for lunch, lead him or carry him to the table, still chatting with him about the thing that was on his mind before. When you see signs that he needs to go to the bathroom, lead him there or bring the potty chair to him. Start undoing him without even mentioning what you're up to.

You might get the idea that I am advising you to swoop down on him and give him the "bum's rush." I don't mean exactly that. In fact, every time you take a child away from something he's absorbed in, it helps to be tactful. If your 15-month-old is busy fitting one hollow block inside another at suppertime, you can carry him to the table still holding his blocks and take them away when you hand him his spoon. If your 2-year-old is playing with a toy dog at bedtime, you can say, "Let's put doggie to bed now." If your 3-year-old is chugging a toy automobile along the floor when it's time for the bath, you can suggest that the car make a long, long trip to the bathroom. When you show interest in what he's doing, it puts him in a cooperative mood.

As your child grows older, he'll be less distractible, have more concentration. Then it works better to give him a little friendly warning. If a 4-year-old has spent half an hour building a battleship of blocks, you can say, "Put the guns on soon now; I want to see them shooting before you go to bed." This works better than pouncing on him without warning when the most exciting part of the play is still to come, or giving him a cross warning as if you never did see anything in battleships except the mess they make on the floor. All this takes patience, though, and naturally you won't always have it.

485. Don't give the small child too many reasons. You sometimes see a child between the ages of 1 and 3 who becomes worried by too many warnings. The mother of a certain boy 2 years old always tries to control him with ideas. "Jackie, you mustn't touch the doctor's lamp, because you will break it, and then the doctor won't be able to see." Jackie regards the lamp with a worried expression and mutters, "Doctor can't see." A minute later he is trying to open the door to the street. His mother warns him, "Don't go out the door. Jackie might get lost, and Mummie couldn't find him." Poor Jackie turns this new danger over in his mind and repeats, "Mummie can't find him." It's bad for him to be hearing about so many bad endings. It builds up a morbid imagination. A 2-year-old baby shouldn't be worrying about the consequences of his actions. This is the period when he is meant to learn by doing and having things happen. I'm not advising that you never warn your child in words, but only that you shouldn't always be leading him out beyond his depth with ideas.

I think of an overconscientious mother who feels she should give her 3-year-old a reasonable explanation of everything. When it's time to get ready to go outdoors, it never occurs to her to put the child's clothes on in a matter-of-fact way and get out. She begins, "Shall we put your coat on now?" "No," says the child. "Oh, but we want to get out and get some nice fresh air." He is used to the fact that she feels obliged to give a reason for everything, and this encourages him to make her argue for every point. So he says, "Why?" but not because he really wants to know. "Fresh air makes you strong and healthy so that you won't get sick." "Why?" says he. And so on and so forth, all day long. This kind of meaningless argument and explanation doesn't make him a more cooperative child or give him respect for his mother as a reasonable person. He would be happier and get more security from her if she had an air of self-confidence and steered him in a friendly, automatic way through the routines of the day.

When your child is young, rely most heavily on physically removing him from dangerous or forbidden situations by distracting him to something interesting but harmless. As he grows a little older and learns the lesson, remind him by a matter-of-fact "No, no" and more distraction. If he wants an explanation or a reason, give it to him in simple terms. But don't assume that he wants an explanation for every direction you give. He knows inside that he is inexperienced. He counts on you to keep him out of danger. It makes him feel safe to have you guiding him, provided you do it tactfully and not too much.

486. Temper tantrums. Almost any baby has a few temper tantrums between 1 and 3 years. He's gotten a sense of his own desires and individuality. When he's thwarted he knows it and feels angry. Yet he doesn't usually attack the parent who has interfered with him. Perhaps the grown-up is too important and too big. Also, his fighting instinct isn't very well developed yet.

When the feeling of fury boils up in him, he can't think of anything better to do than take it out on the floor and himself. He flops down, yelling, and pounds with his hands and feet and maybe his head.

A temper tantrum once in a while doesn't mean anything; there are bound to be some frustrations. If they are happening regularly, several times a day, it may mean that the child is getting overtired or has some chronic physical trouble. Frequent tantrums are more often due to the fact that the mother hasn't learned the knack of handling the child tactfully. There are several questions to ask: Does he have plenty of chance to play freely outdoors in a place where his mother doesn't have to keep chasing him, and are there things for him to push and pull and climb on there? Indoors, has he enough toys and household objects to play with, and is the house arranged so that his mother doesn't have to keep forbidding him to touch things? Is she, without realizing it, arousing his balking by telling him to come and get his shirt on instead of slipping it on without comment, asking him if he wants to go to the bathroom instead of leading him there or bringing the potty to him? When she has to interrupt his play to get him indoors or to meals, does she frustrate him directly, or get his mind on something pleasant? When she sees a storm brewing, does she meet it head-on, grimly, or does she distract him to something else?

You can't dodge all temper tantrums. A mother would be unnatural if she had that much patience and tact. When the storm breaks, you try to take it casually and help to get it over. You certainly don't give in and meekly let the child have his way; otherwise he'd be throwing tantrums all the time on purpose. You don't argue with him, because he's in no mood to see the error of his ways. Getting angry yourself only forces him to keep up his end of the row. Give him a graceful way out. One child cools off quickest if the parent fades away and goes about her own business, matter-of-factly, as if she couldn't be bothered. Another with more determination and pride sticks to his yelling and thrashing for an hour unless his mother makes a friendly gesture. She might pop in with a suggestion of something fun to do, and a hug to show she wants to make up, as soon as the worst of the storm has passed.

It's embarrassing to have a child put on a tantrum on a busy sidewalk. Pick him up, with a grin if you can force it, and lug him off to a quiet spot where you can both cool off in private.

Breath-holding spells, in which a child may turn blue and even lose consciousness momentarily, can be an expression of temper. They are alarming to a mother, but she should try to learn to manage them sensibly, as in the discussion above, in order to keep the child from deliberately using them more and more.

487. Is punishment necessary? The only sensible answer is that a great majority of good parents feel that they have to punish once in a while. On the other hand, a few parents find that they can successfully manage their children without ever having to punish. A lot depends on how the parents were brought up. If they were punished occasionally for good cause, they naturally expect to have to punish in similar situations. And if they were kept in line by positive guidance alone, they are apt to find that they can do the same with their children.

To keep the record straight, it should be realized that there are also a fair number of poorly behaved children. The parents of some of them punish a lot and the parents of others never do. So we can't say either that punishment always works or that lack of it always works. It all depends on the nature of the parents' discipline in general.

Before we go further with the subject of punishment, we ought to realize that it is never the main element in discipline —it's only a vigorous additional reminder that the parent feels strongly about what he says. We have all seen children who were slapped and spanked and deprived plenty, and yet remained ill-behaved. Many chronic criminals have spent half their adult years in jail, and yet each time they get out they promptly become involved in another crime.

The main source of good discipline is growing up in a loving family—being loved and learning to love in return. We want to be kind and cooperative (most of the time) because we like people and want them to like us. (Habitual criminals are people who in childhood were never loved enough to make much difference to them, and many of them were abused, besides.) A child gradually lessens his grabbing and begins to share, somewhere around the age of 3 years, not primarily because he is reminded by his mother (though that may help some) but because his feelings toward other children —of enjoyment and affection—have developed sufficiently.

Another vital element is the child's intense desire to be as much like the parent as possible. He works particularly hard at being polite and civilized and responsible in the 3-to-6-year-old period (Sections 512, 513). This is the time when the boy acquires much of his desire to be cooperative with men, brave in danger, courteous to women, faithful to a job, just as his father is. This is the age when a girl is inspired to be helpful in the home, devoted to babies (including dolls), tender to other members of the family, just as her mother is.

Though children do the major share in civilizing themselves, through love and imitation, it still leaves plenty for parents to do, as all of you know. In automobile terms, the child supplies the power but the parents have to do the steering. The child's motives are good (most of the time), but he doesn't have the experience or the stability to stay on the road. The parents have to be saying, "No, crossing the street is too dangerous," "You can't play with that, you'll hurt someone," "Say thank you to Mrs. Griffin," "You have to come in now because lunch is ready," "You can't take the wagon home because it belongs to Harry," "You have to go to bed to grow big," etc., etc. How well the guidance works depends on such factors as whether the parent is reasonably consistent (nobody can be completely consistent), whether she means what she says (is not just sounding off), and whether she is directing or prohibiting the child for a good reason (not just because she's feeling mean or bossy).

The everyday job of the parent, then, is to keep the child on the right track by means of firmness. (You don't sit by and watch a small child destroy something and then punish him afterward.) You come to punishment (if you use it at all) once in a while when your system of firmness breaks down. Maybe your child, sorely tempted, wonders whether you still mean the prohibition that you laid down a couple of months ago. Or maybe he is angry and misbehaves on purpose. Perhaps he breaks something that's very precious to you, by foolish carelessness. Or he's slightly rude to you at a moment when you are tense about another matter. Maybe he narrowly escapes being run over because he didn't look. Indignation or righteous anger wells up in you. At such a moment you punish, or at least you feel like punishing.

The best test of a punishment is whether it accomplishes what you are after, without having other serious effects. If it makes a child furious, defiant and worse behaved than before, then it certainly is missing fire. If it seems to break the child's heart, then it's probably too strong for him. Every child reacts somewhat differently.

There are times when a child breaks a plate or rips his clothes because of accident or carelessness. If he gets along well with his parents, he feels just as unhappy as they do, and no punishment is needed. (In fact, you sometimes have to comfort him.) Jumping on a child who feels sorry already sometimes banishes his remorse and makes him argue.

If you're dealing with an older child who is always fooling with the dishes and breaking them, it may be fair to make him buy replacements from his allowance. A child beyond the age of 6 is developing a sense of justice and sees the fairness of reasonable penalties. However, I'd go light on the legalistic, "take-the-consequences" kind of punishment before 6, and I wouldn't try to use it at all before 3. You don't want a small child to develop a heavy sense of guilt. The job of a parent is to keep him from getting into trouble rather than act as a severe judge after it's happened.

In the olden days children were spanked plenty, and nobody thought much about it. Then a reaction set in, and many parents decided that it was shameful. But that didn't settle everything. If an angry parent keeps himself from spanking, he may show his irritation in other ways: for instance, by nagging the child for half the day, or trying to make him feel deeply guilty. I'm not particularly advocating spanking, but I think it is less poisonous than lengthy disapproval, because it clears the air, for parent and child. You sometimes hear it recommended that you never spank a child in anger but wait until you have cooled off. That seems unnatural. It takes a pretty grim parent to whip a child when the anger is gone.

Some parents find that putting a child in his room works well. One theoretical disadvantage is that it may make his room seem like a prison. Having the young child sit in a special chair for a few minutes is an effective reminder in some families.

Avoid threats as much as possible. They tend to weaken discipline. It may sound reasonable to say, "If you don't keep out of the street with your bicycle, I'll take it away." But in a sense a threat is a dare—it admits that the child may disobey. It should impress him more to be firmly told he must keep out of the street, if he knows from experience that his mother means what she says. On the other hand, if you see that you may have to impose a drastic penalty like taking away a beloved bike for a few days, it's better to give fair warning. It certainly is silly, and quickly destroys all a parent's authority, to make threats that aren't ever carried out or that can't be carried out. Scary threats, such as of bogeymen and cops, are 100% wrong in all cases.

488. Parents who can't control their children or who have to punish frequently need help. A few parents have extreme difficulty controlling their children. They say their child "won't obey" or that he's "just bad." The first thing you see when you watch such a parent (let's say it's a mother, so we can refer to her as "she") is that she doesn't appear to be really trying, even though she wants to and thinks she is. She threatens or scolds or punishes frequently. But one such mother almost never carries out a threat. Another, though she punishes, never in the end makes the child do what she said he had to do. And another makes him obey once, but 5 minutes later and 10 minutes later she lets him get away with it. Another laughs in the middle of a scolding or punishment. Another just keeps shouting at the child that he's bad or asks a neighbor, right in front of the child, whether she ever saw a worse one. Parents like these unconsciously expect the child's bad behavior to go right on and can do nothing effective to stop it. They are inviting it, without realizing it. Their scolding and punishing is only an expression of frustration. In their complaints to neighbors they are only hoping to get some comforting agreement that the child is truly impossible. Frustrated parents like these have often had an unsatisfactory childhood during which they never received sufficient assurance that they were basically good and well behaved. As a result they don't have enough confidence in themselves or in their children. They need a lot of help from a child guidance clinic or from a family social agency (Sections 577, 578).

JEALOUSY AND RIVALRY

489. Jealousy can be helpful as well as hurtful. It is a strong emotion even in grown-ups. It can be more disturbing to the very young child because he doesn't know just what has hit him.

If it is intense, it may sour his outlook on life for quite a while. But jealousy is one of the facts of life and can't be completely prevented, so parents shouldn't expect to accomplish the impossible. However, they can do a great deal to minimize it and to help the child convert it into other feelings that are painless and constructive. If he comes to realize that there is no reason to be so fearful of a rival, it strengthens his character so that he will be better able to cope with rivalry situations later in life, at work and at home.

490. Helping the child to feel more grown-up at this time. A great majority of young children react to a baby's arrival by yearning to be a baby again, at least part of the time, and this is quite normal. They want a bottle occasionally. They may wet their bed and pants, and they may soil themselves. They may relapse into baby talk and act helpless about doing things for themselves. I think a parent is wise to humor the craving to be a baby at those moments when it is very strong. They can even good-naturedly carry a child up to his room and undress him, as a friendly game. Then he can see that he is not being denied these experiences, which he imagines are delightful but which may prove disappointing.

However, I think the parents can help the child more by appealing, most of the time, to the side of him that wants to grow up. They can remind him of how big, strong, smart or skillful he is. I don't mean that you should give him one big overenthusiastic sales talk but that you should hand him a sincere compliment whenever it is appropriate. From time to time the parent can refer to some aspect of the baby's helplessness in a tone of pity.

You'll notice that I'm not suggesting direct comparisons that imply that the parents definitely prefer the other child to the baby. To feel that he is the favored child may gratify a child temporarily. But in the long run he will feel insecure with parents who are partial—they might change their preference. The parents should, of course, let their love of the baby be evident. I'm only emphasizing the importance of giving the older child chances to feel proud of his maturity and to remember that there are lots of disadvantages to being a baby.

Encouraging the child to be grown up should not be pushed too hard, however. If the parent is constantly calling all the things that the child temporarily yearns to do "babyish" and all the things that he's temporarily reluctant to do "grown up" he can only come to the conclusion that he wants to be a baby for sure.

491. Turning rivalry into helpfulness. One of the ways in which a young child tries to get over the pain of having a younger rival is to act as if he himself were no longer a child, competing in the same league with the baby, but as if he were a third parent. Of course, when he's feeling very cross with the baby, he may act the disapproving parent. But if he's feeling more secure, he can be the kind of parent who teaches the baby how to do things, gives him toys, wants to assist in feeding and bathing and clothing him, comforts him when he's miserable, protects him from dangers. He tries to slip into the parental role even without much help from the parents. But the parents can assist him tremendously by suggesting how he can help them at times when it wouldn't occur to him, and by showing their real appreciation of his efforts. As a matter of fact, mothers of twins who were desperate for real help have told me they were amazed to find how much honest-to-goodness help they received from a daughter as young as 3 years, so it doesn't all have to be pretend. Even a young child can fetch a bath towel, a diaper, or a bottle from the refrigerator. He can pretend to help the baby, "watch" him while the mother is out of sight.

A small child almost always wants to hold the baby, and a mother is apt to hesitate for fear he may drop it. But if the child sits on the floor (on a carpet or blanket) or in a large stuffed chair or in the middle of a bed, there's little risk, even if the baby is dropped.

In such ways the parents can help a child to actually transform resentful feelings into cooperativeness and genuine altruism.

Usually the left-out feeling is more apt to be experienced by the first child when the second baby arrives, because he has been used to the spotlight and has had no practice in sharing the parents' love with others. A middle child doesn't have to decide between being a parent and being a baby when a new one arrives. He can see that he's still just one of the children, as he has always been. I believe that the greater need of the average first child to think of himself as a parent helps to explain why so many first children later enjoy being parents and are so apt to go into professions like teaching, social work, nursing, medicine, which are concerned with caring for others.

492. Preparing the way for the baby. It is good for a child to know ahead of time that he is going to have a baby brother or sister, if he is old enough to understand such an idea at all, so that he can get used to the idea gradually. (Don't promise him it's going to be a girl or a boy; a child takes a promise like that seriously.) The question of where the baby is coming from is discussed more fully in "The Facts of Life" (Sections 530–534). Most educators and child psychologists believe that it is wholesome for a child to know that the baby is growing inside his mother and to feel it move. It's hard to explain much to a child under 2.

The arrival of the baby should change a child's life as little as possible, especially if he has been the only child up to that time. It is better to make all possible changes several months ahead of time. If his room is to be given over to the baby, move him to his new room several months ahead, so that he feels that he is graduating because he is a big boy, not because the baby is pushing him out of his own place. The same applies to graduating to a big bed. If he is to go to nursery school, he should start a couple of months beforehand. Nothing sets a child's mind against nursery school so much as the feeling that he is being banished to it. But if he is already well established in nursery school, he goes on liking it, and his satisfying life there keeps him from being as much disturbed by what's going on at home.

How a child gets along while his mother is in the hospital makes a big difference in his feelings toward her and the baby when they come back. Most important is who takes care of him. This is discussed in Sections 501, 773, 778.

493. When the mother brings the baby home. It's usually a hectic moment when the mother comes back from the hospital. She is tired and preoccupied. The father scurries about, being helpful. If the older child is there, he stands around feeling troubled and left out. So this is the new baby!

If it's likely to be like this, it may be better for him to be away on an excursion if this can be arranged. An hour later, when the baby and the nurse and the luggage are all in their place and when his mother has at last relaxed on the bed, is time enough for the child to come in. His mother can hug him and talk to him and give him her undivided attention. Let him bring up the subject of the baby when he is ready to.

It's tactful to play down the new baby in the early weeks. Treat her casually. Don't act too excited about her. Don't gloat over her. Don't talk a lot about her. As far as is convenient, take care of her while the older one is not around. Fit in her bath and some of her feedings when he is outdoors or taking his nap. Many young children feel the greatest jealousy when they see the mother feeding the baby, especially at the breast. If he's around, he should be allowed in freely. But if he is downstairs playing happily, don't attract his attention to what's going on.

If he wants to drink from a bottle, too, I'd suggest cheerfully fixing him one. It's a little sad to see an older child trying a bottle out of envy of the baby. He thinks it's going to be heaven. When he gets up his courage to take a suck, disappointment spreads over his face. It's just milk, coming slowly, with a rubber taste. He may want a bottle off and on for a few weeks, but there's not much risk that he'll want to go on with it forever if his mother gives it to him willingly and if she is doing the other things she can to help him with his jealousy.

A child usually feels a mixture of love and jealousy of the baby.

Other people play a part in jealousy, too. When the father comes home from work, he should suppress the impulse to ask the child, "How's the baby today?" Better to act as if he has forgotten there is a baby, sit down and pass the time of day. Later he can drift on to have a look at her when the older one is interested in something else. Grandma, who used to make a big fuss over the child, can be a problem, too. If she meets him in the front hall with a big package tied up in satin ribbon, and says, "Where's that darling baby sister of yours? I've brought her a present," then his joy at seeing her turns to bitterness. If a mother doesn't know the visitor well enough to coach her in how to act, she can have a box of ten-cent-store presents on the shelf and produce one for the child every time a visitor comes with one for the baby.

Playing with dolls may be a great solace to the child, whether girl or boy, while his mother is caring for the baby. He wants to warm his doll's bottle just the way his mother does, and have a reasonable facsimile of the other pieces of clothing and equipment that his mother uses. But doll play shouldn't take the place of helping care for the real baby; it should only supplement it.

494. Jealousy takes many forms. If a child picks up a large block and swats the baby with it, the mother knows well enough that it's jealousy. But another child is more polite. He admires the baby for a couple of days without enthusiasm and then says, "Now take her back to the hospital." One child feels all his resentment against his mother, grimly digs the ashes out of the fireplace and sprinkles them over the living-room rug in a quiet businesslike way. One with a different makeup becomes mopey and dependent, loses his joy in the sand pile and his blocks, follows his mother around, holding onto the edge of her skirt and sucking his thumb. He may wet his bed again at night or even wet and soil in the daytime. Occasionally you see a small child whose jealousy is turned inside out. He becomes preoccupied with the baby sister. When he sees a dog, all he can think of to say is, "Baby likes the dog." When he sees his friends riding trikes, he says, "Baby has a tricycle, too." He's bothered, all right, but he doesn't admit it even to himself. This child needs help even more than the one who knows exactly what he resents.

A parent sometimes says, "We found that we didn't have to worry about jealousy at all. Johnny is **fond** of the new baby." It is fine when a child shows love for the baby, but this doesn't

mean that jealousy should be ignored. It may show up in indirect ways or only in special circumstances. Perhaps he's fond
of her indoors but is rude when strangers admire her on the
street. A child may show no rivalry for months until one day
the baby creeps over to one of his toys and grabs it. Sometimes this change of feeling comes on the day the baby begins
to walk.

A mother may say, "Johnny seems very affectionate with
the baby. In fact, he often hugs her so tight that she cries."
This isn't really an accident. His feelings are mixed.

It's wise to go on the assumption that there is always some
jealousy and some affection, whether they both show on the
surface or not. The job is not to ignore the jealousy or to try
to forcibly suppress it or to make the child feel deeply
ashamed about it, but to help the feelings of affection to come
out on top.

495. How to handle different kinds of jealousy. When
the child attacks the baby, a mother's natural impulse is to
act shocked and to shame him. This doesn't work out well for
two reasons. He dislikes the baby because he's afraid that his
mother is going to love her instead of him. When she threatens
not to love him any more, it makes him feel more worried and
cruel inside. Shaming also may make him bottle up his feelings of jealousy. Jealousy does more harm to his spirit and
lasts longer if it is suppressed than if it is allowed to stay out
in the open.

There are three jobs: to protect the baby, to show the child
that his mother will not permit him to carry out his mean
feelings in action, and to reassure him that his mother still
loves him. When she sees him advancing on the baby with a
grim look on his face and a weapon in his hand, she must jump
and grab him, tell him firmly that he can't hurt the baby.
(Whenever he succeeds in being cruel, it makes him feel guilty
and more upset inside.) But she can occasionally turn the
grab into a hug and say, "I know how you feel sometimes,
Johnny. You wish there weren't any baby around here for
Mother to take care of. But don't you worry, Mother loves you
just the same." If he can realize at a moment like this that his
mother accepts his angry feelings (not actions) and still loves
him, it is the best proof that he doesn't need to worry.

As for the child who spreads the ashes around the living
room, it's natural for his mother to feel exasperated and angry,
and she will probably reprove him anyway. But if she realizes

that he did it from a deep sense of despair and bitterness, she may later feel like reassuring him, too, and try to remember what she did that he just couldn't take any longer.

The child who turns mopey in his jealousy, being of a more sensitive and in-turning nature, needs affection, reassurance and drawing out even more than the child who eases his feelings by violence. With the child who doesn't dare show directly what's bothering him, it may actually help him to feel better if his mother can say understandingly, "I know that sometimes you can feel cross at the baby, and cross at Mommy because I take care of her," and so on. If he doesn't respond after a while, his mother may want to get a temporary helper for the baby even though she decided beforehand that she couldn't afford it. If it works and helps him get back his old joy in life, it will have a permanent value far beyond the expense involved.

It is worthwhile consulting a children's psychiatrist about the child who has turned all his jealousy inside and been curdled by it, whether it takes the form of moping or of being obsessed with the baby. The psychiatrist may be able to draw

The jealous one must be restrained, but he also needs reassurance.

the jealousy back to the surface again, so that the child can realize what's biting him and get it off his chest.

If the jealousy comes out strongly only after the baby is old enough to begin grabbing the older one's toys, it may help a great deal to give him a room of his own, where he can feel that he and his toys and his buildings are safe from interference. If a separate room is out of the question, his father or a carpenter can build him a big chest or cupboard for his things, with a mighty padlock. Not only does this protect his toys, but having a key of his own in his pocket and a grown-up lock to open gives him a great sense of being important.

Should he be urged or compelled to share his toys with the baby? Not compelled. A suggestion that he give the baby a plaything that he has outgrown may appeal to him a lot and foster his generosity. But generosity that has any meaning must come from inside, and a person must feel secure and loving first. Forcing a child to share his possessions when he is insecure and selfish makes those traits stronger and more lasting.

Generally speaking, jealousy of the baby is strongest in the child under 5, because he is much more dependent on his parents and has fewer interests outside the family circle. The child of 6 or more is drawing away a little from his parents and building a position for himself among his friends. Being pushed out of the limelight at home doesn't hurt so much. It would be a mistake, though, to think that jealousy doesn't exist in the older child. He, too, needs consideration and visible reminders of love from his mother, particularly in the beginning. The child who is unusually sensitive or who has not found his place in the outside world may need just as much protection as the average small child. Even the adolescent girl, with her growing desire to be a woman, may be unconsciously envious of her mother's new parenthood.

There's one caution that I'd like to add here that may sound contradictory. Conscientious parents sometimes worry so much about jealousy and try so hard to prevent it that they make the older child less secure rather than more so. They may reach the point where they feel positively guilty about having a new baby, feel ashamed to be caught paying any attention to it, fall all over themselves trying to appease the older child. If a child finds that his parents are uneasy and apologetic toward him, it makes him uneasy, too. It reinforces his own suspicion that there is dirty work afoot and inclines him to be more mean to both baby and parents. In other words, the parents should be as tactful as possible to the older child but should not be worried or apologetic.

496. Doesn't the new baby need some attention, too? We have certainly been thinking exclusively about the older child's jealousy of the baby and even talking about ignoring the baby at times for the sake of the other child. The new baby needs attention and affection, too. But in his early days and months, he sleeps three-quarters of the time, and the minutes of the day when he's ready for fondling are few. This fits in with the needs of the older child. It's in the early days and months that he needs extra attention and demonstrations of affection. If the job is done well in the beginning, he gradually accustoms himself to the baby and loses his alarm. By the time the baby needs his full share of the family's attention, the older child should feel secure enough to permit it.

497. Jealousy between older children. There is almost bound to be some jealousy, and if it is not severe, it probably helps children to grow up more tolerant, independent and generous.

In a general way, the more agreeably parents get along with the children, the less jealousy there is. When each child is satisfied with the warm affection he receives, he has less reason to begrudge attention to his brothers and sisters.

Basically, the thing that makes each child secure in the family is the feeling that his parents love him and accept him for himself, whether he is boy or girl, smart or dull, handsome or homely. If they are comparing him with his brothers or sisters, either openly or in their thoughts, he senses it, feels unhappy inside, resentful toward the other children and the parents.

A harassed mother who is trying hard to treat her jealous boys with perfect justice may say, "Now, Jackie, here's a little red fire engine for you. And Tommy, here is another, just exactly the same, for you." But each child, instead of being satisfied, suspiciously examines both toys to see if there is any difference. Her remark has called attention to their rivalry. It's as if she said, "I bought this for you so you wouldn't complain that I was favoring your brother," instead of implying, "I bought this for you because I knew you'd like it."

The fewer the comparisons, complimentary or uncomplimentary, between brothers and sisters, the better. Saying to a child, "Why can't you be polite like your sister?" makes him dislike his sister, his mother and the very idea of politeness.

And if you say to an adolescent girl, "Never mind if you don't have dates like Barbara. You're much smarter than she is, and that's what counts," it doesn't help her feelings.

It generally works better if a mother keeps out of most of the fights between children who can stand up for themselves. When she concentrates on pinning the blame, it leaves one warrior, at least, feeling more jealous. To a greater or lesser degree, children squabble because of their jealousy, because each would like to be favored by the parents. When a parent is always ready to take sides, in the sense of trying to decide who is right and who is wrong, it encourages them to quarrel soon again. Each one hopes each time to win the parents' favor and to see the other scolded. If a mother has to break up a fight, to save life or to prevent rank injustice or to restore quiet for her own sake, it's better to simply demand an end to the hostilities, to refuse to listen to arguments, to act uninterested in discrimination (unless it is quite clear that one child was outrageously to blame), and to concentrate on what's to be done next and let bygones be bygones. In one case she can casually but firmly suggest a compromise, in another case distract them to a new occupation.

The Two-Year-Old

WHAT HE'S LIKE

498. The 2-year-old learns by imitation. In a doctor's office he solemnly places the stethoscope bell in different spots on his chest. Then he pokes the ear light in his ear, and looks a little puzzled because he can't see anything. At home he follows his mother around, sweeping with a broom when she sweeps, dusting with a cloth when she dusts, brushing his teeth when she does. It's all done with great seriousness. He is making giant strides forward in skill and understanding by means of constant imitation.

He may be quite dependent around 2. He seems to realize clearly who it is that gives him his sense of security, and shows it in different ways. A mother complains, "My 2-year-old seems to be turning into a mother's boy. He hangs onto my skirts when we're out of the house. When someone speaks to us, he hides behind me." It's a great age for whining, which is a kind of clinging. He may keep climbing out of bed in the evening to rejoin the family, or calling from his room. He may be timid about being left anywhere by his mother. He's apt to be upset if a parent or other member of the household goes away for a number of days or if the family moves to a new house. It's wise to take his sensitivity into account when changes in the household are being considered.

499. Two is the age to encourage sociability. At 2, children don't play much with each other, cooperatively. However, they love to watch each other's occupations, and enjoy playing alongside each other. It's worth a lot of trouble to bring a 2-year-old every day if possible, or at least several times a week, to where other children are playing. A 2½- or 3-year-old child won't get the hang of sharing, of rough and

Playing near and watching come before playing together.

tumble, unless he's already spent months becoming used to other children.

WORRIES AROUND TWO

500. Fear of separation. Here's what happens occasionally when a sensitive, dependent child of 1¾, 2, 2¼—particularly an only child—is separated abruptly from his mother. Perhaps she has to go out of town unexpectedly for a couple of weeks. Or she decides that she has to go to work, and arranges for a stranger to come in and take care of the child during the day. Usually the child makes no fuss while the mother is away, but when she returns, he hangs onto her like a leech and refuses to let the other woman come near. He becomes panicky whenever he thinks his mother may be leaving again. Separation anxiety is worst at bedtime. The terrified child fights against being put to bed. If his mother tears herself away, he may cry in fear for hours. If she sits by his crib, he lies down only as long as she sits still. Her slightest move toward the door brings him instantly to his feet.

In some of these cases there is also worry about urinating. The child keeps saying "Wee wee" (or whatever word he uses). His mother brings him to the bathroom, he does a few drops, and then cries "Wee wee" again just as soon as he is back in bed. You might say that he just uses this as an excuse to keep her there. This is true, but there is more to it. Children like this one are really worried that they might wet the bed. They sometimes wake every 2 hours during the night thinking about it. This is the age period when the mother is apt to be showing disapproval when there is an accident. Maybe the child figures that if he wets, his mother won't love him so much, and will therefore be more likely to go away. If so, he has two reasons for fearing to go to sleep.

501. Avoiding fears at this age. Children who from infancy have been around different people and who have been allowed to develop independence and outgoingness are less apt to develop such fears.

If your child is around 2, be careful about drastic changes. If it's almost as easy to wait 6 months for a trip or to take a job, better wait, especially if it's your first child. If you have to go now, arrange for the child to get thoroughly used to the person who is going to take care of him, whether it's a friend, a relative, a maid or foster mother. (If the child is going to be staying at the other person's house, it's even more important for him to get used to the new person and the new place by gradual steps.) Allow 2 weeks anyway. Let the new person just be around the child for a number of days without trying to take care of him, until he trusts and likes her. Then let her take over gradually. Don't leave him for a full day at first. Start with half an hour and work up. Your quick reappearance reassures him that you always come back soon. Don't go away for a month or so after you have moved or after another member of the household has left. A child at this age needs a long time to adjust to each of these changes separately.

In "The Working Mother" (Sections 772–778), there is more discussion about what arrangements should be made by a mother who is going to be away from her child.

502. How to help a fearful 2-year old. If your child has become terrified about going to bed, the safest advice, but the hardest to carry out, is to sit by his crib in a relaxed way until he goes to sleep. Don't be in a hurry to sneak away before he is asleep. It alarms him again and makes him more wakeful. This campaign may take weeks, but it should work in the end. If he was frightened because you left town, try to avoid going away again for many weeks. If you have to go away each day to work, say good-bye affectionately, but cheerfully and confidently. If you have an anguished, unsure-whether-you're-doing-the-right-thing expression, it adds to his uneasiness.

Making the child more tired by keeping him up later or omitting his nap, or having the doctor prescribe a sedative, may help a little but usually won't do the whole job. A panicky child can keep himself awake for hours even though he's exhausted. You have to take away his worry, too.

If your child is worried about wetting, keep reassuring him that it doesn't matter if he does wee wee in his bed—that you'll love him just the same.

503. Overprotectiveness increases children's fears. A child who is frightened by separation—or anything else—is very sensitive to whether his mother feels the same way about it. If she acts hesitant or guilty every time she leaves his side, if she hurries into his room at night, her anxiety reinforces his fear that there really is great danger in being apart from her.

This may sound contradictory after I've said that a mother must reassure a frightened 2-year-old by sitting by his bed as he goes to sleep and by not going away on any more trips for a number of weeks. I mean that she must give him this special care the way she gives special consideration to a sick child. But she should try to be cheerful, confident, unafraid. She should be looking for signs of the child's readiness to give up his dependence, step by step, and encourage him and compliment him. This attitude of hers is the most powerful factor in getting him over his fear.

This connection between overprotective feelings in the parent and overdependence in the child applies to many other fear situations, sleep problems and spoiling problems in infancy and childhood.

Overprotective feelings occur mostly in very devoted, tenderhearted parents who are too inclined to feel guilty when there is no realistic need for it (Sections 27, 480). Most important of all, in a majority of cases, is the parent's inability to admit that he or she is sometimes resentful or angry toward the child (Section 21).

The parent and child who are afraid to recognize that there are naturally moments when they have mean feelings toward each other, when each wishes that something bad would happen to the other, have to imagine instead that all the dangers in the world come from somewhere else, and grossly exaggerate them. The child who is denying the meanness in his mother and in himself places it all in bogeymen or witches or robbers or dogs or dinosaurs or polio or lightning, depending on his age and experience. And he clings tightly to his mother—for protection for himself and to reassure himself that nothing is really happening to her. She suppresses her occasional mean thoughts and exaggerates the dangers of kidnappers or whooping cough or home accidents or inadequate diet. She has to stay close to the child to make sure the dangers don't strike, and her anxious expression convinces the child that his fears are well founded.

Of course, the answer is not for parents to take out all their angriest feelings on the child or to let him be abusive toward them. Neither of these would help. But it certainly is helpful for parents to recognize the inevitability of their occasional mean feelings toward their child and to admit them jokingly to each other. It helps to clear the air if a parent occasionally admits to a child how angry he felt—especially if the angriness was not quite fair—and it doesn't interfere with good discipline if it's done in a sensible way. It's good to say to a child once in a while, "I know how angry you feel toward me when I have to do this to you."

When it comes to the management of the child's fear, a lot depends on how important it is for him to get over it in a hurry, from a practical point of view. There's no great necessity for an anxious child to be hurried into making friends with dogs or going into deep water in the lake or taking a bus trip by himself. He'll want to do these things as soon as he dares. On the other hand, if he has already started in nursery school, I think it's better to insist that he go unless he's deeply terrified. At night a child should not be allowed to come into his parents' bed; he should be trained to stay in his own bed. A school-age child with a phobia must get back to school sooner or later; the longer it is put off the harder it is for him. In these various separation fears, it is wise for a mother to try to see whether her own protectiveness is playing a part and to overcome it. Both steps are difficult to accomplish alone, and the mother is certainly entitled to help from a child guidance clinic or family agency (Sections 577, 578).

504. Mild bedtime difficulties. I don't want to leave the impression that every 2-year-old who objects to being put to bed should be sat with. Far from it. Severe separation anxiety is rare, but mild reluctance to be separated is very common. There are two varieties. The first consists of trying to keep the mother in the room. The child urgently says, "Wee wee!" though he went to the bathroom just a few minutes ago. This puts the mother in a quandary. She knows it's an excuse, but on the other hand she wants to encourage cooperation from the child by being cooperative herself. So she says, "Once more." As soon as he's back in bed and she starts to leave, he cries, "Drink of water!" looking as pathetic as a man dying of thirst. If his mother complies, he keeps alternating these two requests all evening. I think that such a child is feeling just slightly worried about being left alone. Usually the best and most practical way for his mother to reassure him is to remind him in a friendly, firm and breezy tone that he's just had a drink and been to the bathroom, and then to say good night and leave his room without hesitation. If she allows herself to be detained or looks troubled and uncertain, it's as if she were saying, "Well, maybe there is something to be nervous about." Even if he whimpers or cries for a few minutes, I think it is wiser not to go back. It's much easier on him to learn the lesson right away with a little unhappiness than to have the struggle drag on for weeks.

The other type of mild bedtime anxiety is when a 2-year-old learns to climb out of his crib soon after being put to bed and appears at the parents' side. He's smart enough to be very charming at such a time. He's happy to chat or to be cuddled —things he has no time for during the day. This makes it very hard for the parents to be firm. But firm they have to be, and promptly, too. Otherwise repeated climbing out of bed may develop into an unpleasant battle lasting an hour or more every night.

When a climbing-out-of-bed problem in a 2-year-old has gotten completely out of hand, parents sometimes ask if it is all right to lock the child's door. I don't like the idea of a child crying himself to sleep at a locked door. Less objectionable, I think, is to rig a string netting over the top of the crib. You can buy a badminton net at a sporting-goods store. It's too long and narrow, but it can be cut in half and the two pieces sewed together side by side. Then it can be bound with firm cord to the top rail of the side of the crib next to the wall, and also partway along the top of the head and foot of the crib.

The front half of the net can be folded back to let the child in. Then the entire front edge can be tied firmly with several tapes or cords to the springs, way under the bed, out of reach.

I am not sure that such a net is harmless from a psychological point of view, but I think it is better than repeated angry scoldings every night. It should never be spoken of as a punishment or a threat. The mother can suggest it cheerfully as a top on the bed to make a cozy house for the child to stay in and sleep in, and ask the child's help in tying it on. Most children of 2 are intrigued with the idea, allow themselves to be put in willingly, do a little poking around to see if they can make an exit, and then go to sleep. I would not keep the child in this if he acted frightened, and I would not use it for a 3-year-old, who is more apt to develop claustrophobia.

I think it's sensible to keep a 2-year-old in his crib as long as he has not learned to climb out of it, even if another crib has to be bought for a new baby. I've heard too many stories of 2-year-olds who became evening wanderers just as soon as they were graduated to youth beds. By the time they can climb out of the crib, it doesn't make any difference.

If the child is afraid to go to bed, it sometimes solves the problem to have either an older or younger brother or sister sleep in his room.

505. Children use separation anxiety to control. A child clings to his mother because he has developed a genuine fear of being separated from her. But if he finds that she is so concerned about his fear that she will always do anything he wants for reassurance, he may begin to use this as a whip. There are 3-year-olds, for instance, who are anxious about being left at nursery school and whose mothers not only stay at school for days but stay close to the children and do what they ask, to reassure them. After a while you can see that such children are exaggerating their uneasiness because they have learned to enjoy bossing their mothers around. A mother can say, "I think you are grown up now and aren't afraid to be in school. You just like to make Mommy do what you want. Tomorrow I won't need to stay here any more."

CONTRARINESS

506. Balkiness between 2 and 3. In the period between 2 and 3, children are apt to show signs of balkiness and other inner tensions. Babies begin to be balky and "negativistic" way back when they are 1 year old, so this is nothing new. But it reaches new heights and takes new forms after 2. The 1-year-old contradicts his mother. The 2½-year-old even contradicts himself. (Gesell and Ilg bring this out clearly in their discussion of the 2½-year-old in *Infant and Child in the Culture of Today*.) He has a hard time making up his mind, and then he wants to change it. He acts like a person who feels he is being bossed too much, even when no one is bothering him. He is quite bossy himself. He insists on doing things just so, doing them his own way, doing them exactly as he has always done them before. It makes him furious to have anyone interfere in one of his jobs, or rearrange his possessions.

It looks as though the child's nature between 2 and 3 is urging him to decide things for himself, and to resist pressure from other people. Trying to fight these two battles without much worldly experience seems to get him tightened up inside, especially if his parents are a little too bossy. It's similar to the 6-to-9-year-old period, when the child tries to throw off his dependence on his parents, takes over a lot of responsibility for his own behavior, becomes overfussy about how he does things, and shows his tenseness in various nervous habits.

It's often hard to get along with a child between 2 and 3. Parents have to be understanding. The job is to keep from interfering too much, from hurrying him. Let him help to dress and undress himself when he has the urge. Start his bath early enough so that he has time to dawdle and scrub the tub. At meals let him feed himself without urging. When he is stalled in his eating, let him leave the table. When it's time for bed, or going outdoors, or coming in, steer him while conversing about pleasant things. Get things done without raising issues. Don't be discouraged; there's smoother sailing ahead.

507. The child who can't stand two parents at once. Sometimes a child around 2½ or 3 can get along with either parent alone, but when the other one comes onto the scene he flies into a rage. It may be partly jealousy, but at an age when he's sensitive about being bossed and trying to do a little bossing himself, I imagine he feels outnumbered when he has to take on two important people at once. It's more often the father who is particularly unpopular at this period, and he sometimes gets the feeling he's pure poison. He shouldn't take it too seriously. It will help the child to play with his father alone, at times, so that he can know him as an enjoyable and loving person, not just an intruder. But the child must also learn that the parents love each other, want to be with each other and will not be bullied by him.

STUTTERING

508. Stuttering is common between 2 and 3. We don't entirely understand stuttering or stammering, but we know several things about it. It often runs in families, and it's much commoner in boys. This means that it is easier for certain individuals to develop it. Trying to change a left-handed child to right-handed sometimes appears to start it. The part of the brain that controls speech is closely connected to the part that controls the hand that a person naturally prefers. If you force him to use his wrong hand, it seems to confuse the nervous machinery for talking.

We know that a child's emotional state has a lot to do with stuttering. Most cases occur in somewhat tense children. Some stutter only when they are excited or when they are talking to one particular person. Here are some examples. One little boy began to stutter when a new baby sister was brought home from the hospital. He didn't show his jealousy outwardly. He never tried to hit or pinch her. He just became uneasy. A girl of 2½ began to stutter after the departure of a fond relative who had been with the family a long time. In 2 weeks the stuttering stopped for the time being. When the family moved to a new house, she was quite homesick and stuttered again for a period. Two months later the father was called into the Army. The family was upset, and the little girl started again. Mothers report that their children's stuttering is definitely worse when the mothers are tense. I think children who, during too much of the day, are being talked to and told stories, urged to talk and recite, shown off, are especially liable. Stuttering may start when a father decides to be stricter in his discipline.

Why is stuttering so common between 2 and 3? There are two possible explanations. This is the age period when a child is working very hard at his talking. When he was younger, he used short sentences that he didn't need to think out: "See the car," "Wanna go out," etc. But when he gets past 2, he tries to make up longer sentences to express new ideas. He starts a sentence 3 or 4 times, only to break off in the middle because he can't find the right words. His mother, worn out by his constant talking, doesn't pay too much attention. She says, "Uh huh," in an absentminded way while she goes about her business. So the child is further frustrated by not being able to hold his audience.

It is also possible that the balkiness that is a part of this rather tense stage of development affects his speech, too.

509. What to do for stuttering. You may be especially distressed if you yourself or some relative has had a lifelong struggle to overcome stuttering. But there is no cause for alarm. I think nine out of ten of the children who start to stutter between 2 and 3 outgrow it in a few months' time if given half a chance. It's only the exceptional case that becomes chronic. Don't try to correct the child's speech or worry about speech training at 2½. Look around to see what might be making him tense. If he was upset by being separated from you for a number of days, try to avoid further separations for a couple of months (Sections 501, 502). If you think you have been talking at him or urging him to talk too much, try to train yourself out of it. Play with him by doing things instead of by always talking things. Is he having plenty of chance to play with other children with whom he gets along easily? Does he have toys and equipment enough, indoors and out, so that he can be inventing his own games without too much bossing? I don't mean that you should ignore or isolate him, but when you're with him be relaxed and let him take the lead. When he talks to you, give him your attention so that he doesn't get frantic. If jealousy is upsetting him, see whether you can do more to prevent it. Stuttering in most cases lasts a number of months, with ups and downs. Don't expect it to go right away; be content with gradual progress. If you can't figure what, if anything, is wrong, talk it over with a children's psychiatrist. A tongue-tie has nothing to do with stuttering, and should not be cut.

Some schools and hospitals have special speech classes or clinics, in which older children can receive special training. This is often helpful, but by no means always. It is most valuable for the school-age child who wants assistance. For the child who is of a distinctly nervous type, it might be better to consult a children's psychiatrist first to see if it's possible to discover and remove the causes of tenseness (Section 577).

NAIL BITING

510. Nail biting is a sign of tenseness. It is more common in relatively high-strung, worrisome children. They start to bite when they are anxious—for instance, while waiting to be called on in school, while watching a scary episode in a movie. It isn't necessarily a serious sign in a generally happy, successful child, but it is always worth thinking over.

Nagging or punishing a nail biter usually doesn't stop him for longer than half a minute, because he seldom realizes he is doing it. In the long run, it may increase his tension. Bitter medicine on the nails rarely helps.

The better course is to find out what some of the pressures on the child are and try to relieve them. Is he being urged or corrected or warned or scolded too much? Are the parents expecting too much in the way of lessons? Consult the teacher about his school adjustment. If movie, radio and TV adventures make him much more jittery than the average child, he'd better be kept away from the worst programs.

A girl beyond the age of 3 may be helped by a manicure set, and perhaps some nail polish, if they are offered in a co-operative spirit.

Three to Six

DEVOTION TO THE PARENTS

511. Children at this age are usually easier to lead.
Boys and girls around 3 have reached a stage in their emotional development when they feel that their father and mother are wonderful people. They pay their parents the compliment of wanting to be like them, do what they do, wear what they wear, use the same words. The 2-year-old girl who sees her mother sweeping wants to do it, too, but she's thinking mostly of the broom. The 5-year-old girl wants to dress up in her mother's clothes, but she's not thinking so much of the clothes as of looking and feeling like her mother. She is actually beginning to be like her mother, even when she isn't trying. This is called identification.

The automatic balkiness, the hostility that was just below the surface in the 2½-year-old period seem to lessen after 3 in most children. The feelings toward the parents aren't just friendly; they are warm and tender. However, the child is not so devoted to his parents that he always obeys and behaves well. He is still a real person with ideas of his own. He wants to assert himself, even if it means going against his parents' wishes at times.

While I'm emphasizing how agreeable children usually are between 3 and 6, I ought to make a partial exception for 4-year-olds. There's a lot of assertiveness, cockiness, loud talk and provoking that comes out around 4 years in many children and that requires a firm hand in the mother.

512. A boy now wants to be like his father. By the age of 3 a boy is beginning to realize more clearly that he is a boy and will grow up to be a man like his father. This gives him a special admiration for his father and other men and boys. He watches them carefully and works hard to be as much like them as he can, in appearance and behavior and interests. In his play he concentrates on propelling toy trucks, trains and planes, pretending his tricycle is a car, being a policeman or fireman, making deliveries, building houses and bridges. He copies his father's remarks in his father's tone of voice. He takes on his father's attitude toward other males and toward women. He is preparing himself to play a man's part in the world, spiritually, occupationally, socially, by means of his love and admiration of his father and other men.

513. A girl wants to be like her mother. The girl at this age realizes that it is her destiny to be a woman, and this makes it particularly exciting and challenging for her to try to be like her mother and other women. She turns with more concentration to housework and baby (doll) care if these are her mother's occupations. In caring for her dolls, she takes on the very same attitudes and tone of voice her mother uses toward children. She absorbs her mother's point of view toward men and boys.

Boys and girls now become fascinated with all aspects of babies. They want to know where they come from. When they find out that babies grow inside mothers they are eager to carry out this amazing act of creation themselves—boys as well as girls. They want to take care of babies and love them, the way they realize they were cared for and loved. They will press a younger child into the role of a baby and spend hours acting as father and mother to him, or they'll use a doll.

It's not generally recognized that little boys are as eager as girls to grow babies inside themselves. When their parents tell them that this is impossible, they are apt to refuse to believe it for a long time. "I will too grow a baby," they say, really believing that if they wish something hard enough they can omnipotently make it come true. In a country like ours, where boys are shamed as sissies for wanting to be like a girl in any way, this desire to grow a baby is eventually suppressed. But in some primitive parts of the world, when a woman goes into labor her husband does, too, and is taken to the men's labor hut, moaning and writhing, by his sympathetic male friends. In our kind of society we believe that the frustrated desire of boys to make a baby becomes part of men's urge to create things: buildings, bridges, machines, inventions, books, plays, music and pictures.

514. Boys become romantic toward their mother, girls toward their father. Up to this age, a boy's love for his mother has been predominantly of a dependent kind, like that of a baby. But now it also becomes increasingly romantic, like his father's. By the time he's 4, he's apt to insist that he's going to marry his mother when he grows up. He isn't clear just what marriage consists of, but he's absolutely sure who is the most important and appealing woman in the world. The little girl who is growing normally in her mother's pattern develops the same kind of love for her father.

These strong romantic attachments help children to grow spiritually and to acquire wholesome feelings toward the opposite sex that will later guide them into good marriages. But there is another side to the picture that creates unconscious tension in most children at this age. When a human male, old or young, loves a woman very much, he can't help wanting her all to himself. He can't help feeling jealous of the love that exists between her and some other man. And so, of course, the boy of 3 and 4 and 5, as he becomes more aware of his possessive devotion to his mother, also becomes aware of how much she already belongs to his father. This irritates him underneath, no matter how much he loves and admires his father. At times he secretly wishes his father would get lost, and then he feels guilty about such disloyal feelings. Reasoning as a child does, he imagines that his father has the same jealous and resentful feelings toward him. He tries to push these scary thoughts out of his mind, since his father, after all, is so much bigger and stronger, but they are apt to come to the surface in his dreams. We believe that these mixed feelings—of love, jealousy and fear—toward the father are the main cause of the bad dreams that little boys of this age are so apt to have—of being chased by giants, robbers, gorillas and other frightening figures.

The little girl, if she is developing normally, also becomes more possessive in her love for her father. She wishes at times that something would happen to her mother (whom she loves so much in other respects) so that she could have her father for herself. She may even say to her mother, "You can go away for a long trip, and I'll take good care of Daddy." But then she imagines that her mother is jealous of her, too, and subconsciously worries about this.

These fears of children—that their parents are angry with them—get mixed up with their worries about why boys and

men are shaped differently from girls and women. This will
be discussed in Section 522.

Since all small children, we believe, go through this phase,
it shouldn't make parents worry unless a child becomes excessively fearful or antagonistic to the parent of the same sex
or much too close to the parent of the opposite sex. In that
case, it's wise to get the help of a child guidance clinic.

**515. The attachment isn't meant to become too com-
plete.** This romantic attachment to the parent of the opposite
sex in the years between 3 and 6 is what you might call Nature's way of molding a child's feelings in preparation for his
eventual life as husband and father or wife and mother. But
Nature doesn't want the attachment to go so far or get so
strong that it lasts through life or even through childhood.
Nature expects that the child by 6 or 7 will become quite
discouraged about the possibility of having the parent all to
himself. The unconscious fears about the parent's supposed
anger and about genital differences will turn his pleasure in
dreaming about romance into an aversion. From now on, a
boy will shy away from his mother's affectionate kisses. His
interests turn with relief to impersonal matters such as
schoolwork and science. He tries to be just like the other boys
instead of just like his father.

The previous intense attachments to his two parents will
have served their main constructive purpose and will be progressively outgrown. (Freud called this shift the resolution
of the Oedipus complex.)

So a father who realizes that his young son sometimes has
unconscious feelings of resentment and fear toward him does
not help the boy by trying to be too gentle and permissive
with him or by pretending that he, the father, doesn't really
love his wife very much. In fact, if a boy was convinced that
his father was afraid to be a strong man, a firm father and a
normally possessive husband, the boy would sense that he
himself was having his mother too much to himself and would
feel really guilty and frightened. And he would miss the inspiration of a manly father, which he must have in order to
develop his own manliness and courage.

In the same way a mother, even though she knows that
her young daughter is sometimes jealous of her, best helps her
daughter to grow up by being a self-confident mother who
doesn't let herself be pushed around, who knows how and

when to be firm, and who isn't at all afraid to show her affection and devotion to her husband.

You can see why it complicates life for a boy if his mother is a great deal more permissive and affectionate toward him than his father is. The same is true if she seems to be closer and more sympathetic to her son than she is to her husband. Such attitudes have a tendency to alienate a boy from his father and to make him too fearful of him. In a corresponding manner, the father who is putty in his daughter's hands and is always undoing the mother's discipline, or the father who acts as if he enjoys his daughter's companionship more than his wife's, is being unhelpful not only to his wife but to his daughter. This interferes with the good relationship that a daughter should have with her mother in order to grow up to be a happy woman.

Incidentally, it is entirely normal for a father to be a bit more lenient toward his daughter and a mother toward her son, and for a son to feel a little more comfortable with his mother and a daughter with her father, because there is naturally less rivalry between male and female than between two males or two females.

I don't want to get fathers and mothers so concerned about these relationships that they become self-conscious or inhibited or worried. In the average family there is a healthy balance between the feelings of father, mother, sons and daughters that guides them through these stages of development without any special effort or conscious thought. I bring these points up only to give some clues for those families whose relationships have gotten out of kilter—families in which, for instance, the parents are constantly at odds about disciplining the children, or a boy is becoming timid toward all boys and men, or a girl is excessively defiant of her mother.

516. Parents can help children through this romantic but jealous stage by gently keeping it clear that the parents do belong to each other, that a boy can't ever have his mother to himself or a girl have her father to herself, but that the parents aren't shocked to realize that their children are mad at them sometimes on this account.

When a boy declares that he is going to marry his mother, she can act pleased with the compliment but she can also explain that she's already married and that when he grows up he'll find another girl his own age to marry.

When parents are being companionable together, they

needn't and shouldn't let a child break up their conversation. They can cheerfully but firmly remind him that they have things to talk over and suggest that he get busy, too. Their tactfulness will keep them from prolonged displays of affection in front of him (as it would if other people were present), but they don't need to spring apart guiltily if he comes into the room unexpectedly.

When a boy is being rude to his father because he's feeling jealous, or to his mother because she's the cause of his jealousy, the parent should insist on politeness. But at the same time the parent can ease the child's feelings of anger and guilt by saying that he knows that the child is cross at him. See Section 482.

517. Sleep problems at 3, 4 and 5. Many of the sleep problems in 3-, 4- and 5-year-old children that have been studied in child guidance clinics are found to be caused by romantic jealousy. The child wanders into the parents' room in the middle of every night and wants to get into their bed because subconsciously he doesn't want them to be alone together. It's much better for him as well as for the parents if they promptly and firmly, but not angrily, take him back to his own bed.

CURIOSITY AND IMAGINATION

518. The child's curiosity at this age is intense. He wants to know the meaning of everything that meets his eye. His imagination is rich. He puts two and two together and draws conclusions. He connects everything with himself. When he hears about trains, he wants to know right away, "Will I go on a train someday?" When he hears about an illness, it makes him think, "Will I have that?"

519. A little imagination is a good thing. When a child of 3 or 4 tells a made-up story, he isn't lying in our grown-up sense. His imagination is vivid to him. He's not sure where the real ends and the unreal begins. That is why he loves stories that are told or read to him. That is why he is scared at the movies and shouldn't go to them.

You don't need to jump on him for making up stories occasionally, or make him feel guilty, or even be concerned yourself, so long as he is outgoing in general and happy with other children. On the other hand, if he is spending a good part of each day telling about imaginary friends or adventures, not as a game but as if he believes in them, it raises the question whether his real life is satisfying enough. Part of the remedy may be finding him children his own age to play with and helping him to enjoy them. Another question is whether he is having enough easygoing companionship with his parents. A child needs hugging and piggyback rides. He needs to share in his parents' jokes and friendly conversations. If the adults around him are undemonstrative, he dreams of comfy, understanding playmates as the hungry man dreams of chocolate bars. If the parents are always disapproving, he invents a wicked companion whom he blames for the naughty things he has done or would like to do. If a child is living largely in his imagination and not adjusting well with other children, especially by the age of 4, a psychiatrist should be able to find what he is lacking.

Occasionally a mother who has always lived a great deal in her imagination and who is delighted to find how imaginative her child is overfills him with stories, and they both live for hours in fairyland. The games and stories that the other children make up are poor in comparison to hers. The child may be weaned away from his interest in real people and things and have a harder time later adjusting to the world. I don't mean that a mother should be afraid of fairy stories or of a little make-believe, but only that it should be in moderation.

520. Why does an older child lie? The older child who tells a lie to deceive is a different problem. The first question is: Why does he have to? Everyone, grown-up or child, gets in a jam occasionally when the only tactful way out is a small lie, and this is no cause for alarm.

A child isn't naturally deceitful. When he lies regularly it means that he is under too much pressure of some kind. If he is failing in his schoolwork and lying about it, it isn't because he doesn't care. His lying shows that he does care. Is the work too hard for him? Is he confused in his mind by other worries so that he can't concentrate? Are his parents setting too high standards? The job is to find out what is wrong, with the help of the teacher, or the guidance teacher, or the school psychologist, or a psychiatrist (Section 577). You don't have to pretend that he has pulled the wool over your eyes. You might say gently, "You don't have to lie to me.

Tell me what the trouble is and we'll see what we can do."
But he won't be able to tell you the answer right away because he probably doesn't know it himself. Even if he knows
some of his worries, he can't break down all at once. It takes
time and understanding.

FEARS AROUND THREE, FOUR AND FIVE

521. Imaginary worries are common at this age. In
earlier sections we discussed how anxieties are different at
different age periods. New types of fear crop up fairly often
around the age of 3 or 4—fear of the dark, of dogs, of fire
engines, of death, of cripples. The child's imagination has
now developed to the stage where he can put himself in other
people's shoes and picture dangers that he hasn't actually experienced. His curiosity is pushing out in all directions. He
wants to know not only the cause of everything but what
these things have to do with him. He overhears something
about dying. Quickly he wants to know what dying is, and
as soon as he gets a dim idea he asks, "Do I have to die?"

These fears are commoner in children who have been made
tense from battles over such matters as feeding and toilet
training, children whose imaginations have been overstimulated by scary stories or too many warnings, children who
haven't had enough chance to develop their independence
and outgoingness, children whose parents are too protective
(Section 503). The uneasiness that the child has accumulated before now seems to be crystallized by his new imagination into definite dreads. It sounds as if I mean that any
child who develops a fear has been handled badly in the past,
but I don't mean to go that far. I think that some children
are born more sensitive than others; and all children, no matter how carefully they are brought up, are frightened by
something. Read Section 514 about children's feelings about
their parents.

If your child develops a fear of the dark, try to reassure
him. This is more a matter of your manner than your words.
Don't make fun of him, or be impatient with him, or try to
argue him out of his fear. If he wants to talk about it, as a
few children do, let him. Give him the feeling that you want
to understand but that you are sure nothing bad will happen
to him. This is the time for extra hugs and comforting reminders that you love him very much and will always protect

him. Naturally you should never threaten a child with bogey-men or policemen or the devil. Avoid movies and scary TV programs and cruel fairy stories. The child is scared enough of his own mental creations. Call off any battle that you might be engaged in about feeding or staying dry at night. Keep him behaving well by firm guidance rather than by letting him misbehave and then making him feel guilty about it afterward. Arrange to give him a full, outgoing life with other children every day. The more he is absorbed in games and plans, the less he will worry about his inner fears. Leave his door open at night if that is what he wants, or leave a dim light on in his room. It's a small price to pay to keep the goblins out of sight. The light, or the conversation from the living room, won't keep him awake so much as his fears will. When his fear subsides, he will be able to stand the dark again.

Realize ahead of time that questions about death are apt to come up at this age. Try to make the first explanation casual, not too scary. You might say, "Everybody has to die someday. Most people die when they get very old and tired and weak and they just stop being alive." Some parents like to express it in religious terms: "He was very, very sick, and God took him to Heaven to take care of him." Remember to hug him and smile at him and remind him that you're going to be together for years and years.

All healthy people of every age have some degree of fear and resentment of death. There is no way to present the matter to children that will get around this basic human at-titude. But if you think of death as something to be met eventually with dignity and fortitude you'll be able to give somewhat the same feeling about it to your child.

A fear of an animal is common at this period, even though the child has had no bad experiences. Don't drag him to a dog to reassure him. The more you pull him, the more you make him feel he has to pull in the opposite direction. As the months go by, he will try himself to get over his fear and ap-proach a dog. He will do it faster by himself than you can ever persuade him. That reminds me of fear of the water. Don't ever pull a child, screaming, into the ocean or pool. It is true that occasionally a child who is forced in finds that it is fun and loses his fear abruptly, but in more cases it works the opposite way. Remember that the child is longing to go in even though he has a dread of it. Let him build up his own courage at his own speed.

With fears of dogs and fire engines and policemen and other concrete things, a child may try to get used to his worry and overcome it by playing games about it. This acting out of a fear is a great help if the child is able to do it. A fear is meant to make us act. Our bodies are flooded with adrenaline, which makes the heart beat faster and supplies sugar for quick energy. We are ready to run like the wind or to fight like wild animals. The running and the fighting burn up the anxiety. Sitting still does nothing to relieve it. If a child with a fear of a dog can play games in which he pounds the stuffing out of a toy dog, it partly relieves him. If your child develops an intense fear, or a number of fears, or frequent nightmares, or sleepwalking, you ought to get the help of a children's psychiatrist (Section 577).

522. Fear of injury. I'd like to discuss separately the fear of bodily injury in the age period between 2½ and 5, because there are special things you can do to prevent or relieve it. A child at this age wants to know the reason for everything, worries easily and applies dangers to himself. If he sees a crippled or deformed person, he first wants to know what happened to him, then puts himself in the other's place and wonders if that injury might happen to himself. Children develop these fears not only about real injuries. They even get mixed up and worried about the natural differences between boys and girls. If a boy around the age of 3 sees a girl undressed, it may strike him as queer that she hasn't got a penis like his. He's apt to say, "Where is her wee wee?" If he doesn't receive a satisfactory answer right away, he may jump to the conclusion that some accident has happened to her. Next comes the anxious thought, "That might happen to me, too." The same misunderstanding may worry the little girl when she first realizes that boys are made differently. First she asks, "What's that?" Then she wants to know anxiously, "Why don't I have one? What happened to it?" That's the way a 3-year-old's mind works. He may be so upset right away that he's afraid to question his mother.

This worry about why boys are shaped differently from girls shows up in different ways. I remember a boy just under 3 who, with an anxious expression, kept watching his baby sister being bathed and telling his mother, "Baby is boo-boo." That was his word for hurt. His mother couldn't make out what he was talking about until he got bold enough to point. At about the same time he began to hold onto his own penis in a worried way. His mother was unhappy about this and assumed it was the beginning of a bad habit. It never occurred to her that there was a connection between these two developments. I remember a little girl who became worried after she found out about boys, and kept trying to undress different children to see how they were made, too. She didn't do this in a sly way; you could see she was fearful. Later she began to handle her genitals. A boy 3½ first became upset about his younger sister's body, and then began to worry about everything in the house that was broken. He would ask his mother nervously, "Why is this tin soldier broken?" There was no sense to this question, because he had broken it himself the day before. Everything that he saw damaged seemed to remind him of his fears about himself.

It's wise to realize ahead of time that a normal child is likely to be wondering about things like bodily differences between 2½ and 3½, and that if he isn't given a comforting explanation when he first gets curious, he's apt to come to worrisome conclusions. It's no use waiting for him to say, "I want to know why a girl isn't made like a boy," because he won't be that definite. He may ask some kind of question, or he may hint around, or he may just wait and get worried. Don't think of it as an unwholesome interest in sex. To him it's just like any other important question at first. You can see why it would work the wrong way to shush him, or scold him, or blush and refuse to answer. That would give him the idea he was on dangerous ground, which is what you want to avoid. On the other hand, you don't need to be solemn as if you were giving a lecture. It's easier than that. It helps, first of all, to bring the child's fear out into the open by saying that he (or she) probably thinks a girl had a penis but something happened to it. Then you try to make it clear, in a matter-of-fact cheerful tone, that girls and women are made differently from boys and men; they are meant to be that way. A small child gets an idea more easily from examples. You can explain that Johnny is made just like Daddy, Uncle Harry, David and so on, and that Mary is made like Mommy, Mrs. Jenkins and Helen (listing all the individuals that the child knows best). A little girl needs extra reassurance because it's natural for her to want to have something that she can see. (I heard of a little girl who complained to her mother, "But he's so fancy and I'm so plain.") It will help her to know that her mother likes being made the way she is, that her mother loves her just the way she's made. This may also be a good time to explain that girls when they are older can grow babies of their own inside them and have breasts with which to nurse them. That's a thrilling idea at 3 or 4.

DIFFERENT CAUSES FOR HANDLING THE GENITALS

523. In the infant it's wholesome curiosity. Babies in the last half of the first year discover their genitals the way they discovered their fingers and toes, and handle them the same way, too. The 1¼-year-old baby, sitting on the potty, explores himself with definite curiosity for a few seconds at a time. This won't come to anything or start a bad habit. You can distract him with a toy if you want, but don't feel that you've got to. It's better not to give him the idea that he is bad or that his genitals are bad. You want him to go on having a wholesome, natural feeling about his entire body. If he is scared about any part of himself, it draws his attention to it, gets it on his mind, and may have bad results later. Furthermore, if you try to stop a year-old baby by saying, "No, no," or slapping his hand, or yanking it away, it's apt to make him more determined.

524. At 3 it's related to his feelings. Children between 3 and 6 are surprisingly grown up in lots of ways. They love intensely and romantically those who are close to them, especially their parents.

We realize now that there is a childish kind of sexual feeling at this period, which is an essential part of normal development. (In former times people believed that nothing of this sort occurred until adolescence, probably because they themselves had been brought up worried about sex and they wanted to avoid recognizing it in their children as long as possible.) Children of 3, 4 and 5 are physically affectionate. They cling to their favorite grown-ups and lean against them. They are interested in each other's bodies, occasionally have the desire to see and touch each other. This is one reason why they like to play doctor.

If you realize that this early interest in sex is a natural part of the slow process of growing up and that it occurs to a degree in all wholesome children, you can take a sensible view of it. If a child is not preoccupied with sex, if he is generally outgoing, unworried and has plenty of other interests and playmates, there is no cause for concern. If not, he needs to be helped.

If you discover your small child in some sort of sex play alone or with others, you'll probably be at least a little bit surprised and shocked. In expressing your disapproval it's better to be firmly matter-of-fact rather than very shocked or angry. You want him to know that you don't want him to do it, but you don't want him to feel that he's a criminal. You can say, for instance, "Mother doesn't want you to do that again," or "That isn't polite," and shoo the children out to some other activity. That's usually enough to stop sex play for a long time in normal children. It's sensible for a mother to keep some track of a group of small children who are in a period of occasional interest in sex, and make sure they have plenty of other things to do. The principal reason is that some children are upset and worried by what is done and said, especially if there is an older child with an exaggerated interest leading them on. Naturally, parents should not become suspicious snoopers or make accusations.

525. A lot at 3 may be due to worry. In Section 522 there were examples of children in the neighborhood of 3 years who handled themselves a great deal, in a preoccupied manner, after they became worried about why girls aren't made the same as boys. It's important for parents to know that the fear that something will happen or has happened to the genitals is one of the commonest causes of excessive handling or masturbation in young childhood.

To tell such a child that he'll injure himself makes matters worse. To tell him that he's bad and that you won't love him any more gives him a new fear. The wise thing is to try to take away his fear as soon as you see it developing. If the mother of the little boy who said, "Baby is boo-boo," had known that this misunderstanding and this worry are common, she could have started to reassure him the first time he said it. The same thing applies to the mother of the little girl who anxiously tried to undress the other children.

526. After 6 there's a stronger effort to control it. Between the ages of 6 and puberty, it seems as if the child, by his own nature, makes an effort to suppress the impulse to masturbate or to become involved in sex play with others. Children get the idea that masturbation is considered wrong, whether their parents have told them so or not, and this is the period when their conscience is becoming strong. But it doesn't stop altogether in all children. Occasionally a child is drawn into it in the group because the others are doing it. It's a time in his life when he's striving with might and main to become a "regular guy."

527. It may be a sign of tenseness and worry at any age. At any age there are a few children who handle their genitals a great deal, sometimes in public. They hardly seem to be aware of what they are doing. They are usually tense or worried children. They aren't nervous because they are masturbating; they are masturbating because they are nervous. The job here is to find out what's causing the tenseness, instead of attacking the masturbation directly. An 8-year-old boy is terrified that his ill mother is going to die. He can't put his mind on schoolwork but absentmindedly handles his genitals in school as he gazes out the window. Another child is thoroughly maladjusted, doesn't know how to get along with other children, has no close connection with the world around him. Cut off from the outside, he must live within himself Such children and their parents need the help of a psychiatrist or child guidance clinic (Section 577).

Many children hold their genitals when they need to urinate. especially the procrastinators, and this has no special significance.

528. Why threats are harmful. Most of us heard in childhood the threat that masturbation would lead to insanity. This belief is untrue. It grew up because certain adolescents and young adults who are becoming seriously ill mentally masturbate a great deal. But they aren't becoming insane because they are masturbating. The excessive masturbation is just one symptom of the nervous breakdown. This is an example of the fact that frequent masturbation is due to something else going wrong in the child's life or in his spirit. The job is to find the cause.

What's wrong with telling a child that masturbation will make him sick, or injure his genitals, or mark him as an evil person? First of all, none of these things is true. In the second place and more important, it's risky and it's wrong to put deer fears into a child's mind. The self-confident, tough-minded child may not be much affected by these threats. But the sensitive child takes them to heart. He may develop such a morbid fear of anything sexual that he will grow up maladjusted, afraid, or unable to marry or have children.

Though masturbation doesn't lead to nervousness, excessive worry about it can certainly cause nervousness. I think of an adolescent boy whose parents were morbidly afraid of masturbation. They hired a companion for their son, whose job it was to stay close to him 24 hours a day to make sure he didn't do it. This reminded him of masturbation constantly, and at the same time gave him a monstrous fear of it. This is an exaggerated case, but it's an example of how unwise it is to attack the problem blindly. It's important that parents not only avoid serious threats but also avoid getting the child's mind on it.

All these reasons for avoiding severe methods of repression don't mean that a parent should try to ignore masturbation or other sex play. We were all brought up to be disturbed by it, and we can never unlearn that. We can't be comfortable with our children if they are doing things we dislike. Even if we would magically get over our disapproval (which I don't think would be desirable), the fact would remain that our children live in and must adapt to a society that disapproves. Furthermore, there is lots of evidence that all children feel guilty about masturbation whether or not their parents have found out about it or said anything about it. So I think it's quite appropriate when a mother discovers a child in sex play to give him the idea that she doesn't want him to do it any more, in a tone that implies that this will help him to stop. With the child who seems to need reassurance, the mother can explain that most boys and girls want to do it sometime or other but they can usually stop when they try.

529. Why there is more at adolescence. Among adolescents there tends to be an increased urge to masturbate for reasons that are easy to understand. Glandular changes are taking place that transform boy into man, girl into woman. The increased function of the glands doesn't affect just the body. It also affects the thoughts and emotions. The child becomes increasingly aware of his sexual and romantic feelings, not because he wants to but because his glands say he has to. Yet he is nowhere near ready, in the early part of adolescence, to express his feelings openly. When he is more grown up, the same impulses find expression in dates, romantic companionship, dancing and flirting. Later still, they lead to falling in love in earnest and marriage.

Some conscientious adolescents feel excessively guilty and worried about masturbation, even when it's just a thought, and need reassurance. If a child seems to be generally happy and successful, doing well in school, getting along with his friends, he can be told that all normal young people have these desires and do their best to control them. This won't take away all his feeling of guilt, but it will help. If, on the other hand, he is wrapped up in himself, or unable to enjoy friendships, or is getting into trouble with his schoolwork, then it is time to find help from someone who understands adolescents well. The best person would be a children's psychiatrist. If that's not possible, talk to the guidance teacher or counselor in the high school. In an unhappy child, frequent masturbation, or preoccupation with it, is only one symptom of a larger problem.

"THE FACTS OF LIFE"

530. Sex education starts early whether you plan it or not. It is common to think that sex education means a lecture at school or a solemn talk by a parent at home. This is taking too narrow a view of the subject. A child is learning about "the facts of life" all through his childhood, if not in a good way then in an unwholesome way. Sex is a lot broader than just how babies are made. It includes the whole matter of how men and women get along with each other, and what their respective places are in the world. Let me give you a couple of bad examples. Suppose a boy has a father who is disagreeable and abusive to the mother. You can't educate the boy with a lecture at school telling him that marriage is a relationship of mutual love and respect. His experience tells him differently. When he learns about the physical side of sex, whether it's from a teacher or from other children, he will fit it into the picture he has of a man being disagreeable to a woman. Or take the example of a girl who grows up feeling unwanted because she thinks her parents prefer her younger brother. She is going to resent men, because she believes that they get all the breaks—that women are always the victims. It won't matter how many books or talks you give her about sex and marriage. Whatever she hears or experiences she will fit into the pattern she has fixed in her mind: it's the man taking advantage of the woman. Even if she marries, she won't adjust to it.

So a child begins his sex education as soon as he can sense how his mother and father get along with each other in general, and how they feel about their sons and daughters.

531. A normal child asks questions around 3. A child begins to get more exact ideas about the things that are connected with sex around the ages of 2½, 3, 3½. This is the "why" stage, when his curiosity branches out in all directions. He probably wants to know why boys are made differently from girls (which is discussed in Section 522). He doesn't think of it as a sex question. It's just an important question. But if he gains the wrong impression then, it will become mixed up with sex later and give him distorted ideas.

532. Where do babies come from? This question is also pretty sure to come up in the period around 3. It's easier and better to begin with the truth, rather than tell him a fairy story and have to change it later. Try to answer the question as simply as he asks it. For instance, you can say, "A baby grows in a special place inside his mother." You don't have to tell him more than that for the time being if it satisfies him. But maybe in a few minutes, maybe in a few months, he wants to know a couple of other things. How does the baby get in and how does he get out? The first question is apt to be embarrassing to the mother (or father). She may jump to the conclusion that he is now demanding to know about conception and sex relations. Of course, he has no such idea. He thinks of things getting into the stomach by being eaten and perhaps wonders if the baby gets in that way, too. A simple answer is that the baby grows from a tiny seed that was in the mother all the time. It will be months before he wants to know what part the father plays. Some people feel that the child should be told at the time of his earlier questions that the father contributes by putting his seed in the mother, too. Perhaps this is right, especially in the case of the little boy who feels that the man is left out of the picture. But most experts agree that at 3 or 4 years it is not necessary to try to give him an exact picture of the physical and emotional sides of intercourse. It's more than the child bargained for, you might say, when he asked his question. All that's necessary is to satisfy his curiosity at the level of his understanding.

To the question of how the baby gets out, a good answer

is something to the effect that when he is big enough he comes out through a special opening that's just for that purpose. (It's just as well to make it clear that it is not the opening for bowel movements or for urine.)

533. Why not the stork? You may say, "Why isn't it easier and less embarrassing to tell him about the stork?" There are several reasons. We know that a child as young as 3, if he has a pregnant mother or aunt, may have a suspicion of where the baby is growing from observing the woman's figure and from bits of conversation that he overhears. It's apt to mystify and worry him to have his mother nervously telling him something different from what he suspects is the truth. Even if he doesn't suspect anything at 3, he is surely going to find out the truth or the half-truth when he's 5 or 7 or 9. It's better not to start him off wrong and have him later decide that you're something of a liar. And if he finds that for some reason you didn't dare tell him the truth, it puts a barrier between you, makes him uneasy. He's less likely to ask you other questions later, no matter how troubled he is. Another reason for telling the truth at 3 is that the child is satisfied with simple answers. You get practice for the harder questions that come later.

Sometimes a small child who has been told where the baby is growing confuses his parents by talking as if he also believed the stork theory. Or he may mix up two or three theories at the same time. This is natural. Small children believe part of everything they hear because they have such vivid imaginations. They don't try, like grown-ups, to find the one right answer and get rid of the wrong ones. You must also remember that a child can't learn anything from one telling. He learns a little at a time, and comes back with the same question until he feels sure that he has gotten it straight. Then at every new stage of development he's ready for a new slant.

534. A step at a time usually satisfies. Realize ahead of time that your child's questions will never come in exactly the form or at the moment you expect. A parent is apt to visualize the scene at bedtime when the child is in a confidential mood. Actually, the question is more apt to be popped in the middle of the grocery store or while you are talking on the street with a pregnant neighbor. If it does, try to curb that impulse to shush the child. Answer him on the spot if you can. If that is impossible, say casually, "I'll tell you later. These are things we like to talk about when other people aren't around." Don't make too solemn an occasion of it. When he asks you why the grass is green or why dogs have tails, you answer in an offhand way that gives him the feeling that it is the most natural thing in the world. Try to get the same spirit of naturalness into your answers about the facts of life. Remember that even if this subject is charged with feeling and embarrassment for you, it is a matter of simple curiosity to him. The question, "Why don't babies come until you are married?" or "What does the father do about it?" may not come until the child is 4 or 5 or older unless he observes animals. Then you can explain that the seed comes out of the father's penis and goes into the place where the baby will grow. It may be some time before he tries to visualize this situation. When he is ready for that, you can bring in something in your own words about loving and embracing.

A young child is very apt to stumble on some evidence of menstruation and to interpret this as a sign of injury. A mother should be ready to explain that all women have this discharge every month and that it doesn't come from a hurt. Something about the purpose of menstruation can be explained to a child of 4 or older.

535. The child who hasn't asked. What about the child who has reached the age of 4 or 5 or more and hasn't asked any questions at all? Parents sometimes assume that this means the child is very innocent and has never thought of these questions. Most people who have worked closely with children would be inclined to doubt this. It is more likely that the child has gotten the feeling, whether the parents mean to give it or not, that these matters are embarrassing. You can be on the lookout for indirect questions and hints and little jokes that a child uses to test out his parents' reaction. I think of several examples. A child of 7 who was not supposed to know anything about pregnancy kept calling attention to his mother's large abdomen in a half-embarrassed, half-joking way. Here was a good chance, better late than never, for the mother to explain. A little girl who is at the stage of wondering why she isn't made like a boy sometimes makes valiant efforts to urinate standing up. The mother then has an opportunity to give a reassuring explanation, even though the child hasn't asked a direct question. There are occasions almost every day, in a child's conversation about humans and animals and birds, when a mother on the lookout for indirect questions can help the child to ask what he wants to know.

536. How the school can help. If a child's mother and father have answered his earlier questions comfortably, he keeps on turning to them as he grows older and wants more exact knowledge. But the school has a chance to help out, too. Many schools make a point of letting children in kindergarten or first grade take care of animals, such as rabbits, guinea pigs or white mice. This gives them an opportunity to become familiar with all sides of animal life—feeding, fighting, mating, birth and suckling of the young. It is easier in some ways to learn these facts in an impersonal situation, and it supplements what the child has learned from his parents. But what he finds out in school he probably wants to discuss and clear up further at home.

By the fifth grade, it is good to have biology taught in a simple way, including a discussion of reproduction. At least some of the girls in the class are entering the puberty stage of development and need some accurate knowledge of what is happening. The discussion from a somewhat scientific point of view in school should help the child to bring it up more personally at home.

537. The right slant at adolescence. Girls. You might get the idea from articles on this subject that it's easy for parents to talk about it if they are wholesome people. This is simply not so. The adolescent's acute awareness of his sexuality, his rivalry with his parent make such a discussion embarrassing in many cases, especially between son and father. Many fathers and sons can't get to it at all, nor can quite a few mothers and daughters. Then the information— or misinformation—comes from friends, older brothers or sisters, books. A sound book made available by a parent can be helpful, either alone or, better still, backed up by the parent's answers to questions.

A girl needs to be told by the beginning of puberty development that during the next 2 years her breasts will develop, hair will grow in the genital region and under the arms, that she will grow rapidly in stature and in weight, that her skin will change its texture and may become liable to pimples, that in about 2 years she will probably have her first menstrual period. How you tell her about her monthly periods makes a difference. Some mothers emphasize what a curse they are. But it is a mistake to stress that part to a child who is still immature and impressionable. Other mothers emphasize how delicate a girl becomes at such times and how careful she must be. This kind of talk makes a bad impression, particularly on those girls who have always been somewhat resentful that they weren't boys anyway and on those who are inclined to worry about their health. The more doctors and women's educators have learned about the periods, the more convinced they have become that most girls and women can live perfectly normal, healthy, vigorous lives right through them. It is only the occasional girl who has cramps severe enough to keep her out of activities. Incidentally, it's the girl who has developed a worried attitude about health and menstruation who is more apt to have severe cramps.

When a girl is on the threshold of womanhood, it's good for her to be looking forward to it happily, not feeling scared or resentful. The best thing to emphasize about menstruation is that the uterus is being prepared for the time she will be a mother.

It helps put the child in the right mood during the months she is waiting for her first period to give her a belt and a box of napkins. This makes her feel as if she is grown up and ready to deal with life rather than waiting for life to do something to her.

538. Boys, by the time they are in the stage of puberty development, need to be told about the naturalness of erections and nocturnal emissions. Fathers who know that nocturnal emissions are certain to occur if a boy is normal, and that there will probably be a strong urge to masturbate at times, sometimes tell the boy that these things are not harmful if they don't happen too often. I think it's a mistake for a parent to set a limit, even though it may sound sensible. The trouble is that an adolescent easily becomes worried about his sexuality, easily imagines he is "different" or abnormal. Being told, "This much is normal, that much is abnormal," is apt to get his mind more preoccupied with sex.

539. Keep the tone wholesome. It's natural in most families for the father to talk to the son and the mother to the daughter. This shouldn't be considered an absolute rule, though, and if it comes much more easily to the other parent, then that's the best way. It's preferable, just as in earlier

childhood, for talk about sex to come up easily from time to time rather than be one big solemn lecture. The parent has to be willing to bring it up early in puberty, though, since the child so often doesn't.

One mistake that is easy to make, especially if the parents themselves were brought up in fear of sex, is to concentrate on all the dangerous aspects of sex. A nervous mother may make her daughter so scared of becoming pregnant that the poor girl has a terror of boys under all circumstances. Or the father may overfill his son with dread of venereal disease. Of course, the child who is moving into adolescence should know how pregnancy takes place and that there is danger of disease in being promiscuous, but these disturbing aspects of sex shouldn't come first. The adolescent should think of it as primarily wholesome and natural and beautiful.

What worried parents find hard to believe, but what people who have studied young people know well, is that the happy, sensible, successful adolescent doesn't get into trouble with sex just because he hasn't been warned sternly enough. All the common sense, self-respect and kindly feeling toward people that he has built up through the years keep him on an even keel even when he is sailing through an entirely new phase of development. To turn it around the other way, the adolescent who gets into trouble with the wrong kind of companions is usually a child who for years has been mixed up with himself and others.

The danger of scaring a sensitive child about sex is partly that you make him tense and apprehensive at the time, partly that you may destroy his or her ability to adjust to marriage later.

540. How much modesty in the home? In half a century, Americans have made a full swing from the excessive modesty of the Victorian period to the partial nudity of sports clothes and to complete nudity in quite a few homes today. Most people agree (and I certainly do) that today's casual attitude is a lot healthier. Nursery school teachers, children's psychiatrists and psychologists generally agree that it's wholesome for **young** children of both sexes to see each other undressed at times in the home and at the beach.

However, there's evidence that at least some young children get upset by regularly seeing their parents naked. The main reason is that young children's feelings for their parents are so intense. A boy loves his mother much more than he loves any little girl. He feels much more rivalrous with his father and more in awe of him than he feels toward any boy. So the sight of his mother may be a little too stimulating, and the chance to compare himself so unfavorably with his father every day may make him feel like doing something violent to his old man. (Nudist fathers have told me about snatching gestures their 3- and 4-year-old sons have made during morning shaving.) Then the boy feels guilty and fearful. A little girl who regularly sees her father nude may be too much stimulated.

I don't want to claim that all children are bothered by parental nudity. No study has been made of normal children. But since we know that it's a possibility, I think it's a little wiser for parents to give their children the benefit of the doubt and, as a general rule, keep reasonably covered and keep children out of the bathroom while a parent is bathing or using the toilet. This doesn't have to be carried to extremes. A parent is caught off guard occasionally, and he shouldn't then act shocked or angry. It's only necessary to say, "Will you wait outside until I get dressed?" After the age of 6 or 7, most children begin to want a little more privacy for themselves, at least at times, and I think it's good to respect this.

NURSERY SCHOOL

541. A good nursery school doesn't take the place of home; it adds to it. Most children would benefit from a good nursery school, but it certainly isn't necessary in every case. It is particularly valuable for the only child, for the child without much chance to play with others, for the child who lives in a small apartment, for the child whose mother finds him difficult to manage for any reason. Every young child by the age of 3 needs other children his own age, not just to have fun with but also to learn how to get along with. This is the most important job in his life. He also needs space to run and shout in, apparatus to climb on, blocks and boxes and boards to build with, trains and dolls to play with. He needs to learn how to get along with other grown-ups besides his parents. Few children nowadays have all these advantages in their own home. Nursery school doesn't take the place of home; it just adds to it.

542. **What's the difference between a day nursery and a nursery school?** For many years there have been day nurseries—good, bad and indifferent—where mothers who have to work can leave their babies and small children. The good ones have been run by people who try to understand children's needs, love them, give them attention, affection, things to play with, freedom to develop. The poor ones have been run by people who think the main job is to discipline children into being good, or who think all a child needs in the way of care is cleanliness and enough food.

The people who started the nursery school idea said, "All small children need a chance to be with other children, not just the ones whose mothers are working. All young children need space, music, paints and clay to enrich their spirits." Furthermore, they said, "It isn't enough that a person who is going to take charge of young children should just love them; she must understand them, too; and that means going to a training school for nursery school teachers."

But don't get the idea that any place that calls itself a nursery school is wonderful, for some of them are second-rate and just use the name because it's popular. And there are some day nurseries that have kept up with progress and are running excellent nursery schools with trained teachers under the old label. When you are thinking of placing your child in a nursery or nursery school, you want to know, What is the attitude of the teachers toward the children? Almost as important is the question, Have the teachers had real training? Next, How many children to a teacher? (It's hard to do a good job with more than 8 to 10 children to a teacher.) Finally, Is there enough play and rest space, indoors and out, enough equipment, toys, blocks, paints, clay, etc.?

You should be able to find out about nursery schools in your neighborhood by consulting a family social agency.

543. **At what age to start nursery school?** Most nursery schools begin with 3-year-olds, and this is a good age to start if your child seems ready for it. Some parents have the idea that the only good the child derives from school are skills like cutting out pictures and counting. I have heard mothers say, "I think I'll wait to put him in nursery school till he is 4 years old when he can get more out of it." This is a mistake. Skills are a very small part of what a good nursery school can give. Learning how to enjoy other children's company, to co-operate, to think up projects and work them out, and having

the freedom to romp and dance and sing, are much more important. A child needs these experiences at 3 just as much as he needs them at 4. The longer they are postponed, the harder it is to pick them up easily.

A few nursery schools start with 2-year-olds. This may work very well if the child is fairly independent and outgoing (many are still quite dependent up to 2½ or 3), if the class is small (not more than 8), and if the teacher is so warm and understanding that she quickly makes children feel secure.

But lots of children are really too young to go to school regularly at 2. They are still dependent on their mothers, timid with other children and grown-ups. I don't mean that such children should be kept tied to their mothers' apron strings forever. They need every opportunity to be around where other children play so that they can become accustomed to them, interested in them, and wean themselves from their dependence. But this takes a little time. If you are in doubt about your child's readiness for nursery school, talk it over with a good nursery school teacher.

There are a few children who are considered unready for steady schooling because they have been unusually sickly or because they easily become exhausted with a group. We have to admit that a child is apt to have more colds staying indoors with a group of children than if he just played outdoors with one or two regular friends. This is no reason for keeping a robust child out of nursery school, because he can stand a few more colds without any serious harm. All the other benefits from nursery school more than offset the disadvantage of the colds. It's a different proposition with the frail child whose colds are always severe. As for fatigue, a certain number of children are overstimulated and overtired at the beginning of nursery school in the fall. But in a few weeks most of them become adjusted to it and take it in their stride. The child who doesn't get used to it should try a shorter schedule.

544. The first days at school. The 4-year-old who is outgoing takes to nursery school like a duck to water. He doesn't need any gentle introduction. It may be quite different with a sensitive 3-year-old who still feels closely attached to his mother. If she leaves him at school the first day, he may not make a fuss right away, but after a while he may miss her. When he finds she isn't there, he may become frightened. The next day he may not want to leave home. With a dependent child like this, it's better to introduce him to school gradually.

For several days his mother might stay nearby while he plays, and then take him home again after a time. Each day the mother and child stay for a longer period. Meanwhile, he is building up attachments to the teacher and other children that will give him a sense of security when his mother no longer stays. Sometimes a child seems to be quite happy for several days, even after his mother has left him there. Then he gets hurt and suddenly wants her. In that case, the teacher can help the mother decide if she should come back for a number of days. When a mother is staying around the school, she ought to remain in the background. The idea is to let the child develop his own desire to enter the group, so that he forgets his need for his mother.

Sometimes the mother's anxiety is greater than the child's. If she says good-bye three times over, with a worried expression, it gives him the idea, "She looks as if something awful might happen if I stay here without her. I'd better not let her go." It's natural for a tenderhearted mother to worry about how her small child will feel when she leaves him for the first time. Let the nursery school teacher advise you. She's had a lot of experience.

When a child becomes reluctant or fearful about returning to a good school with understanding teachers, I think it is usually better for the parents to act quite confident and firm and explain that everybody goes to school every day. In the long run, it's better for the child to outgrow his dependence than to give in to it. When the child is having great difficulty separating from his mother at school, it often works better to have the father take him for a few weeks. If the child's terror is extreme, the situation should be discussed with a psychiatrist or child guidance clinic. The connection between overprotectiveness and fears is discussed in Section 503.

545. Reactions at home. Some children make hard work of nursery school in the early days and weeks. The large group, the new friends, the new things to do get them keyed up and worn out. If your child is too tired at first, it doesn't mean that he can't adjust to school, but only that you have to compromise for a while until he is used to it. Discuss with his teacher whether it would be wise to cut down his school time temporarily. In one case, coming to school in the middle of the morning is the best answer. Taking the easily tired child home before the end of the school day works less well because he hates to leave in the middle of the fun. The problem of fatigue in the early weeks is further complicated in the all-day school by the fact that a certain number of children are too stimulated or nervous to go to sleep at naptime at first. Keeping the child at home 1 or 2 days a week may be the answer to this temporary problem, too. Some small children starting nursery school preserve their self-control in school in spite of fatigue, but let loose on the family when they come home. This calls for extra patience and a discussion with the teacher.

A well-trained nursery school teacher ought to be, and usually is, a very understanding person. A mother shouldn't hesitate to talk over the child's problems with her, whether or not they are connected with school. A teacher gets a different slant. She has probably faced the same problems before in other cases.

546. How to get nursery schools. You may say, "I believe in the importance of my child's going to nursery school, but there is none in my community." Nursery schools aren't easy to start. Well-trained teachers, plenty of equipment, indoor and outdoor space are all necessary and all cost money. Good schools are never cheap, because a teacher can satisfactorily take care of only a small number of children. They have most commonly been formed on a private basis, with the parents paying the full expense; or by churches, which provide the space; or by women's colleges, for the training of students in child care. In many cities, groups of parents have formed cooperative nursery schools. They engage a trained head teacher and take turns in acting as assistant teachers under her supervision. In the long run, a sufficient number of nursery schools will be created, as a part of the public school system, only if the citizens of the community convince the local government and school authorities that they want them, and vote for candidates for office who pledge themselves to work for them.

From Six to Eleven

FITTING INTO THE OUTSIDE WORLD

547. There are lots of changes after 6. The child becomes more independent of his parents, even impatient with them. He's more concerned with what the other kids say and do. He develops a stronger sense of responsibility about matters that he thinks are important. His conscience may become so stern that it nags him about senseless things like stepping over cracks. He is interested in impersonal subjects like arithmetic and engines. In short, he's beginning the job of emancipating himself from his family and taking his place as a responsible citizen of the outside world.

Back in Section 515 I mentioned Freud's explanation of what happens in the child's unconscious feelings that makes him change so much. Between 3 and 5 years he was, generally, a cozy, affectionate family child who proudly patterned his activities, his table manners and his speech after his parents. The boy was trying all day to be like his admired father and he had a strong romantic attachment to his mother. For the girl it was the other way round. But the possessive, romantic feelings bring an increasingly uncomfortable sense of rivalry with the parent of the same sex. The unconscious fear of this parent's resentment and worry about genital differences eventually cause a revulsion of feeling. The former pleasure in romantic daydreaming turns to aversion. The boy now usually squirms when his mother tries to kiss him. His aversion spreads to all girls; he calls them silly or disgusting. He groans when there are love scenes in movies. This is what makes him so eager, we believe, to turn to such impersonal and abstract subjects as reading, writing, arithmetic, mechanics, science, nature study. This is part of the explanation of why children are so emotionally ready for schoolwork at this age.

Another way of viewing the psychological changes that take place in children about 6 or 7 is to see how they are related to the evolution of man from his prehuman ancestors. Each individual as he passes through the 6-to-12-year-old period is retracing, I think, that particular stage of evolution. Millions of years ago our prehuman ancestors used to acquire full growth and full instincts by about 5 years of age. In their attitude toward family life, when full grown, they were probably much like our 5-year-old children: happy to continue to live with their family, even after growing up, happy to give obedience to the old man of the family, striving to be like him and learn from him. In other words, these prehumans were tied together for life by close personal family ties. It was only much later in the course of evolution that our ancestors developed the ability to become more independent of their parents, learned to live in a larger society by means of cooperation, rules, self-control, thinking things out. It takes years for each individual to learn how to get along in this complicated, grown-up way. Probably that's the reason human beings are held up so long in their physical growth. The infant increases rapidly in size like an animal, and so does the older child in the puberty period. But in between he slows down more and more, particularly in the 2 years just before puberty development begins. It's as if his nature were saying, "Whoa! Before you can be trusted with a powerful body and full-grown instincts, you must first learn to think for yourself, control your wishes and instincts for the sake of others, learn how to get along with your fellows, understand the laws of conduct in the world outside your family, study the skills by which people live."

548. Independence of parents. The child after 6 goes on loving his parents deeply underneath, but he usually doesn't show it so much on the surface. He's cooler toward other adults, too, unless he's sure they're swell people. He no longer wants to be loved as a possession or as an appealing child. He's gaining a sense of dignity as an individual person, and he'd like to be treated as such.

From his need to be less dependent on his parents, he turns more to trusted adults outside his family for ideas and knowledge. If he mistakenly gets the idea from his admired science teacher that red blood cells are larger than white blood cells, there's nothing his father can say that will change his mind.

The ideas of right and wrong that his parents taught him have not been forgotten. In fact, they have sunk in so deep that he now thinks of them as his ideas. He is impatient when his parents keep reminding him what he ought to do, because he knows already and wants to be considered responsible.

549. Bad manners. The child drops the extra-grown-up words out of his vocabulary and picks up a little tough talk. He wants the style of clothes and haircut that the other kids have. He may leave his tie off and shoelaces untied with the same determination with which people wear party buttons during a political campaign. He may lose some of his table manners, come to meals with dirty hands, slump over his dish, and stuff more in his mouth. Perhaps he kicks the leg of the table absentmindedly. He always throws his coat on the floor. He slams doors or leaves them open. Without realizing it, he is really accomplishing three things at once. He's shifting to his own age for his models of behavior. He's declaring his right to be more independent of his parents. He's keeping square with his own conscience, because he's not doing anything that's morally wrong.

These "bad manners" and "bad habits" are apt to make good parents unhappy. They imagine that the child is forgetting all that they taught him so carefully. Actually, these changes are proof that he has learned for keeps what good behavior is—otherwise he wouldn't bother to rebel against it. It will come to the surface again when he feels he has established his independence. Meanwhile, understanding parents can be reassured that their child is growing up normally.

I don't mean that every child is a hellion during this age period. One who gets along happily with easygoing parents may show no open rebelliousness at all. Most girls show less than boys. But if you look carefully, you will see signs of a change of attitude.

What do you do? After all, the child must take a bath once in a while, get neatened up on Sunday. You may be able to overlook some of his minor irritating ways, but you should stick to your guns in matters that are important to you. When you have to ask him to wash his hands, try to be matter-of-fact. It's the nagging tone, the bossiness, that he finds irritating and that spurs him on unconsciously to further balkiness.

Manners may seem to be lost.

550. Gangs and clubs. This is the age for the blossoming of clubs and gangs. A number of kids who are already friends decide to form a secret club. They work like beavers making membership buttons, fixing up a meeting place (preferably hidden), drawing up a list of rules. They may never figure out what the secret is. But the secrecy idea probably represents the need to prove they can govern themselves, unmolested by grown-ups, unhampered by other more dependent children.

It seems to help the child, when he's trying to be grown up, to get together with others who feel the same way. Then the group tries to bring outsiders into line by making them feel left out or by picking on them. It sounds conceited and cruel to grown-ups, but that's because we are accustomed to using more refined methods of disapproving of each other. The children are only feeling the instinct to get community life organized. This is one of the forces that make our civilization click.

551. Helping a child to be sociable and popular. These are some of the early steps in bringing up a child to be sociable and popular: not fussing over him in his first years; letting him be around other children his size from the age of a year; allowing him freedom to develop independence; the fewest changes possible in where the family lives and where he goes to school; letting him, as far as possible, associate with, dress like, talk like, play like, have the same allowance and other privileges as the other average children in the neighborhood, even if you don't approve of the way they are brought up. (Of course, I don't mean letting him take after the town's worst scoundrel. And you don't have to take your child's word about what the other children are allowed to do.)

How happily a person gets along as an adult in his job, in his family and social life depends a great deal on how he got along with other children when he was young. If parents give a child high standards and high ideals at home, these form part of his character and show up in the long run, even though he goes through a period of bad English and rough manners in the middle period of childhood. But if parents are unhappy about the neighborhood they live in and the companions their child has, give him a feeling that he is different from the others, discourage him from making friends, the child may grow up unable to get along comfortably with anyone. Then his high standards won't be of much use to the world or to himself.

If a child is having trouble making friends, it helps most if he can be in a school and in a class where the program is flexible. Then the teacher can arrange things so that he has chances to use his abilities to contribute to class projects (Section 564). This is how the other children learn to appreciate his good qualities and to like him. A good teacher who is respected by the class can also raise a child's popularity in the group by showing that she appreciates him. It even helps to put him in a seat next to a very popular child, or to let him be partners with him in marching, going on errands around the school, etc.

There are things that the parents can do at home, too. Be friendly and hospitable when your child brings others home to play. Encourage him to invite them to meals and then serve the dishes that they consider "super." When you plan week-end trips, picnics, excursions, movies and other shows, invite another child with whom your child wants to be friends (not necessarily the one you would like him to be friendly with). Children, like adults, have a mercenary side, and they are more apt to see the good points in a child who provides treats for them. Naturally, you don't want your child to have only "bought" popularity; that kind won't last anyway. But what you are after is to prime the pump, to give him a chance to break into a group that may be shutting him out because of the natural clannishness of this age. Then, if he has appealing qualities, he can take over from that start and build real friendships of his own.

SELF-CONTROL

552. He becomes strict about some things. Think of the games a child enjoys at this age. He's no longer so interested in make-believe without any plan. He wants games that have rules and require skill. In hopscotch, jacks and mumblety-peg, you have to do things in a certain order, which becomes harder as you progress. If you miss, you must penalize yourself, go back to the beginning and start over again. It's the very strictness that appeals. This is the age for starting collections, whether it's stamps or cards or stones. The pleasure of collecting is in achieving orderliness and completeness.

At this age the child has the desire at times to put his belongings in order. Suddenly he neatens his desk, puts labels on the drawers, or arranges his piles of comic books. He doesn't keep his things neat for long. But you can see that the urge must be strong just to get him started.

553. Compulsions. The tendency toward strictness becomes so strong in many children around 8, 9 and 10 that they develop nervous habits. You probably remember them from your own childhood. The commonest is stepping over cracks in the sidewalk. There's no sense to it, you just have a superstitious feeling that you ought to. It's what a psychiatrist calls a compulsion. Other examples are touching every third picket in a fence, making numbers come out even in some way, saying certain words before going through a door. If you think you have made a mistake, you must go way back to where you were absolutely sure that you were right, and start over again.

The hidden meaning of a compulsion pops out in the thoughtless childhood saying, "Step on a crack, break your grandmother's back." Everyone has hostile feelings at times toward the people who are close to him, but his conscience would be shocked at the idea of really harming them and

"Step on a crack, break your grandmother's back."

warns him to keep such thoughts out of his mind. And if a person's conscience becomes **excessively** stern, it keeps nagging him about such "bad" thoughts even after he has succeeded in hiding them away in his subconscious mind. He still feels guilty, though he doesn't know what for. It eases his conscience to be extra careful and proper about such a senseless thing as how to navigate a crack in the sidewalk.

The reason a child is apt to show compulsions around the age of 9 is not that his thoughts are more wicked than previously, but that his conscience is just naturally becoming stricter at this stage of development. He is now worrying, perhaps, about his suppressed desire to hurt his brother or father or grandmother when they irritate him. We know that this is an age when the child is also trying to suppress thoughts about sex, and these sometimes play a part in compulsions, too.

Mild compulsions are so common around the ages of 8, 9 and 10 years that it's a question whether they should be considered normal or a sign of nervousness. I wouldn't worry too much about a mild compulsion, like stepping over cracks, in a child around 9 years who is happy, outgoing, doing well in school. On the other hand, I'd call on a psychiatrist for help (Section 577) if a child has compulsions that occupy a lot of his time (for instance, excessive hand-washing, precautions against germs) or if he is tense, worried, unsociable.

554. Tics. Tics are nervous habits such as eye-blinking, shoulder-shrugging, facial grimacing, neck-twisting, throat-clearing, sniffing, dry coughing. Like compulsions, tics occur most commonly around the age of 9, but they can come at any age after 2. The motion is usually quick, and it is repeated regularly and always in the same form. It is more frequent when the child is under tension. A tic may last off and on for a number of weeks or months and go away for good, or a new one may take its place. Blinking, sniffing, throat-clearing, dry coughing often start with a cold but continue after the cold is gone. Shoulder-shrugging may begin when a child has a new loose-fitting garment that feels as if it were falling off. A child may copy a tic from another child, but he wouldn't have picked it up if there hadn't been a tenseness already waiting in him.

Tics are more common in tense children, with fairly strict parents. There may be too much pressure at home. Sometimes the mother or father is going at the child too hard, directing him, correcting him, whenever he is in sight. Or the parents may be showing constant disapproval in a quieter way, or setting standards that are too high, or providing too many activities such as dancing, music and athletic lessons. If the child were bold enough to fight back, he would probably be less tightened up inside. But being, in most cases, too well brought up for that, he bottles up his irritation, and it keeps backfiring in the tic.

The child should not be scolded or corrected on account of his tics. They are practically out of his control. The whole effort should go into making his home life relaxed and agreeable, with the least possible nagging, and making his school and social life satisfying. Tics must be distinguished from chorea and general restlessness (Section 693).

TELEVISION, MOVIES AND COMICS

555. Brutality in television, movies and comics. Back in Section 462 I said that I believed that parents should keep their children from watching brutality on television, and the same goes for movies. Comic books are not quite as corrupting because what is shown does not seem as real, but the same principles apply.

If we rule out the comics and other stories that are brutal and obscene, there is still the question—for parents with high aspirations—whether the other kinds, which are merely vulgar or preposterously heroic or filled with fighting which is not particularly brutal, will hurt their children's characters or ruin their taste for good literature. I don't think there is much to worry about in these respects. I've known hundreds of children who went through a long stage of fascination with comics of these types and who finally outgrew them.

556. Obscenity. As children become old enough to buy comic books and other literature, and to go to movies, the problem of obscenity also comes up. There used to be considerable protection for children in the precensorship of movies in Hollywood and in the various states, and also in the respect for obscenity laws on the part of film exhibitors and sellers of literature. However, the Supreme Court has removed the ban on all but the most deliberate pornography, so parents must now be the guardians.

I explained in Section 13 that the idealism and creativity of human beings is related to the inhibition and sublimation of sexuality which takes place all through childhood but particularly in the 6-to-12-year-old period, more so when the parents set high standards. To be specific, I believe that the potentialities of children for productivity in their future life work and for achieving soundly spiritual marriages may be impaired—at least slightly—if they get a consistently coarse picture of sexuality in childhood. I'm not referring here to a few accidental, unfortunate glimpses, despite the parents' best efforts, such as we all experienced. I mean that children shouldn't get the impression that their parents view sex crudely or that their parents don't care what impression their children get from others.

I believe that parents should let their children go only to movies and buy only literature which the parents know for sure—from reviews or from neighbors—have a moral and spiritual tone of which they approve.

557. The hours for watching television should be limited. There is a problem with the child who is glued to the set from the minute he comes in, in the afternoon, until he is forced to go to bed at night. He doesn't want to take time out for supper or for his homework or even to say hello to his family. It's better for the parents and child to come to a reasonable but definite understanding about which hours are for outdoors, for homework, for meals and for programs, and then for everyone to stick to the bargain. Otherwise the parents are apt to be nagging him about his duties whenever they catch him at the set, and he is turning it on whenever he thinks they aren't paying attention. Some adolescents and adults can work just as well with the radio on (they say better), though this is less likely with talking programs than with musical programs. There is no objection to this if the child is keeping up with his homework.

558. Fearfulness about movies and television. Movies are a risky business under the age of 7. You hear of a program, let's say an animated cartoon, that sounds like perfect entertainment for a small child. But when you get there, you find, three out of four times, that there is some episode in the story that scares the wits out of little children. You have to remember that a child of 4 and 5 doesn't distinguish clearly between make-believe and real life. A witch on the screen is just as alive and terrifying to him as a flesh-and-blood burglar would be to you. The only safe rule that I know is not to take a child under 7 to a movie unless you, or someone else who knows small children well, has seen it and is positive that it contains nothing upsetting. Don't even take an older child to the movies if he gets frightened easily.

There are sensitive children who are also upset by fairy stories, adventure stories and Western dramas on television. They shouldn't be allowed to watch them.

STEALING

559. Taking things in early childhood. Small children of 1, 2 and 3 take things that don't belong to them, but it isn't really stealing. They don't have any clear sense of what belongs to them and what doesn't. They just take things because they want them very much. It's better not to make a small child feel wicked. The mother needs only to remind him that the toy is Peter's, that Peter will want to play with it soon, and that he himself has lots of toys at home.

560. What stealing means in the child who knows better. Stealing that means more occasionally crops up in the period between 6 and adolescence. When a child at this age takes something, he knows he is doing wrong. He is more apt to steal secretly, to hide what he has stolen, and to deny that he has done it.

When a parent or a teacher finds that a child has stolen something, she is pretty upset. Her impulse is to jump on him hard and fill him with a sense of shame. This is natural enough, since we have all been taught that stealing is a serious crime. It scares us to see it coming out in our child.

It is essential that a child know clearly that his parents disapprove of any stealing and insist on immediate restitution. On the other hand, it isn't wise to scare the daylights out of him or act as if his parents will never love him again.

Let's take first the child around 7 who has been carefully brought up by conscientious parents, who has a reasonable number of toys and other possessions, and who gets an allowance. If he steals something, it's apt to be small amounts of money from his mother or from classmates, or his teacher's pen, or a pack of trading cards from another child's locker. Often there's no sense to the stealing because he may own these things anyway. We can see that he's mixed up in his feelings. He seems to have a blind craving for something, and tries to satisfy it by taking an object he doesn't really need. What does he really want?

In most cases, the child is unhappy and lonesome to some degree. He doesn't have a sufficiently warm relationship with his parents, or he doesn't feel completely successful in making friends with children his own age. (He may feel this way even though he is actually quite popular.) I think the reason that stealing occurs more often around 7 is that the child at this age may be feeling particularly distant from his parents. Then, if he hasn't the knack of making equally warm and satisfying friendships, he gets into no-man's land and feels isolated. This explains why some children who steal money use it all to try to buy friendship. One passes out dimes and nickels to his classmates. Another uses it to buy candy for the class. It's not just that the child is drawing away a little from the parents. The parents are apt to be more disapproving of him at this less appealing age.

The early part of adolescence is another period when some children become more lonely, because of increased self-consciousness, sensitiveness and desire for independence.

A craving for more affection probably plays some part in stealing at all ages, but there are usually other individual factors, too, such as fears, jealousies, resentments. A girl who is deeply envious of her brother may repeatedly steal objects that are linked in her unconscious mind with boys.

561. What to do for the child who steals. If you are pretty sure that your child (or pupil) has stolen something, tell him so, be firm about knowing where he got it, insist on restitution. In other words, don't make it easy for him to lie. (If a parent accepts lies too easily, it's as if he were condoning the theft.) The child should take the object back to the child or store from which he took it. If it's a store, it may be tactful for the parent to go along to explain to the salesman that the child took it without paying and wants to return it. A teacher can return an article to its owner to spare the child from public shame. In other words, it's not necessary to humiliate the child who steals, only to make it crystal-clear that it can't be permitted.

It is time to think over whether the child needs more affection and approval at home, and help in making closer friendships outside (Section 551). This is the time to give him, if possible, an allowance of about the same size as that of the other children he knows. It helps him to establish himself as "one of the boys." The parents should get help from a child guidance clinic or a children's psychiatrist if the stealing persists or if the child seems maladjusted in other ways (Section 577).

The next type of stealing is entirely different. There are plenty of neighborhoods where the kids think of swiping things as the daring and manly thing to do. It's not proper, but it's not vicious and it's not a sign of maladjustment. The boy of conscientious parents who lives in such a neighborhood may need an understanding talk, but should not be treated as a criminal because he joined in one of these adventures. He was only obeying a normal instinct to make his place in the group. The cure lies in better economic conditions, better schools, better recreational facilities.

Finally, there is the stealing of the aggressive child or adult who has little conscience or sense of responsibility. A person gets this way only through a childhood quite lacking in love and security. His only hope is in good psychiatric treatment and being able to live with kind, affectionate people.

Schools

WHAT A SCHOOL IS FOR

562. The main lesson in school is how to get along in the world. Different subjects are merely means to this end. In the olden days, it used to be thought that all a school had to do was make children learn to read, write, figure and memorize a certain number of facts about the world. I heard a great teacher tell how, in his own school days, he had to memorize a definition of a preposition that went something like this: "A preposition is a word, generally with some meaning of position, direction, time or other abstract relation, used to connect a noun or pronoun, in an adjectival or adverbial sense, with some other word." Of course, he didn't learn anything when he memorized that. You learn only when things mean something to you. One job of a school is to make subjects so interesting and real that the children want to learn and remember.

You can go only so far with books and talk. You learn better from actually living the things you are studying. Children pick up more arithmetic in a week from running a school store, in making change and keeping the books than they learn in a month out of a book of cold figures.

There's no use knowing a lot if you can't be happy, can't get along with people, can't hold the kind of job you want. The good teacher tries to understand each child so that she can help him overcome his weak points and develop into a well-rounded person. The child who lacks self-confidence needs chances to succeed. The troublemaking show-off has to learn how to gain the recognition he craves through doing good work. The child who doesn't know how to make friends needs help in becoming sociable and appealing. The child who seems to be lazy has to have his enthusiasm discovered.

A school can go only so far with a cut-and-dried program in which everyone in the class reads from page 17 to page 23 in the reader at the same time and then does the examples on page 128 of the arithmetic book. It works well enough for the average child who is adjusted anyway. But it's too dull for the bright pupils, too speedy for the slow ones. It gives the boy who hates books a chance to stick paper clips in the pigtails of the girl in front. It does nothing to help the girl who is lonely or the boy who needs to learn cooperation.

563. How schoolwork is made real and interesting. If you start with a topic that is real and interesting, you can use it to teach all manner of subjects. Take the case of a third-grade class in which the work of the year revolves around Indians. The more the children find out about Indians, the more they want to know. The reader is a story of the Indians, and they really want to know what it says. For arithmetic they study how the Indians counted and what they used for money. Then arithmetic isn't a separate subject at all but a useful part of life. Geography isn't spots on a map; it's where the Indians lived and traveled, and how life on the plains is different from forest life. In science study the children make dye from berries and dye cloth, or grow corn. They can make bows and arrows and Indian costumes.

People are sometimes uneasy about schoolwork's being too interesting, feeling that a child needs to learn, most of all, how to do what's unpleasant and difficult. But if you stop to think of the people you know who are unusually successful, you'll see that in most cases they are the ones who love their work. In any job there's plenty of drudgery, but you do the drudgery because you see its connection with the fascinating side of the work. Darwin was a wretched student in all his subjects in school. But in later life he became interested in natural history, performed one of the most painstaking jobs of research that the world has ever known, and worked out the theory of evolution. A boy in high school may see no sense in geometry, hate it and do badly in it. But if he is in the Air Force and sees what geometry is for, realizes that it may save the lives of the whole crew, he works at it like a demon. The teachers in a good school know well that every child needs to develop self-discipline to be a useful adult. But they have learned that you can't snap discipline onto him from the outside, like handcuffs; it's something that he has to develop inside, like a backbone, by first understanding the purpose of his work and feeling a sense of responsibility to others in how he performs it.

564. How a school helps a difficult child. A flexible, interesting program does more than just make schoolwork appealing. It can be adjusted for the individual pupil. Take the case of a boy who had spent his first 2 years in a school where teaching was done by separate subjects. He was a boy who had great difficulty in learning to read and write. He had fallen behind the rest of the class. Inside, he felt ashamed about being a failure. Outwardly he wouldn't admit anything except that he hated school. He had never gotten along too easily with other kids anyway, even before his school troubles began. Feeling that he was a dumbbell in the eyes of the others made matters worse. He had a chip on his shoulder. Once in a while he would show off to the class in a smarty way. His teacher used to think that he was just trying to be bad. Of course, he was really attempting, in this unfortunate way, to gain some kind of attention from the group. It was a healthy impulse to keep himself from being shut out.

He transferred to a school that was interested in helping him not only to read and write but to find his place in the group. The teacher learned in a conference with his mother that he used tools well and loved to paint and draw. She saw ways to use his strong points in the class. The children were all painting together a large picture of Indian life to hang on the wall. They were also working cooperatively on a model of an Indian village. The teacher arranged for the boy to have a part in both these jobs. Here were things he could do well without nervousness. As the days went by, he became more and more fascinated with Indians. In order to paint his part of the picture well, in order to make his part of the model correctly, he needed to find out more from the books about Indians. He **wanted** to learn to read. He tried harder. His new classmates didn't think of him as a dope because he couldn't read. They thought more about what a help he was on the painting and the model. They occasionally commented on how good his work was and asked him to help them on their parts. He began to warm up. After all, he had been aching for recognition and friendliness for a long while. As he felt more accepted, he became more friendly and outgoing.

565. Linking school with the world. A school wants its pupils to learn at firsthand about the outside world, about the jobs of the local farmers and businessmen and workers, so that they will see the connection between their schoolwork and real life. It arranges trips to nearby industries, asks people from the outside to come in and talk, encourages classroom discussion. A class that is studying food may have an opportunity, for example, to observe some of the steps in the collecting, pasteurizing, bottling and delivery of milk, or in the transportation and marketing of vegetables.

High school and college students have further opportunities to learn about the world by attending summer work camps. A group of students and teachers may work in a factory or in a farming area, discuss together and come to understand better the problems of various occupations and industries and how they are solved.

566. Democracy builds discipline. Another thing that a good school wants to teach is democracy, not just as a patriotic motto but as a way of living and getting things done. A good teacher knows that she can't teach democracy out of a book if she's acting like a dictator in person. She encourages her pupils to decide how they are going to tackle certain projects and the difficulties they later run into, lets them help figure out among themselves which one is to do this part of the job and which one that. That's how they learn to appreciate each other. That's how they learn to get things done, not just in school but in the outside world, too.

Actual experiments have shown that children with a teacher who tells them what to do at every step of the way do a good job while she is in the room, but when she goes out a lot of them stop working, start fooling. They figure that lessons are the teacher's responsibility, not theirs, and that now they have a chance to be themselves. But these experiments showed that children who have helped choose and plan their own work, and have cooperated with each other in carrying it out, accomplish almost as much when the teacher is out of the room as in. Why? They know the purpose of the job they are on and the steps ahead in accomplishing it. They feel that it is their job, not the teacher's. Each one wants to do his share because he is proud to be a respected member of the group and feels a sense of responsibility to the others.

This is the very highest kind of discipline. This training,

this spirit, is what makes the best citizens, the most valuable workers and even the finest soldiers.

567. Cooperating with other child specialists. Even the best of teachers can't solve all the problems of their pupils alone. They need the cooperation of the parents through parent-teacher association meetings and individual conferences. Then parent and teacher will understand what the other is doing, share what they know about the child. The teacher should even be able to get in touch with the child's scoutmaster, minister, doctor, and vice versa. Each can do a better job by working with the other. It's particularly important in the case of a child with a chronic ailment that the teacher know just what it is, how it's being treated, what she can do or watch for in school. It's just as important for the doctor to know how the disease is affecting the child in school hours, how the school can help, and how he can prescribe treatment so as not to work against what the school is trying to accomplish with the child.

There are children who have problems that the regular teacher and the parents, no matter how understanding, can solve better with the help of specialists in child guidance. Few schools as yet have a psychiatrist. Some, though, have guidance counselors, psychologists or visiting teachers, trained to help children, parents and classroom teachers in understanding and overcoming a child's school difficulties. Where there is no guidance counselor or psychologist, or when the teacher finds that the problem is deep-rooted, it is wise to turn to a private children's psychiatrist or to a child guidance clinic, if such is available.

568. How to work for good schools. Parents sometimes say, "It's all very well to talk about an ideal school that makes the work interesting and finds a way to bring out the best in every child. But the school that my child goes to is pretty cut-and-dried, and there's nothing I can do about it." That isn't true. Every town and city has the kind of schools its citizens want. If they know what good schools are and insist on having them, they can get them. That's how democracy works.

Parents can join their local parent-teacher association, go to meetings regularly, show the teachers and principals and superintendents that they are interested and will back them up when they are using sound methods. They can also vote for local officials who will work for constant improvement in the schools. No school system is ever perfect, and even the best of schools will go downhill unless the citizens stay interested.

There are lots of people who don't realize how much fine schools can accomplish in developing useful, happy citizens. They object to increasing the school budget for smaller classes, better-paid teachers, carpentry shops, laboratories and afternoon recreation programs. Not understanding the purpose or value of these proposals, they naturally think of them as "unnecessary frills" just to amuse children or make jobs for more teachers. Even from a strictly cash point of view, that's penny wise and dollar foolish. Money spent wisely for better child care pays back the community a hundredfold. First-rate schools that succeed in making each child feel he really belongs, as a useful and respected member of the group, reduce drastically the number of individuals who grow up irresponsible or criminal. The value of such schools shows even more in all the other children (who would never be criminals anyway), who take their places in the community as better workers at their jobs, more cooperative citizens, happier individuals in their own lives. How better can a community spend its money?

TROUBLE WITH LESSONS

569. There are many causes for failure in schoolwork. Individual problems are more common when a school is using rigid teaching methods, when the attitude toward the children is regimenting and harsh, when the classes are too large for individual attention.

In children themselves there are various reasons for poor adjustment. On the physical side, there are eye defects, deafness, occasionally fatigue or chronic illness. On the psychological side, there is the child unable to read because of a special difficulty in recognizing words, the child who is too nervous and worried about other things, the one who can't get along with teacher or pupils. There is the child who is too smart and the one who can't do the work because his intelligence isn't up to it. (The slow child is discussed in Section 799.)

Don't scold or punish the child who is having difficulties. Try to find out where the trouble lies. Consult with the principal or teacher. Get the help of the school guidance counselor if there is one. Have the child tested by the school psychologist if that seems the next step. Consult a child guidance clinic or a private psychiatrist or psychologist if no specialists are available at the school (Section 577). Have him examined physically, including his vision and hearing.

570. The extra-bright child. In a class in which everyone does exactly the same lessons, the child who is smarter than others of his age may be bored because the work is too easy. The only solution seems to be to skip a grade. This may not work out too badly if the child is large for his age and advanced socially. But if not, he's apt to become socially isolated and lost, especially when his classmates get to the adolescent years. He may be too small to compete in games or be popular at dances. He's apt to have younger interests than the other members of his class, which keep him from mixing easily. What good is it for him to enter high school or college at a very young age if he is going to turn into a lonely person?

It is much better in most cases for the bright child to stay in a class that is close to him in age, provided the school has a flexible program that can be "enriched" for the pupils who are more advanced. He, for instance, is the one to read the more difficult reference books in the library. When a bright child is working for marks and to please the teacher, the other kids are quick to call him "Smarty" and "Teacher's Pet." But if he is working on group projects, they appreciate him all the more because of the extra help he can provide.

Even if you think your child is extra-smart, never try to get him into a more advanced grade than the school advises. Usually a teacher knows best about placement. It's cruel for a child to be placed beyond his capacities. In the end he does poorly or is left back again later.

That brings up the question of teaching a bright child to read and figure at home before he starts first grade. A parent may say that the child is asking questions about letters and numbers and practically insisting on being taught. This is true to a degree with some children, and there is no harm in casually answering their questions.

But there is another side to it in many such cases. It often turns out that the parents themselves are more ambitious for their child than they perhaps realize, more eager to have him excel. When he is playing childish games or roughhousing, they pay only a normal amount of attention. But when he shows an interest in reading at an early age, their eyes light up and they help him enthusiastically. The child senses their delight and responds with greater interest. He may be weaned away from the natural occupations of his age and turned into something of a scholar before his time.

Parents wouldn't be good parents if they weren't delighted with their children's fine qualities. But it's necessary to distinguish between which are the children's interests and which are the parents' eager hopes. If parents who are naturally ambitious can honestly admit this to themselves and be on guard against using their ambition to run their children's lives, the children will grow up to be happier, abler and more of a credit to their parents. This applies not only to early reading and writing but to putting pressure on a child at any age, whether it's in schoolwork, music lessons, dancing lessons, athletics or social life.

571. Poor schoolwork because of "nervousness." All kinds of worries and troubles and family frictions can interfere with a child's schoolwork. Here are some examples, though they don't cover all the possibilities by any means:

A 6-year-old girl who is burned up with jealousy of a younger brother may be tense, "distracted," unable to pay attention, and make sudden attacks on other children for no good reason.

A child may be worried about illness at home or a threatened separation of the parents or misunderstandings about sex. In the early grades especially, he may be afraid of a bully or a barking dog on the way to school, of the school janitor, of a severe-looking teacher, of asking permission to go to the toilet, of reciting before the class. These seem like small matters to an adult, but to a timid 6- or 7-year-old they may be terrifying enough to paralyze his thinking.

The child around 9 years old who is nagged and corrected excessively at home may become so restless and tense that he can't keep his mind on anything.

The "lazy" child who won't try to do his lessons usually isn't lazy at all. The young animal of all species is born to be curious and enthusiastic. If he loses that, it's because it's been trained out of him. Children appear to be lazy in school for a number of reasons. One is balky from having been pushed too much all his life. You'll find him eager enough about his own private hobbies. Sometimes a child is afraid to try in school (or anywhere) for fear of failing. This may be because his family has always been critical of his accomplishments or set too high standards.

Strange as it may seem, an occasional child may do poor schoolwork from being overconscientious. He keeps going over the lesson that he's already learned or the exercises that he's already finished for fear that something is incomplete or incorrect. He's always behind, fussing.

The child who has been severely deprived of love and security in his early years typically reaches school age as a tense, restless, irresponsible creature with little ability to get interested in schoolwork or to get along with teachers or pupils.

Whatever the cause of a child's difficulty in school, the problem should be attacked from two directions. Try to find the underlying cause, as suggested in Section 569. But whether or not you can discover what's bothering him inside, it should be possible for teacher and parents, by sharing their knowledge of a child, to use his interests and good qualities to draw him gradually into the group and the things they are working on.

572. Poor reading because of slow development of visual memory. To you and me the word "dog" looks entirely different from the word "god." Most young children, when they are just beginning to read, think these words look much the same because each spells the other backward. They occasionally read "was" for "saw" and "on" for "no." In writing they sometimes reverse letters, especially those like small "b" and small "p," which are confused with "d" and "q." But as the months go by, they learn to perceive and remember more accurately and these mistakes become infrequent by the end of second grade.

But there are about 10% of children—most of them boys—who have much more than the average difficulty recognizing and remembering the appearance of words. They continue to reverse many words and letters for several years. It takes them a lot longer to learn to read reasonably well and some of them remain poor spellers for life, no matter how much they are drilled.

Such children quickly get the idea that they are dumb and often come to hate school because they cannot keep up with the others. They need to be reassured by parents and teachers that this is a special memory problem (just the way some children can't carry a tune); that they are not stupid and not lazy; that they will learn to read and write and spell as soon as they are able.

Most of these children can be helped by extra practice in phonics, in which they sound the letters and the syllables of words, and point at them with their fingers at the same time. In this way, they can make up for some of their weakness in recognizing words. If the school can't provide extra help, the parents should consult the teacher or principal about whether it would be desirable to try tutoring outside of school hours, either with a tactful tutor or a very patient parent. It is also sensible to consider a checkup by a child psychiatrist or guidance clinic; especially if the child has other emotional problems, since these can play a large part in a reading disability.

573. Helping a child in his lessons. Sometimes a teacher advises that a child needs extra tutoring in a subject that he's falling behind in, or the parent has the idea himself. This is something to be careful about. If the school can recommend a good tutor that you can afford, go ahead. Too often a parent makes a poor tutor, not because he (or she) doesn't know enough, not because he doesn't try hard enough, but because he cares too much, is too upset when his child doesn't understand. If a child is already mixed up in lessons, a tense parent is the last straw. Another trouble is that the parent's method may be different from that being used in the class. If a child is already baffled by the subject in school, the chances are that he will be more baffled when it's presented in a different way at home.

I don't want to go so far as to say that a parent should never tutor a child, because in an occasional case it works very well. I'd only advise a parent to talk it over thoroughly with the teacher first, and then quit right away if it isn't a success.

What should you do if your child asks for help with his homework? If he is puzzled once in a great while and turns to you for clarification, there's no harm in straightening him out. (Nothing pleases a parent more than to have a chance occasionally to prove to his child that he really knows something.) But if a child is asking you to do his work for him because he can't understand it, better consult the teacher. A good school prefers to help the child understand, and then let him rely on himself. If the teacher is too busy to straighten him out, you may have to lend a hand; but even then help him to understand his work, don't do it for him.

574. School phobia. Occasionally a child develops a sudden and unexplainable fear of going to school. This often happens after he has been absent for a few days because of an illness or accident, especially if the illness began or the accident happened at school. Typically, the child hasn't any idea of what it is he fears at school. Child guidance studies of such cases show that often the real cause has little to do with school. The child has become more dependent on his mother because of his feelings of guilt over his unconscious antagonistic feelings toward her (Section 503). The illness at school and staying at home with her have brought this nearer the surface. If the child is freely allowed to stay home, his dread of returning to school usually gets stronger. It's increased by his fear that he is behind in his work and that the teacher and other children will criticize him for his absence. So it usually works best for the parents to be very firm about getting him back to school promptly and to refuse to be dissuaded by his physical complaints or to try to get the doctor to excuse him. (Of course, he needs to be checked by the doctor.) The child and parent should have child guidance help if this can possibly be arranged. The child guidance clinic usually considers such a case an emergency, knowing how time makes it worse (Section 577).

575. The child who can't eat breakfast before going to school. This problem comes up occasionally, especially with first- and second-graders, at the beginning of school in the fall. It's the conscientious child who is so overawed by the big class and the sovereign teacher that he can't eat the first thing in the morning. If his mother forces him to, he is only too likely to vomit on the way to school or after he's there. This adds a feeling of disgrace to his other troubles.

The best way to handle this is to let the child alone at breakfast time; let him take only his fruit juice and milk if that is all he can comfortably swallow. If he can't drink, let him go to school empty. It's not ideal for a child to start the day hungry, but he'll become relaxed and able to eat breakfast sooner if you leave him alone. Such a child usually eats fairly well at lunch, and then makes up for all he has missed with a huge supper. As he gets used to school and his new teacher, his stomach gradually becomes hungrier at breakfast time, provided he doesn't have to struggle against his mother, too.

Even more important for the child who is timid at the beginning of school is for the mother to talk things over with the teacher so that the latter can understand and work to overcome the difficulty at school. The teacher can make a special effort to be friendly with the child, and help him, in the projects they are working on, to find a comfortable place in the group.

576. Parent and teacher. It's easy to get along with a teacher if your child is her pride and joy and doing perfectly in class. But if he is having trouble, the situation is more delicate. The best parent and the best teacher are both very human. Each has pride in the job she is doing. Each has a possessive feeling toward the child. Each secretly feels, no matter how reasonable she is, that the child would be doing better if the other would only handle him a little differently. It's helpful for the parents to realize at the start that the teacher is just as sensitive as they are, and that they will get further in a conference by being friendly and cooperative. Some parents realize that they are scared of facing a teacher, but they forget that just as often the teacher is afraid of them. The parents' main job is to give a clear history of the child's past, what his interests are, what he responds to well, what badly, and leave it to the teacher how best to apply this information in school. Don't forget to compliment her on the parts of the class program that are a great success with the child.

CHILD GUIDANCE

577. Psychiatrists, psychologists and child guidance clinics. Parents are apt to be confused about what psychiatrists and psychologists are for and what the difference between them is. A children's psychiatrist is a physician trained to understand and treat all kinds of behavior problems and emotional problems of children. Back in the nineteenth century, psychiatrists were mainly concerned with taking care of the insane, and for that reason some people are still reluctant to consult them. But as psychiatrists have learned how serious troubles usually develop out of mild ones, they have turned more and more attention to everyday problems. In this way they do the most good in the shortest time. There's no more reason to wait to see a psychiatrist until a child is severely upset than to wait until he is in a desperate condition from pneumonia before calling the regular doctor. In larger cities there are child psychiatrists in private practice. Ask your family doctor.

Psychologist is a very general title used for people, not physicians, who specialize in one of the many branches of psychology. Psychologists who work with children are trained in such subjects as intelligence testing and aptitude testing, and the causes and treatment of learning problems in school.

In a **child guidance clinic** (or children's psychiatric clinic) the psychiatrist is the doctor who takes charge of the case, gets to know the child and where his worries are coming from, helps him to understand and outgrow them. He may call on the psychologist for mental tests to see what the child's weak points and strong points are, or to give the child remedial teaching if, for instance, he has a reading problem. A psychiatric social worker may be asked to visit the school to find out from the teachers more exactly what difficulties the child is having there, and to give the teacher the benefit of the understanding of the problem that has been gained in the clinic. Either the social worker or the doctor has interviews with the parents to find out more about the child and to help the parents in managing him. Some child guidance clinics are connected with hospitals; others are independent.

In a few cities there are child guidance clinics connected with the board of education, staffed with psychiatrists, psychologists, social workers, to deal with all kinds of behavior problems. Some states have traveling clinics that visit different communities. Many other school systems, local and state, have psychologists for the testing and remedial teaching of children who are having school problems.

In a city you can inquire about a child guidance clinic, or a private children's psychiatrist, or a psychologist for testing, through your regular doctor or a large hospital, through the school principal or superintendent, through a social service agency. Or you can look in the telephone book to see if there is a local Mental Hygiene Committee or Society. If you have no luck or live in a smaller place, you can write to the National Association for Mental Health, 10 Columbus Circle, New York City, and they will tell you the nearest place you can get help. If there is no child guidance clinic, a family social agency may be able to give you the guidance you need.

Someday I hope there will be psychiatrists and psychologists connected with all school systems, so that children, parents and teachers will be able to ask for advice on all kinds of minor problems as easily and as naturally as they can now inquire about inoculations and diet and the prevention of physical disease.

578. Family social agency. Most cities have at least one family social agency, and some large cities have Catholic, Jewish and Protestant agencies. They are staffed by social workers trained to help parents with all the usual family problems—child management, marital adjustment, budgeting, chronic illness, housing, finding jobs, finding medical care.

Many parents have grown up with the idea that a social agency is for destitute people only and mainly provides charity. This is the opposite of the truth today. The modern family agency is just as glad to help solve small problems as large ones (they're easier), as glad to assist families who can afford to pay a fee as those who can't (that way they can expand their services).

If you have a problem with a child and you can make an appointment soon with a private child psychiatrist or a child guidance clinic, that may be the most direct approach. But if there is no clinic available or if there is a long waiting list, it may be wiser to consult a family agency. If the problem is one that they can deal with satisfactorily, they will continue with your case. If they think it requires child guidance treatment, they may be able to expedite an appointment.

Inquire at the Community Chest or, in a rural area, at County Welfare.

Puberty Development

PHYSICAL CHANGES

579. Puberty development in girls. By **puberty development** I mean the 2 years of very rapid growth and development that come before "maturing." A girl is said to mature at her first monthly period. In the boy there is no such clear-cut event. So let's discuss puberty development in the girl first.

The first thing to realize is that there is no regular age at which puberty begins. The largest number of girls begin their development at around the age of 10 and have their first period about 2 years later, at 12. But a fair number begin their development as young as 8. Late developers may not even begin until 12. There are extreme cases of girls starting as early as 7 or as late as 14.

The fact that a girl starts her puberty development much earlier or later than average usually doesn't mean that her glands aren't working right. It only means that she is working on what you might call a faster or slower timetable. This individual timetable seems to be an inborn trait. Parents who were late developers are more apt to have children who are late developers, and vice versa.

Let's trace what happens in the case of the average girl who starts her puberty development at 10. When she was 7 years old, she was growing 2 to 2½ inches a year. When she was 8 years old, her rate of growing slowed down to perhaps 1¾ inches a year. Nature seemed to be putting on the brakes. Suddenly, at about 10, the brakes let go. She begins to shoot up at the rate of 3 or 3½ inches a year for the next 2 years. Instead of putting on 5 to 8 pounds a year as she used to, she now gains between 10 and 20 pounds a year, without becoming fatter. Her appetite becomes enormous to make this gain possible.

414

But other things are happening, too. At the beginning of this period her breasts begin to develop. First the areola (the dark area around the nipple) enlarges and gets slightly puffed out. Then the whole breast begins to take shape. For the first year and a half it has a conical shape, but as her first menstrual period nears, it rounds out into more nearly a hemisphere. Soon after the breasts begin to develop, the pubic hair starts to grow. Later, hair appears in the armpits. The hips widen. The skin changes its texture.

At 12 the average girl has her first menstrual period. By now she has a woman's body. She has acquired most of the height and weight she will ever have. From this time on, her growing slows down rapidly. In the year after her first period she will grow perhaps 1½ inches, and in the year after that perhaps ¾ of an inch. In many girls the periods are irregular and infrequent for the first year or two. This is not a sign that something is wrong; it seems only to represent the body's inexperience.

580. Puberty begins at different ages. We have been talking about the average girl, but only a certain number of girls come near the average in any one particular. Many start their puberty development earlier than the average and many later. The child who begins at 8 is naturally apt to feel awkward and self-conscious when she finds herself the only girl in her class shooting upward and acquiring the shape of a woman. This experience isn't painful to every early developer. It depends, of course, on how well adjusted she was before and on how ready and eager she is to grow up. The girl who gets along well with her mother and wants to be like her is inclined to be pleased when she sees she is growing up, whether or not she is ahead of her schoolmates. On the other hand, the girl who resents being a girl—for instance, because of jealousy of her brother—or the child who is afraid to grow up is apt to be resentful or alarmed by early signs of womanhood.

Also bothered is the girl on a slow timetable. The 12-year-old who has shown no signs of puberty development has seen practically all her classmates grow rapidly taller and develop into women. She herself is still in the period of extra-slow growth that precedes the puberty spurt. She feels like an underdeveloped runt. She thinks that she must be abnormal. She needs to be reassured, to be told that her growth in height and her bodily development will be coming along just as surely as the sun rises and sets. If her mother and other relatives were late developers, she needs to be told that, too, in explanation. She can be promised that when her time comes, she will have 7 or 8 more inches of height before she stops growing altogether.

There are other variations besides the age at which puberty development begins. In some girls the pubic-hair growth comes months before the breasts start to develop. And once in a while hair in the armpits is the earliest sign of change instead of a late one. The length of time between the first signs of puberty development and the coming of the first period is usually about 2 years, but the girls who begin developing young are apt to have a shorter, quicker period of development, occasionally less than a year and a half. On the other hand, the girls who begin their puberty development later than average are more apt to take longer than 2 years to reach their first menstrual period. Occasionally one breast begins to develop months before the other. This is fairly common and nothing to worry about. The earlier-developing breast tends to stay larger throughout the puberty stage of development.

581. The average boy starts 2 years later than the girl. The first thing to realize about puberty development in boys is that the average boy begins 2 years later than the average girl, at 12 in contrast to her 10. The earlier developers among boys begin as early as 10, a few younger still. Plenty of slow developers start as late as 14, and there are a few who wait longer. The boy may grow in height at double the rate he was growing before. The penis, the testicles and the scrotum (the sac in which the testicles lie) all develop rapidly. Pubic hair begins to grow early. Later comes the hair in the armpits and on the face. The voice cracks and deepens.

At the end of about 2 years' time, the boy's body has fairly well completed its transition to that of a man. In the following 2 years, he will creep up 2 or 2½ inches altogether and then practically stop.

The boy, like the girl, may go through a period of some physical and emotional awkwardness as he tries to gain control of his new body and new feelings. The way his voice keeps breaking down and up is an example of how he is both boy and man and yet not either.

This is a good moment to mention the difficulties of social life in school during puberty development and adolescence.

Adolescence comes at different ages.

The boys and girls in a class are of approximately the same age. And yet between the ages of 10 and 14, particularly, the average girl is 2 full years ahead of the average boy in development—towering over him in size and more grown up in interests. She's beginning to want to go to dances and be treated as if she were glamorous, while he is still an uncivilized little boy who thinks it would be shameful to pay attention to her. During this whole period it is better for social functions to include different age groups for a better fit.

The boy who is on a slow timetable of development, who is still a "shrimp" at 14 when most of his friends have turned into grown men, needs reassurance even more than the slow-developing girl. Size and physique and athletic ability count for a lot at this age. What happens sometimes is that the boy, instead of being reassured that he will start developing in time and grow something like 8 or 9 inches in the process, is taken by his worried parents on a hunt for a doctor who will give gland treatment. This helps to convince him that something is really wrong with him. There are glandular preparations that bring on the signs of puberty at whatever age they are given. But it seems wiser and safer, when the boy is normal, to let his inborn pattern unfold in its proper order.

582. Skin troubles in adolescence. Puberty changes the texture of the skin. The pores enlarge and secrete more oil. Blackheads are formed by the combination of oil and dust and dirt. These plugs enlarge the pores further. Then it is easy for ordinary germs to get in under a blackhead and cause a small infection or pimple.

Adolescent children have a tendency to be self-conscious anyway, and to worry about any defects in their appearance. They fret about pimples and are apt to finger them and squeeze them. The trouble is that when a pimple is broken, the germs are spread in large numbers onto the surrounding skin and onto the fingers. Then when the child touches another part of his face, he inoculates the germs into other blackheads and starts new pimples. Squeezing a pimple often makes it larger and deeper and therefore more likely to leave a scar. Some adolescents, worried about sex, imagine that their pimples are caused by guilty thoughts or masturbation.

Parents commonly accept their children's pimples fatalistically, assuming that nothing but time will bring a cure. This is too pessimistic a view. With modern methods of treatment, great improvement can be made in many cases and some improvement in the others. A child is entitled to all the help he can get from his regular doctor or a skin specialist, for the sake of improving his present appearance and spirits, and to prevent the permanent scars that sometimes develop.

Whatever the specific methods are that the doctor prescribes, there are also general measures that are believed to be helpful. Vigorous daily exercise, fresh air and direct sunshine seem to improve many complexions. The frequent eating of chocolate, candy and other rich, sweet foods has been suspected of favoring pimples, but this has never been proved in experiments. It has been the common practice to recommend thorough washing of the face twice a day, though skin specialists have doubts about it in some cases. The usual procedure is to thoroughly but gently clean the face with a washcloth and a soap containing hexachlorophene, then rinse with hot and cold water. It is certainly important to make it clear to the child why he should keep his hands away from his face at all times except when he is washing it, and why he should never squeeze a pimple. If a whitehead has formed and is bothering him, he can soak it off with a piece of wet absorbent cotton, being careful not to spread the pus around when it breaks.

Another skin change at adolescence is a more profuse and strong-smelling perspiration in the armpits. Some children, and parents, too, are not aware of the odor, but it may cause unpopularity with schoolmates. It calls for thorough daily washing with soap and the regular use of a suitable deodorant, in all adolescents.

PSYCHOLOGICAL CHANGES

583. Self-consciousness and touchiness. As a result of all the physical and emotional changes, an adolescent becomes much more self-conscious. He may exaggerate and worry about any defect. If a girl has freckles, she may think they make her look "horrible." A slight peculiarity in the adolescent's body or how it functions easily convinces him that he is "abnormal."

He may not manage his new body with as much coordination as he used to, and the same applies to his new feelings. He is apt to be touchy, easily hurt when criticized. At one moment he feels like a grown-up and wants to be treated as such. The next he feels like a child again and expects to be cared for.

584. Rivalry with parents. It isn't often realized that the rebelliousness of adolescents is mainly an expression of rivalrousness with parents, particularly the rivalry of son with father and girl with mother, which first developed back in the 4-to-6-year-old period. This rivalrousness becomes much more intense in the adolescent because he has stronger emotions and because he senses that as an almost adult person he is ready to compete in the parents' own league, you might say. It's now his turn to challenge the world, to fascinate the opposite sex, to be the head of a family. So he feels like elbowing the has-been parent off the seat of power. Subconsciously the parent senses this and, understandably, doesn't feel too gracious about it.

Rebellious rivalry takes many forms. A mountaineer's son may suddenly at the age of 16 become angry at his father in an argument and, without premeditation, knock him down. He then realizes that it's no longer dignified to stay on in his father's house, so he abruptly leaves home to look for a job. Another boy may continue to get along well enough on the surface with his father but he displaces his defiance onto the school authorities or the police.

In university-level families father and son are apt to be so self-disciplined that they keep their anger under control and deal with each other by reasonableness. When a boy from such a background feels angry rivalrousness underneath, he may have difficulty finding a legitimate complaint against his considerate father. In families like this, rivalry is sometimes expressed unconsciously through unexpected school failure— in high school or college or graduate school—even though the boy has a high degree of intelligence, conscientiousness and an excellent previous school record. He is sincere in saying he has no idea why he can't study or hand in papers or take examinations, whichever the problem may be. When such a youth seeks help through psychoanalysis it may be discovered that, if he is planning to work in the same field as his father, he is afraid unconsciously either that he will ignominiously fail to come up to his father's level or, conversely, that he might outstrip his father and make him very angry. In either case the boy's school failure is the worst kind of blow to the parents; but he doesn't have to feel responsible for it because he has no conscious control. (Some, not all, of the youths who leave school because of unexpected failure find that they regain their academic efficiency and a heightened ambitiousness after working at a job or being in the Army for a couple of years; i.e., they outgrow the unconscious fear. A more purposeful method is psychoanalysis.)

Other boys may express their anxious competitiveness by steering very clear of their father's occupation though some of them swing around to it later when they have matured enough to overcome the irrational fear.

Psychoanalysis has also revealed that many boys who feel overawed by their father suppress their resentment and antagonism toward him and displace it onto their mother. flaring up at her over quite reasonable requests or imagined slights.

If youths were not rebellious, they would lack the motive to leave home and make their own way in the world. Rivalrousness also provides the motive power for young people who try to improve the world, find new methods that will supersede the old, make discoveries, create new art forms, displace old tyrants, right wrongs. A surprising number of scientific advances have been made and masterpieces of various arts created by individuals just on the threshold of adulthood. They were not smarter than the older men in their fields and they were admittedly less experienced. But they were critical of traditional ways. biased in favor of the new and the untried, and that happened to be enough to do the trick. This is how the world makes progress.

An adolescent girl is much less often overawed by her mother than a boy is by his father, so her rivalrousness is more apt to be expressed openly around the house, not often in academic failure. A girl can even be flirtatious with her father right under her mother's nose or reproach her mother for not being nice enough to her father. Few boys would dare taunt their father in such ways.

585. Identity. A central problem for the adolescent and the young adult is to find out what kind of person he is going to be, doing what work, living by what principles. It's partly a conscious but even more an unconscious process. Erik Erikson has called this the identity crisis and exemplified it in his biography of Martin Luther.[1]

A youth has got to separate himself emotionally from his parents in order to find out who he is and what he wants to be. Yet he is basically made from his parents—not just in the sense that he has inherited his genes from them but that he has been deliberately patterning himself after them all his life. So he must pry himself apart. The eventual outcome will be influenced by three factors: the pull of his dependency, the intensity of his rebelliousness and the kind of outside world he finds and what it seems to ask of him.

In groping to find his identity an adolescent may try out a variety of roles: dreamer, man of the world, cynic, wit, leader of lost causes, ascetic.

[1] *Young Man Luther* (New York: Norton, 1958).

As he tries to emancipate himself from his parents, he is apt to have a great need to find compensation in intimate ties to friends his own age; more often ties to those of his own sex at first, because of the residual taboos against the opposite sex. These friendships, within or across the sexes, help to lend a youth some external support—like the timbers that are sometimes used to prop a building up during alterations—while he is giving up his identity as his parents' child and before he has found his own.

A youth finds himself through finding something similar in his friend. He mentions that he loves a certain song or hates a certain teacher or craves to own a certain article of apparel. His friend exclaims with amazement that he has always had the very same attitude. Both are delighted and reassured Each has lost a degree of his feeling of aloneness, of peculiarity, and gained a pleasurable sense of belonging.

Two girls talk fast all the way home from school, talk for another half hour in front of the house of one, finally separate. But as soon as the second reaches her home she telephones and they resume the mutual confidences.

A majority of adolescents help to overcome their feelings of aloneness by a sometimes slavish conformity to the styles of their classmates—in clothes, hairdos, language reading matter, songs, entertainers These styles have to be different from those of their parents' generation. And if their own styles irritate or shock their parents, so much the better. It is revealing, though that even those youths who adopt extreme styles to differentiate themselves from their parents must still conform to the styles of at least a few of their friends.

A majority of adolescents become ashamed of their parents for a few years particularly when their friends are present. This is partly related to their anxious search for their own identities. Partly it is the extreme self-consciousness of the age period. Most of all it is the intense need to be just like their friends and to be accepted totally by their friends. What youths choose to deplore in their parents is sometimes ludicrous. But the parents shouldn't accept discourtesy. Their best cue, when they find themselves with their children's friends, is to be agreeable but not talk too much. It's most important, from their children's point of view, that they not try to talk or act as if they are young themselves.

Youths in trying to achieve emotional independence are on the lookout for evidences of hypocrisy in their parents. To the extent that their parents are obviously sincere in their ideals, their children feel under obligation to continue to adhere to them. But if they can find hypocrisy, this relieves them of some of the moral duty to conform. It also gives them a welcome opportunity to reproach their parents.

586. Demands for freedom and fear of freedom. A common reproach of adolescents is that their parents don't allow them enough freedom. It's natural for a child nearing adulthood to insist on his rights, and his parents need to be reminded that he is changing. But parents don't have to take every claim at its face value. The fact is that any adolescent is also scared of growing up. He is unsure about his capacity to be as knowledgeable, masterful, sophisticated and charming as he would like. But his pride won't allow him to recognize this. When he's unconsciously in doubt about his ability to carry off some challenge or adventure, he's quick to find evidence that his parents are blocking his way. He reproaches them indignantly. Or he blames them when talking with his friends. Parents can particularly suspect this unconscious maneuver when he suddenly announces a plan of his group for some escapade—like an evening at an unsavory roadhouse— which is way beyond anything he's done before. He may be asking to be stopped.

587. Withdrawal, eccentricity, radicalism. It sometimes takes a youth 5 or 10 years to truly find his own positive identity. Meanwhile he may be stalled at a halfway stage characterized by a passive resistance to and withdrawal from ordinary society (which he equates with his parents) or an excessively rebellious radicalism.

He may decline to take an ordinary job. He may emphasize his unconventional dress, grooming, acquaintances, residence. These seem like evidence of vigorous independence to him. But by themselves they don't add up yet to a positive stand on life or a constructive contribution to the world. They are essentially a negative protest against the parents' conventions. But even when the striving to be independent shows up only in the form of eccentricities of appearance it should be recognized as an attempted step in the right direction, which may go on to a constructive, creative stage later. As a matter of fact, the young people who have to strain so visibly to be free are apt to come from families with unusually strong ties and high ideals.

Other youths, who are idealistic and altruistic in character, often take a sternly radical or purist view of things for a number of years—in politics or in the arts or in other fields. Various tendencies of this age period operate together to draw them into these extreme positions—heightened criticalness, cynicism about hypocrisy, intolerance of compromise, courageousness, willingness to sacrifice. A few years later, having achieved a satisfactory degree of emotional independence from parents and having found out how to be useful in their chosen fields, they are more tolerant of the frailties of their fellow men and more ready to make constructive compromises.

588. Sexuality and romance are strained for the adolescent for several reasons. (I use the word "sexual" when I put the emphasis on glands and crude inborn instinct, the word "romantic" when I mean the tender, highly personal, idealistic aspects of love between the sexes, which are mainly learned during a childhood with parents whose love is of this kind. I realize that this usage has various inaccuracies; also that to call anything romantic nowadays makes it seem to some people insipid or bogus.) The adolescent has emerged from two earlier, contradictory phases which were described briefly way back in Section 13 and described in more detail in the Chapters "Three to Six" and "From Six to Eleven." Between 3 and 6 years the child grew spiritually by overidealizing his two parents; and he became interested in romance, sex and babies. Between 6 and 12, through a complex interaction of emotions, he repressed his interest in romance, turned away from his parents and became absorbed in the impersonal outside world of schooling, social adaptation, laws and legends.

In adolescence the glandular pressures compel the child to be preoccupied with sexual and romantic interests again. But the revived sexual drives will continue to be in conflict with the earlier taboos for several more years, causing internal embarrassment and guilt, and external awkwardness. The simplest example is the young adolescent's shyness in dealing with the opposite sex.

The conflicting emotions also cause trouble in the child's relations with his parents. When the rush of strong romantic feeling wells up in adolescence, it first starts—like a spring flood running down a dry riverbed—toward the parent of the opposite sex. Yet the adolescent realizes subconsciously that this is not right at all. So his initial job at this age is to steer his feelings away from his parent toward someone outside the family. He actually covers up the positive feelings with negative ones. This is at least a partial explanation of why a boy so often picks fights with his mother and why a daughter may be surprisingly antagonistic toward her father at times.

At first the adolescent doesn't know at all clearly where his feelings belong. He becomes generally intense and romantic in his attitudes toward different kinds of people. Yet he may be nowhere near the time where he can show these feelings toward an individual of the same age and opposite sex, especially if he is shy and idealistic. He may develop a great admiration for a teacher of the same sex, or a hero of fiction. It's only gradually that the barriers between the sexes are broken down. Perhaps the adolescent first dares to think romantically of someone in Hollywood. Then boys and girls in the same school can dream about each other; but it may take some further time before the shy ones can show their interest face to face.

Even after an adolescent's instincts have broken through the inhibitions of the earlier period and involved him in dating, a portion of this energy will still be held in reserve and invested in idealistic yearnings. Some part of this will ensure that his attitude toward the opposite sex is romantic and chivalrous. But another part, even at this relatively late stage of development, will still be sublimated into aspirations which on the surface seem unrelated to sex or even romance—to create things of beauty, for example, or to become a benefactor of mankind.

In the very beginning of his interest in members of the opposite sex the adolescent may be unable to recognize any sexual feeling towards a person for whom he feels respect and tenderness, only for those who seem debased in some way. (For a few individuals this dissociation unfortunately lasts for life.)

Before a child has become secure about his sexuality or integrated it into his personality it remains a rather awkward, compelling, crude, separate instinct. He feels a nagging curiosity about what sex is in the ultimate and a compulsion to find out by experimentation. These feelings run counter, of course, to his idealistic emotions. In fact, he may be tenderly in love with one person and still find himself impelled to make advances—hesitant or bold—to others, in a rather impersonal, promiscuous spirit.

A child in the early teens is apt to experience a series of intense infatuations, in each of which the sense of being in love is intense. But he can fall out of love as quickly as he falls in. He discovers that he and his beloved really have little in common. Sometimes the reason is that one or both have changed. More often it's that they had originally fallen in love with the ideal they saw in each other, which had little to do with the reality. As the years pass they become more cautious, and more realistic about what kind of person they need and can get along with. As they gradually mature they also have more to give to each other—a vital ingredient of true love.

589. Parental guidance of adolescents. Being a wise parent to adolescents has always been a difficult job. If the child is made of good stuff he is bound to feel rivalrous and rebellious, whether or not the parent is being reasonable. The job is greatly complicated in the twentieth century by the fact that parents have all read psychology of one kind or another and have been made uneasy about the theoretical possibility of doing harm by well-intentioned efforts. This is too bad, because in most cases it's better to do the supposedly wrong thing with an air of confidence than the supposedly right thing with a hesitant or apologetic manner. Then there's also the fact that many children today have the bit in their teeth and have their parents on the run.

Most adolescents are not the enemies of parents, though. They are reasonable a good part of the time. This is remarkable considering the inner emotional storms they are experiencing and the dozens of new adjustments they are having to make between their new selves and the new life they are being called on to live, the heavy academic schedules that most of them are carrying.

The first and most important point—by far—is that adolescents need and want guidance from their parents—and even rules—no matter how much they argue against them. (Their pride won't let them admit the need openly.)

Trusted schoolteachers and child guidance workers have all heard adolescents say, "I wish my parents would make definite rules for me, like my friend's parents do." They sense that it's one aspect of parents' love to want to keep their children from misunderstandings and embarrassing situations out in the world, from giving the wrong impression or gaining an unfortunate reputation, from getting into trouble through inexperience.

This doesn't mean that parents can be arbitrary or overbearing. Adolescents have too much dignity and indignation for that; they want to discuss the issues on an adult-to-adult basis. If the argument comes out a draw, though, the parent shouldn't be so scrupulously democratic that he assumes the child is as likely to be right as he is; the parent's experience should be presumed to count for a lot. In the end, the parent should confidently express his judgment, his request and, if appropriate, his order. He owes his child this clarity and definiteness.

But, parents ask, what if the child openly defies the order or quietly disobeys? If the child-parent relationship is halfway sound, the child will not defy or disobey in the early years of adolescence. Even in the later years he may not. In the later years the parent may even consider it wise on occasion to give a youth permission to go against the parent's judgment; this doesn't mean that the parent has no confidence that his judgment is right.

A parent's attitude should indicate, without his necessarily saying so in words, that he realizes the youth will be out of his sight most of the time and therefore will be obeying because of his conscience and his respect for his parent, not because the parent can make him obey or watch him.

Even if an older adolescent defies or disobeys a parent's direction, this does not mean that the direction did no good. It certainly helps an inexperienced person to hear all sides. If he decides not to take his parent's direction he may of course be making a reasonably sound decision, perhaps being in possession of knowledge or insights that the parent lacks. Certainly as he progresses into adulthood he must be prepared to reject advice on occasion and to take the responsibility for his decision. If a youth rejects his parent's direction and gets into trouble, this experience will increase his respect for his parent's judgment, though he probably won't admit it.

Suppose the parent doesn't know what to say or think about some issue. He can discuss it not only with his child but with other parents, perhaps get the PTA to have a general session on it. In some cities there have been official conferences between parents and adolescents which have led to a fairly uniform code of behavior that was a comfort to all concerned.

But individual parents should not feel bound in advance to adhere to other people's code even if they are the only parents who disagree. In the long run parents can only do a good job if they are convinced they are doing right. And what is right for them is what they feel is right, after hearing the arguments.

590. Specific suggestions. I myself have strong opinions about the general principles of parental guidance but I'd be hesitant to convert these into arbitrary specifics. Times change. Customs vary in different parts of the country and in different groups in the same community. Individual children vary greatly in their maturity and reliability.

There are some simple rules, I think:

Adolescents, like adults, out of respect for themselves as well as others, should bathe regularly, wear clothes that are clean and considered reasonably attractive by their age group. The style of clothes, hairdo, can be left to their choice as long as these are not so deliberately provocative that they outrage parents, neighbors, school authorities.

Individually and in groups they should be expected to be civil to people generally and definitely cordial to their parents, family friends, teachers and the people who serve them. It is natural for youths to have at least a mildly hostile attitude underneath toward adults, with whom they are inevitably rivalrous, whether or not they are aware of this. But it does them no harm to have to control this hostility and be polite anyway. Their politeness certainly makes a great difference to the adults concerned.

Youths should have serious obligations in helping their families—in regular chores and in special additional jobs. This benefits youths by giving them a sense of dignity, participation, happiness, as well as helping the parents.

591. Dating. I believe myself (and I was brought up in a strict, old-fashioned way) that it's better that younger adolescents—up to the age of 16 or 17, let's say—not have individual dates or go steady. In recent decades children have been dating and going steady at younger and younger ages. There have probably been a number of causes for this shift. Since the turn of the century, sexual standards have been progressively relaxed—for all ages. There has been a widespread tendency to question the certainty of old religious and moral teachings and to substitute the findings of biology and psychology, as if Nature were perhaps the only reliable guide. Many parents, on the basis of their interpretation of child psychology, have been hesitant to use the same rules that were applied to themselves in childhood, for fear of the reproach of being old-fashioned or of making their children unhappy. Some mothers have gone along with permissive standards because they wanted their daughters, above all, to be socially successful. A few mothers have enjoyed vicariously coaching their young daughters in dating and then hearing the results from them.

I feel that early dating and going steady often cheapen love, make it seem mainly biological rather than a spiritual relationship. A majority of young adolescents just don't have the maturity yet to love tenderly, generously, companionably, devotedly. They are too inclined to exploit a member of the opposite sex for their own curiosity and gratification, and for finding out whether they can master their own roles as beginning lovers. When they become involved in regular dating, the physical, experimental aspects of sex are apt to get a head start and crowd out the companionable and spiritual possibilities.

When going steady at a young age has become the local custom, many girls want regular boyfriends not really to love but so that they can have regular partners at parties and be considered socially successful. They encourage or permit physical intimacy to hold the boy's interest. This often leads to pregnancies, which seriously hurt them and their boyfriends—emotionally, socially, academically. (Illegitimate pregnancies have tripled in the last twenty years.)

By contrast, when a mature boy and girl are becoming more deeply in love, because they are right for each other, the physical desire increases but it is always integrated with and under the control of the tender and generous feelings.

The girl with high aspirations is particularly apt to want to reserve her full response and final intimacy for the boy she is sure she will love totally and permanently—even though this impulse is in conflict with her physical desire and curiosity. Many boys with high ideals have the same wish. When a true love is in the early stages of development it is usually the girl who, because of needing to be sure, keeps the progress of physical intimacy under control. And the boy is willing to let his ardor be controlled because of the tenderness and respect he feels for her.

592. Parental supervision of dating. Parents should specify, without being overbearing about it, the hour at which their children are to come home from parties and dates, where they can and can't go. They should know and approve of the others with whom their children are going out, and who is to drive. Parents don't need to be put off when children point out that they could just as easily get into trouble before midnight as after, which is a plausible argument. But the very fact that the parents set a certain hour, and are waiting for them then, reminds children that the parents are genuinely concerned with their conduct and reputations. Parents can explain correctly, too, that neighbors tend to judge propriety by the hour of homecoming, and that reputations have importance. When children have a party at home, the parents should be there.

Parents don't have to sound like suspicious detectives in asking about the plans and the cast of characters when their children are going out for the evening. In the 13-to-15-year-old period they will know inevitably. After that they can continue to indicate indirectly that they still expect to know. If they have to ask directly and the child asks why they want to know, they can answer that good parents feel completely responsible for their children, at least up to the time when they go away to college or to work; society expects them to maintain that responsibility. "Suppose," parents can say, "there is some accident which delays you. We ought to know where to inquire or to search." Or the parents can say, "Suppose the parents of another child in the group calls us because, according to their understanding, their child is overdue; we would appear irresponsible if we had to answer that we had no idea where you were or when you were coming home." Incidentally, if there is a delay or a change in plan, adolescents should call home to explain, before they are overdue.

These suggestions of mine might imply to some parents that they can't trust their children and will have to admit this to them. Adolescents who are supervised carefully will surely reproach their parents for not trusting them. To admit to a child that you don't trust his morals, his character, is definitely unwise. In a sense it gives him permission to be bad. He can say, "If that's all they think of me, there's no point trying to be good." Child guidance workers have learned how often an adolescent's delinquent behavior began in response to a parent's accusation or implication that he was seriously misbehaving when he really wasn't.

But it is not an expression of lack of trust in a child's character or morals when his parents are keeping supervision over his parties and dates and hours. It's only a recognition that he is still relatively inexperienced about the many pitfalls of the adult world and still needs guidance, though he is at a stage in life when his pride and aspirations won't let him admit this. In order to make this distinction convincingly, parents must be ready for the reproach (about lack of trust) and answer up briskly, because hesitancy encourages children to press their arguments and reproaches with more determination.

The intensity of young love and the present style of early marriage sometimes confront parents with serious crises these days. If I had a daughter of 16 or 17 who wanted to marry someone she'd known only a few months, I wouldn't think I could persuade her that this love wasn't the real thing or that her beloved wasn't worthy—all her dignity and her loyalty to him would be arrayed against my argument. But I would earnestly ask her to wait until she had been engaged for a year, to make sure that their personalities and tastes had stopped changing.

Some parents and professional people take an attitude about adolescent sexuality and dating which is quite different from mine. They say that we moderns have at last emancipated ourselves from old-fashioned puritanical attitudes toward sex, that adolescence is meant to be a time for sexual experimenting, that the availability of various efficient forms of contraception removes the last reasons for concern and disapproval. They advocate, for example, that all girls in their later teens be instructed in the use of the diaphragm or the pill so that there will be no misfortune of pregnancy.

This view is appealing but I think it is too simple to be true or workable. The wish that some idealistic young people have, to reserve sexual intimacy for the person he will love deeply, is not just American puritanism. It has been characteristic of idealistic young people for many centuries in Western countries. There is evidence that the best aspects of civilization—the creation of all forms of beauty, the pursuit of science, the advances of technology—are fostered by the partial repression and sublimation of sexual interests in childhood and adolescence.

One reason why I stress this point is that psychiatrists in universities report that girls and boys who find themselves not ready, not wanting to become sexually involved at this stage are, in today's atmosphere, made to feel abnormal by the taunts of their less idealistic friends. And if adolescents are routinely instructed in contraception, on the initiative of their parents or schools, this is an invitation to casualness in sexual relations. (During the past half century, mature young people who decided to have relations but were not yet ready for marriage managed to secure contraceptives in one way or another.)

Some people assume that when a psychologist or physician

speaks of the inhibition of sexuality in those raised with high standards he means that they will have less sexual pleasure when they are ready for true love. This is not what is meant. They will have at least as much physical pleasure; and their marriages will be more inspiring and more long lasting, as the figures show.

593. Juvenile delinquency. This subject is too complex for more than a brief definition and a few examples. The term is confusing because it covers everything for which a youth might be hailed into court, from playing hooky to murder. The aggressiveness of boys in adolescence is such that a majority of them engage in offenses such as truancy, petty theft (hubcaps, for instance) or mischief (breaking windows in a vacant building), at one time or another in adolescence, though most of them don't get caught. Such offenses are usually of no great psychological significance if a boy commits them only once or twice, and in a group. But society has to disapprove of them firmly and parents should, too. However, repeated offenses of such kinds in the case of a boy brought up in a strict neighborhood mean either that he has a definite neurotic problem (compulsive stealing, for example) or that he has never been loved adequately and doesn't care much what his parents and society think of him; or that his parents have unconscious delinquent tendencies, despite their conventional exteriors, and are vicariously enjoying his escapades. The same kind of repeated mild delinquencies in a tough neighborhood may mean only that a youth is proving his manhood by defying the police.

Offenses that have a lot of grasping aggression in them (robbery) or destructiveness (wrecking a schoolroom at night) or cruelty (a sexual attack; or beating people up for no good reason) mean that a child was raised not only without much love but was subjected to a lot of hostility or cruelty in addition.

On the other hand, the peeping tom or the boy who cautiously tries to make a pass at a strange girl sitting next to him in a movie theatre usually has no excess aggressiveness—often quite the contrary. He is restricted to an incomplete expression of sexuality because of an excessive repression and perhaps also an abnormal shyness.

Girls have on the average less aggressiveness than boys and their delinquency usually does not take the form of defying the authorities or attacking people. Instead they make their parents miserable. A moderately serious form of feminine delinquency is running away from home. It occurs in girls who are immature and unstable, and there has usually been a long history of disharmony with the parents.

An example of a more harsh and serious delinquency is when a girl engages in promiscuous sexual behavior, in her parents' community, to scandalize and enrage them, and spitefully to give the whole family a bad name. The parents call on the police to arrest her because they can't control her. Usually there are serious conflicts throughout the family and a deficiency in the parents' love of the girl.

In one sense any girl who becomes illegitimately pregnant is delinquent in that she has defied her parents and society. But in most cases she is trying to hide her affair and is involved with only one man. So of course the parents don't call on the police. But psychiatric study often shows—not always, by any means—that this was not a love affair in which the girl was carried away; she has reacted to angry quarreling with her parents by involving herself rather cold-bloodedly with a man for whom she had little affection, and neglected precautions against pregnancy, with the unconscious purpose of hurting her parents. Girls who are not resentful toward their parents and who are involved in affairs because of infatuation or true love are extremely careful in most cases to avoid pregnancy, which has so many unfortunate results.

The main point I want to make about the more serious forms of delinquency is that they don't appear suddenly in adolescents who were well adjusted before. They occur in unstable families where relations between the parents and between child and parents have been way out of line for a long time, where there has been very little love and where the child's behavior showed serious aberrations long before adolescence. The prevention of delinquency consists, of course, in the early child guidance treatment of the child who is distinctly maladjusted.

594. Drugs. The habituation or addiction to drugs is largely confined to the period from midadolescence to about the age of 30, during which many individuals are groping for a positive identity—for a place and an active function in the world.

It occurs most often in youths who are somewhat immature, self-centered, passive, and have little sense of direction in life as yet. But several characteristics of normal adolescents favor experimentation with drugs:

They have a powerful curiosity to find out all there is to know about life—especially about what seem like the mysterious aspects.

Many, especially males, have an impulse to sacrifice themselves, in the sense of taking wild chances, accepting dangerous dares, being proud of burning the candle at both ends, proving their courage. (This is one reason why they bravely take up smoking while older people are striving to give it up.)

At the same time they are secretly afraid of facing new, difficult situations. A drug may, like alcohol, give a promise of numbing inhibitions, erasing apprehensions, increasing courage sufficiently to get a youth over the threshold—of lovemaking, for example.

There is a particularly strong appeal to a youth to follow the style of his peers; and if that style worries or angers parents, so much the better.

Marijuana is the least dangerous drug in terms of addiction and of psychiatric disturbance but it is not harmless by any means. Adolescents make a big point of the fact that it is no more dangerous than alcohol, which is a dig at their parents. But alcoholism is a common and extremely destructive disease.

If my adolescent child raised the subject of drug use, obviously to see my reaction, I'd firmly condemn it as medically and emotionally unsound. But I wouldn't keep harping on this theme, which would imply that I had no confidence that I'd gotten my message across.

Problems of Feeding and Development

THIN CHILDREN

595. Thinness has various causes. Some children seem to be thin by heredity. They come from thin stock on one or both sides of the family. From the time they were babies they have been offered plenty to eat. They aren't sickly, and they aren't nervous. They just never want to eat a great deal, especially of the rich foods.

Some children are thin because their appetites have been taken away by too much parental urging (Section 597). Other children can't eat for other nervous reasons. The child who is worrying about bogeymen, or death, or his mother's going away and leaving him, may lose a lot of his appetite. The jealous younger sister who is driving herself all day long to keep up with her older sister burns up a lot of energy and gives herself no peace at mealtime, either. As you can see, the tense child is thinned out by a two-way process. His appetite is kept down, and his restlessness uses up extra energy.

There are many children throughout the world who are malnourished because their parents can't find or afford the proper food. There are a few chronic physical diseases that cause malnutrition. But children who become thin during an acute illness usually recover their weight promptly if during convalescence they are not urged to eat until their appetite recovers.

596. Care of a thin child. A thin child should, of course, have regular medical checkups. This is more important if he acts tired or if he has lost weight or if he has failed to gain a reasonable amount.

Thinness, failure to gain weight and fatigue come more

often from emotional troubles than from physical causes. If your child is nervous or depressed, try to consult a child guidance clinic or a family social agency. Talk over his situation with his schoolteacher. In any case, it's wise to think over again his relations with parents, brothers, sisters, friends and school. If you have gotten involved in a feeding problem, try to undo it.

Eating between meals is helpful for those thin children whose stomachs never seem to want to take much at a time but are quite willing to eat often.

A healthy child may stay thin despite a large appetite, and this is probably the way he was meant to be. In many of these cases, the child prefers relatively low-calorie foods, like meat, vegetables and fruit, and shies away from rich desserts.

Finally, if your child doesn't seem to be any kind of problem, has been slender since infancy, but gains a reasonable amount of weight every year, relax and let him alone. He is probably meant to be that way.

FEEDING PROBLEMS

597. Where feeding problems begin. Why do so many children eat poorly? Most commonly because so many mothers are conscientious about trying to make them eat well. You don't see many feeding problems in puppies, or among young humans in places where mothers don't know enough about diet to worry. You might say jokingly that it takes knowledge and many months of hard work to make a feeding problem.

One child seems to be born with a wolf's appetite that stays big even when he's unhappy or sick. Another's appetite is more moderate and is easily affected by his health and spirits. The first child seems to be cut out to be plump; the second is apparently intended to stay on the slender side. But every baby is born with enough appetite to keep him healthy, keep him gaining at the proper rate for him.

The trouble is that a child is also born with an instinct to get balky if he is pushed too hard, and an instinct to get disgusted with food that he's had unpleasant experiences with. There's one further complication: a person's appetite doesn't always go out to the same things. For a while he feels like eating a lot of spinach or a new breakfast cereal. Next month it may not appeal to him. Some people always go in heavily for starches and sweets; others are fed up with a little bit. If you understand these points, you can see how feeding problems begin at different stages in a child's development. The baby becomes balky in his early months if his mother often tries to make him finish more of his bottle than he wants, or, when the first solid food is introduced, he isn't given a chance to get used to it gradually. Many become more picky and choosy after the age of a year because they aren't meant to be gaining so fast, because they are more opinionated, and perhaps because of teething. Urging them reduces the appetite further and more permanently. A very common time for feeding problems to begin is at the end of an illness. If an anxious mother begins pushing food before the child's appetite returns, it quickly increases his disgust and gets it firmly fixed.

All feeding problems don't start from urging. A child may stop eating because of jealousy of a new baby or worries of many kinds. But whatever the original cause, the mother's anxiety and urging usually make it worse and keep the appetite from returning.

Put yourself in the child's place for a minute. To get in the mood, think back to the last time you weren't very hungry. Perhaps it was a muggy day, or you were worried, or you had a stomach upset. (The child with a feeding problem feels that way most of the time.) Now imagine that a nervous giantess is sitting beside you, watching every mouthful. You have eaten a little of the foods that appeal to you most and have put your fork down, feeling plenty full. But she looks worried and says, "You haven't touched your turnips." You explain that you don't want any, but she doesn't seem to understand how you feel, acts as if you are being bad on purpose. When she says you can't get up from the table until you've cleaned your plate, you try a bit of turnip, but it makes you feel slightly sick to your stomach. She scoops up a tablespoonful and pokes it at your mouth, which makes you gag.

598. A cure takes time and patience. Once a feeding problem is established, it takes time and understanding and patience to undo. The mother has become anxious. She finds it hard to relax again as long as the child is eating poorly. And yet her concern and insistence are the main things that are keeping his appetite down. Even when she reforms, by a supreme effort, it may take weeks for the child's timid appetite to come back. He has to have a chance to slowly forget all the unpleasant associations with mealtime.

His appetite is like a mouse and the mother's anxious urging is the cat that has been scaring him back into his hole. You can't persuade the mouse to be bold just because the cat looks the other way. The cat must leave him alone for a long time.

Dr. Clara Davis found that babies who hadn't built up any prejudices about foods naturally picked well-balanced diets in the long run when offered a variety of natural foods (Section 416). But you can't expect a child who has been fighting against certain foods—vegetables, for example—for months or years to suddenly turn to those foods just because his mother gives him a free choice. He might at a camp where everyone else is eating the vegetables, where he's hungry, and where no one cares whether he eats them or not. But at home those vegetables have too many associations in his mind. Just as soon as he sees them, his spirit and his stomach say, "No!"

599. A mother has feelings, too. And they are strong feelings by the time she has a chronic feeding problem on her hands. The most obvious one is anxiety—that the child will develop some nutritional deficiency or lose his resistance to ordinary infections. Her doctor tries to reassure her again and again that children with feeding problems are not more susceptible to diseases, but this is hard for her to believe.

She is apt to feel guilty, imagining that her relatives, her husband's relatives, the neighbors, the doctor, consider her a neglectful mother. Of course, they don't. It's more likely that they understand because they have at least one child in the family who's a poor eater, too.

Then there's the inevitable feeling of frustration and angriness at a whippersnapper who can completely foil all his mother's efforts to do right by him. This is the most uncomfortable feeling of all, because it makes the conscientious mother feel ashamed of herself.

It's an interesting fact that many parents who have feeding problems in their children recall having been a feeding problem themselves in their own childhood. They remember only too well that urging and forcing work in the wrong direction, but they find themselves powerless to do otherwise. In such cases, the parent's strong feelings of anxiety, guilt and irritation are partly leftovers from the same feelings implanted in him in childhood.

600. There's rarely danger for the child. It's important to remember that children have a remarkable inborn mechanism that lets them know how much food and which types of food they need for normal growth and development. It is extremely rare to see serious malnutrition or vitamin deficiency or infectious disease result from a feeding problem. The child's eating pattern should be discussed with the doctor at the time of checkups, of course.

601. Make mealtime pleasant. The aim is not to make the child eat but to let his natural appetite come to the surface so that he wants to eat.

Try hard not to talk about his eating, either with threats or with encouragement. I wouldn't praise him for taking an unusually large amount or look disappointed when he takes little. With practice, you should be able to stop thinking about it, and that's real progress. When he feels no more pressure, he can begin to pay attention to his own appetite.

You sometimes hear the advice, "Put the food before the child, say nothing, take it away in 30 minutes, no matter how much or little has been eaten. Give nothing else until the next meal." This is fine if it's carried out in the right spirit—that is to say, if the mother is really trying not to fuss or worry about the child's eating and remains agreeable. But an angry mother sometimes applies the advice this way. She slaps the plate of dinner in front of the child, saying grimly, "Now, if you don't eat this in 30 minutes, I'm going to take it away and you won't get a thing to eat until supper!" Then she stands glaring at him, waiting. This threatening hardens his heart and takes away any trace of appetite. The balky child who is challenged to a feeding battle can always outlast his mother.

You don't want your child to eat because he has been beaten in a fight, whether you have been forcing him or taking his food away. You want him to eat because he feels like eating.

Start with the foods he likes best. You want his mouth to water when he comes to meals so that he can hardly wait to begin. The first step in building up that attitude is to serve for 2 or 3 months the wholesome foods he likes best (offering as balanced a diet as possible), and to omit all the foods that he actively dislikes.

If your child has a limited feeding problem, dislikes only one or another group of foods but eats most kinds fairly well, read Sections 437–447. They explain how one food can be substituted for another until a child's appetite swings around or until he loses his suspiciousness and tenseness at meals.

602. The child who likes few foods. A mother might say, "Those children who dislike just one type of food aren't real problems. Why, my child likes only hamburgers, bananas, oranges and soda pop. Once in a while he'll take a slice of white bread or a couple of teaspoonfuls of peas. He refuses to touch anything else."

This is an unusually severe feeding problem, but the principle is the same. You could serve him sliced bananas and a slice of enriched bread for breakfast; hamburger, 2 teaspoonfuls of peas and an orange for lunch; a slice of enriched bread and more banana for supper. Let him have seconds or thirds of any of the foods if he asks for them and you have them. Serve different combinations of this diet for days. Hold down firmly on his soda pop. If his stomach is awash with syrup, it takes away what little appetite he has for more valuable foods.

If at the end of a couple of months he is looking forward to his meals, add a couple of teaspoonfuls (not more) of some food that he sometimes used to eat—not one he hated. Don't mention the new addition. Don't comment if he leaves it. Try this one again in a couple of weeks, and meanwhile try another. How fast you go on adding new foods depends on how his appetite is improving and how he's taking to the new foods.

603. Make no distinctions between foods. Let him eat four helpings of one food and none of another if that's the way he feels (as long as the food is wholesome). If he wants none of the main course but wants his dessert, let him have his dessert in a perfectly matter-of-fact way. If you say, "No seconds on meat until you've eaten your vegetable," or "No dessert until you've cleaned your plate," you further take away his appetite for the vegetable or the main course and you increase his desire for meat or dessert. These results are the exact opposite of what you want.

It's not that you want your child to go on eating lopsided meals forever. But if he has a feeding problem and is already suspicious of some foods, your best chance of his coming back to a reasonable balance is to let him feel that you do not care.

I think it's a great mistake for the parent to insist that a child who is a feeding problem eat "just a taste" of a food he is suspicious of, as a matter of duty. If he has to eat anything that disgusts him, even slightly, it lessens the chance that he will ever change his mind and like it. And it lowers his enjoyment of mealtimes and his general appetite for all foods by one more degree.

Certainly, never make him eat at the next meal food that he refused at the last meal. That's looking for trouble.

604. Serve less than he will eat, not more. For any child who is eating poorly, serve small portions. If you heap his plate high, you remind him of how much he is going to refuse and you depress his appetite. But if you give him a first helping that is less than he is willing to take, you encourage him to think, "That isn't enough." You want him to have that attitude. You want him to get to think of food as something he is eager for. If he has a really small appetite, serve him miniature portions: 1 teaspoonful of meat, 1 teaspoonful of vegetable, 1 teaspoonful of starch. When he finishes, don't say eagerly, "Do you want some more?" Let him ask, even if it takes several days of miniature portions to give him the idea.

605. Getting him to feed himself. Should the mother feed a poor eater? A child who is given proper encouragement (Section 423) takes over his own feeding somewhere between 12 and 18 months. But if an overworried mother has continued to feed him until the age of 2 or 3 or 4 (probably with a lot of urging), it won't solve the problem simply to tell her, "Stop!" The child now has no desire to feed himself; he takes being fed for granted. To him it's now an important sign of his mother's love and concern. If she stops suddenly, it hurts his feelings, makes him resentful. He is liable to stop eating altogether for 2 or 3 days—and that's longer than any mother can sit by doing nothing. When she feeds him again, he has a new grudge against her. When she tries another time to give up feeding him, he knows his strength and her weakness.

A child of 2 or more should be feeding himself as soon as possible. But getting him to do it is a delicate matter that takes several weeks. You mustn't give him the impression that you are trying to take a privilege away. You want him to take over because he wants to.

Serve him his favorite foods meal after meal and day after day. When you set the dish before him, go back to the kitchen or into the next room for a minute or two, as if you had forgotten something. Be away a little longer each day. Come back and feed him cheerfully with no comments, whether or not he has taken anything himself. If he gets impatient while you are in the next room and calls you to come and feed him, come right away, with a friendly apology. He probably won't progress steadily. In a week or two he may get to the point of eating one meal almost entirely himself, and the next meal want to be fed from the beginning. Don't argue at all during this process. If he eats one food, don't urge him to try another, too. If he seems pleased with himself for doing a good job of self-feeding, compliment him on being a big boy, but don't be so enthusiastic that he smells a rat.

Suppose for a week or so you have left him alone with good food for as long as 10 or 15 minutes and he's eaten nothing. Then you ought to make him hungrier. Gradually, in 3 or 4 days, cut down to half what you customarily feed him. This should make him so eager that he can't help starting in himself, provided you are being tactful and friendly.

By the time the child is regularly feeding himself as much as half a meal, I think it's time to encourage him to leave the table rather than feed him the rest of the meal. Never mind if he has left out some of his foods. The hunger will pile up and soon make him eat more. If you go on feeding him the last half of the meal, he may never take over the whole job. Just say, "I guess you've had enough." If he asks you to feed him some more, give him two or three more mouthfuls to be agreeable and then suggest casually that he's through.

After he has taken over completely for a couple of weeks, don't slip back into the habit of feeding him again. If some day he's very tired and says, "Feed me," give him a few spoonfuls absentmindedly, and then say something about his not being very hungry. I make this point because I know that a mother who has worried for months or years about a child's eating, who spoon-fed him much too long, and finally let him feed himself, has a great temptation to go back to feeding him again the first time he loses his appetite or the first time he is sick. Then the job has to be done all over again.

606. Should the mother stay in the room while he is eating? This depends on what the child is used to and wants, and how well the mother can control her worry. If she has always sat there, she can't suddenly disappear without upsetting him. If she can be sociable, relaxed and get her mind off the food, it's fine for her to stay (whether or not she is eating her own meal). If she finds that even with practice she can't get her mind off the child's eating, or stop urging him, it may be better for her to retire from the picture at mealtime, not crossly, not suddenly, but tactfully and gradually, a little more each day, so that he doesn't notice the change.

607. No acts or bribes. Certainly the parents shouldn't put on acts to bribe the child to eat, such as a little story for every mouthful or a promise from Father to stand on his head if the spinach is finished. All this kind of persuasion seems at the moment to be making the child eat a few more mouthfuls. But in the long run it takes his appetite away more and more. The parents have to keep raising the bribe to get the same results. They end up putting on an hour's exhausting vaudeville for five mouthfuls.

Don't ask a child to eat to earn his dessert, or a piece of candy, or a gold star, or any other prize. Don't ask him to eat for Aunt Minnie, or to make his mother happy, or to grow big and strong, or to keep from getting sick, or to clean his plate. Let's state the rule more briefly: Don't ask a child to eat.

There is no great harm in a mother's telling a story at suppertime, or playing the radio if that has been the custom, so long as it is not connected in any way with whether the child is eating or not.

608. It isn't necessary to be a doormat. I have said so much about letting a child eat because he wants to, that I may have given the wrong impression to some parents. I remember a mother who had been snarled up for years in a feeding problem involving her 7-year-old daughter, urging, arguing, forcing. When she understood the idea that the child probably had, underneath, a normal appetite and a desire for a well-balanced diet, and that the best way to revive it was to stop battling over meals, she swung to the opposite extreme and became apologetic. The daughter by this age had a lot of resentment in her from the long struggle. As soon as she realized that her mother was all meekness, she took advantage of her. She would pour the whole sugar bowl on her cereal, watching out of the corner of her eye to see her mother's silent horror. The mother would ask her before each meal what she wanted. If the child said, "Hamburger," she obediently bought and served it. Then the child, as like as not, would say, "I don't want hamburger. I want frankfurters," and the mother would run over to the butcher's to get it.

There's a middle ground. It's reasonable for a child to be expected to come to meals on time, to be pleasant to other diners, to refrain from making unpleasant remarks about the food or declaring what he doesn't like, to eat with the table manners that are reasonable for his age. It's fine for the mother to take his preferences into account as much as is possible (considering the rest of the family) in planning meals, or to ask him occasionally what he would like, as a treat. But it's bad for him to get the idea that he's the only one to be considered. It's sensible and right for the mother to put a limit on sugar, candy, sodas, cakes and the other less wholesome foods. All this can be done without argument as long as the mother acts as if she knows what she is doing.

609. Gagging. The child beyond the age of a year who can't tolerate anything but pureed food has usually been fed forcibly, or at least urged vigorously. It isn't so much that he can't stand lumps. What makes him gag is having them pushed into him. The mothers of gagging children usually say, "It's a funny thing. He can swallow lumps all right if it's something he likes very much. He can even swallow big chunks of meat that he bites off the bone." There are three steps in curing a gagger. The first is to encourage him to feed himself completely (Section 423). The second is to get him over his suspiciousness about foods in general (Sections 601–607). The third is to go unusually slowly in coarsening the consistency of his food. Let him go for weeks—or even months if necessary—on pureed foods, until he has lost all fear of eating and is really enjoying it. Don't even serve him meats, for instance, during this time if he cannot enjoy them finely ground.

In other words, go only as fast as the child can comfortably take it.

A few babies have such sensitive throats that they gag even on pureed foods. In some of these cases, the cause seems to be the pasty consistency of the food. Try diluting it a little with milk or water. Or try chopping vegetables and fruits fine without mashing them.

FAT CHILDREN

610. The treatment depends on the cause. Many people think the cause is gland trouble, but actually this is rarely the case. There are several factors that make for overweight, including heredity, temperament, appetite, happiness. If a child comes from a stocky line on both sides of the family, there is a greater chance of his being overweight. The placid child who takes little exercise has more food calories left over to store in the form of fat. The most important factor of all is appetite. The child who has a tremendous appetite that runs to rich food like cake, cookies and pastry is naturally going to be heavier than the child whose taste runs principally to vegetables and fruits and meats. But this only raises the question of why one child does crave large amounts of rich foods. We don't understand all the causes of this, but we recognize the child who seems to be born ("constitutionally") to be a big eater. He starts with a huge appetite at birth and never loses it afterward, whether he's well or sick, calm or worried, whether the food he's offered is appetizing or not. He's fat by the time he's 2 or 3 months old and stays that way at least through childhood.

611. Unhappiness is sometimes a factor. Of the excessive appetites that develop later in childhood, some at least are due to unhappiness. This happens, for instance, around the age of 7 in children who are somewhat unhappy and lonely. It is the period when the child is drawing away from his close emotional dependence on his parents. If he doesn't have the knack of making equally close friendships with other children, he feels left out in the cold. Eating sweet and rich food seems to serve him as a partial substitute. Worries about schoolwork or other matters sometimes make a child seek comfort in overeating, too. Overweight often develops during the puberty stage of development. The appetite normally increases at this time to take care of the increased rate of growth, but it's probable that loneliness plays a part in some cases, too. It is the period when the child may become more turned-in and self-conscious because of all the changes he is experiencing, and this may lessen his ability to get along enjoyably with his fellows.

Obesity may become a vicious circle, no matter which factor caused it in the beginning. The fatter the child, the harder it is for him to enjoy exercise and games. And the quieter he is, the more energy his body has to store as fat. It's a vicious circle in another way, too. The fat child who can't comfortably enter into games may come to feel more of an outsider, and he is liable to be kidded and ridiculed.

Fatness is complicated.

Obesity is a most serious problem for any child. Since it's apt to become a vicious circle, it should be combatted as soon as it appears. If a baby is becoming unusually plump during his first year, this shouldn't be considered cute. It should be treated with dietary shifts right away. Often it's possible to satisfy such a child fairly well with a lot of protein, vegetables, fruits, and to hold way down on his sweets, starches, fats.

612. Mild overweight is common between 7 and 12. But I don't want to leave the impression that every child who turns plump is unhappy. There seems to be a normal tendency for many children, including the cheerful and successful ones, to put on extra weight in the 7-to-12-year-old period. Very few of these become excessively obese. They are just slightly overpadded. Most of them stay plump during the 2 years of very rapid puberty development and then slender down as they get further into adolescence. Many girls, for instance, become slimmer around 15 years of age without great effort. It's good for parents to know that this mild school-age obesity is common and that it often goes away later, so that they won't make too much of an issue about it.

613. Dieting is difficult. What is there to do about a fat child? Right away you would say, "Diet him." It sounds easy, but it isn't. Think of the grown-ups you know who are unhappy because of their weight and who still aren't able to stick to a diet. A child has less will power than an adult. If the mother serves the child the less fattening foods, it means either that the whole family must go without the richer dishes or that the fat child must be kept from eating the very things his heart craves most while the rest of the family enjoys them. There are very few fat children reasonable enough to think that that's fair. The feeling of being treated unfairly may further increase the craving for sweets. Whatever is accomplished in the dining room may be undone at the refrigerator or candy store between meals.

But the prospects of dieting are not so black as I have made out. A tactful mother can do a good deal to keep temptation away from her fat child without making an issue of it. She can serve rich desserts less frequently. She can stop having cakes and cookies always around in the kitchen, and provide fresh fruit for between-meals nibbling. She can serve frequently the less fattening foods that are his favorites. If the child shows any willingness to cooperate in his diet, he should certainly be encouraged to visit the doctor, preferably alone. Talking to the doctor, man to man, may give him the feeling of running his own life like a grown-up. Anyone can take dietary advice better from an outsider. A child should never take any medicine for reducing without a doctor's recommendation, and unless he can return at **regular** intervals for checkups.

Since overeating is often a symptom of loneliness or maladjustment, the most constructive thing is to make sure that the child's home life, schoolwork and social life are as happy and satisfying as possible (Section 551).

If, despite your efforts to help him, a child's obesity is more than mild or if he is gaining weight too rapidly, you should certainly get medical and psychiatric assistance. Obesity is a serious problem for any child.

614. Dieting should be supervised by a doctor. Self-dieting sometimes becomes a problem and a danger in the adolescent period. A group of girls excitedly work themselves up to going on some wild diet that they have heard about. Within a few days, hunger makes most of them break their resolutions, but one or two may persist with fanatical zeal. Occasionally a girl loses alarming amounts of weight and can't resume a normal diet even when she wants to. The group hysteria about dieting seems to have awakened in her a deep revulsion against food, which is usually a hangover from some unsolved worry of early childhood. Another girl in the early stages of puberty declares hectically, "I'm getting much too fat," even though she is so slender that her ribs are showing. She may be emotionally unready to grow up and secretly disturbed by the development of her breasts. The child who becomes obsessed with dieting should have the help of a children's psychiatrist.

If either your child or you think he should be on a diet, the first step, for a number of reasons, is to consult a doctor. First, he will determine whether dieting is necessary or wise. Secondly, the adolescent is more apt to accept the doctor's advice than his parents'. If it is agreed that a diet is wise, it should certainly be prescribed by the doctor. He will take into account the child's food tastes, the family's usual menus, in order to work out a diet that is not only sound nutritionally but practical in that particular home. Finally, since weight loss puts some strain on health, anyone who is planning to reduce should be examined at regular intervals to make sure that the rate is not too fast and that he remains strong and healthy.

If it is not possible to have the supervision of a doctor, the parents should insist that a child who has the bit in his teeth must take at least the following foods daily: a pint and a half of milk, meat or poultry or fish, an egg, a green or yellow vegetable, fruit twice. The child can be assured that these foods in reasonable servings do not cause weight gaining and that they are essential to prevent the muscles, bones and organs of his body from being dangerously depleted.

Rich desserts can be omitted without risk, and should be, by anyone who is obese and trying to reduce. The amount of plain, starchy foods (cereals, breads, potatoes) taken is what determines, in the case of most people, how much they gain or lose. Any growing child needs some, even though he is trying to lose weight. It is not wise for even a fat person to lose more than a pound a week, unless a doctor is carefully supervising.

GLANDS

615. Glandular disturbances. There are several definite glandular diseases, and there are a few glandular medicines that have a definite effect on human beings. For example, when the thyroid gland is not secreting sufficiently, a child's physical growth and mental development are definitely slowed down. He is sluggish, has a dry skin, coarse hair and a low voice. His face may appear puffy. (Insufficient thyroid secretion does not cause obesity.) His basal metabolism, which means the rate at which his body burns fuel when resting, is below normal. The proper dose of thyroid medication brings about remarkable improvement.

Some people who have read popular articles on glands assume that every short person, every slow pupil, every nervous girl, every fat boy with small genitals, is merely a glandular problem who can be cured by the proper tablet or injection. This enthusiasm is not justified by what is known scientifically at the present time. It takes more than one symptom to make a glandular disease.

In many cases when a boy is heavy during the years before puberty development, his penis appears smaller than it really is because his plump thighs are so large in comparison and because the layer of fat at the base of his penis may hide three-quarters of its length. Most of these boys have a normal sexual development at puberty, and many of them lose their excess weight at that time. See Sections 522 and 616 on the harm of worrying a boy about his genitals.

Certainly every child who is not growing at the usual rate or in the usual shape, or who appears dull or nervous or out of line in any other way, should be examined by a competent physician. But if the doctor finds that the child's stature is only his inborn constitutional pattern, or that his mental state is due to real troubles in his daily life, then what he needs is assistance in his adjustment to life, not a further search for magic.

UNDESCENDED TESTICLES

616. Undescended testicles. In a certain number of new-born boys, one or both testicles are not in the scrotum (the pouch in which the testicles normally lie) but are farther up in the groin or inside the abdomen. Most of these undescended testicles come down into the scrotum soon after birth. A great majority of the rest of them descend during the stage of puberty development, which begins in the average boy at about 13. There are only a very few cases in which the testicles don't ever come down by themselves, and in these there is some obstruction or abnormality.

The testicles are originally formed inside the abdomen and move down into the scrotum only shortly before birth. There are muscles attached to the testicles that can jerk them back up into the groin, or even back into the abdomen. This is to protect the testicles from injury when this region of the body is struck or scratched. There are lots of boys whose testicles withdraw on slight provocation. Even chilling of the skin from being undressed may be enough to make them disappear into the abdomen. Handling the scrotum in an examination frequently makes them disappear. Therefore, a parent shouldn't decide that the testicles are undescended just because they are not usually in sight. A good time to look for them is when the boy is in a hot bath, without handling his body.

Testicles that have been seen at any time in the scrotum, even if only rarely, need no treatment because they will surely settle down in the scrotum by the time puberty development is under way.

Sometimes just one testicle is definitely undescended. Though this may require treatment, there is no cause for great concern because one testicle is sufficient to make a boy develop properly and become a father, even in the unusual case in which the other one doesn't appear later.

If one or both testicles have never been seen in the scrotum by the time a boy is 2 years old, this should be discussed with the doctor.

If your child appears to have undescended testicles, try not to worry yourself and don't worry him. It is important not to make the child self-conscious by anxious looks and frequent examinations. It is really harmful to a boy's emotional development for him to get the idea that he is not formed properly. If glandular injections are recommended, the parents should speak of this treatment casually, in a way that is least likely to raise doubts in the boy's mind.

POSTURE

617. The treatment of bad posture depends on the cause. Good or bad posture is made up of a number of factors. One—perhaps the most important—is the skeleton the child is born with. You see individuals who have been round-shouldered from babyhood, like their father before them. Some children seem to be born with a relaxed set of muscles and ligaments. They run to knock-knees no matter how much vitamin D you give them. Another child looks tightly knit, in action or at rest. It's hard for him to slump. There are diseases that affect posture, such as rickets, infantile paralysis and tuberculosis of the bones. Chronic illness and chronic fatigue, from any cause, that keep a child under par may make him slump and sag. Overweight sometimes produces swayback, knock-knees and flat feet. Unusual tallness makes the self-conscious adolescent duck his head. A child with poor posture needs regular examinations to make sure that there is no physical disease.

Many children slouch because of lack of self-confidence. It may result from too much criticism at home, or from difficulties in school, or from an unsatisfactory social life. The person who is buoyant and sure of himself shows it in the way he sits and stands and walks. When parents realize how much feelings have to do with posture, they can handle it more wisely.

The natural impulse of a parent, eager to have his child appear well, is to keep after his posture: "Remember the shoulders." "For goodness' sake, stand up straight." But the child who is stooped over because his parents have always kept after him too much won't be improved by more nagging. Generally speaking, the best results come when he receives posture work at school, or in a posture clinic, or in a doctor's office. In these places the atmosphere is more businesslike than at home. The parents may be able to help him greatly in carrying out his exercises at home, if he wants help and if they can give it in a friendly way. But the main job for them is to help the child's spirit by aiding his school adjustment, fostering a happy social life and making him feel adequate and self-respecting at home.

Illness

FEVER

618. What's fever and what isn't? Taking the temperature is a bugaboo to many mothers. They find a thermometer hard to read. They are confused by the difference between mouth, axillary (armpit) and rectal temperatures.

It might be easier for you to get someone else to show you how to read one, but here goes. Most thermometers are engraved the same. They have a long mark for each degree and a short mark for each fifth of a degree. Only the even degrees—94, 96, 98, 100, 102, 104—are numbered on the thermometer, because of lack of space. There is an arrow pointing to the "normal" mark, 98⅗. Many thermometers are marked in red above the normal point.

The first thing to realize is that a healthy child's body temperature doesn't stay fixed at 98⅗°. It is always going up and down a little, depending on the time of day and what the child is doing. It's usually lowest in the early morning and highest in the later afternoon. This change during the day is only a slight one, however. The change between rest and activity is greater. The temperature of a perfectly healthy small child may be 99⅗° or even 100° right after he has been running around. (On the other hand, a temperature of 101° probably means illness whether the child has been exercising or not.) The older child's tem-

453

perature is less affected by activity. All this means that if you want to know whether your child has a slight fever due to illness, you must take his temperature after he has been really quiet for an hour or more.

In most feverish illnesses the temperature is apt to be highest in the late afternoon and lowest in the morning. But there is nothing to be surprised at if a fever is high in the morning and low in the afternoon. There are a few diseases in which the fever, instead of climbing
and falling, stays high steadily. The commonest of these are pneumonia and roseola infantum. A below-normal temperature (as low as 97°) sometimes occurs at the end of an illness, and also in healthy babies and small children on winter nights. This is no cause for concern so long as the child is feeling well.

Now about the difference between mouth, axillary (armpit) and rectal temperatures. That of the rectum is highest because it is well inside the body where the body is thick. That of the mouth is lowest because the mouth is cooled by the air being breathed through the nose. There is usually less than one degree's difference in temperature between the rectum and the mouth. The temperature of the axilla is in between.

619. The thermometer. The only difference between a mouth and a rectal thermometer is in the shape of the bulb. The bulb of the rectal thermometer is round so that it won't be so sharp. A mouth thermometer has a long slender bulb so that the mercury can be warmed more quickly by the mouth. The markings on the two thermometers are exactly the same and mean the same thing. (In other words, they are not marked differently to allow for the difference of temperature between the mouth and rectum.) You can use a clean rectal thermometer perfectly well in the mouth, and a mouth thermometer in the rectum, if inserted gently.

Most thermometers register well enough in a minute in the rectum. If you watch a thermometer sometime when it is in a baby's rectum, you can see that it goes up very rapidly at first. It gets within a degree of where it is going to stop in the first 20 seconds. After that it barely creeps up. This means that if you are nervous taking the temperature of a struggling baby, you can take the thermometer out in less than a minute and have a rough idea what the temperature is.

It takes longer to register the correct temperature in the mouth—1½ to 2 minutes. This is because it takes the mouth a while to warm up after being open and because the bulb is partly surrounded by air. It takes 4 minutes to take an accurate axillary temperature but you can get a rough idea in a couple of minutes.

620. Taking the temperature. Before taking a temperature, shake the thermometer down. You hold the upper end of the thermometer (the opposite end from the bulb) firmly between your thumb and finger. Now shake the thermometer

vigorously, with a sharp, snapping motion. You want to drive the mercury down at least as far as 97°. If it doesn't go down, you aren't snapping hard enough. Until you get the hang of it, shake the thermometer over a bed or couch. Then if it slips out of your hand, it won't be broken. The bathroom is the worst place of all to shake a thermometer because of the hard surfaces.

If you are taking a rectal temperature, dip the bulb of the thermometer into petroleum jelly or cold cream. The best position for a baby is on his stomach across your knees. He can't squirm out of this position very easily, and his legs hang down out of the way. Insert the thermometer gently into his rectum. Push it in with a light touch, letting the thermometer find its own direction. If you hold it stiffly, it may poke him inside. Once the thermometer is in, it is better to shift your grip off the end of the thermometer, because if the baby struggles, the twisting might hurt him. Instead, lay the palm of your hand across his buttocks, lightly holding the thermometer between two of the fingers, the way you'd hold a cigarette.

You can also take the rectal temperature with the child lying on his side on a bed with his knees up a little. It is harder to find the rectum when a child is lying flat on his stomach. The worst position is with the child lying on his back. It is hard to get to his rectum, and his féet are in position to kick your hand accidentally or on purpose.

By the time a child is 1 year and older, it's psychologically preferable to take his temperature in his armpit (axilla). He is beginning to be aware of his body, his dignity, his security. He's apt to be bothered or even alarmed by having something poked into his rectum. You can get a satisfactory temperature by placing the bulb of the thermometer in his axilla and then holding his arm flat against his chest. There should be no clothes between his arm and his chest, of course, just the bulb of the thermometer. You can use a rectal or mouth thermometer in the axilla.

After the age of 5 or 6 a child can usually cooperate in keeping the thermometer bulb under his tongue and his lips closed. Then you can take temperature by mouth or axilla, whichever is more convenient.

Reading the thermometer is very easy once you get the knack. Most thermometers are somewhat triangular in cross section, with one edge sharper than the rest. This sharp edge should point toward you. In this position the marks of the degrees are above and the numbers are below. Between them is the space in which the mercury shows. Roll the thermometer very slightly until you see the band of mercury. Don't worry

too much over the fractions of degrees. It makes little difference if the temperature is 99⅖° or 99⅗°. What the doctor will be interested in is **about** what the temperature is. When you report the temperature to the doctor, tell him what the thermometer actually says, and then add "by mouth", "by axilla" or "by rectum." I say this because sometimes a mother who has the mistaken idea that the mouth temperature is the only correct one takes a temperature by rectum and then tells the doctor what she figures the mouth temperature would be. Usually the best times to take the temperature are in the first part of the morning and late in the afternoon.

The next question is how many days to go on taking the temperature. Here is what happens occasionally. A child has a bad cold with fever. The doctor sees him or gets reports regularly and has the mother take the temperature twice a day. Finally the fever is gone, the child is convalescing well, has only a mild cough and running nose. The doctor tells the mother to let the child outdoors as soon as the cold is gone completely. Two weeks later the mother telephones to say that she and the child are getting desperate staying indoors, that the running nose and cough have been completely gone for ten days, that the child looks wonderful and eats well, but that the "fever" is still going to 99.6° each afternoon. As I explained earlier, this is not necessarily a fever in an active child. The 10 days of staying indoors and of worrying over the temperature have all been a waste and a mistake. When the temperature has stayed under 101° for a couple of days, it's a good general rule to forget about the thermometer unless the doctor asks you to continue or unless the child seems sicker in any way. Don't get in the habit of taking a child's temperature when he is well.

621. Emergency treatment of high fever. Between the ages of 1 and 5 years, children may develop fever as high as 104° (sometimes even higher) at the onset of mild infections, such as colds, sore throats, grippe, just as often as with serious infections. On the other hand, a dangerous illness may never have a temperature higher than 101°. So don't be influenced too much, one way or the other, by the height of the fever, but get in touch with the doctor whenever your child appears sick in any way.

If on the first day of an illness a child's temperature is 104° or higher, and if it will be an hour or more before you can speak to the doctor, even on the telephone, it's wise, as an emergency measure, to bring the fever down a little with a wet rub and aspirin—1 tablet of "baby" aspirin (1¼ grains) under a year; 2 baby tablets (2½ grains) between 1 and 5 years; 3 baby tablets (3¾ grains) for a 6-to-12-year-old. (Be sure to keep aspirin out of your child's reach.)

The purpose of the wet rub is to bring the blood to the surface by rubbing and to cool it by the evaporation of the water off the skin. (Alcohol has traditionally been used in a wet rub, but if it is applied very freely in a small room, too much may be inhaled. Anyway, water is just as good even if it doesn't smell so important.)

Undress the child and cover him with only a sheet or light blanket. Wet your hand in a basin of water. Expose one of his arms and rub it gently for a couple of minutes, wetting it again any time it becomes too dry. Then put it back under the sheet. Proceed, in turn, to the other arm, each leg, the chest, the back. Take the temperature again in half an hour, and if it isn't under 104° give the child cold fluids by mouth and place him in a tepid bath for 15 minutes or so. You prefer to keep the temperature under 104° until the doctor comes because a small child who develops a sudden high fever the first day of an illness may become trembly or even have a convulsion (Section 716). When a child's fever is very high and he is flushed, use only light covers at ordinary room temperature, perhaps as little as a sheet. You can't get his temperature down very well if he's heavily covered.

Many parents assume that the fever itself is bad and want to give medicine to bring it way down, no matter what degree it is. But it's well to remember that the fever is not the disease. The fever is one of the methods the body uses to help overcome the infection. It is also a help in keeping track of how the illness is progressing. In one case the doctor wants to bring the fever down because it is interfering with the child's sleep or exhausting him. In another case he is quite willing to leave the fever alone, and concentrate on curing the infection.

GIVING MEDICINES AND ENEMAS

622. Giving medicine. It's sometimes quite a trick getting a child to take his medicine. The first rule is to slip it into him in a matter-of-fact way, as if it has never occurred to you that he won't take it. If you go at it apologetically, with a lot of explanation, you convince him that he's expected to dislike it. Be talking about something else when you put the spoon in his mouth. Most young children open their mouths automatically, like birds in their nest.

Tablets that don't dissolve can be crushed to a fine powder and mixed with a coarse, good-tasting food like applesauce.

Mix the medicine with only 1 teaspoonful of the applesauce, in case he decides he doesn't want very much. Bitter pills can be mixed in a teaspoonful of sugar and water, or honey, or maple syrup, or jam. Eye ointments and drops can sometimes be applied during sleep.

When giving medicine in a drink, it's safer to choose an unusual fluid that the child does not take regularly, such as grape juice or prune juice. If you give a queer taste to his milk or his orange juice, you may make him suspicious of it for months.

Getting a small child to swallow a whole tablet or a capsule is difficult. Try putting it in something lumpy and sticky like banana and follow the teaspoonful quickly with a drink of something he likes.

623. Don't give medicine without a doctor's advice and don't continue it without keeping in touch with him. Here are some examples of why not. A child has a cough with his cold, and the doctor prescribes a certain cough medicine. Two months later he develops a new cough, and the mother has the prescription renewed without consulting the doctor. It seems to help for a week, but then the cough becomes so bad that she has to call the doctor anyway. He realizes right away that the disease this time is not a cold but whooping cough. He would have suspected it a week before if he had been consulted. In that case the child could have been isolated immediately and would not have exposed unnecessarily a lot of other children.

A mother who has treated colds or headaches or stomach-aches a few times in the same way comes to feel like an expert, which she is in a limited way. But she's not trained, as a doctor is, to first consider carefully what the diagnosis is. To her, two different headaches (or two stomachaches) seem about the same. To the doctor, one has an entirely different meaning from the other and calls for different treatment. People who have been treated by a doctor with one of the sulfa drugs or one of the antibiotics (such as penicillin) are sometimes tempted to use it again for similar symptoms. They figure that it produces wonderful results, is easy to take, and they know the dosage from the last time—so why not?

Serious reactions occasionally develop from the use of these drugs—fevers, rashes, anemia, bleeding from the kidney, obstruction to the flow of urine. These complications, fortunately, are rare, but they are more liable to occur the more often the drugs are used, especially if they are used improperly. That is why they should be given only when a doctor has decided that the danger from the disease and the likelihood of benefit from the medicine outweigh the risks of treatment. Even the continued use of as common a drug as aspirin can occasionally cause serious trouble.

Cathartics (drugs to make the bowels move) should not be used for any reason—especially not for stomachache—without consulting a doctor. Some people have the mistaken idea that stomachache is frequently caused by constipation, and want to give a cathartic first of all. There are many causes of stomachache (Sections 704–706). Some, such as appendicitis and obstruction of the intestines, are made worse by a cathartic. Therefore, since you don't know for sure what is causing your child's stomachache, it is dangerous to give a cathartic.

624. Enemas and suppositories. A doctor sometimes prescribes an enema or suppository when a child becomes suddenly constipated, particularly if he is sick. During some illnesses these are safer than a cathartic given by mouth because they will not cause vomiting or irritate the small intestines.

A parent should not give an enema or suppository for constipation or illness or pains until the doctor has made the diagnosis and prescribed the treatment. It's particularly important not to give enemas or suppositories repeatedly for a tendency to constipation, because eventually they focus a child's mind on his anus and bowels.

A suppository for constipation is slipped all the way into the rectum, where it dissolves. It contains a mildly irritating material which draws moisture into the rectum and encourages a movement.

The doctor will tell you what to put in the enema. A soapy enema is made by stirring a piece of mild toilet soap in the water until it is slightly milky. This is a little irritating and is less often given to an infant. Enemas can also be made with a half teaspoonful of table salt, or a teaspoonful of bicarbonate of soda, added to an 8-ounce cup of water. The water should be at about body temperature. You can give 4 ounces to a small infant, 8 ounces to a 1-year-old, a pint to a 5-year-old.

Place a waterproof sheet on a bed and lay a bath towel

over it. Have the child lie on this on his side with his legs pulled up. Have a potty close at hand.

For an infant or small child, it is easiest and safest to use a rubber ear syringe with a soft tip of the same material. Fill the bulb completely, so that you won't be injecting air. Grease the tip with petroleum jelly, cold cream, or soap; gently insert it an inch or two. Squeeze the bulb slowly and not too forcibly. The slower you put it in, the less liable it is to make the baby feel uncomfortable and expel it. The bowel contracts and relaxes in waves. If you feel a strong resistance, wait until it "gives" rather than push harder. Unfortunately, a baby is apt to push as soon as he feels something in his anus, so you may not get much in.

As you pull the tip out, press his buttocks together to try to hold the water in a few minutes to do its job of softening the movement. If the water has not come out in 15 or 20 minutes, or if it has come out without much movement, you can repeat the enema. There is no danger from an enema's staying in.

With an older child who will cooperate, you can use a syringe or enema bag or enema can with a rubber tube and a small, hard-rubber tip. Don't hang the bag higher than 1 to 2 feet above the level of the rectum (the height determines the pressure). The lowest height that makes the water run in slowly causes the least discomfort and brings the best results.

HANDLING AN INVALID

625. Spoiling is easy. When a child is really sick, you give him lots of special care and consideration, not only for practical medical reasons but also because you feel sorry for him. You don't mind preparing drinks and foods for him at frequent intervals or even putting aside a drink he refuses and making another kind right away. You are glad to get him new playthings to keep him happy and quiet. You ask him often how he feels, in a solicitous manner.

A child quickly adjusts to this new position in the household. If he has a disease that makes him cranky, he may be calling and bossing his mother like an old tyrant.

Fortunately, at least 90% of children's illnesses are on the way to recovery within a few days. As soon as the mother stops worrying, she stops kowtowing to the child when he is unreasonable. After a couple of days of minor clashes, everyone is back to normal.

But if a child develops a long illness or one that threatens to come back, and if the parents have a tendency to be worriers, the continued atmosphere of overconcern may have a bad effect on his spirit. He absorbs some of the anxiousness of those around him. He's apt to be demanding. If he's too polite for that, he may just become excitable and temperamental, like a spoiled actor. It's easy for him to learn to enjoy being sick and receiving pity. Some of his ability to make his own way agreeably may grow weaker, like a muscle that isn't being used.

626. Keep him busy and polite. So it's wise for parents to encourage themselves to get back into normal balance with the sick child as soon as possible. This means such little things as having a friendly, matter-of-fact expression when entering his room rather than a worried one; asking him how he feels today in a tone of voice that expects good news rather than bad (and perhaps asking him only once a day). When you find out by experience what he feels like drinking and eating, serve it up casually. Don't ask him timidly if he likes it or act as if he were wonderful to take a little. Keep strictly away from urging unless the doctor feels that it is necessary. A sick child's appetite is more quickly ruined by pushing and forcing than a well child's.

If you are buying new playthings, look particularly for the ones that make him do all the work and give him a chance to use his imagination (blocks, sets for building, sewing, weaving, bead-stringing, painting, modeling, stamp collecting). These make demands on him and occupy him for long periods, whereas toys that are merely beautiful possessions quickly pall and only whet his appetite for more presents. Deal out one new plaything at a time. There are lots of homemade occupations, like cutting pictures out of old magazines, making a scrapbook, sewing, whittling, building a farm or town or doll's house of cardboard and glue.

If a child is going to be laid up for a long time, but is well enough, get a teacher or a tutor or the best teacher in the family to start him on his schoolwork again for a regular period each day, just as soon as possible.

If he's human, he wants company part of the time, and you can join in some of his occupations or read to him. But if

*A child is allowed up when he feels well enough, with rare
exceptions.*

he wants more and more attention, try to avoid arguments
and bargaining. Have regular times when he can count on
your being with him and others when he knows you are going
to be busy elsewhere. If he has a disease that isn't catching
and the doctor lets him have company, invite other children
in regularly to play and for meals.

It all adds up to letting the child lead just as normal a life
as is possible under the circumstances, expecting from him
reasonable behavior toward the rest of the family, and avoiding worried talk, looks and thoughts.

GOING TO THE HOSPITAL

627. How to help the child. There's no perfect way to
handle the business of taking a child to a hospital. There's
usually some disease or risk that worries the parents.

Between the ages of 1 and 4 years, the child is most worried about being separated from his parents. He feels as if he
is losing them forever when they first leave him and at the
end of each hospital visit. Between visits he may remain
anxious and depressed. When the parents come to see him,
he may silently reproach them by refusing to greet them at
first.

After the age of 4 the child is apt to be more fearful about what's going to be done to him, the injury to his body and the pain. It won't do for the parents to promise that the hospital will be a bed of roses, because if unpleasant things happen, the child loses confidence in his parents. On the other hand, if he is told everything bad that might happen, he is apt to suffer more in anticipation than he will when he is there.

The most important thing is for the parents to show all the calm, matter-of-fact confidence they are capable of, without forcing it so much that it sounds false. Unless the child has been a hospital patient before, he tries anxiously to imagine what it will be like, perhaps feeling the worst. The parents can set his mind at rest better by describing hospital life in general than by arguing with him whether it's going to hurt a lot or a little. You can tell him how the nurse will wake him in the morning and give him a bath right in bed, how the meals will come on trays and be eaten in his own bed, how there will be time to play, how he may use the bedpan or urinal instead of the bathroom, how he can tell the nurse if he needs someone. You can tell him about visiting days and about all the other children to keep him company in the ward.

If he's going to be in a private room, you can talk about what favorite toys and books he's going to bring, and about renting a TV set with remote control, or whether there is a small radio to take from home or to borrow. He'll be interested in the electric button for calling the nurse.

It's fair to dwell on these everyday, pleasanter aspects of hospital life because even at the worst the child will spend most of his time amusing himself. I wouldn't keep away from the medical program altogether, but let the child see that it's a small part of hospital life.

If he's going to have his tonsils out, you can tell him about the mask they will put up to his nose, and how he will breathe and breathe until he goes to sleep; how he will wake up in an hour and find that his throat is sore (the way it was last winter when he had tonsillitis); that you will be there when he wakes up (if that is true), or that you will come to get him the next day.

628. Let him tell you his worries. More important than telling your child what occurs to you is giving him chances to ask questions and tell you what he imagines. Young children view these things in ways that never occur to adults.

In the first place, they often think they have to be operated on or taken to the hospital because they have been bad—because they haven't worn their rubbers or haven't stayed in bed when sick or have been angry with other members of the family. They may imagine that their necks have to be cut open to remove their tonsils or their noses removed to get at the adenoids. Because of their worries and misunderstandings about the physical differences between boys and girls, children—particularly between 3 and 6—often fear subconsciously that an additional operation may be performed on the genitals, especially if they feel guilty about masturbation. So make it easy for your child to raise questions, be ready for strange fears and try to reassure him about these.

629. Let him know ahead of time. If you know days or weeks ahead of time that a child will be hospitalized, it brings up the question of when to tell him. If there is no chance of his finding out, I think it is kinder to wait to tell a small child until a few days before it's time to leave. It won't do him any good to worry for weeks. It may be fairer to tell a 7-year-old some weeks ahead if he's the kind who can face things reasonably, especially if he has some suspicions. Certainly, don't lie to a child of any age if he asks questions, and never lure a child to a hospital pretending it's something else.

If your child is going to have an operation and you have a choice in the arrangements, you can discuss the matter of anesthetists and anesthesia with the doctor. How a child accepts the anesthesia is apt to make the biggest difference in whether he is emotionally upset by an operation or whether he goes through it with flying colors. Often in a hospital there is one or another anesthetist who is particularly good at ensuring confidence in children and getting them under without fright. It is worth a great deal to obtain the services of such an anesthetist if you have a choice. In some cases, there is also a choice in the kind of anesthetic that the doctor is considering, and this also makes a difference to the child psychologically. Generally speaking, it is less frightening to the child to start with gas than to start with ether, which is uncomfortable to breathe. The type of anesthetic that is given by a small enema (into the rectum)—even before the child starts for the operating room—is least likely to frighten him, but is not suitable medically in all cases. Naturally, the doctor is the one who knows the factors and has to make the decision. It's when he feels that there is an equal choice medically that the psychological factor should be considered carefully.

630. Visiting. The parent should stay in the hospital with a child between the ages of 1 and 5 years if at all possible, especially in the daytime. At least, a parent should visit daily. Visits create difficulties with the small child. The sight of the parents reminds him how much he has missed them. He may cry heartbreakingly when they leave or even cry through the entire visiting period. The parents are apt to get the impression that he is miserable there all the time. Actually, young children adjust surprisingly well to hospital life when the parents are out of sight, even though they are feeling sick or having uncomfortable treatments. I don't mean that the parents should stay away. The child is getting security of a kind from the visits even though they upset him, too. The best the parents can do is to act as cheerful and unworried as possible. If the parents have an anguished expression, it makes the child more anxious.

The chance that a child will be emotionally upset by an operation is greatest in the first 5 years of life. This is a reason for postponing an operation if the doctor feels that there is no particular hurry, especially if the child is already dependent or worrisome or subject to nightmares.

DIET DURING ILLNESS

Diet during diarrhea is discussed in Section 316.

631. Diet for a cold without fever. Your doctor will tell you what diet to use in each of your child's illnesses, taking into account the nature of the disease and the child's taste. What follows are some general principles to guide you in emergencies when you are unable to get medical help.

The diet during a mild cold without fever can be entirely normal. However, a child may lose some of his appetite even with a mild cold because he's indoors, because he's not taking his usual amount of exercise, because he's a little uncomfortable and because he's swallowing mucus. Don't urge him to take more than he wants. If he is eating less than usual, offer him extra fluids between meals. There is no harm letting a child drink all that he feels like drinking. People sometimes have the idea that the more fluid, the better the treatment. Excessive amounts of fluid don't do any more good than reasonable amounts.

632. Diet during fever (emergency advice until you can consult the doctor). When a child has fever above 102° with a cold, grippe, sore throat or one of the contagious diseases, he usually loses most of his appetite in the beginning, especially for solids. In the first day or two of such a fever, don't offer him solid food at all, but offer fluids every half hour or hour when he's awake. Orange juice, pineapple juice and water are most popular. Don't forget water. It has no nourishment, but that's unimportant for the time being. It's for this very reason that it often appeals to the sick child most. Other fluids depend on the child's taste and his illness. Some children love grapefruit juice, prune juice, lemonade, pear juice, grape juice, weak tea with sugar. Older children like carbonated drinks, like ginger ale, sarsaparilla, fruit-flavored sodas and the cola drinks. Some cola drinks contain small amounts of caffeine, a stimulant, so should preferably not be given within a couple of hours before sleep time.

Milk is hard to make a rule about. The sick baby usually takes more milk than anything else. If he takes it without vomiting, it is the right thing. The older child may reject or vomit it. Offer it if it is desired and held down. With fever of over 102°, milk is digested more easily when it is skimmed (the top cream poured off). It's the butterfat that is hardest to digest.

When a fever continues, a child is apt to have a little more appetite after the first day or two. If your child is hungry in spite of a high fever, he may be able to take simple soft solids like toast, crackers, cereal, custard, gelatin, junket, ice cream, applesauce, soft-boiled egg.

The foods that are usually not wanted and not well digested during fever are vegetables (cooked or raw), meats, poultry, fish, fats (such as butter, margarine, cream). However, Dr. Clara Davis in her experiments on diet found that children often crave meats and vegetables during convalescence—after the fever is gone—and digest them well.

One rule more important than any other is not to urge a sick child to eat anything that he doesn't want unless the doctor has a special reason for urging it. It's only too likely to be vomited, or to cause an intestinal upset, or to start a feeding problem.

633. Diet when there is vomiting (emergency advice until you can consult the doctor). Of course, vomiting occurs in many different diseases, especially at the beginning when there is fever. The diet depends on many factors and should be prescribed by the doctor. However, if you cannot reach the doctor immediately, you can follow these suggestions. Vomiting occurs because the stomach is upset by the disease and is not able to handle the food.

It's a good idea to give the stomach a complete rest for at least a couple of hours after vomiting. Then **if the child is asking for it,** give him a sip of water, not more than half an ounce at first. If this stays down and he begs for more, let him have a little more, say 1 ounce in 15 or 20 minutes. Increase gradually up to 4 ounces (half a glass) if he craves it. If he has gone this far all right, you can try a little orange juice or pineapple juice or a carbonated drink. It is better not to go beyond 4 ounces at a time the first day. If several hours have gone by since the vomiting and the child is begging for solid food, give something simple like a cracker, or a tablespoonful of cereal or applesauce. If he is asking for milk, skim it.

If he vomits again, be more strict. Give nothing at all for 2 hours, and then start with a teaspoonful of water or cracked ice. In 20 minutes let him have 2 teaspoonfuls. Work up cautiously again. **If a child who has previously vomited doesn't want anything to drink even several hours later, don't offer anything.** It would almost certainly be vomited. The reason you play safe is that every time he vomits he is apt to lose more than he has drunk.

The vomiting that goes with a feverish illness is most apt to occur on the first day and may not continue even if the fever goes on.

Small specks or streaks of blood sometimes show in the vomited material when a child is retching violently. This is not serious in itself.

634. Avoiding feeding problems at the end of illness. If a child has a fever for several days and wants little to eat, he naturally loses weight rapidly. This worries a mother the first time or two that it happens. When the fever is finally gone and the doctor says it's all right to begin working back to a regular diet, she is impatient to feed him up again. But it often happens that the child turns away from the foods that are first offered. If the mother urges, meal after meal and day after day, his appetite may never pick up.

Such a child has not forgotten how to eat or become too weak to eat. At the time his temperature went back to normal there was still enough infection in his body to affect his stomach and intestines. Just as soon as he saw those first foods, his digestive system warned him that it was not ready for them yet.

When food is pushed or forced onto a child who already feels nauseated because of illness, his disgust is built up more easily and rapidly than if he had a normal appetite to start with. He can acquire a long-lasting feeding problem in a few days' time.

Just as soon as the stomach and intestines have recovered from the effects of most illnesses and are in condition to digest food again, a child's hunger comes back with a bang—and not just to what it used to be. He usually is ravenous for a week or two in order to make up for lost time. You sometimes see such a child whimpering for more, 2 hours after a large meal. By the age of 3, he may demand the specific foods that his starved system craves most.

The parent's course at the end of illness is to offer the child only the drinks and solids he wants, without any urging, and to wait patiently, but confidently, for signals that he is ready for more. If his appetite has not recovered in a week, the doctor should be consulted again.

COLDS

635. The cold virus, and the germs that make complications. Your child will probably be sick with colds ten times as much as with all his other illnesses combined. We only partly understand colds at the present time. A cold is started by a "filtrable virus." This is a germ so small that it can pass (filter) through unglazed porcelain, so small that it cannot be seen through an ordinary microscope. It is believed that the virus can cause only a mild cold with a clear nasal discharge and perhaps a slight scratchy feeling in the throat. If nothing else happens, the virus cold goes away in about 3 days. But something else often does happen. The cold virus lowers the resistance of the nose and throat, so that other germs that cause more trouble get going, germs such as the streptococcus, the pneumococcus and the influenza bacillus. They are called "secondary invaders." These regular bacteria are often living in healthy people's throats during the winter and spring months, but do no harm because they are held at bay by the body's resistance. It's only after the

cold virus has lowered the resistance that these other germs get their chance to multiply and spread, causing bronchitis, pneumonia, ear infections and sinusitis. That's why it is a good idea to take care of a child who has just a cold.

The best thing that you can do to avoid a cold is to keep away from anyone who has one.

636. Resistance to colds. Many people believe that they are more susceptible to colds when tired or chilled, but this has never been proved. A person is less apt to be chilled if he has built up his resistance by regularly going out in cold weather. A bank clerk is more easily chilled when he gets outdoors than a lumberjack. That is why children of all ages should be outdoors several hours a day in winter. It's also the reason they shouldn't be overdressed outdoors or too heavily covered in bed.

Houses and apartments that are kept too hot and dry during the winter season parch the nose and throat, and this may lower resistance to germs. The air in a room that's 75° is excessively dry. Many people hopefully try to moisten the air by putting pans of water on the radiators, but this method is almost completely worthless. The right way to keep enough moisture in the air in winter is to keep the room temperature down to 70° or below (68° is a good figure to aim at); then you won't need to worry about the humidity. Buy a reliable indoor thermometer. (See if it corresponds with several of the best thermometers your dealer has—an inexpensive one may be 4 degrees off, which makes it useless.) Then train yourself to glance at the thermometer several times a day. Turn the heat off every time the temperature goes above 68°. It will seem like a chore at first, but after living for a few weeks in a temperature below 70°, you will be trained to it and will feel uncomfortable in a hotter room. If you can't control the steam heat, you can use a cold-mist humidifier.

What is the effect of diet on resistance to colds? Naturally, every child should be offered a well-balanced diet. But there is no proof that a child who is already receiving a reasonable variety will have fewer colds if he gets a little more of one kind of food or less of another.

What about vitamins? It is true that a person who is receiving a shockingly small amount of vitamin A in his diet may be more liable to colds and other infections. But this danger doesn't apply to children who are taking a decent diet, because vitamin A is plentiful in milk, butter, eggs, vegetables.

It is believed that a child who is suffering from rickets (because of too little vitamin D) is more susceptible to the complications of colds, such as bronchitis. But if a child has no rickets and is receiving a satisfactory dose of vitamin D, there is no reason to believe that he will have fewer colds if **more** vitamin D is stuffed into him. There should be a sufficient amount of vitamin C in the diet (Section 428).

637. Age is a factor in colds. Children between 2 and 6 get more colds, have them longer and with more complications. (The average is 7 a year in northern cities in the United States—more if there are children in the family attending school.) After the age of 6 years, the frequency and the severity grows less. A 9-year-old is apt to be laid up only half as much as he was at 6, and the 12-year-old only half as much as at 9. This should comfort the parents of a small child who seems to be forever sick.

638. The psychological factor in colds. Psychiatrists feel quite sure that **certain** children and grown-ups are much more susceptible to colds when they are tense or unhappy. I think of a boy 6 years old who was nervous about school because he couldn't keep up with the class in reading. Every Monday morning for several months he had a cough. You may think he was putting it on. It wasn't so simple as that. It wasn't a dry, forced cough. It was a real, thick one. The cough would improve as the week went by and by Friday it would be all gone, only to reappear again Sunday night or Monday morning. There's nothing mysterious about this. We know that one person has cold, clammy hands when he is nervous; an athlete may have diarrhea before a race. So it's perfectly possible that nervousness may interfere with the circulation of the nose or throat so that germs have a better chance to flourish there.

639. Exposure to other children. There is another factor that influences the number of colds a child has. That's the number of children he plays with, especially indoors. The average single child living on an isolated farm has few colds because he is exposed to few cold germs. On the other hand, the average child in a nursery or elementary school has plenty, even though the school is careful to exclude every child who has symptoms. A person can probably give his infection to others for at least a day before he shows signs of it himself, and at times he can carry cold germs and pass them on to others without ever showing symptoms himself. There are some lucky children who rarely catch cold, no matter how many colds there are around them.

640. Can the spread of infection in a family be checked? Most colds that are brought into a family are caught by the younger children in at least a mild form, especially if the house is small and everyone has to use the same rooms. Not only do the germs of colds and other infections get passed from one person to another in large doses on the spray of sneezes and coughs, but they also float around in the air of the room in fair numbers just from being breathed into the air. Tests have shown that a gauze mask worn over the nose and mouth doesn't keep most germs from getting into the air. All of this means that there's no great advantage in the mother's wearing a mask or in trying half-heartedly to keep young children apart. Babies catch fewer colds, and it may be worthwhile for the mother—especially if she has a sore throat—to avoid sneezing, coughing or breathing directly into a baby's face and to wash her hands with soap before handling things that will go into the baby's mouth—the bowl of the spoon, the mouth part of a nipple, a teething ring, finger foods—to prevent the transfer of large numbers of bacteria.

Under special circumstances, it may be worthwhile to go to extra lengths to protect a baby or small child who is frail or particularly susceptible to infections—if the house is large enough so that the baby can be kept in a separate room with the door closed and if there is one adult without symptoms who can care for him. It is probably preferable that this adult, who is also mixing with the rest of the family and who is therefore carrying some germs, not sleep in the baby's room or stay there when the baby doesn't need attention.

If an outsider has any suspicion of a cold or any other illness, be very firm about not letting him in the same house with the baby, or within a couple of yards of the carriage outdoors. Say that the doctor told you to keep people with colds away.

What about chronic nose colds or sinusitis? If a person has had such an infection for 2 weeks or more, it's probably no longer important to keep him out of the same room. I would still suggest the other precautions: hand-washing, keeping his face turned away when doing anything for the baby.

641. X ray for anyone with a chronic cough. Anyone in a household who has a chronic cough should be examined by a doctor and X-rayed to be sure it is not tuberculosis. This rule is particularly important if there is a baby or small child in the home, or if one is expected. If you have a baby or child and are hiring a maid or nurse, she should be examined and have a chest X ray before becoming a member of the household.

642. Colds in the infant. If your baby has a cold during his first year, the chances are that it will be mild. He may sneeze in the beginning; his nose will be runny or bubbly or stuffy. He may cough a little. He is not likely to have any fever. When his nose is bubbly, you wish you could blow it for him. But it doesn't seem to bother him. On the other hand, if his nose is obstructed with thick mucus, it may make him frantic. He keeps trying to close his mouth and is angry when he can't breathe. The stuffiness may bother him most when he tries to nurse at the breast or bottle, so much so that he refuses altogether at times.

Bubbling and obstruction can often be relieved by sucking the mucus out with a nasal syringe. Compress the bulb, insert the tip into his nose and release the bulb.

Extra moisture in his room (Section 646) helps prevent stuffiness. If it is severe, the doctor may prescribe the shrinking kind of nose drops for use just before nursing, or medication by mouth. In other respects the baby may not lose much of his appetite. Usually the cold is gone in a week. Sometimes, though, a small baby's cold can last an unbelievably long time even though it stays mild.

Of course, a baby's cold can become severe. He can have bronchitis and other complications, but these are less common during the first year than later. If he has a frequent cough or a deep cough or a wheezy cough, he should be examined by a doctor, even if he has no fever. The same rule applies if he looks sick with a cold. In other words, a baby can be quite sick and not have fever.

643. Colds and fever after infancy. Some children go on having the same mild colds, without fever or complications, that they had during infancy. It's more common, though, when a child gets to be 1 or 2 years old, for his colds and throat infections to act differently. Here is a common story. A child of 2 is well during the morning. At lunchtime he seems a little tired and has less appetite than usual. When he wakes up from his nap he is cranky and his mother notices that he is hot. She takes his temperature, and it's 102°. By the time the doctor examines him, the temperature is 104°. The child's cheeks are flushed and his eyes are dull, but otherwise he doesn't seem particularly sick. He may want no supper at all, or he may want a fair amount. He has no cold symptoms, and the doctor hasn't found anything definite except that his throat is perhaps a little red. The next day he may have a little fever, but now his nose may begin to run. Perhaps he coughs occasionally. From this point on, it's just a regular mild cold that lasts anywhere from 2 days to 2 weeks.

There are several variations of this typical story. Sometimes the child vomits at the time his fever is shooting up. This is particularly apt to happen if his mother has unwisely tried to get him to eat more of his lunch than he wanted. (Always take a child's word for it when he loses his appetite.) Sometimes the fever lasts several days in the beginning, before the cold symptoms appear. One reason that the nose doesn't run at first is that fever dries it up. Sometimes the fever lasts for a day or two and then goes away without any running nose or cough taking its place. In this case, the doctor may call it grippe or flu. These terms are commonly used for infections that have no local symptoms (like running nose or diarrhea), only generalized symptoms (such as fever or a sick-all-over feeling). You suspect that this kind of 1-day fever is sometimes a cold that was stopped in its tracks: the child seems perfectly well for a day or two after his fever is gone, and then promptly starts a running nose or cough when he is taken out in cold weather.

I am making the point that children over the age of 1 year often start their colds with sudden high fever so that you won't be too alarmed if this happens. You should, of course, always consult the doctor whenever your child falls ill with a fever because it occasionally means a more serious infection.

When a child is 5 or 6, he's more apt to be starting his colds without much fever again.

Fever that begins after a cold is well under way has a different meaning entirely from the fever that comes on the first day. It usually indicates that the cold has spread or become worse. This isn't necessarily serious or alarming. It only means that the doctor should see the child again to make sure that the ears, bronchial tubes and urinary system are still healthy.

THE HANDLING OF A CHILD WITH A COLD

644. Calling the doctor. You should call the doctor when your child's first cold appears. He will decide whether he needs to see the child, and outline the treatment. You may not need to call him every time another mild cold begins, but you certainly should call him every time an unusual symptom appears, every time there is fever of 101° or more, and every time the cold is more than just a mild one. (If you happen to find in the middle of the night that your child has a temperature of 101°, you don't have to call the doctor then, as long as the cold is mild. Call him in the morning.)

645. Keep him evenly warm. Chilling often makes a cold worse. That is why it is generally recommended that a child stay indoors and away from drafts until the cold is over. It's not quite so important in warm weather, but it is still advisable, especially for the young child. Wind cools one part of the body more than another, and it's this uneven coolness that seems to make the cold worse.

A mother is usually anxious to get her child outdoors again, and a doctor hears the following story many times each winter. The mother says, "His cold was so much better, and it was such a beautiful day, that I decided it would do him good to be outdoors. But tonight his cough is much worse, and he is complaining of an earache." There is no proof that sunshine does a cold any good, and there's plenty of evidence that chilling does harm.

There are lots of children who are never kept in when they have a cold, and nothing serious seems to happen. But this doesn't cover all the cases. A doctor sees the ones that become worse. Perhaps that makes him overcautious. It is safer to keep a young, susceptible child indoors for 1 or 2 full days after the last signs of the cold are gone, then let him out for 20 or 30 minutes in a sheltered spot. If the cold doesn't come back after the first day out, let him out for his usual length of time the second day. You don't have to be so fussy with an older child.

Most doctors nowadays don't advise keeping a child in bed unless he feels sick enough to want to be there. (There are a few exceptions, such as orthopedic conditions and hepatitis.)

Clothing during a cold is important. Aim to keep your child evenly, comfortably warm. If he is sitting up in bed, he should wear a light sweater or warm bathrobe over his pajamas to keep the upper half of his body as warm as the lower. Don't put too many blankets over his legs. In a warm room one is sufficient. You don't want him to be in a warm perspiration below and a cool perspiration above. The same principle of even warmth applies if he is up and around the house. He should have as much on his legs as on his chest. (The air is coolest and draftiest near the floor.) The best way to achieve this is with long overalls. A pair of long stockings or long underwear also does the job.

The temperature of the room in which the child plays might be kept around 72° (compared with the 68° that is ideal when he is healthy). It's better to keep the room comfortably warm during the night, too. This means keeping the windows closed. Then there is no danger of drafts or of chilling if he gets uncovered. Cold air is health-giving when a person is well, but when he has a cold it is somewhat risky. If you're worried about the stuffiness of the room, leave the door open into the hall, or give the room an airing by opening the window for a couple of minutes.

646. Keeping the air moist in an overheated room. The doctor sometimes recommends humidifying or steaming the room during a cold. It counteracts the dryness of the air and soothes the inflamed nose and throat. It is particularly valuable in the treatment of a tight, dry cough or croup. Extra moisture is less necessary in warm weather when the heat is off.

By far the best equipment is a **"cold-mist" humidifier,** which blows moisture into the room. A good humidifier of this sort costs approximately 20 dollars but will be used many times and prove its worth.

An **electric steam vaporizer** gets moisture in the air by boiling water, by means of an electric heating element which

fits into a large glass jar of water. It is much less expensive. But it is also less efficient in getting moisture into the child's chest, less comfortable because it heats up the room, and less safe because a small child may touch it or knock it over. If you buy one of these steam vaporizers, get a large size that holds a quart or more and turns itself off when the water boils away.

In a pinch you can boil water in a saucepan on an electric burner in the child's room or bring him to the kitchen; or hang wet towels on the radiator or wet sheets on a line. In an emergency, in the case of croup, carry the child into the bathroom and turn on the hot water in the bathtub or shower—to make steam, not to put the child into.

647. Nose drops. The doctor may prescribe nose drops. Generally speaking, they fall into two groups. There are the mild antiseptics to kill germs. Their usefulness is limited because they can't kill the germs that are below the surface. The other general class of nose drops are the solutions that shrink the tissues in the nose. This opens up more space for breathing and gives the mucus and pus a better chance to drain. The main drawback is that after the tissues have been shrunk a reaction sets in and they expand again. This may leave the nose more stuffy than ever and may be irritating to the delicate membranes if it's done too often. There are three situations in which the shrinking kind of nose drops are useful. The first is when a baby is so stuffed up that he is frantic. He can't nurse without suffocating, and his sleep is interrupted. (This condition may be relieved by suction with a nasal syringe alone.) The second is in the late stages of a bad cold or sinusitis, when the nose is filled with a thick secretion that does not discharge by itself. The third is when the doctor wants to open up the eustachian tube, which connects the ear with the throat, during an ear infection.

Nose drops do a lot more good if they get back into the inner and upper passages of the nose. Suck out the mucus in the front of the nose with a nasal syringe. Then have the child lie on his back across a bed with his head hanging well down over the side. Insert the drops and try to keep him in this position for half a minute while the drops work back and up.

Medicine to take internally to shrink the nose tissues is now available.

Nose drops should be used only on a doctor's recommen-

dation, no more often than every 4 hours. Don't use them for more than a week unless the doctor says to go on. One disadvantage of nose drops is that many small children fight them. There are only a few conditions in which nose drops do enough good to be worth getting the child all upset.

There are a number of commercial ointments for rubbing on the chest. The idea is to stimulate the skin of the chest to relieve a cough, or to help the nose with the aromatic oils that are wafted upward. There is no proof of the benefit of this kind of treatment, but if it seems to help, there is no harm in its use.

648. Cough medicines. No cough medicine can cure a cold, in the sense of killing the germs. It can only make the windpipe less ticklish, so that coughing is less frequent, or loosen up the mucus. A person who has an infection in his windpipe or bronchial tubes should cough once in a while to bring up the mucus and pus. It is particularly important that a baby's cough not be suppressed too much. The doctor prescribes a cough medicine to keep the cough from being so frequent that it tires the person out or interferes with his sleep or irritates his throat. Any child or grown-up who has a cough that is that frequent should be under the care of a doctor, and he is the one to prescribe the right cough medicine.

EAR INFECTIONS

649. Mild ear infections are common in young children. Some children have inflammation of the ears with most of their colds, and others never do. The ears are much more apt to be infected in the first 3 or 4 years of life. In fact, there is a slight ear inflammation in a majority of colds at this age, but it usually never comes to anything, and the child has no symptoms.

Usually the ear doesn't become inflamed enough to cause pain until after a cold has been going for several days. The child over 2 tells what is the matter. A baby may keep rubbing his ear or just cry piercingly for several hours. There may or may not be fever. The doctor is apt to find at this stage that there is only a mild inflammation of the upper part of the eardrum. This is not an abscess. Most ear infections of this degree get well again in a few days with proper treatment. Incidentally, many early mild inflammations of the ear

cause pain and tenderness behind the ear, in the mastoid region, but this does not mean an infection of the mastoid bone and is not a serious sign at this stage. I mention these points so that you will not begin worrying about an abscess or a mastoid infection the first time an earache develops.

With prompt treatment with modern drugs, few ear infections get even as far as an abscess, and mastoiditis is rare.

Any time that your child has an earache, you should get in touch with the doctor that same day, particularly if there is any fever. The drugs that are used when necessary work much better in the early stages of ear infections.

Suppose it will be several hours before you can reach the doctor. What can you do to relieve the pain? A hot water bottle or an electric heating pad helps some. Small children are impatient with them. Aspirin relieves a certain amount of pain (Section 621). What will help even more, if you happen to have it on hand, is a dose of a cough medicine containing codeine that the doctor has prescribed for that particular child. (A medicine prescribed for an older child or adult might contain too much of the drug.) Codeine is an efficient pain killer as well as cough remedy. If the earache is severe, you can use all these remedies together.

Once in a while an eardrum breaks very early in an infection and discharges a thin pus. You may find the discharge on the child's pillow in the morning without his ever having complained of pain or fever. Usually, however, the drum breaks only after an abscess has been developing for several days, with fever and pain. In any case, if you find your child's ear discharging, the most that you should do is to tuck a loose plug of sterile absorbent cotton into the opening to collect the pus, wash the pus off the outside of the ear with soap and water, and get in touch with the doctor. If the discharge leaks out anyway and irritates the skin, wash the pus off and protect the skin with petroleum jelly.

It is quite common for a child to become deaf after a few days of even a moderate ear infection. In practically all cases, this deafness clears up if the infection is promptly and correctly treated.

BRONCHITIS AND PNEUMONIA

650. Bronchitis. There are all degrees of bronchitis, from very mild with no fever, to severe. Bronchitis simply means that a cold has spread down to the bronchial tubes. There is

usually plenty of cough. Sometimes you can hear faraway squeaky noises as the child breathes, and feel the vibration of the mucus as you touch his chest.

A very mild bronchitis, without fever, without much cough, without loss of appetite, is only a little more serious than a nose cold. However, if the child acts sick, or coughs frequently, or has a fever of 101°, the doctor should be reached that same day, because modern drugs are of great benefit in cases that require them.

The young infant who has a frequent cough should be examined whether he has a fever or not, because in the first month or two of life there can be serious infections without fever. In the meantime, you don't need to worry if his appetite and general appearance are satisfactory.

651. Pneumonia. Pneumonia usually comes on after a child has had a cold for several days, but it may start without any previous warning. You suspect it when the temperature climbs up to 103° or 104°, the breathing becomes rapid and there is a cough. Vomiting often occurs at the beginning, and there may even be a convulsion in a small child. Modern drugs bring about a prompt cure of the ordinary types of pneumonia if treatment is started early. Naturally, you call the doctor if your child develops a fever and cough.

There are also unusual types of pneumonia, most of which are probably caused by filtrable viruses. In many of these "atypical" pneumonias, the child is less sick, though the disease may last a long time.

CROUP

652. Spasmodic croup without fever. Croup is the word commonly used for various kinds of laryngitis in children. There is usually a hoarse, ringing, barking cough (croupy cough) and some tightness in the breathing.

The commonest and mildest type, **spasmodic croup without fever**, comes on suddenly during the evening. The child may have been perfectly healthy during the day or have had the mildest kind of cold without cough. Suddenly he wakes up with a violent fit of croupy coughing, is quite hoarse and is having difficulty breathing. He struggles and heaves to get his breath in. It's quite a scary picture when you see it the first time, but it's not so serious as it looks. You should call the doctor promptly for any kind of croup.

The emergency treatment of croup, until the doctor can be reached, is moist air. Use a cold-mist humidifier if you have one. See Section 646 for other ways to humidify. A small room is preferable because you can humidify it faster. If the water runs hot, you can take the child into the bathroom and run hot water into the tub (to make steam, not to put the child in). If there is a shower, that will work best of all.

When the child breathes the moist air, the croup usually begins to improve rapidly. Meanwhile, the air in the room where he will go back to bed should be moistened. An adult should stay awake as long as there are any symptoms of croup, sleep in the same room with the child for 3 nights, and wake herself 2 or 3 hours after the croup is over to make sure that the child is breathing comfortably.

Spasmodic croup without fever sometimes comes back the next night or two. To avoid this, have the child sleep in a room in which the air has been moistened for 3 nights. This form of croup is apparently caused by the combination of a cold infection, a child with a sensitive larynx, and dry air.

653. Severe croup with fever (laryngobronchitis). This is a more severe form of croup, which is usually accompanied by a real chest cold. The croupy cough and the tight breathing may come on gradually or suddenly at any time of the day or night. Steaming only partly relieves it. **If your child has hoarseness with fever or tightness of breathing with fever, he must be put under the close, continuous supervision of a doctor without delay.** If you cannot reach your doctor right away, find another doctor. If a doctor cannot reach you, you should take the child to a hospital.

654. Diphtheria of the larynx is still another cause of croup. There is a gradually increasing hoarseness, cough, difficulty in breathing and moderate fever. There is practically no danger of this form of croup developing if a child has received diphtheria inoculations.

However, with any form of croup, a child should be seen promptly by a doctor. The urgency is greatest when hoarseness and tight breathing are persisting, even mildly, and when there is fever of 101° or more.

SINUSITIS, TONSILLITIS AND SWOLLEN GLANDS

655. Sinusitis. The sinuses are cavities in the bones surrounding the nose. Each sinus cavity connects with the interior of the nose through a small opening. The maxillary sinuses are in the cheekbones. The frontal sinuses are in the forehead, just above the eyebrows. The ethmoid sinuses are up above the inner passages of the nose. The sphenoids are farther back, behind the nasal passages. The maxillary and the ethmoid sinuses are the only ones that are well enough developed in the early years of childhood to be infected then. The frontals and sphenoids develop gradually after the age of 6. When there is a severe or prolonged cold in the nose, the infection may spread from the nose into these various sinus cavities. Sinus infections usually last longer than simple nose colds, because they are more closed in, can't drain so well. A sinus infection may be very mild and show itself only by a chronic discharge of pus from the back of the nose into the throat (called a postnasal drip). This sometimes causes a chronic cough when the child lies down in bed or when he first gets up in the morning. On the other hand, sinusitis may be severe, with high fever and pain. When a doctor suspects sinusitis, he sometimes investigates further by X-ray pictures or by shining a light through the sinuses in a dark room. He uses various treatments, such as nose drops, nose packs, suction, drugs, depending on the case.

Whatever specific method the doctor is using, remember that the general care of the child is important, too. A sinus infection is, after all, only a more advanced and persistent form of a cold. Like a cold, it is helped by keeping a child indoors, in a warm, even-temperatured room with moist air. The child should be evenly clothed and the windows should be kept closed at night.

656. Tonsillitis. Serious tonsillitis is most often caused by the streptococcus. The child usually has high fever for a number of days and feels sick. Headache and vomiting are common. His tonsils become fiery red and swollen. After a day or two, white spots or white patches appear on them. An older child may complain of such a sore throat that he can hardly swallow. Young children may be bothered surprisingly little by the sore throat.

You should consult the doctor for a case of tonsillitis, however mild. It is important to treat it promptly and thoroughly with one of the antibiotic drugs that are so effective in overcoming the infection and preventing complications. The drug should be given in a manner which will continue the treatment for 10 days. Convalescence is often slow. If the neck glands become swollen, if the child continues to look washed out or to run a low fever, treat him as an invalid and keep in touch with the doctor. Other complications, which usually occur only in untreated cases, are ear infections, anemia, rheumatic fever, inflammation of the kidney with smoky urine.

657. Other throat infections. There are all kinds and degrees of throat infections, caused by a variety of germs. The medical term for them is pharyngitis. Many people feel a slight sore throat at the beginning of every cold. Often the doctor, in examining a child with a fever, finds a slightly red throat as the only sign of disease. The child may or may not notice any soreness. Most of these are soon over. The child should stay indoors until the sore throat is all gone. The doctor should be called if there is any fever, or if the child looks sick, or if the throat is more than slightly sore (even if there is no fever). If the doctor suspects a streptococcal infection, he may take a throat culture or treat it anyway with one of the effective drugs, to prevent possible complications.

658. Swollen glands. The lymph glands that are scattered up and down the sides of the neck sometimes become infected and swollen as a result of any disease in the throat, mild or severe. The commonest cause is tonsillitis. It can develop in the middle of the tonsillitis or a week or two later. If the glands are swollen enough to be visible, or if there is fever of 101° or more, the doctor should certainly be called. Treatment with drugs may be called for in certain cases and is most valuable if begun early.

Slightly enlarged neck glands may last for weeks or even months after some throat infections. They can come from other causes, too, such as infected teeth, scalp infections and general diseases, like German measles. You should consult your doctor about them. But if he finds the child generally healthy, don't worry about slightly swollen glands.

TONSILS AND ADENOIDS

659. The tonsils and adenoids are meant to be there unless they are causing trouble. Tonsils and adenoids have been blamed for so many things in the last half century that many people think of them as villains that have to be removed eventually, and the sooner the better. This is the wrong way to look at them. They are there for the purpose of helping to overcome infection and build up the body's resistance to germs.

The tonsils and adenoids are made of what is called lymphoid tissue, and are similar to the glands in the sides of the neck, the armpits and the groin. Any of these glands, including the tonsils and adenoids, become swollen when there is infection nearby, as they labor to kill germs and build resistance.

660. The tonsils. In normal, healthy children, the tonsils gradually become larger until the age of 7 or 8 or 9, and then gradually decrease in size. In former times it was believed that all abnormally enlarged tonsils were diseased and should be removed. Nowadays it is believed that the size is unimportant. It is only extremely rarely that tonsils (or adenoids) need to be removed.

Recurrent tonsillitis, frequent colds, ear infections, rheumatic fever, chorea are not reasons for tonsillectomy. There is no need to remove the tonsils, even when they are large, in a child who is perfectly healthy and has few nose and throat infections. There is no reason to operate because of a feeding problem, or stuttering, or nervousness; in fact, the operation may make the child worse.

661. The adenoids. The adenoids are clusters of lymphoid tissue up behind the soft palate, where the nose passages join the throat. When they become greatly enlarged they may block this passageway from the nose and cause mouth breathing and snoring. They may prevent the free discharge of mucus and pus from the nose, and thus help to keep bad colds and sinus infections going. These conditions were usually considered reasons for removal of the adenoids in previous times. Nowadays, however, they are often successfully treated medically: with internal and external preparations to shrink the tissues, antibiotics to treat the infections.

Removing the adenoids does not necessarily make a child breathe through his nose. Some children are mouth breathers

because of habit (they seem to be born that way) and not because of obstruction. And some children's noses are obstructed not by adenoids but by swollen tissues in the front of the nose (for instance, by hay fever or other forms of allergy). Removing the adenoids has little or no effect on the frequency of ear infections.

If the tonsils are removed, the adenoids are sometimes cut out, too. On the other hand, there may be reason to take out the adenoids alone if they are causing persistent obstruction, and to leave the tonsils.

The adenoids always grow back to some extent, and the body always tries to grow new lumps of lymphoid tissue where the tonsils used to be. This isn't a sign that the operation was done incompletely or that it has to be done again. It shows only that the body means to have lymphoid tissue in that region and tries hard to replace it.

In Sections 627–630 there are suggestions about handling operations.

ALLERGIES

662. Allergic nose troubles, including hay fever. You probably know someone who has ragweed hay fever. When ragweed pollen gets in the wind in mid-August, he starts to sneeze and his nose begins to be stuffed up and itch and run. This means that his nose is **allergic,** or oversensitive, to the pollen, which doesn't bother other people at all. Some people have hay fever in spring because they are allergic to certain tree pollens, and others have it in early summer from certain grasses. If your child develops a running, itching nose that lasts for weeks, at the same time every year, you should take it up with your doctor. From the appearance of the nose in the season and from skin tests with the suspected pollens, he can tell whether it's hay fever. The treatment often consists of frequent injections carried out over a long period. The doctor can usually give temporary relief with medicine.

But there are nose allergies aside from seasonal hay fevers that may be less dramatic but more troublesome. There are noses that are sensitive to the feathers in pillows, or to dog hair, or to house dust, or to any number of other substances. Such year-round allergies as these may keep a child stuffy or running at the nose, breathing through his mouth, month in and month out. The chronic obstruction may make him more susceptible to sinus infections. If your child is much bothered

this way, your doctor, or an allergy specialist whom he recommends, may be able to find the cause. The treatment is different in each case and depends on the causes. If it's goose feathers, you change the pillow. If it's dog hair, you may have to give away the dog and substitute some other plaything. If it's something hard to avoid, like house dust, the doctor may give injections of the offending substance over a long period. He is likely to recommend "stripping the room" to lessen the dust there, especially if the symptoms occur mainly at night or the first thing in the morning. You remove the rugs and curtains for good and give the room a wet-mopping every day. You eliminate all wool from the room and also the stuffed toys. You either buy dustproof coverings for the mattress and pillow, or use ones made of foam rubber, or use a canvas cot with no pillow at all.

Allergy symptoms usually can't be eliminated completely. You have to be satisfied with partial improvement.

663. Asthma. Asthma is another kind of allergy. Instead of the sensitive organ being the nose, as in hay fever, it is the bronchial tubes. When the irritating substance reaches the small bronchial tubes, they swell, thick mucus is secreted, and the passageways for air are so narrowed that breathing becomes difficult, labored and wheezing. Coughing occurs.

When an older child has chronic asthma, it's apt to be due to substances that float in the air, such as horse dander, dog hair, molds, etc. Allergists call these "inhalants." In a very young child, allergy to foods is more likely to be the cause or to play a part.

The child who has chronic asthma of more than slight degree is usually tested to discover the offending substances, and then treated. If the disease is neglected, the repeated attacks may have a harmful effect on the structure of the lungs and chest. The treatment depends on the cause and is different in each case. Foods that the child is sensitive to are eliminated from the diet. When inhalants are the cause, the treatment is much the same as in year-round allergies of the nose (Section 662).

Asthma is not simply a matter of allergy to certain substances. A person has an attack at one time and not at another, even though he's in the same place leading the same life. Attacks are more common at night. Season of year, climate, temperature, exercise, state of mind play a part in different cases. Colds often start an attack. Certain children are

apt to have attacks of asthma (or other allergies) when they are anxious—consciously or unconsciously—about separation from a parent, for instance, or about conflict with a parent, or about conflict between the parents. They may be greatly improved when their troubles are straightened out, perhaps with a psychiatrist's help. In other words, you try to treat the whole child, not just the asthma.

The treatment of the individual attack of asthma depends a lot on how severe it is, and on what the doctor finds is helpful for that case. There are drugs given by mouth or injection for temporary relief when the child is having real difficulty breathing.

If your child develops asthma for the first time when you are out of reach of a doctor, don't be alarmed. The condition is rarely as dangerous as it looks. Keep him in bed if the breathing is very difficult. If it's winter and the house is heated, get extra moisture into the air (Section 646). If he is coughing much and you have cough medicine that was prescribed for him before, you can give him a dose. Get him occupied in play or reading while you go about your own work, or read to him yourself. If you hover over him anxiously, it keeps him more frightened and may actually make the asthma worse. If he continues to have spells, you can try stripping his room (Section 662), until you are able to consult a doctor.

It is impossible to predict about asthma. Cases that start early in childhood are more apt to clear up in a few years than those that start later. A certain number go away by the age of puberty. But sometimes hay fever takes the place of the asthma.

664. Asthmatic bronchitis should be mentioned separately. An occasional baby or small child has spells of wheezing, difficult breathing, not at any old time, as in typical chronic asthma, but only when he has a real cold. This tendency is most common in the first 3 years of life. It's discouraging to have a baby who regularly has this much trouble with his colds, but there is a brighter side to the picture. The tendency to asthmatic bronchitis is usually well on its way to disappearing in a couple of years. The doctor should be called, of course. The infection and the cough may need treating as much as the wheezing. If the house is heated, it may help to get extra moisture in the air (Section 646). The injections and medicines to open up the bronchial tubes that are often help-

ful in ordinary asthma have little effect in asthmatic bronchitis.

665. Hives. Hives are considered, at least in some cases, to be due to allergy of the skin. The commonest kind consists of raised welts. They are often pale in the raised part, because the blood has been pressed out by the swelling. They itch, sometimes unbearably. A few individuals get hives repeatedly, or even most of the time. But many people have them only once or twice in a lifetime. They are occasionally found to be caused by sensitivity to some food. They also come from serum injections and at the end of certain infections. In many cases the cause cannot be discovered.

A household remedy for itching hives is a hot bath to which has been added bicarbonate of soda (baking soda). Use a cupful for a small tub, 2 cupfuls for a large one. The doctor can usually relieve the attack of hives with medicine or an injection.

666. Eczema. Eczema is a rough, red rash that comes in patches. It is caused by allergy, like hay fever and asthma. In hay fever the nose is allergic (sensitive) to a pollen, like ragweed. In eczema the skin may be allergic to some food in the diet. When that food gets into the blood and reaches the skin, the skin becomes inflamed. In another case the skin may be allergic to some material, like wool, silk, rabbit's hair, or some substance, like orrisroot in powder, that comes in direct contact with the skin. A baby is more likely to have eczema if he has relatives who have asthma, hay fever, hives or eczema.

Even when eczema is primarily due to allergy to foods, two other factors may play a secondary part. The first is irritation of the skin from the outside. One baby has eczema only when his skin is irritated by cold weather, another only in hot weather from the irritation of perspiration, still another only in the diaper region from the irritation of the urine. If a baby has eczema only where wool comes in contact with his skin, it may be that he is really allergic to wool directly, or it may be that he is allergic to some food and the wool merely acts as a simple irritant.

Another factor in eczema is the baby's fatness and rate of gaining weight. There is much more eczema in fat babies than in medium-weight babies. Thin babies rarely get it.

You need a doctor, of course, to diagnose and treat the condition. The easiest eczema to describe is the kind that comes in patches of rough, red, thick, scaly skin. When eczema is mild or just starting, the color is apt to be a light red or tannish pink, but if it becomes severe, it turns a deeper red, usually itches, and the baby scratches and rubs it. This causes scratch marks and "weeping" (oozing). When the oozing serum dries, it forms crusts. When a patch of eczema is healing, even after the redness has all faded away, you can still feel the roughness and thickness of the skin.

The commonest place for eczema to begin in a young baby is on the cheeks or the forehead. From there it may spread back to the ears and neck. The scaliness looks from a distance as if salt has dried there, especially on the ears. Near a year of age, eczema may start almost anywhere—the shoulders, the diaper region, the arms, the chest. Between 1 and 3, the most typical spots are the creases in the elbows and behind the knees. Severe eczema can be a very trying disease to take care of. The baby is wild with the itching. The mother is wild trying to keep him from scratching. It can last for months.

667. There are several angles to the treatment. What a doctor does in studying and treating a case depends on many factors, including the baby's age, the location and character of the rash, his fatness and the rate at which he is gaining, the history of what new foods were introduced before the rash began, and how he responds to different forms of treatment. Many cases can be cured by lotions and ointments alone. In the more persistent ones, an effort is made to find what food or foods the child is allergic to. In the young infant, fresh cow's milk is often found to be the cause. Then a shift to evaporated milk sometimes helps, because any food is less likely to cause allergy when it is thoroughly cooked. Evaporated goat's milk occasionally succeeds when cow's milk fails. A few babies can be cured only by giving up real milk altogether and shifting to one of the artificial milks, such as those made from soybeans. Eliminating orange juice often helps.

In severe eczema in older babies and children who are eating a number of foods, the doctor experiments carefully by eliminating various ones from the diet. In severe and persistent cases he may do "skin testing" by injecting samples of different foods. Hives develop around the injections of foods to which the child is sensitive. If a baby is fat or gaining rapidly, it may help to remove much of the sugar and starches from the diet.

When an external irritant seems to be playing a part, that needs attention, too. Wool is very commonly irritating to eczema, and it is usually eliminated from the clothing. If the eczema is all in the diaper region, it is worthwhile to take all the precautions discussed in Section 319 on diaper rashes. If cold, windy weather brings out the eczema, find a sheltered place for outings. Soap and water are sometimes irritating to eczema, in which case the baby can be cleaned with mineral oil on absorbent cotton.

If for the time being you are out of reach of a doctor and your young baby develops a severe itching eczema, it will do no harm, and it may help, to shift from a fresh-milk to an evaporated-milk formula. You can also eliminate the sugar from his formula and limit his cereal, so that he won't gain so rapidly. If you are in the same situation with an older baby who, for instance, develops a severe eczema after starting on egg, leave out the egg until you can get advice. It may take 2 weeks or more for the improvement to show. Wheat is another common offender. It is a mistake, though, for a parent to begin eliminating a number of foods from the diet, and not even one food should be eliminated by the parent if it is possible to get a doctor's help. The reason is this: a case of eczema varies from week to week even with the same diet. When you are changing the diet around yourself you are apt to think that first one food, then another, is the cause. Every time the eczema becomes worse again, you become more confused. The danger is that you will make the diet so lopsided that the child's nutrition will suffer. If the eczema is not bothering the baby much, don't try any changes in the diet until you can get help.

Parents are upset about a severe eczema and are impressed by the necessity of keeping the baby from scratching himself. This combination may make them afraid to cuddle and stroke him. But he needs this kind of closeness and visible affection.

The thing to remember about eczema is that it's a tendency inside the child, not an infection, like impetigo, that you can get rid of completely. In most cases you have to be satisfied if you can just keep the rash mild. A majority of the eczemas that start early in infancy clear up completely, or at least become much milder, in the following year or two.

SKIN DISEASES

668. Distinguishing the common rashes. This section isn't meant to make you a diagnostician. If your child has a rash, you need your doctor's help. Rashes due to the same cause vary so in different individuals that even a skin specialist sometimes has a job diagnosing them. They confuse less expert people very easily. The purpose of this section is only to give you a few general pointers about the commoner rashes of children to relieve your mind until you can reach your doctor.

Measles. Fever and cold symptoms appear 3 or 4 days before the rash begins. It consists of flat, pink spots that begin around the ears and work down. The fever is high when the rash begins (Section 677).

German measles. Flat, pink spots, often faint, that rapidly spread all over the whole body. Little or no fever. No cold symptoms, but swollen glands on the back of the head and neck (Section 678).

Chicken pox. Separate raised pimples. Some of these develop tiny, delicate blisters on top, which break within a few hours, leaving a small crust. The pimples come out a few at a time, beginning on the body or face or scalp. The doctor, to make the diagnosis, searches among all the crusted pimples for a few fresh tiny blisters (Section 681).

Scarlet fever. The child is sick for a day before the rash comes out, usually with headache, fever, vomiting and sore throat. The rash, which is a red blush, starts in the warm, moist parts of the body, armpits, groin and back (Section 684).

Prickly heat. Comes in babies in the beginning of hot weather. Starts around the shoulders and neck. It is made up of patches of many small tan-pink pimples, some of which develop tiny blisters (Section 321).

Diaper rash. All in the area that is wet with urine. Pink or red pimples of various sizes, or patches of rough, red skin (Section 319).

Eczema. Patches of red, rough skin, which in the beginning come and go. If it is bad, it becomes scaly, itchy and crusted.

Apt to start on cheeks in the very young infant, later in the first year on the trunk. Common spots after a year are behind the knees and in the elbow folds (Section 666).

Hives. Welts scattered pretty evenly over the entire body. They itch (Section 665).

669. Insect bites. There are many different kinds, from big, puffy swellings, the size of a half dollar, down to a simple blood-crusted spot without any swelling. But there are two common characteristics of most bites. There is a tiny hole or tiny bump in the center where the stinger went in. And the bites are located on the exposed parts of the skin, in most cases.

Any insect bite that is itching (mosquito bite, for instance) or stinging may be partly relieved by applying a paste made by running a few drops of water into a teaspoonful of bicarbonate of soda. For a **bee sting,** remove the stinger, if visible, with tweezers and apply bicarbonate of soda. More effective for a **wasp** or **hornet sting** is to rub a drop of vinegar into the spot.

670. Scabies. Groups of pimples topped with scabs, and a lot of scratch marks from the incessant itching. Located on parts of the body that are frequently handled: backs of hands, wrists, penis, abdomen. Not on the back. It is contagious, needs treatment.

671. Ringworm. Circular patches of rough skin, most commonly about nickel size. The outer rim is made up of little bumps. In ringworm of the scalp, there are round patches of scaly skin in which the hair is broken off short. Ringworm is a fungus infection that is contagious, has nothing to do with worms, requires treatment.

672. Impetigo. In a child past infancy there are scabs or crusts, partly brown, partly honey-colored. In fact, any scabs on the face should first be suspected of being impetigo. The infection is apt to start with a pimple with a yellowish or white blister on top, most often on the face, but this soon gets rubbed off and the scab takes its place. Other spots develop on the face and on any part of the body that the hands can carry the infection to. You should have the doctor see it promptly for diagnosis and treatment. It spreads easily if neglected, and is contagious to others.

In the newborn infant, impetigo is different. It starts with a very delicate small blister that contains yellowish fluid or white pus and is surrounded by reddened skin. The blister is easily broken and leaves a small raw spot. It does not develop a thick crust as in the older child. It's apt to start in a moist place, such as the edge of the diaper or in the groin or armpit. New spots may develop. It should be treated promptly by a doctor. If you cannot reach a doctor, the best method is to carefully wipe off the blister with a piece of cotton (so as not to spread the pus onto the surrounding skin), and then leave the raw spot exposed to the air. Arrange the clothing and bedclothes so that they do not cover the spot or spots, and keep the room warmer than usual if necessary. During impetigo, disinfect the diapers, sheets, underclothing, nighties, towels and washcloth every day. Ordinary hypochlorite bleach works well.

673. Poison ivy. Clusters of small blisters of various sizes, on reddened, shiny skin. It itches, comes on the exposed parts of the body, in spring and summer. Consult your doctor about treatment if it is extensive.

674. Head lice. It's easier to find the eggs than the lice. They are tiny, pearly-white, egg-shaped objects, each one firmly cemented to a hair. There may be itching red pimples where the hair meets the back of the neck.

675. Birthmarks. Most babies have a collection of red, mottled spots on the backs of their necks when they are born. These also commonly occur in two other places: between the eyebrows and on the upper eyelids. These blotches disappear gradually in most cases, and nothing needs to be done for them.

"Port wine stains" are areas of skin that have a deep-red coloring but are flat and otherwise normal. They are similar to the red spots on the neck and eyelids mentioned in the first paragraph, but they occur on other parts of the body, are apt to be larger, deeper-colored and more permanent. Some of them do fade, particularly the lighter-colored ones. There is no easy treatment for them.

"Strawberry marks" are fairly common. These are raised and are of an intense, deep-crimson color. They look very much like a piece of the outside of a shiny strawberry. They may be small at birth and later increase in size, or they may not appear at all until after birth. They are apt to grow for a while and then stop. As the years go by, most of them shrink back to nothing without treatment. They can be treated if the doctor thinks it necessary.

"Cavernous hemangiomas" are fairly large blue-and-red marks caused by a collection of distended veins deep in the skin. Sometimes they can be removed if they are disfiguring.

Moles can be of all sizes, smooth or hairy. They can be removed surgically if they are disfiguring or irritated by the clothing.

676. Warts. There are different types of ordinary warts that develop on the hands, soles of the feet, face. They are mildly contagious and should be seen by a doctor. In addition, there is a special type known as "contagious warts." At first they are round, smooth, waxy, the size of a pinhead, and white or pink in color. They multiply, enlarge and become concave in the center. They should be treated to avoid spreading.

MEASLES, GERMAN MEASLES, ROSEOLA

677. Measles. Measles for the first 3 or 4 days has no rash. It looks like a bad cold that is becoming worse. The eyes are red and watery. If you pull the lower lid down, you see that it is angry red. There is a hard, dry cough that becomes frequent. The fever usually goes higher each day. The rash comes out about the fourth day, when the fever is high, as indefinite pink spots behind the ears. They spread gradually over the face and body, becoming bigger and darker-colored. The day before the rash comes out, "Koplik's spots" appear on the inside of the cheeks, next to the lower molar teeth. They are minute white spots surrounded by redness, but are hard to recognize unless you know them.

The fever stays high, the cough frequent (in spite of medicine), and the child feels pretty sick while the rash comes out full, which takes 1 to 2 days. Then everything should improve rapidly.

You suspect a complication if the fever stays high more than 2 days from the time the rash begins, or if the fever goes down for a day or more and then comes back again. The commonest complications are ear abscesses, bronchitis and pneumonia. You will be calling the doctor at least once during a case of measles, whether you suspect the disease or not, because of the cough and fever. You must call him back promptly or bring the child to a hospital if the fever stays up or comes back after 2 days of the rash. The complications can be serious, and unlike the measles itself, can be successfully treated by modern drugs.

During the feverish part of the disease, the child almost completely loses his appetite. The most he usually takes is fluids, which should be offered frequently. The mouth needs to be gently cleaned three times a day. It used to be thought necessary to keep the room very dark to protect the eyes. But now it is known that there is little danger. All that is necessary is to darken the room somewhat if the light makes the child uncomfortable. The room should be kept comfortably warm to prevent chilling. The child is usually let out of bed 2 days after the fever is gone. It is safe to let him outdoors and to play with other children a week after the rash began, provided all cough and other cold symptoms are completely gone.

The first symptoms of measles begin anywhere from 9 to 16 days after exposure. It is contagious to others from the very beginning of the cold symptoms. No one with a cold or sore throat should come anywhere near a child with measles, since it is cold germs that cause the complications. It is unusual for a person to catch real measles twice.

Measles can and should be prevented by vaccination at 1 year of age. But if a child who has not been protected is exposed, the attack can still be prevented or made milder if gamma globulin is given in time. It's a good idea to prevent measles before the age of 3 or 4, because that is the time when complications are more frequent and more severe. It is also wise to prevent it in an older child who is run-down or ill. Get in touch with your doctor immediately to discuss globulin while it will still be effective. The protection of globulin lasts for only a couple of weeks.

678. German measles. The rash of German measles looks much like the rash of real measles, but the two diseases are entirely separate. In German measles there are no cold symptoms (running nose or cough). There may be a little sore throat. The fever is usually low (under 102°). The person may hardly feel sick at all. The rash consists of flat, pink spots, which usually cover the body the first day. The second day they are apt to fade and run together, so that the body looks flushed instead of spotty. The most characteristic sign is swollen, tender glands on the back of the skull, behind the ears and on the sides of the neck, toward the back. These glands may swell before the rash comes out, and the swelling is apt to last some time after the disease is over. In some cases the rash is so slight that it is not noticed.

German measles usually develops from 12 to 21 days after exposure. The child usually doesn't need to be kept in bed. A doctor should make the diagnosis, because German measles is easily confused with real measles, scarlet fever and certain virus infections.

It is bad for a woman to have German measles during the first 3 months of pregnancy because of the chance of her baby acquiring some defect from the disease. If she is exposed at this time, she should promptly discuss with her doctor the advisability of gamma globulin, though its value has never been proved. Many doctors feel that girls should be deliberately exposed to this disease so that they have it before marriage. There is now a test that will tell whether a person has previously had the disease.

679. Roseola. The proper name for this disease is exanthem subitum, but it's easier to call it roseola, short for roseola infantum. It is a less well-known contagious disease. It usually occurs between the ages of 1 and 3, rarely afterward. The child has a steady high fever for 3 or 4 days without any cold symptoms, and usually without seeming to be very sick. (Occasionally there is a convulsion on the first day because of the fever.) Suddenly the fever falls to normal, and a pinkish flat rash, something like the rash in measles, comes out on the body. By this time the child no longer looks ill but may be cranky. The rash is gone in a day or two, and there are no complications to worry about.

680. Other infectious diseases with rashes. In recent years it has been learned that there are several kinds of respiratory diseases (colds) caused by viruses (with names like adenovirus, ECHO, Coxsackie) which often have rashes that resemble measles.

CHICKEN POX, WHOOPING COUGH, MUMPS

681. Chicken pox. The first sign of chicken pox is usually a few of the characteristic pimples on the body and face. These pox are raised up like ordinary small pimples, but some of them have tiny yellow water blisters on top. The base of the pimple and the skin around it are reddened. The delicate blister head breaks within a few hours and dries into a crust. When a doctor is trying to make the diagnosis, he searches among all the crusted pimples to find a fresh one that still has the blister. New pox continue to appear for 3 or 4 days.

An older child or adult may feel sick and have headache the day before the pox appear, but a small child doesn't notice these symptoms. The fever is usually slight at the beginning, but may go higher the next day or two. Some children never feel sick, never have a temperature of more than 101°. Others feel quite sick and have high fever. The pox usually itch.

You should call a physician to diagnose and treat your child if he has a rash, certainly if he has a fever or feels sick. (Chicken pox, for instance, can be confused with smallpox and other diseases.) The child is usually kept in bed as long as new pox are appearing. The itching can be relieved by placing him in a warm starch or soda bath for 10 minutes 2 or 3 times a day. Use a starch that dissolves in water, or bicarbonate of soda (1 cupful for a small tub, 2 for a large one). Do not rub the scabs off. The only common complication is boils, which come from infecting the pox by scratching. Wash his hands 3 times a day with a soap containing hexachlorophene, and keep his fingernails very short.

Chicken pox usually develops between 11 and 19 days after exposure. The usual rule is to let a child out and back to school a week after the disease began, or 2 days after new pox have stopped appearing. The dried scabs are not contagious and should not be a reason for keeping the child quarantined. However, some schools insist that he stay away until all the scabs have fallen off.

682. Whooping cough. There's nothing about whooping cough in the first week to make you suspect that disease. It's just like an ordinary cold with a little running nose and a little dry cough. Toward the end of the week the mother usually thinks that the cold is about over and sends the child back to school. "There was just a little dry cough left." It is during the second week that the first suspicion arises. Now it's noticed that the child is beginning to have long spells of coughing at night. He coughs 8 or 10 times on one breath. One night, after several of these long spells, he gags and vomits. Or maybe he whoops. The whoop is the crowing noise he makes trying to get his breath back after a spell of coughs. In these days, when whooping cough shots are so widely used, many cases never are bad enough to reach the whooping stage, and in some there isn't even vomiting. The diagnosis is then based on the character of the cough in the second week (cough, cough, cough, cough, cough, cough, cough, cough—a string of coughs in rapid succession, without a breath in between) and on the fact that there are other cases in the neighborhood.

You should never jump to the conclusion that your child has whooping cough because he develops a bad cough in the first few days of a cold. In fact, a bad cough in the beginning of a cold argues against the diagnosis of whooping cough.

Whooping cough lasts for weeks and weeks. In an average case, the whooping stage lasts 4 weeks, in a severe case 2 or 3 months. A doctor thinks of whooping cough whenever a dry cough lasts a month.

When there is a doubtful case and it is important to make the diagnosis, there are three laboratory tests that sometimes help. The first is a "cough plate." The doctor has the child cough into a laboratory plate containing a special gelatin on which whooping cough germs grow easily. If he finds the germs, he is sure it is whooping cough. But if he doesn't find the germs, it doesn't prove that it isn't whooping cough. This test is most reliable in the first week or two of the disease. The second test is a blood count. In some cases the result is definite, especially in the third and fourth week; in others it is no help. The third is a "fluorescent antibody" test, on material from a throat swab, which is available only in certain medical centers.

Whooping cough can be a serious disease, especially in a baby under 2. It's a disease to avoid like the plague if you have a baby in the household. The main danger at this age is exhaustion and pneumonia.

Your doctor will prescribe treatment, based on the age of the child and the severity of the case. Cough medicines are always used but often have only a small influence. Most cases do better when in cold air, day and night, but naturally the child must be protected against chilling. Robust children are sometimes allowed to play outdoors throughout the disease as long as they have no fever. Naturally, they should not play with other children. Some children have many fewer coughing spells when they are kept in bed. When vomiting is a problem, frequent small meals stay down better than the regular three full meals. The safest time of all to feed a child is right after he has vomited, since he usually won't have another bad spell for some time. A tight abdominal binder may give relief to the exhausted abdominal muscles.

Since whooping cough is sometimes a serious disease, especially in babies and young children, it is important to call a doctor promptly when there is a suspicion. There are two main reasons: to make sure of the diagnosis, if possible; and to prescribe the right treatment. Special treatment is called for and is valuable in infants.

Quarantine regulations are different in different communities. Usually a child is kept out of school until 5 weeks after the beginning of the disease and until he has stopped vomiting. The contagiousness of whooping cough does not cease suddenly after a certain number of weeks. It gradually diminishes, sooner in a light case. For home purposes, you can count a child as being no longer much danger to others when his cough has been much improved for 2 weeks. Whooping cough takes from 5 to 14 days to develop after exposure. If an infant who has not yet had his whooping cough shots is exposed to the disease, a serum can be given to prevent the disease or make it lighter.

683. Mumps. Mumps is principally a disease of the saliva glands, most commonly the parotid glands, which lie in the hollow just under the lobe of the ear. First the gland fills in the hollow, then it swells the whole side of the face. It pushes the lobe of the ear upward. If you run your fingers up and down the back part of the jawbone, you can feel that the hard swelling runs forward, covering part of the jawbone.

When a child has a swelling in the side of the neck, the question always comes up, Is it mumps (a specific infection of the parotid saliva gland), or is it one of the other, rarer diseases of the parotid gland (which may recur repeatedly), or is it an ordinary swollen gland (one of the lymph glands in the side of the neck)? The ordinary lymph glands that sometimes swell after a sore throat are lower down on the neck, not tucked up under the ear lobe. The hard swelling does not cross the jawbone.

When a small child develops mumps, the swelling under the ear is usually the first thing noticed. An older child may complain of pain around his ear or in the side of his throat, especially on swallowing or chewing, for a day before the swelling begins. He may feel generally sick. There is often little fever in the beginning, but it may go higher on the second or third day. Most commonly the swelling begins on one side first, but spreads to the other side in a day or two. Sometimes it takes a week or more to spread to the other side and, of course, in some cases the second side never swells.

There are other saliva glands besides the parotids, and mumps sometimes spreads to these, too. There are the sub-maxillary glands, tucked up under the lower part of the jaw-bone. The sublinguals are just behind the point of the chin. Occasionally a person gets one of the complications of mumps without having had a swelling in any of the saliva glands.

A very mild mumps swelling may go away in 3 or 4 days. The average swelling lasts a week to 10 days.

Mumps can spread to the testicles in men and boys who have reached the age of puberty. This usually involves only one testicle. But even when both are inflamed, this does not usually cause sterility (inability to have children). However, it is preferable for boys to have mumps before puberty, and some doctors recommend deliberate exposure. Adolescent boys and men should avoid exposure. Mumps sometimes causes a special kind of mumps meningitis. The child has high fever, a stiff neck, and is delirious. This is seldom dangerous. Infection of the pancreas gland in the abdomen may cause severe abdominal pain and vomiting.

Sometimes a person who believes he had mumps previously will again get a swelling of a parotid gland. Most doctors believe that one or the other such attack was caused by some other germ than the mumps virus or by a tiny stone obstructing the salivary duct; they think that a person can't have mumps twice because they believe that one attack confers immunity for life. Whether or not a person can ever have mumps twice, he can certainly catch real mumps after thinking he had it before. Therefore I'd advise fathers and boys who have reached puberty not to expose themselves unnecessarily when there is mumps in the family.

A mumps immune globulin is available but it efficacy is doubtful. There is a skin test which is fairly reliable in telling whether a person is immune or susceptible and this can aid the decision whether an exposed father should take the globulin anyway.

You should call the doctor for a suspected case of mumps. It is important to be certain of the diagnosis. If it turns out to be a swollen lymph gland, the treatment is quite different.

The child is usually kept in bed until the swelling is gone. Some people can't take tart-tasting foods like lemon juice during mumps (it hurts the inflamed glands), but others continue to enjoy them. So a lemon or pickle is no test of mumps. Mumps takes 2 to 3 weeks to develop after exposure.

SCARLET FEVER, DIPHTHERIA, POLIOMYELITIS

684. Scarlet fever. Scarlet fever usually begins with some of these symptoms: sore throat, vomiting, fever, headache. The rash is not apt to appear for a day or two. It begins on the warm, moist parts of the body, such as the sides of the chest, the groin, the back if the child has been lying on his back. From a distance it looks like a uniform red flush, but if you look at it more closely, you can see that it is made up of tiny red spots on a flushed skin. It may spread over the whole body and the sides of the face, but the region around the mouth stays pale. The throat is red, sometimes very angry, and after a while the tongue usually gets red, first around the edge. You should, of course, call the doctor if your child has fever and sore throat.

Nowadays scarlet fever is not apt to be so severe as it used to be. It is not an entirely separate disease with a germ of its own, like measles. It is caused by one type of the common streptococcus, which produces sore throats, swollen glands, ear abscesses, in other people. Scarlet fever is just one form that a streptococcus infection can take, most commonly between 2 and 8 years of age. In the olden days, before it was known to be a form of streptococcus infection, scarlet fever was dreaded because cases developed far away in time and distance from other cases. Thinking that one case must come from another, people would blame the contagion on a toy that had been played with by another scarlet-fever patient a year before. Now we understand that a child who develops scarlet fever probably picked up a germ from someone who just had a sore throat or was carrying the streptococcus without feeling its effect at all.

Scarlet fever should be treated promptly and carefully with one of the antibiotic drugs that shorten the disease and greatly lessen the chances of complications. The drug should be given in a form which continues the treatment for 10 days. The common complications are ear infections, swollen glands in the neck, nephritis (which produces blood in the urine), rheumatic fever. They may begin any time in the disease, but most commonly 10 to 15 days after the fever has come down, when the child seems to be completely recovered. That is why a scarlet fever case is watched for a full 3 weeks. Report promptly any new symptoms.

Though scarlet fever may spread easily in an institution, it is not very contagious in ordinary day schools. You should not be alarmed if you receive a notice from your child's school that he has been exposed. His chances of catching it are small. (Consult your doctor about the need for throat culture or treatment.) When it does develop, it is usually within a week after exposure. Quarantine regulations vary a great deal in different localities.

685. Diphtheria. Diphtheria is a serious but completely unnecessary disease. If your child is given 3 injections in infancy and booster shots at 1 year and then every 4 years, there's practically no chance of his catching it. It begins with feeling sick, sore throat and fever. Dirty-white patches develop on the tonsils and may spread to the rest of the throat. Occasionally it begins in the larynx, with hoarseness and barking cough; the breathing becomes tight and difficult. In any case, you should have a doctor promptly when your child has sore throat and fever, or when he has any croupy symptoms. The treatment of any case of suspected diphtheria is the immediate use of serum along with other drugs. The disease develops within a week after exposure.

686. Infantile paralysis (poliomyelitis). This disease has been almost eliminated wherever polio vaccine has been systematically used. Every child should be protected in early infancy against the three types of polio, with the Sabin oral vaccine

The disease begins, like so many other infections, with a general sick feeling (malaise), fever and headache. There may be vomiting, constipation or a little diarrhea. Most cases do not go on to paralysis, and a fair number of those that do recover completely. If there is any paralysis remaining after the acute stage of the infection is over, it is vitally important that the child continue to have regular, expert medical attention. The National Foundation stands ready to help families obtain this care.

If there are cases in your community, it is sensible to keep your child away from crowds, especially in closed places like stores and movies, and away from swimming places that many people use. On the other hand, it's out of proportion, from what we know at present, to keep him from seeing his regular friends. If you were going to be that careful with him the rest of his life, you wouldn't ever let him cross a street. Doctors suspect that chilling and exhaustion make a person more susceptible to the disease, but it's sensible to avoid these at any time.

QUARANTINE

687. Quarantine or isolation for contagious diseases. On general principles, it's a good idea to keep a child with a contagious disease away from all other members of the household except the one person who is taking care of him. This is, first of all, to prevent others—either adults or children—who have not had the disease from catching it unnecessarily. If your other children were exposed before you knew what the disease was, they will most likely catch it anyway, but it is just as well for them not to be continually overexposed. Another reason is so that they will not carry the germs to others outside the home. To be sure, the risk of a healthy person's carrying the germs to other outsiders is slight in measles, chicken pox and whooping cough, though it occasionally occurs if less than half an hour elapses. In the case of scarlet fever, it is more important for only one adult to be in the child's room because the streptococcus that causes it can be carried in the throat for long periods. The fewer people who pick it up from the child, the less chance of its being spread around the community. Another reason for keeping the sick child isolated is so that he will not be picking up new germs from others to complicate his illness.

How do you maintain a good quarantine? You keep the child in one room and keep everyone else out except the one grown-up who is taking care of him. She slips on a smock that is kept hanging in the room just for this purpose. This keeps her regular clothes from collecting germs. She takes it off every time she leaves the room. She washes her hands every time she leaves the room. All the drinking and eating utensils that leave the room should be carried to the kitchen in a dishpan and boiled in it before being handled or washed or mixed with the utensils for the rest of the family.

In the case of scarlet fever, diphtheria and some other serious diseases, further precautions are required by some health departments.

In most places, grown-ups in the family—except those who are schoolteachers or food handlers—are not restricted about leaving the home or going to business in **any** of the diseases. You have to use your own good sense, though, about visiting families who have susceptible children. The chances of your carrying the germs to other children are practically zero as long as you keep away from them. Just the same, you're not going to be very welcome if the mother is fussy, especially if the disease is one that is dreaded, such as mumps for a man, whooping cough for a baby, scarlet fever. She'll blame you if anyone in her family catches that disease any time in the next year. On the other hand, don't hesitate to go if the disease is one of the less feared ones, like measles, chicken pox and German measles, and if you have had the disease, and if a friend who doesn't worry and whose children are out of the way asks you over for the evening.

Other children in the home who have had the disease in question are practically always allowed to go to school during the quarantine period if it is one of the less serious diseases. The rules about brothers and sisters may be stricter for such diseases as scarlet fever, diphtheria, meningitis, poliomyelitis, etc. The rules about other children in the family who **haven't** yet had the disease vary in different localities and in different schools. For the sake of other small children and your own conscience, keep your child away from the neighbor's small children at the time when he is due to come down with a disease.

TUBERCULOSIS

688. Tuberculosis is different in infants, children and adults. Most people think of tuberculosis as it occurs typically in adults. A "spot," or cavity, develops in the lung, and produces such symptoms as fatigue, loss of appetite, loss of weight, fever, cough, sputum.

Tuberculosis in childhood usually takes other forms. In the first 2 years of life, resistance is not so good as in later years, and there is more chance of the infection's spreading to other parts of the body. That is why you never take the slightest chance of exposing a baby to a known case of tuberculosis unless the doctor and the X ray guarantee that the person has been completely cured. It's a reason also why anyone in a household who has a chronic cough should be examined and

X-rayed, and why it's wise to have a new maid or nurse examined and X-rayed.

In later childhood, tuberculous infection is fairly common and less likely to cause serious trouble. This is not a reason to treat it lightly or take any chances. Tuberculin tests show that in some cities as many as 50% of all children have had a slight infection with tuberculosis by the time they are 10 years old. Most of these cases have been so mild that no one suspected that anything was wrong at the time. An X ray shows at most a little scar where the infection healed in the lung or in the lymph glands at the roots of the lungs.

Sometimes, however, a childhood type of tuberculosis is active enough to cause symptoms, such as fever, poor appetite, poor color, irritability, fatigue and perhaps a cough. (There isn't much sputum, and what there is, is swallowed, of course.) The infection may be in other parts of the body, such as the bones or the neck glands, but most commonly it's in the lungs and in the lymph glands at the roots of the lungs. In most of these active cases, healing gradually takes place over a period of 1 to 2 years if the child is well cared for, and only a scar is left. With proper treatment with special drugs, healing is fostered and a serious spread of infection is prevented.

As the child reaches adolescence, he becomes more liable to develop the serious, adult type of tuberculosis. This should be kept in mind whenever an adolescent or young adult is run-down, tired, loses appetite or weight, whether or not there is any cough.

689. The tuberculin test. A few weeks after tubercle bacilli have gotten into a person's body, he becomes "sensitized" to them. After that, if the doctor injects tuberculin (material from dead tuberculosis germs) into his skin, a red spot develops. This is a positive tuberculin test. (Nowadays the "tine test" is used for routine office tests. The tines are several tiny sharp plastic points coated with tuberculin which protrude from a plastic base and which are pressed briefly into the skin; so the more painful hypodermic needle doesn't have to be used.) The red spot shows that the body has already had experience with tuberculosis germs and reacts against them. If no red spot develops, it shows that the body has not contained the germs before. Generally speaking, if a person has ever had a tuberculous infection, he will react with a positive test the rest of his life, even though the infection was healed long ago.

Doctors often give tuberculin tests in routine examinations —at 1, 2, 3, 4 years of age, and perhaps every other year after that. The test is also made when a child isn't doing well, or has a chronic cough, or when tuberculosis is discovered in another member of the family.

If your child is ever found to have a positive tuberculin test (which is not impossible when you consider how many children are positive), you have to keep a sense of balance. There's no need to be alarmed, since a great majority of the cases discovered throughout middle childhood have either healed already or will heal gradually with care. On the other hand, you don't want to neglect any precautions.

The first step is the doctor's investigation of the child's case. X ray of the lungs is essential in all cases to see if there are any signs of active infection or of healed scars. Sometimes the doctor orders other tests: X rays of other parts of the body, washing out of the stomach to see if there are tubercle bacilli in sputum the child has swallowed, taking of temperatures for a period. If the doctor is convinced that the infection is already well healed, he may recommend that the child lead an entirely normal life. However, he will want to take further X rays at regular intervals to be sure. He advises also taking precautions to avoid measles and whooping cough for several years if possible, since these diseases sometimes stir up recently healed tuberculosis.

Modern drug therapy is generally effective and free from serious side effects. It is usually continued for a year or more.

Aside from the child himself, the doctor checks every other member of the household (and any other adult that the child regularly comes in contact with) to discover, if possible, where the tuberculosis germs came from, and to find out if other children in the household have been infected, too. Other children should all have tuberculin tests. Any child with a positive test should be examined and have his lungs X-rayed. It doesn't matter how healthy the other members of the household feel or how unnecessary they think all the fuss is. Many times no disease is found in any adult in the household, and it has to be assumed that the child picked up the germs from some source outside the home. On the other hand, an active case of tuberculosis is sometimes found in the least suspected adult in the house. It's a lucky thing for him to have his disease discovered at an early stage, and it's lucky for the rest of the family to have the danger removed. No person with active tuberculosis should stay in a house with children; he should go promptly to a sanitarium, where he has the greatest chance of being cured and the least chance of infecting others.

RHEUMATIC FEVER

690. It takes many forms. Rheumatic fever is a disease that affects the joints, the heart and other parts of the body. Doctors believe that it is a reaction in some part of the body (a joint or the heart, for instance) to a streptococcus infection in the throat. When not treated promptly and adequately, an attack is apt to last for weeks or months. Furthermore, it is a disease that has a tendency to recur again and again throughout childhood, whenever the child has another streptococcal throat infection.

Sometimes it takes a very acute form with high fever. In other cases, it smolders along for weeks with only a little fever. When there is severe arthritis, it travels around from joint to joint, causing them to become swollen, red and exquisitely tender. In other cases, the arthritis may be mild—just an aching off and on in one joint or another. If the heart is being affected severely, the child is visibly prostrated, pale and breathless. In another case, it is discovered that the heart has been damaged by some past attack that was so mild it was not noticed at the time.

In other words, rheumatic fever is an exceedingly variable disease. Naturally, you consult your doctor if your child develops any of the symptoms in a severe form. But it's just as important to have a child examined who has vague symptoms, like paleness, tiredness, slight fever, mild joint pains.

Nowadays we have several drugs that are effective in clearing up streptococcal infection in the throat—the root of the disease—and in hastening the end of the rheumatic inflammation in the joints or the heart. As a result, heart valves are no longer so likely to be damaged in the first attack. More important still, the child who has had one attack of rheumatic fever can usually be kept from having further attacks—and further heart damage. He must continue indefinitely, under the doctor's continuing supervision, to take medication by mouth or by injection (to prevent new streptococcal infections) **absolutely regularly.**

691. Joint and "growing pains." In the olden days, it was thought natural for children to complain of "growing pains" in their legs and arms, and nobody worried about them. Ever since it was discovered that rheumatic fever pains could be very mild, doctors have had to consider them as a possibility in every case of pains in the limbs. But parents sometimes assume that rheumatic fever is the only cause for all of them, and worry unnecessarily.

There are, for instance, leg pains caused by flat feet and weak ankles, which occur most commonly toward the end of the day when the child is tired. Then there is the child between the ages of 2 and 5 who wakes up crying, complaining of pain around his knee or his calf. It happens only during the evening, but may recur each night for weeks on end. On investigation, it usually proves not to be due to rheumatic fever. It is often believed to be caused by cramps in the calf muscles.

There are many other causes for pains in the arms and legs, and you can see that you need a doctor to examine, test and decide in every case.

692. Heart murmurs. The words "heart murmur" have an alarming sound to parents. It's important to realize that a great majority of heart murmurs don't mean anything serious. Generally speaking, there are three kinds—acquired, congenital and functional (or "innocent").

Most acquired murmurs in childhood come from rheumatic fever, which inflames the valves and may leave scars on them afterward. This causes them either to "leak" or to obstruct the proper flow of blood. When a doctor hears a murmur in a child's heart that wasn't there before, it may mean, on the one hand, that active rheumatic inflammation is going on. In this case, there are other signs of infection, such as fever, rapid pulse, elevated blood count and sedimentation rate. The doctor treats such a child with drugs until all signs of inflammation go away—even if it takes months. On the other hand, if there have been no signs of active infection for some time, the murmur may be due to old scars left over from a previous attack.

In former years, the child with an old murmur was sometimes treated as a semi-invalid for years, forbidden to play active games or sports, even though there were no signs of active infection. A doctor's tendency nowadays is to let the child who is **completely** over the stage of active inflammation go back gradually to as normal a life as possible (including the games and sports that he can do easily), if the healed scars do not noticeably interfere with the efficient working of the heart. There are two reasons for this. The muscles of the heart, as long as they are not inflamed, are strengthened by ordinary activity. Even more important is keeping the child's spirit healthy—preventing him from feeling sorry for himself, from feeling that he is a hopeless case, that he's different from everyone else. Such a child should be receiving **absolutely regular medication**, however, to prevent further streptococcus infection.

A murmur caused by **congenital heart disease** is usually discovered at birth or within a few months afterward (occasionally not till several years later). Such a murmur is usually not caused by inflammation but means that the heart was improperly formed in the first place. The important thing is not so much the murmur itself but whether the malformation interferes with the efficiency of the heart. If it does, the baby may have blue spells, or breathe too hard, or grow too slowly.

A baby or child with a congenital heart murmur needs a careful investigation by specialists. Some cases that are serious can be cured by operation.

If a child with a congenital murmur can exercise without turning blue and without becoming abnormally out of breath, and grows at the normal rate, it is important for his emotional development that he not be thought of or treated as an invalid but that he be allowed to lead a normal life. He does need to avoid unnecessary infections and to be well cared for during illnesses, but so do all children.

The term **functional** or **innocent murmur** is just a clumsy way of saying that a child has a murmur that doesn't come from a congenital malformation or from rheumatic fever. These innocent murmurs are very common in the early years of childhood. They tend to fade out as the child reaches adolescence. Your doctor tells you about an innocent murmur in your child so that if it is discovered later in childhood by a new doctor, you can explain that it has been there all along.

693. Chorea. Chorea, or Saint Vitus's dance, is a nervous disease in which there are twitching or writhing movements of different parts of the body, which may last for months. They may be very obvious or so slight as to be hardly noticeable. Twitches of the muscles of the face produce irregular grimacing. A shoulder may shrug, first in one direction and then in another. Twitchings of the trunk muscles make the body lurch slightly. The hands and fingers may twitch or writhe. The child's handwriting may become poor, and he may drop things. The movements come **irregularly,** first in one muscle, then in another. No two movements are exactly the same.

Some children who have attacks of chorea also have definite attacks of rheumatic fever in the sense of heart disease and arthritis. This has made many doctors assume that chorea is just another form of rheumatic fever. But other children have one or more attacks of chorea without ever having another symptom of rheumatic fever. Therefore some doctors believe that these are two separate kinds of chorea—one rheumatic and the other not.

Most attacks of chorea occur between the age of 7 years and the beginning of adolescence. Other nervous traits, such as **tics** and **general restlessness,** are common in this age period, too, and are often confused with chorea. A child with a tic nervously and repeatedly makes exactly the same motion, such as eye-blinking, throat-clearing, shoulder-shrugging (Section 554), whereas the movements of chorea are skipping around and always different. General restlessness is something else again. By that I mean the activity of a child who is constantly squirming in his chair, shuffling his feet around, fiddling with his hands, etc.

During an attack of chorea, a child is apt to be unstable. He cries easily, laughs easily, flies off the handle on slight provocation. You have to make allowances for this in handling him at home because he can't help it. A child with chorea should be under a doctor's care. The chorea will surely go away in time, even if there are several attacks. But the child must be examined regularly to make sure that no other signs of rheumatic fever develop. If they do, they should be carefully treated.

URINARY DISTURBANCES

694. Late bed wetting (enuresis). There are a number of different causes. A very few cases are due to physical disease. In these there are usually symptoms, such as inability to control the urine in the daytime, that make the doctor suspicious. The great majority of cases are due to tensions of a wide variety of sorts in a child's feelings.

There are situations that upset a young child in such a way that unconsciously he wants to retreat into babyhood again. A 3-year-old who has been dry for 6 months may begin to wet again when he moves to a new house for the summer. Even though he is happy in his new surroundings, he evidently feels homesick underneath. When the children of London were removed to the country at the beginning of World War II, away from family, friends and familiar surroundings, bed wetting was common, even in adolescent children. It is frequent in some orphanages. Children are also apt to wet after an exciting experience, like a birthday party or an afternoon at the circus.

The commonest occasion in early childhood is the arrival of a new baby in the home.

It's important to realize that in these situations children are not wetting deliberately. After all, they are sound asleep. It is their unconscious feelings that take over at night and that express themselves in dreams. Bed wetting often occurs during dreams in which the child is in a distressing situation and feels powerless to do anything. The child who wets when he is homesick or upset by the new baby may be dreaming that he is a lost baby himself, looking for the mother who will care for all his bodily needs without complaint, the way she used to.

In the case of the homesick small child, the parent's job is to be around him a little more for a few days to ease his loneliness and help him find the joys of the new place. If there is a new baby, the job is to reassure the child that he doesn't have to feel displaced (Sections 490–496). There is no need to scold or shame him for wetting; he usually feels bad about it. It helps him if you express confidence that he will soon be staying dry again.

What about the child of 3 or 4 or 5 who has never become dry in the first place? (A majority of children become dry at night somewhere between 2 and 3 years of age.) In some of these cases, there has been tension over daytime toilet training. The child resisted for a long while, and the mother became more impatient. He eventually accepted daytime training, but it looks as if his resistance is continuing in his unconscious mind at night, along with a guilty feeling that he is still a naughty baby. It's wise to try to eliminate any conflict about daytime training if it still exists, and any shaming about bed wetting. In most cases, it is advisable to stop picking the child up in the evening because he is apt to interpret this as a reminder that he's only a baby. What he needs is the confidence of his parents and himself that he's growing up and that someday he will be able to stay dry all by himself.

Excitement of various kinds can play a part. A girl's romantic possessiveness toward her father may be raised to a high pitch if he responds too enthusiastically. A boy may become wildly excited every evening by roughhousing with his father (which arouses a combination of fear and pleasure) or by roughhousing with his sister (which overstimulates his aggressiveness and his unconscious sexuality).

695. A common type in boys. Some psychiatrists who have studied bed wetting in children believe that one of the commonest types in boys (and 80% of enuretics are boys) is the following: The boy is somewhat insecure and too easily convinced that he's inadequate. He may be afraid to compete with other boys or to stand up to them. He's inclined to feel dominated by his mother. She is devoted to him, but for his particular personality she is at times too impatient, too interfering. He is too strictly brought up to fight back openly. He resists passively by procrastinating or by just being irritating. Then his mother can't help feeling more dissatisfied with him. Often in these cases the father is not giving the boy enough moral support. See Sections 467 and 483.

The measures that parents sometimes use for enuretics of this type may work in the wrong direction. To pull a groggy child out of bed (enuretics seem to be particularly heavy sleepers) and push him into the bathroom each night only convinces him further that he is a baby. Restricting a child's fluids after 5 o'clock usually makes him imagine he is thirsty right away (it would be the same with you and me) and almost guarantees a running argument between him and his mother all evening, which isn't good for either of them. Making a boy wash and hang out his sheets fills him with dread that other boys will learn of his disgrace. It isn't lack of shame that causes his enuresis. Any boy over 5 would give a million dollars to overcome the problem. He wants to cooperate, but he has little control over the unconscious feelings that produce the wetting in his sleep.

What the enuretic boy needs is more confidence that he is a competent person, and this can be gained only gradually, with help. The most direct way is through a child guidance clinic or a child psychiatrist, especially if the child has a variety of troubles. But if this is not possible, there are a number of things the parents can do, depending on circumstances. Their general attitude should be one of encouragement. They can explain that they have learned that quite a few boys have this problem but that practically all of them overcome it in time. They can express their confidence that he will, too.

I think it is preferable in most cases to give up such methods as getting the boy up at night and restricting fluids.

Pasting gold stars on a chart is occasionally helpful for a 5-, 6- or 7-year-old but usually not for an older boy. A reward that has great appeal—skates, bicycle, sports equipment—may be worth a trial. Even better, I think, though it may not sound sensible to you, is to give the boy, right away, a possession that he has yearned for but that his parents have been withholding until he becomes dry. The idea is to make him begin to feel equal with other boys as soon as possible.

If the father has been too self-effacing at home, it helps a lot for him to take a more active part in managing the child and, if possible, to find some hobby that he can enjoy with the boy occasionally. If his mother has been pushing and prodding him in other areas, such as homework, or getting dressed in the morning (Section 476), she can try to ease up. A conference with the teacher should produce a useful comparing of notes.

696. Enuresis in girls. The commonest picture in enuresis in girls is quite different from that in most boys. The girl is more apt to be a spunky sort, perhaps a tomboy who is competing with a brother and also competing with her mother. (She may feel, for instance, that she can take care of her father and keep him company better than her mother can.) In such cases, the job is to help her feel more comfortable about being a girl, to lessen the causes of rivalry with her brother, for her parents to show her they love her most as a girl, for her father to demonstrate that he loves her as a daughter but that he shares his concerns and interests primarily with his wife. Child guidance or psychiatric help is most valuable in these cases, too, not just to get the girl over her enuresis but to get her ready to enjoy her life as a woman.

697. Daytime wetting. Late daytime wetting (say after the age of 3) is, once in a great while, due to physical disease.

In such a case, the child usually just dribbles a small amount at frequent intervals. He needs a thorough check-up by the doctor. The urine should be examined in all cases of late wetting.

In most cases of daytime wetting there is bed wetting, too, and much that was said in Sections 694–695 about the importance of various kinds of nervousness could be repeated here.

But there are two factors that ought to be emphasized. Most of the children who go on wetting in the daytime have a tendency to balk and to procrastinate. Watching such a child, you can see that one half of him knows perfectly well that his bladder is uncomfortable—he's prancing around restlessly and crossing his legs. But the other half of him is absorbed in play and refuses to do anything about it. There's nothing to be concerned about if a slight "accident" occurs once in a while with a small child when he's deeply absorbed. But if he's stalling and procrastinating all the time, about everything, it's usually a sign that he's being pushed and bossed too much. It's become such a habit to resist that he does it not just when his parents but when his own insides tell him there is something he ought to be doing. This is often called laziness, but actually it requires a lot of effort. It's like a car being driven with the brakes on.

A few children, even happy, well-adjusted ones, have trouble controlling the bladder when they are excited or frightened or laugh suddenly. At these times, they find themselves wetting without any warning. This is not a disease, and it's not an entirely strange thing. Many animals automatically empty the bladder when they are alarmed. The child needs only to be reassured that he has done nothing to be ashamed of.

698. Frequent urinating. Frequent urinating has several possible causes. When it develops in a child who was not frequent before, it may mean some disease, such as an infection of the urinary system or diabetes. The child and a urine specimen should be examined promptly by the doctor.

A few individuals, even calm ones, seem to have bladders that never hold as much as the average, and this may be the way they were made. But most of the children (and adults, too) who regularly have to urinate frequently are somewhat high-strung or worried. In one case it's due to a temporary strain; in another it's a chronic tendency. Even the healthy, normal athlete is apt to have to go to the toilet every 15 minutes just before a race. The parents' job, then, is to find out what, if anything, is making the child tense. In one case it's the handling at home, in another it's his relations with other children, in another still it's school. Most often it's a combination of these. A common story involves the timid child and the teacher who seems severe. To begin with, the child's apprehensiveness keeps his bladder from relaxing sufficiently to hold much urine. Then he worries about asking permission to be excused. If the teacher makes a fuss about his leaving the room, it's worse still. It's wise to get a note from the doctor, not simply requesting that the child be excused, but explaining the child's nature and why his bladder works that way. If the teacher is approachable and the parent is tactful, a personal visit will help, too.

699. Difficult urination. Once in a great while a baby, usually a boy, is born with such a small urinary passage or opening that he has to push hard to pass his urine, or the urine comes only in a small stream or dribble. The urinary passage needs to be enlarged promptly by a doctor. It is harmful to the inner passages and the kidneys to have the urine obstructed.

Occasionally in hot weather, when a child is perspiring a great deal and not drinking enough, he may pass his urine infrequently, perhaps not for 12 hours or more. What does come is scanty and dark and it may burn. The same thing may happen during a fever. A child in hot weather or when feverish needs plenty of chances and occasional reminders to drink between meals, especially when he is too small to tell what he wants.

A fairly frequent cause of painful urination in girls is an infection of the vagina that inflames the lower urinary passage, too. This may make her feel as if she has to urinate frequently, though she may be unable or too scared to do anything, or pass only a few drops. The doctor should be consulted and a urine specimen examined. Until he can be reached, she can be relieved by sitting several times a day in a shallow warm bath to which has been added a cup of bicarbonate of soda. After gently blotting dry the urinary region, a thick dab of petroleum jelly, boric-acid ointment, zinc ointment or plain cold cream can be applied to it to soothe and protect it.

700. Sore on the end of the penis. Sometimes a small raw area appears around the opening, or "meatus," of the penis. There may be enough swelling of the tissues here to close up the meatus and make it difficult for the boy to pass his urine. This little sore is a localized diaper rash, caused by ammonia (which can be smelled in the bed in the morning). The ammonia is not passed in the urine but is manufactured from urine by bacteria in the diaper, night clothes and bedclothes. This ammonia sore occurs most often when the baby is over a year old and the mother has stopped using the diaper service. The bacteria have accumulated in the pajamas, sheets and pads, and they set to work making ammonia just as soon as the child wets himself in the evening. The important thing in treatment is to boil the diapers, pajamas, sheets and pads every day or treat them with a diaper antiseptic (Section 319) as long as any sore exists. Meanwhile, the sore can be soothed and protected by frequent application of zinc ointment or other ointment, especially before going to bed. If the child is in pain from being unable to urinate for many hours, he can be sat in a warm bath for half an hour. If this doesn't make him urinate, the doctor should be called.

701. Infections of the urinary tract (pyuria, pyelitis, pyelonephritis, cystitis). Infections in the kidneys or the bladder may cause a stormy illness with a high, irregular fever. On the other hand, infection is sometimes discovered by accident in a routine urine examination in a child who hasn't felt sick at all. An older child may complain of frequent, burning urination, but most often there are no signs pointing to the urinary tract. These infections are commoner in girls, and in the first 2 years of life. Prompt medical treatment is necessary, and usually is successful.

A urine specimen should be examined any time a child has a fever without a known cause. It should also be examined any time a fever lasts more than a few days, even if there is a cold or sore throat to explain the temperature, since an infection elsewhere in the body may spread to the urinary system and keep the fever going.

If there is a lot of pus, the urine may be hazy or cloudy, but a little may not show to the naked eye. On the other hand, a normal child's urine may be cloudy, especially when it cools, due to ordinary minerals in it. So you can't tell definitely from looking at the urine whether it is infected or not.

If a urinary infection does not clear up satisfactorily, or if the child ever has a second urinary infection, his whole urinary system should be investigated thoroughly with special examinations. Urinary infections are more common in children who have abnormally formed urinary passages. If there is anything pointing to such an abnormality, it should be corrected before permanent harm is done to the kidneys. For this reason it is wise, after a child has had a urinary infection, to check his urine again 1 and 2 months later to make sure the infection has not come back, even though he appears well. Infections are usually treated thoroughly for a month or more. Then there are several follow-ups, over a period of time, to see whether pus or bacteria have reappeared in the urine.

702. Pus in a girl's urine may not mean urinary infection. There is always the possibility that pus in a girl's urine is coming from a vaginal infection, even one so mild that there is no visible inflammation or discharge. For this reason, it should never be assumed, without further investigation, that pus in an ordinary specimen means an infection of her urinary system. The first step is to secure a "clean" urine specimen. That means to separate the labia, sponge the genital region briefly and gently with a piece of wet absorbent cotton, and blot dry with a soft towel or a piece of dry absorbent cotton, before letting her pass urine for the specimen. If the clean specimen also shows pus, then the doctor, to be absolutely sure, can pass a catheter (a small rubber tube) into her bladder to obtain a specimen that has not touched her skin outside at all.

VAGINAL DISCHARGE

703. Treat it considerately. It is fairly common for young girls to develop slight vaginal discharges. A majority of these are caused by unimportant germs and clear up in a short time. A thick, profuse discharge that is irritating may be caused by a more serious infection and needs prompt medical treatment. A mild one that persists for days should be examined, too. A discharge that is partly pus and partly blood is sometimes caused by a small girl's having pushed some object into her vagina, which remains there, causing irritation and infection. If this is found to be the case, it is natural and sensible for her mother to ask her to please not do this again; but it's better not to make the girl feel really guilty or to imply that she has hurt herself seriously, or might have. The exploring and experimenting she has done is not too different from what most children do at this age. As explained in Section 522, little girls may be upset about genital differences and sometimes conclude that the reason they are not like boys is because they have injured themselves in handling their genitals. Parental accusations, either about masturbation or about genital injury, may reinforce these fears.

If there is delay in reaching the doctor, the burning sensation from a slight discharge can often be relieved without fuss by sitting the child twice a day in a shallow bath to which half a cup of bicarbonate of soda has been added.

STOMACHACHES AND UPSETS

Diarrhea is also discussed in Sections 315–317, vomiting in Sections 305, 306 and 633.

704. Call the doctor. Don't give cathartics. You certainly should get in touch with the doctor for any stomachache that lasts as long as 1 hour, whether it is severe or not. There are dozens of causes. A few of them are serious; most are not. A doctor is trained to distinguish between them and prescribe the right treatment. People are apt to jump to the conclusion that a stomachache is due either to something that has been eaten or to appendicitis. Actually, neither of these is a common cause. Children can usually eat strange foods or an unusual amount of a regular food without any indigestion.

It is wrong to give a cathartic before the doctor has seen the child because there are some stomachaches for which a cathartic is dangerous. Before you call the doctor, take the child's temperature so that you can tell him what it is. The treatment, until you reach him, should consist of putting the child to bed and giving him nothing to eat. If he's thirsty, give him small sips of water.

705. Common causes of stomachache. In the early weeks of life, stomachache is common in indigestion and colic. These are discussed in Sections 292, 293 and 307.

There is an uncommon condition called **intussusception** in which the intestine "telescopes" into itself and becomes obstructed. The two most prominent symptoms are vomiting and intermittent abdominal cramps in a baby who has seemed otherwise healthy. In one case the vomiting is more prominent, in another the pain. The vomiting is more copious and repetitious than the usual "spitting" of a baby. The cramps are sudden and usually severe. They come a number of minutes apart, and between them the baby may be fairly comfortable. Vomiting is apt to occur and be repeated. After a number of hours (during which there may be normal or loose movements), a movement is passed containing mucus and blood—a "currant jelly" or "prune juice" stool. This condition occurs most commonly between the ages of 4 months and 2 years, though it may occur outside this age period. Though uncommon, it requires emergency medical treatment, without delay, and that is why it is mentioned here.

Also rare but serious are other types of **intestinal obstructions.** A part of the intestine gets kinked and stuck in a pocket in the abdomen—most frequently in an inguinal hernia (Section 709). There is usually vomiting and sharp cramps.

After the age of a year, one of the commonest causes of stomachache is the onset of a simple **cold** or **sore throat** or **grippe,** especially when there is fever. It is just a sign that the infection is disturbing the intestines as well as other parts of the body. In the same way, almost any infection may cause vomiting and constipation, especially in the beginning. A small child is apt to complain that his tummy hurts when he really means that he feels nauseated. He often vomits soon after this complaint.

There are many different kinds of **stomach** and **intestinal infections** that cause stomachache, sometimes with vomiting, sometimes with diarrhea, sometimes with both. These are often loosely called "intestinal flu" or "intestinal grippe," or "a virus," meaning a contagious disease caused by an unknown germ. These infections often pass through several members of a family, one after the other. Some epidemics of "intestinal flu" turn out to be dysentery or paratyphoid infections. There may or may not be fever with any of them.

"**Food poisoning**" is caused by eating food that is heavily contaminated with poisonous bacteria. The food may or may not taste queer. Food poisoning seldom occurs from food that has been thoroughly and recently cooked, because the cooking kills these germs. It's caused most often by pastries filled with custard or whipped cream, and poultry stuffing. Germs multiply readily in these substances if they remain out of the refrigerator for many hours. Another cause is improperly home-canned foods.

The symptoms of food poisoning are usually vomiting, diarrhea and stomachache. Sometimes there are chills and sometimes fever. Everyone who eats the contaminated food is apt to be affected by it to some degree at about the same time, in contrast to an "intestinal flu," which usually spreads through a family over a number of days.

Children with **feeding problems** often have stomachaches when they sit down to a meal or after they have eaten a little. The parents are apt to think the child has made up the stomachache as an excuse not to eat. I think that it's more likely that his poor stomach is all tightened up by his tense feeling at mealtimes, and that the stomachache is real. The treatment here is for the parents to handle mealtimes in such a way that the child enjoys his food. See Sections 601–608.

Children who have never been feeding problems but who have other **worries** can have stomachaches, too, especially around mealtime. Think of the child who is nervous about starting school in the fall and has a stomachache instead of an appetite for breakfast, or the child who feels guilty about something that hasn't been found out yet. All kinds of emotions, from fears to pleasant excitement, can affect the stomach and intestines. They can cause not only pains and lack of appetite, but vomiting and diarrhea and constipation. Pain in such cases tends to be in the center of the abdomen.

A few children who have **worms** seem to have stomachaches from them, but most aren't affected that way.

There are other infrequent causes of stomachache, too: chronic indigestion with gas, intestinal allergies, inflamed lymph glands in the abdomen, rheumatic fever, kidney disturbances and so on. As you can well see, a child who has pains—whether they are acute and severe, or mild and chronic—needs a thorough check-up by the doctor.

706. Appendicitis. Let me at the start contradict some common notions about appendicitis. There isn't necessarily any fever. The pain isn't necessarily severe. The pain doesn't usually settle in the lower right side of the abdomen until the attack has been going on for some time. Vomiting doesn't always occur. A blood count doesn't prove that a stomachache is or isn't due to appendicitis.

The appendix is a little offshoot from the large intestine, about the size of a short earthworm. It usually lies in the central part of the right lower quarter of the abdomen. But it can be lower down, or over toward the middle of the abdomen, or as far up as the ribs. When it becomes inflamed, it's a gradual process, like the formation of a boil. That's why a sudden severe pain in the abdomen that lasts a few minutes and then goes away for good isn't appendicitis. The worst danger is that the inflamed appendix will burst, very much as a boil bursts, and spread the infection all through the abdomen. This is called peritonitis. An appendicitis that is developing very rapidly can reach the point of bursting in less than 24 hours. That's why any stomachache that persists for as long as 1 hour should be seen by a doctor, even though 9 out of 10 cases prove to be something else.

In the most typical cases, there is pain around the navel for several hours. Only later does it shift to the lower right side. There is apt to be vomiting once or twice, but it doesn't always occur. The appetite is usually diminished, but not always. The bowels may be normal or constipated, rarely loose. After it's gone on a few hours, the temperature is apt to be elevated to 100° or 101°, more or less, but it's possible to have real appendicitis without any fever at all. The person may feel more pain when he pulls his right knee up, or when he stretches it way back, or when he walks around. You can see that the symptoms of appendicitis vary a lot in different cases and that you need a doctor to make the diagnosis. The doctor is guided most by whether he finds a tender area in the right side, as he feels deeply but gently into every part of the abdomen. You will notice that he doesn't ask whether it hurts every time he pokes, but on the contrary tries to distract the child from what he is doing. This is because many children with a pain in the stomach, especially young ones, are delighted to say, "Yes, that hurts," every time they are asked. When the doctor finds a tender spot in the right side of the abdomen, he is suspicious of appendicitis, but he sometimes likes to have a blood count to help him decide. A raised blood count just says there is infection somewhere. It doesn't say where.

It's often impossible for the most expert of doctors to be absolutely sure whether or not a child has appendicitis. When there is much suspicion he advises operation, and for a very good reason. If it is appendicitis, it is dangerous to delay.

If it is not appendicitis, it is unlikely that any harm will be done by prompt operation.

707. Chronic and intermittent diarrheas. There are several different digestive diseases that cause chronic diarrheas in infants and young children. They were once all considered the same condition. They are still not completely understood.

Cystic fibrosis. The two commonest symptoms of this disease are foul diarrhea and cough, but there is great variation in the symptoms. There may be frequent bowel movements which look normal in early infancy but become loose and foul smelling after solid foods are introduced. The baby is apt to have had a low birth weight and to gain slowly but his appetite is good. He may eventually become severely malnourished. Sooner or later he develops a persistent bronchitis. In the mildest cases there is no digestive trouble but the persistent bronchitis develops later in childhood.

This disease involves several types of glands of the body—the glands of the pancreas, which make digestive juices, the mucous glands of the bronchial tubes and the sweat glands. (The sweat has an excessive salt content and the test for this is most useful in diagnosis.) In its severe form, without treatment, this disease is very dangerous in infancy and early childhood. In later childhood the danger lessens. The digestive symptoms are treated with a high-protein diet, extra vitamin A. Vaporized-mist therapy and antibiotics are vital for the bronchitis.

Celiac disease is characterized by frequent, loose, foul bowel movements, which may appear intermittently toward the end of the first year but become chronic in the second year. There may be intermittent constipation. The appetite worsens and the nutrition suffers. The intestines are unable to handle fats and this disability is exaggerated when the child eats gluten, the protein in wheat, rye and barley.

A first step in treatment may consist simply in eliminating all gluten from the diet (any foods containing wheat, rye or barley). If this does not bring about marked improvement, the child may be tried on a diet containing at first only skimmed or "protein" milk, cottage cheese and ripe banana. When the movements and appetite are much improved, other foods are added cautiously, one by one, over a period of months: lean meats, fruit juices and fruits, nonstarchy vegetables. A good dose of a multivitamin preparation is important from the start. The condition lasts a long time and has many ups and downs even when treatment is going well.

Other malabsorption conditions have been recognized in recent years, the best known being inability to digest certain ordinary sugars. These cause bowel movements that are loose but not evil smelling.

708. Worms are no disgrace, but need treatment. It horrifies a mother to find worms in her child's movement, but there is no reason to be distressed or to decide that the child has not been properly cared for.

Pinworms, or threadworms, are the commonest variety. They look like white threads, a third of an inch long. They live in the lower intestine, but come out between the buttocks at night to lay their eggs. They can be found there at night or in the bowel movement. They cause itching around the anus, which may disturb the child's sleep. In former days worms were thought to be the chief cause for children's grinding their teeth at night, but this is probably not so. Save a specimen of the worms to show the doctor. There is an efficient treatment for pinworms, which a doctor should supervise.

Roundworms look very much like earthworms. The first suspicion comes when one is discovered in the bowel movement. They usually don't cause symptoms unless the child has a great number of them. The doctor will prescribe treatment.

Hookworms are common in some parts of the southern United States. They may cause malnutrition and anemia. The disease is contracted by going barefoot in soil that is infested. A doctor can prescribe treatment.

HERNIAS, RUPTURES, HYDROCELE

709. Hernias, or ruptures. The commonest hernia of all, protruding navel, is taken up in Section 244.

The next commonest is what doctors call inguinal hernia. There is meant to be a small passage from inside the abdomen, down along the groin, into the scrotum (in the case of a boy), for the blood vessels and nerves that go to the testicles. This passageway has to pass through the layers of muscle that make up the wall of the abdomen. If these openings in the muscles are larger than average, a piece of intestine may be squeezed out of the abdomen and down the passageway when the child strains or cries. If the intestine goes only partway down, it makes a bulging in the groin. If it goes all the way down into the scrotum (the pouch for the testicles behind the penis), the scrotum looks very enlarged for the time being. Inguinal hernia does occur, though less commonly, in girls. It appears as a protrusion in the groin.

Rupture is a bad name for a condition like this, because it sounds as though something breaks when the intestine is pushed down during straining. This idea makes a mother worry unnecessarily about her baby's crying. Actually nothing breaks. The overlarge passageway is present at the time the baby is born; it is the way he is made.

In most hernias the intestine slips back up into the abdomen when the baby or child is lying down quietly. It may push down every time he stands up, or it may go down only once in a great while when he strains hard.

Occasionally an inguinal hernia becomes "strangulated." This means that the intestine has stuck in the passage and that the blood vessels have been kinked and shut off. It is a form of intestinal obstruction. This causes abdominal pain and vomiting. It calls for emergency surgical care.

Strangulation of an inguinal hernia occurs most often in the first 6 months of life. Usually it is a hernia that has not been noticed before. The mother changes the baby because he is crying so hard and notices the lump in his groin for the first time. (The groin is the groove between the abdomen and the thigh.) It is not wise to try to push the lump down with the fingers. However, while waiting for the doctor or while driving the baby to the hospital, you can elevate his hips on a pillow, give him a bottle to stop his crying, and apply an ice bag (or crushed ice in a sock) to the hernia. These procedures together may make the intestine slip back into the abdomen.

If you suspect a hernia in your child, you should, of course, report it to the doctor right away. Nowadays inguinal hernias are usually repaired promptly by surgery. It is not a serious operation, it is almost always successful, and the child is soon out of bed.

710. Hydrocele, or swelling around the testicle. Hydrocele is often confused with hernia or rupture because it also causes a swelling in the scrotum. Each testicle in the scrotum is surrounded by a delicate sac that contains a few drops of fluid. This helps to protect the testicle. Quite often in new-

EYE TROUBLES • 525

born babies there is an extra amount of fluid in the sac that surrounds the testicle, and this makes it appear to be several times its normal size. Sometimes this swelling takes place at a later period.

A hydrocele is nothing to worry about. The fluid in most cases diminishes as the baby gets older, and then nothing needs to be done for it. Occasionally an older boy has a chronic hydrocele, which should be operated on if it is uncomfortably large. You should not try to make the diagnosis yourself. Let the doctor decide whether it's hernia or hydrocele.

EYE TROUBLES

711. Reasons for seeing the eye doctor. A child needs to go to an eye doctor if his eyes turn in (cross-eyes) or out (walleyes) at any age (Section 325); if he is having any trouble with his schoolwork; if he is complaining of aching, smarting or tired eyes; if his eyes are inflamed; if he is having headaches; if he holds his book too close; if he cocks his head to one side when looking at something carefully; or if his vision is found to be defective by the chart test at school. However, just because a child can read a chart satisfactorily in school does not mean for sure that his eyes are all right. If he is having symptoms of eyestrain, he should be examined anyway. To be completely sure, it is a good idea to take a child to the oculist by the age of 4. Chart testing, at school or the doctor's, should be done each year after 5.

Nearsightedness, which is the commonest eye trouble that interferes with schoolwork, develops most often in the age period between 6 and 10. It can come on quite rapidly, so don't ignore the signs of it (holding the book closer, having trouble seeing the blackboard at school) just because the child's vision was all right a few months before.

Inflammation of the eye (conjunctivitis) can be caused by many different infections or by allergy. Most of the mild cases are caused by ordinary cold germs, and accompany colds in the nose. You should be more suspicious of inflammation when there is no nose cold. It is a good idea to get in touch with your doctor anyway, but particularly when the white of the eye becomes reddened or when there is pus.

712. Harmful fluids in the eye. If a child is accidentally squirted in the eye by something in a spray can or some possibly harmful fluid is splashed in his eye, flush the eye promptly by laying the child on his back and squeezing water freely into his eye from an eye dropper or washcloth.

713. Specks. Specks in the eye should be removed promptly. It is always preferable to let a doctor do this if possible. It is absolutely necessary to go to a doctor if the speck has not been removed in half an hour. A speck that stays imbedded over the pupil or iris for several hours may cause a serious infection. There are three methods you can try if it is difficult to reach the doctor. The first is to draw the upper eyelid down and away from the eye, holding it by the lashes. This gives the tears a chance to wash the speck out. Next, you can use an eyecup, containing a sterile 2% solution of boric acid (2 level teaspoonfuls of boric acid powder in a cupful of boiled water). The child tips his head down, applies the filled eyecup to his eye, straightens his head up, blinks several times with the cup against the eye. The third method is to examine the inside of the upper lid. This is where most specks lodge. You need a clean cotton swab (made on a toothpick or matchstick) and a plain match or toothpick. Tell the child to look down and keep looking down. This relaxes the upper lid. Take hold of the eyelashes of the upper lid, pull the lid down as far as it goes, lay the matchstick horizontally across the middle of the lid, and fold the eyelid back over the matchstick. While you hold the lid firmly folded back, reach for the cotton swab. If you see the speck on the lid, gently wipe it off with the swab. You need a good strong light. If you can't find the speck and the pain goes on, or if the speck is lodged on the eyeball, go to an eye doctor promptly. Don't try to remove a speck from the eyeball yourself.

714. Styes. A stye is an infection in a hair follicle of the eyelashes, and is similar to a pimple anywhere else. A stye is caused by ordinary pus germs that happen to be rubbed onto the eyelid. The stye usually comes to a head and breaks. The doctor may prescribe an ointment to promote healing and prevent spreading. An adult with a stye feels more comfortable if he puts on hot applications, and this may hasten its coming to a head and breaking, but it makes no great difference. A child doesn't want to be bothered. The main trouble with a stye is that one often leads to another, probably because when the first one breaks the germs are spread to other hair follicles. This is a reason for trying to keep a child from rubbing or fingering his eyelid at the time a stye is coming to a head or discharging. If a child has several styes in succession, he should be examined by his doctor and have a urine analysis. Styes occasionally mean that a person has some condition that lowers his resistance.

A mother with a stye should wash her hands thoroughly before doing things for a baby or small child, especially if she has touched her stye, because the germs are easily passed from person to person. A father or brother with a stye had better not handle the baby temporarily.

715. Things that don't harm children's eyes. Watching television, sitting too close to the set, reading an excessive amount, holding the book close will not harm the eyes. (If the book is held close, the eyes should be checked for nearsightedness, though.)

CONVULSIONS

716. A convulsion is a frightening thing to see in a child, but in most cases it is not dangerous in itself. Most convulsions stop in a short time, whether or not any treatment is used.

Telephone for the doctor. If you cannot reach him immediately, don't worry. The convulsion is usually over anyway and the child asleep by the time the doctor can get there.

Keep the child from hurting himself. If he is biting his tongue, you can try to keep his jaws separated with a clothespin or with the small end of a fountain pen or with a pencil.

Don't try to get him into a tepid bath; it won't make that much difference.

If the child has a high fever, give him a wet rub to get his temperature down. Take off his clothes. Wet your hand in water and rub one arm for a couple of minutes, then the other arm, each leg, the chest, the back. Keep wetting your hand as necessary. The gentle rubbing brings the blood to the surface, and the evaporation helps in the cooling. If the convulsions continue or if the temperature stays above 103°, you can continue to rub. Don't cover him with blankets when you are trying to get the temperature down.

In most convulsions, the child loses consciousness, the eyes roll up, the teeth are clenched, and the body or parts of the body are shaken by twitching movements. The breathing is heavy, and there may be a little frothing at the lips. Sometimes the urine and bowel movement are passed.

Convulsions are brought on by irritation of the brain from a number of different causes. The causes are different at different age periods. In the newborn baby they are usually due to injury to the brain.

717. In the young child, between 1 and 5, the commonest cause is sudden fever at the onset of colds, sore throats and grippe. Fever coming on so quickly seems to make the nervous system irritable. Lots of children of this age are trembly at the start of their fevers, even though they don't have convulsions. So if your child around 2 or 3 has a convulsion at the onset of a fever, it doesn't necessarily mean that he has a serious disease, and it doesn't mean that he's going to have more convulsions in later life. Convulsions are rare after the first day of fever.

718. Epilepsy is the name given to convulsions that occur repeatedly in the older child, without any fever or other disease. Nobody knows the real cause. There are two different forms of epilepsy. In "grand mal" attacks, the person loses consciousness completely and has convulsions. In "petit mal," the attack is so brief that the person doesn't fall or lose control of himself; he may just stare or stiffen momentarily.

Every case of epilepsy should be investigated by a doctor familiar with the disease. Though the condition is usually a chronic one, there are several drugs that are helpful in stopping or reducing the frequency of the spells.

There are other causes of convulsions less common than these that have been mentioned.

First Aid

CUTS, HEMORRHAGE AND BURNS

719. Soap and pure water for cuts and scratches. The best treatment for scratches and small cuts is to wash them with soap and pure water on a piece of absorbent cotton or clean cloth. Then rinse the soap off with plenty of clear water. Ask your doctor whether the water you use is pure enough to wash wounds with. If not, you can keep a bottle of 3% hydrogen peroxide to use for this soaping and rinsing.

An antiseptic is less important than careful washing, and some doctors prefer that no antiseptic be used. Don't use iodine. Cover with a bandage. The only purpose of the bandage is to keep the cut reasonably clean.

For large cuts that gape open, you should, of course, consult your doctor. It is good to have expert care for cuts on the face, even when they are small, since scars are more noticeable there, and also for cuts on the hand and wrist, because of the danger of cut nerves and tendons.

Wounds that might be contaminated by any street dirt or soil that contains manure should be reported to your doctor. Manure frequently carries the germs of tetanus (lockjaw). The doctor may recommend a tetanus toxoid booster shot or antitoxin, especially for deep cuts or puncture wounds.

Animal bites. Get in touch with the doctor promptly. Meanwhile, first aid is the same as for cuts. The important thing is to keep track of the animal to be sure he is not developing rabies. If the animal does develop rabies or if he cannot be traced, the doctor gives rabies inoculations.

720. Bandaging. What you use for bandaging depends on the size and location of the scratch or cut. Small prepared sterile bandages are good for most small wounds. They won't stick on the palm. For larger cuts and scratches, use a gauze square that comes sterile in an envelope, or a folded piece of clean cotton cloth. It can be held in place by narrow strips of adhesive. (A small child can loosen a bandage in no time at all.) Any bandaging has to be snug to do any good.

Don't wrap adhesive all the way around the arm or leg (so that it overlaps itself) because this might shut off the circulation. If the foot or hand becomes at all swollen or darker in color after the leg or arm has been bandaged, it means that the bandage is too tight. It should be loosened right away. It's all right to wrap a small prepared bandage around a finger if it's not too tight. Strips of adhesive to hold a bandage in place have more chance of staying if you make them plenty long.

A wound heals quicker and is less apt to become infected if you don't disturb the bandaging too often. If it becomes too loose or dirty-looking, apply a new layer on top of the old. Take a bandage off very gently. Peel the inner layer back in the same direction as the cut runs. (For instance, if the line of the cut runs up and down the arm, peel the bandage up or down the arm.) In this way there is less likelihood of pulling the edges of the cut apart. If a bandage sticks, soak it off with 3% hydrogen peroxide. A cut may throb the first day and night, and this doesn't mean much. If it becomes increasingly painful later, it may be due to infection. Then the bandage should be removed to see what is happening. If there is swelling or redness, the doctor should see it.

Barked knees, after being washed, are best left unbandaged until a dry scab is formed. Otherwise the bandage gets stuck and pulls off the scab when it is changed.

If a small child has a cut near the mouth, it may stay cleaner without any bandage (to catch food and saliva).

721. Bandaging a finger. A child's finger is the part most frequently bandaged and the most difficult to bandage. Use a prepared bandage wrapped around the finger if this will cover the cut. If not, wrap the finger with a sterile gauze square or a strip of clean cloth. Hold this in place with a couple of strips of adhesive that circle the finger.

Now take a narrow strip of adhesive tape about a foot long, apply one end to the base of the bandage on the palm side, run to the end of the finger, over the end, up the back side of the bandage, up the back of the hand, and halfway up the arm. When you are sticking the adhesive to the back of the hand and arm, have the child's finger and wrist partly bent over; otherwise the adhesive acts as a halter holding the finger up straight. With another piece of adhesive, circle the middle of the bandage once more, snugly, to hold it together and to keep the lengthwise strip of adhesive from coming loose.

722. Bleeding (hemorrhage). Most wounds bleed a little for a few minutes, and this is good because it washes out some of the germs that were introduced. It's only profuse or persistent hemorrhage that needs special treatment.

Bleeding of the hand, arm, foot or leg stops sooner if the part is elevated. Have the child lie down, and put a pillow or two under the limb. If the wound continues to bleed freely, press on it with a sterile gauze square or any clean cloth, until it stops or until you decide to bandage it. Clean and bandage the wound while the limb is still elevated.

If the wound was made in a clean way (with a knife, for instance) and bled freely, don't try to wash the cut but clean around it gently (soap and water, or soap and hydrogen peroxide on sterile cotton). If the wound still contains dirt, clean inside the cut, too.

When bandaging a cut that has bled a lot or is still bleeding, use a number of gauze squares (or folded pieces of clean cloth) on top of each other so that you have a thick pad over the cut. Then, when you snugly apply the adhesive or gauze roll bandage, it exerts more pressure on the cut and makes it less likely to bleed again. This is the principle of the "pressure bandage."

723. Severe bleeding. If a wound is bleeding at an alarming rate, don't wait to find the right bandages. Stop the bleeding with pressure immediately and wait for someone else to bring the bandages. Elevate a limb if possible. Make a pad of the cleanest material you have handy, whether it's gauze squares, a clean handkerchief or the cleanest piece of clothing on the child or yourself. Press the pad against the wound, and keep pressing until help arrives or until the bleeding stops. Don't remove your original pad. As it is soaked through, add new material on top. If the bleeding is easing up and you have suitable material, apply a pressure bandage. The pad over the wound, made of a number of gauze squares or folded material of the cleanest available, should be thick enough so that when it is bandaged it presses on the wound. A small pad is enough for a finger, but a thick dressing is necessary for a thigh or abdominal wound. Bandage snugly with gauze bandage or adhesive tape or long strips of any kind of material. If the pressure bandage doesn't control the bleeding, continue hand pressure directly over the wound. If you have no cloth or material of any kind to press against a wound that is bleeding alarmingly, press with your hands on the edges of the wound, or even in the wound.

A great majority of even serious hemorrhages can be stopped by simple direct pressure. If you are dealing with one that can't and if you have learned in a first aid class how to apply a tourniquet, then go ahead. It's seldom necessary, though, and it's nothing that a novice should try to learn for the first time in an emergency. It must be loosened every 30 minutes.

724. Nosebleeds. There are a number of simple remedies for nosebleed. Just having a child sit still for a few minutes is often sufficient. To avoid his swallowing a lot of blood, have him sit up with his head bent forward, or if he's lying down, turn his head to the side so that his nose points slightly down. Keep him from blowing his nose or from pressing and squeezing it with his handkerchief. It's all right to hold the handkerchief gently against the nostril to catch the blood, but moving the nose around helps to keep up the bleeding.

Cold applied to any part of the head constricts the blood vessels and helps to stop a hemorrhage. Place something cold against the back of the neck, or the forehead, or the upper lip. A cloth wrung out in cold water, an ice bag or a cold bottle from the refrigerator will do.

If the nosebleed continues for 10 minutes in spite of these measures, get in touch with the doctor. If you have a bottle of nose drops of the kind that shrink the tissues, wet a small, loose wad of cotton with the nose drops and tuck it into the front part of the nostril. Nosebleeds usually occur from the front part of the nose. You can sometimes stop a severe hemorrhage by gently pinching the lower part of the nose for 10 minutes. Let go slowly and gently.

Nosebleeds occur most frequently from blows on the nose, from picking the nose, and from colds and other infections. If a child has repeated hemorrhages from no apparent cause, he needs to be examined by a doctor to make sure he has none of the general diseases that sometimes cause nosebleeds. If no disease is found, it may be necessary to cauterize (burn) the exposed blood vessel that is always breaking. The proper blood vessel to cauterize can be discovered only right after a hemorrhage.

725. Burns. The treatment of burns has changed a lot in recent years and is continuing to change. It is a good idea to ask your doctor ahead of time what he recommends in case of emergency.

In case of a burn, call the doctor for instructions before doing anything else. If he is not there, ask the office to reach him and have him call you as soon as possible. Meanwhile, give first aid treatment. Then, if the burn is severe and it looks as though you can reach a hospital sooner than you will hear from the doctor, start for the hospital.

One satisfactory first aid treatment for a small burn is to apply plain petroleum jelly (petrolatum) and cover loosely with a clean bandage. If you have no petrolatum, you can use clean vegetable fat (shortening) or even butter.

Another method, clumsier than ointment, is to cover the burn with clean gauze pads wet with bicarbonate of soda solution (a level teaspoonful to a cup of water). Hold them in place with loose bandaging and moisten from time to time with more of the solution, until you can get ointment for a small burn or get a doctor for a larger one.

It is much safer to consult a doctor for any burns that cause blisters or raw spots. Some of the blisters are apt to break, and infection easily occurs under the edges of a broken blister.

If you have to deal with one or two small, unbroken blisters without the help of a doctor, don't open them or try to puncture them with a needle. There is less danger of infection if you leave them alone. Small blisters sometimes reabsorb without ever breaking; or if they break after several days, the new skin is pretty well formed underneath. When a blister does break, it is better to cut all the loose skin off. Use a pair of nail scissors and a pair of tweezers, both of which have been boiled for 10 minutes. Then cover with a sterile bandage coated with petroleum jelly. If a blister becomes infected, as shown by pus in the blister and redness around the edge, you should certainly consult your doctor. If this is impossible, cut away the blister and use wet dressings (Section 711).

Never put iodine or any similar antiseptic on a burn of any degree. It makes matters worse.

726. Sunburn. The best thing for sunburn is not to get it. Severe sunburn is painful, dangerous and unnecessary. A half hour of direct sunshine at a beach in summer is enough to cause a burn on a fair-skinned person who is unused to exposure.

Better to take too little sun the first days on the beach or in the country than too much. You can't tell when the skin's had enough from looking at it or feeling it. It takes hours for a burn to show. A good rule for the first few days at the beach is to keep the child's face, body and legs covered or shaded except when he is actually going into the water. That means a hat to shade the forehead and nose, a shirt to cover the shoulders, and overalls to protect the legs, especially the back of the knees while lying on the stomach.

"Tanning" lotions that promise to make a nice tan without burning may help somewhat, but they can't protect against a large amount of sunshine.

For relief of sunburn, you can apply plain cold cream or petroleum jelly. With a moderately severe burn, a person may have chills and fever and feel sick. Then you should consult a doctor, because sunburn can be just as serious as a heat burn. Keep sunburned areas completely protected from sunshine until the redness is gone.

727. Wet dressings for skin infections until you can reach the doctor. If a child has a boil, or an infection of the end of his finger, or around his fingernail or toenail, or an infected cut, or any similar type of infection under his skin, it should be seen by the doctor. Meanwhile, the child should be quiet, preferably in bed, with the limb elevated on a pillow.

If there is an unavoidable delay in reaching the doctor, the best first aid treatment is to apply a continuous wet dressing. This softens the skin, hastens the time when it breaks to allow the pus to escape, and keeps the opening from closing over again too soon.

You can make a solution by boiling a cupful of water and adding a tablespoonful of Epsom salts, or magnesium sulfate, or table salt.

Make a fairly thick bandage over the infection and pour enough of the salt solution into the bandage to make all of it wet. Every few hours, when it begins to dry, add more solution.

You can keep it wet longer, especially at night, and keep the child's clothes and bedclothes dry, by covering the whole dressing with a piece of waterproof material, such as the plastic bags that are used in refrigerators, or plastic wrapping. Use a large enough piece to extend beyond the edges of the bandaging, and hold it in place with strips of adhesive tape. (Don't run adhesive tape tightly around an arm or leg—it may cut off the circulation.)

If a child has fever with a skin infection, or if there are red streaks running up his arm or leg, or if he has tender lymph glands in his armpit or groin, the infection is spreading seriously and should be considered a real emergency. Get the child to a doctor or a hospital, even if you have to drive all night. Modern drugs are vitally important in combating serious infections.

SPRAINS, FRACTURES, HEAD INJURIES

728. Sprains usually need examination and treatment. If your child sprains his ankle, have him lie down for a half hour or so and elevate the foot on a pillow. This keeps the deep hemorrhage and swelling to a minimum. If swelling occurs, you ought to consult your doctor, because it is possible that a bone has been cracked or broken.

A sprained knee should always be seen by a doctor and treated carefully. A neglected knee sprain in which a cartilage has been injured may not heal properly and may give trouble for years. If a child has fallen on his wrist and it remains painful, either when it is still or when it is moved, you have to suspect a fracture, even though there is no crookedness or swelling.

You can say, then, that any sprain that continues to be painful or that swells should be examined. This is not only because of the possibility of fracture, but also because most sprains are much more comfortable if they are splinted or bandaged correctly. Many sprains and partial fractures are numb for an hour or so and then become more and more painful.

If a limb continues to be painful or if a child uses it strangely, whether or not there has been a known injury, the doctor is apt to want X rays, often of both limbs for comparison.

729. Fractures. The brittle bones of adults really break. The softer bones of children are more apt to bend and splinter a little ("greenstick" fractures). Another type of fracture in a child is the loosening or breaking off of the growing end of a bone. This is particularly apt to happen at the wrist. (The picture that occurs when the growing end of a bone [epiphesis] becomes loosened may not be apparent at first, even on X ray.) When a child has had a severe fracture, it is easy enough for anyone to see. But there are some common fractures that don't look especially deformed. A broken ankle can look straight enough, but there is considerable swelling and pain. A black-and-blue spot appears after a number of hours. Only a doctor can distinguish between an ankle that is severely sprained and one that is broken, and he often needs an X ray to tell. A wrist can be broken without being out of line enough for you to realize it. Finger bones are often chipped when a ball is caught on the end of a finger. There is only swelling and later some blueness. A vertebra (one of the bones in the spine) is sometimes slightly crushed when a child falls on his behind. Nothing shows outside, but he complains of pain when he curves his body forward or when he jumps and runs. In a general way, suspect a fracture if pain in a limb continues, or if there is swelling, or if a black-and-blue mark appears.

Avoid further injury in a suspected fracture. Don't move the injured limb around. Don't let the child move it. If he's in a halfway comfortable place and you can get a doctor soon, keep him quiet where he is. If he has to be moved, put some kind of splint on first.

A splint to do any good must extend far enough up and down the limb. For an ankle injury, the splint should reach to the knee; for a break in the lower leg, it should go up to the hip; for a break in the thigh, you need a board that goes from the foot to the armpit. For a broken wrist, the splint should go from the fingertips to the elbow; for a broken lower or upper arm, it should go from the fingertips to the armpit. You need a board to make a long splint. A short one for a small child can be made by folding a piece of cardboard.

Move the limb with extreme gentleness when you are applying the splint to it, and try to avoid any movement where the break is. Tie the limb to the splint snugly in 4 to 6 places, using handkerchiefs, strips of clothing, or bandages. Two of the ties should be close to the break, on either side of it, and there should be one at each end of the splint. For a back injury, it is even more important to leave the patient where he is if he can possibly be made comfortable there. If he must be moved, use a stretcher or a door. In picking up a person with a back injury, keep his back straight or arched inward (so that it is "hollow"). Never let his back curve outward. That means that when he is picked up, or if he has to be carried on a mattress or other makeshift stretcher that sags, he should be on his stomach. In case of a neck injury, the neck should be kept straight or, if curved at all, curved backward. (His head should not bend forward.) For a broken collarbone (at the top of the chest in front), make a sling out of a large triangle of cloth and tie it behind the neck, so that it supports he lower arm across the chest.

If a person with a serious injury has to be kept for some time in a cold place, protect him reasonably with blankets or with other clothing. Put a blanket under him. It is no longer considered wise to try to make a person in shock really warm with many hot blankets or hot water bottles.

730. Head injuries. A fall on the head is a common injury from the age when a baby can roll over (and thereby roll himself off a bed). A parent usually feels guilty the first time this happens. But if a child is so carefully watched that he never has an accident, he is being fussed over too much. Bones may be saved, but his character will be ruined.

If, after a fall on the head, a baby stops crying within 15 minutes, keeps a good color, and doesn't vomit, there is little chance that he has injured his brain. He can be allowed to resume his normal life right away.

When a blow on the head is more severe, the child is apt to vomit, lose his appetite, be pale for a number of hours, show signs of headache, fall asleep easily but be able to be roused. If a child has any of these symptoms, you should get in touch with your doctor. He may want to examine the child or have his skull X-rayed. The child should be kept as quiet as possible for 2 or 3 days and any new symptoms reported to the doctor immediately. It's a good idea to rouse the child twice during the first night after the fall to make sure that he's not unconscious. If he is not feeling his usual self the next day, the doctor should be notified again.

If a child loses consciousness either right after a fall or later, he should certainly be examined by a doctor immediately. The same rule applies even without unconsciousness if the child continues to complain of headache, trouble with his vision, or if he vomits later.

A swelling that puffs out quickly on a child's skull after a fall doesn't mean anything serious in itself if there are no other symptoms. It is caused by a broken blood vessel just under the skin.

SWALLOWED OBJECTS AND CHOKING

731. Swallowed objects. Babies and small children swallow prune pits, coins, safety pins, beads, buttons—in fact, anything you can mention. They seem to be able to pass most of these things through their stomachs and intestines with the greatest of ease, even open safety pins or a little broken glass. The objects that are more dangerous are needles and straight pins.

If your child has swallowed without discomfort a smooth object, like a prune pit or a button, you don't have to worry or give him bread to push it along. Just watch the movements for a few days to reassure yourself that it has come out. Naturally, if he develops vomiting or pains in the stomach, or if an object gets painfully stuck in his gullet, or if he has swallowed a sharp object such as an open safety pin or a needle, you should consult the doctor immediately.

Never give a cathartic to a child who has swallowed an object. It won't do any good and it may do harm.

732. Choking. When a child breathes or coughs something into his windpipe and is choking, hold him upside down and slap him vigorously on the back of his chest. If he keeps on choking and begins to turn blue, rush him to the nearest hospital or doctor's office. Let someone else telephone ahead. Don't wait for anything.

A sharp object stuck in the throat, like a fishbone, though very uncomfortable and gagging, is not dangerous like an object that is obstructing the breathing. You should reach the doctor as soon as possible, but it isn't a matter of life or death. Lots of times the object can't be found when the doctor examines the throat, though the child keeps saying it's there. In these cases the fishbone, or whatever it is, has been swallowed, but the child is still feeling the scratches left in his throat.

ARTIFICIAL RESPIRATION

733. Artificial respiration.

If person has drowned, first drain water from lungs by laying him on stomach for 10 seconds with hips a foot higher than head (over your knee, a box, etc.).

A person may stop breathing because of smothering, drowning, electric shock, inhaling gas. Start artificial respiration promptly. Keep it up until he continues to breathe by himself or until help comes, as long as 2 hours. **Never give it to a person who is breathing.**

It is vital to open the air passages by raising neck, tilting head way back.

Then keep victim's **chin pressed upward all the time,** to keep the passages open.

With a child's small face you can breathe into nose and mouth together. (With adult, breathe into mouth or nose, and keep the other pinched shut.)

Breathe into victim, using only mild force. (A small child's lungs cannot contain your entire exhalation.) Remove your lips, allowing his chest to contract while you inhale your next breath. Breathe into victim again.

Each of your breaths goes into the victim. With an adult, breathe at your natural speed. With a child use slightly quicker, shorter breaths.

OBJECTS IN THE NOSE AND EARS

734. Objects in the nose and ears. Small children often stuff things like beads and wads of paper into their nose or ears. The important thing is not to push the object any farther in, in your efforts to take it out. Don't try to go after a smooth, hard thing. You are almost certain to push it in farther. You may be able to grasp a soft object that isn't too far in, with a pair of tweezers.

With objects in the nose, have the child blow his nose. (Don't try this if he is so young that he sniffs in when told to blow.) He may sneeze the object out in a little while. If the object stays in, take him to your doctor or a nose specialist. Foreign objects that stay in the nose for several days usually cause a bad-smelling discharge tinged with blood. A discharge of this kind from one nostril should always make you think of this possibility.

POISONS

735. On the skin or in the eye: Flush off the skin with plenty of plain water. If you have no eye dropper, you can squeeze water from a sponge or washcloth into the eye.

736. Swallowed substances: First **telephone your doctor,** hospital emergency ward or Poison Information Center for advice.

If there's no hospital or poison center and your doctor's not in his office, ask his secretary or the telephone operator to find him or another immediately. Ask her to let you know within 10 minutes if no doctor can be reached. Then stay off the line so that doctor or secretary can call you back.

While you wait, consider whether the substance is one for which you should or should not induce vomiting.

DO NOT INDUCE VOMITING FOR THESE

kerosene	turpentine	ammonia
gasoline	liquid auto polish	lye; drain cleaners
benzene	liquid furniture polish	caustic lime
cleaning fluids	insect sprays	bleach

strong acids (sulfuric, nitric, hydrochloric, carbolic)

Petroleum products are most harmful when breathed or choked into the lungs and vomiting might cause this. Acids and caustic cleaners may burn the throat again coming up.

Do not induce vomiting in a person who is in coma or having a convulsion.

737. If you haven't heard from the doctor in 10 minutes and if the substance is not a petroleum product or a caustic, try to induce vomiting.

Get your child to drink as much milk or water as he'll take in a hurry. Have him lie across a bed with his head hanging over the edge. Put a large pan on the floor to catch the vomitus for the doctor to analyze.

Run your finger down the back of his throat in an unhesitating way; keep it in motion there for a few seconds, to make sure he gags thoroughly. A brief gag won't be enough. If you hesitate on the way in or out you may be bitten. But he can't bite while he's gagging.

If you couldn't get him to vomit that way, give him a full tablespoonful (3 teaspoonfuls) of syrup of ipecac if you have it available. (Two teaspoonfuls if he's under 2 years). Repeat in 15 minutes if no vomiting has occurred. (Don't give it a third time; twice is enough).

Persist in your efforts to reach a doctor or take your child to the hospital, even if he seems well or you made him vomit. The effects of many poisons (aspirin, for instance) take hours to show.

738. Some substances which are dangerous though they may not seem so: tobacco (one ingested cigarette is dangerous for a 1-year-old); iron, quinine and strychnine pills; boric acid; aspirin.

Some frequently ingested substances which are only mildly harmful (call the doctor anyway): ink; mercury in liquid form from a broken thermometer; tincture of iodine.

Special Problems

TRAVELING WITH A BABY

There are several methods of preparing and carrying formula when traveling. Which one is most convenient for you depends on the facilities you will have and on how long you will be away from a kitchen and refrigerator.

Ask your doctor, well ahead, whether he has any recommendations. Ask a railroad or airline whether they can provide you with refrigeration, and for how many bottles.

739. Buy prepared, sterile formula in disposable bottles or cans if they are available and your doctor says that one of them is suitable. They have all the conveniences: They don't have to be refrigerated. The bottle and nipple can be thrown away after each feeding so there is nothing to wash or sterilize.

740. Bringing your own formula. If you can't get prepared formula and if you are going to be traveling for 24 hours or less, you can prepare your regular formula at home, get it well chilled in your refrigerator, then keep it cold in a picnic icebox in your car or in the refrigerator on a plane or train. You can save space by carrying the whole 24-hour quantity in 1 quart bottle. (Sterilize the formula in this bottle.) At each feeding fill a nursing bottle through a funnel. After feeding, wash the bottle, nipple and funnel with soap and brush before using them again; or bring enough clean bottles and nipples to last the trip. Or if you have space in the car for a large picnic icebox, you can carry the nursing bottles already filled with formula, packed in ice cubes with perhaps a few bigger chunks. (The smaller the pieces of ice, the quicker they melt.)

You can make the ice in your picnic icebox last longer by wrapping all but the lid of the box in ten or more layers of newspaper. It's a good insulator. If you are carrying only 1 or 2 bottles, prechilled, in an insulated bottle bag, you can first wrap each bottle in newspaper for added insulation.

741. Making up each bottle, on a long trip. If you can't buy prepared, sterile formula and your baby is on an evaporated milk formula, the easiest method is to prepare each bottle just before feeding, using the small, 6-ounce cans of evaporated milk. Then nothing has to be refrigerated. You carry as many of these cans as there will be feedings during the trip. Bring a jar of sugar or a bottle of corn syrup. The most convenient way to carry water for formula is to buy a half gallon of sterile distilled water at the drugstore. Another bottle can be bought wherever you go, and it will be sterile and the same composition. (It's tasteless to drink!) Or you can boil your own water at home and bring it in bottles or a jug. (It's better not to use water from the train or from faucets along the route. It will have to be boiled. Also, changes of water may upset a baby's bowels temporarily.) You'll need your funnel, measuring spoon, can opener, bottle brush, enough clean bottles and nipples to last until you can wash them again.

At each feeding pour into a clean bottle the proper amount of syrup or sugar, water and evaporated milk from a freshly opened can. Put on the nipple and shake until well mixed. Your doctor can tell you the proportions for each bottle. For instance, if the usual total formula is 13 ounces evaporated milk, 19 ounces water, and 3 tablespoonfuls corn syrup, divided into 5 bottles, then each bottle would be made with 2 teaspoonfuls of corn syrup, 4 ounces water, 2½ ounces evaporated milk.

If you give your baby warmed formula, you can warm the bottle in a washstand in a train. The waiter on a railroad diner, the stewardess on a plane, the waitress or cook in a roadside diner or restaurant will warm the bottle for you. If you will be traveling by car, you can buy a bottle warmer made to plug into the cigarette lighter or you can bring a Sterno burner along.

Since you probably won't be able to boil the bottles and nipples, you should wash them and the funnel carefully—as soon as you get a chance—with soap and a bottle brush. Rinse and drain dry. The reason you can use a clean but unboiled bottle again is that there is no formula in it between feedings, for bacteria to multiply in.

742. Solid foods. Most solid foods should be in jars or cans. The baby can be fed directly from them. Don't worry about providing everything that the baby usually gets (potatoes, for example). Just bring enough of the things he likes best and digests most easily. Many traveling babies do not want so much as they would be taking at home. Don't urge anything that he doesn't want even if he is taking much less than usual. He may want to be fed small amounts at more frequent intervals.

743. Food for a child. It's better to keep a small child from drinking train water (bring some in a bottle) and eating unusual foods. When buying food for him in public places, avoid particularly cakes and pastries with moist fillings, milk puddings, cold meats, cold fish and cold eggs, creamy salad dressings (including sandwiches and salads that contain them). These are the foods that are most easily contaminated with poisonous bacteria if carelessly handled or not properly refrigerated. Better stick to hot foods, fruit that you peel yourself, milk in separate containers. (Of course, you can put up your own sandwiches at home, such as peanut butter, jelly, tomato.) Even if you are expecting to feed a child at roadside restaurants, or in the diner, or on the meals provided in a plane, bring a bag of food for snacks or in case meals are delayed—a box of salted crackers (said to be helpful for car sickness), cheese and hard-boiled eggs in the shell (if enjoyed), fruit, a Thermos bottle of milk, a jar of pureed prunes in case of constipation.

744. Other tips. It is worthwhile, with a baby, to travel by the best accommodations that you can afford. You will get more service on a first-class railroad ticket, and if you can afford it, you will feel a lot more comfortable in a compartment when the baby is fussing.

Disposable diapers are a great help, especially the type in which a disposable pad fits into a cover.

With a small child, don't forget to have handy the cuddly toys that he takes to bed. They will be an extra comfort in traveling. In addition to his favorite toys, it is wise to bring a few new playthings of the kind that take a lot of doing—miniature cars or trains, a small doll with several articles of clothing or other equipment, a coloring or cut-out book, a new picture book, cardboard houses or other objects to fold and assemble, a pad of paper, pencil and crayons. A child of 3 or over likes to pack his favorite toys in his own small suitcase.

A large box of **cleansing tissues** is essential. A couple of large **plastic tablecloths** are valuable, one for protecting the mattress from bed wetting, another to cover the carpet if a small child is eating in a hotel room or a baby is sitting on the floor, or to cover a bed on which a baby is being changed.

In car travel, it is wise to stop, not only at regular meal-times, but also in midmorning and midafternoon, for a snack and for a chance for children to run around for a few minutes in a place, perhaps a field or a playground in a city park, where they don't have to be constantly warned to keep off the road.

For a small child, it may be important to carry along the **toilet seat** he is used to.

The leg space for the back seat of a car can be filled with luggage and covered with a pad so that a crawling baby or small child has room in which to roam or fall asleep. If children insist on standing, they should stand on the floor, not on seats; the back of the front seat can be padded to lessen injury in case of a sudden stop.

A baby's **auto bed** or a basket made into a bed is extremely helpful for car, plane or train. You can move the baby around in it without waking him up, and it's more comfortable for the mother, even if she has to hold it in her lap at times.

A good rule for car travel is to plan to always stop for the night by 4 P.M., so you'll have more chance of finding a motel room and avoid driving on for hours with tired children. Many a man gets the bit in his teeth about making a certain distance and refuses to stop even though it's getting late. But if he solemnly agrees before the trip to a certain stopping hour, there's more chance of his being reasonable.

THE PREMATURE BABY

A baby weighing much under 5 pounds will probably be taken to a hospital where an incubator and expert care are available.

The information in this chapter is given only to cover those rare emergency situations in which a premature baby has to be cared for, temporarily, by the family until he is taken to the hospital.

745. Keep the baby warm. A premature baby loses body heat rapidly when exposed to cool air, and his body's ability to make heat and to keep an even temperature is poor.

Wrap him in a warm cotton receiving blanket and then in a soft acrylic or wool baby blanket the minute he is born (even before the cord is cut) and keep him in a warm place. The cord should not be tied and cut until it stops beating. This is to make sure he receives all the blood available from the placenta.

The room temperature should be 80° day and night. This means a very warm room. Other things being equal, it is easier to keep a small room warm than a large one—if you are using an electric or kerosene heater, for instance.

If the baby is going to stay at home for more than a few hours during the steam-heating season, you should get extra moisture into the air by one of the methods described in Section 646.

The bed can be an ordinary bassinet, a wooden box or a cardboard carton. If you have no baby's mattress, you can use a pile of folded newspapers topped with a folded pad or small blanket. It should not be a pillow; it's too soft.

Here is one way to arrange the bed. Line it with a wool or acrylic blanket, crib or adult size. You can let the ends hang down outside. Cover it in the bottom with a piece of waterproof sheeting. This should be cut small or folded so that it doesn't have to be tucked in—you want to be able to change it easily without undoing the whole bed. Use a folded diaper for a sheet—it shouldn't be tucked in, either.

Place the baby, still loosely wrapped in only the blankets, in the bed, on his back. Now another ordinary acrylic or wool blanket, crib or adult size, should be stretched over the top of the bed in such a way that it does not lie on the baby's body and does not cover his head. The edge of the blanket toward his head should dip down to his neck (to close in his body and leave his head out).

Don't remove the baby from the bed. You change his special diaper and the sheet and waterproof sheeting under him. The simpler the clothing, the easier it is to change. Just keep him wrapped in the receiving blanket and a wool or acrylic baby blanket. You can cut them to make them small enough. You can cut small diapers for him, or you can lay a piece of absorbent cotton covered by a layer of gauze under his buttocks (inside the blanket or gown) to absorb urine and bowel movements, and throw it away when it is soiled.

746. Going to the hospital. When you can reach the doctor, he will decide when and how the baby will go to the hospital.

If you are not able to get in touch with the doctor right away, don't take the baby to the hospital until you can get a traveling incubator or until you have a heated car (unless it is summer). It is much safer for a baby to stay warm at home for a few hours or even a couple of days than to get chilled.

747. Feeding the premature baby when it is impossible to have a doctor's advice. The feeding of a premature baby is the most difficult part of his care. It is also the most dangerous because he is so apt to choke and stop breathing in his first few days. If there is a chance of getting a baby to a hospital by the time he is 5 days old, it is safer **not to feed him anything** at home.

If you have to continue to care for your baby at home, **you should not begin to feed him until he is 72 hours old,** which is the beginning of his fourth day of life. This gives him a chance to get used to breathing well first.

If he still sounds as if he has mucus in his bronchial tubes or is having any other trouble breathing, wait another day, or even 2 days, before starting to feed him.

The premature baby can take only small amounts at first, chokes easily and yet, in most cases, needs a good intake of milk to gain weight. Until he weighs about 5 pounds, he is usually too weak to suck at a nipple so must be fed by **medicine dropper.** The medicine dropper should be boiled each time before it is used again.

Breast milk is much safer and better, if it can be procured. The mother's breasts should be carefully emptied every 3 or 4 hours (Sections 148–151). At feeding time, the correct amount of breast milk can be poured from the bottle in which it has been kept in the refrigerator, into a clean cup.

If no milk has been obtained by the fourth day, it will be necessary to use a cow's-milk formula until the breast milk comes in.

You can use the following formula:

evaporated milk .... 6 ounces
water ....12 ounces
corn syrup .... 2 tablespoonfuls

The directions for making a formula are in Sections 181–183, and for liquefying powdered milk, in Section 169.

Prepare your formula daily and put 6 ounces in each of 3 bottles. At each feeding, measure out the amount you need with a measuring teaspoon into a small cup. Throw away what you do not need at the end of 24 hours. Prop the baby's head and shoulders up with a small pillow at feeding time. For the first 2 or 3 days of feedings, particularly with a baby under 4 pounds, go very slowly in dropping the milk into his mouth. Put in only a couple of drops at a time, and wait until he swallows. Don't worry if each feeding takes the better part of an hour at first. As he gets more used to it, he will swallow sooner and you can go faster.

The formula is given every 3 hours, day and night. The usual hours are 6 A.M., 9 A.M., 12 noon, 3 P.M., 6 P.M., 9 P.M., 12 midnight, 3 A.M. That's 8 feedings a day.

On the fourth day of life give 1 teaspoonful of breast milk or formula at each feeding, on the fifth day 2 teaspoonfuls at each feeding, and so on up to 7 teaspoonfuls or about 1 ounce each feeding on the tenth day. By then you will know whether you have to keep on increasing at this slow speed or can go a little faster.

He may not begin to gain weight until he gets up to a total of about 16 ounces of formula a day, which is 2 ounces in 8 feedings.

By the time he weighs about 5 pounds it's time to try him on breast or bottle, and now he may be able to go 4 hours between feedings at night. Then you divide his total formula into 7 feedings.

748. Other needs of the premature baby. He needs a full dose of vitamins D and C by the time he is 10 days old. Give 0.6 cc a day of an A, C and D combination.

By the age of a month he may need an iron prescription to prevent anemia.

Most premature babies develop quite normally, allowing for their prematurity. They usually gain and grow more rapidly for a while to make up for the slow gaining at first. Naturally, they cannot make up for their youngness. The baby who was born 2 months early and has become "1 year old" should be thought of as really a 10-month-old.

749. It's hard to get over your anxiety. By the time a premature baby weighs 6 pounds, he needs no more coddling or worrying than any baby, but this is very hard for the parents to believe. In the beginning the doctor himself cautioned them against being too optimistic, and he only gradually became more reassuring. The baby probably had to be in an incubator, watched constantly by nurses and doctors, and probably had to be fed by tube. The parents weren't able to get near him most of that time. The mother had to go home from the hospital without him, and both parents then lived a strange kind of parental life for a number of weeks, knowing in a theoretical way that they had a baby but not feeling as if they did. As such parents say, "It was the hospital's baby, not ours."

It's no wonder that when the doctor finally says, "Now you can take him home," the parents feel quite frightened and unready. They find that they don't yet have all the clothing and equipment (the mother had counted on more time at the end of her pregnancy). They find that one or the other has a slight cold. All kinds of small reasons seem terribly important reasons why they can't take him yet.

When the baby at last comes home, all the worries that all new parents experience—about room temperature, baby temperature, breathing, hiccups, burps, bowel movements, formula-making, schedule, crying, colic, spoiling—hit the parents of a premature with triple force. It may take weeks before they gain self-confidence and months before they are convinced that the baby is as healthy, husky and advanced as any other conceived at the same time.

750. Worrisome neighbors. Meanwhile, other troubles may come from the outside. Neighbors and relatives often act more anxious, more awe-struck, more preoccupied, than the parents. They question, they exclaim, they fuss, until the parents can hardly stand it any longer. A few of them insist on telling the parents all the wild stories they have heard about how frail and susceptible prematures remain. This kind of talk would be bad enough for the parents to hear if it were true. It's particularly unfortunate for them to be subjected to untruths of this sort at a time when they are trying to overcome their own anxiety.

751. Feeding. If your baby is about 5½ pounds when you bring him home, he probably wants feedings about every 3 hours in the daytime and every 4 hours at night. The average amount desired per feeding is about 2½ ounces, but there is considerable variation. By the time he weighs 7 or 8 pounds, the interval will sometimes be 4 hours, sometimes 3 or 3½. If he is on a regular schedule, I'd change him to 4 hours by the time he weighs 8 to 9 pounds.

Somewhere between 7 and 10 pounds, most babies are ready to give up one of the night bottles. They show it by sleeping through at 10 P.M. and waking at 11 or 12.

I would encourage the mother of a premature to be looking for this readiness and to take advantage of it by waking and feeding the baby just before she retires, hoping that he will then sleep through till 4 or 5 A.M. By helping him to give up this feeding, she will be convinced in one more respect that he is growing up normally. Each time a feeding is dropped, the same total formula is then divided into fewer bottles.

The main thing to be on guard against in the beginning is attempting to get the baby to take more milk (and, later, more solids) than he wants. This is a great temptation because he looks so slender. You feel that if you could squeeze a little more in, he would fatten up faster and thus be better able to throw off any germs. But resistance to disease has nothing to do with fatness. Your baby, like every other, has his individual pattern of growth and an appetite to take care of it. If you push food beyond what he is eager for, you only take away his appetite and slow up his weight gaining.

A premature particularly needs his vitamins with regularity. The doctor has to watch him for anemia because he has inherited little iron from his mother. Solids can be started by the time he's been home 6 to 8 weeks. Because of the parents' anxiety about growth, it's important here, too, to be tactful, to give him plenty of time to get to like solids, and to increase them only as he shows his enthusiasm. In other words, avoid feeding problems.

752. No other precautions. He can have a tub bath as soon as he weighs 6 or 7 pounds, and I'd encourage the mother to start them by 7 pounds. Like any baby, he can go for outings and have his window open when he weighs 8 pounds.

The parents certainly don't need to wear masks even when he first comes home. He has to get used to the ordinary family germs. He shouldn't be exposed to outsiders with colds or other infections any more than any baby or child should, but otherwise no special precautions are necessary or wise.

THE RH·FACTOR

753. If you have an Rh problem in the family, you need the help of your doctor in understanding how it applies to your particular situation. This is just a very abbreviated discussion of a complicated subject for general information.

A majority of people have the "Rh-positive factor" in their blood. A minority have the "Rh-negative factor." There is no problem if a man and wife are both Rh positive or both Rh negative or if the wife is positive and the husband is negative.

But difficulty sometimes arises if the man is positive and the wife is negative. In this situation, which occurs in about 1 marriage in 8 in the United States, some of the children inherit the Rh positive factor from their father. Then if an Rh-positive baby is growing in the uterus of an Rh-negative mother, a little of his blood may get into the mother's blood through the placenta, especially during labor. The mother's system may then develop protective antibodies that destroy these alien blood cells—just as we all develop antibodies against the germs of measles to destroy them if they try to attack us a second time. But if the mother develops antibodies against her baby's Rh-positive cells, her antibodies go back through the placenta into the baby's circulation and destroy some of his own blood cells there. If a lot are destroyed, the baby becomes anemic soon after birth, and the material from the destroyed cells makes him jaundiced and sick.

A mother's blood won't develop antibodies in time to destroy blood cells in her first Rh-positive baby, but each such baby may sensitize her blood to a greater degree, so there may be increasing difficulty after the first. However, the mother may have developed antibodies even before her first pregnancy if she has had transfusions with Rh-positive blood.

The important things to keep in mind are that only 1 marriage in 8 is between an Rh-positive man and an Rh-negative mother, and even in such a marriage there is only 1 chance in 20 that a baby's blood will be destroyed to a serious degree. In other words, it's the exception rather than the rule.

TWINS

I once made an appeal to mothers of twins to tell me what solutions they had found for their problems, so that I could pass them on. I got 200 wonderfully helpful letters. As you might expect, they showed sharp differences of opinion in some respects, great unanimity in others.

754. Help! All mothers of twins agree that the work is terrific, especially at first, but that the rewards are great.

You need all the help you can get, for as long as you can get it. If possible, hire somebody, even though you have to go into debt. Or beg your mother or another relative to come for a month or two. When there is no room and no privacy in the house, parents have even turned the garage into a bedroom for the helper, in suitable climates. Part-time assistance is a lot better than none at all: a high-school student after school, a cleaning woman or a sitter once or twice a week. Encourage the neighbors to help regularly with certain feedings. It's surprising how much assistance can be gotten from even a 3-year-old sister of the twins.

Of course, the most important helper by far is the father of the twins—in spelling the mother in giving night feedings (alternate feedings or alternate nights) or suppertime baths, making formula, doing some of the household chores that the mother never finds the time for during the day. Even more important to the mother than the practical help is her husband's moral support—patience, appreciation, sympathy, affection. The father of twins has the greatest opportunity that ever comes to a husband to show his devotion and his caliber.

755. Laundry. Mechanical aids become triply valuable. Now is the time, if at all possible, to get an automatic washer and dryer, especially if no diaper service is available. They save hours of work and produce dozens of clean, dry diapers, sheets, pads, shirts, nighties, even in rainy weather.

The babies' wash can be done daily or every other day, depending on what suits the mother's wishes. Frequency of change of sheets and pads can be decreased by placing a small additional waterproof sheet under the baby's hips.

Diaper service is a greater bargain than ever. Laundry service, complete or partial, for the rest of the family is also an important saver of time and energy.

The diaper load can be reduced by changing diapers only once at each feeding, either before or after.

756. Shortcuts. Any mother of twins simply has to find shortcuts in housework. She can go through her house, room by room, stripping it of unessential furnishings and furniture that prolong housecleaning. Furthermore, she should clean only half as often as before. She can select clothes for the family that don't muss and soil quickly, that launder easily and that, as far as possible, don't need ironing. She can select foods that require the minimum of preparation and attention, let dishes soak clean in suds, let them drain dry.

757. The right equipment for the twins can be enormously helpful. Many mothers find a single crib, with a partition across the middle designed by the father, very practical for the first couple of months until the twins become too large and active. Cribs with springs that can be elevated save parents' backs and energy, can serve as diapering and dressing tables. An extra bassinet in which one fussing baby can be wheeled into another room helps to keep the other baby asleep. A great convenience in a two-story house is extra cribs and stores of clothing downstairs for the daytime, eliminating constant stair climbing. Much of the equipment can be borrowed or bought secondhand.

A hospital table on wheels or a tea table on wheels may be convenient, with certain room layouts, for holding stacks of diapers, clothing, sheets, etc. It can be wheeled from crib to crib or room to room.

A double baby carriage is too wide for most doors, and two babies sleeping that close together begin to disturb each other within a few months. On the other hand, a double stroller usually proves valuable for many months. A back-to-back stroller goes through doors more easily. Two car beds are useful. Two inclined seats are really essential.

758. Bathing can be skimped a great deal, if care is taken. Faces can be kept clean with plain water on a washcloth. The diaper area can be washed daily with a soapy washcloth and the soap wiped off twice with a rinsed washcloth. Then, as long as the skin stays in good condition, the all-over bath can be cut down to every other day, twice a week, or even once a week. The complete bath can be given with a washcloth on a waterproof sheet (a sponge bath) if more convenient. It's hard to finish baths for two babies soon enough to avoid a lot of crying from one or both. There are several solutions: a helper to feed the baby who is bathed first; baths in the evening so that the father can help; different bath days or bath hours for different babies. If a tub bath is given (in sink, washstand or fabric tub) and if the babies can wait long enough, it's time-saving to bathe one right after the other in the same water. All bath equipment, clothing, crib and bottles must be ready and close at hand before the bath is started.

759. Breast feeding is practical and possible. From letters I received, I believe that twins are breast-fed for a number of months as often as single babies. (This proves again that there is no set limit to the amount of milk a mother can produce. The breasts supply whatever the baby or babies demand if the mother is going about it with the right method and attitude.) If the babies are too small to nurse well or if they stay in the hospital longer than the mother, then it is a job to establish the breast milk supply by means of manual expression. But as soon as the babies can nurse at the breast, they can both be put to breast together. The mother must have a comfortable chair with good arm support. There are at least three possible positions. If the mother can half recline, or recline, a twin can lie along each of her arms. If she sits up fairly straight, with pillows at each side, the babies can lie along each side, feet toward her back, heads held up to her breasts with her hands. It's also possible to lay the babies across the mother's lap, one more or less on top of the other, but with heads at opposite sides of the mother. The underdog doesn't object in these circumstances.

760. The making and storing of formula for two is cumbersome. Twins are usually small at birth and may need feedings every 3 hours, which adds up to 16 bottles every 24 hours. Two sterilizing pails are necessary to avoid doing that job twice. If refrigerator space is a real problem, the formulas can be sterilized in two dairy milk bottles (quart size), which are stored in the refrigerator. Then at each feeding, 2 sterilized nursing bottles are filled with the correct amount of formula. The nursing bottles can be sterilized once a day by boiling or, if more convenient, by baking in the oven for 15 minutes at about 250°. The nipples should be boiled, not baked.

Some mothers swear by the disposable thin plastic "bottles." They come in long strips already sterilized, occupy less refrigerator space, warm up easily. Only the nipples need to be sterilized.

761. Feeding schedule. A great majority of mothers of twins have found that it is essential to get onto a regular schedule as soon as possible and to feed both babies at once, or one right after the other. Otherwise feeding is going on at all hours of the day and night. (A few mothers find a modified demand schedule is practical. They wait for the first baby to wake and cry, but they wake up the second baby as soon as the first is finished.) Most babies can be accustomed to regularity within a few days. If a baby wakes and fusses before feeding time, you stall for a while, hoping he will go back to sleep. If he gets crying hard, you may have to compromise and feed ahead of schedule, but each day you get stricter, counting on the baby's digestive system to become habituated to the schedule. A pacifier is usually a great help in keeping a baby happy until feeding time. In a few cases, with very irregular, fretful babies, scheduling doesn't work. Then it's easier to feed on demand for a few weeks, however irregularly, rather than have to listen to crying for long periods.

Twins are often premature and small. Then they may require a 3-hour schedule, at least in the daytime, until they weigh 6 or 7 pounds. If one twin is much smaller, he may require a 3-hour schedule for a few weeks while the other is fed every 4 hours, but the smaller one may still be able to go 4 hours at night.

762. How to give bottles. How do you feed bottles to two babies at the same hour? There are several methods. If you have a regular helper, you can each feed a baby. A few mothers have trained one cooperative baby to wake half an hour after the other. But most mothers find that both babies wake together and that there is nothing more nerve-racking than to feed one while the other howls. One solution in the early weeks is to lay the twins on a sofa or bed on either side of the mother, their feet toward her back; in this position she can give two bottles at the same time. Another method is to use a bottle holder for one while she holds the other, alternating babies each feeding.

But some mothers find that a bottle holder (or propping

a bottle on a folded diaper) doesn't work that well, at least in the early weeks. Either the baby loses the nipple and cries, or he chokes. Then the mother has to hurriedly drop the other baby, who cries, while she rescues the first. These mothers find it more practical to use bottle holders or propping for both babies simultaneously, with the babies in inclined seats. They sit close by or between the babies, with both hands free to give whatever help is needed. As these mothers correctly point out, they save enough time with bottle holders to be able to give the twins more and better cuddling at less hectic times.

If there is much irregularity in the early weeks in the amounts or times of feedings, it is necessary to keep a record of how much formula each baby has taken at what hour, and also data on weights and baths. Otherwise you forget too much or try to feed one twin twice and burp the one with the empty stomach. A notebook or a blackboard serves the purpose, or a cardboard clock face for each crib, with elastic bands for minute and hour hands.

Many twins, like single babies, burp themselves if laid on their stomachs after feeding. Remember, too, that though some babies will be uncomfortable unless the bubble is gotten up, others don't seem to feel any difference and then there is no need to make the effort.

763. Feeding of solid food has to be done efficiently, too. When it's all new to the twins, many mothers spoon-feed one baby while the other takes the bottle, and then reverse the process. Additional time can be saved in two other ways: You can bunch the solids so that they are all given in 2 feedings a day instead of 3. You can also give the solids (cereal and fruit, for instance) at one of the daily feedings in the bottle of formula, with a nipple hole as large as the head of a pin. This leaves the other feeding each day in which the babies learn how to swallow solids from a spoon. By the time the twins are skillful at taking solids, they can be propped up in the corners of bassinet, crib or armchair, and spoon-fed together. Or there is an infant feeding table that comes in twin size, with seats that can be adjusted to a semireclining position for babies who can't sit up yet; mothers find it extremely useful.

It is a great time-saver to spoon-feed twins simultaneously. One has just time enough to swallow his mouthful while the mother is loading the spoon and offering it to the other. It may not seem hygienic or polite to use one dish and one spoon, but it's so much more practical.

With twins, there's extra reason for an early start with finger foods (zwieback, bread, wholesome crackers, chopped cooked vegetables, chopped meats) and for relying on them heavily. There's also reason to encourage self-feeding by spoon at least by the age of 12 months.

764. A playpen is particularly valuable for twins (it's impossible to watch two crawling babies at once), and fortunately they are happy in it for longer hours and until a later age than single babies because of each other's company. (It can even be used as a double crib in traveling.) They should be put in it for play period by 2 or 3 months, so that they won't become accustomed to freedom first. Heavy or sharp toys must be avoided because twin babies whack each other without realizing that it hurts. Later, if they begin to be bored in the pen together, one can be moved to a walker, then the other. Such variations interest even the one in the playpen.

After the age of a year it's a great convenience to have a separate room for the twins to play in, with a gate at the door. It can be furnished so that the children can't easily hurt it or themselves (twins are ingenious, cooperative and lightning fast in getting into mischief), and they will play happily in it much longer than a single child would.

765. Clothes and toys: similar or dissimilar? Some mothers point out that since there is usually only one kind of playsuit, for instance, in a store that appeals to the mother in terms of design, warmth, price, it is difficult if not impossible to dress twins differently. And their twins, they say, usually insist on wearing similar clothes at the same time. Other mothers emphasize—about dresses, for instance—that it's usually impossible to buy two of a kind, so twins are compelled to dress differently. Still other mothers say that since the twins have to wear mostly hand-me-down clothes, they have to dress differently from the start and enjoy having their own distinctly different clothes.

Some mothers report that they have had to buy identical toys from the start, or their twins would be rivalrous and miserable. Others say that they usually buy different toys (except for particularly precious possessions like tricycles, dolls), and that twins learn to share happily from an early age.

I suspect that the attitude of the parent makes the biggest difference. If the parent takes it for granted that twins must wear different clothes most of the time and share some of their playthings, either by necessity or on principle, the twins will generally accept this. But if the parent encourages the expectation of identical clothes and toys, and especially if she gives in every time the twins insist, they may well become more insistent with time. Of course, this same principle applies to single children: if parents are firm, children accept; if parents are hesitant, children argue.

It helps twins develop a sense of individuality about their own clothes and a liking for them if each has separate drawer and closet space and if similar garments are marked with names or other markings. Similar garments of different colors preserve some of the advantages of being both twins and individuals. When one twin always has green and the other yellow, this helps everybody keep them straight.

766. Individuality. This brings us finally to the philosophical question of how much to emphasize the twinness of twins and how much to encourage the individuality, especially with identical twins. The whole world is fascinated with twins, makes a fuss over them, likes them to look alike and be dressed alike, asks the parents silly questions about them ("Which is smarter?" "Which do you love best?"). It's hard for the parents not to play up to the world's sentimental or morbid interest. Why not? The trouble is that this may give the twins the feeling that their only source of attraction is their cuteness as a look-alike, dress-alike pair. This may seem appealing at 3 years of age. But if it ends up, as it occasionally does, in two women still trying to attract attention by dressing alike at 30, so dependent on each other that they can't fall in love or marry, the result is not cute but sad.

Now, this doesn't mean that the parents should be afraid of ever dressing the twins alike or should be ashamed to enjoy the world's attention to their children. Twinness is fun for the twins and for the parents.

Twins, in fact, develop special strength of personality from being twins: early independence of parental attention, unusual capacity for cooperative play, great loyalty and generosity toward each other.

But to avoid overemphasis on twinness, it's wise for parents, particularly with identical or very similar twins, to keep away from very similar names (it's hard enough to call the right twin even when the names are dissimilar), to refer to them by their names rather than as "the twins," to dress them alike only part of the time, to introduce them early and regularly to other children before they become used to each other's company exclusively, to let them make separate friends to the degree they wish, to encourage the neighbors to feel free to invite one of them over to play or to a party occasionally (while the other twin has a chance to have his parents all to himself for a change).

In an occasional case, one twin becomes so dependent on the other in schoolwork that it is wise to separate them. But it seems foolish and cruel to have an arbitrary rule about separation when there is no need.

767. Don't worry about favoritism. One further word of advice. Some conscientious parents become too worried at the start that they may give a bit more attention to one baby or always serve him first—because he's smaller, for instance, or more responsive. Such strict impartiality is not necessary —in fact, it encourages a too mechanical, too forced kind of attention. Every child wants and needs to be loved naturally for his own lovable qualities. He is satisfied if he knows that he has a good niche of his own in his parents' hearts and does not worry then about what love his brother or sister is getting. But in the long run he will sense the hollowness of forced attention. A legalistically equal treatment will focus his attention on his rights and make him argue for them like a lawyer. Avoid systems like "Mother puts A's shirt on first, then B's pants on first," or "Today is A's chance to sit next to Daddy."

768. Twin language. Twins often develop a private language between themselves—glances, grunts, foreign-sounding words—which may lead to delay in speaking the family's language and may even cause temporary backwardness in school. Some parents have had to insist that the twins' demands not be met unless they were expressed in English.

SEPARATED PARENTS

769. Is separation necessary? Parents who are considering separation sometimes ask a doctor whether it is better for the children if the parents separate for the sake of peace, or if they hold the family together in spite of friction. Of course, there is no general answer to this. It all depends on why the parents don't get along and the chances of their working out their differences.

It's usually true that when a couple are disagreeing, each one feels that the other is mostly to blame. Yet an outsider can often see that the trouble is not that one or the other is a villain but that neither seems to realize how he or she is acting. In one case, each spouse unconsciously wants to be pampered by the other, like an adored child, instead of being willing to contribute his or her share in a partnership. In another case, a bossy spouse has no idea how much he or she is trying to dominate the other; and the one who is being nagged may be asking for it. Very often in the case of unfaithfulness, the faithless one is not really falling in love with an outsider but, rather, running away from a hidden fear or unconsciously trying to make the spouse jealous. If husband, wife or both are willing to make a real effort to save the marriage, a good psychiatrist or social worker or a wise and tolerant minister should be able to help them to analyze where the trouble lies.

770. Let the child stay loyal to both. How much a separation will damage the child's security depends very largely on how the whole matter is handled. The children should certainly be told soon after the parents have made their decision. Children are always disturbed by a family crisis anyway, and more so if it is kept a mystery. The important things to let the children understand are: (1) Even though the parents separate, the children will still belong to both and will always be able to see both regularly. (2) That neither parent is the good one or the bad one. This is the hardest rule for the parents to abide by. It is only human for each to feel that the other is at fault and to want to get the children to agree with him. It's terrible for a child to become convinced that one of his parents is bad. The child of a divided home needs to believe in both of his parents just as much as the child of a happy family. But there is another danger, even for the parent who has won the child over to his side. When the child reaches a later stage of development, most often in adolescence, when his feelings toward the people who are close to him are going through all kinds of upheavals, he may suddenly turn against the parent he has been loyal to all along and switch sides completely. In other words, each parent has a better chance of keeping a child's love and respect if the child is never encouraged to take sides.

In what words can you explain the separation to a child? It depends on the age of the child and what he wants to know. The mother of a small child may say, "Your Daddy and I argue and fight too much, just the way you and Peter Jenkins do. So we've decided that we'll all have a better time if we don't try to live in the same house. But Daddy will still be your Daddy and I'll still be your Mummy." This is explaining it at the level of the small child who knows well what arguing and fighting are. The older child will want to see the reasons a little more clearly than this. I would try to give him answers that satisfy him, but steer away from pinning blame.

Arguments aren't shameful. Parents who are disagreeing often make a great point of trying to conceal their arguments from their children and even imagine that they don't suspect that anything is up. It is certainly better to carry on heated fights when the children are out of the way, but it's a mistake to think that they aren't aware of family tensions. When a child stumbles in unexpectedly on a scene, I think it's much better for the parents to admit humanly that they have been having an argument than to suddenly become silent and severe and order the child out of the room. It helps to clear the air for everyone to admit that fights are one of the facts of life, even among grown-ups, that people can fight at times and still love and respect each other, that a fight doesn't mean the end of the world.

771. Living arrangements for the child's benefit. What arrangements are made for the children's spending time with each parent depends on circumstances. If the parents live within a reasonable distance of each other and if the children spend most of the time with their mother, the best arrangement may be to have them visit their father on weekends and during those vacations that he can share with them. Whether the visits occur once a week or once a year, it's better for them to be regular, and it's very important for the father not to miss or postpone them.

An arrangement whereby the children stay 6 months of the year with one parent and then 6 months with the other usually works out badly. It breaks up their schooling, separates them for too long a time from the other parent, and gives them a feeling that their lives are chopped in two in a very arbitrary way.

It's a mistake for either parent to pump the child about what happened while he was visiting the other parent or to criticize the other parent. This only makes the child uneasy when he's with either parent. In the end, it may backfire and make him resent the suspicious parent.

In all cases, but especially if the parents can't agree on a reasonable sharing of the child or if he himself dislikes visiting one of them, it is better for the parents to consult a children's psychiatrist (Section 577) about what will work out best for the child, instead of fighting for his custody, like dogs fighting for a bone.

THE WORKING MOTHER

772. To work or not to work? Some mothers have to work to make a living. Usually their children turn out all right, because some reasonably good arrangement is made for their care. But others grow up neglected and maladjusted. It would save money in the end if the government paid a comfortable allowance to all mothers of young children who would otherwise be compelled to work. You can think of it this way: useful, well-adjusted citizens are the most valuable possessions a country has, and good mother care during early childhood is the surest way to produce them. It doesn't make sense to let mothers go to work making dresses in a factory or tapping typewriters in an office. and have them pay other people to do a poorer job of bringing up their children.

A few mothers, particularly those with professional training, feel that they must work because they wouldn't be happy otherwise. I wouldn't disagree if a mother felt strongly about it, provided she had an ideal arrangement for her children's care. After all, an unhappy mother can't bring up very happy children.

What about the mothers who don't absolutely have to work but would prefer to. either to supplement the family income or because they think they will be more satisfied and therefore get along better at home? That's harder to answer.

The important thing for a mother to realize is that the younger the child the more necessary it is for him to have a steady, loving person taking care of him. In most cases. the mother is the best one to give him this feeling of "belonging," safely and surely. She doesn't quit on the job, she doesn't turn against him, she isn't indifferent to him, she takes care of him always in the same familiar house. If a mother realizes clearly how vital this kind of care is to a small child, it may make it easier for her to decide that the extra money she might earn, or the satisfaction she might receive from an outside job, is not so important after all.

773. What children need most from parents or substitutes. The things that are most vital in the care of a child are a little bit different at different age periods. During the first year, a baby needs a lot of motherly care. He has to be fed everything he eats, he eats often, and his food is usually different from the adults'. He makes a great deal of laundry work. In cities he usually has to be pushed in his carriage for outings. For his spirit to grow normally, he needs someone to dote on him, to think he's the most wonderful baby in the world, to make noises and baby talk at him, to hug him and smile at him, to keep him company during wakeful periods.

A day nursery or a "baby farm" is no good for an infant. There's nowhere near enough attention or affection to go around. In many cases, what care there is is matter-of-fact or mechanical rather than warmhearted. Besides, there's too much risk of epidemics of colds and diarrhea.

774. Individual care at least until 3. The infant whose mother can't take care of him during the daytime needs individual care, whether it's in his own home or someone else's. It may be a relative, neighbor or friend whom the mother knows and has confidence in. If a new maid or nurse is to come into the home, the mother should know her well before she leaves the baby in her care. Or the mother may decide to leave him in a foster home for "foster day care," that is to say, in the care of a woman who makes a profession of caring for children. But the foster mother should be doing it more because she loves children than for the income it brings. The only safe way to choose a foster home is through a first-rate, conscientious child-placing agency that investigates and supervises the individual homes it recommends. But whoever the mother chooses should be a woman who is gentle and loving, and who is not trying to take care of more than two or, at the very most, three babies or small children.

Between the ages of 1 and 3, the care of a child requires a little less time but a lot more understanding. It's good for him to have other children around. He's a person now, with ideas of his own. He needs more and more opportunity to be independent, has to be steered tactfully. An adult who is too bossy makes him balky and frantic. One who lacks self-confidence may be helpless to control him. One who smothers him with too much attention hampers his development. Furthermore, this is the age when he comes to depend for security on one or two familiar, devoted people, and is upset if they disappear or keep changing. This is the least advisable period for the mother who has always taken care of him to go off to work for the first time, or to make changes in the person who takes her place. Many day nurseries do not have enough nurses or attendants to give each child the feeling of really belonging to someone. And the staff may not have had the expert training in understanding small children to be able to foster their fullest development, spiritually, socially and physically.

So if you have to go off to work when your baby is about a year old, the best solution is individual care, just as it is for the younger infant. But for this age it is particularly important to find a person who has the ability to understand a child and get along with him easily, and who is not likely to quit the job in a few months.

How to get a small child used to a new grown-up is discussed in Section 501.

775. Possibly a nursery school at 3. A good nursery school or day nursery (Section 541), staffed by trained teachers, may become the best solution somewhere between 2 and 3 years of age. If a first-rate school that takes 2-year-olds is available, and the mother can take over for part of the afternoon, I think it is all right to start a 2-year-old who is quite independent, especially if individual care has not worked out well or if the child has had no chance to play with other children. It might be better to wait until 2½ or even 3, if he is a timid, dependent child (though he should be getting used to other children in the meantime) or his mother's working hours mean his staying in school all day long.

But if there is no good nursery school, if the individual care is satisfactory, if the child is having a chance to play with other children anyway, then there is every reason to continue with individual care right up until he starts first grade.

If you live in a city, get the help of a child guidance clinic or of the best child care agency or family agency in town, in deciding about a nursery school or foster day care. Even the best of nursery schools is apt to have two disadvantages for the working mother. The school day may not last until she can take over, and there is the problem of who is to take care of the child when he is sick.

Whatever the age of the child, it is much better for him and for his mother if she can possibly find a job that leaves her part of the afternoon (or any other part of the day) to be with him.

Between 3 and 6, a child still needs plenty of affectionate, understanding care from adults. If his mother is working most of the day and he goes to a nursery school, he must feel he belongs to his teacher, too. This is why she ought not to be taking care of more than 8 or 10 children. However, at this age he is able to adjust to a teacher, and get a sense of security from her, more easily and completely than at 2. He still should find someone dear to him when he comes home from school, whether at noon, or 3 or 6 P.M.

776. The school child should belong somewhere after school. After 6 years, and particularly after 8, the child seeks and enjoys independence, turns more to outside adults (especially to good teachers) and children for his ideals and companionship. He can get along comfortably for hours at a time without having to turn to a close adult for support. After school he still ought to have a feeling he belongs somewhere, even if he forgets to go there. A motherly neighbor may be able to substitute for a working mother until the latter comes home. After-school play centers are valuable for all children, but particularly for those whose mothers work.

777. The temptation to spoil. A working mother may find that because she is starved for her child's company (and perhaps because she feels guilty about seeing him so little), she is inclined to shower him with presents and treats, bow to all his wishes regardless of her own, and generally let him get away with murder. When a child finds that his mother is an appeaser, it doesn't satisfy him—it's apt to make him more greedy It's fine for a working mother to show her child as much agreeableness and affection as comes naturally, but she should feel free to stop when she's tired, consider her own desires spend only what money is sensible, expect reasonable politeness and consideration—in other words, act like a self-confident, all-day parent. He will not only turn out better, he'll enjoy her company more.

778. What to look for in a mother substitute or sitter.
It's easy to make a list of all the virtues you would like the
person who is to take care of your child to have. But when
it comes down to choosing among the actual human beings
available, you have to decide which qualities are more
valuable.

Far and away the most important is the woman's disposition. Toward the child she should be affectionate, understanding, comfortable, sensible, self-confident. She should love
and enjoy him without smothering him with attention. She
should be able to control him without nagging or severity. In
other words, she should get along with him happily. It is a
help when interviewing a prospective mother substitute or
sitter to have your child with you. You can tell how she responds to a child better by her actions than by what she says.
Avoid the person who is cross, reproving, fussy, humorless
or full of theories.

I think the commonest mistake that parents make is to look
first of all for a person with a lot of experience. It's natural
that they should feel more comfortable leaving a child with
someone who knows what to do for the colic or the croup.
But illnesses and accidents are a very small part of a child's
life. It's the minutes and hours of every day that count. Experience is fine when it's combined with the right personality.
With the wrong personality, it's worth hardly anything.

Cleanliness and carefulness are a little more important
than experience. You can't let someone make the baby's formula who refuses to do it correctly. Still, there are many
rather untidy people who are careful when it's important.
Better a nurse who is too casual than one who is too fussy.

Some parents feel that the education of a nurse or mother
substitute has an influence on the child, but I think it's unimportant compared with other qualities, especially for a young
child. Even if he learns to say "ain't," he'll surely drop it later
if it's not used by his parents and friends.

A common problem is that a grandmother or regular sitter
may favor the youngest child in the family, especially one who
was born after she joined the household. She calls him **her**
baby. If this is a joke and she really is just as devoted to the
older children and they know it, there's no harm. But if the
older children feel discriminated against and show it in their
spirits, it's a bad business and she should not stay. It does
irreparable harm to leave a child in the care of a person who
does not give him security.

A word about boy sitters. They can be entirely satisfactory and they have an added value in a fatherless family. But males on the average have a more insistent sexuality than females. Little girls, between 3 and 6 years particularly, have an instinctive seductiveness, even in the most proper families. If an adolescent boy and a little girl (or a couple of little girls) who enjoy each other's company are together for hours, exciting play can easily lead around to sex play without anybody planning it that way. This is much less likely to happen if there are children in the family beyond 7 or 8 years, who usually have strong consciences.

THE FATHERLESS CHILD

779. When the father's away. If a father is far away when his baby is born and growing up, it doesn't mean he can't have a feeling of taking part in the baby's care, or that the child will be seriously deprived. Far from it. The father needs lots of news and pictures. When a mother is writing, she's apt to think of the facts that are important to her: The baby is healthy, he's gaining weight at a good rate, he has two teeth, the doctor says he's normal—in fact, very advanced. The father wants to know these things, but even more he wants to know the little details that the mother takes for granted. Tell him how loud the bubble burp is and how dignified the baby looks when he lets it out. Jot down all the things he does for 10 minutes: how he scrambles for a magazine, settles back on his behind, tastes the cover, puckers his face and shudders at the bitter taste, leans way forward to gaze at a picture as if he recognized something, tears it apart, rubs the shreds in his hair, crawls off with a piece in his hand, stops at the radio to bat it solemnly. You'll be amazed at how much there is to tell, and the father will grin all over when he pictures it. With a little practice you can remember some of a small child's remarks word for word until you get a chance to write them down. The most skilled author can't make up a child's conversation that's half as amusing or heartwarming as what any small child says any old time.

Take as many snapshots as you can, and send along any that don't look like midnight. A proud mother feels like holding back on the pictures that make the baby or her look homely or silly or cross. But a father trying to imagine his family doesn't want all smiling faces any more than a hungry man wants all candy. Keep sending a few pictures regularly, rather than a big bunch infrequently.

There's another point that's a little more serious and important. A father (like a mother) wants to feel that he's necessary and that he's helping. If the mother, to keep him from worrying, tells him only about how easily she has settled all the questions that have come up and how she has everything under control, he can't help feeling unnecessary. On the other hand, it won't help him to hear all the mother's secret worries about the baby that he can't do anything about. But there are always plenty of reasonable questions in a mother's mind: Should she spend the money to take him to the country on a holiday? Should he go to nursery school next fall? Should he be allowed to tear his clothes and endanger his limbs by climbing trees? These are questions that a father would naturally help to decide if he were at home. He may see them from new, helpful angles that haven't occurred to the mother, and it gives him a real sense of closeness if he is given a chance to share in deciding them.

A mother may feel that she's having a hard enough time as it is, making wise decisions—that it would only complicate matters to get opinions from her husband. But for better or worse, the bringing up of a child has to be shared by both parents in the long run. If a father, during a long absence, comes to feel that the mother is getting off the beam, that there is a lot he will have to undo when he gets home, it will complicate things for a long time after he arrives. It sometimes works out better in the long run if the mother (or father) agrees to a decision that she doesn't think is the right one.

780. Making it up to the child. It would be foolish to say that his father's absence or death makes no difference to a child, or that it's easy for a mother to make it up to him in other ways. But if the job is well handled, the child, either boy or girl, can continue to grow up normal and well adjusted.

The mother's spirit is most important. She may feel lonely, imprisoned or cross at times, and she will sometimes take it out on the child. This is all natural and won't hurt him too much. The important thing is for her to go on being a normal human being, keeping up her friendships, her recreations, her outside activities, as far as she can. This is hard if she has a baby or child to take care of and no one to help her. But she can ask people in, and take the baby to a friend's house for an evening if he can adjust to sleeping in strange places. It's more valuable to him to have his mother cheerful and outgoing than to have his routine perfect. It won't do him any good to have her wrap all her activity and thoughts and affection around him.

A child, whether he's young or old, boy or girl, needs to be friendly with other men if the father is not there. With the baby up to the age of a year or two, a good deal is accomplished if he can just be reminded frequently that there are such creatures as agreeable men, with lower voices, different clothes and different manners than women. A kindly grocer or milkman who just grins and says hello helps even if there are no closer friends. As the child goes on toward 3 and over, the kind of companionship with men is increasingly important. Whether he is boy or girl, he needs chances to be with and feel close to other men and older boys. Grandfathers, uncles, cousins, scoutmasters, men teachers at school, the minister, old family friends or a combination of these can serve as substitute fathers if they enjoy the child's company and see him fairly regularly. Any child of 3 or over builds up an image of his father that is his ideal and inspiration, whether he remembers him or not. The other friendly men he sees and plays with give substance to the image, influence his conception of his father, make his father mean more to him. The mother can help by being extra hospitable to male relatives, sending her son or daughter to a camp that has some men counselors, picking a school, if she has a choice, that has some men teachers, encouraging a child to join clubs and other organizations that have men leaders.

The boy without a father particularly needs opportunity and encouragement to play with other boys, every day if possible, by the age of 2, and to be mainly occupied with boyish pursuits. The temptation of the mother who has no other equally strong ties is to make him her closest spiritual companion, getting him interested in clothes and interior decoration, in her opinions and feelings about people, in the books and other recreations she enjoys. If she succeeds in making her world more appealing to him, easier to get along in, than the world of boys (where he has to make his own way), then he may grow up precocious, with feminine interests. It's all to the good if a mother can spend time and have plenty of fun with her boy, provided she also lets him go his own way, provided she shares in his interests rather than having him share too many of hers. It helps to invite other boys to the house regularly and to take them along on treats and trips.

THE HANDICAPPED CHILD

781. Treat him naturally. A child with a handicap may need treatment of the defect. But even more he needs to be treated naturally, whether the handicap is mental slowness, crossed eyes, epilepsy, deafness, shortness, a disfiguring birth-mark, or a deformity of any other part of the body. This is easier said than done. A defect quite naturally upsets the parents to some degree. Here are examples of different re-actions they may have.

782. His happiness depends on his attitude, not on his defect. A boy has been born with only a thumb and one finger on his left hand. At 2½ years he is happy and can do almost as much with his left hand as with his right. His 6-year-old sister is fond and proud of him, wants to take him with her everywhere she goes, never seems to worry about his hand. The mother, however, is very conscious of the miss-ing fingers. She winces when she sees a strange child catch sight of his hand and stare. She thinks it is fairer to the child to keep him at home where he won't be subjected to curiosity and remarks, makes excuses when he wants to go shopping with her. Which attitude is better for him, the mother's or the sister's? We first have to answer another question. Does a defect in itself make a child seriously self-conscious and ashamed? Generally speaking, No.

Of course, all of us are slightly self-conscious, and we all focus on what we think are our weakest features. Those with defects naturally worry about them some. But anybody who has known many cripples, for example, realizes that some of those with the worst handicaps are just as outgoing, happy and unworried as anyone with sound limbs. And at the other extreme, you can probably think of one acquaintance who is miserably self-conscious, for instance, about the prominence of her ears, when actually they are not noticeable at all.

In other words, the seriousness of a defect has little to do with whether a person grows up feeling self-conscious, ashamed, unhappy.

The important factors that make a person (**with or without defects**) grow up happy and outgoing are having parents who thoroughly enjoy and approve of him, who do little worrying, urging, fussing, criticizing; having opportunities to learn the fun of give and take with other children from an early age. If the parents from the beginning are unhappy or ashamed about a child's appearance, always wishing he were different, overprotecting him, keeping him from mingling with others, he is apt to grow up turned in on himself, dissatisfied, feeling that he is queer. But if they take his disfiguring birthmark or deformed ear as of no great importance, act as if they consider him a normal child, let him go places like anyone else, don't worry about stares and whispered remarks—then the child gets the idea he is a regular guy and thinks little of his peculiarity.

As for the stares and pointing and whispered remarks, the child with a noticeable defect has to get used to them, and the younger the easier. If he is hidden most of the week and gets one stare on Sunday, it is more disturbing than ten stares every day, because he is not accustomed to them.

783. He'll be happier without pity. A 6-year-old boy has a birthmark that covers half his face. His mother has taken this hard and feels a lot of pity for him. She is strict with her two older daughters but excuses the boy from household tasks, lets him get away with rudeness to her and meanness to his sisters. He's not too popular with his sisters or other children.

It's understandable why parents of a handicapped child are inclined to feel too sorry for him for his own good and to expect too little of him. Pity is like a drug. Even if it's distasteful to a person at first, he's likely to come to depend on it. Naturally, a child with a defect needs understanding, and he often needs special handling. The slow child should never be expected to do a job that is beyond his mental development, and one with stiff hands shouldn't be criticized for poor penmanship. But the child with a defect can be reasonably polite, take turns, do his share of the chores. Everyone is happier and more pleasant when he knows he's expected to be considerate. The child with a handicap wants to be treated the same, held to the same rules as other children.

784. Fairness to the whole family. A 4-year-old child has been found to be very slow in his mental and physical development. The parents have taken him from doctor to doctor and clinic to clinic. Each time they hear the same story. It is not a mental defect for which there is any curative treatment, though there are many things to be done to bring him up happy and useful. The parents naturally want more than this, and they end up traveling long distances and paying exorbitant fees to a quack who promises a magical cure. As a result, the other children in the family receive less than their share of attention. The parents, however, feel much happier spending the money and making the effort.

It certainly is right and normal for parents to want to do whatever has a reasonable chance of helping a child with a handicap. But there's another hidden factor. It's human nature for them to feel, underneath, that they are somehow to blame—even though all the doctors and books explain that the condition is a pure accident of nature. All of us in our upbringing have been made to feel guilty about things we did and things we ought to have done. If we have a handicapped child, this guiltiness left over from youth is apt to get focused on the handicap.

This unreasonable sense of guilt often drives parents, especially if they are very conscientious people, to do something even if it's not sensible. It's a kind of penance, though they don't think of it that way.

If parents are on the lookout for this tendency, they are better able to choose the right treatment for the child and, incidentally, spare their other children (and themselves) unnecessary deprivation.

785. Love him for himself. A certain child at the age of 10 is distinctly shorter than average, even shorter than his 8-year-old sister. The parents feel that this is a real tragedy and keep taking him to new doctors, all of whom agree that there is no deficiency disease—he is merely a child who seems to have been born with a small pattern. The parents show their concern in other ways, too. They frequently urge him to eat more so that he will grow faster. When there is any allusion to his size compared to his sister's or to other boys', they eagerly remind him how much smarter he is.

There is enough rivalry among boys so that an individual who is short feels some disappointment anyway. But the two factors that make the biggest difference are the boy's general happiness and self-confidence, and how easily the parents accept his shortness.

Being told to eat reminds him of how worried his parents are and is more likely to take his appetite away than to improve it. Being compared favorably to his sister and friends in other qualities doesn't make him feel better about being short, and it only emphasizes the idea of competition and rivalry. There are times when the parents sense that a short child, or a homely one, or a nearsighted one wants to be told how unimportant his handicap is. Confident reassurance is then a great help. But if the parents are the uneasy ones, always bringing up the subject, it convinces the child that he must be in a bad way.

786. Brothers and sisters take their attitude from the parents. A child, now 7 years old, was born with cerebral palsy. His intelligence has not been affected at all, but his speech is hard to understand and his face and limbs are constantly making strange contortions over which he has little control.

His mother has a sensible attitude toward his handicaps. She treats him the same as her younger boy except that she takes him several times a week to a special clinic, where he receives massage, exercises and training in control of his limbs and speech. His younger brother and the children in the neighborhood are all devoted to him because of his friendly nature and enthusiasm. He gets in all their games and, though he often can't keep up, they make allowances. He goes to the regular neighborhood school. He is naturally handicapped in some ways, but since the program is flexible and the children take a part in planning and working out their projects, his good ideas and cooperative spirit make him a popular member of the class. His father, who is more of a worrier, thinks the boy might be happier in the long run if he were sent away to a special boarding school, among others with similar handicaps. He also fears that when the younger boy grows older, he will be embarrassed by the other's peculiar appearance.

If the parents accept a handicapped child wholeheartedly and matter-of-factly, the brothers and sisters are apt to do so also. They are not too upset by the remarks of other children. But if the parents feel embarrassed and tend to conceal him, he will be on the minds of the brothers and sisters just as much as if he were in sight.

787. Changes in the parents' feelings. Many parents who discover that they have a child with a serious handicap go through much the same stages of feelings. First is the painful shock and the natural resentment. "Why does this have to happen to our family?" Then so often comes the guiltiness (discussed in Section 784). "What did I do wrong or what did I not do that I should have done?" The doctor keeps explaining, "You could not have prevented this condition." But it takes a long time for the parents to begin to feel convinced on the inside.

A difficulty that arises now and later is that various relatives and acquaintances keep coming forward with tales they have heard of experts and new treatments all over the world. They insist that the parents consult each in turn. They act shocked when their advice is not followed. They are well-meaning, but they keep the parents troubled.

The next stage is often one in which the parents become so preoccupied with the handicap and its treatment that they partly lose sight of the child as a person. They fail to enjoy all his other good qualities, which are quite unimpaired. Then as they gradually get back into focus and begin to think of him as another nice human being who just happens to have a particular difficulty, they can't help being irritated by those relatives and friends who still can't talk about anything but the child's handicap.

It helps parents in going through these painful stages to know that hundreds of thousands of other good parents have had the same experience.

788. Most parents need some help, too. Caring for a child with a handicap usually means extra effort and extra strain. To make the best plans for him requires real wisdom, which is hard to come by when you are upset and have little experience. All this adds up to the fact that you who are parents of handicapped children often need guidance and you are certainly entitled to it. I am thinking not just of medical advice. I'm thinking of opportunities to discuss the management of the child at home, the problems created for the other members of the family, the pros and cons of the local school compared with schools farther away, the frustrations and resentment of the parents themselves. To get such matters clarified usually takes many long talks, over a period of years, with a counselor who is experienced in the field and is comforting to deal with.

There are usually social workers in state bureaus for the blind, deaf, crippled and retarded, and also on the staffs of the schools and clinics that care for such children. In a rural district there may be a county welfare worker. In cities there are social workers in family and children's social agencies. To find the right person to help you with your problems, write, if you live in the country or a small town, to the department of welfare in your state capital. If you live in the city, call the Community Chest. They can tell you the right agency.

In recent years, the parents of children with various handicaps have organized themselves into local chapters and national associations. There are several purposes, all worthwhile. They share their special problems and solutions. They hear talks by professionals in the field. They exert their influence to get better facilities for their children. They raise funds for research and treatment.

You may be able to get information from the following national organizations:

United Cerebral Palsy Associations, Inc.
　　321 W. 44th Street, New York, N. Y. 10036
Muscular Dystrophy Associations of America, Inc.
　　1790 Broadway, New York, N. Y. 10019
Cystic Fibrosis Foundation
　　202 E. 44th Street, New York, N. Y. 10017
United Epilepsy Association, Inc.
　　111 W. 57th Street, New York, N.Y. 10019
National Association for Retarded Children, Inc.
　　420 Lexington Avenue, New York, N. Y. 10017

789. Where to live, where to go to school, where to get special training. Suppose a child has a defect that does not interfere with his getting to the regular neighborhood school and does not handicap him in learning in a regular class. Examples would be minor crippling, healed heart disease that does not seriously limit a child's activity, peculiarities of appearance such as birthmarks. It's best for such a child to go to the regular neighborhood school. He will be living the rest of his life among average people, and it's best for him to start out that way, thinking of himself as average in almost all respects.

790. Regular school when possible. In previous times it was believed that children with handicaps that interfere with ordinary classroom learning—such as impaired hearing or vision, for instance—should be sent from the start to specialized day schools in their own community or, if none were available, to specialized boarding schools. In more recent years it has been realized that though the education of the handicapped child is extremely important, even more important is his adjustment and his happiness. This means keeping in mind the sociability he will acquire from being with unhandicapped as well as handicapped children, the wholesome view he will take of the world and of himself if he grows up thinking of himself as a regular guy in most respects, the security he will gain from being part of his family. It is certainly preferable that a child live at home if possible. The younger a child is (especially up to the age of 6 or 8), the more he needs the close, loving, understanding kind of care, the sense of really belonging, that he is more likely to get at home than in even the best of boarding schools. So there has been an increasing effort to provide for handicapped children in regular neighborhood day schools wherever that is possible and, when appropriate, to keep them in regular classes as much of each day as is possible. This means increasing school budgets and training more specialized teachers so that local schools can have such facilities. It means in one case that the handicapped child may spend part of each day in a special class and other periods in the regular classroom with unhandicapped children. In some cases a specialized teacher can coach the regular classroom teacher in how to teach a subject so that the handicapped child can comprehend and participate.

How the philosophy works out in any community or school depends on many factors: the number and skill of the special teachers, the size of classes and classrooms, the kind of handicap, the severity of the handicap, the age and the previous training of the handicapped child.

791. The slightly or moderately hard-of-hearing child needs primarily lip reading instruction, speech correction and probably a hearing aid. With the assistance of these he can usually take his place in a regular local school.

792. The child who is more severely deaf cannot get much from a regular class until he has learned how to communicate with others. This requires long training at a special school for the deaf. In the cities where there are day schools for the deaf it is important for children to begin attending between 2 and 3 years of age, when their capabilities are flexible and their eagerness to learn is great. It is much better for young children to be living at home if this is at all possible, where their special needs for love and for belonging can be satisfied. But if there is no local school and the family cannot move, a boarding school should be considered by the time a child is 4.

There has been much controversy about whether, in order to favor lip reading and speech training, the deaf child should be prevented from using sign language and finger spelling. Parents who of course would like their child to be able to comprehend and speak in the company of hearing people and are eager that he not appear different, have naturally favored the philosophy of no sign language or finger spelling.

But lip reading is an incomplete, inexact form of comprehending for even the most apt pupil. Different sounds have exactly the same mouth movements, so there has to be a lot of guessing. Many children—including bright ones—never become even fairly good lip readers, despite the most expert schooling. The teaching of speech to severely deaf children is painfully slow and often far from satisfactory. Nowadays it is recognized that when children are forbidden to use sign language and finger spelling in order to encourage lip reading and speaking, it is more likely to slow them down in all aspects of their learning. To put it the other way around, it is helpful to allow and encourage **all** forms of communication for the deaf; sign language and finger spelling will supplement and encourage lip reading and speaking.

793. A blind child may be able to get a great deal from the regular school class (or regular nursery school) even though he needs some special instruction at the same time. It is amazing and inspiring to see how well even a 3- or 4-year-old blind child can get along in a class of seeing children. The inexperienced teacher, just like the parent, tends to be anxiously overprotective at first, but gradually comes to realize that overprotection is not necessary and only gets in the child's way. Of course, sensible precautions have to be taken and allowances made. The other children accept the handicapped one easily after a little questioning. They usually make allowances and give help in a very sensible manner. Information about special classes and schools for blind children can be obtained from your State Board of Education or State Commission for the Blind.

794. Some children with cerebral palsy or infantile paralysis require not special classes but highly skilled muscle treatment and training that is available in only a few places. Information about classes, schools and other facilities for crippled children can be secured from your State Department of Health, Division of Crippled Children. The very special training that is needed for children with cerebral palsy cannot yet be secured in every part of the country. You can consult the National Society for Crippled Children and Adults, Inc., 2223 West Ogden Avenue, Chicago, Ill. 60612.

If no satisfactory training and treatment can be received where a family lives, they may consider moving.

795. Steady medical care. The parents of a child with any defect should, of course, get expert advice, from a private doctor or from a good hospital clinic. If they don't feel satisfied or if the suggested treatment sounds drastic, they are entitled to request another opinion, in consultation with the first doctor. Occasionally parents who have received what sounds like good advice from one doctor will go to one or two more "just to be sure," but they are apt to be confused by minor differences in treatment or terminology, and end up with more doubts than they started with.

If you have found a skillful doctor who understands your child's problem, stay with him, consult him regularly. The doctor who has known the child and family over a period of time is in a better position to prescribe wisely than the doctor who has just been called in. Psychologically, it is apt to be upsetting to the child with a defect to be taken to one new doctor after another. If you read of a new discovery in the condition your child has, ask your own doctor about it rather than rush to the discoverer. If it has been proved to be beneficial, your own doctor will know or can find out whether it has any promise in your child's case.

796. Mental slowness. You can roughly divide cases of real mental slowness into three groups: organic, glandular and "natural." Organic cases are those in which there is physical brain damage, caused for example, by insufficient oxygen reaching the brain during birth or by encephalitis. Glandular cases are due to deficient functioning of the thyroid gland; if they are diagnosed early and treated correctly, the mental deficiency may be kept to a minimum.

The majority of cases of mental slowness are "natural," in

the sense that they are not caused by disease or injury or by anything that the parents did wrong or failed to do right. The child merely has less than the average degree of intelligence, just the way other children are brighter, shorter or taller than average. His intelligence continues to develop steadily but at a slower rate than average. If a particular child at the age of 4 years has the intelligence of the average 3-year-old, then at 16 he will probably have the intelligence of an average 12-year-old. He is said to have an intelligence quotient (I.Q.) of 75 (3/4 = 12/16 = 75/100). Though there is lots to be done for the naturally slow child, there is no cure, any more than there is a cure for blue eyes or large feet.

797. Being accepted enables him to make the most of his abilities. The behavior problems that a few slow children develop are usually due not to low intelligence but to mistaken methods of handling. If the parents feel that the child is queer or shameful, for instance, their love may not go out to him in sufficiently full measure to give him security and happiness. If they mistakenly believe that they are to blame for his condition, they must insist on unwise "treatment" of all kinds that disturbs him without benefiting him. If they jump to the conclusion that he is a hopeless case who will never be "normal," they may neglect to provide him with the playthings, the companions, the proper schooling that are needed by all children to bring out their best abilities. The greatest danger of all is that the parents, trying to ignore the signs that he is slow, trying to prove to themselves and the world that he is just as bright as the next child, will push him all along the line—try to teach him skills and manners before he is ready, hurry his toilet training, get him into a school class that he isn't up to, coach him at home in his lessons. The constant pressure makes him balky and irritable. Being frequently in situations in which he can't possibly succeed robs him of self-confidence.

Sadly enough, the slow child whose parents have had only an average amount of schooling and are living happily on a modest scale often makes out better than the child who is born into a college-educated family or one that has high ambitions for worldly success. The latter are more likely to assume that it's vital to get good marks at school, to go to college, to go into a profession.

There are many useful and dignified jobs that are best

performed by people who have less than average intelligence. It's the right of every individual to grow up well enough adjusted and well enough trained to be able to handle the best job that he has the intelligence for.

The slow child must be allowed to develop in his own pattern, to have eating habits, toilet habits that are suitable for his stage of mental growth rather than suitable for his age. He needs opportunities to dig and climb and build and make-believe at the periods when he is ready for these activities, playthings that appeal to him, chances to play with children that he can enjoy and keep up with (even if they are a year or more younger in age). When he goes to school, he must go into a class where he can feel that he belongs and is accomplishing something. He needs to be loved warmly and enjoyed for his appealing qualities.

Anyone who has observed groups of slow children knows how natural and friendly and appealing most of them are—particularly the ones who have been accepted naturally at home. And when they are busy at play or schoolwork that is right for them, they have the same eager, interested attitude that average and superior children do. In other words, the "dumb" look comes more from feeling out of place than from having a low I.Q. Most of us would have a stupid look in an advanced lecture on relativity.

The child who is only mildly or moderately slow is, of course, usually cared for at home. This is the place where he, like the average child, gets the most security. It will be good for him to go to nursery school, if possible, where the teachers can decide whether he should be with his own age or younger children.

798. The care of a slow child at home. Parents, when they become convinced that a child is slow in his mental development, are apt to ask the doctor or social worker what special playthings and educational material they should buy and what special instruction they should give the child at home. This is due to people's natural tendency to think, at first, that a handicapped child is very different from other children. To be sure, a retarded child has interests and capabilities that are not up to his chronological age; they correspond to his mental age. He is apt to want to play with children younger than himself, and with toys suitable for that younger age. He won't begin to try to tie his shoe-laces or to pick out letters at 5 or 6, but he probably will become interested in these activities several years later, when his mental age is 5 or 6.

The mother of a child of average intelligence doesn't have to ask a doctor or read a book to find out his interests. Mostly she watches him playing with his own possessions and with the possessions of neighbors and senses what else might appeal to him. She observes what he is trying to learn and helps him tactfully.

It's really just the same with a retarded child. You watch to see what he enjoys. You get him the playthings, indoors and out, that are sensible. You help him locate the children he has fun with, every day if possible. You teach him the skills he wants assistance with.

799. The right school placement is vital. It is wise to get the opinion and guidance of a psychiatrist or psychologist, privately or through a child guidance clinic or through the school system, when it is suspected that a child is slow (Section 577). It is important that he be tested by the time he is 5 or 6 years old, before he enters kindergarten or first grade. He should not get into a class that is beyond him. Every day that he is unable to keep up, his self-confidence is destroyed a little, and being left back a grade or demoted hurts him a lot. If he is only slightly slow and the school program is one in which every child can contribute according to his ability, he may be able to move along with children his own age. But if he is moderately slow, or if the schoolwork is the same for all children in the class, then he should not start first grade until his mental ability is up to it. This may mean waiting 1 or more years. If there is a kindergarten, it may be wise to wait to start this until the year before he is ready for first grade, so that he won't be disappointed if he does not move on to the grades with his class. On the other hand, if the kindergarten is very flexible, it may be better for him to plan to be there for 2 years, especially if he has few children to play with at home.

In a large school system there may be special "opportunity" classes for children who are moderately slow. They start in the special class at 6 or 7 or 8, but postpone book work for several years, depending on what they are ready for.

If the family have determined in advance, with the help of a psychologist, that a child needs to be in a special class, they may be able to move into a neighborhood where such classes exist by the time the child is of school age.

If it is impossible to get the help of a psychologist, discuss the child thoroughly with the teacher or principal, giving her all the facts. If there is any doubt of his readiness, it is better to wait too long than to start too soon.

800. Boarding school if it offers more. The situation can always be reviewed again later to see whether the day school is meeting the needs of the child, in either a regular or special class. If the child is not up to the work in the class that is available and is not happy there, or if his handicap is too upsetting to other members of the family, it may be better for all concerned, at some future stage, to take advantage of the opportunities offered by a state or private boarding school. At least the parents will want to look into this carefully. The waiting list at most state schools is long and there may be a delay of several years between the time application is made and the time the child is accepted. Better to get on a waiting list early and then give up the place later if it is not needed than to delay applying because you are undecided.

801. The more seriously retarded child. The child who at 1½ or 2 years, for instance, is still unable to sit up, who shows little interest in people or things, presents more complicated problems. He will have to be cared for as a baby for a long time. Because of his very limited awareness, he receives less benefit from the family and they find less to respond to in him. Of course, there is no one right answer. It depends on the degree of retardation, the temperament of the child, how he affects other children in the family, whether by the time he is active he can find playmates and activities to keep him happy, whether there is a special class in one of the local schools that will accept him and suit him, the availability and quality of boarding schools. Most of all, it depends on how much his mother can enjoy caring for him or how much he exhausts her physically and emotionally. Some of these questions can't be answered until the child is several years older.

One mother is so constituted that she can take a retarded child in her stride. She can find ways to care for him that don't exhaust her. She is able to enjoy his agreeable qualities, not be upset by the difficulties he presents, and not become too wrapped up in his care. The other children in the family take their cue mainly from her in these respects. The acceptance by the rest of the family brings out the best in the retarded child and gives him a good start in life. He may be able to benefit most by living at home indefinitely.

Another mother who is equally devoted finds herself becoming increasingly tense and impatient in caring for a child with such special needs. This may impair her relationship with her husband and other children, and the children may be upset by the presence of the handicapped child. The mother needs a lot of help from a social worker. This should lead either to a more comfortable attitude or to making some other provision for the child that will be better for all concerned.

Still another mother finds that she can throw herself into the care of a seriously handicapped child without a feeling of undue strain, even with an enjoyable devotion. But an outsider can see that her sense of obligation to the child is so intense that she is not thinking enough of her husband, her other children or her own normal interests. In the long run, this is not healthy for the family as a whole or even for the retarded child. The mother needs help in gaining a sense of proportion and in easing up in her preoccupation (Section 788).

802. Dowd syndrome (Mongolism). This is a special type of organic mental deficiency but there is also a disturbance of bodily growth. The eyes slant upward like an Oriental's and this is how the condition received its earlier name. There are other distinctive characteristics. Physical growth is slow, and the child does not reach full size. Intelligence develops very slowly in most cases, but in a few it develops to a fair degree. In disposition these children are characteristically sweet-natured.

The chances of having a baby with this condition increase toward the end of a woman's child-bearing period. It is caused by an abnormality of the chromosomes, which develops at the start of the life of the embryo. It is not an inherited disease. There are several distinct types of the disease. If a mother has one such child, a study of chromosome patterns in the child and the mother should be carried out by a genetic specialist to determine how much chance there is that any future child of this mother will have the condition. The chromosome study is particularly essential if the mother is young.

As in other forms of mental slowness, the best course for

the future depends on how the child develops, the local opportunities for classes and playmates, how difficult or how comfortable it proves for the mother to carry out her other jobs and this special one, too. Some Mongoloid children are reared at home enjoyably and without undue strain on parents and children. In other cases, it turns out as the child grows older that he and the rest of the family would be happier if he were cared for in a state or private boarding school. With this possibility in mind, it is wise to make tentative application early, because there is usually a waiting list of several years' duration. The application can always be canceled later if it is not wanted. Continued counseling is helpful in arriving at the best decision.

Some doctors recommend to parents who can afford it that the baby be cared for in a private nursing home from birth so that they will not become overattached to a child who is not likely to develop far and so that they can devote all their care to the older children. This may be the better plan in some families, not in others. I think parents should take their time in coming to a decision and that if they are in doubt, it is helpful to get counsel from a family social agency or a psychiatrist. Very few families, however, can afford such private care, year after year. Very few state schools can accept such children before they are 5 years or older because of policy or because of lack of facilities.

ADOPTING A CHILD

803. Both parents should want him very much. A couple should decide to adopt a child only if both of them love children and feel that they just can't get along without them. All children, "own" or adopted, need to feel that they belong to and are loved by both father and mother, deeply and "forever," if they are to grow up secure. It's worse for an adopted child to sense a lack of devotion in one or both parents because he's not quite so secure to begin with. He knows that he was given up for some reason by his true parents, and he may fear secretly that his adopted parents might someday give him up, too. You can see, then, why it's a mistake to adopt when only one parent wants to, or when both parents are thinking of it only for practical reasons, such as to have extra help on the farm or to have someone to take care of them in their old age. Occasionally a woman

who is afraid that she's losing her husband wants to adopt a child with the futile hope that this will hold his love. Adoption for reasons like this is not just unfair to the child. It usually proves to be wrong from the parents' point of view, too. All too often the adopted child who is not deeply loved becomes a serious behavior problem.

It's usually unwise for a single person to adopt a child. This is because boys and girls both need the influence of father and mother in their upbringing, and because the single person may become too wrapped up in the child.

A couple should not wait until they are too old to adopt a child. They are liable to become too set in their ways. They've dreamed so long of a little girl with golden curls filling the house with song as she goes about her daily tasks that even the best of children turns out to be a rude shock. How old is "too old"? It's not a matter of years alone. It's something to discuss with a child-placing agency.

Parents who have a child of their own who is not very happy or sociable sometimes consider adopting another to keep him company. It's a good idea to talk this over with a children's psychiatrist or the child-placing agency before thinking of this very seriously. The adopted child is apt to feel like an outsider compared to the "own" child. If the parents lean over backward to show affection for the newcomer, it may upset rather than help their own child. It's a risky business.

There's sometimes danger, too, in adopting to "replace" a child who has died. If there are other "own" children in the family, an adopted child may feel at a disadvantage. But even if the parents have no other children, they should adopt only because they want a child to love for himself. There is no harm in adopting one who is similar in age and sex and appearance to the child who died, but the comparison should stop there. It is unfair and unsound to want to make one individual play the part of another. He is bound to fail at the job of being a ghost, and he will disappoint the parents and become unhappy. He should not be reminded of what the other child did, or be compared with him out loud or in the parents' minds. Let him be himself. (Some of this applies also to the "own" child who is born after an older one dies.)

804. Adopt through a good agency. Probably the most important rule of all about adoption is to arrange it through a first-rate child-placing agency. It is always risky for the adopting parents to deal directly with the true parents or through an inexperienced third person. It leaves the way open for the true parents to change their minds and to try to get their child back. Even when the law stands in the way of this, the unpleasantness can ruin the happiness of the adopting family and the security of the child. The good agency stands like an impenetrable wall between the two sets of parents, keeps them from ever knowing each other, keeps them from ever making trouble for each other, and thereby protects the child. The agency helps the natural mother and relatives to make the right decision in the first place as to whether to give the baby up or not. It uses its judgment and experience in deciding which couples should be dissuaded from adopting. The agency also watches the child during the probationary period in the new family to make sure that the arrangement is working out well for all concerned. Wise agencies and wise state laws require a probationary period before the adoption becomes final.

At what age should a child be adopted? In a general way, the younger the better. The adopting parents feel that they are starting with a clean slate and can get used to the baby through the same easy stages as if he were their own. However, plenty of successful adoptions have been made later in childhood.

Adopting parents usually wonder about the baby's heredity and how it will affect his future. The more we have learned about personality development, including intelligence, the clearer it becomes that the most important factor by far is the environment in which the child grows up, especially the love he receives and the feeling of belonging that he acquires. There is no evidence that specific social abnormalities like alcoholism, immorality, delinquency or irresponsibility are inherited.

805. Let him find out naturally. Should an adopted child be told he is adopted? All the experienced people in this field agree that the child should know. He's sure to find out sooner or later from someone or other, no matter how carefully the parents think they are keeping the secret. It is practically always a very disturbing experience for an older child, or even an adult, to discover suddenly that he is adopted. It may disturb his sense of security for years. Supposing a baby has been adopted during his first year, when should he be told? The news shouldn't be saved for any definite age. The parents should, from the beginning, let the fact that he's adopted come openly, but casually, into their conversations with each other, with the child and with their acquaintances. This creates an atmosphere in which the child can ask questions whenever he is at a stage of development in which the subject interests him. He finds out what adoption means bit by bit, as he gains understanding.

Some adopting parents make the mistake of trying to keep the adoption secret; others err in the opposite direction by stressing it too much. Most adopting parents have, quite naturally, an exaggerated sense of responsibility at first—as if they have to be letter-perfect to justify the fact that someone else's child has been entrusted to their care. If they go too earnestly at the job of explaining to the child that he's adopted, he begins to wonder, "What's wrong with being adopted anyway?" But if they accept the adoption as naturally as they accept the color of the child's hair, they won't have to make a secret of it, or keep reminding him of it. They should remind themselves that, having been selected by the agency, they're probably darned good parents and the child is lucky to have found them.

Let's say that a child around 3 hears his mother explaining to a new acquaintance that he is adopted, and asks, "What's **adopted**, Mommy?" She might answer, "A long time ago I wanted very much to have a little baby boy to love and take care of. So I went to a place where there were a lot of babies, and I told the lady, 'I want a little boy with brown hair and brown eyes.' So she brought me a baby, and it was you. And I said, 'Oh, this is just exactly the baby that I want. I want to adopt him and take him home to keep forever.' And that's how I adopted you." This makes a good beginning because it emphasizes the positive side of the adoption, the fact that the mother received just what she wanted. The story will delight him, and he'll want to hear it many times.

But somewhere between the ages of 3 and 4, if he is like most children, he wants to know where babies come from in the beginning. The answer is discussed in Section 532. It is best to answer truthfully, but simply enough so that the 3-year-old can understand easily. But when his adopted mother explains that babies grow inside the mother's abdomen, it makes him wonder how this fits in with the story of picking him out from all the other babies at the institution. Maybe then, or months later, he asks, "Did I grow inside you?" Then the adopting mother can explain, simply and casually, that he grew inside another mother before he was adopted. This is apt to confuse him for a while, but he will get it clear later.

Eventually he raises the more difficult question of why his own mother gave him up. To imply that his mother didn't want him would shake his confidence in all mothers. Any sort of made-up reason may bother him later in some unexpected way. Perhaps the best answer and nearest to the truth might be, "I don't know why she couldn't take care of you, but I'm sure she wanted to." During the period when the child is digesting this idea, he needs to be reminded, along with a hug, that he's always going to be yours now.

806. He must belong completely. The secret fear that the adopted child may have is that his adopting parents will someday give him up as his true parents did, if they change their minds or if he is bad. Adopting parents should always remember this and vow that they will never, under any circumstances, say or hint that the idea of giving him up has ever crossed their minds. One threat uttered in a thoughtless or angry moment might be enough to destroy the child's confidence in them forever. They should be ready to let him know that he is theirs forever at any time the question seems to enter his mind; for instance, when he is talking about his adoption. I'd like to add, though, that it's a mistake for the adopting parents to worry so about the child's security that they overemphasize their talk of loving him. Basically, the thing that gives the adopted child the greatest security is being loved, wholeheartedly and naturally. It's not the words but the music that counts.

Index

EMERGENCIES

Animal bites	529	Head injuries ...	537-538
Artificial respira-		Hemorrhage	531-533
tion	539-540	Objects in nose	
Bleeding	531-533	and ears	540
Broken bones ...	536-537	Poisoning	540-542
Burns	533-534	Smothering	539
Choking	538-539	Swallowed objects	538
Concussion	537-538	When to call the	
Convulsions	527-528	doctor	52-53
Fractures	536-537		

Index

A

Abscess
breasts, 99
ear, 478-479
skin, 534-535
Accidents, 529-542; see also
    Emergencies; First aid
animal bites, 529
artificial respiration, 539-540
bandaging, 530-532
bleeding, 531-533
broken bones, 536-537
burns, 533-534
choking, 538-539
concussion, 537-538
cuts, 529
drowning, 539
electric shock, 539
fractures, 536-537
fluids in eyes, 526, 540
gas poisoning, 539
head injuries, 537-538
hemorrhage, 531-532

nosebleeds, 532-533
poisons, 540-542
prevention, 266-269
smothering, 539
sprains, 535-536
stings, 492
swallowed objects, 538
Acid poisoning, 540-541
Adenoids, 484-485
Adolescence, see Puberty devel-
    opment
Adoption, 585-589
Advanced child, 406-407
Aggressiveness, 311, 313-317
biting, 319-320
control of, 313-317
discussing feelings, 332
excessive, 311
language, 317-318
about possessions, 311
Aims in raising a child, 10-17
Air bubble, 68
Airing, 163-164
Alcohol rubs, 457-458

593

Allergies, 485-490
Ammonia
  in diapers, 206-207
  poisoning, 540-541
  rash, 206-207
Anger in child
  in adolescence, 419-421
  causing overdependence, 21-22, 353-354
  jealous of parent, 363-366
  learning control, 313-317
  let him recognize angry feelings, 332, 334-336
  temper tantrums, 334-336
  two parents at once, 357-358
Anger in parents
  causing overprotection, 21-22
  in discipline, 330-332
  in feeding problems, 438
  at fretful baby, 190-191
  naturalness of, 20-22
  in overpermissiveness, 9, 192-193, 328-330
  parents' quarrels, 560-562
  in punishment, 336-339
  some causes, 25-26
Animal bites, 529
Ankles, weakness, 238-239
Antibiotics, 459-460
Antiseptics, 529
Appendicitis, 520-522
Appetite, see Feeding problems
Artificial respiration, 539-540
Ascorbic acid, 291
Aspirin
  in breast feeding, 76-77
  for earache, 478-479
  for high fever, 457-458
  poisoning, 540-542
Asthma, 486-487
Asthmatic bronchitis, 487-488
Athletics
  interest in, 320-321

Attention in infancy, see Enjoying your baby; Permissiveness; Play; Spoiling
Automobile-polish poisoning, 540-541

B

Balkiness at 2 years, 356-357
Bandaging
  for bleeding, 530-532
  for infection, 534-535
Bassinet, 39-40
Bath
  equipment, 40
  fear of, 269
  in infancy, 154-157
  thermometer, 45
Bedding in infancy, 43, 44-45, 162-163
Bedtime, see 166-167, 322-324, also Sleep; Sleep problems
  difficulties at 2 years, 355-356
  fear of separation, 351-356
  in infancy, 166-167
  keeping it happy, 322-324
Bed-wetting, 510-513
  fear of, 351-352
Bee sting, 492
Beets in bowel movement and urine, 136
Benzene poisoning, 540-541
Berries, 299-300
Bibs, 42
Birthmarks, 493-494
  parents' attitude, 572
Bites
  animal, 529
  insect, 492
Biting humans, 319-320

Bladder disturbances, 510-517, *see also* Urinary disturbances

Bladder training, 260-264; *see also* Urine training

Blankets, 44, 162-163

Bleach poisoning, 540-541

Bleeding, *see also* Blood
cuts, 531-533
nosebleeds, 532-533

Blindness, 578; *see also* Handicapped child

Blisters
from burning and chafing, 533-534
in chicken pox, 496-497
in impetigo, 492-493
on lips, 208
in poison ivy, 493

Blood
in bowel movements, *see* Bowel movements
in vomitus, 467-468

Blood poisoning, 534-535

Blue feeling after childbirth, 26-27

Blueness
in breath-holding, 212-213
mottled skin, 205
from nitrates, 129

Boils, 534-535

Booties, 43, 239

Boric-acid poisoning, 540-542

Bottle feeding, *see* Feeding, bottle

Bottles
prepared,
sterilizing, *see* Feeding, bottle
types, 46-47
warmers, 45

Bowel movements, 172-175
beets in, 136

blood
in diarrhea, 203
from fissure, 175, 257-258
in intussusception, 175, 519
from malformations, 175, 257-258
in bottle feeding, 173-174
in breast feeding, 173
changes in infancy, 174-175
vegetables in, 136
constipation, 199-202
in bottle feeding, 200
in breast feeding, 200
chronic, 200-201
from fissure, 257-258
psychological, 201, 252
spastic, 202
at start of infection, 202
temporary, 202
diarrhea
in celiac disease, 522-523
in cystic fibrosis, 522
in digestive diseases, 522-523
emergency treatment, 203-205
in food poisoning, 519-520
in infants, 202-205
in intestinal infections, 519
enemas, 460-461
green stools
in diarrhea, 202-203
from exposure, 174
in indigestion, 199
infrequent in breast feeding, 173
looseness
in bottle feeding, 173-174
in breast feeding, 173
in digestive diseases, 522-523
in indigestion, 199
meconium, 172-173

Bowel movements (cont.)
mucus, 174
sore buttocks, 207
straining in breast feeding, 173
suppositories, 460-461
toilet training, 249-259
vegetables in, 174
Bowel training, 249-259
cause of problems, 258-259
constipation in, 200-201, 252
fear of hard movements, 201, 257-258
imitation of parent, 256
methods of, 254-257
parents' attitudes, 258-259
readiness, 249-252, 253-254
resistance, 252-253, 258-259
training pants, 257
type of seat, 254
Bowlegs, 237-240
Braveness, 320
Bread
in diet, 300-302
starting in infancy, 140-141
Breast feeding, see Feeding, breast
Breasts, see also Feeding, breast
in puberty, 414-416
swelling in infancy, 211
Breathing troubles, 211-213
in asthma, 486-487
breath-holding, 212-213, 336
chronic noisy, 212
in croup, 480-481
faint, 212
mucus in colds, 473
nose obstructed by dry mucus, 157
thymus gland, 213
Broken bones, 536-537
Bronchitis, 479-480
asthmatic, 487

Brush for bottles, 47
Brutality
in play, 313-317
in television, movies and comics, 317, 395-397
Bubbling, 68
Buntings, 42, 162-163
Burns, 533-534

C

Cakes, 302
Calories, 293
Candy, 303
Caps, knitted, 43
Carbohydrates, 292
Carbolic-acid poisoning, 540-541
Carriage, 45
letting him out, 271
safety in, 266
"Castration anxiety," 160-161, 370-371, 373
Caustic poisoning, 540-541
Celiac disease, 522-523
Cephalhematoma, 6
Cereal
in diet, 300
in infancy, 132-134
loss of appetite for, 282
refusal at 1 year, 300
refusal at start, 134
Cerebral palsy, 574, 579
Chair
high, 235, 266
low chair-table, 235, 266
rocking, 78
Cheese in diet, 296
Chicken pox, 496-497
Child-centeredness of Americans, 11-14
Child-guidance clinics, 411-412
Child-health stations, 50

Child psychiatry, 411-413
Choking, 538-539
Chorea, 509-510
Circumcision, 159-161
Cleaning-fluid poisoning, 540-541
Clothing in infancy, 41-43, 162
Cobalamine, 291
Coffee, 305
Colds, 469-478
  bronchitis, 479-480
  causative factors, 469-472
  cough medicine, 478
  croup, 480-481
  in ears, 478-479
  fever, at start, 474
    later, 475
  handling child, 475-478
  humidifier, 470, 476
  in infancy, 473
  in mothers, 472
  nose drops, 477-478
  resistance to, 470-471
  sinusitis, 482
  syringe for mucus, 473
  vaporizer, 476-477
  in young child, 474-475
Colic, 187-191
Colostrum, 72, 81
Comforters, 215-218
  strokable, 217-218
Comforting
  in infancy, 4
  in injuries, 320
Comics, 395-396
Companionship, see Play
Complemental feedings, 93-94
Compulsions, 393-395
Concussion, 537-538
Conjunctivitis, 209-210, 525
Conscience between 6 and 11 years, 393-395
Constipation, 199-202; see also

Bowel movements
Contrariness at 2 years, 356-358
Convulsions, 527-528
Cookies, 302
Corn syrup, 113
Cough
  in adults in household, 472, 473, 504-505
  in asthma, 486
  in bronchitis, 479-480
  in colds, 473, 478
  in croup, 480, 481
  humidifier for, 476
  in measles, 494-495
  medicine, 478
  in pneumonia, 480
  in sinusitis, 482
  vaporizer for, 476-477
  in whooping cough, 497-499
Coverings, 162-163
Cradle cap, 208
Creeping, 236
Crib, 39-40
Cripples, 579
Croup, 480-481
  humidifier for, 481
"Cry-baby," 320
Crying, 183-191
  from bubble, 185
  from colic, 187-191
  common causes in early weeks, 183-191
  from ear pain, 478-479
  from fatigue, 185-186
  fretful baby, 186, 190-191
  on going to bed at 2 years, 351-356
  on going to sleep in infancy, 185-186
  from hunger, 184-185
  hypertonic baby, 186-187, 190-191
  in indigestion, 185, 187, 199

Crying (cont.)
intestinal obstruction, 519
intussusception, 519
"periodic irritable," 187-191
from spoiling, 191-196
from wetness, 185
when hurt, 320
when mother leaves 1-year-
old, 270
Cup, weaning to, 150-153
Curiosity, 366
Cuts, 529-532
Cystic fibrosis, 522
Cystitis, 516-517

D

Dating, in adolescence, 428-432
Davis, Dr. Clara, experiments,
279-281
Dawdling
at 1 year, 275-276
prevention, 326
Day nurseries, 383-387, 564-566
Deafness
in ear infections, 478-479
permanent, 577-578
Death, fear of, 368-369
Deformities, 571-572
Delinquency, 432-433
"Demand" schedule, 60-63
Dentist, 248
Deodorant, 419
Dependence
at 1 year, 270-272
at 2 years, 351-356
Depression in mother, 26-27
Desserts, 302-304
Development, 229-248
attitude toward strangers,
234-235
creeping, 236

differences in, 5-6
emotional, 231
feet and legs, 238-239
hearing, 232
individual fellows race, 229-
230
intelligence, 231, 579-580
left- and right-handedness,
233-234
mental, 231, 579-580
motor, 230-231
parents' attitude, 5-6
right- and left-handedness,
233-234
rolling over, 235
seeing, 232
sitting, 235
slowness of, 230; see also
Mental slowness
smiling, 232
social, 231
standing, 236-237
sucking, 232
talking, 240-242
teeth, 242-248
tenseness in early months,
231-232
use of hands, 233
walking, 237-238
Diapers, 175-177
buying, 42
changing, 175-176
disposable, 176, 545
liners, 42
pail, 40
rash, 206-207
service, 42
washing, 176-177
waterproof pants, 42-43
Diarrhea, see Bowel movements
Diet, see also Feeding in infancy
balance, 293-294

Diet *(cont.)*
  berries, 299-300
  between meals, 305-306
  bread, 300
    in infancy, 140-141
  cakes, 302
  calories, 293
  candies, 303
  carbohydrates, 292
  cereals and substitutes, 300
    in infancy, 132-134
  cheese, 296
  coffee and tea, 305
  cookies, 302
  Davis experiments, 279-281
  desserts, 300-303
  eggs, 297-298
    in infancy, 137
  elements in, 288-294
  fats, 292-293
  in fever, 467
  finger foods, 140-141
  fish, 297
    in infancy, 140
  foods and meals in childhood,
    295-307
  frozen foods, 305
  fruits, 299-300
    in infancy, 134-135
  fuel, 292
  guide to meals, 306-307
  ice cream, 303
  in illness, 466-469
  jams and jellies, 302-303
  less valuable foods, 302-305
  less valuable grains, 304
  lumpy foods before 1 year,
    141-142
  meat soups in infancy, 138
  meats, 297
    in infancy, 137-138
  melons, 299-300
  milk and substitutes, 295-297

minerals, 289
nursing mother, 77-78
at 1 year, 142
pastries, 302
potato, 300-302, 306-307
  in infancy, 140
protein, 288-289
puddings, 300-302
  in infancy, 139
roughage, 292
salads, 298-299
sandwiches, 301
simple guide to elements in,
  294
at 6 months, 138-139
sodas, 303
soups, 298-299, 301
starches, 292-293
substitutions, 296-297, 297-
  298, 299, 300-302
suppers, 300-302
sweets, 303-304
vegetables and substitutes,
  298-299
  in infancy, 135-136
vitamins, 289-291
  in infancy, 127-128
in vomiting, 467-468
water, 292
  in infancy, 128-129
when traveling, 543-545
Dieting, importance of supervision, 448-449
Differences between children,
  5-6, 18, 25
Digestive diseases, 522-523
Diphtheria, 502
  inoculations, 177, 178
  serum, 502
Dirtiness, 327
Discipline, 7-10, 328-339; *see
  also* One-year-old; Man-

Discipline (cont.)
aging young children;
Spoiling
based on love, 336-339
changing theories, 7-10
children prefer to be kept
good, 22-23
confinement in room, 338
correction, 336-339
don't ask child, 333
excessive need to punish, 339
father's part, 332
firmness, 22-23, 331-332
friendliness, 331-332
guidance, 336-339
imitation of parents, 337
misunderstandings, 328-330
need of, 21-23
parental guilt, 330-331
punishment, 336-339
in school, 403-404
spanking, 338
temper tantrums, 334-336
threats, 338-339
unnecessary reasoning, 333-
334
working mother, 566
Diseases, see Illness and under
name of individual dis-
ease
Divorced parents, 560-563
Doctor
getting along with, 50-51
how to choose, 50
in strange city, 54-55
when to call, 52-53
for your baby, 49-55
Dog bites, 529
Dowd syndrome, 584-585
Drain-cleaner poisoning, 540-
541
Dresses, 43
Dressing

impatience during, 235-236
self, 325
Drinking from cup, 150-153
Dropping and throwing, 276-
277
Drowning, 539
Drugs
in adolescence, 433-434
in breast feeding, 76-77
Duties, 324-328
Dwarfs, 573-574

E

Early childhood, 313-317
Ears
care in infancy, 156-157
infections, 478-479
objects in, 540
Eczema, 488-489
Eggs
in diet, 297-298
starting in infancy, 137
Electric shock, 539
Emergencies, see also First aid
artificial respiration, 539-540
choking, 538-539
poisoning, 540-542
when to call the doctor, 52-53
Emetics, 541
Enemas and suppositories, 460-
461
Enjoying your baby, 4-7
Enuresis, 510-513
Epilepsy, 528
Equipment for baby, 39-48
Erections in infancy, 161
Erythroblastosis, 552
Evaporated milk, 108-109, 147-
149
advantages, 108-109
when to change to pasteur-

Evaporated milk *(cont.)*
    ized milk, 148-149
  when to stop sterilizing formula, 147-148
Exanthem subitum (roseola), 496
Eyes
  blindness, 578; *see also* Handicapped child
  care in infancy, 156-157
  conjunctivitis, 209-210, 525
  crossed, 210-211
  drooping lid, 209-210
  harmful fluids in, 526, 540
  nearsightedness, 525
  pink eye, 209, 525
  poisons in, 540
  reasons to see eye doctor, 525
  specks, 526
  stuck lids, 209-210
  styes, 526-527
  tear-duct obstruction, 209-210
  tearing, 209-210

F

"Facts of life," 376-383
Fairy stories, 366-367
  fear of, 369, 397
Family social agency, 412, 413
Fat
  of body, 292-293
  in diet, 292-293
  obesity, 445-450
Father, *see also* Parents
  away from child, 568-569
  child resenting father and mother together, 357-358
  as companion, 320-322
  and daughter, 321-322
  his part in discipline, 332

  hospital period, 28-30, 55-57
  importance to his children, 30-31
  mother's need of, 28, 30
  reaction to pregnancy, 28-30
  rough-housing, 322
  and son, 320-321
  teasing, 322
Fatherless child, 568-571
Fatigue
  in infancy, 185-186
  after nursery school, 386-387
Fatness, 445-450
Fears
  of animals, 369-370
  of bath, 269
  of bed-wetting, 351-352
  of cripples, 370-372
  of the dark, 368-369
  of death, 368-369
  of fairy stories, 369, 397
  of flushing, 254
  of gagging, 141-142
  about genitals, 370-372
  of going to bed at 2 years, 351-352
  of hurts, 370-372
  influence of overprotection, 353-354
  of injury, 370-372
  of movies, 366, 369, 397
  of noisy objects at 1 year, 269
  of nursery school, 385-386
  of operations, 463-466
  of painful movements, 257-258
  of parent's leaving, 351-353
  of school, 407-408, 410
  of separation, 351-356
  of strangers, 234-235, 271-272
  of swimming, 369

Fears (cont.)
  of television, 369, 397
  at 3 years and after, 368-372
Feeding, bottle, 108-126
  avoiding bedtime bottle, 126
  equipment, 46-48
  formula, full strength, 115-116
    modified, 109
    for newborn, 114-115
    for premature, 548-549
    prepared, 109
  giving bottle, 120-126
  nipple holes, 122-123
  poor nursers, 125
  premature, 548-549
  preparation of formula, 116-119
  prepared formulas, 109, 114, 543
  preparing formulas when traveling, 543-545
  propping bottle, 121-122
  purpose of formula, 108
  refrigeration inadequate, 119-120, 125-126
  relief bottle, 91-92
  sterilization, 119
  sugars for formulas, 113-114
  unfinished bottle, 125
  various milks used, 108-113; see also Milk
  warming bottle, 120-121
  weakening formula temporarily, 116
  weaning to cup, 150-153
  when to change to pasteurized milk, 148-149
  when to remove sugar, 144
  when to stop sterilizing, 147-148
Feeding, breast, 72-107
  alcohol in, 76-77
  what angers baby, 80
  apparent fullness of breasts, 84
  appearance of milk, 84
  biting during teething, 99-100
  breast abscess, 99
  breast and bottle, 92-94
  caked breast, 99
  chewing nipple, 79-80
  colostrum, 72, 81
  confidence, 85
  crying is no criterion, 84, 90-91
  different types of babies, 80, 94-96
  drugs, 76-77
  engorged breasts, 97-99
  extra effort, 86-90
  fluids for mother, 88
  friends' attitudes, 89
  getting areola into mouth, 79-80
  getting started, 78-87
  illness in mother, 99
  increasing the milk, 86-90
  insufficient milk, 87-94
  is he getting enough, 84
  manual expression of milk, 100-103
  mother-baby relationship, 75-76
  mother's diet, 77-78
    figure, 73-74
    health, 74-75
    life, 76-77
  nipple care, 85; see also Nipples
  nipple shield, 103
  one or both breasts, 83-84
  pains in abdomen, 96-97
  pains in nipples, 97
  poor nursers, 94-96
  pumping breasts, 103
  questions about, 73-78

Feeding, breast *(cont.)*
  relief bottle, 91-92
  removing nipple from mouth, 79-80
  retracted nipples, 96
  size of breasts, 74
  sore nipples, 97
  tobacco in, 76-77
  twins, 555
  value of, 72-73
  weaning from breast, 103-107; *see also* Weaning
  working mother, 75
Feeding schedule, 60-67
  2 A.M. feeding, 65-66
    when to omit, 66
  3-hour feedings, 65
  3 meals a day, 144-147
  4-hour feedings, 64-65
  10 P.M. feeding, when to give, 66-67
    when to omit, 142-143
  "demand" schedule, 60-63
  regularity and flexibility, 60-64
  working toward regularity, 63-64
Feeding in childhood, 288-294; *see also* Diet
Feeding in infancy, 58-153
  adding solid foods, 131-142, 557-558
  bubbling, 68
  getting enough, 68-71
  meals at 1 year, 142
  meals at 6 months, 138-139
  orange juice, 128
  self-feeding at 1 year, 285-287
  starting coarse, lumpy foods, 141-142
  vitamins, 127-128
  water, 128-129

  what it means to baby, 58-60
  when traveling, 543-545
Feeding problems
  avoidance in bottle feeding, 123-126
  in infancy, 58-59
  in starting solids, 132-133
  balking at first cereal, 134
  bribes, 303-304, 443
  causes, 436-437
  desserts, 302-304
  encouraging child to feed himself, 285-287
  gagging, 141-142, 444-445
  after illness, 468-469
  loss of appetite
    between 1 and 2 years, for vegetables, cereal, milk, 281-283
    3 to 9 months, 143-144
  mother's feelings, 438
  playing at meals, 283-284
  poor nursing on bottle, 125
  poor nursing at breast, 94-96
  refusal to nurse due to bubble, 68
    during menstruation, 77
    in teething, 67
    in thrush, 209
    in weaning from breast, 107
  sweets, 302-304
  treating, 437-445
  variable appetite at 1 year, 278-287
Fever, 453-458
  in colds, 474-475
  dehydration, 59-60
  diet during, 467
  emergency treatment when high, 457-458
  often high at start of infections in young child, 474
Finger foods, 140-141

Firmness, see Discipline
First aid, 529-542
  animal bites, 529
  artificial respiration for
      drowning, 539-540
    electric shock, 539-540
    gas poisoning, 539-540
    smothering, 539-540
  bandaging, 530-532
  bleeding, 531-533
  broken bones, 536-537
  burns, 533-534
  choking, 538-539
  concussion, 537-538
  convulsions, 527-528
  cuts, 529
  emetics, 541
  fluids in eyes, 526, 540
  fractures, 536-537
  head injuries, 537-538
  hemorrhage, 531-532
  nosebleeds, 532-533
  objects in nose and ears, 540
  poisoning, 540-542
  skin infections, 534-535
  splints, 535-537
  sprains, 535-536
  stings, 492
  supplies, 55
  swallowed objects, 538
  wet dressing, 534-535
  when to call the doctor, 52-53
First child, preserving outgo-
      ingness, 311-313
Fish
  in diet, 297
  starting in infancy, 140
Flash bulb, 6
Flexibility in feeding schedule,
      60-64
Fluoridation, 245-246
Fontanel (soft spot), 161

Foods and meals in childhood,
      295-307; see also Diet
Foreskin, 159-160
Formulas, 108-120; see also
      Feeding, bottle
Foster care, 564-565
Fractures, 536-537
Fresh air, 163-165
Fretful babies, 186, 190-191
Friendships, see Outgoingness
Frozen foods, 305
Fruit
  canned, 302-303
  in diet, 299-300
  starting in infancy, 134-135
Funnel, 47
Furniture polish poisoning, 240-
      241

G

Gagging
  on lumps, 141-142, 444-445
  on potato, 140
Gaining weight
  in child, 445-449
  in infancy, 69-71
Gamma globulin, for measles,
      495
Gangs and clubs, 391
Gas
  bubble, 68
  in colic, 187-189
  in indigestion, 199
  poisoning, 539-540
Gasoline poisoning, 540-541
Generosity, 311
German measles, 495-496
Germs in infancy, 55-56, 129-
      130
Glands
  enlarged, 483
  of "internal secretion," 449-
      450

Glands *(cont.)*
swollen lymph glands, 483
thymus, 213
thyroid, 449-450
Grandparents, 31-35
Growing pains, 508
Gum cysts, 209
Gunplay, 313-317

H

Hair of newborn, 7
Handedness, right- and left-, 233-234
Handicapped child, 571-585
blindness, 578
cerebral palsy, 574, 579
cripples, 579
deafness, 577-578
deformities, 571-572
Dowd Syndrome, 584-585
duties, 572
effect on brothers and sisters, 574
epilepsy, 528
fostering happiness, 571-574
hard-of-hearing, 577
help for parents, 575-576
infantile paralysis, 502, 579
medical care, 579
mental slowness, 572-573, 579-585
mongolism, 584-585
national associations, 576, 579
parents' feelings, 574-575
pity, 572
schooling, 576-577, 582
shortness, 573-574
social agency, 575-576
Handling genitals, 372-383
Hands, use of, 233-234
Hay fever, 485-486

Head
injuries, 537-538
-rolling and -banging 227-228
Hearing, development of, 232
deafness
permanent, 577-578
temporary, 478-479
Heart disease and murmurs, 507-509
Hemangiomas, 493-494
Hematoma, 6
Hemorrhage, *see* Bleeding; Blood
Hernias
inguinal, 523-524
strangulated, 524
umbilical (naval), 158-159
Hexachlorophene soap, 40, 155, 419, 497
Hiccups, 197
High chairs, 235, 266
Hives, 488
Hoarseness, 480-481
Hornet stings, 492
Hospital
for delivery, 55-57
preparing child for, 463-466
Hot-water bottle, 189
Houseworker
health of, 473, 504-505
to help new mother, 36-38
personality, 564, 567-568
Humidifier, 470, 476, 481
Hydrocele, 524-525
Hypertonic babies, 186-187, 190-191

I

Ice cream, 303
Identity, in adolescence, 421-423
Illness, 453-528

Illness (*cont.*)
avoiding feeding problems, 468-469
avoiding invalidism and spoiling, 461-462
care of sick child, 453-469
common rashes
in childhood, 491-497
in infancy, 205-208
diet, 466-469
diseases, *see* name of individual disease
emergency treatment of high fever, 457-458
finding doctor in strange city, 54-55
giving enema, 460-461
giving medicine, 458-460
handling child with cold, 475-478
hospitalization, 463-466
how long to take temperature, 454-455
medicine cabinet, 55
playthings during, 462-463
quarantine, 503-504
taking temperature, 455-457
vaporizer, 476-477
what's fever, 453-454
Imagination, 366-367
Impetigo, 492-493
Independence
at 6 months, 215-218
at 1 year, 270-272
after 6 years, 389-390
Indigestion, *see also* Stomach-aches and upsets
in celiac disease, 522-523
colic, 187-191
hiccups, 197
in infancy, 197-199
mild, 199
spitting, 197-198

vomiting, 197-199
Infantile paralysis, *see* Poliomyelitis
Injuries, *see also* First aid
comforting, 320
fears of, 370-372
Ink poisoning, 540-542
Inoculations, 177-182
diphtheria, 177-178, 502
D.P.T. (combined), 177-178
lockjaw, 177-178, 178-180, 529
measles, 180-181, 495
pertussis, *see* Whooping cough
poliomyelitis, 180, 502-503
rabies, 529
smallpox, 181-182
tetanus, 177-178, 178-180, 529
vaccination, 181-182
whooping cough, 177-178, 497-499
Insect bites, 492
Insect-spray poisoning, 540-541
Intelligence
bright child, 406-407
development, 231
slowness, *see* Mental slowness
tests, 231, 579-580
Intestinal disturbances
bowel movements, diarrhea, 202-205
colic, 187-191
indigestion in infancy, 197-199
stomach-aches and upsets, 518-523
Intussusception, 519
Invalidism, avoiding, 461-463
Iodine
as antiseptic, 529
poisoning, 540-542

Ipecac, syrup of, 55, 541
Iron
  in cereals, 133-134
  in diet, 289
  poisoning, 540-542

J

Jams and jellies, 302-303
Jaundice, 6
Jealousy, 339-349
  between older children, 348-349
  bringing baby home, 342-344
  can be constructive, 339-340
  desire to be baby, 340-341
  fostering helpfulness, 341-342
  fostering maturity, 340-341
  management, 345-348
  needs of new baby, 348
  of new baby, 339-348
  of parents, 357-358, 363-366
  about playthings, 348-349
  preparation for baby, 342
  various forms, 344-345
Joint pains, 508
Jouncing, 227-228
Junior foods, 140-142

K

Kerosene poisoning, 540-541
Kidding by father, 322
Kiminos, 41
Knock-knees, 237-240

L

Language
  "bad," in small child, 317-318

rough, after 6, 390
speech development, 240-242
Laryngitis, 480-481
Laryngo-tracheo-bronchitis, 481
"Latency period," 6 to 11 years, 388-399
Layette, 39-48
Laziness, 407-408
Left-handedness, 233-234
Lice, head, 493
Lips, blisters on, 208
Lockjaw, inoculations, 177-178, 178-180, 529
Lotion, 46, 157
Lye poisoning, 540-541
Lying, 367-368
Lymph glands, 483

M

Maid, *see* Houseworker
Make-believe, 366-367
Managing young children, 308-328; *see also* Discipline; Jealousy; One-year-old; Spoiling
  aggressiveness, control of, 313-317
  arranging house, 273
  avoiding accidents, 266-269
  bad language, 317-318
  balkiness at 2 years, 356-357
  bedtime at 2 years, 355-356
  biting, 319-320
  comforting, 320
  dawdling, 275-276, 326
  dirtiness, 327
  distracting, 272-273
  dressing self, 325
  duties, 324-328
  father's companionship, 320-322

Managing young children (*cont.*)
    generosity, 311
    going to bed, 322-324
    gunplay, 313-317
    how much sleep, 323-324
    kidding, 322
    manners, 327-328
    naps at 1 year, 278
    outgoingness, *see* Outgoingness
    play, 308-311
    putting things away, 325-326
    rough-housing, 322
    selfishness, 311
    sissiness, 318-319
    timidity, 318-319
    toys, 308-310
        in bed, 322-323
    training not to touch, 273-275
Manliness, 320-321
Manners
    learning, 327-328
    worse after 6 years, 390
Manual expression, breast milk, 100-103
Masks, 56
Masturbation, 372-376
Mattress, 39-40
Meals
    in childhood, 295-307; *see also* Diet
    at 1 year, 142
    at 6 months, 138-139
Measles, 494-495
    gamma globulin for, 495
    German, 495-496
    vaccination, 180-181, 495
Measure for formula, 47
Meat
    in diet, 297
    soups, 138
    starting in infancy, 137-138

Meconium, 172-173
Medicine
    cabinet, 55
    for cough, 478
    giving, 458-460
Melons, 299-300
Menstruation
    effect on breast feeding, 76-77
    in puberty, 414-416
    in sex education, 380-381
Mental slowness
    causes, 579-580, 584-585
    Dowd Syndrome, 584-585
    management, 579-585
    Mongolism, 584-585
    parents' guilt feelings, 572-573
    schooling, 582-583
    tests, 231, 579-580
Mercury poisoning, 540-542
Messing, 237
Milk, 108-113
    artificial, 113
    breast, 72-73, 84; *see also* Feeding, breast
    in diet, 294, 295-296
    evaporated, 108-109, 147-149
    formulas, 108-120; *see also* Feeding, bottle
    half-skimmed, 110-111
    homogenized, 109-110
    lactic-acid, 112-113
    loss of appetite for, 282
    modified evaporated, 109
    modified powdered, 109
    pasteurized, 109, 147, 148-149
    powdered, 111
    prepared formula, 109
    raw, 110
    rich, 110
    skimmed, 111
    substitutes in diet, 296-297

Milk (cont.)
  vitamin D, 110
  whole, 110
Mineral oil, 201
  in breast feeding, 76-77
  for skin, 46, 157; see also
    Lotion
Minerals, 289
Modesty, 382-383
Moles, 493-494
Mongolism, 584-585
Moral values, 12-17
  in adolescence, 421-433
  in childhood, 395-399
Mother, see also Parents
  depression, 26-27
  need of help, 36-38
  substitute for, 37-38, 564-
    565, 567-568
  working, 563-568
Mouth
  care in infancy, 156-157
  gum cysts, 209
  thrush, 209
Movies, 395-397
  fears of, 366, 369, 397
Mucus
  in bowel movements, 174
  in colds, 473
  dry, in nose, 157
Mumps, 499-500
  globulin for, 500
  skin test for, 500

N

Nail-biting, 360
Nail-cutting, 156-157
Naps
  giving up, 323-324
  at 1 year, 278

Navel
  care in infancy, 158
  hernia, 158-159
  infection, 158
  protrusion, 158-159
  strapping, 159
Nearsightedness, 525
Neatness
  let him get dirty, 327
  putting his toys away, 325-
    326
  between 6 and 11 years, 393
Nervousness
  causing school problems, 407-
    408
  chorea, 509-510
  compulsions, 393-395
  fears, see Fears
  head-rolling and -banging,
    227-228
  jouncing in infancy, 227-228
  jumpiness in infancy, 213
  movements, see Chorea;
    Compulsions; Tics; Rest-
    lessness
  nail-biting, 360
  psychiatric help, 411-413
  restlessness, 510
  St. Vitus' dance, 509-510
  startling in infancy, 213
  tenseness in early months,
    231-232
  tics, 395, 510
  trembling in infancy, 213-214
Net over crib, 355-356
New baby, see Jealousy; Preparing child for new baby
Niacin, 290
Nicotine poisoning, 540-542
Nicotinic acid, 290
Nightgowns, 41
Nipples, mother's, see Feeding,
  breast

Nipples, rubber, 47
  right-sized holes, 122-123
Nose
  allergies, 485-486
  bleeds, 532-533
  care in infancy, 156-157
  drops, 477-478
  objects in, 540
  obstructed by dry mucus
    157
  syringe for mucus, 40, 473
Nurse
  in early weeks, 36-38
  health of, 473, 504-505
  mother's feelings toward, 28
  practical, 36-37
  public health, 50
  qualities needed, 36-37, 564,
    567-568
  visiting, 50
Nursery school, 383-387
  while mother works, 564-566

O

Obesity, 445-450
Objects in nose and ears, 540
Obscenity, 396
"Oedipus complex," 364-365,
  388-389
Oil, mineral, 201
  in breast feeding, 76-77
  for skin, 46, 157; *see also*
    Lotion
One-year-old, 265-287
  arranging house for, 273
  dawdling, 275-276
  dependence and independ-
    ence, 270-272
  developing a will, 265
  distractibility, 272-273
  dropping things, 276-277

  encouraging sociability, 271-
    272
  explorer, 265-266
  fear of strangers, 271-272
  feeding self, 285-287
  loss of appetite for vege-
    tables, cereal, milk, 281
  managing him, 272-277
  nap changes, 278
  out of carriage, 270-271
  outgrowing play pen, 271
  playing at meals, 283-284
  preventing accidents, 266-
    269
  preventing frights, 269-270
  toilet training, 249-254
  training not to touch, 273-
    275
  variations in appetite, 278-
    287
Operations, preparing child for,
  463-466
Orange juice, 128
Outgoingness
  first child, 311-313
  fostering friendships, 391-393
  generosity, 311
  at 1 year, 270-272
  at 2 years, 350-351
Overprotection, 353-354

P

Pacifier, 224-227
Pads, 44-45
Pain in abdomen, 518-523; *see
  also* Stomach-aches and
  upsets
Pants, waterproof, 42-43
Parents, 17-35; *see also* Mother;
  Father; Play; Discipline;
  Managing young chil-
  dren

Parents (cont.)
  adopting child, 585-589
  anger, 20-22, 25-26
  deprivations, 18-19
  feelings for different children, 25-26
  feelings about pregnancy, 23-25, 28-30
  and grandparents, 31-35
  guilt undermining discipline, 330-331
  with handicapped child, 574-576
  love for baby comes gradually, 24-25
  needs, 17-18
  nudity, 382-383
  relations with adolescents, 419-423, 426-432
  rights, 19-20
  self-confidence, 3-4
  self-sacrifice, 19
  separated and divorced, 560-563
  spoiling, see Spoiling
  and teachers, 411
  worries, 6, 28
Pastries, 302
Pellagra, 290
Penis
  care of, 159-161
  circumcision, 159-161
  erections, 161
  fears about, 370-372
  sore on end of, 516
Permissiveness, 7-10; see also Spoiling; Discipline; Managing young children
Pertussis, see Whooping cough
Pharyngitis, see Sore throat
Photographing, 6
Pillow, 39-40

Pink eye, 209, 525
Plastic seat, inclined, 40
Play, 308-311
  baby's visitors, 36
  boys playing with dolls, 318-319
  at child's own level, 310
  control of aggression, 313-317
  in dirt, 327
  excessive aggressiveness, 311, 313-317
  with father, 320-322; see also Father
  fatherless boy, 568-571
  gangs and clubs, 391
  gunplay, 313-317
  identification with parents, 361-362
  imaginary playmates, 366-367
  in infancy, 169-171, 192
  with other children, 391-392, 398-399; see also Outgoingness
  sex, 372-376
  with toys, 308-310; see also Playthings
Play pen
  when to get, 171-172
  when's enough, 271
Playthings
  the best kind, 308-310
  boys playing with dolls, 318-319
  child's own level, 310
  comforters, 215-218
  guns, 313-317
  in illness, 462-463
  in infancy, 170-171
  in jealousy, 348-349
  putting away, 325-326
  slow child, 581-582
Pneumonia, 480

Poison ivy, 493
Poisoning
  first aid, 540-542
  poisonous substances, 268, 541, 542
  prevention, 267-269
Poliomyelitis
  inoculations, 180, 502-503
  symptoms, 502-503
  vaccine, 180, 502-503
Politeness, 327-328
Popularity, 391-393
"Port-wine stains," 493-494
Posture, 451-452
Potato
  in diet, 300-302, 306-307
  gagging on, 140
  starting in infancy, 140
Powder, 46, 157
Pram, 45
Pram bag, 42
Pram suit, 42
Pregnancy
  father's feelings, 28-30
  mother's feelings, 23-25
Premature baby, 546-552
  anxieties about, 550
  feeding, 548-549, 551
  going to hospital, 548
  keeping him warm, 547-548
  taking him home, 550
Preparing child for new baby, 339-348
Prickly heat, 208, 491
Procrastinating, 326
Protein, 288-289
Psychiatrist, 411-413
Psychologist, 411-413
Puberty development, 414-434
  the age varies, 415-418
  in boys, 416-418
  dating, 428-432

  parental supervision, 429-432
  defiance of parent, 426-427
  delinquency, 432-433
  deodorant, 419
  disobedience, 426-427
  drugs, 433-434
  eccentricity, 423-424
  freedom, 423
  in girls, 414-416
  identity, 421-423
  masturbation, 375-376
  parental guidance, 426-432
  physical changes, 414-419
  privileges, 423
  psychological changes, 419-423
  radicalism, 423-424
  rivalry with parents, 419-421
  romance, 424-426
  sex education, 380-382
  sexuality, 424-426, 428-429, 431
  skin troubles, 418-419
  withdrawal, 423-424
Puddings
  in diet, 300-302
  in infancy, 139
Punishment, 336-339; see also Discipline
Putting things away, 325-326
Pyelitis, 516-517
Pyelonephritis, 516-517
Pyloric stenosis, 198-199
Pyridoxine, 290
Pyuria, 516-517

Q

Quarantine, 503-504
Quart measure, 47
Quinine poisoning, 540-542

R

Rabies, 529
Rashes, see also Skin
  common in child, 491-497
  common in infant, 205-208
Reading problems, 408-409
Refrigeration
  inadequate, 119-120, 125-126
  when traveling, 543-544
Relief bottle, 91-92
Resistance to sleep in infancy,
  194-196
Retardation, mental, see Mental
  slowness; Handicapped
  child
Rh factor, 552
Rheumatic fever, 507
Rhythmic habits, 227-228
Riboflavin, 290
Rickets, 291
Right- and left-handedness,
  233-234
Ringworm, 492
Rivalry, see also Jealousy
  in adolescence, 419-421
Rocking, 4-5
  rocking chair, 78-79
  rocking self, 228
Rolling over, 235
Room
  for baby, 168-169
  locking in, 355-356
  as punishment, 338
  temperature of, 161
Rooming-in, 56-57
Roseola infantum, 496
Roughage, 292
Rough-housing, 322
Rubber pants, 42-43
Ruminating, 224
Ruptures, see Hernias

S

Sabin vaccine, 180, 502
Sacks, 41
St. Vitus' dance (chorea), 509-
  510
Salads, 298-299
Salk vaccine, 180
Salt, 136
Sandwiches, 301
Scabies, 492
Scales, 45
Scalp
  bathing, 155-156
  cradle cap, 208
  head lice, 493
  ringworm, 492
Scarlet fever, 501-502
Schedules (feeding), see Feeding, schedule
School problems, 405-411
  breakfast trouble, 410-411
  coaching, 409-410
  cooperating with teacher, 411
  extra-bright child, 406-407
  laziness, 407-408
  left-right confusion, 408-409
  mental slowness, 582-583
  nervousness, 407-408
  physical causes, 405-406
  poor reading, 408-409
  poor visual memory, 408-409
  psychological causes, 405-411
  school phobia, 410
  tutoring, 409-410
  vomiting, 410-411
Schools, 400-411
  for handicapped, 576-577,
  582-583
  purposes, 400-405
Scurvy, 291
Seborrheic rash, 208
Sedative for colic, 189

Seeing, development, 232
"Self-demand" schedule, 60-63
Selfishness at 2 years, 311
Separated parents, 560-563
Separation anxieties, 351-356;
     see also Fears
Serum, see also Inoculations
     diphtheria, 177-178, 502
     lockjaw, 177-178, 178-180,
          529
     measles, 180-181, 495
     poliomyelitis, 180, 502-503
     tetanus, 177-178, 178-180,
          529
     whooping cough, 177-178,
          497-499
Sex education, 376-383
Shampoos, 155-156
Sharing, 311
Sheeting, waterproof, 44-45,
     162-163
Sheets, 45
Shirts, 41
Shock, electric, 539
Shoes, 239-240
Shortness, 573-574
Shots, see Inoculations
Sibling rivalry, 339-349; see
     also Jealousy
Sickness, see Illness
Sinus disease, 482
Sitters, 37-38, 564-565
     boy sitters, 568
     personality, 564-565, 567-568
Sitting up, 235
Six to eleven years, 388-399
     aiding popularity, 391-393
     bad manners, 390
     comics, 395-396
     compulsions, 393-395
     gangs and clubs, 391
     independent of parents, 389-
          390

movies, 395-397
     obscenity, 396
     self-control, 393-395
     slow growth, 388-389
     television, 395-397
     tics, 395
Skin
     in adolescence, 418-419
     ammonia rash, 206-207
     birthmarks, 493-494
     bites, 492
     blisters on lips, 208
     bluish mottling, 205
     boils and other infections,
          534-535
     common rashes in childhood,
          491-497
     common rashes in infancy,
          205-208
     cradle cap, 208
     diaper rash, 206-207
     eczema, 488-490
     hemangiomas, 493-494
     hives, 488
     impetigo, 492-493
     lice, head, 493
     lotion for, 46, 157
     moles, 493-494
     oil for, 46, 157
     poison ivy, 493
     "port-wine stains," 493-494
     powder for, 46, 157
     prickly heat, 208, 491
     ringworm, 492
     scabies, 492
     seborrheic rash, 206
     "strawberry marks," 493-494
     warts, 494
Sleep
     amounts at different ages,
          166-167, 323-324
     back or stomach, 167-168
     giving up naps, 323-324

Sleep (cont.)
  in infancy, 166-169
  naps at 1 year, 278
  out of parents' bed, 169
  out of parents' room, 168-169
  training baby to sleep later
      in A.M., 168
Sleep bags, 43, 162-163
Sleep problems
  delaying bedtime at 2 years,
      355-356
  fear of going to bed at 2
      years
    mild, 355-356
    severe, 352-353
  getting out of bed at 2 years,
      355-356
  going to bed in infancy, 194-
      195
  between 3 and 6 years, 366,
      368-370
  waking at night in infancy,
      195-196
Sleep walkers, 43, 162-163
Slowness, see Development;
      Mental slowness
Smegma, 159-160
Smiling, development of, 232
Smothering, 539
Sneezing in infancy, 211-212
Soap, 40, 155
  hexachlorophene, 40, 155,
      419, 497
Sociability, see Outgoingness
Social agency, 412, 413
Sodas, 303
Soft spot (fontanel), 161
Solid foods
  in infancy, 131-142
  shortcuts, 557-558
  traveling, 545
Sore throat
  in diphtheria, 502

in pharyngitis, 483
in scarlet fever, 501-502
in tonsillitis, 482-483
Soups, 298-299, 301
  in infancy, 138
Spanking, 338
Specks in eye, 526
Speech development, 240-242
  stuttering, 358-359
Spinach chapping, 135-136
Spitting in infancy, 197-198
Splints, 536-537
Spoiling, see also Managing
      young children; Disci-
      pline
  baby, 191-196
  changing theories, 7-10
  don't worry at first, 4-5
  eager parents, 192
  from misery in early months,
      191-192
  from misunderstandings
      about discipline, 328-330
  going to bed in infancy, 194-
      195
  guilty parents, 330-331
  in illness, 461-462
  makes unhappy child, 331-
      332
  only child, 192-193
  other causes in parents, 192-
      193
  permissiveness, 7-10
  submissive parents, 192
  unspoiling, 193-194
  very polite parents, 329-330
  vomiting, 198
  waking at night in infancy,
      195-196
  working mother, 566
Spoon
  for infant, 132
  for 1-year-old, 285-287

Sprains, 535-536
Standing up, 236-237
Starches, 292-293
Stealing, 397-399
Steaming room, 476-477
Sterilizer, electric, 47
Sterilizing
  equipment, 47
  formula, *see* Feeding, bottle
  water, 128-129
  what doesn't need it, 129-130
  when to stop, 147-148
Stings, 492
Stockings, 43
Stomach-aches and upsets, 518-
    523
  appendicitis, 520-522
  celiac disease, 522-523
  in colds and other infections,
    519
  colic, 187-191
  common causes, 518-520
  cystic fibrosis, 522
  from feeding problems, 520
  food poisoning, 519-520
  indigestion in infancy, 197-
    199
  "intestinal flu" and "grippe,"
    519
  intestinal obstruction, 519
  intussusception, 519
  strangulated hernia, 519, 523-
    524
  worms, 520, 523
  from worries, 520
Storytelling, 366-367, 369, 397
Strabismus, 210-211
Strangers, baby's attitude to-
    ward, 234-235
"Strawberry marks," 493-494
Stretch suits, 41
Strictness, 7-10; *see also* Spoil-

ing; Discipline; Man-
    aging young children
Stridor, 212
Stroking comforters, 216-218
Strychnine poisoning, 540-542
Stuttering, 358-359
Styes, 526-527
Sucking
  need, 59
  pacifier, 224-227
  thumb and finger, 215-224;
    see also Thumb-sucking
  tongue, 224
Sugar for formulas, 113-114
  brown, 113
  corn syrup, 113
  dextrin and maltose prepara-
    tions, 113-114
  granulated, 113
  lactose, 114
  when to remove, 144
Sugar water, 129
Sulfa drugs, 459-460
Sun baths, 165-166
Sunburn, 165-166, 534
Sunshine, 165-166
Superstitions between 6 and 11
    years, 393-395
Supper suggestions, 300-302
Supplemental feedings, 93-94
Suppositories, 460-461
Swabs, 40
Swallowed objects, 538
Sweaters, 41
  putting on, 162
Swings, 172
Syrup, corn, 113

T

Talking, 240-242
Teasing by father, 322

Teeth, 242-248
  care of, 246-247
  decay, 246
  dentist, 248
  fluoridation, 245-246
  formation, 245
  permanent, 248
Teething, 242-248
  age of, 242-243, 248
  chewing, 244-245
  illness during, 243
  order of, 243, 248
  refusal to nurse during, 67
  symptoms of, 242-244
  wakefulness, 244
Television, 395-397
  brutality in, 314-315, 395-396
  fears of, 397
  limiting hours for watching, 396-397
Temper tantrums, 334-336
Temperature
  of baby's hands and feet, 162
  of baby's room, 161
  how long to continue taking, 455-457
  taking it in child, 455-457
Testicles
  hydrocele, 524-525
  undescended, 450-451
Tetanus inoculations, 177-178, 178-180, 529
Thermometer
  axillary, 453-457
  mouth, 453-457
  rectal, 453-457
  for room, 163-164
Thiamin, 290
Thinness, 435-436
Threats
  about genitals, 374-375
  of punishment, 338-339
Three-month colic, 187-191

Three- to six-year-old, 361-387
  affectionateness, 361-362
  curiosity, 366
  detachment from parent, 364
  "facts of life," 376-383
  fear of injury, 370-372
  identification with parents, 361-362
  imaginary fears, 368-370
  imagination, 366-367
  jealousy of parent, 363-366
  lying, 367-368
  normal interest in sex, 372-373
  romantic feelings, 363-366
  sleep problems, 366, 368-369
Throat infections, see Sore throat
Throwing and dropping, 276-277
Thrush, 209
Thumb-sucking, 215-224
  in bottle-fed baby, 220-221
  in breast-fed baby, 220
  comforters, 215-218
  in early months, 218-220
  effect on teeth, 221
  in older child, 222-224
  pacifier, 224-227
  restraints, 222
  stroking comforter, 217-218
Thymus gland, 213
Thyroid deficiency, 449-450
Tics, 395, 510
Timidity, 318-319
"Tine test," 505-506
Tiredness, see Fatigue
Toeing out and in, 238-239
Toilet training, 249-264; see also Bowel training; Urine training
Tomato juice, 128

Tongue sucking, 224
Tongue tie, 359
Tonsillitis, 482-483
Tonsils, 484
Tourniquet, 531-532
Toys, see Playthings
Training, see also Discipline
  toilet, 249-264; see also
    Bowel training; Urine
    training
Training pants, 257
Traveling, 543-546
Tuberculin test, 505-506
Tuberculosis, 504-507
Tutoring, 409-410
Twins, 553-560
Two-year-old, 350-360
  bedtime problems, 351-356
  dependence, 351-356
  fear of separation, 351-352,
    356
  imitativeness, 350
  importance of sociability,
    350-351
  sensitiveness to changes, 352

U

Umbilicus, see Navel
Underweight, 435-436
Urinary disturbances, 510-517
  boy who won't stand up, 263
  cystitis, 516-517
  difficult urination in infancy,
    515
  difficult urination from infec-
    tion, 516-517
  difficult urination in vaginitis,
    515, 517
  enuresis, 510-513
  frequent urination, 514-515
  inability to urinate in strange
    places, 262

  malformations, 516-517
  pus from infection, 516-517
  pus from vaginitis, 517
  pyelitis, 516-517
  pyelonephritis, 516-517
  redness from beets, 136
  sore on end of penis, 516
  wetting bed, 510-513
  wetting in daytime, 513-514
Urine training, 260-264
  methods, 261-262
  night control, 263-264
  readiness, 260
  standing to urinate, 263

V

Vacations
  with baby, 543-546
  risk around 2 years, 352
Vaccinations, 181-182; see also
  Inoculations
Vagina
  discharge, 517-518
  objects in, 517-518
Vaporizer, 476-477
Vegetables
  in bowel movement, 136
  in diet, 298-299
  loss of appetite for, 281
  starting in infancy, 135-136
  substitutes for, 299
Visitors
  for child in hospital, 466
  for mother, 35-36
Vitamins, 289-291
  A, 289-290
  ascorbic acid, 291
  B_1, 290
  B_2, 290
  B_6, 290
  B_{12}, 291

Vitamins (cont.)
  B complex, 290
  C, in diet, 291
  C, in infancy, 127
  C, in orange juice and to-
      mato juice, 128
  cobalamine, 291
  D, in diet, 291
  D, for infants, 127
  D, for mothers, 77-78
  in infancy, 127-128
  multivitamins, 128
  niacin, 290
  pyridoxine, 290
  riboflavin, 290
  thiamin, 290
Vomiting
  blood in, 467-468
  diet in, 467-468
  in food poisoning, 519-520
  forcible in infancy, 198-199
  inducing in poisoning, 540-
      541
  in infancy, 197-198
  in intestinal infections, 519
  in intussusception, 519
  projectile, 198-199
  before or at school, 410-411
  sour, 197-198
  from spoiling, 196
  at start of infections, 474-475
  in strangulated hernia, 523-
      524

W

Wakefulness in infancy, 194-
    196
Walkers, 172
Walkers, sleep, 43, 162-163
Walking, 237-238

Warts, 494
Washing machine, 37
Wasp stings, 492
Water in diet, 292
  in infancy, 128-130
Waterproof pants, 42-43
Waterproof sheeting, 44-45,
    162-163
Weaning from bottle, 150-153
  avoiding a bedtime bottle,
      126
  the baby's pace, 152-153
  cups for, 151-152
  indulgent mother, 153
  readiness, 150-153
  reluctant mother, 153
  resistance, 152-153
Weaning from breast, 103-107
  to cup, 104-105
  formula for, 91-92
  gradually to bottle, 105-106
  if little milk, 103-104
  refusal of bottle, 107
  suddenly to bottle, 104
Weighing
  in hospital, 59-60
  how often, 70-71
Weight
  gaining in infancy, 69-70
  loss in newborn, 59-60
  underweight, 435-436
Well-baby clinic, 50
Wet rub, 457-458
Wetting, 510-514; see also
    Urinary disturbances
Whooping cough, 497-499
  inoculations, 177-178
  vaccine, 178
Working mother, 563-568
  precautions with child around
    2, 352
Worms, 520, 523

t

Worries, *see* Fears
Wounds, 529-532
    tetanus inoculations, 177-178,
        178-180, 529

Z

Zinc ointment, 46
Zwieback in infancy, 140-141